SOMALI-ENGLISH

AND

ENGLISH-SOMALI DICTIONARY.

SOMALI-ENGLISH

AND

ENGLISH-SOMALI

DICTIONARY.

BY

REV. FR. EVANGELIST DE LARAJASSE,

MISS. APOST. ORD. SS. FRANCISCI CAP. PROVINCIÆ LUGDUNENSIS ALUMNUS.

LONDON:

KEGAN PAUL, TRENCH, TRÜBNER & CO., LTD.,

PATERNOSTER HOUSE, CHARING CROSS ROAD.

1897

LONDON:
PRINTED BY GILBERT AND RIVINGTON, LIMITED,
ST. JOHN'S HOUSE, CLERKENWELL, E.C.

PREFACE.

The few books published on the Somali language being insufficient for anyone wishing to learn it, we, in order to have a basis for a further and thorough study of it, have committed to print this Somali-English and English-Somali Dictionary, although it is not as yet perfect and complete.

For writing Somali phonetically we have employed, firstly, the Roman characters with their Latin pronunciation; secondly, some signs used in the Syrian alphabet (S. J. Beyrouth) for the transliteration of Arabic into Roman characters, and letter đ, as explained in the following alphabetical table :—

Letters.	Sounds.		Letters.	Sounds.		Letters.	Sounds.	
	Latin.	English.		Latin.	English.		Latin.	English.
a	a	ah	ḫ	as *ch* in German		{ s	es	ess
b	be	bay	k̆	ke	kay	{ sh		shay
{ d	de	day	i	i	e	t	te	tay
{ đ	cerebral.		j	dje	jay	u	u	oo
e	e	ay	l	el	ell	w	as in English.	
f	ef	ayff	m	em	emm	y	ie	e-ay
g	g	gay	n	en	enn	‘aa‘ ‘ee‘ }	Sounded	
{ h	he	hay	o	o	o	‘ii‘ ‘oo‘ }	as with ع	
{ ḥ	strong aspirate.		r	er	air	‘u u‘ }	Arabic.	

The letters **a**, **e**, **i**, **o**, **u**, **w**, are vowels; **ai**, **ei**, **au**, **aw**, **ow** are diphthongs; **w**, however, is only a vowel when following the letters **a** and **o**, forming with them the diphthongs **aw** and **ow**. All the other letters are consonants.

OF THE PRONUNCIATION OF THE LETTERS.

Pronunciation of the Vowels.

Simple Vowels.

a

is either long or short:
when long it is pronounced as in English "father."
,, short ,, ,, ,, "cat, mat."

e

has the sound of *a* in such words as "face, space"; but when this vowel stands before a consonant ending a syllable, it has nearly the sound of *a* in the word "care." Ex. **ader**, "paternal uncle," pronounced *ah-dare.*

i

is either long or short.
When long it is pronounced as *i* in "ravine."
,, short ,, ,, "spin."
When **i** is either preceded or followed by **ḥ**, or when marked with ʻ (ʻi and iʻ) it has nearly the sound of *e*.

o

is sounded like *o* in the word "tone," when it is long.
,, ,, ,, "Tom" ,, short.
Ex. **sōr**, "food," pronounced *sore*; **kol**, "time," pronounced *koll.*

u

has the sound of *oo* in the word "pool" when long, and that of *u* in the word "pull" when short. Ex. **gūr**, "marriage," pronounced *goore*; **gur**, "pick up," pronounced *goor*. When **u** is either preceded or followed by hard consonants, as **ḥ**, **ẖ**, it is sometimes pronounced nearly as *u* in "tusk."

ع ('aïn)

The Arabic guttural sound of ع (the pronunciation of which can be learnt only from a native) being of frequent occurrence in the Somali language, the vowels **a**, **e**, **i**, **o**, **u** when having that sound are marked with a reversed comma (‘), either on their right or their left, as shown in the table.

Pronunciation of the Diphthongs.

ai

is pronounced by some as *i* in the word "Bible," and as *ai* in the word "paint" by others.

In a few words these two letters must be sounded separately; in that case the letter **i** will be marked with two dots (ï).

ei

has the sound of *ei* in the English "feign."

au

is sounded as *ow* in the word "cow."

aw

has the same sound as **au**, but is used to represent that sound in words where other vowels follow, and also in attributive verbs.

ow

This diphthong has a kind of hollow sound like that of *oh-oo* pronounced in an empty cask.

Consonants.

b

is sounded as in English "baby," but more forcibly and with a sort of *p* sound.

d

has a clear and distinct sound as in the English "did."

ḋ

is the cerebral *d* of the Sanscrit. Some Somal pronounce this consonant nearly as *rd* in English "hard," "card"; its proper pronunciation can be attained only by practice. There is, however, not very much difference between the pronunciation of **d** and **ḋ** at the commencement and at the end of words. In pronouncing **d** the tongue is allowed to appear between the teeth, whereas to pronounce **ḋ** the tongue must be somewhat curved against the front of the palate.

f

as in English "for," "if."

g

is invariably hard, as in English "gamble," "give," "get."

ḥ

is an aspirate strongly breathed out from the chest, like the Arabic ح "ha."

h

as in English "hare."

ḫ

represents the sounds of the three Arabic letters غ ق خ. Most Somal pronounce any one of those sounds like the German *ch* as pronounced in Switzerland in the words "chirurg," "hochzeit," "loch," the guttural pronunciation not being the same everywhere. In order to avoid confusion and multiplication of sounds we have adopted this sign, although we know that nearly two-thirds of these words commence with the Arabic ق.

k

as in English "kite"; it is interchangeable with g.

j, l

as in English "jump," "lily."

m, n

as in English "mammon," "noon."

r

This consonant is generally strongly sounded, like *rr* in "parrot." There are a few exceptions where it is sounded nearly as cerebral ḋ.

s

is a strong sibilant resembling *ss* in English "hiss."

sh

as in English "shore."

t

is sounded as in English "tattoo," and is interchangeable with **d**.

w

as in English "walk."

y

as in English "yes," "York." In some words this letter is pronounced like *th* in the English "loathe." Ex. **maya**, "no," pronounced *matha.*

The consonants **p**, **v**, and **z** do not exist in the Somali alphabet as separate letters, but their sounds have a reciprocal correspondence to those of the letters **b**, **f b**, and **s**—**p** to **b**, **v** to **f** and **b**, **z** to **s**.

With a view to economize space, indefinite nouns to which either the definite article or the endings of indefinite plural is added, will be represented by the sign (—). When there is no possibility of confusion, the word at the head of an article is also represented by the sign (—) in the phrases and locutions explained, as also in compound words formed from it by the addition of a syllable, particle, or another word when they follow in the same paragraph.

In Somali, for a great number of nouns, the gender is quite arbitrary, as in French, and can be known only by the definite singular article; therefore, with each noun, except with those ending in **o** (which are mostly of feminine gender, and in taking the article **di** change final **o** into **a**), we indicate the article, as **wil**, *m.n.*, "a boy," **—ki**. **gabad**, *f.n.*, "a girl," **—di**.

Polysyllabic or dissyllabic nouns ending with a consonant generally form their indefinite plural by adding **o**; those ending in i by adding **yo**; those ending in **a**, **ai**, and **eh** by adding **yal**; feminine monosyllabic nouns by adding **o**; and dissyllabic or polysyllabic feminine nouns ending in **o** by adding **in**. Masculine monosyllabic nouns form their plural by repeating the final consonant preceded by the vowel a. Ex. **der**, "gazelle"; **derar**, "gazelles."

For all nouns not following the rules given above, the *def. art.* and *plur.* will be indicated thus:

> **gabad**, *f.n.*, "a girl"; **—di**, **gabdo** (plur.)
> **ilig**, *m.n.*, "a tooth"; **—gi**, **ilko** (plur.)

The root or simplest form of the Somali verb being the second person singular of the imperative, all the verbs will be given in that form, to which we add the forms of the second person plural of the imperative and that of the aorist when they are not regularly formed according to the abridged rules below; for from these three forms the other principal tenses of the verb may be formed by the addition of terminations (*see* Gram.).

Rules.

1st. Verbs ending with a consonant generally form the second person plural of the imperative by adding a, and the aorist by adding i, to the root.

Ex. **abur**, "create," "produce (thou)"; —a, "create (ye or you)"; wan —i, "I will create."

2nd. Verbs ending in i, ai, ei, form the second person plural of the imperative by adding **ya** to the root, and the aorist by adding **n**.

Ex. **badi**, "increase"; **—ya**, "increase (ye or you)"; **wan —n**, "I will increase."
adai, "clean"; **—ya**, "clean (ye or you)"; **wan —n**, "I will clean."

3rd. Verbs ending in **o**, **aw**, **ow**, form the second person plural of imperative in **ada**, and the aorist in **an**.

Ex. **hubso**, "meditate"; **hubsada**, "meditate (ye or you)"; **wan hubsan**, "I will meditate."
wanaksanaw, "be (thou) good"; **wanaksanáda**, "be (ye or you) good"; **wan wanaksanan**, "I will be good."
ḥumow, "be (thou) bad"; **ḥumada**, "be (ye or you) bad"; **wan ḥuman**, "I will be bad."

N.B. Exceptions to the above rules will be indicated as follows:—*i.e.*, the whole word given when there is any change in the root, and the root represented by the sign (—) when there is none.

Ex. **tag**, "go"; **—a**; **wan tegi**.
madow, "be black"; **—ba**; **wan —bi**.
sido, "take and carry"; **sita**; **wan sidan**.
daḥamow, "be chilly"; **daḥamoda**; **wan daḥamon**.
'aï, "curse," "abuse"; **—a**, or **'aïtama**; **wan 'aï**.

Somals have taken a great number of words from the Arabic. These words they use with their own article, particles, and pronouns as real Somali words. Ex. **albab**, "the door" in Arabic, is used by Somals in this way: **albab**, "a door"; **albabyo**, "doors"; **albabki**, "the door"; **albabyadi**, "the doors." They do the same with any words which they adopt from other languages.

The character of the Somali language being so very different from that of the English, we give one or more examples in the case of words which present some difficulty.

Article, demonstrative and possessive adjectives and pronouns, personal pronouns, and particles are given at the commencement of their appropriate letters.

Somali is an accentuated language. As for its pronunciation it is of great importance to know upon what vowel or syllable the stress of the voice is to be laid, we mark those vowels with an accent (′). Vowels which of themselves are long are marked with the sign (¯). As a general rule the accent falls on the penultimate syllable; consequently words which follow this rule are not marked.

The Somali words are here given as they are used and pronounced in Berberah. We indicate first the root or chief word, and afterwards the derivatives, without paying any attention to alphabetical sequence; and this in order to facilitate the study of the language. In the Alphabetical Table the letter **k** immediately follows **ḫ**, because their sounds are nearly alike.

We give in a Supplement the new Somali words used in the English-Somali part, because we have found them after having sent the Somali-English part to press.

For some words in very common use, we have given as many sentences as possible, that the student may be able to find out either what word or sentence he has to use for expressing his idea.

EXPLANATION OF THE ABBREVIATIONS.

Definite		*def.*
indefinite		*indef.*
gender		*gend.*
masculine		*m.*
feminine		*f.*
Article		*art.*
Noun		*n.*
singular		*sing.*
plural		*pl.*
Adjective		*a.*
,,	possessive	*a.p.*
,,	demonstrative	*a.d.*
,,	verbal	*a.v.*
Numeral	cardinal	*n.c.*
,,	ordinal	*n.o.*
,,	indefinite	*n.i.*
,,	distributive	*n.d.*
Pronoun		*prn.*
,,	personal	*p.pers.*
,,	demonstrative	*dem.prn.*
,,	possessive	*pos.prn.*
,,	interrogative	*int.prn.*

Pronoun	reflexive	*p.ref.*
,,	relative	*p.rel.*
Verb		*v.*
,,	transitive	*v.tr.*
,,	intransitive	*v.int.*
,,	passive	*v.p.*
,,	causative	*v.c.*
,,	reflexive	*v.r.*
,,	attributive	*v.att.*
,,	impersonal	*v.imp.*
,,	defective	*v.def.*
Adverb		*adv.*
Preposition		*prp.*
Conjunction		*conj.*
Interjection		*int.*
Particle		*part.*
,,	interrogative	*part.int*
,,	negative	*part.neg*
affix		*aff.*
chapter		*ch.*
grammar		*gram.*
See		*see.*

ERRATA.

PART I.—SOMALI-ENGLISH.

PAGE	
1	Read **anigu, adigu, ainu,** instead of **anigo, adigo, aino.**
3	,, **abud,** instead of **abud.**
3	Under **'ad,** read **'ad'ad, 'ad'adki,** instead of **'adad, 'adadki.**
5	,, **afimād,** read **ha wa ladnahai,** instead of **ha wa ladnahai.**
7	,, **'ala'al,** read **'ala'alkisi bu i siyai,** instead of **'ala'alkisi bu i syiai.**
10	,, **ardah,** the article must be **—gi,** instead of **—hi.**
22	,, **bohun,** read **nef an,** instead of **nefan.**
25	,, **dabbalo,** read **wan dabbalan,** instead of **wan dabbahan.**
30	,, **danan,** read **faraska danana,** instead of **faraska danan.**
35	Read **digrin,** instead of **di grin.**
47	Under **fofi,** read **holihi ban so fofiyai,** instead of **holihi ban so fofai.**
51	,, **so gelis,** read **wilka so geliskisu,** instead of **wilka so gelis kisu.**
57	Read **gududonni,** instead of **gududouni.**
63	Under **ḥal,** read **wa run o waḥ ḥun ban kugu falai, lakin iminka ḥal ban ka sinaya,** instead of **wa run o waḥ ḥun ban kugu falaiyai, lakin iminka ḥal ban ka siyai.**
63	Read **hallau,** instead of **hallan.**
67	In the examples given under **hebel,** read **'unai,** instead of **unai.**
71	For **hog,** *v.tr.*, 'extort,' read **ḥog,** instead of **hog.**

ERRATA.

PAGE	
74	In the examples given under **ḫabo**, read **i la ḫabo**, instead of **ila habo.**
76	Under **ḫaib**, *ad.*, 'well,' read 'tell me, him, us, all well,' instead of 'tell me, him, us, all is well.'
77	,, **ḫamis**, *f.n.*, 'Thursday,' read **ḫamista dambe**, instead of **hamista dambe.**
81	,, **ḫorin**, read **inanka ḫorinkisu** ..., instead of **inanka fartisu** ....
85	,, **ma karo**, read **ḫadi kari wah**, instead of **ḫudi kari wah.**
86	,, **kibis**, read **kibis ḫabow**, instead of **kibis habow.**
90	,, **idlow**, read **dauga Bulahar** ..., instead of **danga Bulahar** ....
91	Read **ka 'il hel**, instead of **ka 'il bel.**
96	Under **jer**, 'time,' read **sadeḥ jer**, instead of **sadeh jer.**
98	Read **kaga jiriḫi**, instead of **kaga jirihi.**
102	Under **ma'anaiso**, read **sunkorta ḫawahha ku ma'anaiso**, instead of **sunkorta ḫawahha kuma'anaiso.**
105	,, **malin**, read **malintan todobadkeda**, instead of **malintan todobad keda.**
105	Read **manṭo leili**, instead of **manto laili.**
106	Under **mari**, read **darka birrta mari**, instead of **darka birrta**, 'iron the clothes.'
113	Read **nolan**, instead of **nolau.**
127	Under **sibrar**, read **shagul**, instead of **chagul.**
133	,, **tiri**, read **mid mid u**, instead of **midmidu.**
139	Read **la wah**, instead of **lah wah.**
143	,, **weirweir**, instead of **weiweir.**

Part. II.—English-Somali.

Careful as we have been in revising the proofs, there are nevertheless some words not quite correct, especially in the use of the letters **d̈** or **d**, and **h, ḥ, ḫ**, and sometimes the sign ' before the vowels. But the reader will, either by the help of the Dictionary itself or by the context, easily detect these mistakes.

Here, therefore, we give only the most important corrections.

PAGE

150 Under *about*, read **sidi hore lo yid̈i**, instead of ... **idi.**
151 ,, *absolutely*, read **ḫaib**, instead of **haib.**
154 ,, *after*, read **beri dambe**, instead of **beri beri dambe.**
155 ,, *alive*, read **nol, jira**, instead of **nol jira.**
156 ,, *altar*, read **madbaḥ**, instead of **masbaḥ.**
157 ,, *amuse*, read **jalbebo, — bebta**, instead of **jalbebo, bebta.**
158 ,, *approach*, read **u —, ku d̈owai**, instead of **u ku d̈owai.**
160 ,, *as*, read **sidu u hodmai**, instead of ... **odmai.**
160 ,, *asleep*, read **bad̈na wa so jedai**, instead of **ba d̈na** ....
165 ,, *bark*, read **maïdaḥ**, instead of **maidah.**
168 ,, *beneficent*, read **deḫ badan**, instead of **deḥ badan.**
173 ,, *break*, read **ka dangalaḥsi** instead of **dangalashi.**
175 ,, *browse*, read **ad̈igi wa** ..., instead of **adigi** ....
175 ,, *buckle*, read **ḫadabo**, instead of **ḥadabo.**
175 ,, *bugalow*, read **ḫanjad**, instead of **ḫanyad.**
178 ,, *care*, read **ilali, jir**, instead of **ilali jir.**
180 ,, *cheat*, read **ḫ** (**ḫayano**), instead of **h.**
182 ,, *clamour*, read **sawaḫan**, instead of **sawahan.**
185 ,, *commit*, read **shuḫulkas adan kugu**, instead of ... **hugu.**
193 ,, *deprive*, read **da'anaw, ha laga ḫado**, instead of **da'anaw ha laga** ....

ERRATA.

PAGE

194 Under *difference*, read **maḥa idin deḥaiya**, instead of ... **deḥaiga.**

196 ,, *dog*, do not read *hyæna* alone, but *hyæna dog.*

199 ,, *earth*, read **if,—ki**, instead of **il,—ki.**

206 ,, *film*, read **maskaḥdenu**, instead of **mas ka‘denu.**

216 ,, *go*, read **haggá u ka‘**, instead of **hagga‘ u ka‘.**

225 ,, *hunger*, read **ḫaḫad**, instead of **harḫad.**

227 ,, *inhospitability*, read **marti ḫadis**, instead of **morti** ....

229 ,, *issued*, read **bah**, instead of **baḥ.**

232 ,, *law*, read **ḫaul**, instead of **haul.**

237 ,, *male*, read **ḫod,—di**, instead of **ḫododi.**

241 ,, *mystification*, read **luggoyo**, instead of **uggoyo.**

246 ,, *participate*, read **ḫaibso**, instead of **haibso.**

249 ,, *plain*, read **mel wasa‘ah, doho**, instead of ... **wasa‘ah doho.**

253 ,, *proverb*, read **mahmah**, instead of **maḥmaḥ.**

254 ,, *race*, read **ḫolo**, instead of **holo.**

272 ,, *straight*, read **ḫiyas** and **ḫumi**, instead of **hiyas, humi.**

Part I.

SOMALI-ENGLISH VOCABULARY

SOMALI-ENGLISH VOCABULARY.

A.

a, *df.art.*, the, (*aff.*) used with its support.

á, *ad.*, this, that, (*aff.*) used with its support.

a, *aff.*, pointing out indefiniteness.

ai, a, aya (ayo), *a.p.*, my, thy, ours (*aff.*).

an (aná), ani, aniga (anigo), *p.pers.*, I *or* me.

ad (ada), adi, adiga (adigo), *p.pers.*, thou *or* thee.

ai, *p.pers.*, she *and* they.

anno (aino), annaga, *p.pers.*, we *or* us.

aidin, or **adin**, *p.pers.*, you (*aff.*).

a'al, or **aḥal**, *f.n.*, slime or viscous matter mixed with blood (in dysentery).—**shi**.

'ab, *v.tr.*, drink (this verb is used for any liquid except milk, coffee, and broth); **biyaha 'ab**, drink water; **dawada 'ab**, drink the medicine; **biyo 'ab o ḥamri iss ka da**, drink water and not wine; **biyaha la 'ab**, the water is drunk.

'absi, *v.c.*, cause or give to drink; **i 'absi**, make me *or* give me to drink.

'abad, *m.n.*, camel's grunting (while its burden is fastened on).—**ki**; **aur 'abadked ma je'li**, I do not like the camel's grunting.

abah, *m.n.*, time of birth.—**hi**; **hashi nerig bai abahha ku dashai** or **dalatai**, the she-camel brought forth her young one.

abaho, *f.n.*, coupling of camels.

abaḥ, *m.n.*, lean animal.—**hi**; **aurkasi wa geli abaḥah**, that camel is lean.

abaḥ, *v.i.*, be lean; **wu abiḥi**, he will be lean.

abiḥi, *v.c.*, cause to be lean.

'abai, *v.tr.*, load a gun; **bunduḥa 'abai**, load the gun.

abāl, *m.n.*, gratitude, acknowledgment, remuneration, requital.—**ki**; **abālka an ku** (*pl.* **idin**) **ḥabo** or **haiyo weligi wu jiri**, my gratitude for you will last for ever; **hadiyadda an ku so diro wa abālkan ku ḥaba**

or **haiya**, the gift I send you is an acknowledgment; **wa abālká**, it is your requital; **abāl u ḥab**, be grateful; **abāl ban ād ugu ḥabai** or **abāl āda yan u ḥabai**, I was very grateful to him; **waḥhasi wa abālkai**, it is for my gratitude.

abālgud, *m.n.*, reward.—**ki.**

(u) **abālgud**, *v.tr.*, reward; **i abālgud**, reward me; **wan ku abālgudai**, I rewarded you.

abālgudi, *v.tr.*, reward (only used by some, especially by people from the west).

abālgudah or **abālgudleh**, *a.*, grateful.

abālmari, *v.tr.*, be grateful, thank, reward.—**ya** or **abalmarsha, wan —n**; **aniga abbaha abālmariyai**, I was grateful to the father.

abār, *f.n.*, drought, sterility, famine.—**ti**; **bilad somalied abār ba ka da'dai** or **bilad somalied o ḋami abār wa lehyahai**, there is everywhere drought in the Somali country; **wa abār**, there is famine; **abārta meshas ka da'dai ād ba lo ogyahai**, the sterility of that place is well known.

abār, *v.tr.*, famish, kill, starve.

abba, *m.n.*, father.—**hi**; **aiya abba**, or **abbai**, or **abbo**! O my father.

abban, *m.n.*, friend, protector, guide, conductor.—**ki**; (guest and host are **abban**;) **abban dulai**, *m.n.*, chief, leader.

abbanso, *v.r.*, become friend with; **ninkas abbanso**, put yourself under the protection of that man, *or* become friend with that man.

'abbar, *m.n.*, moment, short time, a while.—**ki**; **'abbar jog**, wait a moment; **'abbar la ḥadso**, sit a moment with him.

abeiso, *f.n.*, kind of (short) poisonous snake.

abguri, *f.n.*, kind of (large) poisonous snake.—**di.**

abḥad, *f.n.*, small box made with the bark of trees tacked together.—**di.**

abḥi, *v.i.*, preach, scold.

abḥo, *f.n.*, fruit of a thorny tree called **ḥuda'**, of which sheep and goats are very fond.

abid and **abki**, *ad.*, never (these words are never employed alone as given, but inflected according to the person speaking or spoken of (*s. gram.*).

abōdi, *m.n.*, large bird of prey, having a red beak and red legs.—**gi**

abor, *m.n.*, species of white ants making their hills or houses in the desert.—**ki.**

'absi, *f.n.*, fear, danger, peril, unsafety.—**di.**

'absi, *v.tr.*, frighten, deter, menace.

'abso, *v.i.*, be afraid or frightened. —**da, wan —n.**

'absila, *a.*, fearless, without danger.

'absileh, *a.*, dangerous, perilous;

war! mel 'absileh ina gei, take us to a dangerous place.

abti, *m.n.*, maternal uncle.—**gi**; or **hoyada walalked,** the mother's brother.

abtiri, *v.i.*, give the genealogy.

abtirso, *v.i.*, give your genealogy.

abtirsinyo, *m.n.*, genealogy.—**hi**; **'Issa abtirsinyihisi,** the genealogy of Jesus.

'abud, *v.tr.*, adore; **ha lagu 'abudo,** be thou adored.

'abudnin, *f.n.*, adoration, worship, —**ti.**

abud, *v.tr.*, shut, close (employed for small boxes), cork a bottle; **abhadda abud,** shut or close the box; **haruradda abud.**

'abud, *v.tr.*, suffocate (**'abudi** is also used by some).

'abudan, *v.p.*, be suffocated; **'abudma, wan 'abudmi.**

abur, *m.* or *f.n.*, behaviour, conduct, temper.—**ki** or —**ti**; **aburkisu wa side?** how does he behave? **aburkisu wa sida,** he behaves so; **abur fi'an,** good temper; **abur hun,** bad temper.

abūr, *v.tr.*, produce, create.

abūran, *v.p.*, be produced, created; **abūrma, wan abūrmi, wan abūrmai,** I was created.

abūreh, *m.n.*, creator.—**hi.**

abūran, *m.n.*, creation.—**ki**; **aburnin.—ti,** *f.n.*, is also used.

abūran, *a.v.*, created; **wah abūran,** a created thing.

ād, *a.* and *ad.*, well, nice, good, loud, strong (this word is an adverb when **u** is added to it. **Ex. kitabkas wa ād,** that book is nice; **ād u tol,** sew well; **ād u hadal,** speak well or loudly; **ād u adkai,** make it strongly; **ād u dis,** build well.

'ad, *m.n.*, piece of meat, flesh. —**ki** (the plural **'adad** is not used by all); **'adki i dib,** give me the piece of meat; **'adki i wada ken** or **'adadki i ken,** bring me the pieces of meat.

'ad, *a.*, white.

'adai, *v.tr.*, brighten, clean, polish, whiten.

'adan, *m.* and *f.n.*, whiteness, fairness.—**ki** or —**ti.**

'adaw, *v.att.*, be, become white (no imperative); **wan 'adan.** (When this verb is used in the imperative it is a kind of curse.)

'adaisnaw, *v.att.*, remain *or* be white, clean; **distigu wa 'adaisanyahai,** the kettle is made white *or* cleansed.

'adaisan, *a.v.*, made white, cleansed; **maro 'adaisan,** clean linen.

'adaisnan, *f.n.*, cleanliness.—**ti.**

'adāb, *f.n.*, hell.—**ti.**; **'adāb yar,** purgatory.

dab 'adābed, *m.n.*, hell fire.—**ki.**

'adab or **'adib,** *v.tr.*, torment, torture; **'adab** means also condemn to hell.

'adad, *f.n.*, kind of acacia tree with stiff and bended thorns, gum-tree.—**di.**

adad, *m.n.*, excresence of flesh in a sore.—**ki.**

'adadi, *m.n.*, cash (of brass money). —**gi.**

'adādi, *v.tr.*, press. (In the jungle Somals, when making their enclosure or fence round their huts, press together the trees cut for that purpose, in order that the branches may be straight, so as to form a close and tough hedge.)

'adādis, *m.n.*, prĕssing.—**ki.**

adág, *a.*, dear (price), fast, firm, hard, strong, light, tough, permanent. (This word is used for things only.)

adkai, *v.tr.*, fasten, strengthen, tighten, make strong.

ha lagu ádka, *v.p.*, be fastened.

adkaw, *v.att.*, be firm, strong, fastened.

ka adkaw, *v.a.*, overcome him, her; **ka adka**, he overcomes, overcame him; **ka adkatai**, she overcomes, overcame; **wa laga adka, adkadai**, he, she is overcome.

adaḥ, *f.n.*, spine or backbone ridge.—**di.**

adaï, *m.n.*, arak tree (*Capparis sodata*), small stick used by Somals for cleaning their teeth.—**gi.**

'adaisimo, *f.n.*, a camel without load

'adanyo, *f.n.*, itching, irritation.

'adanyo or **'adanyod**, *v.i.*, have an itching.—**da, wan —n.**

'adar, *m.n.*, wandering clouds.—**ki.**

'adar, *m.n.*, haziness, hazy weather, drizzling rain.—**ki** (no *plur.*); **'adar da**, it drizzles *or* drizzling rain is falling.

adār, *m.n.*, earthen pot with two handles in which food is cooked. —**ki.**

'addo, *f.n.*, itch, nettle-rash.

'addo, *f.n.*, moonlight (no *plur.*).

'ad'ed, *f.n.*, rays of the sun, sun. —**di; eg! 'ad'eddi da'dai**, look! the sun is setting; **war! 'ad'eddi so baḥdai, ina kena, mesha ka so'onai**, the rays of the sun appear, let us go away from the place.—**di.**

adēr, *m.n.*, paternal uncle.—**ki.**

adéryo, *f.n.*, female koodoo antelope (*Strepsiceros imberbis*).

adéryo 'ari, lesser koodoo antelope (used for both genders).

N.B. Somals generally make no difference between **adéryo** and **adéryo 'ari.** They call the males **godir**, and the females **adéryo.**

adi, *m.n.*, goats and sheep (herd of).—**gi.**

adi ḥal, *m.n.*, butcher.—**ki.**

adi jir, *m.n.*, shepherd.—**ki.**

adin, *m.n.*, limb, member.—**ki.**

adin, *v.tr.*, call to prayer; **adima, wan adimi.**

adimad, *f.n.*, calling to the prayer. —**di.**

'ado, *f.n.*, anger, indignation, rage, wrath (no *plur.*).

'ado, *v.i.*, rage.—**da, wan —n.**

u 'ado, *v.tr.*, rage against.

'adaisan, *a.v.*, angry.

'adaisnaw, *v.att.*, be angry.

'adaisi, with **ka**, *v.c.*, provoke, make him angry, enrage.

adon, *m.n.*, negro, slave.—**ki.**

adon, *f.n.*, negress, slave, concubine.—**ti.**

'adow, *a.* and *m.n.*, cruel, inhuman.

'adownimo, *f.n.*, cruelty (no *plur.*).

af, *m.n.*, mouth, language, dialect, edge.—**ki.**

afayen, *m.n.*, interpreter.

af badan, *a.*, sharp; **mindi af badan,** a sharp knife.

af badnan, *f.n.*, sharpness.—**ti.**

af daran, *a.*, blunt; **mindidi afka daraid i ken,** bring me the blunt knife.

af daran, *f.n.*, bluntness.—**ti.**

afdub, *v.tr.*, close the mouth, gag.

afdub, *m.n.*, closing of the mouth to prevent a man from crying out when they rob his cattle and sheep.—**ki**; **ninkas afdubkisi mid ād u aha,** the gagging of that man was good.

af'eli, *v.tr.*, interpret (this verb is used with **uga, ka,** or **u ka la**); **wan u ka la af'elin,** I interpret *or* I will interpret.

af'elis, *m.n.*, interpreter.—**ki, yo.**

afhun, *a.*, insolent.

aftiro, *v.tr.*, wipe your lips; **aftirta, wan aftiran.** Somals also use **aftiro** for "take some food."

afyahan, *m.n.* and *a.*, eloquent, eloquent man, tame.—**ki; aniga afyahan miihi,** I am not eloquent, *or* not an eloquent man; **faras afyahan,** a tame horse; **dinnad aftahan,** a tame cat; **dinnaddi afkatihin,** the tame cat.

afarr, *n.c.*, four.—**ti; afarr nagod,** four women.

afarrtan, *n.c.*, forty.—**ki.**

afrad, *n.c.o.*, fourth; **ki afrad** (*m.*), the fourth.

afarr iyo tobnad, *n.c.o.*, fourteenth, a fortnight; **afarr iyo tobnadki,** the fortnight.

'affi, *v.tr.*, forgive, pardon.

'affi, *m.n.*, forgiveness, pardon.—**gi.**

war! iss 'affiya, *v.r.*, pardon each other (*plur.*)

afimād, *m.n.*, health.—**ki; ma afimād habta?** are you in good health? **ha wa laduahai,** yes, I am.

afimad, *v.i.*, be in health.

afo, *f.n.*, woman, lady; **afáda serkálka,** the wife of the governor.

afuf, *v.tr.*, blow (with the mouth).

afur, *m.n.*, a small meal taken at about six o'clock in the evening during the time of fasting, while the muezzin is calling Mussulmans to prayer. The other meal, taken from 12 p.m. to 4 a.m. is called **suhur.**

afur, *v.i.*, breakfast (take your breakfast).

afuro, *f.n.*, breakfast.

'ag, *f.n.*, foot.—**ti.**

'agta'ad, *f.n.*, foot-sole; **agti 'adaid,** the sole of the foot.

ag, *ad.*, near (this word is never used alone); **agta, agtaida kalai,** come near (me); **agtisi tag,** go near (to him).

āgan, *f.n.*, bark vessel (shaped

like a double cone, and protected by a light framework of wood called **sāb**).—**ti.**

agon, *m.n.*, orphan boy.—**ki** (the *plur.* for both sexes is **agonadi**).

agōn, *f.n.*, orphan girl.—**ti** (this word is also used for both sexes); **Berberah agonadu wa ku badanyihin,** or **Berberah agontu wa ku badantahai,** or **war! Berberi wa agon badantahai,** there are many orphans in Berberah.

ah, (*root*) *v.*, be (often used as an affix; scarcely ever alone).

ahaw, *v.i.*, be; **ahada, wan ahan, ha ahato,** or **ha ahatai e,** *loc. meaning* nevertheless, never mind, be it so.

ahad, *f.n.*, Sunday.—**di.**

aḥan, *m.n.*, gift left, bequest.—**ki.**

aḥdi, *m.n.*, oath, swearing, alliance, treaty made by an oath.—**gi**; **aḥdi Ebbahai inan ka kausin,** I swear by God that I will kill you.

aḥdi, *v.tr.*, swear, make a treaty, an alliance grounded upon an oath; **wa la iss aḥdiyai o dagal ma jiro,** I made a treaty that we may not fight; **kal hore yainu iss aḥdinai lakin aḥdigi wa adigi beinaiyai,** last year we made a treaty, but you perjured yourself, *or* you did not remain faithful to it.

aḫal, *m.n.*, house, dwelling, room, home.—**ki.**

aḫal horti, *m.n.* façade, house-front.—**ki**; **aḫalka hortisi bai jogan,** or **wa ku joga,** they are before, *or* in front of, the house.

aḫbal, or **ka aḫbal,** *v.tr.*, accept, listen to, receive (in addressing ourselves to God); **Ilahow naga aḫbal,** O God, hear us; **Ilahhai dua'daida ha iga aḫbalo,** or **dua'daida Ilah ha iga aḫbalo,** may God hear our prayers.

aḫbal, with **kaga,** *v.tr.*, kill; **ninki kaga aḫbal,** kill the man (used especially in quarrelling and fighting).

aḫil, *m.n.*, Somali chief, sage, respectable man.—**ki**; **aḫilki Karin yan arkai shalai,** yesterday I saw the chief of Karam; **aḫilo,** or **uḫul,** or **uḫal** are also used.—**ki**; —**shi**; —**shi.**

aḫir, *f.n.*, end.—**ti.**

aḫli, *m.n.*, intellect, understanding, wit.—**gi.**

aḫri, *v.tr.*, read.—**ya, wan —yi.**

'aĭ, *f.n.*, cursing, abuse.—**di.**

'aĭah, *a.c.*, cursed; **eraigi 'aĭdaaha,** the cursed word.

'aĭ, *v.tr.*, curse, abuse.—**a, wan 'aĭ, wan 'aĭtamaya** or **wan 'aĭaya,** I am cursing, abusing him.

'aĭd, *f.n.*, poor man (having nothing at all).—**di.**

aĭmad, *m.n.*, tame beast flying, running away.—**ki.** (They call so a camel which is not yet accustomed to carry loads, and is afraid.)

'aĭn, *f.n.*, wood, forest.—**ti.**

'ain, *m.n.*, kind, sort.—**ki.**

'aïn, *m.n.*, belly-band for camels. —**ki**; **'aïman** (*plur.*).

aïnab, *m.n.*, whitish-grey horse. —**ki**.

aiya! *int.*, used in the place of **warya!** in speaking to the parents or other respectable persons; **aiya abba, abbe,** or **abbo!** O father! **aiya hoyo!** or **ai hoyo!** O mother!

'ajeb, with **la**, *v.i.*, wonder at.

'ajeb, *m.n.*, wonder, astonishment. —**ki**; **'ajayib** (*plur.*).

'ajebi, *v.c.*, astonish, cause to wonder.

'ajibi, *v.tr.*, please, make glad somebody, consent to.

'ajin, *f.n.*, dough.—**ti**.

'ajin, *v.tr.*, knead, bake; **'ajima, wan 'ajimi.**

'ajínleh, *m.n.*, baker.—**hi**.

'ajis, (*m.*) **'ajisad** (*f.*), *n.* and *a.*, indolent, lazy.—**ki**; **'ajisin** (*plur.*), **'ajis**, or **'ajisad ban ahai**, I am lazy.

'ajísnimo, *f.n.*, laziness, sloth.

ajurad, *f.n.*, burnt brick, tile.—**di**.

'al, or **ma'al**, *f.n.*, dew-lap (also used for Somali sheep).

'ala'al, or **'alaan'al**, *m.n.*, regret, sorrow (also the expression of regret you feel at being unable to help someone). **'ala'alkisi bu i syiai**, he expressed to me his regret; **inanka 'alaan-'alkisi ba ku fogadai o la talin kari wainai**, the sorrow of that child was so deep that we could not console him.

'ala'al, with **u**, *v.i.*, regret, repent; **dembigaigi yan ād iyo ād uga 'ala'alsanahai**, I repent heartily of my sins.

'ala'al and **'ala'alsanaw**, *v.att.*, be repentant.

'ala'alsan, *a.*, repentant.

'ala'al, or **'alaan'al**, *f.n.*, palm of the hand.—**shi**.

'ala'al, *m.n.*, a person deprived of all his goods and fortune.—**ki**.

'ala'al, *v.i.*, be deprived of, lose: **bai! bai! 'ala'alaieh ho gai o ho gai!** exclamation of sorrow, the crying of women when beaten, I lost all!

alabo, *f.n.*, baggage, furniture, goods, luggage.

alaḫ, *v.tr.*, hang; **iss —**, hang yourself.

'alal, *m.n.*, rag.—**ki**; *means also* chewing.

'aláli, *v.tr.*, chew.

'alális, *m.n.*, chewing.—**ki**.

'alásho, *v.r.*, chew (yourself).

'alalnáḫsi, *m.n.*, cud-chewing, ruminant.—**gi**.

'alalnāḫso, *v.i.*, chew the cud, ruminate.

alan (*m.*) and **alanad** (*f.*) *n.*, cripple (congenital).—**ki** and —**di**.

'alan, *m.n.*, flag, ensign.—**ki**; **ḫori 'alan**, flagstaff.

albāb, *m.n.*, door, gate.—**ki**, —**yo**.

alēl, *f.n.*, shell.—**shi**.

'alen, *f.n.*, leaf, leaves (also used for tea).—**ti**.

'alid, *v.i.*, fester, grow virulent; **ḫontisu malin walba wa si 'alidaisa**, his sore is growing more virulent every day. (For

a sore becoming worse, *see* **did.** When there is an excrescence of flesh they say **adad.**)
alif, *m.n.,* badge, stripe (from Arabic ا; animals are ordinarily marked with that sign).—**ki.**
alif or **sumad ku jid,** *v.tr.,* stripe or mark the sheep (one only).
alifiyai, *v.tr.,* stripe or mark the sheep (for several).
alikut, or **alakut,** *m.n.,* clipp-springer (with long and somewhat stiff hair).—**ki.**
alol, *m.n.,* roller-blind (made of reeds or bamboos).—**ki.**
'alol, *f.n.,* belly, stomach (generally used also for heart).—**shi.**
'alol ingegan, *a.,* constipated.
'alol ingegnan, *f.n.,* constipation. —**ti.**
'alosha'ad (*see* **haïd**).
alowsho, *f.n.,* forgetfulness (*see* **ilowsho**).
alyo, *f.n.,* saliva.
alya'elis, *m.n.,* cud.—**ki.**
amah, *f.n.,* loan.—**di.**
amahi, *v.tr.,* lend.
amaho, *v.r.,* borrow.
'amal, *m.n.,* character, temper. —**ki.**
amámad, *f.n.,* turban.—**di**; (*see* **imámad**).
amán, *v.tr.,* praise, glorify; **Ilah ban amáni,** I praise God.
amán, *f.n.,* praise, glory.—**ti.**
amána allah! *int.,* farewell! good bye! last adieu before separating.
aman, *v.tr.,* confide, intrust.
amano, *f.n.,* deposit.
amano u dib, *v.tr.,* intrust; **amanan** (for **amano an**) **u dibi** or **ku dibi,** I entrust him *or* thee; **amano ino** or **idin dibai,** he intrusted us *or* you.
amanaiso, *v.tr.,* commit, command; **amanaista, wan amanaisan; Ebbahai neftada ku amanaiso,** commit, command your soul to God.
amar, *m.n.,* haughtiness, pride. —**ki**; **amar ba ku dili,** or **amar bad u diman,** pride will kill you.
amar, *m.n.,* Almighty will, greatness of God.—**ki**; **amarki Ebbahai,** the greatness of God.
amar wein or **amarsan,** *a.,* proud, haughty.
amar weinan, *f.n.,* pride.—**ti.**
amárhádur, *m.n.,* summons, citation.—**ki.**
amárhádur u sar, *v.tr.,* cite, summon.
ambi, *v.tr.,* lose, get rid of; **wilka ambi,** lose the boy in the jungle (*i.e.* to get rid of him); **la'agta wan ambin,** I shall lose the money.
ambo, *v.p.,* be lost; **wilku wu amban,** the boy will be lost; **wilki wa iga ambadai,** I have lost the boy.
'ameiti, or **hameiti,** *f.n.,* gall-bladder, bile.—**di.**
amin, *v.tr.,* believe.
amin, *f.n.,* belief.—**ti.**
(**nin**) **amínah,** *m.n.,* believer.
amin, *f.* and *m.n.,* time, weather (used for the past).—**ti** and

—**ki**; **aminti ainu Bulahar ka nimi ḥumaida**, the weather was bad when we came from Bulahar; **aminti yan tug arkai**, the time I saw the robber.

aminka, or **iminka**, *n.* and *ad.*, now; **iminkada**, the present time; **aminka dabaded**, hereafter; **aminkada**, just now.

amin, *m.n.* and *a.*, careful, honest. —**ki.**

aminahaw, *v.att.*, be careful, honest.

aminimo, *f.n.*, carefulness, honesty.

amūd, *f.n.*, sand, earth.—**di.**

amus, *v.i.*, be quiet, silent.

amusan, *a.*, quiet, silent, civil, humble.

amusnaw, *v.att.*, be, remain, quiet, silent; **sadeḥ sa'adod amusnaw**, be, remain three hours silent.

amusnan, *f.n.*, quietness, silence. —**ti.**

amusi, *v.c.*, cause to be quiet, silent.

amusla, *a.*, never silent (is used for a small child always crying).

an, *part.neg.* (combined with pronouns).

an, *conj.*, that.

'an, *m.n.*, cheek.—**ki**; **'aman** (*plur.*)

'anbur, *a.*, chubby cheek.

anaḥub, *f.n.*, porcupine.—**ti.**

'anbar, *m.n.*, ambergris.—**ki.**

'anbar, *f.n.*, herpes, tetter-scurf. —**ti.**

ándader, *m.* and *f.n.*, spotted hyæna, glutton.—**ki** and —**ti.**

'ando, *f.n.*, udder (of cows, goats).

'anduf, *f.n.*, spittle.—**adi**, —**o**, or —**oin.**

anḥokib, *f.n.*, *Acacia vera.*—**ti.**

'ano, *m.n.*, milk.—**hi.**

ged 'anod, *m.n.*, small-pox.—**ki** (specially used for animals).

anḥau, *m.n.*, ankle.—**gi**, —**yo.**

'antug, *v.tr.*, take a mouthful, gulp.

'antugo, *f.n.*, mouthful, gulp.

'antuji, *v.tr.*, give (him) a mouthful.

ār, *m.n.*, male lion.—**ki.**

'ar ! *int.*, used either to excite, to entice curiosity, or as a provocation to fight (for boys); **'ar ! 'ar ! i dil !** you cannot beat me! **'ar, yel !** work !

araḍub, *m.n.*, kind of spear.—**ki**, —**yo.**

arag, *v.tr.*, behold, perceive, see; **arka, wan arki.**

la árka, *a.*, visible; **markabki ḥatan wa la arka**, the ship is now visible.

la ma árko, *a.*, invisible; **markabki lama arko**, the ship is invisible.

arag, *m.n.*, sight.—**gi**; **araggaigu wa ḥunyahai**, my sight is bad; **ḥatan araggi iga ḥuma**, my sight is bad now.

'arar, *v.i.*, fly, run; **shalai ninki 'ararai**, the man fled away yesterday; **'arar**, he fled away; **'ararai**, they fled away.

'arar, *m.n.*, flight, speed.—**ki.**

arbaḥa, *f.n.*, Wednesday.—**di.**

'arbi, *v.tr.*, make tame, subdue, master.

la **'arbiyai**, *a.*, tame; **wa libaḥ la 'arbiyai**, a tame lion.
'arbun, *f.n.*, security, caution, pledge.—**ti.**
ardah, *m.n.*, kind of verandah.—**hi** (a small place before the hut, surrounded by a fence, where strangers may sleep); **ardahga seḥo**, sleep in the verandah.
ardai, *m.n.*, scholar.—**gi** (learning how to read the Coran for becoming a Wadad).
ardal, *m.n.*, country.—**ki.**
ardal ḥal, *m.n.*, petition, request (of the people).—**ki.**
ardiad, *m.n.*, ground-rent.—**ki.**
ardi, *f.n.*, one pie (the smallest of the Indian brass money).—**di.**
'ari, *m.* and *f.n.*, low tide, ebb.—**gi** and —**ti.**
'ari, or **'arid**, *v.imp.*, retire, ebb; **wai 'arii; bad ya hai'ari**, thou, O sea, retire; **baddu berri wai 'arii**, to-morrow the sea will ebb; **baddi 'aridai**, the sea has retired; **iminka baddu wa 'ari**, the sea is ebbing now.
arim'ad, *m.n.*, hunting chittah.—**ki.**
arin, *f.n.*, suit, sentence.—**ti**; **arinti đamatai**, or **đantahai**, the suit is finished, *or* the sentence is pronounced.
arji, *m.n.*, petition, application.—**gi**; **arji i ḥor**, write an application for me.
'armali, *f.n.*, widow.—**di**; **Berberi wa 'armali badantahai**, there are many widows in Berberah; **'armaliyaha badan e Berberi 'aïd weina**, the numerous widows of Berberah are very poor.
'armo, *f.n.*, grape, creeper clinging to trees (good food for elephants), berries which are red, sometimes eaten by men, and also the boiled leaves.
'aro, *f.n.*, spider.
'aro, *f.n.*, end, point (the highest part of a thing); **'arada waranku wa fiḥantahai**, the point of the spear is sharp.
aror, *v.tr.*, (1) go to drink, water (cattle and sheep); (2) take and carry water (when the flock does not go to the well); (3) go to the well (boy), remain there and watch over the flock; **war! orda arora!** ye men, go and drink; **shalai wa gorti holaha la arori jirai, maḥa la arorin wahyai?** yesterday was the time of watering the flocks, why have they not been watered?
arori, *v.tr.*, go and take the flock to the watering-place.—**ya**; or **arorsha, wan —n**; **shalai iyado ai gorti holaha la arorin jirai tahai** or **ai tahai yannu libaḥ aragnai**, yesterday we saw a lion when we were taking the flock to the watering-place.
aror, *m.n.*, the watering of the cattle.—**ki.**
aror, *m.n.*, declivity, ledge, slope.—**ki**; **arorka si mar o gurada tag** or **u baḥ**, walk along the slope and go to the top.

aror, *f.n.*, morning.—**ti**, —**yo**.
aróryo, *f.n.*, break of day, early morning (this word is the indefinite plur. of **aror**).
aros, *m.n.*, (1) newly-married young man; (2) the name of the house in which the marriage takes place; (3) bridal.—**ki**, —**yo**; **Hassan wa aros**, Hassan is a newly-married young man; **aroska an tagno**, let us go to the house of the new-married couple; **aroska an tagno**, let us go to the bridal, or nuptials.
arosad, *f.n.*, a newly-married girl. —**di**.
'**arrab**, *m.n.*, tongue.—**ki**, —**yo**.
'**arrabla**, *a.*, dumb.
'**arrablaan**, *f.n.*, dumbness.—**ti**.
'**arrab iyo dega ba la**, *a.*, dumb and deaf.
arrin, *m.* and *f.n.*, affair, concern. —**ki** and —**ti**; **wa arrintisi**, it is his affair.
'**arro**, *f.n.*, soil, earth (also salted sand given to the sheep).
arsaḥad, *f.n.*, Godsend, piece of luck.—**di**; **Ebbahai arsaḥad wanaksan bu i sin**, God will make me find a good piece of luck.
'**arsi**, *v.tr.*, take to the shore.
arur, *m.* and *f. pl.n.*, child, ignorant.—**ki** and —**ti**; **ninkasi wa arur o waḥba garan mayo**, that man is ignorant, and he understands nothing.
arúrnimo, *f.n.*, childhood.
arumi, *v.tr.*, make kneel down (the camel).
arun, *v.def.*, kneel down (speaking to a camel); *see* **tu**.
ās, *v.tr.*, bury, thrust (a stake into the ground); **gor dow bainu āsi**, we will bury him soon (in a short time).
āsnin, *f.n.*, burial (not much used). —**ti**.
'**as**, *a.*, red; **dar 'as**, red linen; **maro 'as**, red clothes.
'**asai**, *v.tr.*, redden.
'**asan**, *m.n.*, redness.—**ki**.
'**asal**, *m.n.*, bark of a tree producing red die.—**ki**.
asálba, *ad.*, generally, habitually; **asálba nin ḥun ba tahai**, you are habitually bad.
asarar, *m.n.*, contradiction, denial. —**ki**.
asarar, *v.tr.*, contradict, deny.
(nin) asarar wein, or **asarar midanah**, *m.n.*, contradictor.
ashaḥ, *v.i.*, woo; **wai iss ashaḥen**, they are courting each other.
ashkar, or **ashkir**, *m.n.*, red horse. —**ki**.
askari, *m.n.*, a policeman, soldier, sepoy.—**gi**, **askar**, —**ti** (*plur.*).
'**asho**, *f.n.*, day (of 24 hours); '**asho waḥa jirai**, there was a day.
'**asho**, *f.n.*, supper.
'**ashai**, *v.i.*, take your supper.
ashtako, *f.n.*, complaint.
ashtakai, *v.i.*, complain, appeal.
ashtako, *v.r.*, appeal (for yourself); **ashtakoda, wan ashtakon.**
'**ashur**, *f.n.*, duty, tax.—**ti**; '**ashurtisi ma biḥin**, he has not paid his tax.

'asi, *v.i.*, rebel, revolt.—**ya**, **wan —yi**.

'asi, *m.n.*, disobedient, rebel. —**gi**.

asli, *m.n.*, amber (the substance itself).—**gi**.

aslub, *f.n.*, conduct, behaviour. —**ti**; **wa aslub ḥun**, it is bad conduct.

aslúban, with **si**, *ad.*, well, in a good way, manner; **si asluban u ḥabo**, make it well.

aslúbnaw, *v.att.*, be of good conduct.

'asr, or **'asar**, *m.n.* and *ad.*, evening (from half-past three to the sunset).—**ki**.

astán, *f.n.*, mark.—**ti**; **masarkaiga astántisu wa balladantahai**, the mark on my handkerchief is large.

'asus, *f.n*, reddish colour.—**ti**.

'asúsleh, *a.*, reddish, light brown; **timo 'asusleh**, reddish hair.

'ato, *f.n.*, fatigue, leanness.

'ataisi, *v.c.*, cause him to be tired.

'ataisan, *a.*, tired, fatigued.

'atow, *v.r.*, be fatigued, tired; **'atoba**, **wan 'atobi**.

'ataisnaw, *v.att.*, be fatigued, tired.

au, *f.n.*, leaves of the palm-tree prepared for making mats.—**di**, **awo** (*plur.*).

aud, *v.tr.*, shut, close.

'aul, *m.* and *f.n.*, gazelle (*Gazella Soemmeringi*).—**ki** and —**shi**.

auliad, *f.n.*, saint.—**di**.

aur, *m.* and *f.n.*, camel.—**ki** (*sing.* and *plur.*).—**ti** (*plur.*); **aurki ma yimi?** has the camel come? **aurti ma timi?** have the camels come?

'aus, *m.n.*, grass (green or dried), stubble.—**ki**.

'aus salol, *m.n.*, kind of white reed used for thatching and making mats, and also the mat made of.—**ki**.

'awa, *ad.*, to-night; **'awa yan ku iman**, I will come this night.

'awaisin, *m.n.*, time of supper, end of twilight.—**ki**.

awal or **awel**, *ad.*, ago, before; **awel ḥaggad jirtai**, where were you before? (This word is not much used.)

awawi, *m.n.*, nightmare.—**gi**.

awawi, *v.i.*, talk in sleep.—**ya**.—**yi**.

'awar, *m.n.*, one-eyed person.—**ki**; *means also* a wound, a hurt accidentally received.

'awar, *v.tr.*, hurt (him).

'awaran, *a.*, one-eyed; **wil 'awaran**, a one-eyed boy.

'awaran, *v.r.*, hurt yourself, *or* be hurt; **'awarma**, **wan 'awarmi**.

'awarnaw, *v.att.*, be, remain one-eyed, hurt; **'awaranada**, **wan 'awaran**; **'awarnaw e naga tag**, be one-eyed (*or* hurt) and leave us (kind of curse).

'awi, with **la**, *v.tr.*, help, assist; **war i la 'awi**, help me; *or* **'awin**, **'awima**, **wan 'awimi**.

'awimad, *f.n.*, help, assistance.—**di**; **'awin**.—**ti**, is also used.

'awis, *m.n.*, helper.—**ki**.

awo, *f.n.*, interest, welfare, for your sake, on your behalf.—**di**; **awadāda yad aẖalka ku jogta**, to remain at home is to your interest.
āwada, *prp.*, for.
'awo, *f.n.*, Godsend, piece of luck.—**di**; *means also* the fourth finger, girl's name.
awow, or **awowai**, *m.n.*, grandfather.
ayá? *p.int.*, who? **ayá tahai?** who are you? or of what tribe? **ayá ku dilai?** who beat you?
ayo? *p.int.*, who? **ayo?** who? **ma aniga?** I?
ayo! *int.*, what!
ayaẖ, *m.n.*, locust.—**hi**, —**yo**; **ayaẖ weina eh**, there is a great quantity of locusts.
ayai! *int.*, hop! (for inciting animals); *means also* yes.
ayaiyo, *f.n.*, grandmother.
ayan, *m.n.*, destiny, fate, fortune, luck.—**ki**; **ayankaiga yan ku helai**, I found my destiny.
ayanleh, *a.*, lucky.
ayanla, *a.*, unlucky.
ayan, *f.n.*, day, holiday, feastday.—**ti**; **manta wa ayan ma?** what day is it to-day? **wa ahad**, it is Sunday; **wa ayantaidi**, it is my holiday, my feastday.
āyar, *ad.*, slowly, in a low voice; **āyar hadal**, speak slowly.
'ayar, *v.i.*, play, dance.
ayo, *f.n.*, stepmother, wife of my paternal or maternal uncle (but they add to the word **ayai** the names of **abbai, ader, abti**, and say **ayai abbai, ayai ader, ayai abti**.

B.

b, second letter of the Somali alphabet. It is prefixed to the *p.pers.* in their simple form, and forms **ban**, I; **bad**, thou; **bu**, he; **bai**, she, they; and to the letter **a**, forming **ba**, either used as a pronoun or as for the verb of existence.
ba, *part.* It is added (1) to a noun to show that it is the subject, **aur ba jirai**, there was a camel; (2) to a negative verb to give it more strength, **ha ba 'unin**, do not eat; **aniga 'uni ba mayo**, I will not eat at all; **ha tegin ba**, do not go (I forbid).
ba', *f.n.*, crack, clap.—**di**.
ba, *v.i.*, be unhappy;—**a**, **wan bii**; **war! ba e iga tag**, or **iga tag ba e**, oh! be unhappy and go away from me; **Buniyow ba**, oh! Booni be unhappy! A father will say to his bad son, **ba!** be unhappy (kind of curse); **hebel ba baai**, such a one is unhappy; **kua 'adabta ku jira ba baai**, those who are in hell are unhappy; **kal hore wa la i biiyai**, last year I was unhappy.
baan, *a.*, quarrelsome, wicked.

babah, *a.*, empty, nothing, nothing more; — *v.i.*, be nothing; **gortu maujaddu babahdo**, when the waves retire.

baba'o, *f.n.*, palm of the hand.

babii, *v.tr.*, blot out, efface, abrogate.

babiis, or **babiin**, *m.n.*, abrogation —**ki**, or —**ti**.

bad, *f.n.*, sea, ocean.—**di**; **baddu halai wa buḥdai**, this night the sea was full (high tide).

bad furan, *m.n.*, monsoon, N.E. —**ki**.

bad ḥidan, *m.n.*, monsoon, S.W. —**ki**.

bad̄, half.—**ki**.

bad̄aḥ, *m.n.*, mixture of milk and water.—**hi**.

bad̄aḥ, *v.tr.*, mix milk and water; —**a**, **wan bad̄iḥi**; **'anaha shalai ban bad̄aḥai**, yesterday I mixed the milk with water.

bād̄, *v.tr.*, look for, search, seek; **maḥad aḥalkaiga ka bad̄aisa?** what are you looking for in my room?

bad̄ad̄, *m.n.*, contentment, joy. —**ki**, —**yo**; **bad̄ad̄kà jannada**, the bliss of heaven.

bad̄ad̄, *v.i.*, cheer up.

kaga bad̄ad̄i, or **bad̄ad̄si**, *v.tr.*, rejoice, make joyful.

bad̄ad̄ah, *a.*, wealthy; **nin bad̄ad̄ah**, a wealthy man.

bad̄ád̄san, glad, happy, joyful.

bad̄ád̄sanaw, *v.att.*, be glad.

bad̄ad̄d̄o, *f.n.*, potato.

badag, *m.n.*, goose.—**gi** (most web-footed birds are called so).

bádi, *v.tr.*, augment, increase; **i bádi**, give me more; **u bádi**, give him, her more.

badán, *a.*, much, many, abundant; **ka badan**, more; **ka wada badan**, or **ugu badan**, most.

badnaw, *v.att.*, be abundant, full of; **aniga wa run badnahai**, I am full of truth, truthful.

badnai, *v.i.*, increase.

badso, *v.i.*, abound.

badnan, *f.n.*, abounding.—**ti**.

badbādi, *v.tr.*, lead; **ninka indahala badbādi**, lead the blind man; **ka** —, lead from, preserve from; **adiga bahalka ka badbādi**, preserve the sheep from the wild beasts.

bad̄i, *f.n.*, tail-fat, arse, breech, grease obtained in melting the fat of the tail of a Somali sheep.

baf! *int.*, noise made by something cracking.

baga, *locut.*, it is my will, I have done it purposely (*s.* **ḥushi**).

bagad̄, *m.n.*, hook or staff of a boat.—**di**.

bagaf, *m.n.*, kind of spear.—**ki**, —**yo**.

baḥ, *v.i.*, go out, get out, set out, flow, leak, grow, spring up.—**a**, **wan biḥi**; **biyihi baldigai ka baḥayan**, the water flows out of the bucket, or the bucket leaks; **war! baḥalki muḥu baḥai**, oh! how the radish has grown; **iss ka** —, get out, away; **adiga kolleh iss ka baḥ**, you, by all means, must get out, away; **u** —, go to; **burta dusheda u bah**, go to the top of the mountain; **dibadda u bah**, go outside; **u** —, go at him (for fighting); **wan u bihi**, I will go to him; **shalai ban u bahai o ka adkadai**, yesterday I went to him (for fighting) and I overcame him; **iss** —, independent; **wil iss bah**, an independent boy; **iss bah e naga tag**, may your word fall upon you, but leave us quiet (it is the answer to a man speaking badly or cursing. Arabs say so to the Somals who go them too early in the morning); **so** —, come out with me (from the house); **ka so** —, get out from; **so baha**, grow up, out from (a man having sown something, may say so to the seed thrown on the earth: it is only a wish, but God has the power of speaking so); **u so** —, come for; **wah u so bah**, come out for something; **i so** —, come to me (for fighting), the answer will be **ku so bahai**, I have come.

bah, past participle of the verb **bah**, issued; **Isman wa bah Hadio**, Isman issued from Hadio.

bahsi, *m.n.*, boy, tall boy.—**gi**; **inanki Warsama wa side?** how is the son of Warsama? **wa bahsi**, he is a tall boy (already a young man); **bahsigi me?** where is the boy? (This word is mostly used for boys not yet adult.)

bahso, *v.i.*, escape, fly away; **war! bahso**, or **war! iss ka bahso**, escape, *or* oh! fly immediately.

bahsad, *m.n.*, escape.—**ki**.

u bahso, *v.i.*, run to, for; **serkalka u bahso**, run to the governor, *i.e.*, to request his help.

bahri, *m.n.*, sailor.—**gi**.

bahsan, *a.*, fine, nice, beautiful.

bāho, *f.n.*, gift (this word is used for the act of giving something to a man deprived of his goods by misfortune; everybody of his caste is obliged to give him a gift); **u so bāhi** or **bahai**, give, bring something to him (to the man in want).

u bāho, *v.r.*, be in want.

(nin) bāhan, *a.*, wanting, a man in want; **war! nin bahan, wan u so bāhin**, I will bring something to the man in want.

bahal, *m.n.*, animal, wild beast, cruel.—**ki**; **ninkasi wa bahal**, that man is cruel.

bahal, *m.* and *f.n.*, thing.—**ki**, —**shi**. (This word is often used when the name of the thing is not known or not said.)

bahal hosai, *f.n.*, reptile.—**shi hosai**.

bahi, *f.n.*, appetite.—**di**; **bahidaidu wa wanaksantahai**, my appetite is good.

bah, *v.i.*, fear, be afraid, flee from, funk (this verb has the same meaning as 'abso; meshas ka baḥ libaḥ bai lehdahai, flee from that place, there is a lion.

baḥo, *v.r.*, fear, fly (lest you be overcome); baḥda, wan baḥan. laga baḥo, *a.*, fearful, frightful.

baḥdin, or baḥnin, *f.n.*, peril, risk, danger, dread, fright, terror.—ti.

baji, *v.c.*, cause him to be afraid.

bajis, *m.n.*, cowardice.—ki.

baḥ, *m.n.*, hint, signal, a call, a whistling, a fire or any other sign used by the Somals to recognise themselves in the jungle.—hi ; the watchword also would be called baḥ.

baḥ, *a.*, this name is given to the milk when, the water and the caseous part being separated, it is said to be turned or spoiled ; the Somals throw it away, only beggars drink it ; 'anahasi wa baḥ, this milk is turned, spoiled; 'anaha baḥai, the milk has turned.

bahaïl, *m.n.*, miser.—ki ; ninkasi bahaïl waiyai, that man is a miser ; ninkas wa nin bahaïlah, that man is a miser.

bahaïlad, *f.n.*, miser (*f.*) ; nag bahaïladah.

bahaïlad, *f.n.*, hurricane, storm. —di; war! wa bahaïlad e sehimaduhu ha yai ina ka burburin, oh! there is a storm, do not let the boats be broken (to us).

bahaiya, *m.n.*, eagle.—ihi.

baḥlad, *f.n.*, mule.—di ; baḥlad

lab, he-mule ; baḥlad didig, she-mule.

bahal, *m.n.*, radish.—ki.

bahalya, *m.n.*, species of hawk (small vulture).—hi.

bahbah, *m.n.*, gum (of a blackish colour).— hi, —yo.

baḥlad, *f.n.*, large boat, buggalow. —di.

baḥti, *m.n.*, corpse (especially used for animals).—gi (this word means also death of an animal).

baḥti, *v.i.*, die, extinguish, blow out.—ya, wan —yi.

bakaïla, or bakaïlai, *m.n.*, hare, rabbit.— hi.

baïd, *f.n.*, strap, fastening the camel's pack-saddle under the chest.— di.

baïdbaïd, *m.n.*, zigzag.—ki.

baïdbaïd, *v.i.*, walk like a snake (making zigzags).

bāl, *m n.*, feather, wing, fins (of a fish), page of a book.—ki ; bālka kitabka rog, turn the page of the book.

bal, *part.* of a very common use in Somali ; bal tag, go ; bal kalai, come ; bal i sug, wait for me.

bal an, *part.*, let me, us (this word is ordinarily used with the imperative for asking a permission) ; bal an imado, let me come ; bal an tago, let me go.

bal in, *conj.*, if (this word is ordinarily used in sentences expressing some doubt (indirect

questions); **weidi bal inai fogtahai**, ask if it is far.
balaf, *m.n.*, dislike of food.—**ki.**
balfi, *v.tr.*, refuse the food.
balag, *f.n.*, prepuce, foreskin.—**li.**
balagta ka go, *v.tr.*, circumcise.
balánbalis, *f.n.*, butterfly.—**ti.**
balango, *f.n.*, kind of antelope (water-buck).
balbálo, *f.n.*, shelter, shed (this shelter or shed is ordinarily in front of the hut or tent to protect it from the rays of the sun; the **tumals** (smiths) have a **balbálo** or shed in front of their huts and work under it in order to enjoy the breeze.
balbálai, *v.tr.*, make the shed.
báldi, *m.n.*, bucket, ewer.—**gi.**
bali, *m.n.*, old (only used for things).—**gi.**
ballād, *m.n.*, breadth, also blow given with the flat of a spear. —**ki**; **ballād bu igu duftai**, he beat me with the flat of his spear.
ballādi, *v.tr.*, enlarge, widen.
ballādan, *v.p.*, be enlarged; **ballādma, wan ballādmi.**
ballādan, *a.v.*, broad, large, wide, vast.
ballan, *m.n.*, promise, stipulation, treaty.—**ki.**
ballan, *v.tr.*, fix (a day, a time); **ballama, wan ballami, malinta ballan**, fix the day; **la —**, promise, treat with him; **i la ballan**, promise to me; **an la ballanno**, let us treat; **ka —**, stipulate, state positively, exactly; **faraska gana'disa ka ballan**, state, say exactly the price of the house.
ballami, *v.tr.*, affiance.
balli, *m.n.*, a low place, hole, excavation (forming during the time of rain, pools or wells). —**gi.**
balluḫ, *m.n.*, adult, nubile.—**hi.**
ban, *m.n.*, level ground, plain. —**ki**; **banka Berberi wa balladanyahai**, the plain of Berberah is large.
banan, *m.n.*, collective noun, has the same meaning as **ban.**—**ki.**
banan, *a.*, open (*s.* **furan**).
banai, *v.tr.*, level, make even, plain.
bana'ei, *m.n.*, bellowing and lowing of bulls and cows.—**gi.**
bangad, or **bankad**, *f.n.*, punkah, large fan.—**di.**
bar, *v.tr.*, educate, instruct, teach.
baro, *v.r.*, learn, study; **barta wan baran.**
bara, *m.n.*, instructor, teacher. **hi.**
barad, *m.n.*, pupil, scholar.—**ki,** —**yo.**
barnin, *f.n.*, instruction, education, teaching, learning.—**ti.**
bar, *f.n.*, blot, spot, stain.—**ti**; **baraha 'ad**, white spots; **barbar**, some spots.
baraleh, *a.*, spotted; **shabel wa baraleh**, the leopard is spotted.
bar'as, *m.n.*, leprosy.—**ki.**
bar'asleh, *m.n.*, leper.—**lihi.**
baraf, *m.n.*, ice, snow.—**ki.**
baraḫ, *m.n.*, ease, peace.—**hi**;

baraḥ ba lo yal, they are living in peace; **baraḥ u faḋista**, sit at your ease, or sit down on the ground; **kursiga baraḥ ugu faḋiso**, sit down on the chair.

baraḥad, *f.n.*, a plain surface. **—ḋi.**

barakad, *m.n.*, blessing, benediction.**—di, —yo.**

barakadai, *v.tr.*, bless; **waḥan idinku barakadainaya**, I bless you.

barakadaisan, *a.v.*, blessed.

barakadaisnaw, *v.att.*, be blessed.

barambaro, *f.n.*, blatta indica (in French, cancrelas).

barār, *m.n.*, lamb.**—ki** (generally used for a lamb of one year old, occasionally, however, applied to lambs up to two or three years. When the female sheep is about to bring forth she is called **sabein**).

barar, *m.n.*, swelling.**—ki.**

bararshai, *m.n.*, dropsy.**—hi.**

barárleh, *a.* and *n.*, dropsical person; **nin barárleh**, an hydropic man.

barārug, *v.r.*, rouse (yourself), waken.

bárarug, *m.n.*, glassware, bracelets for women.**—gi.**

bárbar, *m.n.*, young man, youth, time of youth.**—ki**; **anigu weli barbar ban ahai**, I am still a young man; **ninkas barbarkisi mid ḥun bu aha**, that man's youth was bad.

bárbar, *m.n.*, side.**—ki, —yo.**

barḫab, *v.tr.*, male camel (stallion). **—ki, —yo.**

barḫi, *v.tr.*, graze (cattle and sheep) before the milking.

barḫin, or **barḫad**, or **barḫo**, *f.n.*, forenoon (from 9 to 12 o'clock). **—ti**, or **—di**, or **—adi.**

bari, *m.n.*, east; **—gi**; **bari u ka'**, go to the east.

bari, *v.tr.*, beg, beseech, pray. **—ya, wan —yi.**

bariyo, *f.n.*, begging.

bari, *v.i.*, be safe.**—ya, wan —yi**; **ma bariden?** are you safe? (salutation used in the morning); **ha barinai**, yes, we are safe.

baris, or **beris**, or **barid**, *m.n.*, rice.**—ki, —yo.**

barjin, *m.n.*, stool with three legs.**—ki** (*s.* **gambād**).

barki, *m.n*, wooden pillow (having the form of a cresent).**—gi.**

barkimo, *f.n.*, pillow.

barmil, *m.n.*, barrel, cask.**—ki.**

barmil yar, *m.n.*, bucket.**—ki.**

barni, *f.n.*, clean and nice dates, the stones of which are small. **—di.**

baro, *f.n.*, pumpkin, very large vessel for ghee.

barór, *f.n.*, lamentation, crying (only used for women).**—ti.**

baróro, *v.i.*, lament, scream; **barorta, wan baroran.**

ka, or **kaga barór**i, *v.c.*, cause to scream, to lament.

barosin, *m.n.*, anchor.**—ki.**

bartiḫ, *m.n.*, melon, pumpkin. **—hi, —yo.**

barūd, *f.n.*, powder, gunpowder. **—di.**

barūr, *f.n.*, fat, suet, tallow.**—di.**

barwaḫo, *f.n.*, fertility, plenty; **magaladas barwaḫadeda wa la la yaba**, the fertility of this country is wonderful.

barwaḫaisan, *a.v.*, fertile.

bas, *ad.*, enough.

bās, *a.*, bad, wicked, repulsive; **waḫha bās bainu aragnai**, we have seen something bad.

bas, *m.n.*, ticket (for a passage), letter for re-entering a town after having been for a time expelled from it.**—ki.**

basal, *f.n.*, onion.**—shi.**

basbas, or **bisbas**, *m.n.*, pimento. **—ki.**

basha, *m.n.*, pasha.**—hi.**

bassar, *m.n.*, manner, way.**—ki.**

bassarḫun, *a.*, awkward, impolite.

baya mushtari, *m.n.*, trader, merchant.**—gi.**

bauna, *m.n.*, kind of badger. **—hi.**

bed, *ad.*, well (this word is not used alone, and seems to be employed only for "well" when speaking of health; **ma bed ḫabta?** are you well? **wan bed ḫaba ilaḫ maḫdi**, I am well, thanks to God; **ma bed ḫabo**, I am not well.

bedel, *v.tr.*, change, adulterate, sophisticate.

bedelad, *f.n.*, change, adulteration, sophistication.**—di.**

beid, *m.n.*, egg.**—ki**; **albeid! albeid!** cry of egg-sellers.

b'e'id, *m.n.*, antelope, oryx.**—ki** (*s.* **b'i'id**).

bei'di, or **biḫidi**, *m.n.*, kind of spear.**—gi.**

bein, *f.n.*, falseness, lie, perjury, untruth.**—ti.**

beinaleh, or **beinawas**, *m.n.*, liar, impostor.**—hi**, **—ki**, **—yo.**

beinai, *v.tr.*, contradict (not to keep to his promise).

beini, *v.i.*, disprove, prove false.

bein ku dāro, *v.r.*, perjure.

bein sheg, *v.tr.*, lie (tell a lie, an untruth).

beir, *v.tr.*, cultivate, sow.

beir, *f.n.*, cultivation, garden.**—ti**; **beirti Dubahar**, the garden of Dubar.

beir, *f.n.*, tree, plant, vegetable (in a garden).**—ti.**

beira, *f.n.*, musk-deer living in the mountains (seems to be the same as **bair**).**—di.**

beirda, or **beirdai**, *m.n.*, banian-tree (tree and fruit, a kind of fig).**—hi**, **—yal**, or **berdoin** (*plur.*).

beji, *v.tr.*, examine, try.

bejis, *m.n.*, experiment, trial.**—ki**, **—yo**; **gel bejiskisu ma wanaksana**, the trial of the camels was not good.

bel, *v.tr.*, be deprived of, lose.

belbel, *m.n.*, blaze, flame.**—ki.**

belbelli, *v.i.*, inflame, set on fire.

bello, *f.n.*, wicked, bad thing, bad state, condition; **ninka bello ya so gashai**, the man has turned out badly.

bér, *m.n.*, liver.**—ki.**

béryaro, *f.n.*, spleen; **beryarada i ḥanunaisa,** I am suffering from spleen.

bérka dulka sar, *v.tr.*, prostrate; **berka dulka u sar,** prostrate him.

berkad, or **berked,** *f.n.*, cistern, tank.—**di.**

beri, *m.n.* and *ad.*, past time (division of), once.—**gi**; **beri waḥha jirai** . . ., it was once . . .

beri ꝺoweid, *ad.*, lately; **beri ꝺoweid ba abbahai dintai,** my father died lately.

waberi, *ad.*, early morning; **waberi bainu tosnai,** we got up in the early morning.

berri, *m.n.*, earth, land (opposed to water).—**gi.**

berri, *f.n.*, morrow, next day.—**di.**

berri, or **berrito,** *ad.*, to-morrow.

beski, *see* **buksi.**

beyo, *f.n.*, frankincense.

bibíleh, *m.n.*, flute, flageolet, person playing these instruments.—**hi.**

bida, or **bidai,** *m.n.*, slave.—**hi,** —**yal,** or **bidod** (*plur.*).

bidad, *f.n.*, slave (*fem.*).—**di.**

bidar, *f.n*, baldness.—**ti.**

bidarleh, *a.*, bald.

bideḥ, *f.n.*, left hand.—**di**; **bideḥda u jeso,** turn to the left.

bigil, or **bikel,** *m.n.*, bugle, trumpet, or sound of ...—**ki**; **bigilki lagu dufai,** the trumpet has sounded.

biḥi (often used with **u**), *v.tr.*, give, stretch (out), set free, expend, spend (for), pay; **war! waḥ biḥi,** give something (they say so to an avaricious man); **ga'anta u biḥi,** stretch out your hand; **war! ninka biḥi,** set the man free; **abbahai boḥol rubod ban u biḥiyai,** I spent (gave to the poor) 100 rupees (at the death of) for my father; **war! nimanka la'agtoda biḥi,** pay the man, *or* give them their money; **iss ka** —, give, pay: **war! iminka badriga la'agtisi iss ka biḥi,** pay now the money of the father; **so** —, stretch forth, give; **kan i so biḥi,** give that to me; **ka so** —, extract, draw out, get from, save; **war! ninka biyaha ka so biḥi,** draw out, save the man from the water; **dagaḥha 'idda ka so biḥi** or **ruji,** extract that stone from the earth; **u** —, give a name to, call; **waḥhan u biḥin Abdi,** I will call him Abdi.

ha biḥin, *v.tr.* (negative form of the verb **biḥi**), save (money); **la'agtada ha biḥin,** save your money.

beḥis, *m.n.*, expense.—**ki,** —**yo** (*see* **ḥaraj**).

beḥnin, *f.n.*, defence.—**ti**; **'ollki wa fara** or **faro badna o magalada beḥnintedi la ma kar noḥotai,** the enemies were so numerous that the defence of the town was impossible.

biḥimbiḥ, *m.n.*, sigh (of a boy), sham crying.—**hi,** —**yo.**

bihlo, or **bihlai**, *m.n.*, kick (of a horse, mule).—**hi.**

bii, *v.tr.*, blot out, efface, destroy, disgrace; **dinta bii**, destroy religion; **dinti bai magaladi ku biiyen**, they have destroyed religion in the country; **ka** —, corrupt, spoil (in giving bad example); **nafta inanka ka bii**, corrupt that boy (the soul of); **isaga nafta inanka biiyai** or **bashai**, he has corrupted, spoiled the soul of that boy.

b'i'id, *s.* **b'e'id.**

bil, *f.n.*, month, quarter of the moon.—**shi.**

bishi, *ad.*, monthly; **bishi** (or **bil walba**) **Adan ba taga**, I go to Aden every month; **imisa bilod bad Adan fadidai** (or **jogtai**)? how many months have you been in Aden? **imisa bilod bad miyi ka so mahnaid?** how many months have you been absent from the jungle?

bilād, *m.n.*, country.—**ki**, —**yo**; **wa bilādkayaga**, or **dulkayaga**, it is my country.

bilada, or **biladaya**, *m.n.*, mirror. —**hi.**

bilawa, or **bilawai**, *m.n.*, dagger, sword.—**hi.**

bilig, or **biligbilig**, *f.n.*, spark, sparkle, gleam.—**ti**; **baddu wa biligbilig lehdahai**, the sea is covered with phosphorescent gleams; **dabku wa biligbilig lehyahai**, the fire is sparkling.

biligbiligleh, *a.*, sparkling; **eg! awa hediguhu wa wada biligbilig lehyihin**, look! how all the stars are sparkling!

birr, *f.n.*, iron.—**ti**; **birraha na si**, give us the irons; **birr ba lagu hedai**, they have enchained; **nin ba birrku hedan**, a man in chains; **birrta darka la mariyo i ken**, bring me the smoothing-iron.

birrhab, *m.n.*, pincers, iron for marking sheep.—**ki**,—**yo**; **birrhab ku jid**, mark the sheep.

bisbas (*s.* **basbas**), *m.n.*, pimento. —**ki.**

bishil, *m.n.*, wedge.—**ki.**

bisil, *a.*, ripe, cooked; **midkasi wa bisil yahai**, that fruit is ripe; **basashasi wa bisishahai**, that onion is cooked; **hilibka bisil i ken**, bring me the cooked meat; **hilib ki bisla ban siyai**, I gave the cooked meat; **basashi bislaid**, the cooked onion.

bislai, *v.tr.*, cook (not boil), ripen; **ugahanta bislai**, cook the eggs.

bissad, *f.n.*, cat.—**di.**

biyo, *m.n.pl.*, water.—**hi**; **biya! biya!** or **biyaha!** the cry of women selling water; **biyo dānan** (or **hadad**), sour, salted water; **biyo durdur ban 'aba**, I drink river-water; **biyo 'el bainu 'abna**, we drink well-water; **biyo maan**, fresh, sweet water; **biyo 'usboah**, salt water; **biyo rob**, rain-water; **biya garbada ka so dulai**, cascade, waterfall; **biya iss ku waregaya**, whirlpool; **biyaleh**, a woman selling water.

biyow, *v.imp.*, become water; **biyoda** (or **biyoba**) **wu biyon** (or **biyobi**); **ga'anti wa i biyotai**, I have blisters on my hand. (This verb is used for blisters, dropsy...)

bo', *m.n.*, windpipe.—**hi**; **bo'han kugu dufan**, I will strike you on the throat (a Somal would say so to a boy).

bob, *m.n.*, robbery, plunder, pillage, booty.—**ki.**

bob, *v.tr.*, rob, plunder; **wa ḥolo la bobayo, an ḥaibsano**, it is the booty, let us share.

bod, *v.i.*, hop, jump, leap.

bodo, or **bodin**, or **botin**, *f.n.*, jumping.—**di** or —**ti**; **botinta libaḥhu wa la yaba**, the jumping of the lion is wonderful.

bog, *f.n.*, ulcer, ulcerated wound, sore.—**ti.**

bogaleh, *m.n.*, person having a sore.—**hi**, —**yal**; **bogalaha so galai**, or **yimi**, or **yimid**, or **kui bogalaha ya yimid**, the person having the sore has come.

bohol, *f.n.*, a deep cleft between two rocks; a hole made in a plain by heavy rain and overgrown with grass; a deep valley between two plains or table-lands (as the valley of Sodom).—**shi.**

bohun, *a.*, impotent, sterile (not much used); **nefan dali karin** is the loc. ordinarily used.

boḥol, *n.c.*, hundred.—**ki** or —**shi.**

boḥol sanadod, *n.m.*, century; **laba, sadeḥ boḥolo**, two, three centuries.

boḥor, *m.n.*, king.—**ki.** (When a new chief is selected, each tribesman takes a handful of leaves and spreads them over the new chief; after that, he is called **boḥor.**)

boḥor, *v.tr.*, make him king; **boḥra, wan boḥri.**

boḥornimo, *f.n.*, royalty; **wilkasi boḥornimu bu dashai**, that boy was born a king.

boḥortiris, *m.n.*, aide-de-camp of a king, of a leader, of a chief. —**ki, yo.**

boḥor, *m.n.*, woman's belt.

boli, *f.n.*, booty taken from the enemies.—**di**; **shola** —, silver cash.

bōli, *f.n.*, a bush growing near water, having large green leaves. —**di.**

boran, *f.n.*; deep hole in the earth, den, cavern offering a dwelling to wild beasts, as foxes, wolves..., ditch surrounding the **rer**, or village, when there is no wood for making a fence.—**ti.**

bo'shírad, *f.n.*, trade, commerce. —**di.**

botin (*s.* **bodo**); **war hebel botin dera**, such a one (a certain) can jump far.

bowdo, *f.n.*, thigh.

bū, *v.i.*, boast, praise yourself; **war! maḥad la būaisa**, why do you boast? **ninkasi gor iyo**

galab wa būaya, that man always praises himself.

bu, *f.n.*, pupil of the eye.—**di; isha budeda,** the pupil of the eye.

bu'a'ad, plant, with a whitish stem, large round green leaves, exudes a milky fluid, grows in river-beds.—**di.**

bu'amadow, *f.n.*, castor plant (virtues not known by Somals), grows in river-beds, has large green leaves shaped as fig-leaves, which are poisonous when green, but camels eat them when they turn whitish. —**di.**

bub (*root*), *v.imp.*, flee away (only used for animals); **aurteni shalai bubtai,** or **buben,** yesterday our camels fled away.

bubal, *f.n.*, a tame beast become wild.—**shi.**

bud, *m.n.*, club, short thick stick used in fighting.—**ki.**

budai, *v.tr.*, beat, knock down with a club.

budli, *v.tr.*, grind, pound.

bufi, *v.i.*, blow (with the bellows).

bufimo, *f.n.*, bellows.

búg, *m.n.*, belly, stomach, gizzard. —**gi.**

wah búga ku so'oda, reptile (*i.e.*, a thing walking on his stomach).

bug (*root*), *v.tr.*, approve, applaud (used with the *pers. pr.*).

buh, *m.n.*, high tide.—**hi; manta wa buhhi,** it is high tide to-day.

buhi, *v.tr.*, fill; **barmilka wa buha,** the barrel is full.

buhsan, *v.i.*, be filled; **buhsama, wan buhsami.**

buhso, *v.r.*, fill for yourself; **ka —,** fill with, get full of; **dassadada biyaha ka buhso,** fill the cup with water.

buh, *v.i.*, clamour, make a great noise.

buh, *m.n.*, crowd.—**hi; war! bal buhha dai,** look at that crowd.

buhuji, *v.tr.*, suffocate (with a pillow or in a crowd); **wa inanka, buhha la buhujiyai,** the boy was suffocated in the crowd.

buhbuhod, *f.n.*, milk and butter-milk mixed together.—**di.**

buhbuhodi, *v.tr.*, mix together milk and buttermilk.

buk (*root*), *meaning* be sick, remain sick; **wan buki,** I will remain sick.

buka and **bukai,** *a.*, sick, ill.

bukow, *v.i.*, be sick; **bukoda, wan bukon.**

bukaisi, *v.c.*, cause to be sick.

bukan, *m.n.*, sickness, malady. —**ki.**

búksis, —**ki, búksin,** —**ti, búski,** —**gi,** *n.*, cure, healing; **hontada búksintedi wa la la yaba,** the cure of the wound is wonderful.

búksi, *v.tr.*, heal, cure; **bogaha,** or **bog walba daïmahas yan ku búksiya,** I heal every wound with that medicine.

búkso, or **bokso,** *v.i.*, be cured.

bul, *m.n.*, nest, shed, Somali hut. —**ki.**

bulal, *m.n.* (*plur.* of **bul**), hamlet, small village.—**ki.**
bul'aro, *f.n.*, cobweb.
bulhan, *m.* and *f.n.*, clamour; —**ki** and —**ti** for the past.
bulsho, *f n.*, men and black cattle (without either goats or sheep).
bun, *m.n.*, coffee, berry.—**ki.**
bunduh, *m.n.*, gun.—**hi**, —**yo.**
būr, *f.n.*, mount, mountain.—**ti**; **būr yar**, hill.
burow, *v.i.*, grow stout, be or become thick.
buran, *a.*, thick, stout; **nin buran**, a stout man; **niman burburan**, stout men, *means also* a long time, space; **wa buran ba**, it is a long time; **in buran bai u jirta**, it is very far.
bur, *v.tr.*, fasten.
bur, *m.n.*, flour.—**ki.**
bur'ad, *m.n.*, butter.—**ki.**
būrbūr, *m.n.*, kind of infectious disease producing dangerous boils; animals when having that sickness are killed immediately.—**ki.**
burbur, *m.n.*, potsherd.—**ki.**
burburi, *v.tr.*, break (in pieces).
burbur, *v.p.*, be broken, smashed.
burburan, *a.v.*, broken, smashed.
bururi, *v.tr.*, burst, break.
burur, *v.p.*, be burst, broken.
buri, *m.n.*, tobacco.—**gi.**
buro, *f.n.*, wen (kind of tumour).
burobahalad, *f.n.*, wart.—**di.**
buryo, *f.n.*, membrum virile; **buryada ka go**, circumcise.
bushin, *f.n.*, lip.—**ti** (*s.* **debin**).
busta, *m.n.*, blanket.—**hi.**

D. Ḍ.

da, di, du, *f.art.*, the (*aff.*).
da, dan, das, der, di, do, *d.a.*, this, that, that yonder.
dai, daida, *p.pr.*, my.
dá, dada, *p.pr.*, thy.
deda, *p.pr.*, her.
dena, *p.pr.*, our.
dina, *p.pr.*, your.
doda, *p.pr.*, their.
da (for **ḍai**), *v.tr.*, leave, abandon. —**ya, wan dein**; **inanka da**, leave the boy; **iss ka** —, desist, leave; **ta** (or **wahha**) **iss ka da**, leave that; **si** —, let go (from me to a place); **so** —, let go, come (to me).
dā, *f.n.*, age, life, lifetime.—**di**; **dā ma tahai**, what is your age? how old are you? **dādenu wa gabantahai**, our life is short; — **yar**, childhood, infant, small child; — **wein**, old age, aged, old man.
da', *v.tr.*, fall, rob, plunder, cheat; **da'a, wan di'i**; **shalai ban ged ka so da'ai**, yesterday I fell from a tree; **wa la i da'ai**, they have robbed me; **ninkasi wa i da'ai**, that man has cheated me; **so da'da'**, come down (from the tree); **ku** —, fall in, on, plunge; **badda ku da'**, plunge into the sea; **ninka ku da'**, fall on that man; **la** —, beat repeatedly. This verb has also the meaning of "understanding"; **aminka ma ku da'-**

dai? have you understood? (*literally*, have you fallen in?) **i, no da'dai,** I, we have understood.

da'anaw, or **da'an,** *v.att.*, be robbed; **wan da'anahai,** or **wan da'ami** (the verb **da'** in the passive voice with **la, lagu,** has the same meaning).

da'an, *m.n.*, damage.—**ki.**

da', *v.i.*, belch; **da'a, wan da'i.**

da'o, *f.n.*, belch, belching.

da'an, *f.n.*, felled tree used by Somals for shutting the entrance of their enclosure.—**ti.**

da'al, *m.n.*, fringe (of clothes).—**ki.**

da'ar, *f.n.*, bile; aloe about three feet high, red and orange varieties, broad spiked fleshy leaves, spreading out from the ground; is a favourite food of elephants. The variety **da'ar buduḫ** is useful; it is chewed when water is wanting, and allays thirst.—**ti; da'ar badan ba ka timi,** or **da'arti ka timi,** he vomited bile (*lit.* abundant bile has come from).

da'araisan, *a.*, bilious; **ninkasu wa da'araisanyahai,** this man is bilious.

dab, *m.n.*, fire.—**ki; labtaida dab laga shidaya,** my chest is burning.

dab, *v.tr.*, snare, insnare, hunt.

dabád, *m.n.*, hunter, trapper.—**ki, —yo.**

dabin, or **debin,** *m.n.*, snare, trap. —**ki, —mo.**

dabnin, *m.n.*, action of making or placing a snare, a trap.—**ki.**

dāb, *m.n.*, handle, hilt.—**ki.**

ɗab, *v.tr.*, fix, set, stick, pitch.

dāba', or **tāba',** *m.n.*, seal.—**hi, —yo.**

daba', *v.tr.*, seal, print.—**a; wan dabi'i.**

daba'an, *a.v.*, sealed, printed.

dabaḫ, *m.n.*, cover (for jowaree, rice, grain ...).—**hi, —yo.**

dabail, *f.n.*, wind, air, breeze, weather.—**shi; dabail wanaksan,** good wind, fine weather; **dabail ḫun,** bad wind, weather; **dabail ḫabow,** cold wind, weather.

ɗab'al, *m.n.*, miser.—**ki.**

dabal, *m.n.*, post, post-office.—**ki.**

dabaldeg, *m.n.*, fantasia on horses or camels (as Arabs do on feast-days).—**gi.**

dabaldeg, *v.i.*, play a fantasia or participate in it; **war! an dabaldegno,** or **dabaldeg an ḫabsanno,** let us play a fantasia.

ɗaban, *m.n.*, cheek.—**ki, —no.**

dabar, *m.n.*, fetters (for cattle, horses, camels ... at the fore-legs).—**ki.**

ɗabdabar, *v.tr.*, fetter; **ɗabdabra, wan ɗabdabri, aurta ɗabdabra,** fetter (ye) the camels.

ɗabar, *m.n.*, back.—**ki.**

dabbal, *f.n.*, swimming.—**shi.**

dabbalo, *v.i.*, swim, float; **dabbasha, wan dabbahan; ḫorigi wa dabbalaya,** the wood is floating.

dabatag, *f.n.*, antelope, Clarke's roebuck.—**ti.**
dabeir, or **dameir**, *m.n.*, ass.—**ki.**
dabib, *m.n.*, purge, purgation. —**ki**, —**yo.**
dabib, *v.i.*, purge.
dabo, *f.n.*, backside, breech, tail.
dabada, dabaded, *ad.*, after, afterwards (*s.* **haddow**).
daba ḋig, *f.n.*, dysentery.
daba ḥau, *f.n.*, diarrhœa.—**di.**
daba ḥalloḥ, *m.n.*, scorpion.—**hi.**
daba galla, *m.n.*, squirrel.—**hi** (earth squirrel living in holes).
dabagelis, *m.n.*, crupper of a camel's saddle.—**ki, yo.**
dabol, *m.n.*, lid, cover (for anything).—**ki** ; — **deri**, cover of a kettle.
dabol, *v.tr.*, cover, shut.
dabolaw, *v.tr.*, be covered.
dabolan, *a.v.*, covered, shut.
dabsi, *v.i.*, (1) separate a young animal from its mother that it may not suck during the day ; (2) exchange two sucklings (especially camels) ; (3) throw a child (in order to get rid of).
dabsin, *f.n.*, action of separating ..., exchanging ..., throwing ... (a mother throwing away her child is also called **dabsin**).—**ti.**
dabsis, *m.n.*, suckling.—**ki**, —**yo.**
dad, *m.n.*, people, mankind, inhabitant.—**ki** ; **dadki gabowbai**, the old people ; — **ḥun**, *m.n.*, ferocity.—**ki**, —**mo.**
dadḥal, and **dad'un**, *m.n.*, cannibal.—**ki** (*m.*).
dadḥalato, *f.n.*, cannibal.
dād, *m.n.*, deluge, inundation.—**ki.**
dādi, *v.i.*, flow, leak, pour out ; **baldigu bihuhu dādiya**, the ewer (*or* bucket) leaks ; **biyaha dādi**, pour out the water.
ka dādi, *v.tr.*, spill, throw down, overthrow (for all liquids) ; **'anihi la dādi**, the milk is poured out, spilt.
ku dādi, *v.tr.*, sow.
dādsan, *a.v.*, thrown.
dādis, *m.n.*, shedding.—**ki**, —**yo.**
ḋaḋa', *m.n.*, stride.—**hi**, —**yo.**
ḋaḋa', *v.i.*, stride, bestride.—**a** ; **wan ḋāḋi'i.**
dadab, *m.n.*, dream.—**ki**, —**yo.**
dadab, *v.i.*, dream.
ḋaḋab, *f.n.*, a big stone.—**ti.**
ḋaḋan, *m.n.*, taste, flavour.—**ki** ; **harḋaḋkaigi ḋaḋankisi wa ḥunyahai**, I have a bad taste in my mouth.
ḋaḋami, *v.tr.*, taste.
dāf, *v.i.*, go down, descend (in a well, pit) ; **'elka u dāf**, descend, go down into the pit.
dāf, *f.n.*, bottom, below.—**ti** ; **'elka dāftisi ban gaḋai**, I have reached the bottom of the well.
ḋaf, *v.i.*, pass, pass through, pass by (without taking any notice) ; **magalada yan ḋafai**, I passed through the country ; **anigu badrigi ban so ḋafai**, I passed by the father ; **war ! i ḋaf, na ḋaf**, pass, go away, let me *or* us be quiet.

dafi, *v.tr.*, change, exchange, give for; **darka aurkaiga i dafi**, give me clothing for my camel.

dafso, *v.r.*, barter, change (for yourself).

dafsasho, *f.n.*, or **dafsis.—ki**, *m.n.*, exchange.

dafarur, *f.n.*, tree and its fruit (a kind of berry).—**ti.**

dafor, *m.n.*, temples (of the head). —**ki.**

dag, *v.i.*, keep, hold in false security, cause to be careless (as Satan does to sinners); **dadka Shaitan ba daga**, Satan causes people to be careless.

dagan, *a.v.*, deceived.

dagnin, *f.n.*, false security.—**ti.**

dagag, *m.n.*, beggar.—**gi**, —**yo**; **nin dagagah**, a poor man.

dagah, *m.n.*, stone.—**hi**, —**an**, or —**nyo** (*plur.*).

dagah dihed, *m.n.*, pebble.

dagah gubtai, *m.n.*, quick-lime.

dagah madow, *m.n.*, flint, fire-stone.

dagah rob, *m.n.*, hail, hail-stone.

dagah wein, *m.n.*, rock; **dagahnyo wawein**, rocks.

dagal, *v.tr.*, scold, grumble, fight.

dagal, *m.n.*, scolding, battle, combat, fight.—**ki.**

dagalan, *m.n.*, fight.—**ki.**

dagalan, *v.i.*, assail, attack, fight; **dagalama, wan dagalami.**

dagalai, or **degalai**, *f.n.*, javelin. —**di.**

dah, *v.imp.*, rain, it rains; **'erki dah**, or **'erku wa dahaya**, it rains.

dahab, *m.n.*, gold.—**ki**, —**yo.**

dahal, *f.n.*, ear-lap.—**shi.**

dah, *m.n.*, door of a Somali hut (kind of screen or mat hung before the entrance of the hut); **dahha lal**, lift up, *or* open the door; **dahha so da'**, or **so rida**, let fall down the screen, *or* shut the door.

dah, *v.i.*, travel.—**a, wan dihi**; **so —**, come to (in travelling); **si —**, go to (in travelling); **imisad so dahdai**, or **imisa so dahden**, *plur.*, how many days have you travelled? **ashoin badan ban so dahai**, I travelled many days.

dahal, *m.n.*, inheritance.—**ki.**

dahal, *v.tr.*, inherit; **abbahai ban kan dahalai**, I have inherited this from my father.

dahan, *f.n.*, cold, fever.—**ti**; **dahan shalai ban hadai**, I caught a cold, fever yesterday.

dahamow, *v.i.*, catch cold, be chilly; **dahamoda, wan dahamon.**

dähb, *m.n.*, honeycomb. — **ki**; **dahb madan**, an empty honeycomb; **dahb buha**, a full honeycomb.

dah, *v.tr.*, save, economise, lay aside.—**a, wan dihi.**

daho, *v.r.*, lay aside (for yourself). —**da, wan dahan.**

dahasho, *f.n.*, savings.

dah, *v.imp.*, browse, graze; **lo'du wa dahda**, or **lo'di wa dahaisa**, the cows browse, graze.

u dahgei, *v.tr.*, take to graze.

daji, *v.tr.*, graze, feed (cattle); **so** —, take to graze.

daḫad, *f.n.*, window.—**di.**

daḫaji, *v.tr.*, melt, stir.

daḫal, *m.n.*, mast.—**ki.**

daḫar, *m.n.*, every wound received in the head.—**ki.**

daḫar, *v.tr.*, break his head; **daḫra, wan daḫri.**

daḫdaḫaḫ, *m.n.*, movement (slight, nearly imperceptible).—**hi.**

daḫdaḫaḫ, *v.i.*, move; **ha daḫdaḫaḫin,** do not move at all.

daḫdar, *m.n.*, doctor, surgeon. —**ki.**

daḫir, *f.n.*, flour.—**di.**

daḫso, *v.i.*, be quick, make haste; **daḫsada, wan daḫsan.**

daḫso u, *ad.*, quickly; **daḫso u tag,** go quickly.

dakab, *m.n.*, rock, big stone.—**ki.**

dako, *f.n.*, upper part of a skull.

daka'ad, a bald head.

dai, *f.n.*, fresh milk.—**di.**

đai (with **so**), *v.i.*, look; **so — ya, wan so — yi.**

đaimo, *f.n.*, glance.

daibi, *m.n.*, small thorn tree, yellowish stem, very hard wood, used for spear shafts and bows, frames of vessels for liquids. —**gi.**

daïmo, *f.n.* (*s.* **dawo**).

dairi, *v.tr.*, disinherit, disown, exile.

dairis, *m.n.*, disinheritance.—**ki.**

dairsan, *a.v.*, disinherited, exiled; **nin dairsan,** a disinherited, exiled man.

dāl, *m.n.*, fatigue, weariness.—**ki.**

dāl, or **so dāl,** *v.i.*, be fatigued, tired; **inankan galabta ban ku dālai,** this evening I am tired with that boy.

dālan, or **dāshan,** *a.v.*, weary, tired.

dāli, *v.tr.*, annoy, tease, trouble, weary; **wai iss dālinayan,** they tease each other.

dal, *m.n.*, limit, boundary.—**ki.**

daldalasho, *f.n.*, a camel's half-day journey (as from Berberah to Dubar).

đal, *v.tr.*, bear, beget, create, procreate, give birth, bring forth.

đalo, *v.i.*, come to birth, be created (God alone can say so); **wu đalan,** he will come to birth; **ashadan đashai,** the day I was born.

đalin, *f.n.*, birth.—**ti.**

đalinyar, *m.n.*, young man.—**ki,**

đalinyaro, *f.n.*, youth, young people.

đal badan, *a.*, prolific; **nagti đalka badnaid,** the prolific woman. (This word is used for all females.)

ma đalais, *a.*, barren (man or woman).

đal, *m.n.*, young one, suckling (man or animal).

đalasho, *f.n.*, fecundity.

dalab, *v.tr.*, beg earnestly, humbly.

dalbo, *v.r.*, apply, ask for you.

đalal, *v.i.*, shine, glitter, circulate (as blood); **diggu wa đalala,** the blood circulates.

đalal, *m.n.*, brightness.—**ki.**

kaga đalali, *v.i.*, brighten.

dalali, *v.tr.*, melt (wax, butter); **ku** —, melt in.

dálbo, *m.n.*, crookedness of the legs.—**hi.**

(**nin**) **dalbóleh,** *m.n.*, a crook-legged man.

nagti dalbailahaid, *f.n.*, the crook-legged woman.

daldal, *v.tr.*, gather the things and take them to another place.

daldalasho, *f.n.*, taking of things to another place.

dalfo, *f.n.*, gland, fleshy kernel.

dalin, or **dalinbilad,** *m.n.*, highwayman, bandit.—**ki.**

dallayad, *f.n.*, umbrella.—**di.**

dal'o, *f.n.*, heat coming from the rays of the sun at his rising; **dal'adan iss u digaya,** I warm myself in the rays of the sun.

dalol, *m.n.*, hole.—**ki.**

daloli, *v.tr.*, make a hole, bore.

dama', *m.n.*, design, intention, purpose, covetousness.—**hi,** —**yo.**

dama', *v.i.*, determine, intend, purpose, covet; **dama'a, wan dama'i.**

dama'san, *a.v.*, determined.

damad, *m.n.*, sleepy or benumbed person.—**ki.**

damadsan, *a.v.*, sleepy or benumbed; **gabaddas wa damadsantahai,** that girl is sleepy, benumbed.

damas, or **damal,** *m.n.*, timber tree.—**ki,** —**yo; ged damalah,** every large tree (name known or unknown).

dambas, *m.n.*, ashes.—**ki;** —**kulul,** embers.

dambe, or **dambai,** or **dambow,** *ad.*, after (these words are not used alone); **gelin dambe,** afternoon; **kolka,** or **marka dambe,** future; **sa dambe,** the day after to-morrow; **hadda ka dambow,** hereafter, from that time.

dámbai, *v.i.*, remain behind; **ninki ka dambaiya,** the man who is after him, *i.e.*, the successor; **ninki ka dambayai,** the man who was after him; **wa ki ugu dambaiyai** (*m.*), **wa ti ugu dambaisai** (*f.*), it is the last; **wa neifti ugu dambaisai,** it is the last breath.

ugu dambais, *f.n.*, last breath. —**ti; wa ugu dambaistisi,** it is his last breath.

dambaisi, *v.tr.*, leave behind; **ninki ka dambaisi,** leave the man behind the others; **nin iss ka dambaisi,** choose a successor.

dambais, *m.n.*, the remaining after, succession.—**ki; ninkas dambaiskisi 'absileh bu aha,** the succession of that man was dangerous.

dambabid, or **bud,** *m.n.*, kick (of a horse, a mule, an ass...)—**ki.**

dameir, or **dabeir,** *m.n.*, ass, donkey.—**ki; dameir yar,** a young ass, foal; **dameir dibaded,** wild ass.

dameir, *f.n.*, she-ass.—**ti.**

dameiro, *m.n.*, ass (general name). —**hi.**

damin, *f.n.*, security for, pledge. **—ti.**

damino, *v.tr.*, be security or responsible for, bail; **damina, wan daminan; eg! ninkas Warsama damintai**, that man is responsible for Warsama.

damoh, *m.n.*, plaster, poultice. **—hi.**

ku damoh, *v.i.*, put on a plaster, poultice.

dan, *m.n.*, jaw-bone, chin.**—ki; timihi damanka**, whiskers, *or* the hair of the jawbone.

dangalah, *m.n.*, palate, roof of the mouth.**—hi, —yo.**

dangalahsi (with **ka**,) *v.tr.*, break the mouth or the head.

dan, *f.n.*, condition, state, business, want, hurry.**—li; ninkas dantisu wa huntahai**, the condition of that man is bad; **dan mahad lehdahai?** what business have you? **dantaidu wa halkan joniadaha bariskah so gur**, my business is, *or* I am in a hurry to bring all the bags of rice here; **ana dan u leh**, I want to see him.

dan daran, *a.v.*, deprived of all, bad state.

dan daro, *f.n.*, poverty (extreme).

dan, *num.* and *a.*, all, entire, fit, ready; **hilibka wa danyahai**, the meat is ready.

daman, *ind. num.* and *a.*, all, perfect, ready; **imisa sa'adod ya sorta daman donta?** at what o'clock will the food be ready? **sortu gor dow yai daman donta**, the dinner will be soon ready.

damai, *v.tr.*, accomplish, complete, finish.

damaiso, *v.r.*, finish (for yourself;) **damaista, wan damaisan.**

ku damaw, *v.i.*, abut, reach to.

dama, *a.v.*, finished.

dāma (*m.*), **danta** (*f.*), *ad.*, better; **falnin hadal ba dāma**, doing is better than talking.

dāmad.—ki, or **daman.—ti**, *n.*, accomplishment, perfection.

dan, *m.n.*, direction, side.**—ki; daman** (*pl.*); **magalada dankeda shishe**, the other side of the town.

dan, *v.tr.*, drink (milk, ghee); **dama, wan dami.**

dansi, *v.c.*, cause to drink; **arurta dansi**, give *or* make the child drink (ordinarily they say **anaha si**, give milk).

so dami, *v.tr.*, fill; **kussada biyaha ku so dami**, fill the water-pot.

dān, *m.n.*, camel (water-bearer). **—ki.**

danab, *m.n.*, flash of lightning. **—ki.**

danan, *m.n.*, horse's neighing.**—ki,—yo.**

danan, *v.imp.*, neighs, chinks; **faraska danan**, the horse neighs; **ka', ka'! faraski ba dananai**, get up, the horse has neighed; **la'agtu wa dalasha o dananta**, money shines and chinks.

danān, *a.*, salted, sour; **hilib**

đanan, salted meat; **lin đanān,** lemon, citron.
dandánsid or **-sis,** *m.n.*, challenge. —**ki.**
dandánso, *v.tr.*, challenge.
dandul, *f.n.*, skin pail used in digging wells.—**shi.**
dar, *f.n.*, stone house.—**ti.**
dar, *v.tr.*, dip, fill in dipping (dip a pen).
ku dar, *v.tr.*, add to, appoint, settle.
iss ku dar, *v.tr.*, join, mix. (This verb is also used for the joining of letters and sentences.)
iss ku daran, *v.p.*, be joined, gathered.
iss ku daran, *m.n.*, joining (of the flocks), joining, junction (of things).
dar, *root.*
ka si dar, *v.i.*, become worse; **adigu wa ka si daraisa,** you are getting worse; **gidigin wa ka si daraisa e wa side?** you are all getting worse, how is this?
daran, *a.* (This word expresses the privation of some goods or quality, and is never used alone.) **mindi 'af daran,** a blunt knife, *i.e.* a knife whose mouth (**'af**) is deprived of the power of cutting.

N.B.—The word **dar** in **ka si dar** may be considered as the root of **daran,** *meaning* deprived of something.

đār, *f.n.*, oath, faith, fidelity. —**ti.**
đār so mari, *v.tr.*, affirm upon an oath, asseverate.
đāro, *v.i.*, swear; **đārta, wan đāran.**
đāri, *v.c.*, make him swear.
đar, *m.n.*, cloth, clothes (general name), dress.—**ki.**
đarka gasho, *v.i.*, dress yourself.
đarka iss ka đig, *v.i.*, undress.
đar ḫassal, *m.n.*, washerman.
đar tol, *m.n.*, tailor.—**ki,** —**yo.**
đar samai, *v.tr.*, weave.
đar samais, *m.n.*, weaver.—**ki,** —**ti,** —**yo.**
đarab, *m.n.*, dew.—**ki, yo.**
đarabsan, *a.*, dewy; **sāka dulka wa đarabsana,** this morning the earth is dewy.
darad, *f.n.*, interest (for the), sake (for the — of).—**di; daraddai,** for me...
kan daraddi, *c.*, on account of that, therefore.
daraf, *f.n.*, border of a cloth, corners (of the loin-cloth).—**ti,** —**yo; darafta so đigo an hoga barisah kugu shubai,** prepare the corner of your loin-cloth, I will put some rice in it.
daragad, *f.n.*, during the time of rain the Somal prepares branches and boughs in the interior of his hut, so that if the water enters it, he may nevertheless sleep in it without being incommoded by the water. This kind of bed or interior upper floor is called **daragad.**—**di.**
darai, *m.n.*, very large fig-tree, one of the largest trees in Somaliland.—**gi.**
daraj, *m.n.*, means.—**ki.**

daran, *f.n.*, a kind of sour shrub eaten by camels in the jungle. **—ti.**
đarar, *f.n.*, day (the twelve hours of light).**—ti.**
đararta, *ad.*, to-day.
đarar mal, *m.n.*, a person milking during the day. (It is shameful for a Somal to do so.)
đaráro, *v.i.*, dine.
đarárad, *m.n.*, dinner, *or* meal taken during the day.**—ki.**
darbaḥ, *v.tr.*, slap.
darbaḥo, *f.n.*, slap.
dardāran, *m.n.*, legacy, bequest, last words of a dying father. **—ki.**
dardāran, *v.i.*, bequeath, leave to; **dardarma, wan dardarmi.**
dareir, *m.n.*, saliva, spittle.**—ki, —yo.**
daremo, *f.n.*, short and close grass, very good pasture, stubble.
darer, *m.n*, cattle.**—ki.**
dareri, *s.* **fofi.**
dareyo, *f.n.*, chalk.
darkaïn, *m.n.*, kind of cactus, grows in dark groves, its bole has a reddish bark that peels off in diamond-shaped flakes.**—ki.**
dariḥ, *m.n.*, street, road, way. **—hi, —yo.**
darman, *m.n.*, colt, foal.**—ki.**
darman, *f.n.*, filly.**—ti.**
darur, *f.n.*, cloud.**—ti.**
daruran, *a.*, cloudy; **'irku wa daruranyahai**, or **darur bu lehyahai**, the sky is cloudy.
darur, *m.n.*, border, edge, selvedge added to the border of the Somali leather dress or sandals in order to make them strong. **—ki.**
đarūr, *v.tr.*, filter, strain.
đarūr, *f.n.*, filter, colander.**—ti.**
das, *m.n.*, inn, shop, stall.**—ki.**
dāsad, *f.n.*, jug, pot, empty tin pot.**—di.**
dastur, *f.n.*, custom, habit, established manner.**—ti.**
dau, *m.n.*, way, path.**—gi, —yo.**
daudar, *m.n.*, chatting, babbling. **—ki.**
daudar, *v.i.*, chat, babble.
(nin) **daudarah**, *m.n.*, babbler, chatter-box.
daudaula, *m.n.*, kind of woodpecker.**—ki.**
daulad, or **dowlad**, *f.n.*, judge, authority.**—di.**
dauli, or **dowli**, *v.tr.*, draw water from a well.
da'un, *m n.*, cholera **—ki**; **da'unki ba dilai**, cholera killed him
daūr, *m.n.*, a certain number.**—ki.**
đaur, *v.i.*, await, behold, have patience.
iss ka đaur, *v.i.*, be attentive, mind yourself, keep away from.
dawa, *m.n.*, pan.**—hi.**
dawa', *m.n*, male fox.**—ki.**
dawa'o, *f.n.*, fox (general name).
dawād, *f.n.*, inkstand.**—di.**
dawad, *f.n.*, suit, process.**—di.**
dawaḥ, *v.i.*, scream, shout, shriek.
dawaḥ, *m.n*, noise, scream.**—hi, —yo.**
dawan, *m.n.*, small bell.**—ki.**
dawar, *m.n.*, machine.**—ki.**
dawáro, *f.n.*, alms.

dawársi, *m.n.*, begging (of alms).
dawárso, or **dawírso**, *v.i.*, beg (for alms).
dawo, or **daïmo**, *f.n.*, medicine, physic, medicament.
dawai, *v tr.*, give medicine, practise physic.
dawo, *f.n.*, association, company; **dawannu leḥnahai**, we have an association.
la dawaiso, *v.r.*, associate thyself with him; **dawaista**, associate (*plur.*).
daya', *v.tr.*, lose; **daya'a, wan dayi'i.**
dayaḥ, *m.n.*, moon, crescent.—**ha**; **dayaḥ 'usub**, new moon; **dayaḥ badki**, half-moon; **dayaḥ dan**, full moon.
dayan, or **diyan**, *m.n.*, echo.—**ki.**
dayan, or **diyan**, *v.i.*, be echoing, echo; **dayama**, or **diyama, wan dayami; burti wa dayamaisa**, the hill is echoing.
dayi, *m.n.*, fat, tallow under the belly of sheep.—**gi.**
dayimis, or **dayiman**, *m.n.*, eternity.—**ki.**
dayim, or **dayimanah**, *a.*, eternal, everlasting; **Ilaḥ wa dayim**, God is eternal.
de'an, or **da'an**, *m.n.*, juice, gravy, pus, matter, or any humour coming out from a living body.—**ki**; **de'an ba bogtaida ka yimi**, pus comes out from my wound; **de'anka afka maska ka yimada wa urgumo**, the humour coming out from the mouth of the serpent is a venom (poison).

deb'i, *v.tr.*, loose, loosen, slacken.
debi'san, *a.v.*, loose, loosened, slack.
debin, *f.n.*, lip.—**ti**; **debno** (*plur.*).
ded, *v.tr.*, cover him with his sheet (garment).
def, *f.n.*, recompense, reward, salary.—**ti.**
deg, *v.i.*, alight, descend, disembark, land, camp, unload; **ku** —, adhere, stick to, catch hold of.
deji, *v.tr.*, land, disembark; **war! alabadoda deji**, land, disembark your goods; **so** —, go and land; **ku** —, apply (colours), lay to (one thing to another).
so deg, *v.i.*, descend (towards me); **ka** —, get down from; **ku** —, adhere, stick to, catch hold of.
degdeg, *int.*, be quick. (This word is sometimes used as a kind of curse, meaning "hasten to die.")
deg, *f.n.*, ear.—**ti.**
degaiso, *v.i.*, hear, listen to; **degaista, wan degaisan.**
dega, *int.* of surprise, meaning "see!" "hear!"
degala, *a.*, deaf.
dega nugul, *a.*, obedient.
dega adag, *a.*, disobedient.
dega nuglow, *v i.*, be obedient.
dega nuglan, *f.n.*, obedience.—**ti**; **dega nugail.**—**ki** also is used.
degaḥad, or **digaḥad**, *m.n.*, bit of wood used as a broom.—**ki.**
degsar, *m.n.*, armful.—**ki.**
deḥ, *f.n.*, centre, middle —**di.**

deḥda, *ad.*, amidst, among, between.
daḥai, *v.i.*, be in the middle; **u —,** go in the middle; **so —,** come between.
deḥ gal, *v.i.*, intercede, negotiate, settle.
saḥ deḥe, *ad.*, midnight.
ḋeh, *v.tr.*, say (*see* **oḋo**).
deḥ, *f.n.*, generosity.—**di.**
deḥsi, *m.n.*, generous man.—**gi.**
deḥsi ahaw, or **deḥsi noḥo,** *v.att.*, be generous.
deḥ daran, *a.*, ungenerous.
deked, *f.n.*, harbour, pier, wharf. —**di.**
dein, *m.n.*, taking, buying at credit.—**ki.**
dein ḥad, *m.n.*, merchant, borrower.—**ki,** —**yo.**
deïn, *m.n.*, kind of fig-tree, variety of the **darai.**—**ki.**
deir, *m.n.*, dyke, butt (made around a Somali hut to protect it against water).—**ki.**
deldel, *v.tr.*, hang.
dembi, *m.n.*, sin.—**gi.**
dad dembigaleh, *m.n.*, sinner.
denged, *f.n.*, rod used for flogging. —**di.**
dengadai, *v.tr.*, flog, scourge.
ḋer, *a.*, deep, high, long, tall.
ḋerai, *v.tr.*, lengthen, prolong.
ḋerer, *m.n.*, depth, length, height. —**ki,** —**yo.**
ḋereri, *v.tr.*, lengthen; **iss ku —,** lengthen (in adding something to).
der, *m.n.*, he-gazelle.—**ki.**
dero, *f.n.*, gazelle (male and female in general), *gazella nazo.*
derbi, *m.n.*, wall, stone wall.—**gi.**
derder, *v.tr.*, take possession of (a devil); **shaitan ba derderai,** he was possessed of a devil.
derderan, *a.v.*, possessed (of a devil).
derderan, *v.p.*, be possessed of a devil; **derderma, wan derdermi.**
ḋereb, *f.n.*, two skins sewn together; used to carry children. —**ti.**
ḋereg, *m.n.*, satiety, affluence, abundance.
ḋereg, *v.i.*, abound; **ḋerga, wan ḋergi.**
ḋergi, *v.tr.*, make him abound.
ḋerégsan, *a.v.*, satiated.
ḋeregsánaw, *v.att.*, be satiated.
ḋeri, *m.n.*, earthenware pot used as a boiler.
deris, neighbour, inhabitant, subject.—**ki,** — **yo.**
derisnímo, *f.n.*, neighbourhood.
derji, *m.n.*, tailor.—**gi.**
dermo, *f.n.*, mat.
deyib, *f.n.*, Somali pine, mountain cedar.—**ti.**
dhobi, *m.n.*, washerman.—**gi.**
diafad, *f.n.*, banquet.—**di.**
dīb, *ad.*, back, behind; **kasi dīb bu u haḋai,** that one remained behind.
dibad, *f.n.*, back, out, hind part; **dibadda,** outside; **ninkas dibbaddu,** or **dabaddu ka baḥaya,** this man is discharging from behind, *or* has diarrhœa.
dib u haḋ, *v.i.*, remain behind.

dib u jogso, *v.i.*, retire, shrink; **dib ban u**, or **uga jogsan**, I will retire from.
dib u si, *v.tr.*, give back, return.
dib, *m.n.*, tail of a goat.—**ki.**
dib hallow, *m.n.*, scorpion.—**hi,** —**yo.**
dib (with **u**), *v.tr.*, give, bestow; **u dib**, give to him.
diba, *m.n.*, giver.—**hi.**
dibnin, *f.n.*, delivery, giving.—**ti; alabadaidi dibnintedi wa igu humaid**, the delivery of my goods was very difficult.
dibasho, *f.n.*, deposit, pledge, pawn.
u dibo, *v.tr.*, intrust; **amānadas yan ku diban**, I will intrust to you that deposit.
dibin, or **debin**, *f.n.*, lip.—**ti; dibno** (*plur.*).
dibi, *m.n.*, ox.—**gi.**
dibi yar, *m.n.*, bullock.
dibi', *f.n.*, drop, speck, spray.—**di.**
dibow, *m.n.*, kind of euphorbia (as a bush), milky sap.—**gi,**—**yo.**
dibtan, *m.n.*, hard-working man. —**ki,** —**yo.**
dibtan, *v.i.*, work hard; **dibtama, wan dibtami.**
did, *v.i.*, deny, disobey, refuse, forbid; **Ilahhai dembi did**, God forbids sin.
didsan, *a.v.*, disobedient, refusing; **wil didsan**, a disobedient boy; **la didsanyahai**, it is refused.
u did, *v.tr.*, forbid, prevent; **wahhasi wa wah la iss u didai**, that thing is forbidden.
didnin, *f.n.*, disobedience, refusal. —**ti.**
did, *m.n.*, cancerous wound, rotten reddish flesh in a wound.—**ki; hontasi did bai lehda hai**, that wound is cancerous.
didar, *f.n.*, striped hyæna.—**ki.**
didhin, *m.n.*, myrrh-tree.—**ki.**
didib, *m.n.*, peg.—**ki,** —**yo.**
didib, *v.tr.*, peg, put a peg.
didid, *m.n.*, sweat.—**ki,** —**yo.**
didid, *v.i.*, sweat.
didig, *m.n.*, female.—**ki,** —**yo.**
difo, or **dufo**, *v.tr.*, jerk, pull, snatch, take by force; **ka** —, take by force from; **ku** —, fall on, knock, strike; **so** —, take from him to you.
dig, *m.n.*, blood, menses.—**gi; diggu ma ka yimada?** are the menses regular?
dig bah, *v.i.*, bleed;—**a, wan** — **bihi.**
dig ka si da, *v.tr.*, let blood; **dig ban ka si dein**, I will let blood.
dig bah, *m.n.*, bleeding.—**hi.**
dig, *m.n.*, cock.—**gi,** —**ag.**
digag, *m.n.*, cock and hen (general name).—**gi.**
digaga, *f.n.*, hen.—**di.**
dig rin (**'as** or **madow**), *m.n.*, guinea-fowl.—**ki.**
dig (with **u** or **ku**), *v.tr.*, warn, advise.
dignin, *f.n.*, warning.—**ti.**
dignin dir, *v.tr.*, send a warning.
dig, *v.tr.*, place, set, prepare; **miska dig**, prepare the table.
ka dig, *v.i.*, make of, from.
digo, *v.tr.*, keep for you, lay aside, learn.
ku dig, *v.tr.*, write; **warhadda**

ku dig, write the letter; **warhadda ku digai**, I have written the letter.

u **dig**, *v.tr.*, teach.

dig, *f.n.*, bent sticks used for making the frame of a Somali hut.—**ti.**

digdoho, *f.n.*, thorn-tree, horizontal sticks of which huts are made, first stick placed when making a hut.

dig lola, *f.n.*, small boughs or sticks tied together with leathern strings, crossing the bent sticks (or **digo**) on which they are placed and fastened.

digsi, *m.n.*, kettle, boiler.—**gi** (*see* **disti**).

dih, *f.n.*, dry torrent, bed of a river.

dihah, *m.n.*, a woman with child, pregnant.—**hi.**

dihal, *m.n.*, starvation.—**ki.**

dihali, *v.i.*, make him starve.

dihalan, *a.v.*, starving.

dihalanaw, *v.att.*, be starving.

dihi, *f.n.*, grass.—**di.**

dihsi, *m.n.*, fly.—**gi.**

dikri, *m.n.*, bush growing near river-beds, smells like a ripe black currant bush; its leaves are boiled with meat and grease for sick people.

dil, *v.tr.*, beat, strike, kill; **iss —**, commit suicide.

dilan, *v.p.*, be killed; **dilma, wan dilmi.**

dil, *v.tr.*, peel, rind.

dil, *f.n.*, kind of jar made of the fibres of a certain wood first passed through the fire.—**shi.**

dila', *v.imp.*, become worse (this verb is used for sores); **bogtaidi wa dila'dai**, my sore has become worse.

dila', *v.i.*, be torn, burst.

dila'i, *v.tr.*, tear (cloth, paper).

dilal, *m.n.*, broker.—**ki.**

dilal, or **dilal noho**, *v.i.*, broke.

dilif, or **daba dilif**, *m.n.*, sheep's tail below the fat.—**ki.**

dilin, *f.n.*, line.—**ti**, —**mo**, or **dilimoin** (*plur.*).

dillai, *m.n.*, adulterer.—**gi.**

dillo, *f.n.*, adultress, prostitute, harlot.

dillanimo, *f.n.*, adultery.

din, *v.tr.*, diminish, lessen, reduce; **dima, wan dimi.**

diman, *a.v.*, deficient, less; **la'agtu wa dimantahai**, there is not money enough; **la'agti wa dinaid**, the money was not sufficient.

dimad, *m.n.*, death.—**ki**, —**yo**; **dimasho-adi** is also used for death

dimo, *v.i.*, die; **dinta, wan diman.**

dinsan, *a.v.*, mortally wounded.

dīn, *f.n.*, religion.—**ti**, —**mo**; **dimo badan ba jira, mid keliah se hagagsan**, there are many religions, but only one good; **din islamed**, Mohamedan religion.

din, *m.n.*, tortoise.—**ki.**

din baded, *m.n.*, turtle.—**ki**, —**yo.**

dinad, *f.n.*, cat.—**di**; **dinad yar**, kitten.

dinad habishi, *f.n.*, wild cat (*felis cerval*).—**di.**
dinbil, *f.n.*, spark, sparkle.—**shi.**
dir, *v.tr.*, send, despatch ; **la dir,** he has been sent ; **i so dir,** send to me ; **u dir,** send to.
dir, *m.n.*, bark of a tree, a peel, a rind.—**ki.**
dir, *v.tr.*, peel, bark, abrade.
diran, *a.v.*, peeled, stripped, barked ; **gedkasi wa diranyahai,** that tree is barked ; **wan kufai o wai i dirantai,** I fell down and barked myself.
diran, *m.n.*, abrasion.—**ki ; diranka igu yal bog ban ka ḥadai,** my abrasion has turned into a sore.
dirin, *m.n.*, peeling.—**ki.**
dirindir, *f.n.*, caterpillar.—**ti.**
ḋir, *f.n.*, trees (always used in the *plur.*).—**ti.**
dirad, *f.n.*, compass.—**di.**
diraḥ, or **duraḥ,** one of the divisions of the seasons.
dirḥi, *m.n.*, worm, larva.—**gi.**
diri, *v.tr.*, heat, warm.
diran, *v.p.*, be heated, warmed ; **dirma, wan dirmi.**
dirir, *v.tr.*, assail, fight.
dirir, *f.n.*, assault, fight, battle, quarrel, conflict.—**ti.**
dis, *v.tr.*, press, squeeze, push hard.
disan, *a.v.*, pressed, squeezed ; **burigi disan,** the pressed tobacco.
disin, *f.n.*, pressing, squeeze.—**ti.**
ḋis, *v tr.*, build ; **u ḋis,** build for.
ḋiso, *v.r.*, build for yourself ; **ḋista, wan ḋisan.**
ḋisin, or **ḋisnin,** *m.* and *f.n.*, building, construction.—**ki** or —**ti.**
u ḋis, *v.tr.*, give in marriage ; **gabaḋdadu ma i ḋisaisa ?** will you give me your daughter in marriage ?
disti, *m.n.*, kettle, boiler.—**gi.**
ditahab, or **digtab,** *m.n.*, tree of which spear-shafts are made. —**ki.**
diyan (*see* **dayan**).
diyar garai, *v.i.*, make ready (especially used for giving orders).
diyar, *a.*, ready; **ninki wa diyar,** the man is ready.
d'oai, or **d'uai,** *v.tr.*, pray, bless ; **inankaga u d'oai,** bless your son ; **Ilaḥ ha ku d'oaiyo,** may God bless you ; **i d'uai,** pray for me, bless me.
d'oo, or **d'uo,** *f n.*, prayer, blessing.
d'oaiso, *v.r.*, pray for you ; **Ilaḥhow wan d'oaisanaya e iga aḥbal,** O my God, I pray to thee, listen to me.
dob, *f.n.*, sign of a camel's anger (a kind of fleshy ball hanging out of its mouth).—**ti.**
dobleh, *a.*, angry camel (having the sign) ; **aurtasi wa aur dobleh,** that camel is angry.
dobla, *a.*, not angry camel.
dōb, *m.n.*, bachelor, unmarried person.—**ki.**
dof, *m.n.*, sea-voyage, travel, embarkation.—**ki ;** — **af,** or — **yo** (*plur.*).
dof, *v.i.*, sail ; **gormad dofi,** or **dofaisa ?** when will you sail ?

dofi, *v.tr.*, hoist (a sail, a flag). — *v.i.*, embark, travel by sea.
dofsi, *v.tr.*, embark, cause to voyage, send by sea; **adigaigi ban dofsin**, I will embark my sheep.
dofar, *m.n.*, pig, boar, hog, wart-hog.—**ki.**
dog, *f.n.*, green grass.—**ti.**
dogob, *m.n.*, log, a big but short beam.
dogor, *f.n.*, fleece, wool, hair (of goats, cows, horses); always *plur.*—**ti.**
dogor rugmad, *m.n.*, name of a disease (sheep and goats) which makes the fleece become poor and scanty.—**ki.**
dogor rugmad, or **dogorgois**, *m.n.*, moulting.
doḥ, *v.tr.*, disembowel (open the belly).
doḥnin, *f.n.*, rupture, opening of the belly (in cutting).—**ti.**
doḥ, *m.n.*, bed of a river, dry river.—**hi.**
dohana, or **dohanai**, *m.n.*, kind of spear.
doḥbo, *f.n.*, clay, mud, bog.
doḥba haredad, *f.n.*, lime, plaster, —**di.**
doḥb, *v.tr*, plaster (either with mud or lime).
doḥbai, *v.tr.*, defile, pollute, soil, sully.—**dembi naftu doḥbaiya**, sin defiles the soul.
doḥo, *f.n.*, field, large plain or valley covered with grass, stream of water.
doḥon, *m.n.*, blockhead, stupid.—**ki.**
don, *v.tr.*, wish, desire, purpose, seek, search, want, betroth. (This verb is also used as an auxiliary to form certain tenses of the verb; *see Gram.*)
dono, *v.r.*, look for yourself; **donta, wan donan.**
donin, *f.n.*, wish, desire, research, —**ti.**
donin, *m.n.*, betrothing.—**ki.**
donan, *a.v.*, betrothed.
dōni, *f.n.*, large boat.—**di.**
dor, *m.n.*, a bunch of hair left on the top of the head of small boys.—**ki.**
dor, *a.*, nice.
dor, *m.n.*, choice.—**ki**; **wa dor**, it is chosen.
dori, *v.tr.*, barter, change, choose; **i dori**, change with me; **midahas mid iga dori**, choose one of these fruits for me.
doro, *v.r.*, choose for yourself; **dorta, wan doran**; **ka —**, choose from amongst.
dorasho, *f n.*, choice.
dorsan, *a v.*, chosen.
dorsanaw, *v.att.*, be chosen.
iss dori, *v.r.*, disguise yourself.
dorso, *v.tr.*, exchange.
dora, *m.n.*, cock, fowl; —**hi** — **doroin** (*plur.*).
doro, *f.n.*, fowls in general.
doro, word meaning dirt formed on the sexual parts of the body; **doro weinai naga tag**, dirty boy, go away. (This expression is a foul cursing used amongst Somalis, and having the shameful meaning of eating the dirt formed.)

dorrad, *f.n.*, the day before yesterday.—**di**; **dorrad dawan ku siyai,** the day before yesterday I gave you medicine.

đow, *a.*, near, adjacent, recently; **wa i đowyahai,** he is near me.

đowai (with **so**), *v.c.*, cause to approach; **iss u,** or **ku** —, put near each other.

u đowow, *v.i.*, be near, go near; **u đowada, wan đowan.**

so đowow, or **đowo,** *v.i.*, come near, approach; **isagu wa so đowa, kolki kui kaleh 'araren,** he had come near to me when the others fled away.

đowan, *f.n.*, proximity, nearness. —**ti.**

dowdowlai, *v.i.*, shout, bawl.

dowdowleh, *m.n.*, shouter, bawler. —**hi.**

dowli (with **so**), *v.tr.*, draw (water); **biyo so dowliya,** (ye) draw water; **biyo si dowli,** draw water (when I am out).

đowlis, *m.n.*, rope and pail used for drawing water.

druan, *m.n.*, peg-top.—**ki.**

đū, *m.n.*, skin garment worn by women in the jungle.—**gi.**

dub, *m.n.*, human skin.—**ki**; **dubka ka bihi,** skin.

dūb, *v.tr.*, fold, roll up, cover the head; **dūdūb,** fold (*intensive verb*).

dūbnin, *m.n.*, fold, plait, wrinkle, crease.—**ki.**

dub, *v.tr.*, roast on the fire, toast, broil.

dubo, *v.r.*, roast (for you).

duban, *a.v.*, broiled, roasted; **hilib duban,** roasted meat.

đub, *m.n.*, second bark of trees (used for making ropes).—**ki.**

đub, *v.tr.*, point, make acute something; **i đub,** point that for me.

dubalad, *f.n.*, wick.—**di.**

dubbai, or **dubba,** *m.n.*, hammer. —**hi.**

dubba, or **dubbo,** *f.n.*, gourd, kind of pumpkin.—**di.**

dud, *v.i.*, pout. (This verb is also used for a wife having been beaten by her husband; in this case it has two meanings at the same time, of pouting and of running away; **nagti wa dudaisa,** the wife is pouting, and will run away; **nagti wa dudai,** the woman pouted and fled away.

dudmo, *f.n.*, pout.

dud, *m.n.*, mound, embankment. —**ki.**

dūd, *f.n.*, wood, forest.—**di.**

đudun, *m.n.*, fore-arm, wrist, cubit, shank (of camels).—**ki.**

đudumi, *v.tr.*, measure.

dūf, *m.n.*, humour, mucous of the nose (*see* **sin**).—**ki.**

duf, *m.n.*, covering of a Somali hut.—**ki.**

đufan, *m.n.*, castration.—**ki.**

đufan, *v.tr.*, castrate, emasculate.

(nin) đufanan, *m.n.*, eunuch.—**ki.**

đufo (*see* **difo** and **jid**).

dufi, *v.tr.*, allure, attract, entice.

dufso, *v.tr.*, attract, entice to evil.

dufan, *m.n.*, food or grease remaining round the mouth after meal.—**ki**; **war! dufanka iss ka bihi**, clean your lips (mouth).

dug, *v.tr.*, rub, shampoo; **iss ku —**, beat with.

dug, or **dog**, *f.n.*, place where water is found after rain (a kind of pond).—**ti.**

dug, or **tog**, *f.n.*, aim, aiming at (in shooting).

(nin) dug or **tog badan**, *a.*, a man skilful in aiming.

la dugo, or **la togo**, *v.tr.*, aim at; la **dugta, wan la dugan.**

dugag, *m.n.*, animal, beast (general name).—**gi**; **dad iyo dugag**, men and animals.

dugágad, *f.n.*, bracelet (general name), bangle of glass.—**di.**

duh, *m.n.*, marrow.—**hi**, —**yo.**

duhul, *f.n.*, coal.—**shi**; — **nol**, living, or burning coal; — **dableh**, or — **dambasleh**, firebrand; **duhusha!** cry of coal-sellers.

duhul ku reb, *m.n.*, black ant.—**ki.** (After the biting of this ant, a pain resembling that produced by a burning coal remains in the place it has bitten.)

duhur, *m.n.*, noon.—**ki**; **duhurka dabadisa**, the afternoon.

duh, *a.*, aged man, person; **nin-kasi wa duh**, that man is old.

duh, *f.n.*, old age.—**di.**

dug, *a.*, old (only used for things); **darkasi wa dug**, that garment is old.

duh, *f.n.*, game (play).—**di**; **duh ba ku jirta**, or **ku la jirta**, or **duh ban kugu lehyahai**, or **duh ban ka badiyai**, you have lost a game; **duh ban ku derahai**, I have gained one game more than you.

duhfid, *m.* and *f.n.*, last play or play just before dark.—**ki** and **di**; **duhfidki ban ka elai**, or **ka badiyai**, I have gained the last play.

duh, *f.n.*, vagina.—**di.**

duh, *m.n.*, fornication.—**hi.**

duh, *v.i.*, fornicate.

duh, *v.i.*, put the finger in grease or in any other liquid and lick it.

dukan, *m.n.*, shop, public house. —**ki.**

dukis, *a.*, walking slowly, stealthily, as a lame man, a limp.

dukus, *v.i.*, go stealthily, crouch.

duksi, *m.n.*, shelter against the cold, the wind, feeling warm. —**gi.**

duksi, *v.i.*, warm in the sun, prepare a warm place, make the place warm (by shutting the door or windows).

duksiso, *v.r.*, warm yourself.

dul, *f.n.*, top, point, surface.—**shi.**

dul, *ad.*, above, over, up.

dusha, dushi, *prp.*, on, upon, above; **dusha sarai**, higher in place; **dusha gestedi**, upwards.

duled, *m.n.*, outside (of a house) —**di**; **isagu duled ku joga**, he is outside.

dul, *f.n.*, back (especially used for camels).—**shi.**

dūl, *v.i.*, fly (birds).
dūl, *v.tr.*, attack (another tribe).
dul, *m.n.*, nostril.—**ki.**
ɗul, *m.n.*, earth, ground, floor.—**ki.**
ɗul garir, *m.n.*, earthquake.—**ki.**
dulam, or **dulum**, *m.n.*, tyrant, tyranny.—**ki.**
dulan, or **dulun**, *v.i.*, govern as a tyrant; **dulama, wan dulami.**
duldul, *m.n.*, splash, bespattering. —**ki.**
duldul, *v.i.*, bespatter, splash.
dulẖado, *v.i.*, be patient; **u** —, support, be patient with him.
dulẖadsho, *f.n.*, patience; **wa nin dulẖadasho badan**, he is a very patient man.
dullaḥ, *m.n.*, abscess, boil.—**hi,** —**yo.**
dulmadow, *f.n.*, jackal.—**di**; **dawa'o dulmadowa** is also used.
dululuḥ, *m.n.*, pimples covering the skin of goats after rain.—**hi.**
dulun, *v.tr.*, cheat; **dulma, wan dulmi.**
dulun, *m.n.*, cheating.—**ki.**
(nin) dulunah, *a.*, a cheating man; **nin dulman**, a cheated man.
dumar, *m.n.*, womankind, harem. —**ki**; **dumaro** is used when speaking of women in general.
dumashi, *f.n.*, sister-in-law.—**di.**
dumi, *v.tr.*, overthrow, put down, demolish; **aẖalkaiga dumi**, demolish my house.
ɗumi, *v.tr.*, hide, conceal.
ɗumo, *v.r.*, hide yourself; **ɗunta, wan ɗuman.**
ɗumásho, *f.n.*, hiding.

dun, *f.n.*, *plur.*, thread, forefathers. —**ti**; **wa duntaidi**, it is my forefather; **wa dunti rer hebel**, they are the forefathers of such a family.
dundumo, *f.n.*, white ants' hill in the desert.
duni, or **duniyada**, *f.n.*, world. —**di**; **war! duniyada 'iddina ku haɗi maiso**, or **duniyada 'iddina weliged ma jiri dona**, nobody will always remain in the world.
dunyo, *f.n.*, wealth.
dunkal, *f.n.*, poisonous plant, poison.—**shi.**
dunkal si, *v.tr.*, poison, give him poison.
ɗunko, *v.i.*, kiss.
ɗunkad, or **ɗunkasho**, *n.*, kiss, kisses.—**ki**, —**yo** (*m. plur.*); —**adi.**
ɗunyálai, *m.n.*, small mosquito. **hi.**
dur, *m.n.*, grass growing in thick and high feathery clumps, from six to eight feet, excellent pasture when young.—**ki.**
ɗura, *m.n.*, vessel with a handle, used for taking soup or water. —**hi.**
durai, *m.n.*, catarrh, cold.—**gi**; **durai ba i haiya**, I caught a cold.
durai ẖad, *v.i.*, get a cold; — **a wan durihyi.**
durban, *m.n.*, drum.—**ki.**
durdur, *m.n.*, river, stream.—**ki.**
durma, *f.n.*, curb (part of a bridle).—**di.**

duḫsin, *f.n.*, taking out of liquid gum from the hole of a tree, as small boys do in the jungle. —**ti.**

duḫso, *v.i.*, take out the liquid gum...

durug, *v.i.*, move, remove; **durka, wan durki**; **u** —, go near to him; **ka** —, go away from; **si** —, go farther on; **so** —, approach.

durki, *v.t.*, bring forwards, advance, approach.

ḍurwa, *m.n.*, spotted hyæna (name used by the Dhulbahanti.—**gi.**

ḍuryo, *f.n.*, kite (bird).

dus (with **ka**), *v.i.*, sink.

dusi, *v.tr.*, thrust in.

ḍus, *v.i.*, fart, foist.

ḍuso, *f.n.*, fart, foist.

dushin, or **dusin**, *f.n.*, ground, floor.—**ti.**

duti, *v.i.*, limp, go lame.

dutiyai, *m.n.*, lame man.—**hi.**

dutiso, *f.n.*, lame woman.

du'un, *f.n.*, flint stone.

du'un dableh, *f.n.*, steel (of a tinder box).—**ti.**

E.

e, *int. part.*, what? where? (This letter is affixed either to article, noun...)

e, *rel. pr.*, who, which.

e, *conj.*, and.

Ebba, *m.n.*, God. (This word is generally used with the *poss. pron.* in the same way as **abba** — **hi** (*which see*).

ed, *f.n.*, cause, motive, reason.—**di**; **dirirta eddedi wa aurti la ḥadai**, the cause of the attack was the robbery of camels.

ed, *v.tr.*, suffer a loss, have a bad result in a bargain, in changing, in taking a medicine which produces a contrary effect to one's expectation. A robber caught whilst stealing and punished, the unrepentant sinner in hell, will say, **wan edai**, I have been mistaken.

edis, *f.n.*, bad result, reverse, contrary.—**ti.**

edai, *v.tr.*, accuse (generally used in the sense of accusing falsely); **ku** —, accuse him falsely; **ha i edain waḥba ma an ḥadin**, do not accuse me, I have taken nothing.

edan, *m.n.*, prayer call (used among Mussulmans).—**ki**; **edanki ma maḥashai**, have you heard the call.

edib, *f.n.*, politeness.—**ti.**

edbi, *v.i.*, cause to be polite; **war! inamada edbi**, teach the boys to be polite.

edibsan, *a.*, polite.

edibsanaw, *v.att.*, be polite.

eddo, *f.n.*, paternal aunt.

'eḍib, or **'iḍib**, *f.n.*, heel.—**ti**; **'eḍbo** (*plur.*).

'eḍiḍi, or **'iḍiḍi**, *a.* and *m.n.*, narrow, strait: **kursigu wa igu 'eḍiḍi**, the chair is narrow for me; **'eḍidiga nin ba mari**

kara, a man may pass through that narrow place.

'eḍidsan, *a.*, narrow; **mel 'eḍidsan,** a narrow place.

'eḍiḍi, *v.i.*, make it narrow.

'eḍin, *a.*, raw, unripe, not cooked; **midkasi wa eḍin,** that fruit is not ripe.

'eḍin, *m.n.*, rawness.—**ki**; **baris 'eḍinah,** uncooked rice.

eg! ega! erya! *int.*, behold! look!

eg, *v.tr.*, behold, look, see; **berrito barisba la keni, wan egi inu wanaksanyahai,** to-morrow they will bring rice; I will see if it is good.

bal eg, *v.tr.*, look at; **bal an ego, markabka la shegayo,** let me look at the ship they are speaking of; **bal i eg,** look at me; **bal na eg,** look at us; **an so durko, inan bal egi karo,** let me come near, that I may look at it.

iss ka eg, *v.i.*, take care, be attentive. (This word is also used as an interjection, meaning: attention! behold! hark! hist! lo! **war! siradka iss ka eg!** be attentive, that you may not break the lamp.

u eg, *v.i.*, look for him (in the place of, instead of); **i eg,** look for me; **ino eg,** look for us; **warḥaddas i eg,** or **i si eg,** look at that paper for me.

i eg, *v.*, look at me; **ād i eg,** look well at me.

igu eg, look at me with; **ḥoḥadda igu eg,** look at me with the spy glass. (This verb is also used for reproving a man for his not helping another in a moment of danger; **maḥad ninki igu egaisai?** why did you look at the man, instead of helping me?)

so eg, *v.tr.*, go and look; **war! i, ino so eg,** go and look for me, us.

leh eg, *v. imp.*, it suits; **ḥamisku wa i, ku, ina lehegyahai,** the shirt suits me, you, us; **i eg bal in darkani i lehegyahai,** look if those clothes suit me.

iss leh eg, *a.*, alike, the same; **labada kitab wa iss leh egyihin,** the two books are alike.

iss u eg, *v.tr.*, assimilate, compare.

u ekow, *v.tr.*, resemble; **abbihi, hoyadi, bu u egyahai, u eka, u ekadai,** he resembles, resembled, resembled his father, his mother; the past form, **eka,** denotes a resemblance quite past, and **ekadai** a lasting state of resemblance which already formerly existed; **wa iss u egnahai,** we resemble each other.

u ekaisi, *v.tr.*, assimilate, make like; **ushatan tan kaleh u ekaisi,** make this stick like the other.

egmo, *f.n.*, look, glance.

'eḥo (with **ka**), *v.i.*, be partial, favour; **wa naga 'eḥanaya,** he is partial to us; **ninki wa laga 'eḥadai,** the man is under the oppression of an unjust sentence; **ninki laga 'eḥadai Adan**

bu ka ashtakain or **ashtakon,** the man oppressed will appeal to Aden.

gar 'eho, *f.n.*, partial, wrong sentence; **gar 'ehaah nagta dishai,** a partial (unjust) sentence killed this woman.

'ehasho, *f.n.*, partiality, oppression.

eï, *m.a.*, dog.—**gi.**

eiyad, *f.n.*, bitch.—**di.**

'ei, or **'i,** *v.imp.*, cry, bark, bray, cackle (is used for the cry of any animal); **wu 'iyi.**

'eisi (with **kaga**), *v.i.*, cause to cry, vex.

'eib, *f.n.*, loss of reputation, blemish incurred through defamation, defamation.—**ti.**

'eibai, *v.tr.*, defame, blemish.

'el, *m.n.*, well.—**ki.**

'el gun fog, *m.n.*, abyss; **'elki gunta foga,** the abyss.

'elal jog, or **'elal jogjog,** *f.n.*, bustard, dweller at wells (*see* **salalmodleh**).

'eli, *v.tr.*, give back, return (a thing); **ka** —, defend, protect.

iss ka 'eli, *v.tr.*, return, restore (a stolen thing).

so 'eli, *v.tr.*, bring back (as an answer to a letter), restore, re-establish, call again; **dinta ku so 'eli,** re-establish religion.

u 'eli, *v.tr.*, bring back to him, answer.

kala 'eli, *v.tr.*, separate, set apart.

'esho, *v.tr.*, take back again; **ka** —, do not give (keep for yourself).

'elmi, or **'ilmi,** *m.n.*, written book of religion, as Bible, Gospel, Coran; **'elmi bai ahriyahan,** they are reading the written book; **'elmigi bai hayan,** they have the knowledge of the written book.

'emri, *m.n.*, course of life, life; **'emrigagu ha rago,** may your life be prolonged; **'emrigisi bu lastai,** his life is finished (is said of an old man, and also of a young one whose health is ruined).

erai, *m.n.*, word.—**gi.**

eri, *v.tr.*, defeat, drive away, dismiss, discharge, pursue;—**ya, wan — yi; ku eri,** drive; **musmar ku eri,** drive a nail; **ka eri,** drive out.

ergo, *f.n.*, ambassador of peace.

'eyo, or **'iow,** *m.n.*, small owl.

F.

fad, *m.n.*, cloud.—**ki; fadka halka ka so bahai,** look at that cloud rising up there.

fad, *v.tr.*, hollow out.

fadanfad, *m.n.*, mole.—**ki.**

fadi, *v.i.*, sit, stay, abide, dwell, inhabit, reside; —**ya, wan fād yi; Adan bu fadiya,** he is at Aden (abides, dwells, resides).

fadi, *m.n.*, abiding.—**gi.**

fadisi (*see* **farob**), *v.tr.*, congeal milk, curdle; **'anaha fadisi,** curdle the milk; **'anihi fadisiyai,** I have congealed, curdled the milk.

fadiso, *v.i.*, sit, sit down, curdle; **fadista, wan fadisan; 'anihi wa fadisanayan**, the milk curdles.
fadi, *m.n.*, large herd of horses. —**gi**; **fadi ban lehyahai**, I have a large herd of horses.
fah, *m.n.*, consultation, secret word.—**hi**, —**ah**; **fah goniah bannu lehnahai, naga tag**, we have a secret word, a consultation, leave us, go away.
fajas, *v.tr.*, strike (for breaking or splitting), break, split. (This word is principally used in fighting with a sword and for the wound received with a club.
fajaso, *f.n.*, stab of a sword; **eg! fajasada igu da'dai**, look what a stab I have received.
fal, *v.tr.*, act, cause, do.
falnin, *m.* and *f.n.*, action, deed. —**ki** and —**ti**; **ninkas falnintisu wa wada huntahai**, the deeds of that man are all bad.
fāl, *v.t.*, enchant, make incantation.
fāl, *m.n.*, incantation, charm, spell.
wah fāl, *a.* and *m.n.*, incantator, magician, sorcerer; **nin wah fāla**, a sorcerer; **ninki wah fāli jirai**, the sorcerer; **nag wah fāsha**, a sorceress; **nagti wah fāli jirtai**, the sorceress; **anigu wah ban fāla**, I am a magician.
falag, *m.n.*, plaiting (of mats).— **gi**; **falko** (*plur.*).
falki, *v.tr.*, plait (mats).
falah, *m.n.*, pride.—**hi**.
falah, *m.n.*, a proud (man).—**hi**.
(**nin**) **falahah**, *a.*, proud (man).
fallad, *f.n.*, arrow.—**di**.
fallad kulul, *f.n.*, high fever; **ninkas fallad kulul ba haisa**, this man has high fever.
fallad hun, *f.n.*, very strong, violent fever; **ninkasi wa fallad hun yahai**, that man has a violent fever.
falladaha horahda, *f.n.*, sunbeams.
fallad, *num.*, one-eighth.
falti, *f.n.*, cowdung (when liquid, also that of camels when so).— **di**.
fan, *m.n.*, croup, horse's back.— —**ki**.
fān, *v i.*, boast.
fān, *m.n.*, boasting.—**ki**; **fānka iss ka da**, leave off your boasting.
fanah, *m.n.*, knuckle.—**hi**, —**yo**.
fanah, *m.n.*, gap in the front teeth.—**hi**.
fandal, *m.n.*, spoon.—**ki**.
fandal faroleh, *m.n.*, fork (*i.e.*, lit. spoon having fingers).
fānto, *f.n.*, dung (of horses, cows, &c.).
fanto, *f.n.*, small pox.
far, *f.n.*, finger, handwriting.—**ti**.
fárdoho, *f.n.*, middle finger.
faryar, *f.n.*, small finger.—**ti**.
farogorgor, *m.n.*, slap (with the back of the hand).—**ki**.
farabadan, *a.*, numerous.
far, *f.n.*, valley, dale.—**ti**; **labada burod far ba u dahaisa**, there is a valley (small) between the two hills.
farahal, *m.n.*, washing of the hands.—**ki**.

faraḥal, *v.tr.*, wash the hands; **i faraḥal,** wash my hands for me.
faraḥalo, *v.tr.*, wash your hands; **faraḥasha, wan faraḥashan.**
fār, *m.n.*, dry curd, cheese.—**ki.**
fārob, *v.i.*, curdle; **faroba, wan fārobi.**
faraḥ, or **farḥad,** *m.n.*, delight, joy.—**hi; faraḥha jannada,** heavenly delight.
farḥi, *v.i.*, delight, rejoice.
faraḥahaw, *v.att.*, be joyful.
faraḥan, *a.* and *m.n.*, joyful, pleasing, charming, joyfulness. —**ki.**
faraḥsan, *a.*, agreeable.
faraḫ, *m.n.*, fringe, edge.—**hi,**—**yo.**
faral, *m.n.*, standing up (during the Mussulman prayer).—**ki.**
faram, *v.tr.*, ballast; **farma, wan farmi.**
farmi, *m.n.*, ballast.—**gi.**
faras, *m.n.*, horse. — **ki, fardo** (*plur.*).
fardo, *m.n.*, general name for horse, and also herd of horses. —**hi.**
fardoleh, *f.n.*, cavalry.—**di.**
farasjir, *m.n.*, groom, horse-dealer. —**ki.**
farid, *a.* and *m.n.*, clever (boy), man (of wisdom), cleverness, prudence; **ninkasu, wilkasu wa farid,** this man, this boy is clever; **ninka faridkaah, ninki faridkaaha,** the man of wisdom.
farsamo, *f.n.*, ability, cleverness, skilfulness in all kinds of work; **ninkas farsamadisi wa la yabsanyahai,** the skilfulness of that man is wonderful.—**badan,** very clever; **nimankasi wa farsamo badanyihin,** these men are very clever.
farow, *m.n.*, zebra.—**gi.**
farur, *f.n.*, lip (of certain animals whose lips are like those of the hare).—**ti,** —**yo.**
farŭran, *a.*, hare-lipped; **ninka faruran, ninki farura,** the hare-lipped man.
fasaḥ, *m.n.*, leave, leisure, permission.—**hi,** —**yo.**
fasaḥ, *v.i.*, give leave, allow.
fasaḥ ḫado, *v.i.*, get leave; **badriga ka fasaḥ ḫata,** get permission from the father.
fatal, *m.n.*, bawd.—**ki.**
fatalad, *f.n.*, bawd (*fem.*).—**di.**
fatari, *m.n.*, marbles (to play with).—**gi; fatatir.**—**ti,** also is used.
fayido, *f.n.*, advantage, gain, profit; **fayido ma an helin,** I got no profit.
feđ, *v.tr.*, comb (used with the *pron.* **i, ku,** ...).
feđo, *v.r.*, comb yourself; **feđta, wan feđan; iss u** —, comb yourself; **adiga ma ku feđa?** shall I comb you? **maya, ha i feđin,** no, do not comb me.
feiđ, *f.n.*, rib.—**di.**
fēno and **fenfēno,** *v.tr.*, gnaw; **fēnta, wan fēnan; lafta ḫado o fēno,** or **fenfēno,** take that bone and gnaw it.
feyig, foyig, or **fojig,** *a.*, wary, prudent.

fojigla, *a.*, careless.
fojiglaan, *f.n.*, carelessness.—**ti.**
feyigan, *f.n.*, attention, prudence.
feyigow, or **nin fojiganahaw**, *v.i.*, beware.
fi', *m.n.* and *a.*, clever boy, man; **inankasi wa fi'**, that boy is clever; **fi'hasa abalki horai helai**, that clever boy gained the first prize.
fi'an, *a.*, clever, discreet, good, wise, acute, pointed; **nin fi'an**, a clever man; **niman fi'fi'an**, clever man; **ninki fi'ana**, the clever man; **nagti fi'anaid**, the clever woman; **kasi wa ḥalim fi'an**, that is a sharp pen.
fi'nan, *f.n.*, skill, cleverness.—**ti.**
fi'anaw, *v.att.*, be clever, good.
fidin, *m.n.*, man's comb (either a single stick or trident).—**ki.**
fidmer, *f.n.*, bat.—**ti.**
fidnad, or **fidmad**, *m.n.*, fire-brand.
nin fidmad wa leh, or **nin fidnad badan**, fire-brand (in speaking of a man inflaming the passions of others).
fiḥ, *v.tr.*, point, make acute, sweep; **ḥoriga fiḥ**, point that wood:
fiḥan, *a.v.*, pointed, acute, swept; **meshi fiḥnaid**, the swept place.
fiḥi, *m.n.*, schoolmaster.—**gi** (this word is especially used for persons teaching religion).
fiḥsi, or **fuḥsi**, *m.n.*, sip, sup.—**gi.**
fiḥso, *v.tr.*, sip, sup, suck up.
fikir, *m.n.*, thought.—**ki.**
fil, *m.n.* and *a.* (used for very old persons); **iss ku fil bannu naḥai**, we are of the same age.
filow, *v.imp.*, be sufficient; **wai ku filan**, it will be sufficient; **ku filantahai**, it is sufficient.
filan (with **ku**), *a.v.*, sufficient, enough; **igu filan, kugu filan**, sufficient for me, thee; **ku filan**, sufficient for him, her, them; **nagu filan**, sufficient for us; **idin ku filan**, sufficient for you.
filfil, *f.n.*, pepper.—**shi.**
fin, *f.n.*, small bird living on ants and insects.—**ti.**
fin, *m.n.*, pimple, stye.—**ki.**
findi'il, *m.n.*, remaining of food in the teeth.—**ki.**
findi'ilo, *v.r.*, pick off the remains of food ......, **findi'isha, wan findi'ishan.**
findi'ilasho, *f.n.*, act of picking out the remains of food from the teeth.
findi'ilgura or **ai**, *m.n.*, tooth-pick.
finjan, or **fujan**, *m.n.*, cup, bowl. —**ki.**
firash, *m.n.*, carpet.—**ki.**
firid, *m.n.*, scattering, spreading over, propagation.—**ki.**
firdi, *v.tr.*, scatter, propagate.—**ku** —, scatter on.
firdisan, firdadan, or **firdadsan**, *a.v.*, scattered.
fod, *f.n.*, forehead, brow, hole used as a window in the Somali hut.—**di**; **aḥalka foddisa lab**, shut the hole.
fof, *m.n.*, noise made by herds of cattle when on the move.—**ki.**
fofi, *v.tr.*, let go, or take the cattle to graze; **holihi ban so fofai,**

I let go, *or* took the cattle to graze.

fog, *a.*, distant, far; **mel fog**, a distant place; **meshi fogaid**, the far place; **ka —**, farther, more distant; **ka wada —**, the farthest.

fogai, *v.tr.*, remove, avert; **naga fogai**, remove, avert from us.

fogow, *v.i.*, be, *or* go far; **si —**, go farther.

fogan, *f.n.*, distance.—**ti.**

foji, *v.tr.*, remove, separate; **kala —**, open, disjoin, separate.

foḥ, *m.n.*, incense burnt in a room where people are assembled.—**hi.**

fol, *m.n.*, front tooth.—**ki.**

fol marodi, *m.n.*, ivory; **folka marodiga yan haista**, I have ivory.

foldaḫ, or **foldaḫasho**, *m.* and *f.n.*, washing of the face.—**hi.**

foldaḫ, *v.tr.*, wash the face; **i foldaḫ**, wash my face; **u foldaḫ**, wash his face.

foldaḫo, *v.r.*, wash your own face.

forar, or **foror**, *m.n.*, bowing, bending, stooping.—**ki**, **—yo.**

forari, or **forori**, *v.tr.*, bow, reverse, turn upside down.

forarso, or **fororso**, *v.i.*, stoop.

fori, *f.n.*, hiss, whistle.—**di.**

fori, *v.i.*, hiss, whistle; **—ya**, **wan —yi.**

fransis, *m.n.*, Frenchman.—**ki.**

frenji, *m.n.*, European (in general). —**gi.**

fūd, *m.n.*, broth (of meat, rice ...), soup.—**ki**; **fūdka 'ab**, drink the broth.

fūd, *v.tr.*, drink (coffee, soup), smoke (cigar, pipe).

fūd, *f.n.*, a liquid thing (or nearly liquid) become or made dry; **— 'araah**, clod of earth.

fudaid, *m.n.*, lightness, meanness, contempt.—**ki**, **—yo**; **ninkas fudaidkisi waḥba i la ma aha**, that man's contempt is nothing to me.

fudud, *a.*, light, not heavy, mean, contemptible, base.

fududai, *v.tr.*, make like, contemn, despise.

fudfudud, *a.*, agile, active.

fudfudaid, *m.n.*, agility, activity. —**ki.**

fuduḥ, or **furuḥ**, *m.n.*, dislocation.

fudul, *f.n.*, curiosity.—**sha.**

fuduli, *m.n.*, curious man.—**gi.**

fudul badan, or **fuduliah**, *a.*, curious.

ful, *v.i.*, mount, ride, embark.

fuli, *v.c.*, cause to mount, ride.

fulan, *m.n.*, riding.—**ki.**

fulan badan, *a.*, a good riding man.

fulai, or **fula**, *a.* and *m.n.*, coward, bashful.—**hi.**

fulanimo, *f.n.*, cowardice.

fulul, *m.n.*, dung (of cows, goats, sheep, camels).—**ki.**

fur, *v.tr.*, attest, open, develop, unload, divorce; **maḥad furta?** what do you attest? **wahan fura**, I attest, I certify; **u —**, attest, certify to; **ku —**, attest against.

furfur, *v.tr.*, unfold, unload.

furan, *a.v.*, open, free, divorced (only used for women).

furnin, *f.n.*, opening, divorce.—
ti.

fur, *m.n.*, small lid, cork (of a
bottle).—ki.

furai, *v.tr.*, shut, close, cork.

furad, *m.n.*, two skins sewn together and used for carrying
children.—ki, —yo; see dereb.

furuḥ, *m.n.*, small-pox.—hi.

furuḥdan, *m.n.*, pock-mark.—ki,
—yo.

furḥan, Coran.

furo, *v.tr.*, disarm; furta, wan
furan.

futo, *f.n.*, anus.

G.

ga, gi, gu, *def. art.*, the (*aff.*).

gan, gas, ga, go, *dem. a. prn.*,
this, that; yon, yonder (*aff.*).

gai, ga, gis, ged, gen, and gaya,
gin, god, *poss. a. prn.*, my, thy,
his, her, our, your, their (*aff.*).

ga'al, *m.n.*, relations (parents).—
ki; so ga'al na ma liḥid?
have you not any relations?

ga'an, *f.n.*, arm (the whole member), hand.—ti.

ga'an, *m.n.*, elephant's trunk.—ki.

ga'an badan, *a.*, benevolent;
ninkasi wa ga'an badan yahai, that man is benevolent.

ga'anbaded, *m.n.*, arm of the
sea.—ki.

ga'angeli, *v.i.*, interfere.

gāb, *m.n.*, shortness.— ki.

gāb, *v.i.*, be short, delay, be slow.

gābi, *v.tr.*, abridge, shorten, cause
a person to be late.

gāban, *a.*, short; ul gāban, a
short stick; ulo gāgāban, short
sticks.

gabnin, *f.n.*, shortness.—ti.

gabis, *m.n.*, abridgment.—ki.

gabaḍ, *f.n.*, girl, maid, daughter.
—di; gabḍo and hablo (*plur.*);
gabaḍḍi walalkai, my niece;
gabaḍḍi walalkis, his niece.

gabadano, *f.n.* and *a.*, cold (severe); gabadanadi kol hore
dad badan o Somaliah ku dintai, the severe cold killed many
Somal last year.

gabai, *m.n.*, poem, song, verse.—
gi.

gabai, *v.i.*, sing, versify.

gabaya, *m.n.*, poet, singer, min-
strel.—gi.

gabalajif, *f.n.*, last quarter of the
moon.—ti.

gaban, or sa'gabanah, *m.n.*, milch
cow.—ki.

gabati, *m.n.*, first present offered
to a father after he has con-
sented to give his daughter in
marriage.—gi.

gabbal, *m.n.*, light of the day.—
ki; — so baḥ, dawn; gabbalki so beḥ, the dawn; — da',
twilight; gabbalki de', the
twilight.

gabo, *v.r.*, cover yourself with the
shield.

gabasho, *f.n.*, covering with the
shield.

gabariel, *m.n.*, shield-maker.—ki;
see gashan samais.

E

gabow, *a.* and *m.n.*, ancient, old (man, thing).—**gi.**

gabow, *v.i.*, be, become old; **gabowba, wan gabowbi.**

gabowbai, *a.*, old; **kitabki gabowbai i ken**, bring me the old book.

gaboyai, *m.n.*, bow, arrows and quiver (as a whole).—**gi.**

gaboyaileh, *m.n.*, bow-shooter.—**hi.**

gad, *v.i.*, arrive, reach; **so —**, come to him; **í so gad**, come to me.

gadsi, *v.tr.*, reach, make reach, arrive; **i gadsi**, make me reach.

gadnin, *f.n.*, reaching.—**ti.**

gad, *m.n.*, beard.—**ki.**

gadleh, *a.*, bearded.

gadla, *a.*, beardless.

gad ma lehitai or **lahita**, *a.* and *m.n.*, beardless.

gad fed, *m.n.*, comb (for the beard; it is the same as **saḥaf**, woman's comb).—**ki.**

gad madowbai or **madowba**, *a.*, a man in his prime, or a black-bearded man.

gād, *v.tr.*, catch, assail, attack unexpectedly (from an ambush).

gādnin, *f.n.*, going on softly.

gadi, or **gari**, *m.n.*, carriage, cart.—**gi.**

gadiwaleh, *m.n.*, coachman.—**hi.**

faras gadi jidah, *m.n.*, coach-horse; **faraski gadigi jidi jirai**, the coach-horse.

gadid, *m.n.*, the two camels each Somal must have to go from one place to another.—**ki**; **wa gadidla yahai** or **gadid ma leh**, he has not even the two camels (*i.e.* he is a poor man).

gadod, *m.n.*, curdled milk.—**ki.**

gadod, *v.i.*, curdle; **'anihi wa gadodayan**, the milk curdles.

gadodi, *v.tr.*, curdle; **'anaha gadodi**, curdle the milk.

gafanai, *m.n.*, camel's tick.—**hi.**

gafur, *m.n.*, snout, muzzle, nose (for all animals).—**ki.**

gagab, *m.n.*, falling of a man knocked down by the blow of a club on his neck.—**ki.**

gagabi, *v.tr.*, thump, knock down.

gajo, *f.n.*, hunger.

gajaḥun, *f.n.*, a fit of hunger; **gajadi ḥumaid**, the hunger-fit.

gajo, *v.i.*, be hungry.

gajaisan, *a.*, hungry.

gajaisnaw, *v.att.*, become, remain hungry.

gal, *v.i.*, enter, penetrate; **gela, wan gelin**; **so —**, come in; **u so —**, enter for some purpose; **aḥalkisa u so gal**, enter into his house for ...; **so —**, surrender; **no so gal** or **gala** (*plur.*), surrender to us (you cannot fight any longer).

ma galo, *a.* and *v.imp.*, unfit, he is unfit, he cannot; **anigu ma galo**, I am unfit; **ninkasi dagalkas ma galo**, that man cannot go to that battle.

so gal, *m.n.*, entrance.—**ki.**

deḥ gal (with the *prn.* **na**), *v.i.*, negotiate, intercede; **ha na deḥ gasho**, let her negotiate; **wan idin deḥ geli**, I will intercede for you.

biya gal, or **biyo galen**, *m.n.*, pond, lake, place where there is always water.—**ki.**

gal, *m.n.*, sheath, scabbard, case. —**ki.**

gashan, *m.n.*, shield.—**ki.**

gashamo samais, *m.n.*, shield-maker.—**ki.**

gashan ḫad, *m.n.*, a young man able to wear a shield and to get married.—**ki.**

gashan, *f.n.*, a girl able to get married.

galmo, *f.n.*, coition.

geli, *v.tr.*, cause to enter, put in (this word is very often used in a bad sense, as **abbaha inta geli**; **i geli**; **wan ku gelinaya**); **so** —, admit, let enter.

so gelis or **gelin**, *m.n.*, admission. —**ki**; **wilka so gelis kisu wa ino huma**, the admission of that boy was bad for us.

nabad gal, *v.i.*, be in peace; —, **wan geli**; **ma nabad gashai?** were you in peace? **ha nabad galai**, yes, I was in peace; **nabad geliyo**, go, be in peace.

gasho, *v.*, clothe (yourself), to get into a coat, trousers. (This word cannot be used for Somali dresses, but only for European ones.)

gashi, *m.n.*, credit, debt.—**gi.**

ninka gashiga kugu leh, *m.n.*, creditor.

gashiyaisan, *a.* and *m.n.*, debtor; **ninki gashiyaisna**, the debtór.

gāl, *m.n.*, infidel.—**ki** (used for all men not Mussulmans).

gālo, *f.n.*, *plur. of* **gāl.** (This word is used by Mussulmans either for the generality of people not having their belief, or for only one country; as, **habashi o dami wa gālo**, all the Abyssinians are infidels.)

galab, *f.n.*, evening.—**ti**; **galbo** (*plur.*).

galbed, *m.n.*, west.—**ki.**

galabso, *v.tr.*, merit.

galabsi, *v.c.*, cause to merit.

galabildan, or **garabildan**, *m.n.*, phosphorescent gleams of the sea at night.—**ki.**

galaḥ, *m.n.*, breaking.—**hi.**

galaḥsi, *v.c.*, cause to break.

galas, *m.n.*, glass.—**ki**, —**yo.**

gálgalo, *v.i.*, wallow.

galgalásho, *f.n.*, wallowing.

gélgelin, *f.n.*, place trodden by camels or other animals, in which they wallow and form a hole.—**ti.**

gélgelin biyaha, *f.n.*, stagnant water (water remaining in low places after rain).

gálsho, *f.n.*, hole made to receive the remaining water, so that for some days more they may have clear water when the **balli** or **gelgelin biyaha** is finished (*see* **kalshin**).

ga'anta biyo badan ba i galai, *this sentence means* blister on the hand.

gali, *m.n.*, kitchen.—**gi.**

galib, or **dameira galib**, *m.n.*, gad-fly, horse-fly.—**ki.**

galof, *a.* and *f.n.*, barren (for all females).—**ti.**

galol, *m.n.*, fibrous tree producing red dye and very hard wood.—**ki.**

gallow, *m.n.*, bustard (small one). —**gi,** —**yo.**

gama', *v.i.*, sleep; **a, wan gam'i.**

gama', *m.n.*, sleep.—**hi**; **war! gama'hi bu i dilai,** sleep has killed (discouraged) him.

gama'san, *a.v.*, sleeping, sleepy; **nin gama'san ban so marai,** I passed by a sleeping man.

gami' waḥ, *a.*, sleepless, wakeful, in want of sleep; **ninkasi gami' wah,** he is a sleepless man; **ninka buka gami' wah-yai,** the sick man cannot sleep; **nin buka ma gam'o,** a sick man cannot sleep.

gambad, *m.n.*, three-legged stool. —**ki.**

gambo, *f.n.*, coiffure of Somali women (a black linen).

gambo, *f.n.*, anna (silver money).

gamello, *f.n.*, hair of the tail and mane (of horses, camels, ...).

gan, *v.tr.*, aim at (used when hunting with bow and arrows).

ganad, *m.n.*, man aiming at.—**ki.**

ganasho, *f.n.*, aiming.

gān, *a.* and *m.n.*, old, aged, being in age; **ninkasi gān bu joga,** that man is old; **ninkas gān-kisi wa inta,** the age of that man is such.—**ki.**

gana', *f.n.*, cost, price, value.—**di**; **faraskas gana'disu wa konton rubiadod,** the price of that horse is 50 rupees.

gana' adag, *a.*, dear, valuable; **hilibki an so ibiyai wa gana' adka,** the meat I bought is dear.

gana' jebi, *v.tr.*, cheapen.

gana' jaban, *a.*, cheap.

gana' jabnan, *f.n.*, abatement, lowering of the price.—**ti.**

gandafil, *f.n.*, callousness.—**shi.**

gandafilow, *v.i.*, be callous; **gandafiloba, wan gandafilobi.**

gando, *f.n.*, bell; **gandadi kanisada,** the bell of the church.

gango, *f.n.*, snuffling, nasal twang.

gangaleh, *m.n.*, man having a nasal twang, snuffler.—**hi.**

gar, *f.n.*, justice, sentence, claim, plaint, suit.—**ti.**

gar daro, *f.n.*, injustice; **gar daradasi 'adabta yai ku kahain** or **bai ku gein,** that injustice will lead you to hell; **war! gar darada iss ka da,** desist from that injustice.

gar daran, *a.*, unjust.

(nin) gar leh, *a.*, (a man) having gained a suit; **ninki garta laha,** the man who gained the suit.

(nin) gar la, *a.*, (a man) who lost the suit; **ninki garta laa,** the man who lost the suit.

gar eḥo, *f.n.*, wrong *or* partial sentence.

gar goi, *v.tr.*, judge, give judgment.

gar mari, *v.i.*, give the thing he claimed. (This word can only be used after the sentence.)

gar si, *v.i.*, give to him ... (said by someone to the man condemned in order to press him to give the thing claimed); **gar i si**, give the goods I claim.

gar shego, *v.i.*, complain; **wa nin gar sheganaya**, it is a man complaining.

gar u shego, *v.i.*, complain against; **gar ban u shegan**, I will complain against; **nin ban gar u sheganaya**, I am a man complaining against. (The interrogation of the judge will be, **maḥad shegatai?** what do you say, complain of? So for a suit only.)

garai, *v.tr.*, prove; **garai deh**, prove it then; **la garai**, it is proved.

ku garai, *v.i.*, prove against (refute the accusation); **wa ku gar**, it is proved against.

garan, *v.i.*, make a complaint to the governor; **garama, wan garami**; **i garan**, make the complaint for me; **la garan**, make known the complaint to; **serkalki i la garan**, lay the matter before the governor for me.

garansi, *v.c.*, cause the litigants to give *or* pay what they have been sentenced to pay.

garo, *v.i.*, comprehend, know, understand, guess; **maḥad ga'antaida ku hayo 'ar garo**, guess, look what I have in my hand; **maḥad ku garanaisa?** how do you know? **kala —**, *v.tr.*, distinguish.

garasho, *f.n.*, understanding.

(waḥ) an la garan, *a.*, unintelligible; **eraigas wa erai an la garan** or **an la karin**, that word is unintelligible; **ma garanaisa?** do you understand? **ma garatai?** did you understand? **garan mayo**, or **ma garan**, I do not understand.

garad, *m.n.*, good sense, wisdom, age of discretion.—**ki**.

garadleh, *a.*, sensible.

garadyelo, *v.i.*, have good sense, attain discretion, years of discretion.

garad, *m.n.*, chief, king.—**ki**, **— yo**; **ninkasi wa garad**, that man is a chief, a king.

gar, *m.n.*, knot by means of which Somali women tie their garments on the right shoulder, ropes with which the small boughs of the Somali huts are tied together.—**ki**.

garai (with the *prn.* **i, ku, u**), make the knot.

garaiso, *v.i.*, make the knot; **na! garaiso**, Oh! woman, girl! make your knot.

garab, *m.n.*, shoulder.—**ki**; **garbo** (*plur.*); **laf —**, shoulder-blade; **iss —**, shoulder to shoulder, by the side.

garba galai or **gala**, *m.n.*, coat, shirt.—**hi**; **garba galayashini gashada** or **ḥata**, take your shirts.

garbo, *m.n.*, part before the camel's hump, cataract (waterfall), range of mountains; **burta garboho-da**, the range of mountains.

gara dubleh, *m.n.*, small grey squirrel living in holes under ground.—**hi.**

gara', *m.n.*, illegitimate, bastard. —**hi**, —**yo.**

gara', *v.tr.*, beat repeatedly.

garanug, *f.n.*, *Gazella walleri.*—**ti.**

gargar, *v.tr.*, help; **war! ninka gargar**, Oh! help the man; **rag wa ki iss gargara**, men, help each other.

gargor, *m.n.*, stubble or thatch used for making a kind of thick mats or carpets with which Somali huts are covered. —**ki**, —**yo.**

garir, *m.n.*, shivering, ague.—**ki.**

garir, *v.i.*, shiver, tremble.

kaga garirsi or **gariri**, *v.c.*, cause him to shiver, tremble.

gashan, *see* **gal.**

gasirad, *f.n.*, island.—**di.**

gatanur, *v.tr.*, sow slowly.

gaulalo, *f.n.*, tree the bark of which produces red dye.

gebni, *m.n.*, gad-fly, horse-fly; *see* **galib.**

ged, *m.n.*, tree, thing.—**ki.**

ged'ad, *f.n.*, bush with a white flannel-like leaf.—**di.**

gedo, *m.n.*, pasture, grass, any kind of food for animals.—**hi.**

ged'anod, *m.n.*, small-pox.—**ki.**

geda goiyai, *m.n.*, astrologer, dealing with the devil.—**hi.**

geda goiyo, *f.n.*, astrology, the spell itself.

ged ḥajin, *m.n.*, nettle.—**ki.**

ged ma'an, *a.* and *m.n.*, sweet, good; sweet thing (as fruits, sugar, or liquors of which they do not know the name). —**ki.**

geddo, *f.n.*, horse's brisket.

gedi, *m.n.*, camel's journey (of one day).—**gi.**

gegi, gagi, or **gego**, *f.n.*, level ground.—**di.**

gei, *v.tr.*, take to, lead; **i gei**, take me to *or* take for me to such a place; **u** —, *v.tr.*, take *or* bring to him, her, them; **wan u, ku gein**, I will bring to him, to thee; **wad i, no keni**, thou wilt bring to me, to us; (**gei** is used to express a tendency from me to ..., and **ken** for a tendency from a place to me;) **iss u** —, *v.tr.*, add, join, assemble; **war** —, *v.tr.*, proclaim, publish, bring news.

gel, *m.* and *f.n.*, camel (**geli**, *plur.*; **gelal**, *plur.*, is rarely used); **war! gelal ma yimaden?** have the camels come? **ha, gelasheni yimadai**, yes, our camels have come.

gelka'abadis, *f.n.*, kind of lizard. —**ti.**

gelin, *m.n.*, time, division of the day.—**ki**; — **dambe**, afternoon; — **hore**, forenoon; — **dehe**, midnight.

gembissa, *f.n.*, house made of wood and mud or cow-dung.—**di.**

gemo, *m.n.*, horse's mane.—**hi.**

geniyo, *f.n.*, mare.

gerar, *m.n.*, poem which is sung

on horseback.—**ki, —yo** (other songs may also be so called).

gēri, *f.n.*, death (for men only). —**di.**

gerri, *m.n.*, giraffe.

ges, *f.n.*, direction, side.—**ti.**

gesta, *prp.*, beside.

ges, *m.n.*, horn, antler.—**ki**; —**as** or **geso** (*plur.*).

gesi, *a.* and *m.n.*, brave, bold, courageous, warrior, soldier.—**gi**; **nin gesiah**, a courageous man; **ninkasi wa gesi**, that man is a soldier.

gesinimo, *f.n.*, boldness, courage.

gibin or **gaban**, *m.n.*, age.—**ki** (this word is also used for children and small boys, and for small divisions of time); **wil gibinah** or **gabanah**, a small boy; **in gibinah** or **gabanah halka jog**, wait a little while here.

gidi, *num.*, all, whole (inflected with the *poss. prn.*).

girgir, or **jirjir**, *m.n.*, rim, edge, brim.—**ki, —yo**; **'elka girgirkisa ha dowan**, do not go near the edge of the well.

giringir, *f.n.*, wheel, hoop.—**ti.**

go, *v.i.*, be cut, die; **go**, he is dead.

goai, *a.* and *m.n.*, dead; **nin goai**, a dead man; **nag godai**, a dead woman; **dadki dinta**, the dead men; (a man exhausted by work will say: **wa goai**, I am dead).

go, *v.tr.*, cut (generally used for **goi**); **iss** —, cut yourself.

go, *m.n.*, half part (of a fruit), loin-cloth.—**hi.**

gogo, *v.tr.*, cut into many parts, pieces; **basashi i gogo**, cut the onion; **kala** — has the same meaning as **gogo.**

gogoso, *v.tr.*, cut into parts for you; **gogosta, wan gogosan**; **kala gosta**, *v.tr.*, partake with.

kala goi, or **kala go**, *v.tr.*, cut into parts (meat, paper ...), violate, open a girl before her marriage, deflower; **labada melod u kala goi**, cut into two parts; **ha kala goin**, do not violate, open...

gob, *m.n.*, respectable man.—**ki.** (This name is generally given to all Somals except to the **Tumals, Midgans**, and **Yibirs**, who are called **sab**).

gōb, *m.n.*, very large gnarled tree growing in river-beds to height of 50 to 70 feet, leafy, small thorns, and stringy bark. —**ki.**

gobiyahan, *m.n.*, a small red bird with white spots on the wings, a crest on the head, a kind of parrot.—**ki.**

gobo, *f.n.*, circle.

gobai, *v.tr.*, make a circle.

gobabi, *v.tr.*, make a circle, a round, mark the place for a hut.

gobabin, *f.n.*, circle, round made to mark the place for a tent and also its size.—**ti**; **ḥoraḥdu wa gobabin**, the sun is round (a circle).

golaban, *a.*, circular, round.
gobais, *m.n.*, wooden tube used for puffing at the fire, kind of clarionet, fife.—**ki**, —**yo.**
god, *m.n.*, hole (in the earth), pit, den, cavern, burrow.—**ki.**
sogod, *v.tr.*, bend; **ḫanso sogod**, bend a bow.
godgod, *m.n.*, undulation of the land.—**ki**, —**yo.**
godi, *m.n.*, border.—**gi.**
godir, *m.n.*, male koodoo antelope (*Strepsiceros kudu*).—**ki.**
gof, *m.n.*, dry well, dry bed of a river, orbit of the eye.—**ki.**
gog, *m.n.*, large jar made of camel's skin for ghee.—**ki.**
gogol, *f.n.*, bed (complete), bed or mat and blanket.—**shi.**
gogol, *v.tr.*, prepare the bed; **gogla**, **wan gogli.**
gōl, *f.n.*, lioness.—**shi.**
gol, *f.n.*, slope, declivity.—**shi.**
gol, *m.n.*, castrated camel.—**ki.**
gola, *m.n.*, stable for horses. —**hi.**
golab, *v.tr.*, sift.
golab, *m.n.*, sieve.—**ki**, —**yo.**
golli, or **dawa dulmadow**, *f.* and *m.n.*, jackal (with a black back).—**di**, —**ki.**
golli warabais, **golla waraba**, kind of fox.
golmud, *m.n.*, whey.—**ki.**
gomod, *f.n.*, camel's hoof.—**di.**
gomod, *m.n.*, chafe.—**ki.**
gomod, *v.i.*, chafe, be galled by riding.
gomodi, *v.tr.*, chafe, warm by rubbing.

goni, *a.* and *f.n.*, single, alone, solitary.
goniah (mel), *f.n.*, solitude, solitary place; **meshi gonidahaahaid**, the solitude; **mel goniah ban tegi**, I will go into solitude (solitary place).
gor, *f.n.*, time.—**ti**; **gor, gorah kalai** or **gor wanaksan kalai**, come in due time.
gorta, *cnj.*, when.
gortas, *ad.*, then (that time).
halkiyo gorti, *ad.*, since; **halkiyo gorti iss ugu ken dambaisai**, or **an ku arkai, arurti o đami iga wada đamatai**, since we met last time, *or* the last time I saw you, I have lost all my children.
gor badan, or **daur gor**, *ad.*, often.
gor dow, *ad.*, soon; **gor dow kalai**, come soon.
gor walba, or **gor iyo galab**, *ad.*, always, every time.
tan iyo gortan, or **had iyo intan**, *ad.*, till; **jog tan iyo gortan**, or **had iyo intan imanayo**, wait till I come.
laba, sadeḫ ... gor, *ad.*, twice, thrice.
gorma? *ad.*, when?
gorna and **gorra**, *ad.*, at no time.
gora' moḫor, *m.n.*, very large gnarled thorn tree, stringy bark, dark brown flat top.
gora yar, *m.n.*, small thorn tree, stringy bark, and long white thorns.

gorai, *m.n.*, male ostrich (*see* **halda**).—**gi**; **gorayo** (*plur.*).

goráyo, *f.n.*, ostrich (general name).

gorgor, *m.n.*, large black vulture (species of).—**ki**.

gorof, *m.n.*, skin pail used in digging wells, lid having the same form and use as a **hadub**. —**ki**, —**yo**.

gorof leged, *m.n.*, callousness of the camel's hind legs.

goror, *m.n.*, bleeding of the nose. —**ki**.

goror, *v.i.*, bleed from the nose.

gossorad, *f.n.*, bag of dates.—**di**.

gowra', *v.tr.*, behead, slaughter.

gowra', *m.n.*, beheading, slaughter.

gows, *m.n.*, molar tooth.—**ki**.

gu, *m.n.*, year, age, winter, rain during winter.—**gi**.

gub, *v.tr.*, burn, brand, scorch.

gubo, *v.i.*, burn, be consumed, jealous; **muhu u gubanaya**? what is he burning for? *or* why is he so angry *or* jealous?

guban, *a.v.*, burnt.

gūd, *ad.* and *m.n.*, above, over; **gudka tag**, go up, over.

gūdaha, *prp.*, in, within.

gūdihi, *m.n.*, the inside, interior; **ahalka gūdihisi ban ku jira**, I am inside the house.

gūd, *m.n.*, horse's mane.—**ki**.

gud, *v.i.*, travel during night, at night.

gudhur, *a.* and *m.n.*, dark, darkness (when the moon is not shining).—**ki**.

gud, *v.tr.*, circumcise.

gudan, *a.v.*, circumcised; **nin gudan**, a circumcised man; **gabad gudan**, a girl circumcised (sewn).

gudnin, *f.n.*, circumcision.—**ti**.

gudi, *f.n.*, speaker in a secret meeting, vice-chief, taking the place of the chief when he is absent.—**di**.

gud, *v.i.*, be weaned; **arurtasi gudai**, that child was weaned; **afarrta nagod naski ka gud**, these four women have their breasts dried up.

gudi, with **ka**, *v.tr.*, wean, sever; (a mother will say) **wan iss ka gudin**, I will wean, sever from me; **la** —, be weaned, severed.

gudimo, or **gudumo**, *f.n.*, axe (crooked one).

gudubsi, *v.i.*, look for a ford.

gudubsino, *f.n.*, ford.

gudud, *a.*, crimson, scarlet, red.

gududouni or **a**, *m.n.*, lynx.—**gi**.

guh, *v.i.*, buzz, whisper, growl.

gugubod, *m.n.*, medicinal tree.—**ki**, —**yo**.

gugulah, *m.n.*, cuckoo.—**hi**.

gula, *f.n.*, curiosity.—**di**.

gulawa, *m.n.*, a curious man.—**hi**.

gulai, *f.n.*, hoopoe.—**di** (common one).

gulf, *m.n.*, army.—**ki**, —**yo**.

guluf, *v.tr.*, attack; **gulfa**, **wan gulfi** (**gulfa** is generally used, for the singular **ku guluf** is used); **ka** —, get up and run away; **iss ka** —, defend yourself.

gumar, *m.n.*, abdomen.—**ki.**

gumbur, *f.n.*, rock, rising ground, mound.—**ti.**

gumburi, *m.n.*, wild ass.—**gi.**

gun (or **gūn** for the *fem.*), *a.*, advanced in age, old; **gun bad tahai**, you are old.

gumais, *f.n.*, man or woman advanced in age, contemptible person.—**ti.**

gumais, *f.n.*, kind of cuckoo.

gūn, *f.n.*, bottom, root (of a tree), abyss.—**ti.**

'el gūn fog, *f.n.*, abyss; **'elki gūnla foga** or **dera**, the abyss.

gūn ma leh, *a.*, bottomless.

gunud, *v.i.*, knot (make a knot); **gunta, wan gunti.**

guntin, *f.n.*, knot, bundle.—**ti.**

gunti, *m.n.*, knot made for tying the loin-cloth.

gunti (with the *prn.*), gird with the loin-cloth; **wan u guntin**, I will gird him with the loin-cloth; **sunka guntiga igu hegi**, fasten my loin-cloth with the belt.

gunus, *m.n.*, murmur, grumbling. —**ki**, —**yo.**

gunus, *v.i.*, murmur, grumble.

gūr, *v.i.*, depart, migrate, transport (with a caravan).

gūrnin, *m.n.*, departure.

gurguro, *v.i.*, walk on hands and feet, on all fours; **gurgurta.**

gurgurasho, *f.n.*, the walking on hands and feet.

gur, *v.tr.*, pick up, take away; **i gur**, pick up, take away for me; **so gur**, *v.tr.*, bring here (towards me); **kala** —, select.

guro and **gurguro**, *v.r.*, pick up for yourself; **gurata, wan guran**; **so** —, *v.tr.*, go and pick up.

mido la iss u gurai, a gathering of fruits.

gūr, *m.n.*, marriage, matrimony. —**ki.**

u gūri, *v.tr.*, give in marriage.

iss u guri, *v.tr.*, marry (them), it is said so to the khadi.

gurso, *v.i.*, marry; **gursada, wan gursan**; **wa nag la gursadai**, or **wa nag nin leh**, she is a married woman; **nagti ninka lahaid**, the married women; **ninki nagta laha**, the married man.

gura', *m.n.*, wrongness.—**hi.**

gura'an, *a.*, wrong.

gurai, *a.* and *m.n.*, left-handed.

gurgur, *m.n.*, room made in a Somali hut (*see* **ḫollad**).—**ki.**

gurgur, *m.n.*, general name for all Somali vessels.—**ki**; **aḫalka gurgurkisa ḫad** or **gur**, take all the vessels of the house.

gurḫan, *m.n.*, clamour, shout.—**ki.**

guri, *m.n.*, hut, house, large enclosure in which huts are built. —**gi.**

gus, *m.n.*, membrum virile.—**ki.**

guto, *f.n.*, assembly (of men), army.

gu'unso, *f.n.*, ball, any round body.

H, Ḥ.

ha, hi, hu, *art.m.*, the (*aff.*).

ha, han, has, ho, *dem.pro.*, this, that, yon, yonder (*aff.*).

hai, haiga, *poss.a.pr.*, my, mine. (*aff.*).

ha, haga, *poss.a.pr.*, thy, thine (*aff.*).

hi, his, hisa, *poss.a.pr.*, his (*aff.*).

hed, *poss.a.pr.*, her, hers (*aff.*).

haya, hayaga, } *poss.a.pr.*, our,
hen, hena, } ours.

hin, hina, *poss.a.pr.*, your, yours.

hod, hoda, *poss.a.pr.*, their, theirs.

hã, *ad.*, yes.

ha, *part.*, meaning "that"; *conj.* used in the Imperative mood 3rd pers. m. and f. sing. and plur., and in the 2nd pers. sing. and plur. negative form.

ha! *int.*, sigh when feeling pain.

ḥab, *v.tr.*, find your food in the bazaar, streets, anywhere. (Most Somals say so to their small boys; when they are about 5 or 6 years old, they leave them either in Aden, Berberah, or in any other town on the sea-coast and go to their own affairs in the jungle, and their sons grow up thieves and beggars.) 'orod suḥha ḥab, go in the bazaar and find your food.

ḥab, *m.n.*, the finding of food somewhere.—ki.

hábab, *m.n.*, loss of a person (in the way), missing the way.—ki.

hábab, *v.i.*, be lost, go astray; ilmihi habab, the child is lost.

hababi, *v.tr.*, lose (in the way), cause to go astray, bewilder.

habábsan, *a.v.*, lost, gone astray, bewildered; wilki hababsana, the lost boy.

habad, *f.n.*, syphilis.—di.

ḥabag, *f.n.*, gum, glue.—ti; habko (*plur.*).

habaghádi, *m.n.*, false myrrh tree.—gi.

ḥabal, *m.n.*, conception.—ki.

ḥabal, *f.n.*, grave, tomb.—shi; nin walba ḥabal ba haisata, there is a grave for every man.

ḥabalo, *m.n.*, cemetery.—hi.

ḥabal furai, *m.n.*, striped hyæna. —hi.

ḥabār, *v.tr.*, curse.

habãran, or habār ḥaba, *a.v.*, cursed.

habár, *f.n.*, old woman.—ti; habro (*plur.*).

habáryar, *f.n.*, maternal aunt. —ti.

ḥabas, *m.n.*, dust.—ki.

ḥabeib, *f.n.*, aphony, loss of voice. —ti.

habein, *m.n.*, night.—ki; habein bad, midnight.

habeinimo, or hurda habeinimo, *f.n.*, night watch.

habeno, *f.n.*, short sight, privation of sight at night.

habeno ḥaba, *a.v.*, short sighted; ninkasi habena ḥaba, that man is short sighted.

ḥabḥab, *m.n.*, water-melon.—ki, —yo.

hablo, *f.n.plur.*, young girls.
ḥabo, *f.n.*, combustible, fuel, firewood.
habsi, or **habis,** *m.n.*, prison, jail. —**gi,** —**ki.**
had, *f.n.*, time.—**di.**
haddaba, *ad.*, consequently, now, therefore; **haddaba iga tag,** therefore leave us.
haddeh, *conj.*, because.
hadder, or **haddada,** or **haddadatan,** *ad.*, just now, immediately.
hadma? *ad.*, when?
haddai, *ad.*, now; **haddai i da'dai,** now I understand.
hadow, *ad.*, after, after a time.
hadowto, *ad.*, after, afterwards.
hadba, *ind.pr.*, such a one.
had, *m.n.*, midday, noon.—**ki.**
hadimo, *f.n.*, meal (ordinarily taken before noon).
had, *m.n.*, shade, shadow.—**ki.**
hadai, *v.tr.*, shade.
hadaisan, *a.v.*, shady.
had, *v.i.*, remain, stand, stop.
hadnin, or **hadis,** *f.n.*, act of remaining.—**ti.**
had, *m.n.*, remainder, balance.—**ki**; **hadki hadai,** the remainder; **la'agti so hadai ma damā,** the balance of the money is not right; **waḥba ma hadin,** nothing remains.
ḥad, *v.tr.*, steal.
ḥadnin, *m.n.*, theft, stealing.—**ki.**
ḥād, *v.tr.*, sweep.
dul ḥād, *m.n.*, sweeper.—**ki.**
hād, *f.n.*, fowl, poultry, birds (gen. name).—**di.**
hād, *m.n.*, bird, fowl.—**ki.**
ḥādkaadag, *f.n.*, hawk.—**ti.**
hād, *f.n.*, down (of birds).—**di.**
hād, *v.i.*, fly, expire; **ka** —, fly from, expire (used for agony); **ka hādai,** he has expired; **ninki wa ka si hadaisa,** the man is expiring.
kaga hādi, *v.i.*, cause to fly, to expire.
hād, *m.n.*, coward (*see* **fulai**).—**ki.**
hadal, *m.n.*, speech, talk, discourse, deposition, dialogue, discussion.—**ki.**
hal, *m.n.*, word.—**hi,** —**al** (contraction of **hadal**); **sadeh, afarr hal ban lehyahai,** I have to tell you three or four words.
hadal, *v.i.*, speak, talk; **hadla, wan hadli;** **la** —, answer, communicate.
hadal ḥarson, *m.n.*, secret; **hadalki harsona,** the secret.
hadáto, *f.n.*, tickling.
ḥadátai, *v.tr.*, tickle.
ḥadei, *v.tr.*, bless (used of the blessing of God only); **Ilaḥhow i, na hadei,** O God bless me, us; **Ilaḥhi wa ku hadein;** God will bless you; **Ilaḥhi ku hadeiyai,** God has blessed you.
hadi, *conj.*, if, whether, although, either.
hadi ... iyo hadikaleh, *conj.*, whether or not; **hadi magaladu 'absilehdahai iyo hadikaleh ba anigu wa tegi,** whether the country be dangerous or not, I will go.

hadikaleh, *conj.*, otherwise; **arurtaidi yai, wanaksanada, hadikaleh se, jedalkan idin la di'i**, my children, be good, otherwise I will beat you with the stick.
hadiad, *f.n.*, gift, present.—**di.**
ḥadig, *m.n.*, rope, string, cable, *means also* artifice, cheating, fraud, relation.—**gi**; **ḥadko** (*plur.*); **ḥadig bannu iss ku leḥnahai**, we are relations; — **ḥolad**, ropes made of sinews; — **badan**, artful, cheating; **ninki ḥadigga badna**, the artful man.
hadil, *v.tr.*, copy.
hadilad, *f.n.*, copy.—**di.**
ḥadis, *m.n.*, reading or exposition of the Coran, homily.—**ki.**
hadub, *m.n.*, lid covering the jar called **dil**, and which is used to milk sheep and goats; when used for milking she-camels and cows, it is called **hadub gal.**
hadud, or **harud**, *m.n.*, jowari.—**ki.**
ḥafad, *f.n.*, place assigned in a town to each tribe, district, quarter.—**di**; **ḥaffada safarka**, the place (ward) of the caravans.
hafar, *v.tr.*, calumniate; **hafra, wan hafri.**
hafar, *m.n.*, calumny.—**ki.**
hafi, *v.tr.*, drown; **iss** —, drown yourself.
hofo, *v.i.*, be drowned.
hafin, or **hafis**, *f.n.*, drowning.—**ti**; **ninka hafintisi**, the drowning of the man.
ḥafis, *m.n.*, office (as custom-house ...).—**ki**, — **yo.**
dabalḥafis, *m.n.*, post-office.
ḥag, *m.n.*, place.—**gi.**
ḥaggan, *ad.*, here.
ḥagga, ḥaggas, *ad.*, there.
ḥagge? *ad.*, where? whence?
ḥaggi, *prp.*, to.
haga, *m.n.*, hot season.—**gi**, — **yo.**
hagaf, *m.n.*, gardener.—**ki**, —**yo.**
hagaf, *v.i.*, garden (to).
hagag, or **hagag u so'**, *v.i.*, be upright, simple, go straight; **halka ku hagag**, go straight there.
hagag, *m.n.*, uprightness, face, visage.
hagagsan, *a.v.*, upright, just, proper, convenient.
hagagsanaw, *v.attr.*, be upright, just.
hagaji, *v.i.*, make right, well, arrange, settle; **ḥisabta hagaji**, settle the accounts; **kala** —, arrange all well; **waḥ walba i kala hagaji**, put everything in order for me.
hagajiso, *v.i.*, arrange yourself.
hagajis, *m.n.*, arrangement.—**ki.**
hagal, *f.n.*, pit or back of the knee, the arm.—**shi.**
hagag, *f.n.*, stammering.—**ti.**
hagagleh (nin), stammering (man)
ḥago, *v.tr.*, scrape, scratch; **iss** —, scratch yourself.
ḥagḥago, *v.tr.*, scratch in fighting; **iss ḥagḥagta**, scratch

yourselves. (This verb with **iss** is used for women when fighting.)

hagog, *f.n.*, covering of the head and face with the large linen sheet used as a dress by Somalis, linen serving for covering.—**ti.**

u hagog, or **u hagoji**, *v.tr.*, cover the face.

hagogo, *v.i.*, cover your head and face.

haẖ, *a.*, just; **Ebbahai wa haẖ**, God is just.

haẖai, *m.n.*, salary, what is due to me; **haẖaiga i si**, give me my salary.

haẖlei, *m.n.*, disease of lambs (a kind of suffocation).—**hi.**

haẖleh, *m.n.*, *see* **dau'n.**

haẖuẖ, *m.n.*, polish (of a stone).—**hi.**

hakamad, *f.n.*, court-house.—**di**; *see* **mahakamad.**

hakmai or **ma**, *m.n.*, bridle, rein, bit (for horses).—**hi.**

ḥakim, *m.n.*, doctor.—**ki.**

ḥakin, *m.n.*, governor, chief or manager of any government office, judge, a good and truthful man.—**ki.**

hāko, *f.n.*, large spawl (as in the case of a catarrh), glaire.

haï, *m.n.*, white horse.—**gi.**

hai, *v.tr.*, have, keep, possess.

haiso, *v.tr.*, have, keep for yourself.

haisi, *m.n.*, act of keeping.—**gi.**

hais, *f.n.*, container, receptacle.—**ti.**

haibai, or **haïba**, *m.n.*, tree of which rosary beads are made.—**hi.**

ḥaïd, *f.n.*, tallow (grease obtained from the fat around the kidneys and intestines).—**di**; **isha haïd-deda**, the cornea of the eye; **indaha haïddoda**, the cornea of the eyes.

haid alolo, *f.n.*, epiploon (large one).—**di.**

haid mindi'iro, *f.n.*, epiploon (small one).

haïl, *m.n.*, menses.—**ki.**

hail, *m.n.*, kind of spices.—**ki.**

haïmboro, *f.n.*, wooden bracelet *or* bangle.

ḥaj, *m.n.*, pilgrimage.—**ki.**

ḥaji, *m.n.*, pilgrim.—**gi.**

ḥaji, *v.i.*, make a pilgrimage; **hajiya, wan hajiyi.**

ḥajin, *f.n.*, nettle-rash, itch, prickly heats.—**ti.**

hajo, *v.i.*, prove your right; **ha-joda, wan hajon**; **ila hajo**, prove against me.

hal, *root*, place.

hálkan, *ad.*, here.

hálka, halkas, *ad.*, there.

halko, *ad.*, down yonder, up yonder.

halkiyo berri or **berrito**, *ad.*, until to-morrow; **halkiyo berri halkan igu sug**, wait here for me until to-morrow.

hal! *int.*, used in Somali songs when on horseback; it is said also either by the hearers or by the singer himself after each sentence, in the same manner as the word **kow** which is used in conversation to give more force to the sentence.

hal, *m.n.*, amber (the two big pieces of amber fashionable Somals tie to their neck.—**ki**, —**al**.

hal, *f.n.*, she-camel.—**shi**.

hal, *v.tr.*, clean, wash.

ḥal, *m.n.*, asking (for what is due), petition, pardon, reparation, making amends for any fault committed, mischief done to anyone either by acts or in speaking; **wa run o waḥ ḥun ban kugu falaiyai, lakin iminka ḥal ban ka siyai**, it is true, I have done you an injury, but now I make you amends; or **iminka wa ka ḥal marinaya**, but now I am asking your pardon; — **weidiso**, ask pardon.

ardal ḥal, *m.n.*, petition of the people, country.—**ki**.

ḥalmari, *v.i.*, make reparation, *or* give what you owe; **so** —, go and make peace; **iss ḥalmariya o iss daya**, make peace and leave each other.

haladun, *m.n.*, adventure.—**ki**.

halai, *ad.*, last night.

ḣalal, *a.* and *f.n.*, lawful, lawfulness; **wa halal**, it is lawful.

halalai, *v.tr.*, make lawful, circumcise.

halbanleh, *m.n.*, artery. — **hi**; **halbanlihi wa goai**, the artery was cut.

halda, *m.n.*, male ostrich.—**gi**.

halgerri, *f.n.*—**di**; see **gerri**.

hallai, *v.tr.*, lose (especially used for animals and things).

hallan, *m.n.*, loss.—**gi**, —**yo**.

hallan, *v.i.*, be lost; **hallaba, wan hallabi; waḥhasi wa iga hallabi**, that thing will be lost for me.

hallow, *a.v.*, lost *or* is lost; **wilki hallow**, the lost boy, *or* the boy is lost; **gabbaḋdi hallowdai**, the girl is lost.

hallowsan, *a.v.*, lost, defiled, corrupted; **naftu wa hallowsantaḣai**, the soul is lost.

hallavi, *f.n.*, clean and nice dates (*see* **barni**).—**di**.

hallow, *m.n.*, flame, blaze.—**gi**; **hallowga 'adabed kulail o ḋan bu ugu saraiya**, the flames of hell surpass all heat.

halus, *m.n.*, womb, matrix.—**ki**.

halwad, *f.n.*, kind of Arabic cake, the size of a large and thick loaf.—**di**.

ḥamal, *m.n.*, coolie, burden-carrier, porter.—**ki**; **hamallin** (*plur.*).

hamil, *m.n.*, burden.—**ki**; **nagtīs ḥamilkedu wa 'ulusyahai**, the burden of that woman is heavy.

ḥamil ḥad, *m.n.*, strong camel able to carry heavy loads.—**ki**.

ḥamam, *m.n.*, pigeon.—**ki**.

ḣamansi, *m.n.*, gasp, gasping.—**gi**; **hamansi ugu dambaiyai**, agony, last gasp.

hamanso, *v.i.*, gasp.

ḥamar, *m.n.*, chestnut horse.—**ki**; **ḥamar i so ibi**, buy a chestnut horse for me.

ḥamar, *f.n.*, tamarind (tree and fruit).—**ti.**

ḥambar, *v.tr.*, carry (a child).

ḥambaro, *v.i.*, carry (thy child); **ḥambarta, wan ḥambaran.**

ḥambarsan, *f.n.*, carrying (of a child).—**ti.**

ḥambarsanaw, *v.att.*, be carrying (the child).

ḥambaro, *f.n.*, heavy fall.

ḥambarow, *v.i.*, fall heavily; **ḥambaroba, wan ḥambarobi.**

ḥambarai, *v.c.*, make him fall heavily.

hambo, *f.n.*, remainder of food, remnant, food left by the man for his wife.

hamum, or **hamun**, *f.n.*, distress caused by want of tobacco.—**ti.**

hamunsan (nin), *a.*, a man in want of tobacco; **ninki hamunsana**, the man in want of tobacco.

hamunsanaw, *v.att.*, be in want of tobacco.

ḥamumi, *m.n.*, kind of tobacco used in the pipe called **hobble-bobble.**—**gi.**

han, *f.n.*, jar made of bark (for water and milk).—**ti.**

ḥan, *f.n.*, calumny, backbiting, slander.—**ti.**

ḥano, *v.i.*, slander (for calumny and backbiting); **ḥanta, wan ḥanan.**

hanan, *m.n.*, bush.—**ki.**

handaraf, *m.n.*, gallop (full speed).—**ki.**

handaraf, *v.i.*, gallop.

hanfaf, *m.n.*, chip.—**ki.**

hanfi, *m.n.*, hot weather.—**gi**; **manta wa hanfi**, it is hot today.

hangarara, or **hangaraleh**, *m.n.*, scorpion.—**hi.**

hangol, *m.n.*, wooden hook *or* crooked wood used for making the fence round the **rer.**—**ki.**

hanib, *v.tr.*, blame, accuse, mark on the neck.

hanjad, *m.n.*, backbone.—**ki.**

hanjid, *f.n.*, cut *or* burning (made on the heads of sheep when sick).—**di.**

hanjo, *f.n.*, incense, wax, kind of gum.

ḥanshar, *m.n.*, chip, small piece of wood.—**ki.**

ḥantobo, *f.n.*, handful; **ḥantobo barisah**, a handful of rice.

ḥanun, *m.n.*, ache, ailment, pain.—**ki**, —**yo.**

ḥanun, *v.imp.*, feel pain, it pains; **wa i ḥanunaya**, it pains me.

ḥanuni, *v.c.*, cause suffering, make him feel pain, punish, chastise (by beating); **wa i ḥanuninaya** (*mas.*), **wa i ḥanuninaisa** (*fem.*), it pains me.

ḥanunso, *v.tr.*, suffer, feel a pain; **weli ma ḥanunsan**, he has never felt a pain.

ḥanunsan, *a.v.*, afflicted, suffering.

ḥanuji, *v.c.*, cause him pain, correct by striking; **ḥontaidu i hanujinaisa**, my sore causes me pain; **iss** —, cause yourself a pain, regret, repent.

ḥar, *m.n.*, excrement (of men especially, also of animals when no other name for it exists).—**ki.**

ḥar, *v.i.*, purgare ventrem; **ḥarai,** I have gone to the privy.

aḥal ḥarka, *m.n.*, privy.

ḥar gur, *m.n.*, sweeper, giobberti. —**ki.**

ḥar walwal, *m.n.*, beetle, scarabæus (the stinking black one). —**ki.**

hārad, *m.n.*, thirst.—**ki.**

hārad, *v.i.*, be thirsty.

hāradsan, *a.*, thirsty.

hāradsanaw, *v.att.*, be, remain thirsty.

ḥarad, *v.tr.*, carve, engrave; **ḥarda, wan hardi.**

ḥarad, *m.n.*, carving, engraving. —**ki.**

hardan, *a.v.*, carved, engraved.

ḥaraf, *m.n.*, letter of the alphabet.—**ki,** —**yo**; **ḥuruf, ḥurufti** (*plur. Ar.*); **ḥuruf ellija,** alphabet.

harag, *m.n.*, skin, leather (hide of goats and sheep).—**gi**; **hargo** (*plur.* **haragga**) **ka bi'hi,** skin; **haraggan ka bi'hin,** I will skin.

haraidis, *m.n.*, howl.—**ki.**

haraidi, *v.imp.*, howl; **gollidu wa haraidinaisa,** the jackal howls.

ḥaran, *a.* and *f.n.*, unlawful, unjust; **wa ḥaran,** it is unlawful, unjust.

haranta ka go, *v.tr.*, circumcise.

ḥarámi, *m.n.*, rogue, cheat.—**gi**; **ḥarami waiyai,** it is a rogue.

(**nin**) **ḥaramiah,** *a.*, cheating man; **ninki ḥaramigaaha,** the cheating man.

ḥarar, *m.n.*, mat (made with grass and stubble, used for covering the Somali hut, and to put on camels instead of saddles).—**ki.**

ḥarar, *f.n.*, precipice, a place out of reach.—**ti.**

ḥararad, *f.n.*, prickly-heat.—**di.**

ḥarash, *m.n.*, public sale, auction. —**ki.**

harati, *f.n.*, kick (of a camel).—**di.**

ḥarbi, *m.n.*, battle, fight.—**gi.**

ḥarbi, *v.i.*, fight.

ḥardad, *m.n.*, palate (also used for animals).—**ki,** —**yo.**

hardaf, *v.i.*, canter, gallop.

hardafi, *v.c.*, make (the horse) gallop.

hardaf, *m.n.*, galloping, gallop.—**ki,** —**yo**; **faraska hardafkisa,** the gallop of the horse.

hared, *f.n.*, rain-water.—**di**; **baldiga hared ino ka buḥi,** fill the ewer (bucket) with rain-water.

harer, *f.n.*, side.—**ti.**

harero (*plur. of* **harer**), around, on all sides; **Berbera harereheda yan so marai,** I have gone all around Berberah.

hariḥ, *f.n.*, scribble, scribbling.—**ti.**

hariḥ, or **harhariḥ,** *v.i.*, scribble.

ḥarir, *f.n.*, silk.—**ti.**

ḥaro, *v.r.*, mark yourself with the birth sign; **harta, wan haran.** (When a woman has given birth to a child, the seventh day after, coals are ground and mixed with water. This mixture is given to the mother, who traces on her forehead a sign in form of a cross, commencing with the horizontal line; the vertical one is afterwards traced down to the extremity of the nose. Then all say, **wai haratai,** she gave (has given) birth.)

harasho, *f.n.*, birth-sign.—**di**; **Faduman harashadi ku arkai,** I have seen the birth-sign of Faduma.

ḥarrago, *v.r.*, dress yourself with your nicest clothes, array.

ḥarrago, *f.n.*, fashion, fashionable manner.—**di**; **harragadaya-du wa 'ainka,** it is our fashion.

harud (*see* **hadud**), jowari.

harun, or **harei,** or **har,** *n.*, white ant.—**ti,** —**hi,** —**ki.**

ḥarakad, *m.n.*, accent, sign.—**ki.**

ḥas, *m.n.*, family.—**ki.**

ḥasaw, *v.i.*, converse; **ayan** (for **ayo ban**) **la hasawa?** with whom must I converse? **wa hasawaina,** we converse.

hasáwi, *v.c.*, make him converse.

hasawai or **wa,** *m.n.*, conversation. —**hi.**

ḥasau, *f.n.*, iron wire.—**di.**

ḥashin, *f.n.*, skin bag (of two hides sewn together) used for putting all kinds of things into. —**ti.**

hashin, *a.* and *f.n.*, incapable of fighting.—**ti**; **nin, ḥof hashinah,** a man, a person incapable of fighting.

hashish, *m.n.*, grass.—**ki.**

ḥasid, *v.i.*, feel, be jealous, rebel.

ḥasid, *a.* and *m.n.*, disobedient, rebel, envious jealous man, slanderous tongue.—**ki,** —**yo**; **wilki ḥasidkaaha,** the disobedient boy.

ḥadsidnimo, *f.n.*, envy, jealousy. —**di.**

hātan, *ad.*, now, now-a-days.

hatati, *m.n.*, ambush, ambuscade. —**gi.**

ku hatati, *v.tr.*, place in ambush; **ku hatatiya, wan ku hatatiyi, iss** —, place yourself in ambush.

hau, *f.n.*, noise produced in the body either by wind, indigestion, vomiting ...—**di.**

haud, *m.n.*, impenetrability (of a forest).—**ki**; **meshasi wa haud,** that place is impenetrable.

haud, *v.tr.*, close, shut, fill; **dalosha haud,** shut, fill the hole.

haud, *m.n.*, stick, rod.

ḥaudi, *v.tr.*, beat with a stick, flog.

haul, *f.n.*, affair, business, labour, occupation, work, employment. —**shi.**

(**nin**) **haulaisan,** *a.v.*, busy man; **ninki haulaisna,** the busy man; **wa nin haushodai,** he is a busy man.

(**nin**) **haulla,** *a.*, unemployed man; **ninki haushalaa,** the unemployed man.

(**nin**) **haulbadan,** *a.*, a man in a

hurry; **ninki hausha badna,** the man in a hurry.

(nin) hauled, *a.*, an energetic, active, diligent man; **ninki hauled,** the ...

haulyar, *a.*, easy work; **haushi yaraid,** the easy work.

haulyari, *f.n.*, ease, comfort.—**di**; — **ku jir,** *v.i.*, be at ease; **haulyari ban ku jira,** I am at my ease.

haul ḥabo, *v.i.*, serve, work; **haushada ḥabo,** do, execute the work; **haushada ḥabso,** occupy yourself.

hausho, *v.i.*, try, endeavour, make an effort, work; **inad wanaksanato u hausho** or **u haushod,** endeavour to be good.

haurarsan! *int.*, well! all right!

ḥautan, *m.n.*, gush, gushing.—**ki.**

ḥautan, *v.i.*, gush; **diggu wa ḥautamaya,** the blood gushes.

ka ḥautami, *v.c.*, cause to gush.

ḥawaj, *m.n.*, curry-stuff.—**ki**; **ḥawajki me?** where is the curry-stuff?

hawal, *f.n.*, a calm at sea.—**shi.**

ḥawaldar, *m.n.*, sergeant.—**ki.**

ḥawo, *f.n.*, air (the fluid in which we move and breathe).

hayaiya! hayaiya! *int.* (A man on horseback exclaims thus to his companions, who answer in the same manner, **hai! hai! jawis!** When they are near the enemies, in front of them, they cry altogether, **jawis garo ho! ho! hobo! hobo! oh!** — **oh! oh! jawaisa!**

haye! *int.*, yes, all is right!

ḥeb, *f.n.*, shore, sea-shore, coast.—**ti**; **hebta seḥo,** sleep ashore.

heb, *f.n.*, a bad word.—**ti.**

hebel, *n.* and *a.*, certain, such, such a one; **hebel ba yimi,** a certain man has come; **rer hebel,** a certain village; **rerki hebel** or **hebelaha la gub,** such a village has been burnt; **ninki hebel** or **hebelaha me?** where is such a one (man)? **nagti hebelayo medai?** where is such a woman? **ḥaski hebel libaḥ ba unai,** a lion devoured such a family.

ḥedo, *f.n.*, wooden platter, dish; — **sibidi,** *f.n.*, funnel-shaped wooden bowl; — **samai,** *v.tr.*, make wooden plates; — **samais,** *m.* and *f.n.*, wooden plate maker.—**ki,** —**ti.**

ḥedid, or **ḥidid,** *m.n.*, pulse-vein, kindred, kinsman.—**ki,** —**yo,** —**o.**

la ḥedid, *v.i.*, become kin with; **ḥolada la ḥedid,** become kinsman with this tribe; **wainu ḥedidnai,** we are kindred.

ḥedig, or **ḥidig,** *f.n.*, star, hedgehog (so called by the Somal because they believe it to be a star fallen from heaven).—**ti**; — **aroryo,** morning star; — **wa beri,** morning star; — **jaḥha,** pole star.

urur ḥedigaah, *m.n.*, constellation; **ururki ḥedigaaha,** the constellation.

ḥedigiyai, *m.n.*, astronomer.—**hi.**

ḥedin ḥeto, *f.n.*, a whitish-grey bird resembling the lark.

ḥekmad, *f.n.*, Providence.—**di**; **Ebbahai ḥekmaddisa,** the providence of God.

heji, *v.tr.*, hold fast, take strongly.

hel, *v.tr.*, acquire, attain, gain, find, get, obtain.

helhel, *v.i.* (poor parents having nothing to give their child to eat send it out, saying, **helhel,** which means) may God make you find something to eat.

dama' hel, *v.i.*, succeed (in getting ...), to be successful; **isaga dama' helai,** he has succeeded *or* he has been successful.

ka hel, *v.tr.*, conquer, gain.

u hel, *v.tr.*, procure for; **wan u helai,** I procured (found) a good punishment for him; **sorta manta abbaha u hel,** to-day procure the food for your father.

laga hel, *v.pass.*, is deprived of, he has lost, is not successful; **ninki holihi laga hel,** the man is deprived of his property; **nimanka laga helai,** this man was not successful.

helin, *m.n.*, gain.—**ki**; **ninkas helinkisi,** the gain of that man.

heli, or **so heli,** *v.tr.*, return, restore, give back.

helis, or **helin,** *m.n.*, restitution. —**ki**, —**ti.**

ḥelad, *f.n.*, cheating, pretence, excuse.—**di**; **ninka dukankalihi ḥelad bu yaḥan,** the shopkeeper is a cheat.

(nin) ḥeladleh, *a.*, cheated, a man who has always some excuse to give, a swindler; **ninki ḥeladdalaha,** the cheat, the swindler.

ḥéli, *m.n.*, weather.—**gi.**

hensai, *m.n.*, harness.—**hi.**

hensarar, *m.n.*, forked stake thrust in the ground and forming the basis for a Somali hut. —**ki.**

ḥer, *v.i.*, go round, around.

ḥerai, *v.tr.*, surround.

ḥersan, *a.v.*, circular, round.

ḥer, *m.n.*, dyke, dam (to stop water).—**ki.**

ḥero, *f.n.*, enclosure (zereba *or* zariba); this enclosure is made either of trees or of big branches close together, so as to make a fence protecting the tent built within its circuit, and the stable for cattle and sheep.

ḥero ḥodahleh, *f.n.*, enclosure made of thorny trees, zereba of thorns.

ḥero od, *v.tr.*, make an enclosure; **ḥeran odi,** I will make an enclosure.

maḥal ḥerrais, *f.n.*, evening star, time for taking the young animals into the enclosure.

ḥer, *m.n.*, transgression of Somali customs or laws, a case of justice on account of customs or laws. —**ki**; **labada sultan ḥerkodi ya dagalkasi ka daḥai,** the transgression of customs caused that war between the two sultans.

herab, *m.n.*, keel (of a ship).—**ki.**
herar, *m.n.*, crown of hair left on the heads of small girls.—**ki.**
heriyo, *f.n.*, camel's pack-saddle. (Somals put upon the wooden frame of the saddle **kebed, harar,** and **aus salol,** and all those things form the pack-saddle.)
herrib, *f.n.*, wisdom.—**ti.**
(**nin**) **herribleh,** *a.*, wise man; **ninki herribtalaha,** the wise man.
herro, or **herriyo,** *f.n.*, lines of the palm of the hand.
hes, *v.i.*, sing (also used for birds).
hes, *f.n.*, singing, song, hymn, music.—**ti; hesta somalida,** the Somali singing.
heshi, *v.i.*, make peace, be reconciled; **ku —,** agree upon.
heshis, *m.n.*, peace, agreement, accord.—**ki.**
heshisi, *v.tr.*, reconcile; **labadas jal shalai ban heshisiyai,** yesterday I reconciled these two friends; **so —,** arbitrate, settle.
hid (pronounced nearly as **hed**), *v.tr.*, bind, fasten, shut, tie, confine; **iss ku —,** join (two things with thread, rope, wire).
iss ku hidhid, *v.tr.intens.*, tie the camels one to the tail of the other; **eg aurtas iss ku hidhidan,** look, these camels tied one to the tail of the other.
(**nin**) **hidan,** *a.* and *n.*, bound, prisoner; **ninki hidna,** the prisoner.
hidnan, *f.n.*, imprisonment.—**ti.**
hido, *v.r.*, tie (yourself), do the work (yourself); **hidta, wan hidan.**
hidmo, *f.n.*, bale, bundle, parcel; — **habaha,** faggot.
hidmo, *m.n.*, long intestine.—**hi**; — **abahha,** a lean animal.
hidig (*see* **hedig**), *f.n.*, star.—**ti.**
hig, *v.i.*, be near *or* next to, related to; **aurka hig,** be next to the camel; **holadasan higa,** I am related to that family; **holadasanu iss higna,** that family and I are related.
higal, *m.n.*, relation, caste.—**ki.**
higgo, *f.n.*, hiccough.
higmad, *f.n.*, device, stratagem.—**di.**
hijad, *f.n.*, veil of Arab women for hiding their faces.—**di.**
hil, *m.n.*, help, assistance.—**ki** (this word is especially used in the case of a battle).
hili, *v.tr.*, aid, assist, help, relieve, support.
hiliya, *m.n.*, assistant.—**hi; hiliyiheni bu aha,** he was our assistant.
hilhad, *f.n.*, earring, curb (of horses).—**di.**
hil, *m.n.*, shame, shyness, modesty, abuse.—**ki; wa gabad hil badan,** she is a very modest girl.
hil, *v.tr.*, abuse, make ashamed; **wah hilai,** an abusive thing.
hisho, *v.i.*, be modest, shy, ashamed; **ka —,** be ashamed of, dare not.
hishod, *m.n.*, shame.—**ki.**

ḥishodla, *a.*, shameless, immodest; **ninki ḥishodkalaa,** the shameless man.
ḥishodleh, *a.*, modest.
ḣilā, *m.n.*, lightning.—**hi,** —**yo.**
hilā, *v.imp.*, it lightens; *or* **'erku wa hilai.**
hilib, *m.n.*, flesh, meat.—**ki**; **hilbo** (*plur.*); — **idad,** mutton; **hilibki idaha,** the mutton; — **riad,** goat's flesh; **hilibki riaha,** the goat's flesh; — **gel,** camel's flesh; **hilibka gela,** the camel's flesh; — **karsan,** boiled meat; **hilibki karsana,** the boiled meat; — **shilan,** roast meat (in a pan or kettle); **hilibki shilla,** the roast meat; — **duban,** large pieces of meat roasted on the fire itself; **hilibki dubna,** the roasted meat.
hilibdalḥai, *m.n.*, uvula; **hilibdalḥihi,** the uvula.
hilin, *m.n.*, road, trace, way.—**ki.**
ḣin, *v.imp.*, hums, buzzes.
ḣindi, *m.n.*, Indian (native of India).—**gi**; **ard el** —, India (country).
hindis, *v.tr.*, invent, find out.
hindisad, *f.n.*, invention.—**di.**
hindis, *v.i.*, sneeze.
ḥinin, *f.n.*, testicle.—**ti,** —**yo.**
ḣinji, *v.tr.*, lift, lift up.
ḣinrag, *m.n.*, shortness of breath, sigh, puffing.—**gi.**
hinrag, *v.i.*, puff, pant, sigh.
(**u**) **ḥir,** *v.tr.*, shave; **lo ḥir,** it is shaved.
ḥiro, *v.r.*, shave yourself; **hirta, wan ḥiran.**
ḥiran, *a.v.*, shaved; **hiranyahai,** it is shaved.
ḥirib, *f.n.*, eyelash, eyelid, the inside of the eyelid.—**ti**; — **sarai** — **hosai,** eyelids.
ḥirid, *m.n.*, gum (mouth).—**ki.**
ḥirsi, *f.n.*, charm (kind of amulet).—**di.**
ḥisab, *f.n.*, account, arithmetic, judgment of God.—**ti**; **Ilaḥ ḥisabtisa,** the judgment of God.
ḥisab, *v.tr.*, judge (used for God only); **Ilah ba ḥisabi,** God will judge him.
ḥisabi, *v.tr.*, count, account.
ḥisabso, *v.c.*, count yourself.
ḣisti, *m.n.*, mischievous trick.—**gi.**
u ḣisti, *v.i.*, trick, defraud.
ho, (kind of *int.* meaning) take, lay hold of (stretching out the hand); **war! ho!** take; **wan hoi,** I will take (for all the other tenses the verb **ḥad** is ordinarily used).
hod, *v.i.*, fall off, come off; **timihi iga so hodai,** all my hair came off.
ḥodi, *v.i.*, prepare the skin (take off the hair); **haraggi dogorti ka ḥodiyai,** the skin is stripped of its fleece.
hod gudub, *f.n.*, half of the Somali dress.—**ti.**
hodan, *m.n.*, rich man.—**ki.**
hof, *f.n.*, junction of the ribs.—**ti.**

hog, *m.n.*, hole.—**gi.**

hog, *v.tr.*, extort, get by force.

ḥog, *m.n.*, shin (tibia), strength, might, force, violence.—**gi.**

ḥog badan, or **ḥog wein**, *a.*, strong (in fighting and working).

(**u**) **ḥogso**, *v.tr.*, earn, work for your living; **naftada u ḥogso**, earn your living; **naftaidan u ḥogsadai, adigu na naftada u ḥogso**, I have worked for my living, you also earn yours.

hoji, *v.i.*, labour, work.

ḥoga, *num.*, few, little (used with **wa** or **o**); **war! oḥogagaiga i da**, oh! leave to me my little, the little I have; **wa ḥoga biyaah**, a little water.

hogan, *m.n.*, halter (of a camel). —**ki.**

hohob, *f.n.*, jujube tree and fruit (*see* **gob**).—**ti.**

hoḫ, *v.tr.*, scratch, abrade.

ḥoḫad, *f.n.*, spy-glass, telescope. —**di.**

hoi! ho! hoa! *int.*, halloo! hollo! ho! (used alone with **war**, man, and **na**, woman); **war! war hoi!** hollo, man! **na! na hoi!** hollo, woman!

hoio, *v.i.*, halt (at night), pass the night in a place, go home (this last meaning is only used when speaking to small children); **galabta Wager bainu u hoian**, we will halt at Wager this night.

holo, *m.n.pl.*, property, riches (in a general sense), affluence, wealth; — **nol**, living property, cattle; — **badan**, rich man.

hola ba la ima yaḫan, *expression meaning* everybody knows that I have nothing.

holob, *f.n.*, scar in the skull, pellicles.—**ti**, —**yo.**

hololiya, or **hololawa**, *f.n.*, cradle. —**di.**

homādai, *m.n.*, vulture (species of).

hor, *f.n.*, *ad.*, *prp.*, beginning, front, opposite, in front of, before, first (inflected with the *pers.prn.*); **duniyada hortedi**, the beginning of the world; **arur o ɗan nolanta hortedi oidai**, or **wa oida**, at the beginning of life every child cries; **hortaidu jogai**, he was in front of me; **aḫalka aḫalkena ka so hor jeda**, the house which stands in front of ours, *or* which is opposite to ours; **war!. horta kan an ḫabto**, oh! let me do this first; **halkas tol horta**, sew that first.

hor u so'o, *v.i.*, continue, go on; **hor u so'oda, horan u so'on.**

hórai, *v.i.*, go first, advance; **ka** —, go before him; **iga, naga, ka horai**, go before me, us, him, them; **u** —, be first; **nin** —, a superior.

horaisi, *v.tr.*, put before.

hórai, or **hore**, *a.*, first, before, previous, forward; **ki hore**, the first; **marki**—, *ad.*, ago; **kolki**, or **beri**, *ad.*, once, formerly; **sanaddi**, or **kal** —, last year.

ḥor, *v.tr.*, throw; **ku —,** throw at.

ḥor, *m.n.*, camel's milk (when very fresh).—**ki.**

ḥor, *m.n.*, kind of badger (honey-eater), has a white tuft at the end of its tail.—**ki.**

ḥor, *m.n.*, jackal (with a white tail).—**ki.** (Somals call **ḥor** a number of animals and even birds, when they have either white tails or white spots on them.)

ḥor, *m.n.*, calao having a crescent-shaped crest.—**ki.**

horgumo, *f.n.*, panther.

horor, *f.n.*, hyæna, glutton (spotted hyæna, *see* **waraba**).

hōs, *m.n.*, shadow, shade.—**ki.**

hos, *f.n.*, *ad.* and *prp.*, below, down, under.—**ti**; **hosta tag,** go down; **misku hos u yal,** it is under the table; **— u ḥabo,** or **— u hai,** hold lower; **— u hadal,** whisper, do not cry; **hos ban u la hadlai,** I whispered to him.

hosai, *v.i.*, go low, be under, be last; **berigi hore wilashan u hosaiyai, hātan se ana u horaiya,** or **saraiya,** formerly I was the last of the boys, but now I am the first; **ba-hal —,** reptile; **nin —,** an inferior.

hosaisi, *v.tr.*, put under, let down, abase, abate; **isaga u hosaisi,** let him down.

hosaisis, *m.n.*, abasement, humiliation.—**ki.**

hosis, *m.n.*, eclipse of the sun, sun obscured by clouds.—**ki.**

hoyo, *f.n.*, mother; **ber —,** the heart of a mother; **ja'ail —,** maternal love.

hoyanimo, *f.n.*, maternity.

hūb, *m.n.*, arm, weapon (general name).—**ki.**

hūbḥad, *m.n.*, armed man, warrior. —**ki,** —**yo.**

hūbka ka ḥad, *v.tr.*, disarm.

(nin) hūbleh, *a.*, armed (man).

(nin) hūbla, *a.*, unarmed, disarmed (man).

hūbkisa u damai, *v.tr.*, arm.

hub, *v.i.*, be certain; **ma la huba?** is it certain? **wa la huba,** it is certain.

húbso, *v.tr.*, consider, examine, investigate, meditate.

húbsad, *m.n.*, meditation, investigation.—**ki.**

húbsan, *a.v.*, meditating.

ḥub, *m.n.*, film of the brain.—**ki.**

ḥubin, *f.n.*, knuckle, joint, piece. —**ti.**

hudai, or **huda,** *a.* and *n.*, cancerous, cancer, scrofula, king's evil; **ḥontasi wa hudai,** that sore is cancerous.

hudel, *m.n.*, hotel, inn.—**ki.**

ḥudud, *f.n.*, hind part of the arm. —**di.**

ḥudun, or **ḥudin,** *f.n.*, umbilical cord.—**ti.**

huf, *v.tr.*, winnow, blow.

ḥuffi, *v.tr.*, tempt, deceive; **la —,** be tempted; **wa la i ḥuffi,** I shall be tempted.

ḥuffin, *f.n.*, temptation.—**ti.**

hugmi Allaḥ hadai noḥoto, *expression meaning* if it is the will of God, *or* God willing.
huko, *f.n.*, grease of the camel's hump.
ḥukum, *m.n.*, judgment, government, authority.—**ki.**
ḥukum, *v.tr.*, administer, govern, judge, condemn, order, command; **la iss ka ḥukumai,** forbidden; **waḥas wa la iss ka ḥukumai.**
ḥujad, *f.n.*, crime, guilt, case of justice.—**di.**
ḥujad leh, *a.*, guilty.
ḥujadla, *a.*, not guilty, innocent.
ḥul, *v.tr.*, go round, through; **so** —, go through and come back; **si** —, go through when I am off.
ḥulad, or **ḥulod,** *m.n.*, tree felled by means of fire.—**ki.**
ḥulo, and **ka ḥulo,** *v.tr.*, choose from.
ḥumbo, *f.n.*, foam, froth, bubbles.
kaga ḥumbaisi, *v.c.*, make foam.
ḥun, *a.*, bad, ugly, wicked; **nin ḥun, niman ḥunḥun,** bad man, men; **ninki ḥuma,** the bad man; **nagti ḥumaid,** the bad woman.
ka ḥun, *a.*, worse (comparative of **ḥun**).
ka wada, or **ugu wada ḥun,** *a.*, worst (superlative of **ḥun**).
ḥumai, *v.tr.*, make badly (what you have to do); **si** —, aggravate; **u** —, *v.tr.*, trouble, afflict, hurt him; **wilkasi wu ino ḥumain,** that boy will afflict us; **iss** —, afflict yourself.

ḥumo, *a.*, bad (not used alone).
ayanḥumo, *f.n.*, bad luck, misfortune, calamity.
ayanḥun, *a.*, unlucky.
ayan ḥumow, *v.i.*, be unlucky.
ḥumaw, *v.att.*, be bad, ill.
ḥuman, *f.n.*, affliction, adversity, evil, trouble.—**ti.**
ḥundur, *f.n.*, navel.—**ti.**
hunguri, *m.n.*, throat.—**gi** (general name); — **'ad** (*see* **bo'**), windpipe, *or* larynx); — **madow,** throat, pharynx; **hunguri wein,** greedy, glutton.
hunguri weinan, *f.n.*, gluttony. —**ti.**
hunḥa', *v.tr.*, vomit.
hunḥa'o, *f.n.*, vomiting.
hunsho, *f.n.*, vulture (species of), the white one and the black one.
hunug, *m.n.*, bleeding of the nose. —**gi.**
hunug, *v i.*, bleed (nose); **hunga, wan hungi.**
hur, *m.n.*, heat.—**ki.**
huri, *v.c.*, cause him to be warm, cover his head to warm it; **iss** —, cover yourself (with your sheet or dress to get warm).
hur wein, *a.*, hot, very warm.
(nin) hursan, *a.*, perspiring, feeling warm.
hurdan, or **hurdun,** *m.n.*, kick with the heel (in playing).—**ki.**
hurdan, *v.i.*, kick with the heel; **hurdama, wan hurdami.**
hurguf, *v.tr.*, shake off, dust; **la hurguf,** it is shaken off.

huri, *m.n.*, piroque.—**gi.**

ḥuri, *m.n.*, male cat.—**gi.**

ḥuro, *f.n.*, tartar of the teeth.

hurud, *v.i.*, sleep; **hurda, wan hurdi; iss ka** —, remain sleeping.

(nin) hurda, *a.*, sleeping (man), sleeper.

hurdo, *f.n.*, sleep; **hurdadi habenka wa wanaksana,** the sleep of that night was a good one.

huruf, *m.n.*, frown, sour look.—**ki.**

huruf, *v.tr.*, frown, rebuke; **ninka huruf,** rebuke that man.

hurunsho, *f.n.*, a burnt thing (burnt to ashes).

hurunshai, *v.tr.*, burn to ashes.

huryo, *f.n.*, a black bird with yellow beak and feet, the size of a turtle dove, living on larvæ and camel ticks.

ḥusul, *m.n.*, elbow.—**ki.**

ḥusus, *f.n.*, memory, remembrance.—**ti.**

ḥususi, *v.tr.*, remind.

ḥususo, *v.tr.*, remember; **ḥususta, wan ḥususan.**

ḥususnaw, *v.att.*, keep in memory, remember.

huwi, *v.tr.*, cover, clothe.

huwo, *v.r.*, cover, clothe yourself.

Ḫ.

ḫ, 10th letter of the Somali alphabet, used for the Arabic sounds of خ, ق, غ.

ḫab, *v.tr.*, have, take; **ninkas la'agtisi ana ḫaba,** I have the money of that man; **nabad** —, be in peace, be safe; **war** —, a man who receives news, message.

ḫabo, *v.tr.*, catch, hold, keep, seize; **ḫabta, wan ḫaban; ka** —, take from; **iga ḫabo,** take from me; **kaga** —, begin; **ku** —, catch with; **labatan kalun ban shabaggi ku ḫabtai,** I caught twenty fishes with the net; **la** —, aid, assist; **ila habo,** assist me; **so** —, go and catch, run after; **ād u** —, make it well; **ād ban u ḫaban,** I will make it well; **haul** —, occupy yourself, serve, work; **il iss ku** —, or **indaha iss ku** —, *expression meaning* wink, shut your eyes, *i.e.* do not look at a bad thing, turn aside from a bad place *or* thing; **ninkasi ḥishod yu indihi iss ugu ḫabtai,** that man through shame shut his eyes; **hadi u waḥha ku siyo, il iss ku ḫabo,** or **il jebi,** if he gives you that, wink to me, *or* give me a wink.

il iss ku ḫabasho, *f.n.*, a man shutting his eyes (out of shame) when he goes to beg at a house, winking.

ḫabasho, *f.n.*, catching, seizing; **ninka shuḫul ḫabatsi,** employ that man.

ḫabso, *v.tr.*, employ, engage, catch hold of, comprehend; **eraigas ḫabso,** employ that word; **nin-**

ka hebel ḫabso, engage such a man; **marada ḫabso,** catch hold of your loin-cloth; **hadad dinta ād u ḫabsatid bad wanaksanan,** if you well observe religion, you will be good; **ka —,** catch from, get from.

waḫba iga ḫabsadai, *expression meaning* some misfortune has overtaken me.

ḫab, and **ḫabḫab,** *f.n.*, noise.—**ti**; **ḫabḫabta an maḫlayo,** the noise I hear.

allah ḫabai, *m.n.*, an abject, cursed man.—**gi.**

ḫabal, *m.n.*, large oval wooden pan or basin, crib, manger.—**ki.**

ḫabas, *m.n.*, calumniator, tale-bearer.—**ki.**

ḫabasnimo, *f.n.*, calumny.

ḫabbas, *m.n.*, baker.—**ki.**

ḫabil, *v.i.*, support, resist, be strong; **ḫabili maisid,** you cannot do it, *i.e.* you are not strong enough to do it.

ḫabilo, *f.n.*, nation.

ḫabow, *m.n.*, cold.—**gi**; **ḫabowga sāka dadki o dan ya ḫadḫadaya,** on account of the cold of this morning, all people were shivering.

ḫabow, *a.*, cool, gentle, meek, mild; **nin, niman ḫabow,** gentle man, men; **ninki ḫabowba,** the mild man; **nimanki ḫabḫabowba,** the mild men.

ḫabow, *v.i.*, be cool, gentle, meek, mild; **ḫaboba, wan ḫabobi.**

ḫabowji, *v.tr.*, appease, cool.

ḫabowjiso, *v.r.*, appease, cool yourself, bathe; **badda ku so ḫabowjiso,** bathe (take a bath in the sea).

ḫabri, *m.n.*, grave.—**gi.**

ḫabur, *f.n.*, cemetery.—**ti.**

ḫabsin, or **ga'na',** — **hi,** *m.n.*, great gut (intestine).—**ki.**

ḫad, *v.tr.*, take, assume, bear, lift, raise; **la ḫad,** it is lifted up; **robki ḫad,** the rain is over; **ka —,** take from; **la —,** carry, raise with, help, assist; **laga —,** be deprived of; **af kala —,** or **af kala ḫais,** *m.n.*, yawn, yawning.—**ki**; **af kala —,** *v.i.*, yawn; **so —,** fetch, bring; **kor u —,** or **sarai u —,** lift up, raise; **la iss ka —,** *a.*, infectious; **udurkasu wa la iss ka ḫad,** that sickness is infectious; **dein —,** *m.n.*, debtor.—**ki**; **hub —,** *m.n.*, warrior.—**ki, —yo**; **nafta ka —,** *v.tr.*, kill; **naftan ka ḫadi,** I will kill; **war —,** *m.n.*, messenger.—**ki, —yo.**

ḫadi, *v.tr.*, omit, leave; **wilka ḫadi,** leave that boy; **ka —,** leave aside, do not care.

ḫado, *v.tr.*, take for you, endure, support, confess, avow, acknowledge; **ḫata, wan ḫadan; 'udurkaga ḫado,** or **u samir,** endure, support your sickness; **runta sheg o ḫado,** tell the truth and confess; **tugadada ḫado,** acknowledge thy theft; **ho —,** or **ho o —,** take and keep.

ḫadabo, *f.n.*, buckle.
ḫad, *m.n.*, ink.—**ki.**
ḫad, *m.n.*, noise produced by a blow.—**ki.**
ḫadḫad, *m.n.*, ague, pressing hunger.—**ki.**
ḫadḫadiyo, *f.n.*, cold fit, shivering.
ḫadḫad, *v.i.*, shiver.
ḫadab, *m.n.*, fruit, every kind of vegetable.—**ki**, —**yo.**
ḫadabaiso, *v.i.*, eat fruit, vegetables.
ḫadabaisato, or **nin ḫadabaisataah**, or **arah donato**, *f.n.*, eater of fruits, vegetables.
ḫadad, *m.n.*, pit below the skull. —**ki.**
ḫadad, *m.n.*, bitterness, sourness. —**ki.**
ḫadad, *a.*, sour, bitter; **mido ḫadad**, sour fruits; **midihi ḫadada**, the sour fruits.
ḫadafi, or **ḫarafi**, *m.n.*, wooden sandal.—**ki.**
ḫadai, *v.i.*, dine.
ḫadaisi, or **ashaisi**, *v.i.*, give dinner to someone.
ḫadan, *m.n.*, servant.—**ki.**
ḫadari, *m.n.*, estimate (of any work).—**gi.**
ḫadari, *v.tr.*, listen to, confide in; **ninka hadalkisa ban ḫadarin**, I will confide in, listen to what that man says.
ḫadas, *m.n.*, mass (holy sacrifice). —**ki.**
ḫadon, *f.n.*, tree the bark of which produces red dye.—**ti.**
ḫadon, *f.n.*, kind of frankincense. —**ti.**

ḫafila, or **hafilo**, *f.n.*, caravan.
ḫaho, *f.n.*, asthma, consumption (*means also* chest, long breathing); **war! ḫofku ḫaha weina**, oh! how long that man is able to speak, *i.e.* what a chest (lit. what a breathing) he has.
ḫahwa, *f.n.*, coffee (ready for drinking); **ibḫiḫa ḫahwaah**, coffee-pot.
ḫaib, *ad.*, well, completely; **ḫaib igu, ugu, nogu, sheg**, tell me, him, us, all is well; **isagu ḫaibu kugu shegi**, he will tell you well, nicely, strongly.
ḫaïb, *f.n.*, share, portion, division.—**ti.**
ḫaïbi (generally with **u**), *v.tr.*, distribute, divide; **inamada u ḫaïbi**, distribute to the boys; **ku** —, appoint, give; **ninka shuḫulka ku ḫaïbi**, give that work to this man.
ḫaïbso (with **la** in the singular), *v.r.*, partake with.
ḫaïd, *m.n.*, rule, law, commandment.—**ki.**
ḫaid, *m.n.*, loin-cloth (*see* **mahawis**).—**ki.**
ḫaili, *v.i.*, cry, scream, shout, call.
ḫailo, *f.n.*, noise, tumult, shout; **ḫailada iss ka da**, cease that noise.
ḫailo, or **ḫaila gei**, *v.tr.*, go for help (when fighting and near to be overcome, they say so).
ḫaili, *m.n.*, large coloured Somali linen dress (sheet).—**gi.**
ḫair Allaḥ ha ku siyo, *expression*

meaning may God give you a blessing.

ḫaïran, *m.n.*, skin garment for men.—**ki**, —**yo**.

ḫajeila, *ad.*, often.

ḫal, *m.n.*, vinegar.—**ki**.

ḫal, *v.tr.*, cut meat into pieces, slices, butcher; **adi** —, *m.n.*, butcher; **dad**—, *m.n.*, cannibal.

ḫalab, *m.n.*, baggage.—**ki**.

ḫalad, *m.n.*, mixture.—**ki**.

ḫalad, *v.tr.*, huddle, throw into confusion; **iss ku** —, mix.

ḫalaf, *v.imp.*, become coarse, thick, rough, hard; **haraggu wu ḫalafi**, the skin will become rough.

ḫalafi, *v.c.*, cause to become coarse, thick, rough, hard.

ḫalafsan, *a.v.*, coarse, thick, rough, hard.

ḫalalan, *a.*, dry; **wa ḫabo ḫalalan**, it is dry fire-wood; **maro ḫalalan**, dry linen.

ḫalali, or **ḫalaji**, *v.tr.*, dry.

ḫalalif, *f.n.*, boast, humbug, brag. —**ti**.

ḫalalif ka shub, *v.i.*, boast, humbug, brag.

ḫalbi, *m.n.*, heart.—**gi**.

ḫalḫal, *v.tr.*, allure, engage in a bad way, deceive by sophisms or enticements; (fanatic Mussulmans say of the Catholic missionaries,) **badriintu** or **badriyadu wa ina ḫalḫalaisa** or **ḫalḫalayan**, the fathers will deceive us.

ḫalḫal, *m.n.*, allurement, deceit. —**ki**.

ḫalḫalan, *a.v.*, allured, deceived.

nin muḫalḫalah, *m.n.*, impostor. —**hi**.

u ḫalḫal, *v.tr.*, begin, commence, do quickly; **shuhulka hor u ḫalḫal**, do your work quickly. (This word means done disorderly, in a bustle.)

ḫalas, *v.tr.*, finish.

ḫalas, *a.v.*, finished; **ḫalas waiyai**, it is finished.

ḫalḫala, or **ḫalḫalo**, *m.n.*, sack, saddle-bag.—**hi**.

ḫalib, *v.i.*, wish him good luck; **wan ku ḫalibi**, I wish you good luck.

ḫaliban, *a.v.*, fortunate, good luck; **waḫhasi wa ḫalibanyahai**, that is fortunate, lucky.

ḫalim, *m.n.*, pen.—**ki**.

ḫalin, *f.n.*, heifer, young she-camel.—**ti**; **ḫalmo** (*plur*).

ḫalloh, or **ḫalḫalloh**, *m.n.*, curving, bending, bent.—**hi**, —**yo**; **daba** —, scorpion.

ḫallohi, *v.tr.*, bend.

ḫallohan, *a.v.*, crooked, bent, indirect, awry; **ul ḫallohan**, a crooked stick; **ullo ḫalḫallohna**, crooked, bent sticks; **ushi ḫallohanaid**, the crooked, bent stick.

ḫamar, *m.n.*, gambling.—**ki**,—**yo**.

ḫamar, *v.i.*, gamble.

ḫamis, *f.n.*, Thursday.—**ti**; **ḫamista dambe**, the next Thursday.

ḫamis, *m.n.*, long Arab shirt (*see* **garba galai**); Somals use this word for every kind of shirt and even coats.—**ki**, —**yo**; **ḫamsan**, **ḫamsanti** (plural nearly always used).

ḫamir, *m.n.*, yeast, leaven.—**ki.**

ḫamiti, *m.n.*, malevolent, malignant man.—**gi.**

ḫamidnimo, *f.n.*, malevolence, malignancy.

ḫan, *m.n.*, foal (camel, horse, ass, cow).—**ki.**

ḫan, *f.n.*, debt.—**ti**; — **geli**, *v.tr.*, indebt (him), cause him to enter into debt.

(**nin**) **ḫamaisan**, *a.v.*, indebted man, debtor; **ninki ḫamaisna**, the debtor; **wan ḫamaisnahai**, I am indebted.

ḫanan, *v.tr.*, claim, ask for; **ḫanama, wan ḫanami.**

ḫanam, *m.n.*, claim.—**ki**, —**yo.**

ḫanan, *f.n.*, lifting up of the tail, when horses, cows are running. —**ti**; **eg! faras ki wa ka dabadi ḫananta ka digai**, look! there is the horse which has raised his tail.

ḫando, *f.n.*, sudden fit of burning fever; **ḫando ku dishai**, may that burning fit kill you (very bad curse).

ḫangad, *m.n.*, adult.—**ki**, —**yo.**

ḫanjad, *f.n.*, large boat (*see* **doni**). —**di.**

ḫanjaful, or **ḫanjafil**, *f.n.*, hoof of goats.—**shi.**

ḫanjid, *m.n.*, sinew, tendon of the neck, thigh.—**ki.**

ḫanjidai, *v.imp.*, be raw, not cooked (not used for meat); **baris ḫanjidai**, the rice is not cooked.

ḫanjidsan, *a.v.*, unripe, raw, not cooked.

ḫanjidi, *v.tr.*, pinch, nip.

ḫanjido, *f.n.*, pinch, nip.

ḫani, *m.n.*, hold (of a ship).—**gi** (Arabs say **ḫan**); **adiga ḫaniga ku gura**, put the sheep in the hold.

ḫanin, *v.tr.*, bite.

ḫaniyo, *f.n.*, bite, biting, sting (in general).

ḫanso, *f.n.*, bow (for shooting).

ḫanun, or **ḫainun**, *m.n.*, rule, law canon.—**ki.**

ḫar, *num.*, several, some.—**ki.**

ḫar, *m.n.*, mountain range.—**ki**

ḫar hore, *m.n.*, ahead *or* afore, top; **markabka ḫarkisa hore**, the forepart of the ship.

ḫar dambe, *m.n.*, stern, abaft, end; **ḫar hore iyo ḫar dambe**, afore and abaft.

ḫaraf, *m.n.*, match.—**ki**, —**yo.**

ḫaraḥ, *a.*, burst; **mufti'hi ḫaraḥ**, the burst cannon.

ḫaraḥ, *m.n.*, explosion.—**hi.**

ḫaraḥ, *v.i.*, burst; **distigi ba ḫarhai**, the kettle burst.

ḫarai, or **ḫara**, *m.n.*, cudgel, heavy stick.—**hi.**

ḫaraj, *m.n.*, expenses.—**ki**; **bishatan ḫarajku wa badanyahai**, this month the expenses are great.

ḫardas, *f.n.*, amulet, charm.—**ti.**

ḫaren, *m.n.*, affinity.—**ki.**

la ḫarenso, or **u ḫaren noḫo**, or **iss ḫarensada**, *v.i.*, be in affinity.

ḫarendi, *m.n.*, badger.—**gi**, —**di**

ḫarfa, *f.n.*, cinnamon.—**di.**
ḫarḫad, *f.n.*, clout, rag.—**di.**
ḫarḫarsi, *m.n.*, rope tying down a camel's head to his foreleg to prevent it from getting up. —**gi.**
ḫari, *v.tr.*, conceal, hide.
ḫaris, *m.n.*, hiding.—**ki,** —**yo.**
ḫarso, *v.r.*, hide yourself.
ḫarson, *a.v.*, concealed, unseen, secret; **hadal ḫarson,** a secret; **mel ḫarson,** a hiding-place.
ḫariyan, *m.* and *f.n.*, astrologer, sorcerer.—**ki,** —**ti.**
ḫaro, *f.n.*, thickness; **ḫori, ḫoriyo ḫaroleh,** hard wood.
ḫarshi, *m.n.*, thaler, dollar.—**gi**; **nus ḫarshi,** half-dollar.
ḫarurad, *f.n.*, bottle.—**di.**
ḫasa'ad, *f.n.*, snuff-box (of Arabs). —**di.**
ḫasab, or **kasab,** *m.n.*, jowaree plant and its seed.—**ki.**
ḫasab, *v.tr.*, force, oblige; **ḫasba, wan ḫasbi.**
ḫasab, *m.n.*, violence, force.—**ki.**
ḫasaro, *f.n.*, useless expenses, damage.
ḫashar, or **ḫashir,** *m.n.*, coffee husks.
ḫasirad, *f.n.*, fine, penalty.—**di.**
ḫasir, *v.tr.*, fine.
ḫata! *int.* of alarm.
ḫataḫata, or **hadaḫata,** *m.n.*, name given to the Yibir caste, and meaning sorcerer.—**hi.**
ḫatal, *v.tr.*, mislead, blunder, debauch, delude.
ḫatalad, *f.n.*, blunder, fault, mistake.—**di.**
ḫatalan, *v.i.*, be misled, mistaken, err, blunder; **ḫatalma, wan ḫatalmi.**
ḫau! ḫau! *int.* indicating a noise made in striking repeatedly.
ḫaul, *m.n.*, will, word (of God), law.—**ki.**
ḫaw, *f.n.*, brag, deceit.—**di.**
ḫawai, *v.i.*, be deceived, make a mistake.
ḫawaisi, *v.tr.*, deceive, betray, brag.
ḫawayad, *f.n.*, brag, temptation, deceit.
ḫawad, *m.n.*, bawd (*mas.*).—**ki.**
ḫawadad, *f.n.*, bawd (*fem.*).—**di.**
ḫawaja, *m.n.*, gentleman (ordinarily said of Europeans).—**gi.**
ḫawi, *v.tr.*, bare, strip, denude.
(nin) ḫawan, *a.v.*, naked (man); **ninki ḫawana,** the naked man.
ḫawanan, *f.n.*, nakedness.—**ti.**
ḫayaḫayai, *v.i.*, flatter, fawn (upon someone to get money).
ḫayoḫayo, *f.n.*, flattering, fawning.
ḫayoḫayo, *f.n.*, game in which women dance and strike their chest with their hands.
ḫiḫ, *m.n.*, smoke.—**hi**; **ḫiḫ ba ka biḫi,** it smokes.
ḫiḫ, *v.imp.*, it smokes; **dabki wa ḫiḫaya,** the fire smokes.
ḫimad, *f.n.*, barracks.—**di.**
ḫir, *f.n.*, acknowledgment, avowal. —**ti.**
ḫiro, *v.tr.*, acknowledge, avow; **ḫirta, wan ḫiran.**
ḫisas, *f.n.*, retaliation, revenge.—**ti**; **ḫisasta naga si,** give us our revenge.

ḫisas, *v.i.*, pay the retaliation.
ḫiyan, or **ḫiyano,** *m.* or *f.n.*, cunningness, cheating, deceit.—**ki,** —**di**; some also say **ḫaiyan,** or **ḫaiyano.**
ḫiyanleh, ḫiyanoleh, ḫaiyanoleh, *a.*, cunning.
ḫiyanai, *v.tr.*, deceive.
ḫiyar, *m.n.*, cucumber.—**ki.**
ḫiyas, *v.i.*, take the measure (for coat).
ḫiyas, *f.n.* and *a.*, straight, size, target; **wa ḫiyas,** it is straight; **ḫiyas ka dig,** make it straight.
ḫob, *m.n.*, hoof (horse, mule ...). —**ki.**
ḫobad, *f.n.*, small Somali dish, porringer.—**di.**
ḫod, *f.n.*, bold man, male.—**di.**
ḫod, *v.tr.*, dig; **gedka ḫod o so rid,** dig up the tree.
ḫodnin, *m.n.*, digging.—**ki.**
ḫodaḫ, *f.n.*, thorn.—**di; ḫodaḫnyo** (*plur.*).
ḫodaḫleh, *a.*, thorny.
ḫodo, *m.n.*, genitals.—**hi.**
ḫodob, *m.n.*, tacking together.—**ki.**
ḫodob, *v.tr.*, baste, tack together; **ḫodba, wan ḫodbi; kabta i ḫodob,** mend my sandals, *i.e.* put on a piece, or sew; **iss ku—,** join two pieces with nails, sew, mend small holes in the clothes.
ḫodub, or **ḫudub,** *m.n.*—**ki,** or **ḫoto,** *f.n.*, South.
ḫodus, *m.n.*, sanctity (of God).—**ki; nin ḫodusaḫ,** a saint, a saintly man.
ḫodyeḥedo, kind of *int.* expressing a strong affirmation, as truly, just, exactly; **ḫodyeḥedo wa kowdi,** it is exactly one o'clock; **hadanan ḫodyeḥedo ku la dagalamin, nin ba mihi,** truly, if I do not fight with you I am not a man.
ḫof, *m.n.*, person, individual (used for one).—**ki.**
ḫofal, *m.n.*, fetters.—**ki.**
ḫofal, *v.tr.*, fetter.
ḫoḫ, *v.imp.*, it froths.
ḫoḫob, *m.n.*, a hut not built in an enclosure as they are built in each **ḥafad.**—**ki.**
ḫoi, or **ḫo,** *v.tr.*, moisten, soak, wet; **yar ḫoi,** moisten a little.
ḫoiyan, *a.*, damp, moist, wet; **wan ḫoiyanahai,** I am wet; **maradaidu wa ḫoiyantahai,** my garment is wet.
ḫois, *m.n.*, a hut surrounded by an enclosure; when the interior is separated by a kind of screen called **iliḫed** they call the rooms **ḫollad** or **gurgur.**
ḫollad, *f.n.*, room.—**di; ninkas ḫolladisi wa balladantahai,** the room of that man is large.
ḫolli, *f.n.*, turtle-dove.—**di.**
ḫolo, *f.n.*, tribe, caste, descendants, relations.
ḫolof, *f.n.*, scale, cod, husk.—**ti; ḫolfo** (*plur.*).
ḫon, *f.n.*, hurt, sore, wound.—**ti; ḫomo** (*plur.*); **ḫon gibinaḫ,** a small wound; **ḫonti buksatai,** the cured wound, the scar.

ilmaha ka ḫon, *v.i.*, cause to miscarry; **ilmaha wan ḫomi** or **ka ḫomi,** I will cause abortion.

ilmaha iss ka ḫon, *v.i.*, miscarry; **ilmaha wan iss ka ḫomi,** I will miscarry; **ilmaha ka ḫomi,** she will miscarry; **ilmaha ka ḫomai,** she miscarried; **ilma laga ḫomi,** they will make her miscarry; **ilma laga ḫomai,** they made her miscarry.

ilma ka ḫoman, *f.n.*, abortion, miscarriage.—**ti.**

ḫonsi, ḫonsid, or **ḫonsimad,** *m.n.*, discussion, dispute, quarrel, discord.—**di.**

ḫonso, *v.i.*, resent, feel against.

(**u**) **ḫomamai,** *v.i.*, be contrite, regret.

ḫomamais, *m.n.*, contrition, regret. —**ki.**

ḫor, *f.n.*, neck.—**ti.**

ḫorḥid, *m.n.*, necklace (especially for horses).—**ki.**

ḫor, *v.tr.*, write, record, register, *means also* mend (a pen), clean up (a stick), sharpen (a pencil), adapt, cut (a stone).

ḫora, *m.n.*, writer.—**gi,** —**yo.**

ḫoran, *a.v.*, written; **waḥ wa ḫoran,** it is written.

ḫorin.—**ki,** or **far.**—**ti,** writing, handwriting; **inanka fartisu wa wanaksantahai,** that boy's handwriting is good.

ḫornin, *f.n.*, mending (of a pen); sharpening (of a pencil).—**ti.**

ḫori, *m.n.*, wood. —**gi,** —**yo** (general name).

ḫoriah, or **ḫori laga samaiyai,** *a.*, wooden; **abḥadda ḫorigaah,** the wooden box.

ḫori dableh, *m.n.*, fire-brand.

ḫoraḥ, *f.n.*, sun, sunshine.—**di**; — **so baḥ,** sunrise; — **subaḥ,** sun in the morning; — **da'**, sunset; — **galbed,** sun in the evening.

ḫorato, *f.n.*, lizard (small one).

ḫorud, *m.n.*, semen (in general); **biyo baḥ,** semen (*pro homine*).

ḫosh, *v.tr.*, mix, mingle, stir, knead.

ḫosol, *m.n.*, laugh, laughter, smile, grin.—**ki.**

ḫosol, *v.i.*, laugh, smile; **ḫosla, wan ḫosli**; **ku** —, *v.tr.*, mock at, ridicule; **ninki lagu ḫosol,** everyone mocks at him; **wa la igu wada ḫoslai,** they all laughed at me.

ḫoton, *m.n.*, straightness. — **ki** (position of a jar placed in a hole to keep it straight).

ḫoton, *v.i.*, be placed straight; **wa ḫotami,** it will be placed straight.

ḫotomi, *v.tr.*, place straight.

ḫub, *v.tr.*, spill, squander, waste; **la'agtaidi wan ḫubai,** I have squandered my money.

ḫud, *m.n.*, cel.—**ki.**

ḫud, *a.*, sole, single; **nin ḫudiah,** a single man.

u ḫud, *v.tr.*, be inclined to give; **ku ḫudi mayo,** I cannot give to you.

ḫud, *m.n.*, looking at (a man while he is eating, in order to get some food by that importunity.

ḫud, *v.i.*, look at; **maḥad naga ḫudaisa**, why are you looking at us?

ḫudaiyo, or **ḫundanyo**, *f.n.*, ant (very black one).

ḫudda, *m.n.*, large wooden spoon, ladle, skimmer.

ḫudḫudi, *v.tr.*, swallow (water), clip (words).

ḫudḫudis, *m.n.*, swallowing.—**ki.**

ḫudrad, *f.n.*, vegetables.—**di.**

ḫudun, *m.n.*, putrefaction, rottenness.—**ki.**

ḫudun, *v.i.*, putrefy; **ḫudma, wan ḫudmi**; **miyidki ḫudun**, the corpse is putrefied.

ḫudmi, *v.c.*, cause to putrefy, corrupt.

ḫudunsan, *a.*, rotten; **miḋki ḫudusana**, the rotten fruit.

ḫudmun, *m.n.*, stench.—**ki.**

ḫudmun ahaw, *v.att.*, stink, be of bad smell.

ur ḫudmun, *f.n.*, stench; **urti ḫudmunahaid**, the stench.

ḫudunḫuto, or **ḫudḫuto**, *f.n.*, bird (with a long neck and a beak like a horn).

ḫufa', *m.n.*, cough.—**hi.**

ḫufa', *v.i.*, cough.

ḫuful, *m.n.*, lock.—**ki.**

ḫulḫulad, *f.n.*, troublesomeness.—**di**; — **badan**, *a.*, troublesome.

ḫulḫuladai, *v.tr.*, interrupt, trouble.

ḫuliyad, *f.n.*, fairy.—**di** (some also say **ḫuliyad** for a nice-looking person).

ḫulub, *m.n.*, sadness, gloom, sullenness, dejection.—**ki.**

ḫulub, *v.i.*, be sad; **ḫulba, wan ḫulbi.**

ḫulubsi, or **ka ḫulbi**, *v.tr.*, make sad, melancholic.

ḫulubsan, *a.*, sad, gloomy.

ḫulubsanaw, *v.att.*, be gloomy, sad.

ḫumba, or **ḫumbo**, *f.n.*, large skin jar for ghee.

ḫun, *a.*, direct, straight.

ḫun, *v.i.*, be straight; **ḫuma, wan ḫumi.**

ḫun (**u so'o**), *ad.*, directly, straight (walk).

ḫun yar, *ad.*, slow, slowly, a little; **ḫun yar so'o**, walk slowly.

ḫumi, *v.tr.*, make straight.

ḫumanahaw, *v.att.*, be straight.

ḫumati, *m.n.*, straightness, uprightness.—**gi.**

ḫumati u, *ad.*, straight; **miska ḫumati u dig**, place the table straight.

ḫunhani, *m.n.*, drone.—**gi.**

ḫunud, *f.n.*, litany.—**di.**

ḫunudda mari, *v.i.*, recite the litany.

ḫurdan, or **jan**, *m.n.*, upper part of the ear-lobe.—**ki.**

ḫuri, *v.i.*, snore.

ḫuro, *f.n.*, snoring.

ḫuroḥ, *f.n.*, beauty.—**di.**

ḫurḥi, *v.tr.*, make beautiful, nice, beautify.

ḫurḥiso, *v.r.*, make beautiful for you.

ḫuroḥ badan, ḫuroḥ wanaksan,

or **ḥurohsan,** *a.v.*, beautiful, nice; **faraski ḥurohda badna,** the beautiful horse.
ḥururoḥ, *m.n.*, pebbles, gravel.—**hi.**
ḥurunful, *m.n.*, cloves.
ḥus, *v.i.*, dive.
ḥusi, *v.tr.*, duck, make him plunge.
ḥushash, *m.n.*, sweepings, rubbish, chips.—**ki,** —**yo.**
ḥushashad, *f.n.*, rheumatism.—**di.**
ḥushi, *m.n.*, free will, wish, on purpose; **ḥushigai,** my will.
ḥuso, or **iss ka ḥuso,** *v.i.*, despair; **ḥusta, wan ḥusan.**
ḥusad, *m.n.*, despair.—**ki.**
ḥushu', *f.n.*, applause.—**di.**
ḥushu', *v.i.*, be applauded, be merry.
u ḥushu'i, *v.tr.*, applaud.
ḥusur, *a.* and *m.n.*, deep, depth, deepness.—**ki; baddi wa ḥusur,** the sea is deep.
ḥuwad, *f.n.*, power.—**di.**
ḥuwadleh, *a.*, powerful.

K.

ka, ki, ku, *art.*, the (*aff.*).
ká, kí, kér, *dem.a.prn.*, this *or* that;
kán, kás, this *or* that;
kuér, kuás, these *or* those;
kuan, kuakan, these;
kuí, kuí, kuás, those;
kó, kuó, that, those, yon, yonder.
kai, kaiga, kaigi, *poss.adj.prn.*, my, mine; **wa kaigi,** it is mine.
ka, kaga, kagi, thy, thine.
k', kis, kisa, kisi, his.
ked, keda, kedi, her, hers.
kaya, kayaga, kayagi, our, ours (mine and theirs).
ken, kena, keni, our, ours (yours and mine).
kin, kina, kini, your, yours.
kod, koda, kodi, their, theirs.
ke? keba? kuma? kuama? *int. prn.*, who? what? **ninke?** what man?
ku, *pers.prn.*, thee, to him, her, them, by him, her, them.
ku, kugu, *pers.prn.*, to thee, by thee.
ku, *prp.*, to, in, at, for, on, with.
ká, *pers.prn.*, from thee, you, him, her, them; **ka,** *ad.*, than; **ka,** *prp.*, against, from.
ka', *v.i.*, awake, wake, get up, rise; **ka'a, wan ke'i; sara** — and **so** —, get up; **u ka',** get up for, go to.
ke'i, *v.tr.*, wake, awake; **ka** —, awake them all.
kab, *f.n.*, sandal, shoe, boot, slipper.—**ti.**
kab, *v.tr.*, mend, repair (is used for all things).
kabahala, *a.*, bare-footed; **ninki kabahalaa,** the bare-footed man.
kabatol, *m.n.*, shoemaker.—**ki,** —**yo.**

kaba tolai, *m.n.*, shoemaker, *means also* awl, gimlet.—**hi.**
(**nin**) **kabo wein**, *a.*, large-footed man; **ninki kabaha weina.**
kabo weinan, *f.n.*, largeness of feet or of shoes.—**ti**; **kaba weinanta nagaha Somalied eg!** look! how large the Somali women's sandals are.
kabaasaya, *m.n.*, tree producing red dye.—**hi.**
kabad, *m.n.*, stool with three legs (*see* **gambad**).—**ki.**
kabad, *m.n.*, cupboard.—**ki**; **kabadka ku gur**, put in the cupboard.
kabadai, *m.n.*, traveller, peddler. —**hi**; **nin kabadaah**, a man travelling alone in the jungle.
kabadai, *v.i.*, travel.
kabal, *m.n.*, one of the two poles used for making the entrance of a Somali hut.—**ki.**
kaballo, *f.n.* (*plur.* of **kabal**), the two poles (or **dig doho**) tied together thus X, to be put on the camel.
kabtan, *m.n.*, captain of a ship, steamer.—**ki.**
kabubiyo, *f.n.*, cramp, numbness.
kadalob, *m.n.*, sitting on the heels, squatting.—**ki.**
kadalob, *v.i.*, be squat.
kadalobso, *v.r.*, squat.
(**u**) **kadi**, *v.i.*, wait for; **i kadi**, wait for me; **u kadi**, wait for him.
kadsi, *m.n.*, patience, waiting.—**gi.**
kadsileh, *a.*, patient.
kadso, *v.i.*, have patience.
(**nin**) **kadsanla**, *a.*, impatient; **ninkasi wa kadsanlayahai**, that man is impatient.
kādi, *f.n.*, urine.—**di.**
kādi, *v.i.*, piss; **kādsha, wan kādshi**; **so** —, go to ....
kādshahaïs, *f.n.*, bladder.—**ti.**
kadin, *m.n.*, flock, herd.—**ki**; **kadin fardaah, lo'ah, gelah**, a herd of horses, cows, camels.
ka'din, *f.n.*, gallop (at full speed). —**ti.**
ka'dlai, *v.i.*, trot.
ka'dlo, *f.n.*, trot.
kafan, *f.n.*, coffin, white sheet in which Somals tie up their dead. —**ti.**
kafir, or **kofri**, *m.n.*, apostate.—**ki.**
kafar, *v.i.*, apostatize; **kafra, wan kafri.**
kufran, *f.n.*, apostacy.—**ti.**
kaftan, *m.n.*, joke, jest, wit, fun. —**ki.**
kaftan, *v.i.*, joke, amuse, fun; **kaftama, wan kaftami.**
kahai, *v.tr.*, lead, take to (a place, a person); **so** —, take, bring (towards me); **kala** —, separate, detach; **labada nin e dagalamaya kala kahai**, separate the two men who are fighting.
kal (*root*), time, year; — **dambe**, next year; — **hore**, last year.
kala, *ad.*, apart (this word is used for pointing out division, separation); **laba wil o kala amusan**, two sulky boys; **kas iyo**

kan kalana, that and the other.

kalad, *f.n.*, tusk of the wild hog. **—di.**

kalaḥ, *m.n.*, wooden water-cup, mug.**—hi, —yo.**

kalai, *v.i.*, come (used as a call); **kalaiya** (*see* **imo,** come); **ka daba —,** *v.tr.*, follow; **la —,** bring, fetch (only used in the imperative); *see* **ken,** bring.

kaleh, *a.*, other; **ka —, ki —, ku —,** the other; **mid —,** another; **mar —** and **gor —,** again, another time; **mar kaleh ḋeh,** repeat, say again; **o —,** the same, like; **kursigas o kaleh i ken,** bring me a chair the same as that one, *or* like that one; **ku kaleh o la midah i ken,** or **ku kaleh o 'ainkasah i ken,** bring me another of the same kind.

kalil, *f.n.*, hot weather before the S.W. monsoon.**—shi.**

kalshin, *f.n.***—ti** (*see* **galsho**).

kalun, *m.n.*, fish.**—ki.**

kalumaisato, *f.n.*, fishing-boat.

kane'o, *f.n.*, mosquito, gnats, midge.

kanun, *m.n.***—ki** (*see* **ḫanun,** rule).

kar, *v.i.* and *auxil.verb*, (be) able; **wahhad samain kartid samai,** or **intad kartid samai,** do what you can.

ma karo, *n.v.*, I am unable, I cannot; **ma kartid,** thou art unable, thou canst not; **isagu ma karo,** he is unable; **kari wahyai,** I cannot, I could not (they say so only after having tried to do a thing and having failed); **kari wah,** he cannot, he could not; **ḫudi kari wah,** he could not carry.

wah an la karin, *a.*, impossible, unintelligible, *means also* miracle; **eraigas wa waḥ an la karin,** that word is unintelligible.

la ma kar, *a.*, impossible; **wa la ma kar,** it is impossible.

la ma karo, *a.*, impossible (to be done); **waḥhas la ma karo,** that cannot be done.

karnin, *f.n.*, ability, capacity, power.**—ti.**

kar, *m.n.*, boiling.**—ki.**

kar, *v.imp.*, it boils; **gor ḋow biyuhu wai kari,** after a while the water will boil; **'anaha** or **'anuhu wa kari donan,** the milk will boil; **iminka 'anihi** or **'anuhu wa karayan,** now the milk is boiling; **'anahi, biyihi karai,** the milk, the water is boiled.

kari, *v.tr.*, boil, cook.

karsan, *a.v.*, boiled.

deriya karis, or **sor karis,** *m.n.*, cook (man).**—ki, —yo.**

kar, *v.tr.*, mend, patch; **marada kar,** mend the clothes.

karrin, *f.n.*, patch (piece of cloth or linen for mending clothes). **—ti; karrintasa haḋai,** that piece remains.

karamad, *f.n.*, grace.**—di.**

karani, *m.n.*, clerk (in some office).**—gi.**

karan, *v.tr.*, defend, protect, master; **kareba, wan karebi; inankasi dasturta ḥun karau**, master the evil habits of that boy; **iss —**, defend yourself.
karbash, *m.n.*, scourging, flagellation.—**ki.**
karur, *f.n.*, camel's milk become sour.—**ti.**
kashif, *v.tr.*, defame.
kashif, *m.n.*, defamation.—**ki.**
ka'si, *m.n.*, masturbation.—**gi.**
ka'si, *v.i.*, masturbate.
ka'so, *v.r.*, masturbate yourself.
kasta, *num.*, every (has the same meaning as **walba**, but has a more affirmative sense).
katun, *m.n.*, ring.—**ki.**
kau, *f.n.*, killing, or knocking down with a club.—**di.**
ka kausi, *v.tr.*, kill at once.
kaudeh, *v.i.*, die suddenly (used as a curse); **kau ban odan**, I will die suddenly; **kau bu yidi**, he died suddenly; **ha kau yidahdo**, let him die suddenly.
kawir, *v.tr.*, launch; **saḥemada kawira**, take (ye) the boat to the sea.
kebed, *f.n.*, kind of carpet used by Somals for covoring their huts, and as pack saddles for their camels.
kebrid, *f.n.*, match (lucifer), sulphur.—**di**, —**yo.**
kelbad, *f.n.*, hinge (of a door).—**di.**
keli, *num.*, single, alone.—**gi**, —**di**, inflected with the *poss.prn.*; **wa kelidi**, he is a solitary man; **nin keliah**, a single man.
kelli, *f.n.*, kidney.—**di.**
kellyaleh, or **kellya badan**, *m.n.*, a clever, courageous, brave man.
ken, *v.tr.*, bring, fetch (*see* **gei**); **i ken**, bring me; **war —**, inform, bring news; **ka war —**, bring news from, ascertain; **inna kena, inna mariya, inna marsha, inna wada, inna kehaiya**, (all these expressions mean) let us go.
kibir, *v.i.*, be proud; **kibra, wan kibri.**
kibir, *m.n.*, pride, vanity.—**ki.**
kibirsan, *a.v.*, proud, vain; **adigu wa kibirsantahai**, thou art vain.
kibis, *f.n.*, bread, loaf, unleavened bread.—**ti**; some say **kimis.**—**ti**; **kibis diran**, new bread, bread still warm; **kibis kulul**, hot bread; **kibis habow**, stale bread.
kidar, *m.n.*, unleavened bread made of jowaree flour.—**ki.**
kilkilo, *f.n.*, arm-pit, arm-hole.
kintob, *m.n.*, hemorrhoids, piles.—**ki**, —**yo.**
kiro, *f.n.*, rent, hire (of a house).
kirai, *v.tr.*, hire, let.
kiraiso, *v.r.*, hire (for yourself).
kish, *m.n.*, pocket, bag, purse, money-case (of linen), envelope.—**ki.**
kishad, *f.n.*, leathern purse (as Somals ordinarily use).—**di.**
kitab, *m.n.*, book.—**ki**, —**yo** or **kutub.**

kobi, *m.n.*, cabbage.—**gi.**
kobo‘, *a.*, chubby; **ilmahas wa kobo‘,** that is a chubby child; **‘ilma kobai‘,** a chubby child able to sit down and stand.
kod, *m.n.*, eye-brow (hair and bone).—**ki.**
kol, *m.n.*, time, once.—**ki.**
kolka, *conj.*, when.
kolma? *ad.*, when?
kolki hore, *ad.*, formerly.
kolkol, *ad.*, sometimes.
kol badan, *ad.*, often, many times.
kol walba, *ad.*, always, daily.
kol kaleh, *ad.*, twice, another time.
kolleh, and **kollehba,** *ad.*, by all means, absolutely, by no means; **kolleh tag,** you have to go, you must go; **kolleh Adan tegi maisid,** by no means are you to go to Aden (refusal).
kolla, *ad.*, never.
kolai, *m.n.*, basket.—**gi.**
kolombai, or **kulambai,** *m.n.*, a kind of tufted, crested eagle.—**di.**
konton, *num.*, fifty.—**ki.**
kontomad, *num.*, fiftieth.
konton madafto, *f.n.*, phalanx.
kor, *prp.*, over, up; **kor u had,** lift up, take up.
kor, *v.i.*, climb, mount, be educated, grow, grow up; **burta kor,** climb up the mountain.
kor jir, or **kor jog,** *m.n.*, guard, outpost, sentinel, watchman.—**ki,** —**gi,** —**yo.**
la kor, *v.i.*, be brought up, be educated with; **inanki suldanka wan la korai,** I have been brought up with the sultan's son.
kori, *v.tr.*, educate, bring up, adopt; **inankas kori,** adopt that boy.
la koriyai, *a.*, adoptive.
la kori, *v.tr.*, help him to educate; **i la kori,** help me to educate.
koris, *m.n.*, education, training.—**ki.**
korod, *m.n.*, gain, profit, augment. **ki,** —**yo.**
kordi, *v.tr.*, augment, benefit, increase, give *or* put more; **i kordi,** give me more; **bariska i kordi,** give me more rice.
kordiso, *v.r.*, gain (for yourself); **kordista, wan kordisan.**
kordis, *m.n.*, augmentation, gain, increase.—**ki.**
korubodo, *f.n.*, kind of game (nearly the same as draughts).
korai, or **kora,** *m.n.*, saddle.—**hi.**
korai, *v.tr.*, saddle; **faraska i korai,** saddle the horse for me.
kormai, or **korma,** *m.n.*, male horse, stallion.—**hi.**
koron, *m.n.*, big, large *or* fat camel (castrated one), eunuch.—**ki.**
koron koro, *f.n.*, field cricket, locust, grasshopper.
kow, *num.*, one.
kowad, *num.*, first; **ki —,** the first.
kristan, *m.n.*, Christian.—**ki.**

kub, *m.n.*, part of the leg (below the knee).—**ki.**
kubad, or **ḥubad**, *f.n.*, cupola, ball.—**di.**
kubo, *f.n.*, caecum, blind gut.
kūd, *m.n.*, plague, pest.—**ki.**
kūd, *v.i.*, may you die (of pest).
kud, *m.n.*, sodomy.—**ki.**
kud, *v.i.*, practise sodomy; **inanka kud.**
kud! *int.*, used in driving sheep and other animals.
kudkudai or **da**, *m.n.*, camel's tick, sand-bug.—**hi.**
kuf, *v.i.*, fall, tumble; **aurkaigi ba kufai**, or **iga kufai**, my camel fell; **dagaḥ ban ku kufai**, I fell against, on a stone.
kufi, *v.c.*, make him fall.
kufnin, *f.n.*, fall.—**ti.**
kufso, *v.tr.*, violate, break, ravish; **kufsada, wan kufsan**; **gabaddas wa la kufsadai**, that girl was violated.
kufsan, *a.v.*, violated.
kufiad, or **kofiad**, *f.n.*, hat, cap. —**di.**
kug, *f.n.*, upper part of the skull. —**ti** (*see* **dalo**).
kul, *m.n.*, heat.—**ki.**
kulul, or **kulail**, *a.*, warm, hot; **wan kululahai**, I feel warm; **wa kulail**, it is hot.
kulal, *v.r.*, warm yourself.
kulalai, *v.tr.*, heat, make warm, hot.
inda kul, *f.n.*, antimony, collyrium.—**shi.**
kūl, *f.n.*, kind of necklace of the Somali women.—**shi.**
kulan, *f.n.*, kind of tree and its fruit.—**ti.**
kulan, *m.n.*, meeting (act of).—**ki.**
la kulan, *v.tr.*, meet; **la kulma, wan la kulmi**; **hebel ba la kulmai**, I met such a one.
kulli, *num.*, all (*see* **gidi**).
kumbis, *m.n.*, piece of fat meat roasted a little in the **deri.**—**ki**, —**yo.**
kumbul, *m.n.*, blanket.—**ki.**
kun, *num.*, thousand.—**ki.**
kur, *f.n.*, hill.—**ti**; **kurtan u sarai**, I took him to the hill.
kurai, *m.n.*, boy (big).—**gi.**
ku yar, *m.n.*, small boy; **ku yaryar**, small boys; **ki yara**, the small boy.
kurankur, *f.n.*, ankle-bone, kneepan.
kurbo, *v.i.*, shiver, shudder.
kurbad, *m.n.*, shivering, shudder. —**ki.**
kured, *m.n.*, very hard stone used for hammering and driving stakes into the ground, and also for sharpening knives and axes.—**ki.**
kuriyai, *v.i.*, fold sheep and cattle, arrange something in the form of a ball.
kuriyaisan, *a.v.*, spherical.
kuriyaisnan, *f.n.*, sphere.
kurun, *f.n.*, hill, rising ground. —**ti.**
kurundalo, *f.n.*, uneven route, way.
kurus, *m.n.*, camel's hump.—**ki**, —**yo.**

kuruska! *int.*, cry of sellers in the streets.

kursi, *m.n.*, chair.—**gi**; **kurasi** (*plur.* Arabic used by some Somals).

kus, *v.i.*, fold something in the form of a ball.

kus, *m.n.*, lump, mass.—**ki** (*see* **fud**).

kusad, *f.n.*, water-jug.—**di.**

kutan, *f.n.*, bug.—**ti.**

I.

i, used with its appropriate consonant as an affix for *art.* "the"; *dem. a.*, "this, that," and *poss. a.prn.* "his," and with nouns to express generality.

i, *pers.prn.*, me, to me.

igu, *pers.prn.*, to me, by me.

iga, *pers.prn.*, from me.

isagu, isaga, *pers.prn.*, he, him; **isagu isaga wa u tegi dona**, he will go to him.

iyo, iyadu, iyada, *pers.prn.*, she, her.

innagu, innaga, *pers.prn.*, we, us.

idin, idinku, edinka, *pers.prn.*, you.

iyo, iyagu, iyaga, *pers.prn.*, they, them, from them.

'i, *v.i.*, cry, bark, cackle (*see* **'ei**).

'i, *f.n.*, crying, barking, cry of nearly all animals.

ib! ib! ib! iro! *int.*, loud shout (in playing).

ib, *f.n.*, nipple, teat, spring (of water), canal of urine.—**ti.**

ib, *m.n.*, buying, sale, price.—**ki** (there is a great difference between **gana'** (price) and **ib** (price), **gana' ma laha** having no price, in the sense of being useless, or worth nothing); **ib ma laha**, invaluable; **Ebbahai abalgudkisu ib ma laha**, God's reward is invaluable (*i.e.* cannot be paid for).

ibi, *v.tr.*, buy and sell.—**ya** or **ibsha**; **faras ibi**, buy a horse; **faraskaga ibi**, sell your horse; **faraskaiga ma ibin**? will you buy my horse? **faraskaga ma ibin**? will you sell your horse? **so** —, *v.tr.*, go and buy, go and sell; **faraskas so ibi**, go and buy that horse; **ushaida ḥad o so ibi**, take my stick and go to sell it; **basal so ibi**, go and buy onions; **faraskisa ma so ibin**? will you go and buy, *or* will you go and sell his horse; **warmahas ma ibinaisa**? are you buying, *or* are you selling those spears.

ibso, *v.tr.*, buy, sell (for yourself); **kitab ibso**, buy a book; **kitabkas ibso**, sell that book (the money will be for you); **sarrirtatān ma ibsanaisa**? will you sell this bed? **mindiyahas ma ibsanaisa**? will you buy those knives? **so —,** go and buy, *or* sell (for you); **abalgudkagi sarrirtatan u ḥado o so ibso,** for your reward take this bed and sell it.

ibsan, *v.imp.*, be sold; **wai ibsami,** it will be sold.

ibsan, *a.v.*, bought, sold; **wa la ibsan,** it is bought, sold; **faraskaigi wa faras ibsan, e mid an so ḥadai maha,** my horse is a bought horse, and not a stolen one.

ma ibsana, *a.v.*, unsold.

ibsanaw, *v.att.*, be bought *or* sold.

nin waḥ ibiya or **ibsha,** a seller; **ninkí waḥ ibiya,** the seller.

ibādad, *f.n.*, devotion, piety.—**di.**

(nin) ibādad ja'el, or **ibādad badan,** devout, fervent man; **ninki ibādadda ja'la** or **badna,** the devout, fervent man.

ibriḥ, *m.n.*, pot, vessel.—**hi.**

'id, *f.n.*, individual, person, anybody, anyone.—**di**; **'id ma timi?** has anybody come? **'id ma iman,** or **'iddi ma iman,** or **'iddina ma iman,** nobody came; **'iddina ma jogto,** nobody is here.

'idla, *a.*, desert, uninhabited, unoccupied; **burtas wa 'idla,** that mountain is desert, uninhabited.

'idla, or **'idla 'ir sila,** *f.n.*, jungle, desert, *or* calm, tranquillity of the desert.—**di**; **'idladi bahal ba ka buḥai,** the jungle is full of wild beasts.

'id, *f.n.*, sand.—**di.**

'id, *v.tr.*, celebrate (a feast).

'id, *f.n.*, feast (holiday).—**di.**

idan, *m.n.*, censer, vase in which incense is burnt for perfuming.—**ki.**

'idan, *m.n.*, helper, coming to the rescue of combatants.—**ki.**

'idami, *v.tr.*, go, run to the rescue.

'idib, *f.n.*, heel.—**ti** (*see* **'edib**).

idil, *a.*, complete, all, entire; **dad badan idil,** the entire population; **malin o idil,** or **malin idil,** all day long; **shalo idil,** all yesterday.

idlai, *v.tr.*, abolish, accomplish, complete, finish, waste (money); **dinta idlai,** abolish the religion; **shuḥulka idlai,** finish your work; **la'agtada idlai,** waste your money.

idlow, *v.i.*, abut, finish; **danga Bulahar ku idlada,** the way ends at Bulahar.

idlan, or **idlain,** *f.n.*, abolishment, finishing.—**ti.**

an idlan la hain, or **an idlan ha lahain,** endless.

idin, *f.n.*, tanned skin of an antelope or gazelle, used for making charms *or* amulets.—**ti.**

u idin, *v.tr.*, authorize, empower; **idma, wan idmi; ha la idmo,** let him be authorized.

ido, *m.n.*, sheep; **hilib idad,** mutton (flesh).

if, *m.n.*, light, earth.—**ki.**

iftin, *m.n.*, light.—**ki, —yo; iftinki ḥoraḥda,** the sunlight.

iftimi, *v.tr.*, light.
'ifrid, *m.n.*, devil, evil spirit.—**ki.**
il, *f.n.*, eye, fountain, spring (of water).—**shi**; **indo** (*plur.*).
illa, *a.*, one-eyed; **nin illa,** a one-eyed man; **ninki ishalaa,** the one-eyed man.
isha balkeda sarai, and **isha balkeda hosai,** the eyelash (upper and lower).
isha bog ku leh, eyesore.
isha buhdeda, iris of the eye; **indaha buhdoda,** the iris of the eyes.
isha inankeda, or **isha wilkeda,** the pupil of the eye, eye-ball.
il yaro, *f.n.*, *fistula lacrymalis.*
(**nin**) **indala,** *a.*, blind; **ninki indalaa,** the blind man; **nagti indalaid,** the blind woman.
indalaan, *f.n.*, blindness.—**ti.**
(**nin**) **il der,** *a.*, long-sighted.
il deran, *f.n.*, long sight.—**ti.**
(**nin**) **inda fiḥan,** a good-sighted man.
(**nin**) **indo iss dafsan,** a squint-eyed man.
indo ḥallohan, a wry eye.
il ma ḥalul, squinting.
ashḫarah, one-eyed, squint-eyed, *or* goggle-eyed.
indaha ashḫar, *v.i.*, goggle; **wilkasi induhu ashḫari dona,** that boy will goggle; **ninkasi induhu ashḫaraiya,** that man goggles.
il daran, short-sighted, myope, *means also* a dying man, *i.e.* who has already his eyes veiled.
indai, *v.tr.*, observe, look at them; **halaito ḥedigihi ban indaiyai,** last night I observed the stars.
indo (eyes), *m.n.*, observation.—**hi**; **indahaigi,** or **ishaidi,** my observation; **ishayadi,** our observation.
isha ku 'adai, or **isha** or **indo ku tol,** *v.i.*, stare, gaze, look at (fixedly).
il jebi, *v.i.*, make known the things, wink.
'il, *m.n.*, anger, wrath.—**ki**; — **u ḥab,** *v.i.*, be angry; — **u surun,** *v.i.*, be angry, huff, swell with anger, rage.
'il, *v.tr.*, make angry; **'ila, wan 'ila**; **wad i 'ilaisa,** thou makest me angry.
ka 'il bel, *v.i.*, satisfy your anger, take your revenge (until you are satisfied).
'ilan, or **'ishan,** *a.v.*, angry; **ninki 'illa** or **'ishana,** the angry man.
'ilow, or **'isho,** or **u 'isho,** *v.i.*, be angry, abhor; **'ishoda, wan 'ishon**; **wan ku 'ishon,** I will be angry with you; **halaito ban u 'ishodai,** last night I was angry with him.
Ila, or **Ilaḥ,** *m.n.*, God (inflected with the *poss.adj.prn.*); **Ilaḥhai,** my God.
ilā, or **ilāma,** *prp.*, till, up to; **ilā halkas,** till there; **orod ilāma burta gurađeda,** run up to the top of the mountain.
ilaḫtan, *v.i.*, quarrel.

ilais, *m.n.*, fire-light, night-lamp. —**ki**, —**yo**.

ilali, *v.tr.*, take care, protect; **inanka ilali**, take care of the child; **so** —, go and take care; **si** —, continue to take care, to protect.

ilalo, *f.n.*, care, protection, vigilancy.

ilalo, *f.n.*, watchman, guard, sentinel, spy; — **dir**, send a spy; **ilalan diri**, or **ilalo ban diri**, I will send a spy.

so ilalai, or **ilalo tag**, *v.i.*, scout, reconnoitre, spy.

ilaw, or **ilow**, *v.tr.*, forget; **ha ilowbin**, do not forget.

ilowsho, *f.n.*, forgetfulness.

ilḥad, *f.n.*, silver earrings, latch (of a door).—**di**; **albabka ilḥaddisa**, the latch of the door.

ilig, *m.n.*, tooth.—**gi**; **ilko** (*plur.*).

'ilin, *m.n.*, dwarf.—**ki**.

'ilimad, *f.n.*, dwarf (*f.*).—**di**.

illiḥid, *m.n.*, screen (anything used in a hut as a separation). **ki**, —**yo**.

illin, *m.n.*, entrance, gate, door of an enclosure, a stable.—**ki**.

illo, *v.r.*, shoe (yourself), put your feet in shoes, sandals.

'ilmi, *m.n.*, knowledge of the written book (Coran).—**gi**.

ilmo, *f.n.*, tear; **eg! ilmo indihisa ka imanaisa** or **ka oraisa** or **dareiraisa** or **ka da'aisa**, look! a tear flows from his eyes.

ilmo, *m.n.*, child, baby.—**hi**; — **ayal**, or **ilmayaw** (*plur.*).

ilma abti, cousin (from maternal uncle); **ilma abti ya bannu nahai**, we are cousins.

ilma ader, cousin (from paternal uncle); **ilma ader ya bannu nahai**, we are cousins.

ina abtigai, or **ina aderkai**, my cousin; **ilma abtiyashai**, or **ilma aderadai**, my cousins; **ilma abtiyashai**, or **aderadai ban so egaya**, I wish to go and see my cousins.

ilma nasaha jaḥa, sucking child.

ilma koba'ai, chubby child.

ilma dalinah or **dalimah**, spoiled, teasing child.

ilma ḥun, spoiled, corrupted child.

ina, *m.* and *f.n.*, son, daughter; **ina Abdul**, Abdul's son *or* daughter; — **walalkai**, nephew, niece; — **ader**, cousin; **walalkai ba ḍalai**, my nephew; **walashai ba ḍashai**, my niece.

inan, *m.n.*, son, pupil, boy.—**ki**.

inan, *f.n.*, daughter, girl, lady (young).—**ti**.

imāmad, *f.n.*, turban.—**di**.

imāmad, *v.tr.*, arrange his turban (used with the *pronouns*); **wan u, ku imāmadi**, I will arrange his, your turban.

iman, *f.n.*, oath, swearing.—**ti**.

imansi, *v.i.*, swear (used with the *pronouns*); **iman ban ku sin**, I swear to you.

iman, *m.n.*, leader of the Mussulman prayer.—**ki**.

imin.—**ka**, —**ki**, *ad.*, now (*see* **aminka**).

iminkada, *ad.*, just now.

imisa, or **imsa?** *ad.*, how much? how many? **imisa jir bad tahai?** what is your age?

imo, *v.i.*, come (**kalai** is ordinarily used in the 2nd pers. sing. of the imperative mood instead of **imo,** not commonly used); **haddada imo,** come at that time.

imatin, *m.n.*, coming.—**ki.**

imad, *m.n.*, arrival.—**ki.**

in, *conj.*, that; **inan tago,** that I go; **bal —,** if; **bal an ego in Fara so so'odo,** I will see, *or* let me see if Fara is coming.

in, *f.n.*, part, piece, bit, some; **in i si,** give me some.

in yar, *f.n.*, little piece, particle; **inti yaraid,** the particle.

inta, *ad.*, as much, so much, until; **tāgno intan imanaya,** *or* **ila intan imanaya,** remain standing until I come; **intasan haista,** I have so much; **wa inta,** it is so much; **inta leh eg,** like, of that size; **mid inta leh eg,** one of that size, *or* one like that; **intada in leh eg ban haista,** or **intad o kalan haista,** I have as much as you; **intas o kaleh ma haisata,** have you as much? **intas o kalan haista,** I have so much.

intan u, *ad.*, before; **intan u ku odan,** before he told them.

indal, *f.n.*, thong.—**shi.**

indolai, *m.n.*, (all the) skull.—**hi.**

ingeg, *v.i.*, be *or* become dry, wither; **bertasi wa ingegaisa,** that tree becomes dry, *or* is withering.

ingegan, *a.v.*, dry.

(nin) alol ingeganleh, *a.*, a constipated man.

alol ingegnan, *f.n.*, constipation. —**ti.**

ingeji, *v.tr.*, dry; **darka ingeji,** dry the clothes.

ingris, *m.n.*, English.—**ki; ninki ingriskaaha teg,** the Englishman has gone.

inkar, *f.n.*, malediction, abomination.—**ti; Ilah inkartisi ba ku da'dai,** the malediction of God fell upon him.

(nin) inkaran, or **inkarsan,** or **inkar ḫaba,** *a.*, a cursed, abominable man; **Kaïn inkar bu ḫabai,** Cain was cursed.

inkar, *v.tr.*, malediction, curse.

inkir, *v.tr.*, refuse.

inin, *f.n.*, seed, grain.

injil, *m.n.*, Gospel.—**ki; torad iyo injil,** Bible and Gospel.

injir, *f.n.*, louse.—**ti.**

injirbodo, *f.n.*, flea.

'iow, *f.n.*, small owl.—**di.**

'ir, *m.n.*, sky, heaven.—**ki.**

'ir sila, *f.n.*, calm, tranquillity.—**di; habenka 'ir siladisi ba ina bajisai,** the calm of the night frightened us.

'ir, *f.n.*, food contained in the stomach.—**ti; — wein,** greedy, gluttonous; **ninki 'irta weinaid,** the greedy man; **— yar,** abstemious, temperate.

'ir weini, or **'ir weinan,** *f.n.*, greediness, gluttony.—**di, —ti.**

īr, *f.n.*, buttermilk, whey.—**ti.**
īrman, *m.n.*, milch cow.—**ki.**
irbad, *f.n*, needle, pin.—**di.**
'iro, *f.n.*, fog, mist, sand-storm.
'iraisan, *a.*, foggy, misty; **burti 'irasnaid**, the foggy mountain.
'irro, *f.n.*, white, grey beard, grey hair.
'ishai, *m.n.*, fifth time of prayer, at about 7 o'clock in the evening.—**hi.**
islan, *m.n.*, old man.—**ki.**
islan, *f.n.*, wife, old woman.—**ti.**
isnin, *f.n.*, Monday.—**ti.**
iss, *reflex.prn.*, self (this word is also used as a noun, **iss — ki ninkasu iss kisu u so'onaya**, that man is walking of his own accord, but it is especially used with the verb and preposition **ka**); **— la**, the same; **issla magaladi**, the same town, place.
Issa, Jesus.
ital, *m.n.*, strength.—**ki**; **Ilaḥ ba ital u yeli** or **ital sin**, God will give strength; **ital u yel**, give him strength; **Ilaḥ ba ital leh**, the strength belongs to God; **italkaiga waḥ ba ka da'a**, my strength decays; **italka runta**, the force of truth.
iinyo, word used by children in refusing (is the same as **ma dono**, I will not).
iyo, *conj.*, and.

J.

ja'ail, *m.n.*, affection, charity, love.—**ki**; **ja'ailkan Ebbahai u ḥabo**, the love I have for God.
ja'alaw, *v.tr.*, love, like, prefer.
ha ja'alan, *v.tr.*, do not love, dislike; **anigu ma ja'ali**, I do not like.
ja'alan, or **ja'lan**, *f.n.*, affection, friendship, kindness.—**ti.**
iss ja'alan, *f.n.*, self-love, selfishness.—**ti**; **iss ja'alantu**, or **ja'alantisa iss u ḥabo, wa la yaḥan**, or **ād ba lo yaḥan**, his selfishness, *or* the love he has for himself is well known; **ja'alantan iss u ḥabo**, my selfishness.
ma ja'alan, *f.n.*, dislike, aversion. —**ti.**
(**nin**) **dagal ja'el**, *a.*, warlike, pugnacious.
(**nin**) **'ibādad ja'el**, *a.*, devout, fervent, pious.
iss ja'el, *a.*, selfish; **wai iss ja'elyihin**, they are selfish.
ja'elnimo, *f.n.*, friendship.
jāl, *m.n.*, friend, associate.—**ki.**
jab, and **ka jab**, and **jajab**, *v.tr.*, be broken, cheap; **lug ban ka jabai**, or **lug ba i jabtai**, I have broken my leg. (As a kind of curse they use the following expression: **ga'an** or **lug ka jab, Ebbahai ban ku bariyai** or **bariyaya**, I pray God that your hand *or* foot may be broken.)

jaban, *a.v.*, broken, cheap; **garabkisu wa jaban yahai**, his shoulder is broken; **barisku wa jabanyahai**, rice is cheap; **bariski jeb**, rice became cheap.
jab, **jajab**, *m.n.*, potsherd.—**ki**, —**ab**, —**yo**.
jebi, **jejebi**, *v.tr.*, break, and break in pieces.
jabnin, *f.n.*, fracture.—**ti**.
gana' jaban, *a.*, cheap.
gana' jebi, *v.tr.*, cheapen.
jabti, *f.n.*, gonorrhœa.—**di**.
jah, *m.n.*, forehead, visage, countenance.—**hi**, —**yo**.
jahha ururi, or **jahhur**, *v.i.*, frown.
jaḥ, *m.n.*, North pole-star.
jaḥ, or **jeḥ**, half; **gambo iyo jaḥ** or **jeḥ**, one anna and a half.
jaḥas, *f.n.*, crocodile.—**ti**.
jaẖ, *v.i.*, suck (said of children and animals).
jaẖa, *m.n.*, sucking.—**hi**; **inanka jaẖihisa eg!** see! the child is sucking.
jaẖleh, *m.n.*, disease of kids and lambs.—**hi**.
jalahad, *f.n.*, pitcher.—**di**.
jalalaḥ, *v.tr.*, attack, plunder.
jalalaẖa, *m.n.*, attack, plunder.—**hi**.
jalbeb, *f.n.*, amusement, play.
jalbebi, or **jalbebsi**, *v.tr.*, amuse, divert.
jalbebo, *v.i.*, play, amuse yourself; **jalbebta**.
jalilad, *f.n.*, bullet.—**di**.
jama', *m.n.*, congregation of people assembled for prayer.—**hi**.
jamadar, *m.n.*, chief of police.—**ki**.
jamala, *m.n.*, earthen Arab coffee-pot (*see* **jemelad**).
jan, *m.n.*, a plain of dry mud in which there is no sand, burning of the feet (in passing on that plain when heated by the sun).—**ki**.
jan, *f.n.*, sound of footsteps, old and bad shoes or sandals, any piece of leather used for mending the soles of shoes and sandals.—**ti**.
jangeli, or **jingili**, *m.n.*, countryman, churl.—**gi**.
janjed, *m.n.*, irregularity of a line.—**ki**; **kursiga wa janjedah**, the chair is not straight (is awry).
janjed, *v.i.*, be awry.
janjedi, *v.tr.*, put awry.
janno, *f.n.*, heaven, paradise.
jar, *v.tr.*, cut, saw, abrogate, rescind.
jar, *m.n.*, brink of a mountain, cliff, equilibrium of weighing scales.—**ki**.
jar ka da', *v.i.*, lose the equilibrium, come into trouble.
jara', *m.n.*, reed, bamboo.—**hi**, —**yo**.
jarrai, or **jarra**, *m.n.*, halter (of horses).—**hi**.
jarra bar, *v.i.*, master a horse.
jawab, *f.n.*, answer.—**ti**.
jed, *v.tr.*, wait to look at (*root*); **u** —, look at, await, expect; **ninka u jed**, look at that man; **haggad u jeda?** what are you

looking at? *means also* where are you going? **waḫhan u jeda**, I look at something; **mel ban u jeda**, I go somewhere.

so **jed**, *v.i.*, waken, remain awake; **wan so jeda**, I am awake.

jedi, *v.tr.*, turn, distract; **inamada jedi**, distract the boy (that he may not see); **sanduḫha hagga u jedi**, turn the box to that side; **so** —, turn (towards me); **inanka so jedi**, turn the boy to my side; **si** —, turn to a place opposite to me.

jedso, *v.tr.*, look at (for yourself); **hagga u jedso**, look there.

jeso, *v.i.*, turn (yourself); **jesta, wan jesan**; **u** —, turn to; **so** —, turn towards me, us; **si** —, turn away from me.

jedal, *m.n.*, whip, lash (flogging). **ki** (used for women and horses).

jedal, *v.tr.*, flog, whip, scourge; **jedla, wan jedli.**

jedal, *f.n.*, flogging, scourging.—**shi.**

jedali, *v.tr.*, behold.

jegan, *f.n.*, rainbow.—**ti.**

jeḥ, *v.tr.*, rend, tear.

jeḥ, *m.n.*, tearing, cleft, split, crack.—**hi.**

jeḥjeḥ, *v.tr.*, tear into pieces.

jeḥan, *a.v.*, torn, split, ...; **maradi wa jeḥantahai**, the cloth is torn.

jelelo, or **jalelo**, *f.n.*, the senna plant.

jemelad, *f.n.*, earthen Arab coffee-pot.—**di.**

jeni, *m.n.*, foreleg (for all animals).—**gi.**

jeni ḥor, *m.n.*, gallop.—**ki** (lit. throwing the foreleg).

jer, *root*, time; **imisa jer?** how many times? **laba, sadeh jer**, two, three times.

jer, *m.n.*, hippopotamus.—**ki.**

jes, *m.n.*, hut (one family).—**ki**, —**as.** (The plural **jesas** is used for many families living near each other, but not agglomerated.)

jibad, *f.n.*, lion's roar.—**di.**

jibad, *v.imp.*, roar.

jiđ, *m.n.*, body, flesh, lean of meat.—**ki.**

jid, *m.n.*, path, road, way.—**ki.**

jidyaḫan, *f.n.*, guide.—**ti**; **nin jidka yaḫan i ken**, bring me a guide.

jīd, *v.tr.*, draw, pull, row, put up, on; **markabki jīdai**, the steamer is far off, away; **so** —, pull (towards me); **si** —, pull from me to; **la si — adna**, you also pull, draw with, help; **iss** —, come into collision with, run into, against; **labada nin ba iss so jidai**, the two men ran one against another.

jido, *v.i.*, run quick; **jita, wan jidan.**

jif, *f.n.*, top of stiff ascent.—**ti.**

jif, or **iss ka jif**, *v.i.*, rest, remain lying, sleeping.

jifi, *v.c.*, cause him to rest, sleep.

jifso, *v.i.*, go and sleep, lie down and sleep.

jiḥ, *m.n.*, a tree the bark of which is black.—**hi.**

jila', or **jilai'**, *m.n.*, fragility, brittleness.—**hi.**

jilai'san, *a.v.*, brittle, soft; **galas wa jilai'san**, glass is brittle; **ninkasi wa arab jilai'san yahai**, that man is eloquent, intelligent.

jilal, *m.n.*, dry season.—**ki.**

jilbad, *f.n.*, heavy silver necklace (for women).—**di.**

jilbis, *m.n.*, viper, adder.—**ki**, —**yo.**

jilib, or **jilab**, *m.n.*, hook (for fishing).—**ki.** This last word is used by some for the rope or string.

jilab, *v.i.*, fish; **orod o so jilab**, go to fish.

jilabo, *v.i.*, fish (for yourself).

jilabasho, *f.n.*, fishing.

jilib, *m.n.*, knee, tribe.—**ki**, —**yo**, or **jilbo**; **Hussein iss ku jilib bannu nahai**, Hoosein and I are of the same tribe.

jilba jog, *v.i.*, remain on your knees.

jilba jog, *m.n.*, genuflexion.—**hi.**

jilba yaradig, *v.i.*, kneel a little, remain on your knees resting with the back on your heels (sandals).

jilibka dig, *v.i.*, bend the knee.

jilba jogso, *v.i.*, kneel.

jilif, or **jidif**, *f.n.*, bark, husk.—**ti**; **bunka jiliftisa wa ḥashir**, the coffee husks are called **ḥashir.**

jima', **jimai'**, or **juma'**, *m.n.*, Friday.—**hi.**

jimid, *m.n.*, meat, flesh.—**ki.**

jina', *m.n.*, big black ant (the stinking one).—**hi**, —**yo.**

jini, or **jimi**, *m.n.*, genius, demon. —**gi.**

jir, *v.i.* (used for the verb of existence, "be, live," and also as an auxiliary verb, and for the division of time into years, age;) **Adan jir**, or **Adan iss ka jir**, live at Aden; **shalai aurba-jirai . . . .**, there was a camel yesterday; **hebelba Bulahar jogi jirai**, a certain man was living at Bulahar; **adigu imisad jirtai**, or **imisa jir ba tahai?** how old are you? **labatan jir ban ahai**, I am twenty years old; **ma jiro** and **ma jirto**, there is not; **eraigasi ma jiro**, that word does not exist; **manta waḥba ma jiran**, there is *or* there was nothing to-day.

jir, *v.tr.*, take care of, protect (for cattle and sheep); **war! adiga ra' o ād u jir**, hallo! (shepherd), go with the sheep and take good care of them; **manta holihi ma u jiro**, he does not take care of the cattle to-day; **iss** —, take care of yourself (body and soul); **iss ka** —, mind (yourself), take care of yourself (from something); **libaḥha ād issa ga jir**, mind yourself, beware of the lion.

la jir, *v.tr.*, serve, attend.

haulyari ku jir, *v.i.*, be at your

ease; **haulyari ma ku jirta?** are you at your ease? **ha, haulyari ban ku jira,** yes, I am at my ease.

jir, *m.n.*, rat.—**ki**; **jir yar,** a small rat.

jirab, *m.n.*, skin bag.—**ki,** —**yo** (a kind of clothes-bag).

jirid, *f.n.*, root of trees and plants, trunk, stem, stock, log of wood.—**di,** —**o,** or **jirdo** (*plur.*).

jiriḥa, *m.n.*, cricket (insect).—**gi.**

jiriḥsi, *m.n.*, gnashing.—**gi.**

jiriḥso, *v.tr.*, gnash.

kaga jirihi, *v.c.*, make him gnash.

jirjir, *m.n.*, back of the hand, of a blade, of a man.

jirjirad, *m.n.*, all the back.—**ki**; **jirjirad ka iss u rog,** turn yourself on your back; **jirjirad bu u seḥadai,** he is sleeping stretched out full length on his back.

jirjirolai, *m.n.*, cameleon.—**hi.**

ji'sin, *m.n.*, provisions made for travelling, or for one's maintenance at home.—**ki.**

johorad, *f.n.*, gem.—**di.**

jog, *m.n.*, abiding, remaining, staying.—**gi.**

sojog, *m.n.*, air, appearance, countenance of a man.—**gi.**

jog, *v.i.*, used for the verb of existence, be, live, remain, stay, stop; **la** —, remain with; **ka** —, hesitate.

ninka la joga, *m.n.*, the servant; **tag o ninki i la jogai u yed,** go and call my servant.

jogso, *v.i.*, halt, remain, wait, do not go on in your bad way, choke; **waḥ ba i jogsadai,** something choked me; **waḥba kas jogsadai,** something choked him; **ku** —, tread, tread upon, trample; **mahad 'agta iga ga jogsanaisa?** why do you tread upon my foot.

ku jogjogso, *v.i.*, shampoo with the feet (upon the back); **dabarkai hanuni e igu jogjogso,** my back pains me, shampoo it.

jogjogsi, *m.n.*, shampooing with the feet (on the back).—**gi.**

joji, *v.tr.*, detain, impede, intercept, stop; **ku** —, strike him, fix a handle; **iss ku** —, strike yourself, add together.

joniad, *f.n.*, bag.—**di.**

juhula, *m.n.*, ignorant.—**hi.**

juḥ ha odan, do not say a word.

L.

la, particle used for forming the the passive voice; **lo,** contraction of **la** and **u.**

la, *prp.*, with, along with.

laan, *prp.* and *n.*, without.—**ti**; **isaga laanti tag,** go without him. This word is also used as follows: **dan laan bai noḥotai,** that happened by his own fault.

la, for **laï,** *v.tr.*, beat, strike (this word is used when many people are beaten; for a single

person **dil** is used); **—ya, wan laïn**; **inamada la,** beat the boys; **wilka dil,** beat the boy.
la'af, *f.n.*, bait.—**ti.**
la'ag, *f.n.*, money, silver.—**ti.**
lab, male (particle added to names of animals to denote the male sex); **libaḥ lab,** a male lion.
labod, *m.n.*, male.—**ki.**
lab, *a.*, brave, bold; **ninkasi wa nin lab,** this man is brave, bold.
lab, *f.n.*, breast, chest, bosom.—**ti.**
(nin) labla, *a.*, stammering; **wilkasi wa wil labla,** that boy is stammering.
lab, *v.tr.*, fold (one thing). This word is also used for "bend": **jilibka,** or **rugga so lab,** bend the knee; **hunyar lab,** or **so lab,** bend a little.
lablab, *v.tr.*, fold (many things).
laba, *num.*, two; **—di,** both, the two, the pair; **labada nin i so kaḥai,** lead to me both men.
labad, *num.ord.*, second; **kan, ki labad,** the second.
labatan, *num.*, twenty.—**ki.**
laba gor, or **jer,** *ad.*, twice.
labai, *v.tr.*, double.
lāban (with **ku**), *v.tr.*, make again something, return, repeat; **labma, wan ku labmi**; **so —,** *v.i.*, come back.
lāban, *m.n.*, sprain, bruise.—**ki.**
lāban, *a.*, sprained, bruised, curved; **'agta wa lābantahai,** the foot is bruised.
laben, *f.n.*, cream.—**ti.**
lad, *m.n.*, kick (of a man).—**ki.**
lad, *v.tr.*, kick.
ladan, *a.*, in a good state, better, well, wealthy, comfortable; **iss ka warran,** lit. give news from you, *or* how are you? **wa ladnahai,** I am (I feel) better; **abbaha ka warran,** or **abbaha wa side?** how is your father? **wa ladanyahai,** he is better.
ladnaw, *v.att.*, be in a good state, better . . . . .
ladnan, *f.n.*, comfort, ease, rest. —**ti.**
laf, *f.n.*, bone, stone (of fruits), husk.—**ti**; **lafta dabarka,** the backbone; **lafta gad̈ka,** the chin.
lafo, *m.n.*, dice, huckle-bones, osselets.—**hi.**
laḥ, *f.n.*, ewe.—**di.**
laḥad, *m.n.*, limb.—**ki**; **laḥadyada o d̈an go,** cut off all the limbs.
laḥadla, *a.*, cripple.
laḥau, *m.n.*, phthisis, consumption.—**gi.**
lahau ḥabo, *a.*, phthisical, consumptive; **wa nin lahau ḥaba.**
lak, a lakh, or 100,000 Rupees; **lak rubod,** 100,000 Rupees.
laïli, *m.n.*, a young camel not accustomed to carry loads and afraid.—**gi.**
laïli, *v.i.*, quail, tame, master the camel; **laïliya, wan laïliyi.**
laji, or **lajo,** *m.* or *f.n.*, small shells with which Somals adorn their vessels.—**gi, —di**; **kus-**

sadda laji ku samai, adorn the water-jug with shells.

lāl, *v.tr.*, lift up, throw upon (this word is especially used for a mat used as a door in a Somali hut); **dahha lal**, lift up or open the door; **ahalka dushisa mindida ku lal**, throw the knife upon the house.

lalad, *v.p.* and *i.*, hang, be suspended; **ninki gedku ka laladai**, the man was hung on the tree; **modku madahhainu ka so lalada**, death hangs over our heads.

lamai, *v.tr.*, flog, scourge; **ha lagu —**, *v.p.*, be flogged; **wa la lamiyai**, he is flogged.

lān, *f.n.*, branch, bough, stem.—**ti.**

laso, *v.tr.*, finish; **sorta** or **sortada laso**, finish your food; **emrigisi yu lastai**, the course of his life is finished.

layan, *m.n.*, malefactor, a man of a savage or violent temper, highwayman, bloody man.—**ki.**

leb, *m.n.*, shaft of an arrow, wooden arrow used by small boys.—**ki**, **—yo.**

leben, *m.n.*, brick (not burnt). —**ki**; *see* **ajurad.**

lef, *v.tr.*, lick.

leg, *m.n.*, upper part of the belly. —**gi.**

legdan, *v.i.*, wrestle; **legdama, wan legdami**; **la —**, wrestle with him.

legdan, *m.n.*, wrestling.—**ki.**

leged, *v.tr.*, fell (a tree), make him or it fall.

leh, *root*, possessed of (this word is very often used as an affix).

lahaw, *v.att.*, be possessed of.

leh, *num.*, six.—**di**; **lehad**, or **lihad**, sixth; **lehdan**, sixty.

leho, *v.tr.*, turn; **war! leho**, oh! turn yourself; **so —**, turn to (towards me); **u —**, turn to him; **ka —**, turn from.

lei', or **lai'**, *root* not used; **lei'da**, die you (this verb seems to be used only with plural or collective nouns); **berri rag badan ba lai'an** or **lei'an**, to-morrow many men (people) will die; **geli iga wada lai'ai**, all my camels died; **ragi rerkasi wada lai'ai**, all the people of that rer died; **fardihi wa lai'den**, the horses died; **fardihi lai'dai**, the dead horses.

leil, *a.*, complete, entire; **shalai leil**, or **shalai 'o leil**, or **shalo leil**, or **shalaito leili**, all day yesterday; **shalaito o leili yan merai**, I went round all day yesterday.

libah, *m.n.*, lion (gen. name). —**hi**, **—yo**; **libah dadig**, a lioness.

libid, *v.i.*, disappear; **libda, wan libdi.** Parents use this word in cursing their children.

lid, *m.n.*, leathern strap used for fastening charms around the neck.—**ki.**

lif, *m.n.*, quoit (game).—**ki.**

lig, *m.r.* male garanug.—**gi.**

liḥ, *m.n.*, flexibility (of a thing). —**hi.**

liḥah, *a.*, flexible ; **ul liḥah**, a flexible stick.

liḫ, *v.tr.*, swallow, drain off water ; **biyaha liḫ**, drain off the water.

(**nin**) **liḫsan**, *a.*, a drunken man.

lilah (*see* **Ilaḥ**), *m.n.*, God.—**hi.**

lilahi, *f.n.*, truth.—**di** ; **wa lilahi**, by God, it is true ; **lilahi u so'o**, by God, tell the truth ; **nin lilahiah**, a truthful man.

lin, *f.n.*, — **ma'an**, orange ; — **danan**, lemon.—**ti.**

lis, *v.tr.*, sharpen ; **mindida lis**, sharpen the knife.

lissan, *a.v.*, sharp ; **mindidu wa lissantahai**, the knife is sharp.

lissin, *m.n.*, grindstone, whetstone.—**ki.**

liss, *v.tr.*, milk, stroke ; **hashi ban lissai**, I have milked the she-camels.

lo', *f.n.*, cow, herd, flock of neat cattle.—**di**, **la'yan** (*plur.*), —**ga.**

loḥ, *m.n.*, board, plank.—**hi**, —**yo**, or **halwaḥ**,—**di** (*plur.*) ; **halwaḥda aḥalka ku sarab**, floor the house.

los, *m.n.*, arachis, earth-nut. —**ki.**

luf, *m.n.*, slice.—**ki**, —**af**; **lufafki kibista i ken**, bring me the slices of bread.

lug, *f.n.*, leg, hind leg of animals. —**ti.**

(**nin, nag**) **lugla**, *a.*, one-legged (man, woman) ; **nagti lugla laida**, the one-legged woman.

luglawai, *m.n.*, one-legged person. —**hi.**

lug laan, *a.*, cripple (legless).

lugo, *v.p.*, be disappointed.

luggo, *v.tr.*, disappoint, play, prank.

luggoyo, *f.n.*, disappointment, prank, trick.

luḫ, *f.n.*, voice.—**di.**

luḫluḫo, *v.i.*, gargle.

luḫluḫasho, *f.n.*, gargle, gargling.

luḫmad, *f.n.*, bit, mouthful of food.—**di.**

luḫuf, *m.n.*, mockery.—**ki.**

luḫufi, or **luḫfi**, *v.tr.*, mock at.

luki, *f.n.*, hen.—**di.**

lul, *m.n.*, pearl.—**ki.**

lūl, *v.i.*, move, toss, shake milk to and fro to make butter.

lulan, *v.p.*, be tossed ; **lulma, wan lulmi** ; **gor walba dirtu wa lulanta**, the trees are always tossed to and fro.

lulin, *f.n.*, shake, shaking, toss. —**ti.**

lulo, *f.n.*, sleepiness ; — **leh** or — **badan**, sleepy ; **lulo i haisa**, I am sleepy.

lulmo, *v.i.*, be sleepy.

lun, *m.n.*, parchedness (caused by thirst).—**ki.**

lūn, *v.p.*, be lost ; **luma, wan lumi** ; **hadi an raga ra'o la'agtaidu wai lumi**, if I go with these men, my money will be lost.

lumi, *v.tr.*, lavish, squander, annihilate.

(**wil, nin**) **lumai**, *a.*, prodigal.
lumiyai, *m.n.*, debauchee, profligate, corrupter.—**hi.**
lunlumai, *m.n.*, larvæ of gnats.—**hi.**

M.

ma, *neg. part.* (used with verbs and meaning) not; **so ma aha,** it is not.
ma, *interr. part.* (often changed into **mi** and **mu**); **ma?** what? **nin ma?** what man? **so ma aha?** is it not? (this last expression is often used in conversation for asking the hearer if he has well understood).
ma'al, *f.n.*, dewlap (Somali sheep have a dewlap).—**shi.**
ma'alul, *f.n.*, starvation.—**shi; ninkasi ma'alul bu u baḫtiya,** that man is dying of starvation.
ma'an, *a.*, fresh, sweet; **biyo ma'an**, sweet water (*see* **ged ma'an**).
ma'anaiso, *v.tr.*, make sweet, sweeten; **sunkorta ḫawaḫha kuma'anaiso,** sweeten the coffee with sugar.
ma'ash, *m.n.*, brokerage.—**ki.**
ma'ash, *v.tr.*, gain, obtain.
ma'awinad, *f.n.*, help.—**di; ma'awinaddi u ka'**, go for help.
madad, *m.n.*, inkstand.—**ki,—yo.**
madad, *m.n.*, a kind of long thin bag used for loading camels with rice, jowaree, ..., when going into the jungle.—**ki.**
madag, *f.n.*, the two pieces of wood Somals rub one against the other for getting fire in the desert.—**ti.**
madaḥ, *m.n.*, head.—**hi, —yo.**
madaḥ adai, *m.n.*, bald head.—**hi.**
madaḥ ahaw, *v.tr.*, be the head, the superior, the chief; **ana u madaḥah,** I am the head, the chief; **ninki u madaḥah ma jogo** or **teg**, the superior, chief is not here *or* is gone.
madaḥ ḥanun, *m.n.*, headache.—**ki.**
madaḥ wareir, *m.n.*, vertigo, dizziness.—**ki.**
madar, *v.i.*, cry, shout loudly.
mađeđ, *m.n.*, underwood tree and its fruit (as the bean-tree berry). —**ki, —yo.**
mađi, *v.tr.*, empty.
mađo, *v.i.*, be empty; **mađda, wan mađan.**
mađan, *a.v.*, empty, void, hollow.
madar, *m.n.*, water-closet.—**ki.**
madfa', *m.n.*, big gun, cannon.—**hi.**
madow, *a.* and *m.n.*, black.
madowbai, *v.tr.*, blacken.
madow'adan, *a.* and *m.n.*, blue.
madrasad, *f.n.*, college, school.—**di.**
mađūn, *m.n.*, soot.—**ki.**
mafallaḫ, *a.*, extravagant.
ma'fo, *f.n.*, kind of charm tied to a leathern necklace (some wear it round the head and others round the neck).
mag, *m.n.*, attack.—**gi.**

mag, *v.tr.*, attack; **Ebbahai ba ku la magai,** God has decreed that upon you. (This word, as shown by this example, seems also to mean the decree of God.)

maga', *m.n.*, name.—**hi**, —**yo**; **maga'ha?** or **maga'hagu wa mahai?** what is your name? **ninka magi'hisa wa la yaḥan,** or **ad ba lo yaḥan,** the name of that man is renowned.

magalo, *f.n.*, town, country.

magarafad, *f.n.*, hoe.—**di.**

magol, *m.n.*, green trees and grass.—**ki.** (This word is used either when the trees are covered with leaves, or when all is green after rain.)

maha (contraction of **ma aha**), no.

mahae, or **mahe** (contraction of **ma aha e**); **kas mahae wa kan,** it is not that, it is this; **ka mahae, adiga kaleh o dan wada kaḥaiso,** except that one, take for yourself all the sheep.

maḥabis, *f.pl.n.*, prisoners.—**ti**; **mid maḥabistaah,** one prisoner.

maḥai? *int.prn.*, what? **wa mahai?** what is?

maḥai (with **u** before the verb), *ad.*, why? **maḥad** (for **mahai bad**) **u tagtai?** why did you go?

mahad, *f.n.*, thanks.—**di**; **nin nolba wa u mahad**: this expression, very often used, seems to mean, a man still living must be thankful for his life, *or* I am still alive, never mind my sickness.

mahadi, *v.tr.*, thank.

mahad u or **ugu naḥ**, *v.tr.*, thank him; **mahad ban kugu naḥai,** I thank you.

mahadda u naḥ, *v.i.*, say (read) the compliment, thanks; **mahaddi u naḥai,** I have said (read) the compliment.

maḥād, *m.n.*, big needle (used for sewing mats and bags).—**di.**

mahakamad, *f.n.*, court-house.—**di** (some say **hakamad**).

mahawis, or **maḥawis,** *f.n.*, loin-cloth.—**ti.**

maḥmaḥ, *f.n.*, maxim, proverb, saying, aphorism.—**di**; **wa maḥmaḥda wa yelka,** it is the maxim of the ancients.

mahadin, or **maḥadam,** *m.n.*, master, overseer.—**ki.**

maḥal, *m.n.*, hearing.—**ki.**

maḥal, *v.tr.*, hear, heed, listen, obey; **maḥla, wan maḥli**; **maan maḥal,** or **ma maḥal,** I did not hear; **ha maḥlin,** do not listen to, disobey; **ku maḥli ma dono,** he will not listen to you.

maḥashi, *v.tr.*, cause to hear; **na maḥashi,** let us hear.

maḥal, *f.n.*, young (of goats and sheep); *means also* children brought up together, as those in orphanages and seminaries.—**shi**; **wa maḥal badri,** it is a boy of the Padri.

maḥaldad, *m.n.pl.*, small boys.—**ki.**

maḫaldunyo, *f.n.*, children and cattle.
maḫal ḥerais, *m.* or *f.n.*, fold, enclosure for kids and lambs, evening star, time for putting kids and lambs into the enclosure.—**ki** or —**ti.**
maḫal ḥerai, *v.tr.*, fold kids and lambs.
maḫan, *a.*, absent; **wa maḫanyahai**, he is absent.
maḫnaw, *v.i.*, be absent; **todoba 'asho ba maḫnaw e iga tag**, be absent for a week and go away.
maḫnan, *f.n.*, absence.—**ti.**
maḫar, *m.n.*, skin of a dead calf ordinarily filled with grass or anything else; this figure, at the time of milking, is placed beside a cow (the calf of which is dead) in order to make her give her milk.—**ki.**
maḫarsar, *m.n.*, skin of a dead young camel, used for a similar purpose as that of the calf.—**ki.**
maḫar ku mal, *v.tr.*, milk (by taking the skin ...).
maḫari, *m.n.*, tree from which spear-shafts are made.—**gi.**
maḫayad, *f.n.*, coffee-shop.—**di.**
maḫaḥwi, *m.n.*, coffee-shop keeper. —**gi.**
maḫnud, *m.n.*, sodomy, sodomite. —**ki.**
maḫnudnimo, *f.n.*, sodomy.
maḫrib, *m.n.*, evening (sunset). —**ki.**
maḫsin, *m.n.*, apartment, room.—**ki.**
makawi, *m.n.*, amber.—**gi.**
maïd, *v.tr.*, wash, clean (with water); **so** —, go and wash; **si** —, continue to wash; **darka si maïd intan imanayo**, continue to wash the clothes till I come back.
maïdo, *v.r.*, wash yourself; **maïdta, wan maïdan.**
maïdan, *a.v.*, washed, cleansed.
maïdan, *v.p.*, be washed; **maïdma, wan maïdmi.**
maïdasho, *f.n.*, washing.
maïdaḥ, *f.n.*, second bark of the trees used for making ropes.—**di.**
maïdal, *m.n.*, grey horse.—**ki.**
maïdo, *f.n.*, wild date.
maïlin, *m.n.*, measure.—**ki.**
mal, *v.tr.*, milk; **so** —, go to milk.
'ana mal, *m.n.*, day (of 24 hours). —**ki.**
mal, *m.n.*, living property.—**ki.**
māl, *f.n.*, scrofula, king's evil.—**shi.**
mala, *m.n.*, thought, doubt.—**hi.**
malaha, *ad.*, perhaps, probably.
malai, *v.i.*, doubt, guess, suppose, suspect, think.
malaisan, *a.v.*, doubtful, suspected; **markabka imatinkisa manta wa malaisanyahai**, for to-day, the arrival of the ship is doubtful.
malab, *m.n.*, honey.—**ki.**
malaḥ, *f.n.*, pus, matter.—**di.**
malaïko, *f.n.*, angel.
malas, *f.n.*, chalk.—**li.**
malau, *m.n.*, lizzard.—**ki.**

malḫamad, *f.n.*, veil, large kerchief the women sometimes put on their head.—**di.**
malkad, *m.n.*, mortar.—**ki.**
malik, *m.n.*, king; **maliggi**, the king.
malikad, *f.n.*, queen.—**di.**
malin, *f.n.*, day (12 hours of light).—**ti, malmo** (*plur.*); **malintan todobad keda**, this day week; **malin daf**, every other day; **dawada malin daf 'ab**, drink (take) the medicine every other day.
mamus or **namus**, *m.* or *f.n.*, reputation, respect.—**ti**, —**ki.**
(**nin**) **mamusleh**, *a.* (man) of a good reputation.
(**nin**) **mamusla**, *a.* (man) of bad reputation.
mamus, *v.tr.*, respect, honour; **abbaha iyo hoyada mamus**, honour thy father and mother.
mamus jab, *m.n.*, defamation, ignominy, shame.—**ki.**
mamus jebi, *v.tr.*, defame, break the reputation.
man, *m.n.*, bud (of a flower), flowers of trees not bringing forth edible fruits.—**ki.**
man (*root*), day.
manta, *ad.*, to-day.
manto laili, *ad.*, all day long.
manafa'ad, *m.n.*, utility.—**ki.**
ma'nai, *m.n.*, meaning, signification.—**hi**; **eraiga ma'nihisi wa mahai?** what is the meaning of that letter?
mandil or **madil**, *f.n.*, penknife, razor.—**shi.**
manḫas, *m.n.*, scissors.—**ki.**
mantag, *v.i.*, vomit.
mantag, *m.n.*, vomiting, retching.—**gi.**
mantagi, *v.c.*, cause to vomit.
mar, *m.n.*, time.—**ki.**
mar, *ad.*, once.
marmar, *ad.*, sometimes.
marka, *conj.*, when.
marma? *ad.*, when.
markiba, *ad.*, immediately, suddenly, at once; **markiba ban iman**, I come at once.
mar badan, *ad.*, often.
marra, for **marna**, *ad.*, at any time, whensoever.
marki hore, *ad.*, the first time; **marki hore e an arkai ba dilai**, the first time I saw him, I killed him.
mar dambe, *ad.*, a second time; **marki dambe**, the second time.
mar hore, *ad.*, ago, long ago.
mar kaleh, *ad.*, again, another time; **marka ki kaleh**, the other time.
mar, *v.i.*, pass, walk on; **halka mar**, pass here; **hebta** —, walk on the shore; **deḥ** —, pass through, across; **dul** —, go beyond, surpass; **si** —, pass (away from me); **surinka si mar**, pass by that street; **ges** —, pass by on one side; **war! ges mar, ana an gesta kaleh maro**, pass by on one side, and let me pass by on the other; **ges ka** —, pass by (near); **aḫalkan ges ka mari**, I will pass by the house

mar o hel, *v.i.*, succeed, go and find if you can, get rid of somebody; **war! u mar o heli maisid,** oh! you cannot succeed; **wan u mar o helai,** I succeeded.

mari, *v.tr.*, rub, splash, smoothe; **darka sabunta** —, soap the linen; **darka birrta,** iron the clothes.

marso, *v.i.*, splash (yourself), coat, plaster; **doḥbada timaha marso,** splash or coat your hair with clay.

marin, *m.n.*, narrow, small way, path.—**ki.**

mar, *v.tr.*, tie the she-camel's teats (that the young may not suck); **hasha ka agmar,** tie one side, *i.e.*, two teats.

maraḫ, *m.n.*, tow used for closing the she-camel's teats.—**hi,** —**yo.**

maraḫsar, *m.n.*, part behind the camel's hump.—**ki.**

marawahad, *f.n.*, fan.—**di.**

marabi, *f.n.*, tame beast.—**di.**

mardaban, *m.n.*, jar for water.—**ki.**

marḫati, *f.n.*, witness, proof, evidence, testimony.—**di.**

marḫati ku fur, *v.tr.*, certify, testify, prove.

markab, *m.n.*, ship, vessel, steamer. —**ki,** —**yo** or **marakib** (*plur.*).

markab harbiha, *m.n.*, man-of-war; **markabki harbigaaha,** the man-of-war.

maro, *f.n.*, large Somali linen dress in which they wrap themselves; **mara adag,** thick cloth.

marodi, *m.n.*, elephant.—**gi; fol marodi,** ivory.

maroḥ, or **moroḥ,** *f.n.*, tree used for making ropes and baskets. —**di,** —**yo.**

maroji and **marori,** *v.tr.*, curl, wring, twist; **timahá maroji,** curl your hair; **ku** —, *v.tr.*, squeeze (by placing a rope or linen around the neck and wringing it), bore (with a borer or a drill).

marorsan, *a.v.*, curled, bored.

marrin, *m.n.*, brown colour.

marti, *f.n.*, guest, visitor, stranger. —**di.**

marti ḫadis, *m.n.*, inhospitality. —**ki.**

ma'ruf (nin), *a.* and *m.n.*, well known.—**ki; nin ma'rufah,** a well-known man.

mas, *m.n.*, serpent, snake.—**ki.**

masaf, *m.n.*, funnel.—**ki.**

masabid, *v.tr.*, blame, impute falsely.

masabid, *m.n.*, blamer.—**ki; nin la masabido,** *a.*, blaming.

masabidnimo, *f.n.*, blame.

masafiri, *v.tr.*, expel, drive away.

masafiris, *m.n.*, expulsion.—**ki.**

masajid, or **masjid,** *m.n.*, mosque. —**ki.**

masala, or **masalei,** *m.n.*, a skin Somals bear on their shoulders and use for kneeling on while praying.

masalo, *f.n.*, discussion, debate, religious discourse; **masalo badan bannu iss ku ḫabanai,** we had a great discussion.

masbaḥ, *m.n.*, altar.—**hi.**
ma'shar, *m.n.*, lesson.—**ki.**
maskaḥ, *f.n.*, brain.—**di.**
masibo, *f.n.*, misfortune.
masso, or **monso**, *f.n.*, a kind of big lizard. (Somals say that this lizard bleats as a young lamb and so deceives the ewe, drinks her milk, and some say also that it kills the young lamb.
masruf, *see* **musruf.**
masug, *m.n.*, miser (avaricious man).—**gi**, —**yo.**
matan, *m.n.*, twin (*m.*).—**ki.**
matan, *f.n.*, twin (*f.*).—**ti.**
mathal, *m.n.*, allegory, fable, apologue.—**ki.**
mati, *coll.f.n.*, children, boys, cattle, sheep, all that cannot go to fight.—**di**; **mati o dan kalaya o wihina gashan ḥad kaihi halka u so baḥa**, come all ye people and beasts which are unable to bear a shield and stand here by my side.
maujad, *f.n.*, flux, wave.—**di.**
maulid, or **mowlid**, *m.n.*, prayer for the dead.—**ki.**
maya, *ad.*, no (in this word *y* is pronounced in a manner which can be learnt only from a native).
mayad, *f.n.*, tide.—**di.**
mayai, or **ma'ai**, *m.n.*, rain (lasting one).—**hi.**
me and **meyai?** *ad.*, where? (*m.*); **ninki me?** where is the man? **dibigi meyai?** where is the ox?
medai? *ad.*, where? (*fem.*), **hoyadisi medai?** where is his mother?
mel, *f.n.*, place.—**shi.**
meshán, **meshá**, *ad.*, here.
meshás, *ad.*, there.
mesha, or **mesho**, *ad.*, there, yonder.
melma? *ad.*, where?
mel walba, or **mel kasta**, *ad.*, everywhere, wherever.
la mel noḥo, *v.tr.*, hold with (one), side with, take the part of.
meigag, *m.n.*, tree having a black bark.
mer, *v.tr.*, go round.
meri, or **mermeri**, *v.c.*, make him go round.
meraiso, *v.r.*, go (you) round.
mersan, *a.*, round, around.
mersanaw, *v.att.*, stand, be about, around.
mereg, or **murug**, *m.n.*, entanglement.—**gi.**
iss ku mérgi, or **iss ku méreg** *v.i.*, be entangled.
mergi, *m.n.*, muscles.—**gi.**
mera, *m.n.*, camel's hide.—**hi.**
merid, or **mirid**, *m.n.*, rust.
messego and **massego**, *f.n.*, grain (perhaps wheat).
mid, *num.*, one, single.—**ki** (*m.*), —**di** (*f.*).
mid kaleh, *num.*, another.
midka, —**ki kaleh**, *num.*, the other one (*m.*).
midda, —**di kaleh**, *num.*, the other one (*f.*).
midmid, *num.distr.*, one by one.
midla, *num.*, less one.

iss ku mid, *a.*, alike, equal.
kala mid, or **iss ku mid maaha**, *a.*, unlike, unequal, different, or not alike; **wa kala mid; labadatan ulod wa kala mid**, or **iss ku mid maaha**, these two sticks are not alike.
kala mid, *f.n.*, variety.—**di**; **ubaḥ kalamidda** or **ubaḥyada kalamiddoda yab bai ḥaban**, the variety of flowers is wonderful.
midna, *a.*, neither (either), none; **inamada middina waḥ ma barto**, none of the boys learns.
mid, *m.n.*, fruit.—**ki.**
midab, *m.n.*, colour, figure, quality, shape, form, sample.—**ki.**
midab u yel, *v.tr.*, figure, shape, &c.
midan (seems to be) a mixture; **daḥdarka dawadisu wa biyo midan**, or **wa wabayo midan**, the medicine of the doctor is pure water, *or* is pure poison.
midgan, *m.n.*, name of a Somali low caste.—**ki; midgo** (*plur.*), **midgayal** (*int. plur.*). Midgans make bows, arrows, saddles, spoons ...; they also possess the secret for the preparation of the **wabayo**, poison for arrows. They form, so to speak, a separate caste, never touching the things of the other Somals, nor do others eat or drink from the vessel of a Midgan. Some ceremonies, *e.g.*, the circumcision of girls, can be performed only by a Midgan woman.
midḥin, *m.n.*, stone used for grinding the curry-stuff.—**ki.**
mididin, *m.n.*, attendant, servant. —**ki.**
midig, *f.n.*, right hand.— **ti.**
midigta, *ad.*, to the right.
miḥ, *m.n.*, thread taken from the loin-cloth; they use this thread for sewing.—**hi.**
mi'i, *f.n.*, eye-tooth, tusk.—**di.**
milei', *m.n.*, heat and brightness of the sun.—**hi.**
miliḥ, *m.n.*, salt.—**hi.**
min, *m.n.*, bag of dates.—**ki; min gohi**, half a bag.
min, *a.*, each.
mindah, *a.*, perhaps. This word means probability, uncertainty. When asking for a thing and they are not sure it belongs to them, they use this word with the verb in the inter. negative form: **mindah kaigi ma aha?** is it not mine? **maya, ma aha**, no, it is not yours.
mindi, *f.n.*, knife.—**di.**
mindi i'risdab, disease (in the belly) of sheep; they burn them near the navel, otherwise they would soon die.
minfiḥ, *f.n.*, broom.—**di.**
minid, *m.n.*, minute.—**ki**, —**yo.**
minshar, *m.n.*, saw.—**ki.**
mir, *v.tr.*, clear, cleanse, filter; **biyaha mir**, clear, filter the water.
miran, *a.v.*, clear, cleansed.
miran, *v.imp.*, be clear; **wai mirmi**, it will be clear.
miri, *f.n.*, sum given monthly to

the Somali chiefs and their tribes.—**di**; **miridi na si la'agtu bannu donaina**, give us our monthly money, we are in want of it.
mirr, *m.n.*, grazing of horses at night.—**ki**, —**ti**.
so mirr, *v.i.*, graze the horses.
mis, *m.n.*, table.—**ki**.
mis (*pron.* **miz**), *v.tr.*, weigh.
misan, *m.n.*, weight, scales, balance.—**ki**.
misan, *v.tr.*, weigh; **misama**, **wan misami**.
misana, or **misna**, *ad.*, again.
miskin, *m.n.*, beggar.—**ki**; **masakin** (*plur.*).
mismar, or **musmar**, *m.n.*, nail.—**ki**.
musmar, *v.tr.*, nail.
mise, **mase**, **ama** or **amase**, *conj.*, or, else.
missig, *f.n.*, haunch.—**ti**.
miyi, *m.n.*, desert, jungle, country.—**gi**. This word, even when definite, is often used without the article.
miyid, *m.n.*, *pl.* and *s.*, corpse (used for men only).—**ki**.
miyir, *m.n.*, intellect, reason, prudence, fancy.—**ki**.
miyirsan, *a.*, wise, prudent.
miyirla, *a.*, stupid, foolish.
miyirlaan, *f.n.*, stupidity, foolishness.—**ti**.
miyir ḫab, *v.i.*, be prudent, reasonable.
miyir ḫaba, *a.*, intelligent, prudent.
mod, *v.i.*, think, appear.
waḥ la mod, *v.imp.*, seem, appear; **hadi an Adan tago**, or **u ko'o runba waḥba la modi**, if I go to Aden, truth will appear.
mod, *m.n.*, merchandise, property.—**ki**.
mog, **moga**, *a.*, negligent, ignorant (they call a man so who does not know news which everybody knows; this word must be a contraction of **ma ogain**, I did not know).
moji (contraction of **ma ogi**), I do not know.
mohoar madow, *m.n.*, B. Carterii frankincense tree.—**gi**.
moharad, *f.n.*, Boswellia Bhan Dajiana frankincense tree.—**di**.
mos, *v.i.*, heap, pile up the sand around the hut to preserve it from the water.
mos, *m.n.*, bank or hill made around the hut.—**ki**.
mot! *int.*, salutation given when on horseback, to a king, a chief, a governor; exclamation for inciting the horse, and to continue a song.
moyai, or **moya**, *m.n.*, wooden mortar.—**hi**.
moyaitumai, *m.n.*, pestle, stamper.
mu? *ad.*, why? **mu dar i keno**? why does he not bring me a coat?
mu, *m.n.*, time.—**gi**.
muadin, *m.n.*, muezzin.—**ki**.
mu'alim, *m.n.*, schoolmaster.—**ki**.
mud, *v.tr.*, prick, sting, stitch.
mudnin, *f.n.*, pricking, stitching.

muda', *m.n.*, fork.—**hi**, —**yo**. The Somali fork has only one prong, it is used as a bodkin in sewing.
muda'i, *m.n.*, plantiff.—**gi**.
mudali, *f.n.*, defendant.—**di**.
mudal, *m.n.*, miser, hard-hearted man.—**ki**.
muda'nyo, or **mida'nyo**, *f.n.*, kind of tree and its berry.
mudad, *f.n.*, period of time.—**di** (some tribes say, **madal**.—**ki**).
mudakar, *m.n.*, adult, young man.—**ki**.
mudāya', *m.n.*, spendthrift.—**hi**, —**yo**.
mudayo, or **murayo**, *f.n.*, gum tree and its fruit.
mudhi, *v.tr.*, strip off, skin.
mudso, *v.tr.*, suck (fruits, sweets, &c.).
mufo, *f.n.*, oven, hearth, furnace.
mufai, *v.tr.*, bake.
mufta, *m.n.*, key.—**hi**.
mugi, or **mugis**, half (a glass, a pot, a boiler ......); **hadub 'anaha mugi i ken**, bring me half a vessel of milk.
muhuyo, or **muhayo**, *f.n.*, grandmother.
muh, *m.n.*, discovery, vision, sight, appearance.
muhad, or **muhasho**, *f.n.*, apparition, appearance, vision (the thing seen).—**ki**, —**di**.
muho, *v.i.*, appear, seem; **muhda**, **wan muhan**; **u muho**, appear to him; **wa i, ku, u, no, idin muhata**, it appears, seems to me, thee, him, us, you; **wa muhda** or **muhata**, it is visible, apparent, evident, explained; **runta wa muhata**, the truth is evident.
muhalhalah, *m.n.*, impostor.—**hi**.
muhbasad, *f.n.*, unleavened bread (as Arabs and Somals eat).—**di**.
muhmad, *f.n.*, fresh meat cut into pieces, dried in the sun, and afterwards fried with ghee and served in the **hubo**.
muhuni, *v.tr.*, force, oblige, impel.
muhuno, *f.n.*, violence, extortion, compelling.
muhur, *v.i.*, dive.
muhuri, *v.i.*, duck, bathe.
muhurasho, *f.n.*, bath.
muji, *v.tr.*, expose for sale, display, show, point, explain; **i, u, no muji**, explain to me, him, us; **darka i muji**, show the clothes to me.
mujnin, or **mujis**, *f.n.*, exposure of goods, explanation.—**ti**, or —**ki**.
mūmin, *m.n.*, believer.—**ki**; **nin muminah**, a believer.
murayad, *f.n.*, looking-glass, mirror.—**di**.
murku'i, *v.tr.*, cause to sprain.
murko'o, *v.r.*, sprain yourself (in sliding ...).
murkuasho, *f.n.*, sprain, strain, bruise.
murjan, *f.n.*, coral.—**ti** (the red kind, with which they make collars, bracelets ...).
murjo', or **mujo'**, *m.n.*, infant.—**hi**.
murud, *m.n.*, sauce remaining in the plate or boiler.—**ki**.

murdi, *v.i.*, take with the forefinger the remains of sauce or food in a kettle or dish and lick it up.
murdiso, or **murudsato**, or **muruksato**, *f.n.*, forefinger.
muruh, *m.n.*, calf (of the leg), thick part of the arm.—**hi.**
murwad, *f.n.*, esteem, respect.—**di.**
murwad, *v.tr.*, esteem, respect.
mus, *m.n.*, razor.—**ki.**
musanow, *v.i.*, lament, cry, calling for the tribe (**tolai! tolai**); **musanowba, wan musanowbi.** This verb is only used when speaking of men.
mushaharo, *f.n.*, wages.
(**baya**) **mushtari**, trader, merchant (*see* **baya** ...).
mushrik, *m.n.*, two associates, partners; **mushriggi**, the ... ... (generally Somals will use **dawo**).
muslim, *m.n.*, Mohamedan.—**ki.**
musruf, or **masruf**, *m.n.*, food which a father procures for his family.—**ki.**
musruf, or **masruf**, *v.i.*, feed your family.

N.

na, *pers.prn.*, us; **naga**, from us; **no**, to us; **nogu**, by *or* near us.
na, *ad.*, also.
na! *int.* of calling; **na hoi!** ho woman! **na ya Fadumo!** or **na ya hoi!** a father at a distance from his daughter Fatma will so call her.
na', *v.tr.*, abandon, hate, reject, be disgusted; **wan ni'i.**
ne'ban, *f.n.*, hatred.—**ti.**
ne'baw, *v.tr.*, hate; **wa iss ne'byihin**, they hate each other; **wa iss.na'bnahai**, we hate each other.
na'alad or **na'lad**, some also say **na'adal** or **na'dal.—shi**, curse, bad, injurious word; **Allah ku na'lado**, may God curse you; **Ebbahai na'laddisu ha kugu dādo**, may God's curse (or malediction) fall upon you.
na'dal, *v.tr.*, curse.
na'al, *m.n.*, horse-shoe, the thick piece of leather they nail to the heel of the sandals when they are stitched.—**ki.**
nabad, *f.n.*, accord, conciliation, good news, peace.—**di, nabdo** (*plur.*); **nabad gala** (*plur.*), enter, be in peace; **nabad gelyo**, good-bye, farewell; **nabad hab**, be safe; **nabad hado, hata**, make truce; **Badri ma nabad ba?** is there peace, Father? **ha, wa nabad**, yes, there is peace (common salutation); **war ya Warsamow! nabad** or **nabaddi ma jirta?** oh! Warsama, is there peace? **ha, Ilah mahadi**, yes, thanks to God.
nabdi, *v.tr.*, pacify.
nabar, *m.n.*, blow, hurt, scar, stroke, wound.—**ki, —yo.**

nad, *m.n.*, leathern bucket used for watering cattle.
nadi, *m.n.*, a tree (in the jungle) of which they make their riding whips.—**gi.**
nadif, *f.n.*, cleanness.—**ti.**
nadifi, or **nadif ka dig**, *v.tr.*, make clean.
nadifah, *a.*, clean.
nadur, *f.n.*, slime, lime.—**ti.**
naf, *f.n.*, soul, life.—**ti**; **nafi ma ku jirto**, there is no life (a doctor says so when he declares that someone is dead).
nafta ka ḫad, *v.tr.*, kill; **nafti wa ku wareigaisa**, he is in agony.
naftu ha ka baḥdo, *v.i.*, agonize.
nafo, *a.* and *m.n.*, lifelessness.—**ahi**; **adinká nafahaah go**, cut off that lifeless member; **lugtaidi nafahaahaid**, my lifeless leg; **ga'antisu wa nafo**, his arm is lifeless.
naf, *reflex.pers.prn.*, inflected with *poss.prn.*; **naftada u shaḫaiso**, work for yourself; **naftaidan u shaḫaista**, I work for myself.
nag, *f.n.*, woman, wife.—**ti.**
nagnimo, *f.n.*, womanhood.
nāḥ, *v.i.*, become fat.
nāḥsan, *a.v.*, fat; **ninki naḥsana**, the fat man.
nāhi, *v.tr.*, fatten.
naḥ, *v.i.*, start, shrink, be astounded, stunned; **wan niḥi.**
niḥi (with **kaga**), *v.tr.*, stun, astound, startle, affright, alarm; **wan kaga neḥin shekagaiga kaga niḥin**, my story will astound him.
naḥadin, *f.n.*, astonishment, grief felt on receiving the news of some heavy loss, starting, shrinking.—**ti.**
naḥ, *v.i.*, be merciful, charitable; **wan niḥi**; **iga naḥ**, be merciful to me.
naḥadin, *f.n.*, clemency, charity, mercy, pity.—**ti.**
naḥaris, *f.n.*, mercy, pity (especially attributed to God).
naḥaris (with **u**), *v.i.*, have mercy; **no naḥariso**, have mercy on us.
naḥarisla, *a.*, unkind, *or* **naḥarisba ma yaḫan**, who does not know pity.
naḥas, *f.n.*, brass, copper.—**ti.**
naḥwi, *m.n.*, grammar.—**gi.**
naḫ, *v.tr.*, read; **wan niḫi.**
naḫso, *v.r.*, read for yourself.
naḫuda, *m.n.*, captain (of a ship, a buggalow).—**hi.**
naḫwa, *a.v.*, chosen; **mid naḫwaah i ken**, bring me a chosen fruit.
naḫai (with **ka**), *v.tr.*, choose for me.
ka naḫaiso, *v.tr.*, choose.
najar, carpenter (*see* **nijar**).
naïl, *f.n.*, she-lamb.
nana, *m.n.*, sweets, sugar-plums, &c.—**hi.**
nanaïs, *f.n.*, epithet, nickname.—**ti.**
nar, *f.n.*, hell.—**ti**; **dabka narta**, hell-fire.
narjin, **narajin**, or **narjil**, *f.n.*, cocoa-nut.—**ti.**
nas, *m.n.*, breast (of women), bosom (for both sexes).—**ki.**

na's, *m.n.*, blockhead, stupid, foolish, simpleton.—**ki**, —**yo**.

nasab, *m.n.*, a generous man (giving willingly).—**ki.**

nasab, *m.n.*, pedigree (of horses only).—**ki.**

nasi, *v.c.*, make him rest.

naso, *v.i.*, rest, take rest.

nasad, or **nasasho**, *m.n.*, rest, nap.—**ki**, —**di**.

nasib, *m.n.*, luck.—**ki**; **Abdi wa hof nasib ḥun**, Abdi is a person of bad luck.

nashug, *m.n.*, quid, snuff.—**gi.**

so nawil, *v.tr.*, give, deliver, bring the cargo from the ship; **ka nawil ḥebta**, bring the cargo from the shore.

si nawil, *v.i.*, carry your cargo to the ship.

ne'au, *f.n.*, air, breeze.—**di**; **ne'auda an u baḥno**, let us go in the air, breeze.

ne'awi, *v.tr.*, aerate.

nebi, *m.n.*, prophet, saint.—**gi.**

nef, *m.n.*, animal, quadruped.—**ki.**

neif, *f.n.*, breath.—**ti.**

neifso, *v.i.*, breathe.

nejis, *a.* and *m.n.*, cunning.—**ki**, —**yo**. This word is also sometimes used for immodest, immoral.

nejisnimo, *f.n.*, cunningness.

nidar, *v.i.*, vow; **nidra**, **wan nidri.**

nijar, or **najar**, *m.n.*, carpenter. —**ki.**

nijas, or **nejis.**—**ki**, *f.n.*, filthiness.—**ti**; **nin nijasah**, a filthy man.

nimmer, *m.n.*, Arabic name of the leopard.

nin, *m.n.*, man.—**ki.**

nin ūn, somebody, any man; **nin ūn igu yed**, call me a man, somebody.

ninnimo, *f.n.*, manhood.

nin rerod, *m.n.*, foreigner; **ninki rerod**, the foreigner (only women and children use this word for foreigner).

nirig, *m.n.*, young camel.—**gi**; **nirgo** (*plur.*).

nobad, or **nobiad**, *f.n.*, tower.—**di**; **nobad fol marodi laga samaiyai**, a tower of ivory.

noḥo, *v.i.*, go back, happen, occur; **noḥda**, **wan noḥon**; **waḥhai noḥotai**, it happened.

so noḥo, *v.i.*, come back, return; **la** —, go back with it; **la so** —, come back with it.

so noḥod, *m.n.*, return.—**ki.**

nol, *a.*, living, existing; **beir nol**, a living tree.

nolai, *v.tr.*, animate, resuscitate.

nolaw, *v.i.*, revive.

nolau, *f.n.*, life.—**ti**; **nolanta ahiro**, the next life (next world).

nug, *v.tr.*, absorb, suck (especially used for children).

nuji, *v.tr.*, make him suck; **inanka naska nuji**, make the child suck.

'ana nujis, *m.n.*, lactation.—**ki.**

nugail, *m.n.*, cows which must be watered immediately after having been milked.

dega nugul, *a.*, obedient.

dega nuglow, *v.i.*, be obedient.
dega nuglan, or **dega nugail.—ki,** obedience.
nugul, *m.n.*, shivering man.
nurad, *f.n.*, lime, mortar, chunam.
nusked, nisked, or **neski,** half.

O.

ó (used as a *dem.prn.* with its appropriate consonant), yon, yonder.
o, *conj.*, and. Contraction of **iyo**; it is used for joining sentences and parts of sentences: **abbahá iyo hoyadá ba yimadai o na la fadistai,** your father and mother came and remained with us.
ōd, *v.tr.*, obstruct, make a fence, an enclosure.
ōd, *f.n.*, hedge, fence, enclosure made of trees cut in the jungle.—**di.**
ōdan, *a.v.*, shut, obstructed; **dauga wa ōdanyahai,** the road is obstructed.
o'd, *m.n.*, voice.—**ki.**
odai, *m.n.*, old man.—**gi.**
odo (*root*, not used in the imperative mood, they commonly use **deh**), say, tell; **wan odan,** I will say, tell.
odrogad, *m.n.*, a small distance (a ramble, a walk).—**ki.**
ofai, *f.n.*, sea-gull.—**di.**
ofno, *m.n.*, coupling of neat cattle; **wa oftai,** she has been covered.
ōg, *f.n.*, fire (of houses being burnt).—**ti**; **dai ōgta magaladi ka bahaisa,** look! the fire in the town is extending.
og (*root*), *v.*, know; **wa la ogyahai,** it is known; **ya og?** or **ya yahan?** who knows.
ogow, *v.tr.*, know, beware of, remind; **wahhas ād u ogow** (some say) **wahhas ād u oho,** be well aware of, remind well; iss —, take care of yourself.
ogan, *a.*, wilfully, expressly; **ogan ban u falai,** I did that wilfully.
ogaisi, *v.tr.*, communicate, let him know, tell, remind, acquaint, discover; **i, no ogaisi,** tell me, us.
oggol, *m.n.*, will, willing, knowing, complying.—**ki.**
oggolai, *v.i.*, assent, consent.
oggolaisi, *v.c.*, make him consent.
oggolan, *f.n.*, acceptance, compliance, knowledge animals have of those who feed them and that of small children for their parents.—**ti.**
iss oggolan, *f.n.*, accordance, agreement with.—**ti.**
oggolaw, *v.i.*, accept, comply, be willing; **nefkasi wa i oggolyahai,** that animal knows me; **nef oggol,** a tame animal.
ohon (for **ohaw**), *v.tr.*, know; **wa la yahan,** it is known; **ninkas ād lo yahan i so kahai,** lead

that well-known man to me (some use the Arabic word **ma'ruf**, well known; **ninki ma'rufkaaha iga yed**, call me the well-known man).

oḫon, *f.n.*, knowledge, science.—**ti.**

oḫonlaan, *f.n.*, ignorance.—**ti.**

oḫonin, *m.n.*, acquaintance.—**ki**, —**yo.**

oḫonsi, *v.c.*, make him know, be acquainted with.

oḫonso, *v.tr.*, get acquainted with.

oḫli, *m.n.*, bag.—**gi.**

oi, *v.i.*, cry, weep; **oiya**, **wan oiyi**; **maḫal ruḫba oiyaya**, heard a spirit crying.

kaga oi, *v.c.*, make him cry.

oin, *f.n.*, sigh, cry, weeping.—**ti.**

oll, *v.i.*, be lying, remain quiescent, live.

'oll, *m.n.*, adversary, army, enemy. —**ki**; **'oll ahada**, be enemies; **'oll bainu nahai**, we are enemies; **wa 'oll**, or **wa iss u 'oll**, they are enemies.

'ollow (with **la**), *v.i.*, become enemies with; — **'olloba**, become (ye) enemies; **wai 'ollobi**, they will become enemies.

'ollad, *f.n.*, enmity, dispute, feud, revenge, vengeance.—**di.**

'olladi, *v.i.*, revenge, take vengeance.

olol, *v.i.*, growl; **gelu wa olola**, the camel growls.

olol, or **olul**, *m.n.*, flame, blaze.—**ki**, —**yo.**

ololi, *v.tr.*, inflame, light; **dabka ololi**, light the fire.

on, *m.n.*, thirst.—**ki.**

omanaw, *v.att.*, be thirsty; **iss on tir**, or **iss harad tir**, quench your thirst.

onkod, *m.n.*, thunder.—**ki**, —**yo.**

'o'ob, *m.n.*, hole between two hides covering a Somali hut in which they can place or conceal something.—**ki.**

orgi, *m.n.*, he-goat.—**gi.**

orjujun, *m.n.*, cripple.—**ki**; **orjujun ban aha**, I was a cripple.

orod, *v.i.*, run; **orda**, **wan ordi**; — **o tag**, go away; **so** —, come quickly.

orod, *m.n.*, running, speed.—**ki.**

orr, *m.n.*, cry, shout.

orri, *v.i.*, cry, shout.

osob, *m.n.*, spring, verdure.—**ki**; **miyi wa osob**, the jungle is verdant.

owlaled, *a.*, neutral tint, green.

owlan, *a.*, brown, reddish.

ow (*see* **yohow**), *affix meaning* you; **abbihisow kalai**, you, his father, come; **abbahaiow kalai**, you, my father, come.

R.

ra', *v.tr.*, accompany, go along with; **iss** —, go together; **wainu iss ra'i**, we go together; **so** —, come with him.

ríb, *v.tr.*, wish; **maḫad rabta?** what do you wish?

rábsi, *m.n.*, chewing.—**gi.**

rábso, *v.tr.*, chew; **maḥad rabsanaisa?** what are you chewing?
rabrad, or **rarad**, *f.n.*, coffin, bier.—**di.**
rabuḥ, Wednesday (*see* **arbaḥa**).
rad, *m.n.*, footstep, trace.—**ki**; **rad go**, lose the trace; **so rad goiyai.**
radi, *v.tr.*, follow, trace, track.
radis, *m.n.*, follower —**ki.**
rad gur, a man who traces another; **radkisa gur**, trace him; **radkayaga gur**, follow our tracks.
ra'do, *f.n.*, pursuit (of enemies, robbers).
ra'dai, *v.tr.*, pursue.
ra'da reb, *f.n.*, those who remain behind to resist the pursuers. —**ti.**
radaḥ, or **raḥad**, *v.tr.*, grind; **radḥa, wan radḥi.**
radi, *a.*, wishing, willing; **radi ban ku ahai**, I am willing.
raf, *m.n.*, sheep's or goat's hoof (for one separately).—**ki.**
rag, *m.n.*, masculine sex, men.—**gi** (when this word is taken in a general sense, they say **ragi**, men, people).
nin ragah, a brave man, fearing God and telling the truth.
ragnimo, *f.n.*, magnaminity, men, mankind.
rāg, *v.i.*, delay, be late, long; **maḥad ku rāgtai?** why have you been so late?
rāgsan, *a.v.*, late.
rāji, *v.tr.*, adjourn, delay.
rāgnin, *f.n.*, delay, slowness.—**ti.**
rag'ad, *m.n.*, at the finishing of the Mussulman prayers, when on their knees, they touch the ground with their heads, and this stooping is called **rag'ad.** In the morning they have two **rag'adod**, at noon four, and at about 3 or 4 p.m. four; after sunset they have three **rag'adod**, at **ishai** (about 7 p.m.) four.
rah, *m.n.*, frog, toad.—**hi.**
raḥa, raḥo, or **raḥad**, *f.n.*, contentment, plentitude of satisfaction, happiness.—**di**; **raḥad ban ku haista**, or **raḥaddi ban haista**, I have the happiness; **raḥo yu ku jira**, he is in happiness; **nin Ebbahai raḥo u aburai**, God has created man for happiness.
raḥaisi, *v.c.*, cause him to be satisfied.
rahaisan, *a.v.*, happy.
raḥaiso, *v.i.*, be satisfied; **raḥaista, wan raḥaisan.**
rahmad, *f.n.*, mercy, charity.—**di.**
raḥim, *m.n.*, charitable man.—**ki** (**nin raḥimah** is also used).
rahan, *v.tr.*, pawn (give as security); **rahma, wan rahmi.**
rahmad, *f.n.*, pawn, security.—**di.**
raḥan, *f.n.*, flock of quadrupeds, assembly of men.—**ti**; **raḥanti meshi bal inai jogto dai**, look if there is an assembly of men.
raḥ, *v.i.*, bend, stoop for drinking water, lap.

raḥ, *f.n.*, corpse, cadaver.—**di.**
rakāb, *m.n.*, passenger.—**ki.**
rakab, or **rakakab**, *m.n.*, stirrup, brave man, warrior.—**ki, —yo.**
rako', *f.n.*, a profound inclination made in praying.—**di.**
rako', *v.i.*, make a profound inclination.
rai and **rairai**, *v.i.*, rejoice, cheer; **iss ka —**, be glad, rejoice.
rairaisi, *v.tr.*, cheer, rejoice; **kaga —**, make him rejoice.
raïn, *f.n.*, joy, gladness.—**ti.**
raïs, *m.n.*, barber, shaver.—**ki.**
raïs, *m.n.*, wet land, wet soil found in digging and turning over the ground.—**ki.**
ra'is, *m.n.*, prime, the first.—**ki.**
raïs magado, *f.n.*, bridge of the foot, sole.
rajai, *m.n.*, orphan.—**gi** (used especially for one bereaved of mother).
ramash, *m.n.*, fertile place, covered with grass (well watered).—**ki.**
ran, *f.n.*, ringlet of hair.—**ti**; **rantayuhudda**, the curl of hair the Jews have on each side.
rani, *f.n.*, queen at cards.—**di.**
raniyad, *f.n.*, queen (*see* **malikad**).—**di.**
ranji, *m.n.*, colour.—**gi.**
ranji, *v.tr.*, paint; **wan ranjiyi.**
rár, *v.tr.*, load.
rár, *m.n.*, load.—**ki.**
ráran, *a.v.*, laden.
rār, *f.n.*, room (in a house), a place upon a tree where robbers hide the stolen things.—**ti.**
rār, *v.i.*, prepare a place in a house, on a tree ....
rāran, *a.v.*, ready, prepared; **mesha wa rarantahai**, the place is ready, prepared.
rarab, *f.n.*, hand-barrow used for carrying dead bodies.—**ti.**
raran, *m.n.*, embers, sand heated by the sun.—**ki.**
ras and **ras gura**, *m.n.*, ant-hill (of **ḥudanjo**).—**ki, —gi.**
rasās, *f.n.*, lead.—**ti.**
rash, *m.n.*, shot.—**ki.**
rási, *m.n.*, cape.—**gi.**
rásai, *v.tr.*, heap up, accumulate.
rasáisan, *a.v.*, accumulated.
rásais, *m.n.*, accumulation.—**ki.**
rásul, *m.n.*, apostle.—**ki.**
rāti, *m.n.*, he-camel.—**gi.**
rawi, *m.n.*, wealthy.—**gi**; **nin rawiah**, a wealthy man.
reb, *v.tr.*, leave, lay aside, away; **wan kugu rebi**, I will leave it for you; **ku reb**, leave out.
rer, *m.n.*, assemblage of Somali huts within an enclosure, village, family.—**ki**; **rer kani wa rerma?** or **rer ma tihin?** or **war! rerku wa rerma?** whose **rer** is this? A Somal in the jungle, wishing to speak politely to the inhabitants of a **rer** he does not know, asks one of the above three questions.
rer miyi, *m.n.*, a countryman.—**gi.**
rer magala, *f.n.*, people of a town.—**di.**
ri, *f.n.*, she-goat.—**di.**
riyo, *m.n.*, goat (general name).—**hi.**

riyod, or **riyo**, *m.n.*, dream.—**ki**; **wa riyod**, it is a dream.
riyo, *v.i.*, dream.
rial, *m.n.*, thaler, dollar.—**ki** (*see* **harshi**).
rid, *v.tr.*, pitch, throw, upset; **ku** —, put in, throw in, aim at; **wan ku ridai o la wahyai**, I aimed at it and missed it; **kaga** —, shoot; **waraba madahha kaga rid**, shoot that hyæna in the head; **ka** —, conduce.
rif, *v.tr.*, plume *or* pluck (a bird, a fowl).
rifai, *m.n.*, a bold and headstrong man.—**hi**.
rifakal, *m.n.*, a bold man, taking the part or party of the **rifai**.
rih, *v.tr.*, push, shove.
rih, *m.n.*, push, pushing.—**hi**.
rima', or **rimai'**, fraction $\frac{1}{8}$.
rimai, *m.n.*, matrix, womb.—**gi**. This word is not habitually used in speaking of women, although it is the true word for matrix.
rob, *m.n.*, rain.—**ki**; **biyihi 'arrada rogai**, deluge.
rodol, *m.n.*, pound (weight).—**ki**.
rög, *v.tr.*, reverse, turn, set upside down, spill, take ashore, land; **war alabadada rog**, land your goods; **so** —, bring ashore.
rógan, *a.v.*, upside down; **distigi wa roganyahai**, the kettle is upside down.
rogan, *v.i.*, be troubled; **wan rogmi**.
rógmo, *v.i.*, be set upside down; **kolka dunidu rógmato**, when the world will be set upside down, or destroyed.
rognin, *f.n.*, abashment, spoliation, landing.—**ti**.
rōn, *a.*, good, generous; **wa ron**, it is good; **ka ron tahai**, it is better than, *or* it is more; **Yusuf Musa ka ron**, Joseph is better than Moses; **ina ka ahli ron**, he is more intelligent than we are.
ror, *v.i.*, run, palpitate.
ror, *m.n.*, kind of lizard.—**ki**.
rūbab, *m.n.*, marsh.—**ki**, —**yo**.
rubad, *m.n.*, life.—**ki**, —**yo**.
rubad, *f.n.*, the place below the throat, just above the middle of the chest, the thyroid body, trachea.
rubiad, *f.n.*, rupee.—**di**; **rubabi** (*plur.*). In counting, Somals employ the contraction **rubod**, instead of **rubiadod**.
rubi, *m.n.*, 1 shilling, 8 annas.
rug, *f.n.*, abode, dwelling, residence, tent.—**ti**.
rugajso, *v.i.*, live, dwell.
rūg, *m.n.*, knee, callousness of the knees.—**gi**, —**yo**.
rug, *v.tr.*, break the bone in gnawing it.
ruh and **ruhruh**, *v.tr.*, shake, swing.
ruho, *v.i.*, be shaken, tossed; **dabaishi ya i ruhdai**, I was tossed by the wind.
ruhan, *a.v.*, shaken, tossed.
ruhnin, *f.n.*, shake, shaking.—**ti**.

ruḥan, *v.p.*, be crushed down, downcast, exhausted; **ruḥma, wan ruḥmi; wa si ruḥmi,** I shall be exhausted (in going); **wa so ruḥmai,** I was exhausted in coming.
ruḥsad, *f.n.*, permission.—**di; ruḥsad i si,** give me permission.
rukún, *m.n.*, leg (of a chair, a table, a bed).—**ki.**
rūji, *v.tr.*, eradicate, uproot.
rūjin, or **rūjis,** *f.n.*, eradication. —**ti,** —**ki.**
rum, Turkey.
rumi, *m.n.*, Turk.—**gi.**
rumai, *m.n.*, toothbrush, tooth-stick.—**gi.**
run, *f.n.*, truth, certainty.—**ti; wa run, wa runtis, wa runted, wa runtod,** it is true.
rumai, *v.tr.*, ascertain, confirm the truth.
rumaiso, *v.tr.*, believe, take the truth for certain.
rumaisad, *m.n.*, belief.—**ki.**
rushai, *v.i.*, besprinkle water in front of the house after sweeping in order to get fresh air; **u rushai,** water for him.
rushaiso, *v.r.*, water for yourself.

S, Sh.

sā, contr. for **sida,** so; **war! sā fal,** oh! do so; **sā berri an falo,** let me do so to-morrow.
sa (*root*), *meaning* a portion of time; **saka,** this morning; **sa dambe,** the day after to-morrow; **sakub,** or **sakun,** the day after the day after to-morrow.
sa', *m.n.*, cow; **sa'ha, si'hi,** the cow; **sa'yaw,** cows (*plur.*).
sa'ab, *m.n.*, Somali dance (men and women dance together striking their hands), palm of the hand; **sa'abka ku 'un,** eat with the hand.
sa'ad, *f.n.*, hour, clock, watch.—**di; sa'ad badked,** half-an-hour.
sáb, *f.n.*, general name given to the three Somali castes, Tumal, Midgan, Yibir; **Tumal wa sáb.**
sāb, *m.n.*, light wooden basket-work surrounding the jars of ghee and butter, lid used for a **deri,** or **disti.**
sabab, *f.n.*, cause, reason, risk (success as well as failure is called **sabab**).—**ti; waḥhas sababtisi mahai ahaid?** what was the cause of that? **sababti waḥhai ahaid,** the cause was that.
sabab, *v.tr.*, risk; **la'agtada waḥha ku sabab,** risk your money in that affair.
sababo, *v.i.*, adventure, dare.
sabai, *v.i.*, float; **miyidku wa sabainaya,** the corpse is floating.
sabais, *m.n.*, floating.—**ki.**
sabbar, *m.n.*, food.—**ki.**
sabbar, *v.tr.*, feed, nourish.
sabbaro, *v.tr.*, feed, maintain (your children).

sabkah, or **sadkah**, *f.n.*, fruit wrapped up in a pod or husk covered with prickles.—**di.**

sabein, *f.n.*, she-lamb.—**ti.**

sábir, *m.n.*, patience, perseverance.—**ki** (*see* **samir**).

sabo, *f.n.*, wet place becoming muddy by the trampling of camels, clean place made dirty, contagious sickness.—**di.**

sabol, *m.n.*, poor man or woman having just what is necessary for a living; **nin, nag sabolah,** a poor man, woman; **ninki sabolkaaha, nagti sabolkaahaid,** the poor man, woman.

sabti, *f.n.*, Saturday.—**di.**

sabur, *m.n.*, psalms.—**ki.**

sadaho! *int.*, cry of the poor when asking for alms.

sadahad, *f.n.*, alms.—**di; sadahad ban ku sin,** I will give you alms.

sadahadai (with **ku**), *v.tr.*, give alms.

sadahaiso, *v.r.*, give alms (for yourself, for your good).

sadar, *m.n.*, row, line.—**ki; sadar u jogsada,** arrange yourself, sit in a row, line.

sadeh, *num.*, three.—**di; sadeh hal ban ku lehyahai,** I have to tell you three words.

sadehad, *num.ord.*, third, thrice.

sádo, *f.n.*, privilege.

safai, *v.tr.*, clean.

safaisan, *a.v.*, clean, cleansed.

safan, or **daba safan**, *m.n.*, kind of fish.—**ki.**

safan, *f.n.*, chaps (of the heel), especially due to walking on wet grass.—**ti.**

(nin) safanleh, *m.n.*, traveller.—**hi; safanlayashi ba yimadai,** the travellers have come.

sáfar, *m.n.*, caravan, journey (made with a caravan).—**ki; safro** (*plur.*); **annaga o safarah,** our caravan.

sáfar, *v.i.*, travel with a caravan; **safra, wan safri; safarka hore ka so hād o ka dambe ra‘,** leave the first caravan and go with the second.

nin safaráh, a traveller with a caravan.

safiri, or **masifiri**, *v.tr.*, expel, banish; **la masafiri,** he is expelled.

safirsan, *a.v.*, expelled; **ninki safirsana,** the expelled man.

safli, *m.n.*, hide adorned or embellished with rows of shells.—**gi.**

sagal, *num.*, nine.

sagalad, *num.ord.*, ninth.

sagashan, *num.*, ninety.

sagan madon, *f.n.*, nape.—**ti.**

sagaro, or **sakaro**, *f.n.*, sand antelope.

sahai, provisions either for maintenance at home or for travel.—**di.**

sahal, *v.tr.*, bless (*see* **sal**).

sahal, *v.tr.*, render easy, ease.

saharad, *f.n.*, wooden box, case.—**di.**

saharo, *f.n.*, fecal matters, urine.

saharo, or **saharod**, *v.i.*, purga ventrem; **so** —, go and purga ventrem.

sāheb, *m.n.*, master, sir.—**ki.**
sahīb, *m.n.*, companion, friend.—**ki.**
saheh, *m.n.*, signature.—**hi.**
sahima, **sehimad**, or **sihimad**, *f.n.*, boat.—**di.**
sah, *f.n.*, night (time of sleeping).—**di.**
sah dehe, *f.n.*, midnight; **sahda dehe tos**, arise at midnight.
sah, *m.n.*, two annas.—**hi.**
sahaf, *m.n.*, roof.—**ki.**
sahaf, *f.n.*, woman's comb (with ten or twelve teeth).—**ti.**
sahran, *v.i.*, be drunk; **sahrama**, **wan sahrami.**
(**nin**) **sahransan**, *a.v.*, drunk.
kaga sahrami, *v.c.*, make him, cause him to be drunk; **war! igaga sahrami**, oh! you will make me drunk.
sakār, *m.n.*, sternum, breast-bone.—**ki.**
saïd, *v.tr.*, asperse, sprinkle; **iss ka** —, throw; **ku** —, sprinkle on him, them; **nagu saïd**, besprinkle us; **ahalka hortisa biyaha ku saïd**, sprinkle water in front of the house.
saïm, *m.n.*, a fasting man.—**ki**; **saïmin** (*plur.*).
saïn, *f.n.*, hair of a horse's tail, mane of a horse.—**ti.**
sal, *m.n.*, breech, bottom of a vessel, foundation, groundwork.—**ki**; **salka dig**, sit down.
sal, *a.*, true; **wa sal**, it is true; **Eraiga Ilahhi wa sal**, the word of God is true; **eraigasi wa sal**, that word is true.
sāl (*see* **sahal**), *v.tr.*, bless.
salād, *f.n.*, prayer.—**di.**
salah, *m.n.*, deck of a ship.—**hi.**
salah, *v.tr.*, pat, stroke, soothe, smoothe.
salahid, *f.n.*, caress, pat, smoothing.—**di.**
salalmodleh, *m.n.*, bustard (large one).—**hi.**
salam, *v.tr.*, salute, hail.
salam, salutation, hail! **salam alekum**, salutation to a stranger.
salamad, *f.n.*, salutation, farewell (be in safety).—**di.**
salasa, *f.n.*, Tuesday.—**di.**
salid, *f.n.*, oil.—**di.**
salib, *m.n.*, cross.—**ki**, —**yo** (*see* **iss ku talab**).
sallado, *f.n.*, kind of spear.
sallah, *m.n.*, place prepared in a boat for passengers.—**hi.**
sallan, *m.n.*, staircase, ladder.—**ki.**
sālo, *f.n.*, dung (of camels, sheep, goats).
salol, *m.n.*, jowaree.—**ki.**
samah, *f.n.*, pardon.—**di.**
samah, *v.tr.*, pardon, forgive, excuse; **wan samihi**; **i samah**, excuse me; **issa samaha**, pardon each other; **manta wan ku samahaya e mar kaleh ha u nohon**, I pardon you to-day, do not do it again.
samai, *v.tr.*, do, make, construct, repair; **dunidu wahba laga ma samain**, the world is made out of nothing; **la** —, transact, act with.
samaisan, *a.v.*, made.

samaisnaw, *v.att.*, be made.
samaisan, *v.pass.*, be made; **samaisma, wan samaismi; ka samaisma**, is made of, from.
samain, *f.n.*, making, construction.—**ti.**
samais, *m.n.*, maker of everything, constructor.—**ki**, —**yo.**
iss ku samai, *v.tr.*, join with thread, rope, nail.
iss ku samais, *m.n.*, joining; **iss ku samaiski**, the joining.
dar samai, *v.tr.*, weave.
saman, *m.n.*, goods, things.—**ki**; **samanki o dan laga so rog markabka**, all the goods have been brought from the ship.
samar (with **ka**), *v.i.*, give up for lost (it is the word used at the announcement of a death).
sa'maran, *f.n.*, nice dates.—**ti.**
sambab, *m.n.*, lungs.—**ki**, —**yo.**
sambil, *m.n.*, basket.—**ki.**
samir, *m.n.*, patience, perseverance.—**ki.**
samir, *v.i.*, be patient, persevering, endure with patience; **samra, wan samri.**
san, *aff.*, used with **waḥ**; **wa waḥsan**, it is good, well.
san, *m.n.*, nose.—**ki**; **san balladan**, a flat nose.
sanḫaror, *m.n.*, bridge of the nose.—**ki.**
sanḫo, *f.n.*, channel of the nose, twang.
sanḫoleh, *m.n.*, snuffer, a man having a twang.—**hi.**
sān, *f.n.*, hide of camels and of neat cattle.—**ti.**

sānta ka biḥi, *v.tr.*, skin, flay.
sana', *m.n.*, conjuror.—**hi.**
sana'ad, *f.n.*, conjuration.—**di.**
sana'ho, *f.n.*, charm given to a sick person, or words pronounced to conjure his evil, bad spirits.
sanad, *f.n.*, year.—**di**; **sanaddi hore**, the past year, ago (even long ago); **sanaddi dowed**, past year (not long ago); **sanaddan so so'ota**, this coming year.
sanam, *m.n.*, idol.—**ki**, —**yo.**
sanduḥ, *m.n.*, box, chest, trunk. —**hi**, —**yo.**
sanga, or **sangai**, *m.n.*, stallion. —**hi.**
sanḫad, *f.n.*, noise, sound, sound in the desert.—**di**; **degaiso! sanḫad ban maḫlaya**, hark! I hear a sound.
kaga sanḫadi, *v.i.*, make a noise (with something).
sanūnad, *f.n.*, curry.—**di.**
sár, *v.tr.*, place, put on, set on; **so** —, bring away, make go out.
sáran, *a.v.*, placed; **waḥ mel saran**, a thing put in a place.
sarrai, *v.i.*, be (placed) first, go at the head of, before; **inamada u sarrai**, be the first of the boys; **ugu sarrai**, be the first of all, go before; **nagu sarrai**, go before us; **ka** —, be over the others, command, sway.
sarraisi (with **ugu**), *v.tr.*, appoint.
sarsar, *v.i.*, put one over the other.

sara ka', *v.i.*, get up, rise.
sara ka', *m.n.*, a getting up, resurrection.—**hi.**
sár, *v.tr.*, cut, incise.
sársar, *v.tr.*, vaccinate, cut the skin.
sarsar, *m.n.*, vaccination, cutting of the skin.—**ki.** Somals have the habit of cutting the skin of their children when they are sick and especially when they are pot-bellied.
sarmo, *f.n.*, cut, gash, incision.
saro, *v.i.*, copulate, coire; **sarta, wan saran.**
sarab, *m.n.*, row.—**ki.**
sarab (with **ku**), *v.tr.*, put in rows and join; **lohyada ahalka ku sarab**, floor the room (cover with planks); **alwahda sarabkeda**, the flooring.
saran, *f.n.*, groin (of the body). —**ti.**
sarar and **dina'**, fillet (the loins of a horse, an ox ...).—**ti**, and —**hi.**
saren, *m.n.*, corn, flour of wheat.
sarir, *f.n.*, bed.—**ti.**
sarrah, *v.i.*, go free.
sarrahi, *v.c.*, set free (cause to be free).
sarrif, *m.n.*, change of money.—**ki.**
sarrif, *v.tr.*, change; **rubiadda i sarrif**, change me the rupee; **so** —, go and change.
sarruh, *m.n.*, bandit, highwayman.—**hi.**
sasab, *v.tr.*, induce, persuade; **wa la sasabai**, he is persuaded.
sasabo, *v.tr.*, flatter.
sasab, or **sasabnin**, *m.n.*, persuasion, enticement.—**ki**, —**ti.**
sawahan, *m.n.*, clamour, outcry. —**ki.**
sawaheli, *m.n.*, negro, slave.—**gi.**
sawir, *m.n.*, drawing, image, picture, photograph.—**ki.**
sawir, *v.tr.*, draw, picture.
sawiran, *a.v.*, pictured, reproduced in picture, photo, ...
sayad, *m.n.*, fisherman.—**ki.**
sayah, *m.n.*, dew.—**hi.**
sayahsan, *a.*, dewy; **dulku wa sayahsanyahai**, the earth is dewy.
sayah, *m.n.*, goldsmith.—**hi.**
se, *conj.*, but (never used at the beginning of a sentence).
seb, *m.n.*, oar.—**ki.**
sebiyan, *m.n.*, servant.—**ki**; **sebiyan ba lehyahai**, he has a servant.
sefari, *m.n.*, string, twine.—**gi.**
seho, *v.i.*, sleep; **so** —, go to sleep.
sehi, *v.i.*, make (him) sleep, blow, put out; **ilmaha sehi**, make the baby sleep; **siradka sehi**, blow out the lamp.
sehasho, *f.n.*, sleep.
seid, *f.n.*, sinew, tendon.—**di.**
seif, *f.n.*, sword.—**ti.**
sem, *v.tr.*, touch (in playing).
se'ni, or **su'un**, *m.n.*, plate, dish. —**gi**, or —**ti**, —**yo.**
sergad, or **sergan**, *f.n.*, flogging, scourging.—**di**, —**ti.**
serkal, *m.n.*, authority, government.—**ki.**

serkal sarai, *m.n.*, governor; **serkalki sarai**, the governor.
serkal, *m.n.*, gentleman; **sarakishi**, the gentleman.
serji, *m.n.*, brink, hem.—**gi.**
serwan, *f.n.*, rod, stick.—**ti.**
serwanai, *v.tr.*, flog, scourge.
sesa, or **sisa**, *f.n.*, dust, sand (raised up by the galloping of horses), whirlwind or gusty wind.—**di.**
setto, *f.n.*, fetters (for a camel's forelegs).
sha'ab, *m.n.*, coral.—**ki. Sha'ab** is the proper name of the place where the residency of Berberah is built.
shabak, *m.n.*, net.—**gi**, —**yo.**
shabel, *m.n.*, leopard, panther (hunting leopard).—**ki.**
shabuk, *m.n.*, whip.—**gi.**
shaf, *m.n.*, callousness of the camel's chest.—**ki.**
shafi'i, one of the Mohamedan sects. Somals are of the **shafi'i** creed.
shag, *m.n.*, wheel of a carriage. —**gi.**
shah, *f.n.*, a game which Somals are very fond of. It consists in three squares unequal in size, one inside the other, and joined by perpendiculars passing through the middle of each side; each of the two players has twelve stones or shells, which are either of a different colour or kind from those of his opponent, so that they may recognise them easily.
shah, *m.n.*, tea.—**hi.**
shahi, *m.n.*, labourer, workman. —**gi**; **ninki shahigaaha**, a labourer.
shahai, *v.i.*, work.
shahaisi, *v.i.*, make him work.
shahaiso, *v.i.*, work for yourself.
shuhul, *m.n.*, labour, work, business.—**ki.**
shakal, or **shekal**, *m.n.*, fetters (for horses, mules).—**ki.**
shekal, *v.tr.*, fetter, put on fetters.
shakamad, *f.n.*, leathern halter. —**di.**
shaitan, or **shaidan**, *m.n.*, Satan, devil, demon.—**ki.**
shalai and **shalaito**, *ad.*, yesterday.
shama', or **shimai'**, *m.n.*, wax, candle.
shambel, *m.n.*, wild beast about the size of a fox.
shan, *num.*, five.
shanad, *num.ord.*, fifth.—**ki**, —**di.**
shan iyo tobnad, *m.n.*, a fortnight.—**ki**; **shan iyo tobnadkas o dan yu ina ka mahna**, all this fortnight he was absent (from us).
shansho, *f.n.*, part of the leg under the knee.
shár, *m.n.*, evil.—**ki.**
sharad, *m.n.*, bet.—**ki**, —**yo.**
la sharatan, *v.i.*, bet; **la sharatama, wan la sharatami.**
sharer, *m.n.*, forest.—**ki.**
shareri, *v.tr.*, make a forest.
mel shareran, a forest.
sharub, *f.n.*, mustachio.—**ti.**

shash, *m.n.*, fringe.—**ki.**
shaushuga, *m.n.*, greyish red mongoose.—**hi.**
sheg, *v.tr.*, say, relate, tell; **u** —, communicate, tell him; **bein** —, tell, say a lie, be untruthful; **waḥ** —, foretell, predict; **waḥ ban shegi,** I will foretell.
shego, *v.tr.*, demand, claim.
sheko, *f.n.*, history, tale, tradition.
sheko u mari, *v.i.*, narrate, tell a story.
sheḥmad, or **sheḥnad,** *v.tr.*, load, freight.
sheḥnadan, *a.v.*, loaded, laden.
sheḥnad, *f.n.*, cargo, loading.—**di.**
sheklad, *f.n.*, public house (stew). —**di.**
sheiḥ, *m.n.*, sheik, chief, Musulman saint.—**hi.**
shid, *v.tr.*, inflame, light, kindle; **dabka shid,** light the fire.
shidan, *a.v.*, inflamed, lit.
shīd, *v.tr.*, stone.
shīd, *m.n.*, stoning.—**ki.**
shido, *f.n.*, feast in which a goat is killed.
shido, *f.n.*, hurly-burly, bustle, row, clatter.
shidai, *v.i.*, make a noise, caterwaul.
shil, *v.tr.*, fry.
shilan, *a.v.*, fried; **shilan yahai,** it is fried.
shilo, *v.r.*, fry (for yourself); **shisha.**
deriya shil, *m.n.*, a man frying. —**ki.**
shilato, *f.n.*, a woman frying.
shilis, *a.*, fat, stout; **ninki, nimanki shishla,** stout man, men; **nagti shishlaid,** the stout, fat woman; **nagihi shishla,** the fat women.
shishlai, *v.tr.*, make fat.
shishlow, *v.i.*, become fat.
shilin, *f.n.*, tick (the flat one), insect, camel's louse.—**ti.** When this louse bites other animals it causes them to be sick.
shimbir, *f.n.*, bird.—**ti.**
shimbir libaḥ, *f.n.*, owl.—**di.**
shin, *m.n.*, the nine months of pregnancy.—**ki**; **shinki ma aha,** he has not the time; —**dal,** one who is born in his time.
shini, *f.n.*, bee.—**di.**
shir, *m.n.*, assembly, rendezvous, council, assembly of men in the house of a chief.—**ki.**
shirka tag, *v.i.*, go to the council, meeting; **shirkan tegi,** I will go to the meeting.
so shira, *v.i.*, have an assembly, assemble; **wainu so shiri,** we will have an assembly, a meeting.
shirsi, *v.tr.*, reunite.
shira', or **shiraḥ,** *m.n.*, sail of a ship.—**hi,** —**yo.**
shishai, *f.n.*, *prp.* and *a.*, distant, beyond, the following, the last; **halka shishai,** that distant place; **nobadda shishadedu jogo,** he is beyond the tower; **kan maaha, wa ka shishai,** it is not this, it is the next, the following; **adigu u shishai,** be the last of all.

shoï, *f.n.*, a tree and its fruit, which is like a cherry.—**di.**

sholaboli, *f.n.*, cash (silver money), two anna piece.

shub, *v.tr.*, put in, spill, melt, pour out; **so —**, pour out towards me; **si —**, continue to spill; **ku —**, put in; **buradka shub**, melt the butter; **'anihi hanti ku shubai**, I put the milk in the jar; **waḥad igu shubaisid, garan mayo**, I do not understand what you tell me; **wa biyaha la shubayo**, it is spilt water.

shubo, ku shubo, *v.r.*, put in, pour in (for yourself).

shuban, *a.v.*, melted; **bur'ad shuban ban'aba**, I drink melted butter.

shuban, *v.p.*, be melted, be purged; **shubma, wan shubmi; bur'adku ha shubmo**, let the butter be melted; **dabada ka shuban**, take a purge (lit. be purged from the back).

shuban, *m.n.*, effect of a purgative.—**ki.**

shuban, *a.*, straight, nice; **ul shuban i so ibi**, buy a straight stick for me; **nin shuban**, a nice man (tall and of a straight stature).

shuh, *m.n.*, hazy weather.—**hi.**

shukan, *f.n.*, helm.—**ti.**

si, *f.n.*, manner, mode.—**di.**

sida, sidas, sidan, *ad.*, thus, so; **sidas ma tahai?** is it so? *or* are you so? **wa sidas**, it is so; **sidan u samai**, do so (as I say).

sidai, *conj.*, as.

side, *ad.*, how? **wa side?** how is it? **sidan** (for **side**) **ban u gala?** how can I do that?

si un, *ad.*, somehow; **si un u gal o iss kaga tag**, do it somehow (in any manner whatever) and go away.

si kasta, *conj.*, however.

si, *particle*. This particle is often used before the verb to point out either a tendency from me to a place, or the continuity of the action expressed by the verb: **si da**, let go; **si mar**, pass by (from me to ...); **si da'**, continue to plunder; **si shaḥai**, continue to work. When this particle is added to the verb it gives to it a causative sense: **shaḥai**, work; **shaḥaisi**, cause to work.

si, *v.tr.*, give, bestow; **si —**, distribute; **so —**, give to him, buy, take and bring to me; **i so si**, take and bring to me; **wan ku so sin**, I will buy for you; **— so**, buy for yourself; **sista, wan sisan; orod o basal siso**, go and buy onions for yourself; **orod o basal so si**, go and buy onions for me.

siya, *m.n.*, giver.—**hi; ninkasi wa siya, basha, diba, deḥsi**, this man is a giver, generous, benevolent.

sin, *f.n.*, gift, present.

sibaḥ, *m.n.*, dye.—**hi; sibaḥ madow 'adan**, indigo.

sibaḥ, *v.tr.*, dye.

(**nin**) **sibaḥah**, *m.n.*, dyer.—**hi.**

sibibaḥ, *f.n.*, a declivity, slope.—**di**; **mel sibibaḥah**, a sloping place.

sibibaho, *v.i.*, slide.

sibrar, *m.n.*, leathern water-bag, **chagul.—ki.**

sid, *v.tr.*, carry, bring; **war san ban ku sida**, I bring to you good news.

sido, *v.r.*, take and carry for yourself; **sita**; **sortá sido**, or **iss ka sido**, take your food.

sided, *num.*, eight.—**di.**

sidehtan, *num.*, eighty.—**ki.**

sidedad, *num.ord.*, eighth.—**ki**, —**di.**

si'g, *m.n.*, hartebrest or Coke's antelope.—**gi.**

sigo, *f.n.*, sand on the road, sand-storm (*see* **sesa**).

sihin, *f.n.*, melted butter.—**ti.**

sil, *m.n.*, vagina.—**ki.**

silei', *m.n.*, suffering, torment, torture.—**hi.**

silei', *v.p.*, be tortured.

sili'i, *v.tr.*, torment, torture, persecute.

sila'n, *a.*, dull; **shuḥul sila'n**, dull work.

(**nin**) **sila'san**, *a.v.*, tortured man.

silsilad, *f.n.*, chain.—**di.**

silsiladai, *v.tr.*, fetter, enchain.

simbiririho, *v.i.*, slide, slip.

simbiririho, *f.n.*, slide, slip.

simbiririhi, *v.c.*, cause him to slide, slip.

simid, *m.n.*, cement.—**ki.**

sin, or **iss ku sin**, *v.tr.*, flatten, level; **sima**, **wan simi.**

siman, *a.v.*, plain, smooth, straight, parallel; **dilimihi wa simanyihin**, the lines are parallel; **iss ku simanyihin**, they are equal.

siman, or **sinin**, *m.n.*, plane, surface,—**ki**, —**ti.**

sīn, *m.n.*, mucus discharged from the nose.—**ki.**

sīnso, *v.i.*, wipe your nose.

sin, *f.n.*, hip.—**ti**; **sino** or **simo** (*plur.*).

sino, *f.n.*, adultery.

sinaiso, *v.i.*, commit adultery.

sinaisi, *v.c.*, cause to commit adultery.

sindi, *m.n.*, bracelet, armlet (of silver).

singal, *m.n.*, client, a man who comes under the protection of a powerful man.—**ki.**

sinif, *v.tr.*, introduce, produce; **erai 'usub sinif**, create a new word.

sinjibil, *f.n.*, ginger.—**shi.**

sirad, *m.n.*, lamp.—**ki**, —**yo.**

sirad, *v.tr.*, light; **siradka sirad**, light the lamp.

siradan, *a.v.*, lit, lighted; **siradka siradan i ken**, bring me a lighted lamp.

siriri, *v.tr.*, choke, strangle.

siririn, or **siriris**, *m.n.*, strangulation.—**ti**, —**ki.**

sisa, or **sesa**, *f.n.*, dust, sand-storm.—**di.**

sisib, *f.n.*, sliding on a stone.—**ti.**

sisibi, *v.c.*, cause to slide.

sisibo, *v.i.*, slide, slip.

sitah, *m.n.*, necklace or garland (for horses).—**hi**, —**yo**.
siyahad, *f.n.*, ornaments for women, bracelets, necklaces of silver and of precious metals or stones.—**di**.
siyar, *v.i.*, make a feast; **nin la la sahiro ba tahai**, you are a man to feast with us.
siyaro, or **siyarad**, *f.n.*, feast.—**di**.
so, *particle*, used either after or before the verb. When after the verb, it gives to it a kind of reflective sense; when before the verb, it points out either a movement in the action expressed by the verb with a sense of coming back, or a tendency towards me: **u so dib**, give him to bring home; **so heli**, bring back to me; **so durug**, come near.
so', or **kala so'**, *v tr.*, distinguish, separate; **midahas kala so'**, separate those fruits; **inamada Abdi wan ka so'** or **ka deh so'i**, I will separate Abdi from the boys.
so'an, *a.v.*, distinct; **sadehda hof ba kala wa so'an tahai o Ilah keliah iss ku yihin**, the three Persons are distinct one from the other and are only One God.
so'din, *f.n.*, separation, distinction, division.—**ti**.
sod'al, *m.n.*, journey, travel, traveller.—**ki**; **ninká sod'alkisi wah absileh bu aha**, the travel, journey of that man was dangerous; **ninka wein e ad arkaisa wa sod'al**, the big man you see is a traveller.
(**nin**) **sod'alah**, *m.n.*, traveller; **ninki sod'alkaaha**, the traveller.
soda'l, *v.i.*, travel.
soddog, *m.n.*, father-in-law.—**gi**, —**yo**.
soddoh, *f.n.*, mother-in-law.—**di**.
sodon, *num.*, thirty.
sofa, *m.n.*, file.—**hi**.
sofai, *v.tr.*, file, sharpen.
sogsog, *f.n.*, fibrous tree with curved thorns.—**ti**.
sogur, *m.n.*, red mongoose.—**ki**.
soh, *v.tr.*, curl, twist.
sohan, *a.v.*, curled, twisted.
sokai, *a.*, near; **mel sokai**, a near place.
sol, *v.tr.*, broil, grill.
solai, *m.n.*, gridiron.—**gi**. Somals use a stick in the place of iron.
son, *m.n.*, fast, fasting.—**ki**.
(**nin**) **soman**, *m.n.*, fasting, hungry man; **ninki somana**, the fasting man.
so'o, *v.i.*, go on, move, proceed, walk; **so** —, come to me; **si** —, continue to go on; **u so'o**, go, walk for.
so'od, *m.n.*, walk.—**ki**.
so'odsi, *v.tr.*, advance, set forward; **sa'adda so'odsi**, put the clock on.
sor, *f.n.*, food.—**ti**.
soryo, *f.n.*, food given to a stranger on the first day, hospitality.
soryai, *v.i.*, give hospitality.

sow and **show**, particles expressing some doubt, perhaps; **sow sida ma aha?** is it not so? **show wa sidas**, perhaps it is so; **sow markabka ma yimado**, perhaps the ship will not come? **show manta yimadai**, perhaps she has come to-day; **sow sa'addu tobanki maaha?** is it not ten o'clock? **show sa'addu wa tobanki**, perhaps it is ten.
suāl, *v.tr.*, ask, question.
suāl, *f.n.*, question.—**shi.**
subag, *m.n.*, ghee (general name for all melted fat).—**gi.**
subaḥ, *m.* and *f.n.*, morning.—**hi**, —**di**, —**yo.**
subaihi, *m.n.*, police, policeman. —**gi**; **subaihin** (*plur.*).
suf, *m.n.*, rag.—**ki.**
sufur, *m.n.*, brass.—**ki.**
sufur, *f.n.*, dust made by camels on the march.—**ti.**
sug, *v.i.*, wait, have patience, hope.—**ti.**
sugnin, *f.n.*, waiting, patience, hope.—**ti.**
sugninleh, *a.*, patient.
sugninla, *a.*, impatient.
sug, *v.i.*, suffer, beat hard.
sugan, *a.v.*, suffering, beaten hard, severely; **nin sugan**, a suffering man; **wil sugan**, a boy severely beaten.
suḥ, *v.i.*, faint, swoon.
suḥsan, *a.v.*, fainted; **ninki suḥsana ban arkai**, I saw the man in a faint.
suḥdin, *f.n.*, fainting, swoon, epilepsy.—**ti.**
suḥur, *f.n.*, meal taken during Ramadan, between midnight and four o'clock. At midnight a man cries in the streets: **suḥur ya saïmin! suḥur ya saïmin!** eat (meal) you tasting men.
suḥuro, *v.i.*, take your meal.
suḥ, *m.n.*, bazaar, market.—**hi**, —**yo.**
sujud, *f.n.*, profound inclination, consisting in kneeling down and touching the ground with the forehead.—**di.**
sujud, *v.i.*, make the inclination.
sul, *m.n.*, thumb, toe.—**ki.**
suldan, *m.n.*, sultan.—**ki.**
sulub, *m.n.*, soft iron used for making spears.—**ki.**
sumad, *f.n.*, mark, sign, emblem. —**di.**
sumad, *v.tr.*, mark, sign.
sun, *m.n.*, poison.—**ki.**
sūn, *m.n.*, man's belt, waist-band. —**ki**; **suman** (*plur.*).
sunkor or **sonkor**, *f.n.*, sugar.—**ti.**
surin, *f.n.*, street.—**ki.**
surual, *m.n.*, trousers, pantaloons. —**ki**; **sarawil** (*plur.*).
suryo, *f.n.*, noose, a running knot.
suryo, *v.i.*, noose, make a running knot.

T.

ta, ti, tu, *f.art.*, the.
tí, tí, tán, tána, tani, tanu, tás, tasa, tasi, tasu, tẹr, tọ, } *dem.fem.a.prn.*, this, that, yon, yonder.

tai, taida, taidi, taidu, *poss.f.adj.prn.*, my, mine.
tí, tída, tádi, tádu, *poss.f.adj.prn.*, thy, thine.
tis, tisa, tisi, tisu, *poss.m.adj.prn.*, his, his own.
ted, teda, tedi, tedu, *poss.f.adj.prn.*, her, hers.
taya, tayada, tayadi, tayadu, *poss.a.prn.*, our, ours (mine and theirs).
ten, tena, teni, tenu, *poss.a.prn.*, our, ours (yours and mine).
tin, tina, tini, tinu, *poss.a.prn.*, your, yours.
tod, toda, todi, todu, *poss.a.prn.*, theirs.
te? *int.fem.prn.*, what? which? **teba?** which of you?
tuma? *int.fem.prn.*, who? **wa tuma?** who is?
tab, *f.n.*, a kind of play, especially in wrestling.—**ti.**
ta'ab, *m.n.*, torment, pain, suffering.—**ki; ta'abka 'adabtu wa dambaiya hadainan wanaksanain,** the torments of hell are hereafter if we are not good.
tabo, *v.tr.*, touch, feel.
tabsi, *v.c.*, make him touch, feel.
tabasho, *f.n.*, touch, feeling; **tabashadáda ban garanaya,** I feel your touching.
ku taba', *v.tr.*, aspire after, fight for; **wan tabe'i.**
tababar, *v.tr.*, correct, break a horse. subdue.
tabaḥad or **dabaḥad,** *f.n.*, hulk or carcass of a ship.—**di.**
tabalo, *f.n.*, a thing wanted at once and earnestly desired.
tabalaisnaw, *v.tr.*, long for; **la'agtaida wan u tabalaisnahai,** I want to have my money.
tabalaisan, *a.v.*, in want of, wanting; **ninki tabalaisna,** the man in want.
tādbir, *f.n.*, plan.—**ti.**
tag, *v.i.*, go; **wan tegi; teg,** he is gone; **wilki teg,** the boy is gone; **nagti tagtai,** the woman is gone; **iss ka —,** go away; **u —.** go to him; **si —,** go first, I will come after.
tegnin, *m.n.*, departing, going.—**ki.**
tāg, *f.n.*, strength.—**ti.**
tāg, *v.tr.*, fix (a stake firm and straight); **iss —,** halt, stop; **ku —,** prop, shore up.
tāgan, *a.v.*, fixed, firm, straight, upright.
tāgnow, *v.i.*, stand, be standing firm.
tagog or **tagogo,** *f.n.*, fore-arm.
taḥ, *v.i.*, groan, moan.
tah, *m.n.*, groan, moan.—**hi, —yo.**
taḥ, *v.tr.*, put in line, in rows; **wan tiḥi; alelhahá taḥ** or **iss ku taḥ,** arrange, put these shells in a line; **si taḥ,** continue to put.
taḫsir or **taksir,** *f.n.*, offence, guilt. punishment.—**ti.**
taḫsirleh, *a.*, guilty.
taḫsirla, *a.*, not guilty, innocent; **ninkasi wa nin taḫsirla,** or **taḫsir ma leh,** or **taḫsir ma laha,** that man is innocent.

takar, *m.n.*, gad fly.—**ki.**
takfi or **tafki,** *m n.*, flea.—**gi.**
tako, *f.n.*, span.
tal, root.
tali (with **ku**), *v.tr.*, arrange, settle, arbitrate; **waḥha ku tali,** settle that; **la —,** adduce, manage with him, suggest; **iss la —,** settle for yourself; **so —,** go and settle; **u —,** manage, educate; **arurtadá u tali,** educate your children; **u si —,** manage, settle for; **shuḥulkisa u si tali,** direct his work *or* put the work (in place) for him; **ḥoladá u si tali,** settle the affair of that tribe (I say so to a man I send for that purpose).
taliya, *m.n.*, manager, arbitrator. —**hi.**
talo, *f.n.*, management, decision, arrangement, determination, resolution, token, settlement; **talada 'aloshaida ku jirta wa adagtahai,** the decision of my heart is firm; **iss ku —,** having the same manners, feelings; **iss ku talainu** (for **talo yainu nahai**), we have the same feelings; **labada nin wa iss ku talo,** these two men have the same manners.
ūr ku talo, *v.i.*, take your revenge, suffer in your mind, regret.
ūr. ku talo, *f.n.*, revenge, feeling of hatred, suffering in the mind, regret.
tasho, *v.tr.*, think of (what you have to do, either good or bad), examine, consider; **war! horta tasho,** oh! think of, consider before doing; **so —,** go and think of, consider, examine; **la —,** think of with; **'aloshadí la tasho,** consider, think of it within yourself; **'aloshisú la tashanaya,** he is thinking in his heart.
tashi, *m.n.*, thought.—**gi.**
iss ku talo, *f.n.*, arm-bones (the two parts of the arms united to the hand and shoulder), also the bones of forelegs.
talab, *v.i.*, take a step, a pace.
talabi, *v.c.*, cause to march, step, carry over.
talabo, *f.n.*, pace, step, gait.
ka talab, *v.tr.*, cross, pass through.
iss ku talab, *f.n*, cross.—**ti**; **iss ku talabti, Issa Ebbehen wa 'ulus bai ahaid,** the cross of Jesus our Lord was heavy; **iss ku talab samai,** make a cross.
tamanta, *m.n.*, speaking during sleep, dream.—**hi** (*see* **awawi**).
tamashlai, *m.n.*, walk.—**hi.**
tamashlai, *v.i.*, walk, take a walk; **so —,** go to walk; **si —,** continue to walk.
tamuḥ, *f.n.*, level ground, quicksand.—**di.**
tanag, *m.n.*, tin box, the metal itself.—**gi.**
tantomo, *f.n.*, fist.
tanton, *v.tr.*, fist, box, bang; **tantoma, wan tantomi.**
tar, *v.tr.*, render a service, oblige, **war! i tar,** render me a service,

or oblige me (in putting this on your camel); **wan ku tari,** I will render you service, oblige you.

waḥ tar, *m.n.*, use, utility.—**ki.**

waḥ tar, *v.i.*, be of use, useful; **kitabkasu waḥ ba taraya,** that book is useful; **nin waḥ tara ahaw,** be a man of use; **nag waḥ tarta ahaw,** be a useful woman; **waḥba ha tarin,** be of no use.

waḥ ma tarai, *m.n.*, useless man. —**hi**; **waḥba an ma taro,** I am of no use, *or* **nin waḥ ma taraiah ban ahai,** I am a useless man.

an waḥba tarain, *a.*, useless (for things).

tar, *v.tr.*, increase, multiply, get more; **iss ku** —, increase, get more strength, size; **maḥad iss ku taraisa?** why do you increase yourself? *or* why are you boasting of yourself?

taran, *v.i.*, be multiplied, increased; **tarma, wan tarmi.**

tarin, *m.n.*, multiplication, multiplying.—**ki.**

tar, *m.n.*, telegraph.—**ki.**

tariḫ, *m.n.*, era, date.—**hi.**

tarshad, *f.n.*, wave.—**di.**

taurad or **torad iyo injil,** *m.n.*, Bible.—**ki iyo, ki.**

taubad or **tobad,** *f.n.*, penance. —**di.**

taubad or **tobad ken,** *m.n.*, penitent, doing penance.—**ki.**

taubad or **tobad ken** or **yelo,** *v.i.*, do penance, atone for; **Ilahhen Issa dembigaini u taubad kenai,** Jesus our God did penance for (atoned for) our sins.

tebed, *f.n.*, vessel for ghee (made of camel's leather; it is larger than the vessel called **ubo**).—**di.**

tebeda dara, *m.n.*, ladle, used for soup and ghee.—**hi.**

teḥ or **tiḥ,** *m.n.*, shower of rain. —**hi.**

teḥteḥ or **tiḥtiḥ,** *v.imp.*, shower; **wa teḥteḥaya,** it showers.

teri, *m.n.*, kind of big and heavy spear (used by the Gadabursi). —**gi.**

tib, *f.n.*, wooden pestle.—**ti.**

tidi', *v.tr.*, tress, plait (hair, ropes ...); **tida'a, wan tidi'i.**

tido'o, *v.i.*, tress, braid your hair.

tida'an, *a.v.*, braided.

tida'sho, *f.n.*, braid, texture.

tidei', *m.n.*, plait of hair (as Somali girls have).—**hi.**

tifiḫ, *f.n.*, drop.—**di**; **tifiḫ biyaha,** a drop of water.

tiked, *m.n.*, ticket, stamp (ticket of a passenger).—**ki.**

tikso, *v.tr.*, stretch out.

tiksi, *m.n.*, stretching out.—**gi.**

timir, *f.n.*, dates.—**ti.**

tin, *m.n.*, hair.—**ki**; **timo** (*plur.*); **timaha damanka,** whiskers.

tinmod, *m.n.*, hair remaining in the comb.

tir, *v.tr.*, blot out, clean; **iss-ka** —, clean yourself; **sinka iss ka tir,** wipe your nose.

'ada tir, *v.tr.*, appease, calm the anger.

tiri, *v.tr.*, account, calculate, count; **ku** —, add to; **mid-midu** —, enumerate.
tiriya, *m.n.*, accountant.—**hi.**
tiro, *f.n.*, account, calculation, sum, *means also* hundred; **tira adiga au lehyahai**, I have one hundred sheep and goats.
tirso, *v.r.*, count for yourself; **ku** —, account with, add to.
tiro badan, *a.v.*, numerous.
tir, *m.n.*, column, pier.—**ki.**
tiri, *v.tr.*, prop, underpin; **ku** —, lean against something, bend, incline, stoop, recline.
tirso, *v.r.*, lean yourself; **ku** —, lean upon, lounge, stroll; **ha ku tirsan**, do not lounge, stroll.
tōb, *v.tr.*, cup, apply a cupping-glass.
tōbin, *m.n.*, cupping-horn (used instead of a glass).—**ki.**
tōbnin, *f.n.*, cupping.—**ti.**
nin waḥ toba, nag waḥ tobta, a cupper.
tobad (*see* **taubad**).
toban, *num.*, ten.—**ki.**
tobnad, *num.ord.*, tenth.—**ki** or —**di.**
todoba, *num.*, seven.—**di.**
todobad, *num.ord.*, seventh.—**ki** or **di.**
todobatan, *num.*, seventy.—**ki.**
tog, la togo, (nin) tog badan, *see* **dug, la dugo, dug badan.**
toḥob, *f.n.*, pellicles (of the head especially).—**ti.**
tol, *v.tr.*, sew, tack; **ād u** —, sew well; **iss ku** —, join, sew together.
dar tol, *m.n.*, tailor.
kaba tol, *m.n.*, shoemaker.
kaba tolai, *m.n.*, awl, bodkin ... tools of a shoemaker.
tolnin, *f.n.*, sewing, seam.—**ti.**
tol, *m.n.*, tribe, caste, nation, race, kind, sort.—**ki**; **iss ku** —, of the same tribe, of the same kind, sort; **iss ku tol bannu nahai**, we are of the same tribe; **bahalahási wa iss ku tol**, those beasts are of the same kind.
tolmon, *a.*, good, virtuous; **ninki tolmona**, the virtuous man.
tolimo, *f.n.*, goodness, charity.
tolmonow, *v.i.*, be good.
tolmonai, *v.tr.*, make good; **wilka tolmonai**, make the boy good.
ton, *f.n.*, garlic.—**ti.**
torog, *m.n.*, giant, stout man.—**gi**, —**yo**; **torogga dai**, look at that giant.
tos, *v.i.*, arise, get up.
tosi, *v.tr.*, awake, raise.
tosnin, *f.n.*, rising, getting up.—**ti.**
tosnow, *v.i.*, be right.
tos, *a.*, right; **was tos**, it is right; **eragasi wa tos**, that word is right.
tos, *m.n.*, straightness.—**ki.**
tosan, *a.*, straight, upright; **ushasi wa tosantahai**, that stick is straight.
tu, *v.i.*, kneel down (addressing a camel).
tuï, *v.i.*, make the camel kneel down.

tud (with **u**), *v.tr.*, soften, soothe, alleviate, allay.
tudad or **tudnin**, *f.n.*, alleviation.
tuf, *v.i.*, spit.
tufnin, *f.n.*, spitting.
tug, *m.n.*, thief, robber, rascal, rogue, scoundrel, vagabond.—**gi.**
tugo, *f.n.*, robbery, theft, knavery.
tuhun, *m.n.*, suspicion, accusation based only on some probabilities. —**ki.**
tuhun, *v.tr.*, suspect, accuse; **tuhuma, wan tuhumi; nin, ninki la tuhmai**, a suspected man; **Abdi wa un la tuhmai**, Abdi only was accused.
tuhunsan, *a.v.*, suspicious.
tuka or **tukai**, *m.n.*, crow, raven. —**hi.**
tuko, *v.i.*, pray; **so** —, go to pray; **si** —, continue to pray; **u** —, pray for; **la** —, pray with.
tukasho, *f.n.*, prayer.
tukub, *v.i.*, stagger, walk with difficulty (it is said of an old man or of a sick one); **iss ka si** —, continue to ... ; **ku** —, walk with; **ho, usha ku tukub**, take a walk with a stick.
tukabai, *m.n.*, bandy, crutch, stick.—**hi.**
tujad or **tijad**, *m.n.*, hen.—**ki.**
tuji or **tuki**, *v.i.*, be the leader in prayer.—**ki.** (The leader in prayer, or he who stands in front of the Mohamedans, is called **Iman.**)
tuji, *v.tr.*, touch in pressing; **darka tuji**, press the clothes (for washing them). This word is often used in a bad sense as in **naska tuji; iss ku** —, press on; **iss** — or **iss tutuji**, touch yourself; **ga'antada iss ku tuji**, touch yourself with your hand.
tul, *v.tr.*, heap, accumulate.
tumujad, *f.n.*, revolver, pistol.— —**di.**
tumujai, *v.tr.*, thump, box, bang.
tumujo, *f.n.*, blow, bang, box.
tumun, *m.n.*, four annas, $\frac{1}{4}$ of a rupee.
tun, *v.tr.*, forge, grind (with a pestle); **tuma, wan tumi; ku** —, strike upon.
tuman, *a.v.*, forged; **waranku wa tumanyahai**, the spear is forged.
tumal, *m.n.*, smith, blacksmith (name of a low Somali caste). **ki.**
tuman, *m.n.*, eunuch, *see* **dufanan.**
ugad tuman, *m.n.*, gelding.
tur, *v.tr.*, cast, throw; **iss ka** —, throw; **ku** —, throw at, on; **iss u turtura**, throw at each other.
turonturo, *v.i.*, stumble.
turonturo, *f.n.*, stumble, trip.
tūr, *f.n.*, hump, hunch.—**ti.**
tūrleh, *a.*, hunchbacked.
turjuman, *m.n.*, dragoman, interpreter.—**ki.**
turub, *m.n.*, *s.* and *pl.*, cards (a set of).—**ki.**
turub ayar, *v.i.*, play at cards.

tus, *v.tr.*, point out, show; **so —**, go and show; **si —**, show (when you are going).

tusbaḥ, *m.n.*, rosary, chaplet.—**hi**, **—yo**; **ninkasi tusbaḥ iyo massala iyo weiso yu sita**, that man carries a chaplet, a prayer-skin, and a vessel for washing himself (these three things are required for being a saint amongst the Somals).

tutuwai, kind of corrosive medicine (as far as I could make out, it is sulphate of copper mixed with something, I could not find out what).

U.

u, with its appropriate consonant, *def.art.*, the.

u, **usagu**, **wu**, **bu**, **yu**, *pers.prn.*, he.

u, *pers.prn.*, to him.

ugu, *pers.prn.*, to him; **kolkad halka ugu tagto**, when you go to that place to him.

uga, from him.

u, *prp.*, to, for; is also used in forming adverbs.

ubaḥ, *m.n.*, flowers of the trees bearing edible fruits.—**hi**, **—yo**.

ubaḥaiso or **ubohọ**, *v.i.*, flourish, blossom.

ubo, *f.n.*, vessel for ghee, gourd.

'udad, *f.n.*, anvil.—**di**; **'udaddi yaraid**, the small anvil, hand anvil.

'udal, *f.n.*, surety, security, pledge.—**shi**; **'udal i si**, give a security, pledge.

udgon, *m.n.*, perfume, scent.—**ki**.

udgon, *a.*, aromatic.

udgonai, *v.tr.*, perfume; **iss —**, perfume yourself; **la —**, it is perfumed.

ugonow, *v.i.*, be perfumed.

udub, *m.n.*, frame, prop (the two props forming the frame of a Somali tent door).—**ki**, **—yo**.

'udud, *f.n.*, back part of the arm. —**di**.

'udur, *m.n.*, sickness.—**ki**; **wa nin 'udur ḥaba**, it is a sick man.

'udur ḥad, *v.i.*, be sick.

ugadsi, *m.n.*, chase, hunting.—**gi**.

ugadso, *v.tr.*, chase, hunt.

ugad, *f.n.*, game, every kind of wild animal good for eating. —**di**.

ugaḥ, *m.n.*, egg.—**hi**; **ugaḥhan** (*plur.*).

ugas, *m.n.*, chief, king.—**ki**, **—yo**.

ugub, *m.n.*, virgin, girl, maid. —**ki**, **—yo**.

ugubod, *m.n.*, general name for all maids.—**ki**.

'ukad, *f.n.*, skin not cut (as they are sold in Berberah).—**di**.

ul, *f.n.*, stick.—**shi**.

ulai, *v.tr.*, flog.

ulais, *m.n.*, flagellation.—**ki**.

ululi, *v.i.*, stitch across (a bad word, meaning: enter in vagina); **hoyadi ululi** is a very bad curse.

ula'ul, *f.n.*, leech.—**shi.**
ulimo, *see* **ardai**, *f.n.*, reunion, congregation of **wadads.**
'ulus, *a.*, heavy, important; **ninki 'usla**, the important man.
'ulais or **'ulusnimo**, *f.n.*, heaviness, importance.—**ki**, —**di.**
umi, *v.tr.*, warm, perfume a room by burning incense in the vase called **idan**; **iss** —, perfume yourself.
unso, *v.r.*, perfume yourself with incense.
unsi, *m.n.*, act of perfuming.—**gi.**
umi, *m.n.*, vapour clinging to the lid of a kettle when the water boils.—**gi.**
umis, *m.n.*, steam, vapour, warmth.—**ki.**
umul, *f.n.*, a pregnant woman near her deliverance.—**shi.**
umul, *v.i.*, give birth (used only when the time of deliverance is near); **wan umuli**, I will give birth (a mother alone can speak so).
umuli (with **ka**), *v.tr.*, attend to (a woman during her confinement); **kalai o ka umuli**, come to attend to; **iss ka** —, attend to myself.
umulisso, *f.n.*, midwife, nurse.
umur, *f.n.*, wonder, every astonishing thing, prodigy.—**ti.**
umur, *f.n.*, will; **umurta Ebbahai oggolaw**, submit to the will of God.
'umur, *m.n.*, age.—**ki.**
ūn, *v.tr.*, create (for God alone); **Ilaḥ ba náfo ūsub ūmi dona**, God will create new souls; **'asho walba Ilaḥ ba ūma**, God creates every day; **Ilaḥ ba duniyada ūmai**, God has created the world.
ūman, *a.v.*, created; **dadku wa ūman yahai**, man is created; **náfti wa umantahai, jidki se wa dashai**, the soul is created, but the body is generated.
ūmanow, *v.i.*, be created.
ūn, *m.n.*, creature.—**ki**; **dadku wa ūn**, man is a creature; **ūnka o dan wa la hisabi dona**, all the creatures will be judged.
un, *a.v.*, only, soever; **wu un nol yahai**, he only is living; **war! Jama un igu yed**, call me only Jama.
nin un, *rel.prn.*, whosoever, whomsoever.
waḥ un, *rel.prn.*, anything, whatsoever.
mel un, *ad.*, somewhere.
gor un, *ad.*, any time soever.
'un, *v.tr.*, eat; **la** —, it is eaten; **lagu** —, be eaten; **hadu magalada tago, wa la 'uni**, if he goes to the country, he will be eaten; **wa la 'uni**, I shall be eaten; **wa nai la 'uni**, we shall be eaten.
'una, *m.n.*, throat.—**hi**; **'unaha ḫado**, catch him by the throat; **'una ḫabatai**, strangle; **wan ku 'una ḫabatain**, I will strangle you.
'unno, *f.n.*, food, meal, dinner;

'unnadi wa samaisantahai, the dinner is ready.
una'as, *f.n.*, quail.—**ti.**
unun, *m.n.*, wild water-melon (very sour and eaten by goats).—**ki.**
ur, *m.n.*, smell, smelling, odour, scent.
ursi, *v.tr.*, make him smell.
urso, *v.tr.*, smell, snuff.
ur ḥudmun, *a.*, stinking.
ūr, *m.n.*, belly, womb, fœtus.—**ki**; **ūr bai lehdahai**, she is pregnant; **'udur ūrka laga haya**, she has a sickness in the womb.
ūr ḥanun or **'alol ḥanun**, *m.n.*, belly-ache, colic.—**ki.**
ūr ḥumo, *f.n.*, resentment, rancour.
'urad, *m.n.*, eldest son.—**ki.**
'urad ḥigai, *m.n.*, younger son, cadet.—**hi**; **gar u dambais** has the same meaning.
'urdan, *m.n.*, spray, bud, shoot, the fruit remaining after the fall of the flowers.—**ki.**
urgumo, *f.n.*, venom, venomous liquid, poisonous substance, pus, matter.
'uri, *m.n.*, wife, woman, lady. —**di.**
'urian, *m.n.*, palsy.—**ki.**
(nin) **'urianah**, *a.*, paralytic, knock-kneed; **ninki 'urianaha**, the paralytic; **nimanki 'urianaha** or **'uriamadaaha**, the paralytic men.
urur, *m.n.*, assembly, concourse, crowd, mob, meeting.—**ki.**
urur, *v.i.*, be assembled, flock.
ururi, *v.tr.*, assemble, accumulate, collect, combine, gather; **so —**, assemble, gather together; **nimankas halka ku so ururi**, assemble these men here.
ururis, *m.n.*, gathering.—**ki.**
ururaan, *a.v.*, assembled, gathered; **midihi wa ururaanyihin**, the fruits are gathered.
ururaanow, *v.i.*, be gathered.
'ur'ur, *m.n.*, wrist.—**ki.**
us, *m.n.*, dung, excrement.—**ki.**
uslahais, *f.n.*, entrails, intestines. —**ti.**
uslaho or **usloho**, *f.n.pl.*, bowels, intestines.
us! *interj.*, be quiet! silence! (abbreviation of **amus**).
'usboh, *m.n.*, salt.—**hi.**
uskag, *m.n.*, dirt.—**gi.**
uskagleh, *a.*, dirty; **wilkasi uskag bu lehyahai**, that boy is dirty.
uskagai, *v.tr.*, dirt, defile.
uskagaisan, *a.v.*, dirtied, defiled.
'uski, *v.i.*, make him lean, incline, stoop.
'usko, *v.r.*, incline (yourself), lean, stoop.
'uskis, *m.n.*, leaning, stooping. —**ki.**
'usub, *a.*, new; **maradaida wa 'usubtahai**, my cloth is new.
'usub, *a.*, clouded, cloudy (before rain); **'irku wa 'usubyahai**, the sky is cloudy.

W.

w, this letter united to the pers. prn. in its simple form forms other pronouns of very frequent occurrence; **wan**, I; **wad**, thou; **wu**, he; **wai**, she, ...

wa, particle very often used in the Somali language to assist either the subject or the verb in different tenses. Sometimes, also, it performs the office of a pronoun, sometimes that of the verb of existence; **wa ayo**, who is? **wa mahai**, what is? **ḥoraḥdu wa so baḥdai**, the sun is up.

wā, *m.n.*, time, once.—**gi**; **wā waḥ jirai**, or **waḥba wā jirai**, there was once; **wā hore**, **wāgi hore**, formerly, the past time; **wā dambe, wāgi dambe**, afterwards, the time following; **wāgi dambe, ninki dintai**, the man died afterwards.

wa', *f.n.*, noise produced by a sudden blow or thump.—**di.**

wa'al or **we'el**, *m.n.*, natural, illegitimate child.—**ki.**

wa'an, good; **wilki wa'ana**, **wilashi wawa'ana**, the good boy, boys.

wab, *f.n.*, hovel, shed (as that of the tumals).—**ti.**

wabayo, *f.n.*, poison, venom.

wabayai, *v.tr.*, poison; **falladda wabayai**, poison the arrow.

wad, *v.tr.*, row, pull, go on, go before a camel leading it with the rope tied to its head, go along with sheep, leading them; **seḥimmadda wad**, row the boat; **adiga wad**, lead the herd of sheep and goats; **ina kala wad**, go away from us; **so wad**, pull towards me.

wada, *ind.num.*, all; **wada yimadai**, all came; **wada tagai**, all went; **ka wada**, all from; **wada ḥabo**, take, catch all; (this adjective is often used with another adjective meaning all) **kulligod wada ḥabo**, take, catch all.

wadad, *m.n.*, old man, Musulman monk or priest, a man who has passed through all the standards into which the Coran is divided for the students.—**ki.**

wadaf, *m.n.*, sling.—**ki**, —**yo.**

wadfi, *v.tr.*, sling, throw with a sling.

la wadag, *v.i.*, take part, eat from the same dish.

wadān, *f.n.*, leathern bucket, pail for drawing water.—**ti.**

wadi, *m.n.*, river.—**gi.**

wadna or **wadnai**, *m.n.*, heart.—**hi.**

(nin) wadnala, *a.*, heartless; **ninki wadnahalaa**, the heartless man.

wah, *v.i.*, do not find; **wahya**, **wan wahyi** (the past tense of this verb, when used as an auxiliary, gives to the principal verb a past signification, and points out either a want of will or a want of power, ability, and opportunity); **tegi wahyai**, I would not go (I refused); **ana meshi tegi wahyai o ka so noḥdai**, I was not willing to go to that place, and I came back;

tegi kari **wahyai**, I could not go.

wah, *kind of imp.v., meaning* he has not found, he did not find; **Ilaḥ ban bariyai e wah**, I have prayed to God, and that man has not found what he was looking for; **Ali meshi lo dirai wah**, Ali did not find the place he was sent to.

lah wah, *v.imp.*, it is not found, it could not be found.

iss ugu wahan, *expression meaning* have what you deserved, merited; **ana iss ugu wahan**, I have what I have merited; **isaga iss ugu wahna**, he had what he deserved; **iminka edinku iss ugu wahna**, now you have what you merited; **ada iss ugu wahan**, you have what you deserve; **innagu iss ugu wahnain**, we have what we merited. All these expressions are used when a man happens to be disgraced or punished by his own fault.

waḥ, *m.n.*, thing, some, any.—**hi**; **waḥhan**, this thing; **waḥha**, **waḥhas**, that; **waḥho**, **waḥhoi**, that yonder; **waḥho wa mahai?** what is that thing yonder?

waḥ, particle united to the simple pers. prn. in the conjugation of some verbs; **waḥan**, I; **waḥad**, thou; **wuḥu**, he; **waḥai**, she, they; **waḥainu**, we; **waḥaidin**, you.

waḥ un, *a.*, anything whatsoever.

waḥ bug ku so'oda, *m.n.*, reptile, any animal crawling along on its belly; **wiḥhi bugga ku so'odai**, the reptile.

waḥ u 'eli, *v.tr.*, answer, reply, render him something; **waḥ ban u 'elin**.

waḥ sheg, *v.tr.*, foretell, predict.

waḥ sheg, or **nin waḥ shega**, *m.n.*, foreteller, prophet, prediction, prophecy.—**gi**, —**yo**.

waḥ yel, *v.tr.*, abuse, do some mischief, injure.

waḥ yel, *m.n.*, mischievous, malicious person.—**ki**.

waḥ yelo, *f.n.*, mischief, abuse, injury.—**di**; **ninka waḥ yeladisa eg**, look at the mischief of that man.

waḥ, *f.n.*, $\frac{1}{4}$, a quarter.—**di**; **midká waḥdisi medai?** where is the quarter of that fruit?

waha'd, *f.n.*, association, company. —**di**.

la waha'd ḥado, or **la waha'san**, *v.i.*, associate.

wahai, *v.tr.*, make, do; **la wahai**, it is made; **so —**, go and do.

wahan, *v.i.*, be in a gloomy state of mind, melancholic, pensive; **wahama**, **wan wahami**.

wahan, *m.n.*, melancholy, pensiveness.—**ki**.

wahar, *f.n.*, kid.—**ti**.

wahsi, *m.n.*, idleness, sloth.—**gi**.

wahso, *v.i.*, be idle, lazy.

wahsan, *a.v.*, idle, lazy; **wilki wahsan**, the idle boy.

waḥfi, *m.n.*, bracelet (of silver). —**gi**.

waḫhabar, *m.n.*, galaxy, milky way.—**ki.** (Somals call so the white tinge appearing in the sky at night, and they say that it is produced by the garment of a Somal's mother, whom he has been condemned to drag along the sky.)

waḫti, *m.n.*, season, weather, time. —**gi.**

waiyai or **weiyei**, *int.* and *a.*, so it happened, indeed! yes, it is; **ḫalas waiyai**, it is finished.

waladi, *m.n.*, kind of soup made of pieces of meat.—**gi.**

walaḫ, *v.tr.*, stir, move.

walaḫ, *m.n.*, stirring, movement. —**hi.**

walal, *m.n.*, brother.—**ki.**

walal, *f.n.*, sister.—**shi.**

walba, *ind.num.*, every; **gor walba**, every time; **mel walba**, everywhere; **kol walba**, always.

waliba, *ind.num.*, each; **mid waliba**, each one; **mid waliba markisa ha so boḫo**, let each one come at his turn.

walid, *m.n.*, parents and other relations.—**ki**, —**yo.**

walli, *f.n.*, madness, lunacy.—**di.**

wallo, *v.i.*, become foolish, mad; **washa, wan wallan.**

iss walwal, *m.n.*, folly.—**ki**; **iss walwalka dunida**, the follies of the world.

iss walwal, *v.r.*, make yourself a fool.

wallan, *a.*, idiot, lunatic, mad; **ninki walla**, the mad man; **nagti wallaid**, the mad woman; **wu** or **wa wallanyahai**, he is mad.

walo, *f.n.*, kind of kangaroo rat with a trunk.

walo, *f.n.*, kind of Somali game. (They sit down in two rows with their faces opposite to one another, strike first their own hands and chest saying **jawo**, and then they strike the hand of the person opposite.)

walaisi, *v.c.*, make play.

walais (with **la**, in the *sing.*), *v.r.*, play.

wan, *m.n.*, ram.—**ki.**

wan bararah, *m.n.*, he-lamb; **wanki bararkaaha**, the he-lamb.

wanag, *m.n.*, goodness, kindness, niceness.—**gi.**

wanaji, *v.tr.*, make nicely, arrange well in order.

wanajiso, *v.r.*, arrange (yourself), make ...

wanaksan, *a.*, good, nice, kind; **ka wanaksan**, better; **ka wada wanaksan** or **ugu wanaksan**, the best.

wanaksanaw, *v.att.*, be good.

u wanaksanow, *v.i.*, be good for.

wani, *v.tr.*, advise, admonish, preach, teach.

wano, *f.n.*, advice, counsel, preaching.

war! *int. of calling*, ho! hallo! man! boy! **war hoi! war ya! war ya hoi!** (*sing.*); ho! hallo! man! boy! **war yaryahein ka-**

laiya! (*plur.*) hallo! come (ye) men! boys!

war, *m.n.*, news, communication, information, message.—**ki.**

war gei, *v.tr.*, proclaim, publish.

warḫad, *f.n.*, paper, letter, messenger.—**di.**

war ken, *v.i.*, bring news; **ka war ken**, bring news from, ascertain.

war kena, *m.n.*, informant, messenger.—**hi.**

warran, *v.tr.*, announce, inform, acquaint; **warrama, wan warami; waḫhas wan uga warrami**, I will inform him of that; **u** —, communicate; **iss ka** —, inform of yourself, *or* (better) how are you?

warsi, *v.tr.*, communicate.

waraiso or **warso**, *v.c.*, ask the news of him (*means* let him tell you from whence he comes, and who he is); **waraista, wan waraisan**, or **warsada, wan warsan.**

war (*root*).

waren, *v.tr.*, pierce; **warema, wan ku waremi.**

waren, *v.i.*, penetrate into (used as a foul word).

warmo, *f.n.*, intercourse, copulation.

waran, *m.n.*, spear, javelin.—**ki.**

waraba and **wera**, *m.n.*, spotted hyæna (*Hyæna crocuta*). — **hi** (Somals believe the hyæna to be a hermaphrodite).

warabi, *v.tr.*, water, give water to drink; **i warabi**, give me to drink; **faraska, aurka warabi**, water the horse, camel.

waraḫ, *f.n.*, papers, letters (either exposed on a table or tied together).—**di.**

waraḫ, *m.n.*, whining, sigh.—**hi,** —**yo.**

waranus, *m.n.*, big lizard (Abyssinian).—**ki.**

wareg or **iss ka wareg**, *v.tr.*, turn; **ku** —, turn by; **aḫalka ku wareg**, turn by the house; **ku so** —, go round, take a trip.

wareji, *v.c.*, cause to turn, wind up, revolve, spin.

warwareg and **so warwareg**, *v.i.*, wander about, stroll, go to and fro.

warwareji and **so warwareji**, *v.c.*, cause to wander about, make go to and fro.

warwareg, *m.n.*, ramble, rambling.—**gi.**

waregaiso, *v.i.*, move round.

warer, *m.n.*, whirl, giddiness.—**ki; madaḥ warer**, *m.n.*, vertigo.

warer, *v.i.*, whirl.

wareri, *v.c.*, cause to whirl, to get giddy.

warersan, *a.v.*, giddy; **nin warersan**, a giddy man.

warik, *f.n.*, mushroom.—**ti,** —**yo; wa warik**, it is a mushroom.

was, *v.i.*, commit impurity, fornication, adultery, incest; **abbahá was**, filthy expression very often heard amongst the Somals.

wasmo, *f.n.*, impurity.
wasah or **wisih**, *m.n.*, dirt, filth.
wasahai, *v.tr.*, dirty.
wasahaisan, *a.v.*, dirty; **ninki wasahaisna**, the dirty man; **wil yow wasahaisni, iga tag**, you dirty boy, go away.
wasaa', *m.n.*, large plain.—**hi.**
wasiad, *f.n.*, commandment of God.—**di.**
wayel, *m.n.*, old, grown up.—**ki** (this word is used for a man in his prime, and sometimes for women, girls and small boys not doing any house-work).
wayo? *ad.*, why?
wed, *m.n.*, our fate or destiny, God's appointed time, and especially the time of death, as is sentenced by God, according to the Musulman doctrine (or fatalism).—**ki; wedkisi ba galai**, it was his time.
wegered, *m.n.*, girth (for saddle), belly-band (for horses, mules, asses ...).—**ki, —yo.**
wegered 'ad and **madow**, *m.n.*, kind of tree, high, without thorns, and having a white bark.—**ki.**
wehel, *m.n.*, companion, friend, adherent, accomplice, *means also* a man that knows the Coran perfectly.—**ki.**
weheli, *v.tr.*, attend, accompany.
wehesho, *v.i.*, become friend, accompany, **iss weheshada, wan weheshan.**
wehel, *m.n.*, God.—**ki.**

weïd or **weïdnimo**, *f.n.*, leanness, faint-heartedness.
weïdai, *v.c.*, make lean.
weïdow, *v.i.*, be lean, faint-hearted; **weïdoba, wan weïdobi.**
weïdsan, *a.v.*, faint-hearted, feeble, lean; **ninki weïdsana**, the faint-hearted man.
weidi, *v.tr.*, ask, enquire, consult; **iss —**, reflect, ask yourself.
weidis, *m.n.*, demand, request, desire.—**ki.**
weidiso, *v.r.*, apply, ask, demand (for yourself).
weidar, *m.n.*, large and flat Somali spear.—**ki.**
weidaro, *v.i.*, pass by; **weidarta, wan weidaran; wa iss weidaranai**, we crossed each other.
weidari, *v.c.*, cause it to pass.
iss weidari, *v.tr.*, turn round, tie an animal (by crossing the rope); **faraska iss weidari**, turn the horse round, tie the horse.
iss weidar, *m.n.*, crossing one another without seeing or finding.—**ki.**
iss weidar, *m.n.*, fetters tying the right foreleg of an animal to its left one.
weiji, *m.n.*, face.—**gi; weiji bannu iss ku lehnahai**, we are acquainted with each other.
weil, *m.n.*, calf.—**ki.**
weil, *f.n.*, heifer.—**shi.**
weilo, *m.n.pl.*, calves (general name).—**hi.**

weildo, *f.n.*, milk and butter-milk mixed together.

weilalis, *f.n.*, skins sewed together and forming a mat.—**ti.**

wein, *a.*, big, great, large, immense; **ka wein,** bigger, greater; **ka wada wein** or **ugu wein,** the greatest ...; **ninki weina,** the big man.

weinow, *v.i.*, be great, big.

weinai, *v.tr.*, make big ...; **so** —, take and make it big.

weinan, *f.n.*, greatness, stoutness. —**ti.**

weiweir, *m.n.*, affliction, anxiety, discontent.—**ki.**

weirweir or **weilweil,** *v.i.*, be anxious, afflicted, discontented.

weirweirsan, *a.v.*, afflicted; **nebi Job wa nin weirweirsana,** the Patriarch Job was afflicted.

weiso, *f.n.*, vessel containing water for ablutions before prayer.

wel, *m.n.*, vessel (general name for utensils or sets of pots, jars).—**ki.**

weli, *ad.*, yet; **weli ma ḥalas,** not yet finished.

weliba, *ad.*, still, over again, more; **weliba i si,** give me still more.

weliga, weligi, *ad.*, ever, always, never; **weliga wad buki,** you will always remain sick.

weli, *m.n.*, saint.—**gi** (*see* **auliad**).

werar, *m.n.*, attack, assault.—**ki.**

werar, *v.tr.*, assail, assault; **waḥ ka** —, fight with.

lagu werar, *v.pass.*, be attacked; **wa la i werari,** I shall be attacked; **wa lagu werari,** thou wilt be attacked.

weyer, *m.n.*, water (of a well). —**ki.**

wil, *m.n.*, boy, lad.—**ki.**

wiyil, *f.n.*, rhinoceros.—**shi.**

wōb, *m.n.*, yellow colour.—**ki.**

Y.

y, this letter, united to the pers. prn. in its simple form gives the forms **yan,** I; **yad,** thou; **yu,** he; **yai,** she; **yainu,** we (I and you); **yannu,** we (I and he); **yaidiñ,** you; **yai,** they.

ya, *pers.prn.*, *2nd pers.sing.*, thou (used for vocative of address); **war ya!** oh! thou man! **na ya!** oh! thou woman! for the *plur.* they say **waryayahein!** oh! you men! *or* **warya ehein! maḥa donaisan?** oh! you men, what do you want, wish? **waryaehein! niman yohow! waḥha ḥun iss ka daya,** hallo! you men, leave the bad thing.

ya, particle used as **wa** and **ba.**

ya, particle used for the verb of existence.

ya, *int.prn.*, who? contraction of **aya?** and **ya?** what?

ya — da, this word expresses present time in a relation, and means then, and is used for **iyado o; yado ai kolki tuka-**

shada tahai ya na la werarai, when it was the time of prayer, then we were attacked.

ya', *m.n.*, flight, escape, running away.—**hi**; **ya'há dai**, look at that flight.

ya'a, *v.i.*, fly, run away, escape (only used in the plur.); **wainu ya'i**, we will escape, run away, **wainu ya'anai**, we fled; **so** —, fly (ye) towards me.

ya'ai, *m.n.*, boughs put upon and around the **hensarer** to preserve the huts from the sand.

yab, *m.n.*, admiration, marvel, wonder, extraordinary thing. —**ki**.

yab, *v.tr.*, admire; **hadi dadku wah la ma kara arko, wa yabi**, if the people see a miracle, they will wonder, admire.

yabi, *v.tr.*, astonish, amaze.

la yab, *m.n.*, amazement, admiration, astonishment.

la yab, *v.i.*, be astonished, surprised at, wonder.

yaban, yabsan or **la yabsan**, *a.*, wonderful, admirable, extraordinary; **wahhasan la yabsana**, this thing is *or* was wonderful.

la yabsanaw, *v.att.*, wonder at.

yag'ar, *m.n.*, B. frereana gum maieti tree.

yahan (*see* **ohon**), **wa lugu yahan**, you are known.

af yahan, *a.*, eloquent, tame.

jid yahan, *m.n.*, guide.

ya'ni, *expression meaning* that is, that means.

yar, *a.*, small, little; **nin yar**, a small man; **niman yaryar**, small men; **nagti yaraid**, the small woman; **ka yar**, smaller; **ka wada** or **ugu yar**, the smallest, the least.

yarai, *v.tr.*, lessen, diminish, shorten, abate.

yaraiso, *v.r.*, lessen, diminish (for yourself); **sortá yaraiso**, do not take so much food.

yaran, *f.n.*, childhood, littleness, abatement.

yarad, *m.n.*, second and last present given by a young man to the father of a girl he is about to marry (this present is given at the moment of marriage).—**ki**; **yaradki ban hatai**, I have received the gift.

yed, *v.tr.*, call, cry after, aloud; **ugu** —, name, call.

yed and **yednin**, *m.n.*, call, answer to a call.—**ki**, —**ti**.

u yed, *v.tr.*, call for, invite; **ninki lo yed**, the man is called.

ka yed, *v.i.*, call aloud from; **la yed**, call, cry with; **wilka la yed**, cry with the boy.

lagu yed, *v.pass.*, be called; **wa la i yedi**, I will be called; **wa nailo yedi**, we will be called.

yel, *v.i.*, yield, obey, listen to, do; **wahhá abbahá ku dirayo yel** or **abbahá wuhu ku dirayo yel**, do what your father sent you for; **abbaha hadalkisa ban yeli**, I will listen to the word of the father; **wa nin**

hadalkisa la yela, he is a man whose word is obeyed; **iss —,** obey yourself; **iss yel, iss yelyel,** do what you like, do your will; **iss yelyelah,** or **iss yelyelah badan,** opposite, contrary.

yelyel! *int.* do quick and all.

ḥon or **nabar yel,** *v.tr.*, harm, hurt, wound.

waḥ yel, *v.tr.*, injure; **wa nin mel waḥ laga yelai,** he is a man who has received some harm, who has been injured.

waḥ yello, *f.n.*, injury.

yel, *m.n.*, affair, concern (of no consequence, or to which you do not pay any attention); **yelkisa,** it is his affair, never mind; **yelkeda** (*fem.*), **yelkisa naga da, yelka,** it is your affair.

yelo, *v.tr.*, bear, beget, bring forth, produce.

yel, *f.n.*, strap for fastening on the load of a camel.—**shi.**

yel, *v.i.*, sew the sandal-straps; **kabahá i yel,** sew my sandal-straps; **kabahas imisad igu yeli?** how much must I pay for sewing my sandal-straps?

yelo, *v.i.*, take your concern in hand; **la'ag so yelo,** borrow money; **la'ag ban so yelan,** I will borrow money.

yesho, *v.r.*, confide in, have trust (in yourself); **anigu wad yeshon karta;** you may confide in me; **ku —,** trust him with.

yeshod, *m.n.*, confidence.—**ki.**

yeyi, *f.n.*, hyæna dog.—**di.**

yibir, *m.* and *f.n.*, lowest Somali caste, sorcerer, sorceress (giving medicine and amulets).—**ki, —ti; yibro** (*plur.*).

yiḥiḥsi, *m.n.*, disgust.—**gi; yiḥiḥsiga i haya,** I am disgusted.

yiḥiḥsi (with **kaga**), *v.tr.*, disgust.

yiḥiḥso, *v.i.*, be disgusted.

yiḥiḥsan, *a.v.*, disgusting, loathsome.

yi'ib, *f.n.*, almond, almond tree, pistachio.—**ti.**

yiliḥ, *f.n.*, flue, fur.

yohow, *particle*, thou, you; **ninyohow,** thou man; **ragyohow,** you men; **Ilaḥha yohow,** thou God.

yubai, *m.n.*, kind of tree with thorns curved like hooks.—**hi.**

yuhudi, *m.n.*, a Jew.—**gi; yuhud** Jews; **yuhuddi,** the Jews.

yuhudiyad, *f.n.*, Jewess.—**di.**

yur! *int.*, get away!

yurub, *m.n.*, spray.—**ki.**

yusur, *m.n.*, amber beads.—**ki.**

PART II.

ENGLISH-SOMALI VOCABULARY.

ENGLISH-SOMALI VOCABULARY.

A.

a; there is no indefinite article in Somali.

Aaron, *p.n.*, **Arun.**

abandon, *v.tr.*, **da, iss ka da, na'**; — all, **wah kasta ka kalai**; do you abandon me? **ma i na'aisa?**

abandoned, *a.v.*, **la dayai, la na'ai**; **wilki la dayai**, the abandoned boy.

abandoner, *n.*, **hof iss ka dayai** or **na'ai.**

abandonment, abandoning, *f.n.*, **dein,—ti.**

abase, *v.tr.*, **hosaisi.**

abasement, *m.n.*, **hosaisis,—ki.**

abash, *v.tr.*, **rog.**

abashed, *a.v.*, **rogmai, rogmadai**; **nin rogmai**, an abashed man.

abashment, *f.n.*, **rognin,—ti.**

abate, *v.tr.*, **din, hosaisi, joji, yarai, yaraisi, gana' jebi.**

abatement, *f.n.*, **yaran,—ti, gana' jabnan,—ti.**

abbreviate, *v.tr.*, **din, gābi, yarai.**

abbreviation, *m.* and *f.n.*, **gabnin,—ti, gabis,—ki.**

abdomen, *n.*, (lower part of the belly) **gumar,—ki.**

abed, *ad.*; he is abed, **wa hurda, wa jifa.**

abhor, *v.tr.*, **'il u hab, u 'isho, na'.**

abhorrence, *n.*, **'il,—ki, ma ja'alan,—ti, ne'ban,—ti**; **ma ja'alantan dembigaiga u habo wa wein tahai**, the abhorrence I have of my sins is great.

abide, *v.i.*, **fadi, fadiso, jir, jog, rugaiso.**

abiding, *n.*, **fadi,—gi, jog,—gi, rug,—ti.**

ability, *n.*, **farsamo,—di, karnin,—ti.**

abject, *a.*, **bās, allah habai,—gi.**

able, *a.*, **kara**; (skilful) **farsamo badan, wah haban og.**

abjure, *v.tr.*, **dinta did,** or **iss ka did.**

abjuration, *n.*, **didnin dintaah**; **didninti dinta**, the abjuration.

abnegate, *v.r.*, **iss na'.**
abnegation, *n.*, **iss ne'ban,—ti.**
abode, *n.*, **fadi,—gi, jog,—gi, rug,—gi.**
abolish, *v.tr.*, **babii, bii, jar, ka jar.**
abolishment, abolition, *n.*, **babiis, —ki, idlain** or **idlan,—ti.**
abominable, *a.*, **inkaran, inkarsan.**
abominate, *v.tr.*, **'il u ḫab, 'ilow, 'isho, na'.**
abomination, *n.*, (the object of aversion) **inkar,—ti.**
abort, *v.i.*, *see* miscarry.
abortion, *n.*, **ilma ka ḫoman,—ki.**
abound, *v.tr.*, **badnaw, badso, dereg.**
abounding, *n.*, **badin,—ti, badnan,—ti, dereg,—gi.**
about, *prp.*; the soldiers were — him, **askarti wa ku ḫertai**; it was — night, **habenki wa dowa**; when I saw him, he was — to die, **markan arkai inu dinto yu u dowa**; I have no money — me, **anigu la'ag ma sito**; he is somewhere — the house, **aḫalku mel ka joga**; it is — the house, **aḫalkai mel ka tal**; all —, **mel walba,** or **mel kasta**; look — and —, **melaha eg,** or **ka dai**; I visited all the country round —, **magalada o dan ku so waregai**; I am — to go away, **anigu inan iss ka tago ban u dowahai**; look — you, **war! iss jir.**
about, *ad.*; for three leagues round — there is no game, **sadeḫda sa'adod e horai ugaddi ma jogto,** or **ugad arki maisid**; do you know a short cut —? **dau yar mesha ma ka ogtahai?** is there a long (*i.e.* roundabout) way —? **dau wein mesha malehdahai?** drink —, **mid waliba markisa ha 'abo**; a tree of — seven cubits round, **ged todoba dudunah.**
above, *ad.*, **dul, dusha, gudka** as — said, **sidi hore lo idi.**
above, *prp.*; the one sat — and the other below me, **midina wa i dul fadistai ki kaleh na i hos jogai.**
abrade, *v.tr.*, **ḫaḫuḫ, hoḫ.**
abrasion, *n.*, (the act of rubbing off) **hoḫnin,—ti.**
abridge, *v.tr.*, **din, gābi, yarai.**
abridgment, *n.*, **gābnin,—ti; gābis,—ki.**
abroad, *ad.*, **dibadda, mel fog, dul kaleh**; he is —, **dul kaleh yu jira**; to-morrow I will go —, **berri ban mel fog u so'onaya** or **tegi dona.**
abrogate, *v.tr.*, **babii, bii, idlai, jar.**
abrogation, *n.*, **babiis,—ki, babiin,—ti, idlan,—ti.**
abscess, *n.*, **dullaḫ,—hi.**
abscond, *v.i.r.*, **dumo.**
absconding, *n.*, **dumasho,—adi.**
absence, *n.*, **maḫnan,—ti.**
absent, *a.*, **maḫan**; be —, **maḫnaw**; long —, soon forgotten; **nin maḫan gor dow ba la ilow,** a long — man is soon forgotten.

absolve, *v.tr.*, **'affi, ka 'affi, bii, ka bii, fur.**
absolution, *n.*, (an acquittal or discharge) **furnin,—ki**; (an ecclesiastical term) **'affi,—gi.**
absorb, *v.tr.*, **liḫ, 'ab.**
absolutely, *ad.*, **haïb**; I told him — all, **haïb ban ugu wada shegai.**
abstain, *v.i.*, **ha 'unin, ha 'abin, son.**
abstaining, abstinence, *n.*, **'ir yaran,—ti, son,—ki.**
abstemious, abstinent, *a.*, **'ir yar.**
abundance, *n.*, **ḋereg,—gi, badin,—ti, badnan,—ti, dunyo,—adi.**
abundant, *a.*, **badan.**
abuse, *n.*, (an affront) **'aï,—di, waḥyelo,—adi**; (bad custom) **ḥil,—ki.**
abuse, *v.tr.*, **'aï**; *v.c.*, **'aïsi, ḥil.**
abusive, *a.*, **(waḥ) ḥilai.**
abut upon, *v.i.*, (terminate) **ḋamaw, idlaw.**
abutment, *n.*, **idlan,—ti.**
abyss, *n.*, **gun,—ti, 'el gun fog, 'elki gunta foga.**
acacia vera, *n.*, **anḫokib,—ti**; (a kind of) **'adad,—di.**
accent, *n.*, (a sign) **ḥasakab,—ki.**
accept, *v.tr.*, **ho, ḥado, aḫbal, ka aḫbal, oggolaw.**
accepting, acceptance, *n.*, **oggolan,—ti.**
accident, *n.*, (hazard) **ayan,—ti.**
acclaim, *v.tr.*, **bog, u bog.**
acclamation, *n.*, **bog,—gi.**
accommodate, *v.tr.*, (manage) **u tali**; — with, **u ḋig, si.**
accommodate to, *v.i.*, **la heshi, heshiya** (*plur.*).
accommodated, *a.v.*, **(nin) baraḥah**; (well — man) **ladan.**
accommodation, *n.*, **heshis,—ki, baraḥ,—hi, ladnan,—ti.**
accomplice, *n.*, **wehel,—ki.**
accomplish, *v.tr.*, **ḋamai, idlai.**
accomplishment, *n.*, **ḋamad,—ki, ḋaman,—ti, idlan,—ti.**
accord, accordance, *n.*, **heshis,—ki, nabad,—di.**
according to, *prp.*, **'ainka**; **'ainka u samaiyai u samai,** do it — what I did; **Injilka 'aïmada** or **'aïnka rasul Matheos u ḥorai,** — the Gospel of the Evangelist St. Matthew.
accouchment, *n.*, **umusho,—adi.**
account, *n.*, **hisab,—ti, tiro,—adi.**
account, *v.tr.*, **hisabi, tiri**; — with, **ku tiri**; *v.r.*, **tirso, ku tirso.**
accountant, *n.*, **tiriya,—hi.**
account (on your), *prp.*, **awaḋá, daraddá**; in every way you are guilty, **kollei ba ada ḥujadleh**; on no —, **sina.**
accumulate, *v.tr.*, **tul, rasai, ururi.**
accumulated, *a.v.*, **tulan, rasaisan, ururSan.**
accumulation, *n.*, **tul,—ki, rasais,—ki, urur,—ki.**
accurse, *v.tr.*, **habār, inkar, na'dal.**
accursed, *a.v.*, **habāran, habār ḥaba, inkaran, inkar ḥaba.**
accusation, *n.*, **ashtako,—adi.**

accuse, *v.tr.*, **ashtakai**; — falsely, **edai.**
accustom, *v.tr.*, **bar**; **arurta gor horai waḥ bar, inai shuḥulkoda ād u ḥabtan,** or **wanag u ḥabtan,** children must be accustomed early to do their work well.
acerb, *a.*, **ḥadad, danān.**
ache, aching, *n.*, **ḥanun,—ti.**
ache (be in pain), *v.i.*, **ḥanunso**; *v.imp.*, **wu ḥanuni,** it pains; **wa i ḥanunaisa,** it pains me; *v.c.*, **ḥanuni.**
achieve, *v.tr.*, **damai, ḥalas, idlai.**
achievement, *n.*, **damad,—ki, idlain,—ti.**
acid, *a.*, **ḥadad, ḥadada.**
acknowledge, *v.tr.*, (confess, avow) **ḥado, ḥiro**; (be grateful) **abalgud, abalmari.**
acknowledgment, *n.*, **ḥir,—ti, abāl,—ki, abalgud,—ki.**
acolyte, *n.*, **shammas, sham'adani.**
acquaint with, *v.tr.*, **bar, ogaisi, war gei, warran.**
acquaintance, *n.*, **oḥonin,—ki, oḥon,—ti.**
acquainted, *a.v.*, he is — with, **wa ogyahai, wa yaḥan.**
get acquainted with, *v.tr.*, **iss bar, baro, oḥonso, oḥonsada** (*plur.*); *v.c.*, **oḥonsi.**
acquiesce, *v.i.*, **oggolaw, yel.**
acquiescence, *n.*, **oggolan,—ti.**
acquire, *v.tr.*, **hel.**
acquirement, acquiring, acquisition, *n.*, **helin,—ki**; (of instruction) **barasho,—di.**
acquit, *v.tr.*, **fur, si da**; — your debt, **ḥantada iss ka biḥi.**
acquitted, *a.v.*, **la fur, garta laha.**
acquitment, acquittal, *n.*, **furnin,—ti.**
across, *prp.*, pass — the country, — the river, **magalada deh mar, durdurka ka talab.**
act, *n.*, **falnin,—ti.**
act, *v.tr.*, **fal.**
active, *a.*, **hauled (nin), fudfudud.**
acute, *a.*, (subtle) **fi'an**; (pointed) **fiḥan**; make —, **fiḥ, dub.**
adamant, *n.*, **mas** or **almas, daiman,—ki.**
adapt (a stone), *v.tr.*, **ḥor.**
add to, *v.tr.*, **ku dar, iss ku dar, iss u gei, iss ku joji, ku tirso.**
adder, *n.*, **jilbis,—ki.**
addition, *n.*, **tiro,—di.**
address, *v.tr.*, **u dir.**
adduce, *v.tr.*, **la tali.**
adhere, *v.i.*, **ku deg.**
adherent (partisan), *n.*, **wehel,—ki.**
adhesive, *a.*, **ku dega, ku degta**; the leech is an — animal, **'ula-'ushu wa bahal ku degta.**
adieu! *intj.*, **amana Allah.**
adjacent, *a.*, **dow.**
adjoin, *v.tr.*, **la dawaisi, iss u gei, ku tiri.**
adjourn, *v.tr.*, **iss ka da, rāji, u reb.**
adjure, *v.tr.*, **dari**; I — you in the name of God to tell us, **magaha Ebbahai ban ku darinaya e no sheg.**

administer, *v.tr.*, **ḥukum, u tali.**
administration, *n.*, **ḥukum,—ki, talo,—di.**
administrator, *n.*, **ḥakim,—ki, taliya,—hi.**
admirable, *a.*, **yaban, yabsan, la yabsan, yab ḥaba.**
admiration, *n.*, **yab,—ki.**
admire, *v.tr.*, **yab, la yab**; *v.i.*, **la yabsanaw.**
admission, *n.*, **so gelin,—ti, so gelis,—ki.**
admit, *v.tr.*, **so geli.**
admonish, *v.tr.*, **wani, so wani.**
admonishing, admonition, *n.*, **wano,—di.**
adolescence, *n.*, **arurnimo,—di.**
adopt, *v.tr.*, **kori.**
adoptive, *a.*, **la koriyai.**
adorable, *a.*, **la 'ābuda**; God alone is —, **Ilaḥ keliah la 'ābuda.**
adoration, *n.*, **'ābudnin,—ti.**
adore, *v.tr.*, **'abud**; be adored, *v.p.*, **ha lagu 'ābudo.**
adulate, *v.tr.*, **ḥayaḥayai, sasabo.**
adulation, *n.*, **ḥayaḥayo,—di, sasabnin,—ti.**
adult, *n.*, **baluḫ,—hi, ḥangad,—ki, mudakar,—ki.**
adulterate, *v.tr.*, (sophisticate) **bedel.**
adulterer, *n.*, **ḓillai,—gi.**
adulteress, *n.*, **ḓillo,—di.**
adultery, *n.*, **ḓillanimo,—di.**
advance, *n.*, **horan,—ti.**
advance, *v.tr.*, **durki, horaisi, horo u dig, so'odsi.**
advance, *v.i.*, **durug, horai, so'o, hor u so'o, wad.**
advantage, *n.*, **fayido,—di, helin, —ki, koroḓ,—ki.**
advantageous, *a.*, **fayidoleh.**
advent, *n.*, **imatin,—ki.**
adventure, *n.*, **ḥaladun,—ki, sabab,—ti.**
adventure, *v.tr.*, **sabab**; *v.i.*, **sababo.**
adversary, *n.*, **'oll,—ki.**
adverse, *a.*, (contrary) **asarar wein**; (afflictive) **sili'iya, ḥanujiya.**
adversity, *n.*, **ḥuman,—ti, ayan ḥumo,—di.**
advertise, *v.tr.*, **u dig, wani, warran.**
advertisement, *n.*, **dignin,—ti, wano,—di, war,—ki.**
advice, *n.*, (counsel) **wano,—di,** (notice) **war,—ki, dignin,—ti.**
advise, *v.tr.*, **wani, warran, dignin dir.**
advise with (consider, consult), *v.i.*, **hubso, la faḫ.**
advised, *a.v.*, **feïg, fi'an, herribleh, miyirsan, miyir ḥab.**
advocate, *n.*, **Mariam wa ḥof innaga awaden u hadasha,** *lit.* Mary is a person who speaks in our interest, *or* Mary is our advocate; **jannadi 'Issa Kristos ba innaga awaden u hadla,** in heaven Jesus Christ is our advocate.
æra (epoch), *n.*, **ayan,—ti, ayamo,—di, tariḫ,—hi** (commencement of a computation of years).
afar, *ad.*, **mel fog**; it is far, **wa fogyahai.**

affability, *n.*, **wanag,—gi.**
affable, *a.*, **wanaksan, ḫabow.**
affair, *n.*, (concern) **arrin,—ki, yel,—ki**; it is his —, **yelkisa**; (business) **haul,—shi.**
affect, *v.tr.*; **ninka đimashadisi alol ḫumo ayan ku ḫaba,** the death of this man gives me pain, *or* affects me.
affection, *n.*, **ja'ail,—ki, ja'alan, —ti.**
affiance, *n.*, **donanan,—ti, donin,—ki.**
affiance, *v.tr.*, **don, la ballan**; affiance the two, **labada ballami, iss u don.**
affinity, *n.*, **ḫaren,—ki.**
be in affinity, *v.i.*, **la ḫarenso, iss ḫarensada** (*plur.*), **u ḫaren noḫo.**
affirm, *v.tr.*, **rumai, đabai.**
affirmation, *n.*, **đabain,—ti, rumaisi,—gi.**
afflict, *v.tr.*, **u ḫumai, ḫanuji, ḫanuni, sili'i, weirweiri**; *v.r.*, **iss ḫanuji.**
afflicted, *a.*, **ḫanunsan, sila'san, weirweirsan**; be —, *v.i.r.*, **weirweir, iss ḫumai.**
affliction, *n.*, **ḫuman,—ti, weirweir,—ki, silei', sili'hi.**
affluence, *n.*, **đereg,—gi, holo, —ihi.**
afford, *v.tr.*, (produce, give) **biḫi**; the earth produces fruits and plants, **dulku miđo iyo inino yu biḫiya.**
affranchise, *v.tr.*, (to set free) **sarraḫi.**
affray, *n.*, **dirir,—ti.**
affright, *v.tr.*, **'absi, baji, kaga niḫi.**
affront, *n.*, **naḫadin,—ti.**
afore, abaft, *ad.*, **ḫar hore iyo ḫar dambe.**
afraid, *a.*, **'absonaya, baḫaya.**
Africa, *n.*, **Africa.**
after, *ad.*, **dabaded, dambe, dambow, haddow**; look — (search for, take care of), **don, ilali, jir**; (*prp.*) — Sunday, **aḫadda dabadeda**; some while —, **'abbar ka dambow**; he delays day — day, **malin ka malin bu u raga**; go — him, **ka daba tag**; — ages, — times, **beri beri dambe, beri ka dambow**; — supper, **awaisin,—ki** (from 7 p.m.); — to-morrow, **sā dambe**; — noon, **gelin dambe, duḫurka dabadisa, 'asar,—ki** (from 3 p.m. to sunset); after I had gone to the ship, **markan markabka dofaya fulai.**
afterwards, *ad.*, **dabadedba, haddowto, wa,—gi dambe.**
again, *ad.*, **mar, gor, kol kaleh, misana, misna**; give me as much —, **inti in leh eg i si.**
against, *prp.*, **ka.**
age, *n.*, (duration of life, years, interval since birth) **dā,—di, jir,—ti, gu,—gi**; (for aged persons) **fil, iss ku fil, gan, —ki, gumais,—ti**; (tender age) **da yar, gaban,—ki, gibin,—ki, yaran,—ti**; (old age) **dā wein, dādi weinaid, duḫ,—hi.**
aged, *a.*, (person) **ḫof dā wein,**

duḥaḥ; (advanced in age) gun, gumais.

aggravate, *v.tr.*, si ḥumai.

aggregate, *v.tr.*, iss kŭ dar, so ururi.

aghast, *ad.*; he was —, ād bu u naḥai.

aggrieve, *v.tr.*, sili'i.

agile, *a.*, fudfudud.

agility, *n.*, fudfudaid,—ki.

agitate, *v.tr.*, ruḥ, ruḥruḥ, lul, walaḥ.

ago, *ad.*, awal or awel; long —, beri hore; a while —, gor dowaid; some years —, sanado dowa.

agonize, *v.i.*, (die) naftu ha ka baḥdo, or naftu ha kugu waregto, or tadi dambai waiyai e ku dagalan.

agony, *n.* (dying); he is in —, nafti wa ka si baḥaisa, or nafti wa ku waregaisa, or nafti ninka or ninki wadnihi bai kaga jirta or jogta, or wadnihi bai ninki kaga jirta, or ninki wa ka hādaisa, or ninki wa ka si hādaisa.

agree with, *v.i.*, la heshi, heshiya (*plur.*); — upon, in, ku heshi; *v.c.*, heshisi; iyagu sida dinad iyo eï bai u heshiyan, they agree with one another as a cat and a dog.

agreeable, *a.*, baḥsan.

agreed, *a.*; it is —, lagu heshi.

agreement, *n.*, heshis,—ki.

ague (intermittent fever), *n.*, garir,—ki, ḥadḥad,—ki.

ahead, astern, *ad.*, ḥar hore iyo ḥar dambe.

aid, *n.*, 'awinad,—di, 'awin,—ti, gargar,—ti, hil,—ki.

aid, *v.tr.*, 'awi, gargar, la ḥabo, la ḥad, hili.

ail, ailment, *n.*, hanun,—ki.

ail, *v.tr.*, hanuni, hanuji; what ails you? maḥa ku hanujinaya?

aim, *n.*, ḥiyas,—ti, dug,—ti, tog,—ti, togasho,—adi; (intention) dama',—hi.

aim at, *v.i.*, la dugo, la togo, gan, ku rid; be aiming at, dugtan.

aimer (skilful), *n.*, nin dug badan, togasho badan; (ganad,—ki, ganasho,—adi, the aiming).

air, *n.*, (one of the four elements) hawo,—di, dabail,—shi, ne-'aw,—di; (countenance, features) so jog,—gi, jaḥ,—hi, weiji,—gi.

air, *v.tr.*, (aerate) ne'awi.

akin, *a.*, ḥig.

alarm, *n.*, naḥadin; (cry by which men are summoned) ḥata! ḥata!

alarm, *v.tr.*, baji, u ḥaili, kaga nihi.

alight, *v.i.*, ka deg, ka so deg.

alike, *a.*, iss leh eg, iss ku mid; not —, kala mid, iss ku mid ma aha, iss ma leh eka, kan kaleh u ma eka.

aliment, *n.*, sor,—ta.

alive, *a.*, nol jira; he is yet —, wa jira weli.

Alkoran, *n.*, furḥan,—ki.

all, *num.* or *ad.*, dan, daman,—ti, gidi,—gi, kulli,—gi, wada; — men, dadka o dan, or dadki o ɗami, or o wada ɗan; — the world is bad now, dunida o ɗan or o ɗami wa ḥuntahai hatan; God will judge — and every one, Ilaḥhai ba dadka o ɗan o mid walba gonidi u ḥisabi; is that —? ma inta keliah? by — means, kollei; reputation is — in —, mamuskena holo o ɗan ino dama; I was not at — afraid, sina uga ma baḥan; nowhere at —, mela ma jogo, mela ma yal; — the better, wa wanag; — the worse, wa ḥuman; — powerful, ḥuwadleh.

allegory, *n.*, mathal,—ki.

alleviate, allay, *v.tr.*, tud; — my pain, ḥanunka i tud or iga tud.

alleviation, *n.*, tudad,—di, tudnin,—ki.

alliance, *n.*, aḥdi,—gi.

allow, *v.tr.*, fasaḥ.

allowance, *n.*, fasaḥ,—hi.

allure, *v.tr.*, ḥalḥal, sasab, ḥatal.

allurement, *n.*, ḥalḥal,—ki, sasab, —ki.

almighty, *a.*, ḥuwadleh, waḥ walba kara.

almond, *n.*, yi'ib,—ti.

alms, *n.*, sadaḥad,—di; give —, sadaḥadai, sadaḥad si, ku sadaḥadai; give and ask for —, *v.r.*, sadaḥadaiso; sadaḥo! cry of poor people when asking for alms.

aloes-plant, *n.*, da'ar,—ti.

alone, *a.*, goni,—di, keli,—gi or —di.

along, *prp.*; — the shore, hebta dusheda; — the boat, markabka harertisa (mar); go — with, la so'o, la tag, ra'.

alongside, *ad.*, barbar.

aloud, loud, *ad.*; speak —, ād u hadal.

alphabet, *n.*, huruf el hija'.

already, *ad.*, gorti ba, kolki ba yimi.

also, *ad.*, na.

altar, *n.*, masbaḥ,—hi.

alter, *v.tr.*, bedel.

although, *c.*; — you be not good, ya banad wanaksananei; — a big boy, you are not good, wil weina wa tahai, mana (ma se) wanaksanid.

altitude, *n.*, ɗerer,—ki.

altogether, *ad.*, gidi.

always, *ad.*, gor walba, kol walba, gor iyo galab.

amaze, *v.tr.*, yabi.

amazement, *n.*, la yab,—ki.

amber, *n.*, asli,—gi; the two pieces of — they tie to their neck, hal,—ki, makawi,—gi.

ambergris, *n.*, 'anbar,—ki.

ambuscade, ambush, *n.*, hatati, —gi; place in —, ku hatati.

amen, *ad.*, amin, ha lo sida no yel, ha sida ahato.

amend, *n.*, (fine) ḥasirad,—di; make amends, hal mari.

amend, *v.tr.*, (correct) wanaji; *v.r.*, wanajiso; *v.ir.*, iss wanaji.

amiable, *a.*, faraḥanah (*m.*), faraḥanada (*f.*).

amid, amidst, among, amongst, *ad.*, deḥ, deḥda.

amount, *n.*, **ḥisab,—ti, tiro,—adi.**
amuse, *v.tr.*, (divert) **'ayarsi, jalbebi**; *v.i.*, **'ayār, jalbebo, bebta.**
amusement, *n.*, **'ayar,—ti, jalbeb, —ti.**
anathema, *n.*, **inkar,—ti.**
ancestors, *n.*, **dun,—ti.**
anchor, *n.*, **barosin,—ki.**
ancient, *n.*, **nin gabowba, duḥah.**
and, *c.*, **iyo, o, e.**
anecdote, *n.*, **sheko,—adi.**
angel, *n.*, **malaïko,—adi.**
anger, *n.*, **'ado,—adi.**
angry, *a.*, **'adaisan, 'ilan**; be —, **adaïsnaw, 'ilow, 'il u ḥab, 'isho.**
anguish, *n.*, **silei',—hi.**
animal, *n.*, **dugag,—gi, bahal, —ki, nef,—ki**; a lean —, **hidmo abaḥah, neif weidsan.**
animate, *v.tr.*, **nolai**; kindle the fire, **dabka nolai.**
ankle, *n.*, **anḥau,—gi**; ankle-bone, **kurankur,—ti.**
anna (Indian money), *n.*, **gambo, —adi**; two —, **saḥ,—hi**; four —, **tumun,—ki**; eight —, **rubi,—gi.**
annihilate, *v.tr.*, **bii, lumi.**
announce, *v.tr.*, **war gei, war ken, warran.**
annoy, *v.tr.*, **dali.**
annoyance, *n.*, **dal,—ki, dalnin, —ti.**
annual, *a.*, **gu walba wa mar**; this annual feast, **'iddasi gu walba wa mar**, or **gu ba wa kol.**
annunciate, *v.tr.*, **nabad u gei.**
annunciation, *n.*, **nabad,—di.**
anoint, *v.tr.*, **salidda, udgonka mari.**
anonymous, *a.*, **hebel, nin hebel, nin ba.**
another, *a.*, **mid kaleh**; we love one —, **wa iss ja'el nahai.**
answer, *n.*, **jawab,—ti**; — to a call, **yed,—ki, yednin,—ti.**
answer, *v.tr.*, **deh, u'eli, la hadal.**
ant, *n.*, (a black kind) **ḥudanyo** or **ḥudanjo,—adi**; (another kind) **duḥul ku reb,—ki**; (a black kind, big and stinking) **jina',—'ihi**; (a kind of white —) **abor,—ki**; (another kind) **harun,—ti**, or **harei,—ihi**, or **har,—hi**; (name of their nests or hills in the desert) **dundumo, —adi.**
ant-hill, *n.*, **ras,—ki**; **rasgura, —gi.**
anterior, *a.*, **horai** (*m.*), **horaisai** (*f.*).
anthropophagus, *n.*, **dadḥal,—ki** (*m.*), **dadḥalato,—adi** (*f.*).
antichrist, *n.*, **antikristos.**
anticipate, *v.tr.*, **horaisi.**
anus, *n.*, **futo,—adi.**
anvil, *n.*, **'udad,—di**; hand —, **'udad yar,—di yaraid.**
anxiety, *n.*, **weirweir** or **weilweil, —ki.**
anxious, *a.*, **weirweirsan**; be —, *v.i.*, **weirweir**; be —, *v.c.*, **weirweiri.**
any, *a.* or *prn.*, **'id, waḥ**; —body, **'id kasta**; —thing, **'id kasta, walba**; —thing soever, **waḥ un**; in — place, **mel kasta**;

—how, **si kasta**; —body but you, **adiga mahae nin walba**; not —, **'id na**; will you go — further? **ma yar dafi?** I will not put you off — longer, **mar dambe ku rajin mayo**; have you — more to say? **hadal ma u nohon?** or **hadal ma ku hadai?**

apart, *ad.*, **kala**; set —, **kala 'eli.**

apartment, *n.*, **mahsin,—ki.**

aphony, *n.*, **habeib,—ti.**

aphorism, *n.*, **mahmah,—di.**

apologue, *n.*, **mathal,—ki, halalif,—ki.**

apostacy, *n.*, **tarāk,—gi, kufran, —ti, juhud addin** (Ar.).

apostate, *n.*, **jahid,—ki, kāfir, —ki, kufar** (*plur.*), **kafarad, —di** (*f.*), **tarik,—gi.**

apostatize, *v.i.*, **tarak, kāfar, dinta, jahad.**

apostle, *n.*, **rasul,—ki.**

apostolic, apostolical, *a.*, **rasuli, —gi**; the Apostolic religion, **dinta rasuligaah, dinta rasulyada.**

apothecary, *n.*, **bodikeri,—gi.**

apparent, *a.*, **la arka, muhda** (*m.*), **muhata** (*f.*).

apparition, *n.*, **muhad,—ki, muhasho,—di.**

appeal, *n.*, **ashtako,—adi**; *v.i.*, **ashtako, ashtakai.**

appear (become visible), *v.i.*, **muho.**

it appears, *v.imp.*, **wah la moda, wahai la tahai**; — to me, **wahai i la tahai.**

appearance (outside show, figure), *n.*, **muh,—hi**; a fair —, **muh wanaksan.**

appease, *v.tr.*, **habowji, 'ada tir.**

appetite, *n.*, **bahi,—gi.**

applaud, *v.tr.*, **u bog, u hushu'i**; be applauded, **hushu'.**

applause, *n.*, **bog,—gi, hushu', —di.**

application, *n.*, **arji,—gi.**

apply, *v.tr.*, (lay one thing against another) **sar, ku deji, mari**; (address to) **dalbo, weidiso.**

appoint, *v.tr.*, (establish) **ku dar, ku haïbi, ugu sarraisi**; (fix) **ballan.**

appointed, *a.*; **ninki lagu haïbiyai**, the — man; the time —, **gorti la ballamai ba jogta.**

appointment, *n.*, **mushaháro,—adi.**

apprehend, *v.tr.*, (seize) **habo, ku deg**; (fear) **ka' abso, ka bah**; (conceive) **garo**; this I — not, **tasi i ma di'in.**

apprehension, *n.*, **habasho,—adi, bahdin,—ti, garasho,—adi.**

approach, *v.i.*, **dowow, so dowow, so durug**; *v.tr.*, **dowai, u ku dowai durki**; — me, **so dowai, so durug.**

approbation, *n.*, **bog,—gi.**

approve, *v.tr.*, **u bog, 'ajibi.**

Arab, *p.n.*, **Arab.**

Arabian, Arabic, *a.*; **nin arbed, af arbed**, Arabic language; **afka arabta**, the ...

arak-tree, *n.*, **ādaï,—gi.**

arbiter, arbitrator, *n.*, **taliya,—ihi.**

archangel, *n.*, **malaïko ra'isah**; the —, **malaïkada ra'iskaah.**
ardent, *a.*, **kulail, kulul.**
argil (potter's clay), *n.*, **doḥbo, —adi.**
argue, *v.tr.*, (press) **'adadi**; (debate any question) **iss ka ḥeji.**
arise, *v.i.*, **ka', sara ka', tos.**
arithmetic, *n.*, **hisab,—ti.**
arm, *n.*, (all the limb) **ga'an,—ti**; fore —, **đuđun,—ki, tagog, —ti** or **tagogo,—adi**; hind —, **ḥudud**; fore — joined to the upper one, **iss ku taladi hore**; the upper part of the — joined to the shoulder, **iss ku taladi dambe**; the thick part of the —, **muruḥ,—ki.**
armful, *n.*, **degsar,—ki.**
arm-pit,arm-hole, *n.*, **kilkilo,—adi.**
arm of the sea, *n.*, **ga'an baded.**
armlet (bracelet of silver), *n.*, **sindi,—gi.**
arm (weapon), *n.*, **hūb,—ki.**
arm, *v.tr.*, **hūbkisa u đamai.**
armed, *a.*, **hubleh**; — man, **hūbḥad,—ki.**
army, *n.*, **guluf,—ki, guto,—adi, 'oll,—ki.**
aroma, *n.*, **udgon,—ki.**
aromatic, *a.*, **udgon**; an — flower, **ubaḥ udgon.**
aromatize, *v.tr.*, **udgonai.**
around, *ad.*, **ḥer**; *prp.*, **harero, —rihi.**
arouse, *v.tr.*, **ke'i, kake'i, tosi.**
arrange, *v.tr.*, **hagaji, kala hagaji, wanaji, tali.**
arrangement, *n.*, **hagajis,—ki, talo,—adi.**
array, *v.tr.*, (attire) **ḥarrago.**
arrest, *n.*, (arrestation) **ḥabasho, —adi**; (judgment) **ḥukun,—ki.**
arrival, *n.*, **imad,—ki, so so'od, —ki.**
arrive, *v.i.*, **gađ, kalai**; — at that time, **gorta imo.**
arrogance, *n.*, **amar weinan,—ti.**
arrogant, *ad.*, **amarsan, amar wein.**
arrow, *n.*, (shaft) **fallađ,—di, gantal,—shi**; a poisonous —, **ḥāmis,—ki**; when the arrow is poisonous they call it **ḥāmis, kolka fallađdu doḥbantahai, waḥha la yiđahda ḥamis.**
arse, *n.*, **bađi,—gi.**
artful, *a.*, **hađig badan, hikmado badan.**
artifice, *n.*, **hađig,—gi, ḥigmad, —di,** or **hikmad, —di.**
as, *c.*, **sidi, sida** (*past*); I live — I did ..., **sidaidi horai an len nolahai,** or **sidan fali jirai an ...**; — you please, **sidad donto** or **rabtid,** or **sidi had ba ku 'ajibisa**; — I am an honest man, **sidan nin aminah u ahai**; mad — I was, **sidan u walla**; thou good old man, benevolent — wise, **odaiyohow dehsiga ihi e herribtalihi (tolmoni e faridka ihi)**; — sweet — honey, **u ma'an sida malabka**; he is — good — she, **wa wanaksanyahai sideda o kaleh**; I treated him — if he had been my brother, **sida wa-**

lalkai o kaleh u hayai; — the Lord gave to every man, **sida Ebbahai nin walba u siyai**; the history is — follows, **shekadu wa sida an wado** or **shegayo**; do — I bid you, **sidan ku iđahdo fal** or **yel**; he is — a father to me, **isagu wa i abbai**; it were — a play, **sida 'ayar o kaleh**; I will see you — I go by, **sidan ku marayan o ban ku arki**; rich — he is I do not fear him, **sidu u odmai ninka ba ka ma baḫo**; many — they are I do not fear, **in kasta ka ahaden ka biḫi mayo**; — well — I love you, do not think I shall do that, **sidan ku ja'lahai**, or **si kasta an ku ja'lahai, kolla ha modin inan waḫha fali dono**; — sure — it is good that you become a Christian, **sida waḫ-ha la hubo o u fayido u leḫ-yahai, inad Kristan noḫoto đamadai**; — much — you please, **had ba inta dontid**, or **had ba intad biḫin kartid**; — few —, **waḫ yar u dib**; Abdi is — good — Ali, **Abdi sida Ali u wanaksanyahai**; he runs — well — you, **sidadu o kalu u orda**; all such — were chosen, **inti la wada dortai ba serkalki radai**; I took such — I pleased, **waḫan ḫatai had ba kui i 'ajibiyai**; such — it is, **had ba sidai tahai**; — is the beginning, so is the end, **sidai kolka hore tahai bai kolka dambana tahai**, or **sida horanta ba đamanti na tahai**; — for me it is nothing, **anigu waḫba i la maaha**; — soon — I can I will come back, **waḫhan so noḫon had ba kolkan karo.**

ascend, *v.tr.*, **kor.**

ascension, *n.*, **korrin,—ti.**

ascertain, *v.tr.*, (assure) **rumai**; (fix) **đabai.**

ascetic, *a.*, **(nin) du'a ka ragah**; *n.*, **du'a ku rag,—gi.**

ashamed, *a.*, **ḫishod badan**; be —, **ḫisho**; you make me —, **adigu wa i ḫilaisa.**

ashore, *ad.*, **ḥebta**; go —, **deg, hebta u deg**; get —, *v.i.*, **'ari, so 'ari**; get —, *v.tr.*, **'arsi**; a ship —, **markab 'arsan** or **'ariyai.**

aside, *ad.*, **goni**; lay —, **goni u đig, đaḫ, đaḫo**; he took him —, **goni u kaḫaiyai.**

ask, *v.tr.*, **weidi, weidiso, suāl**; —, *v.r.*, **iss weidi**; — for, **ḫanan**; — from, **waraiso, warso.**

asleep, *a.*, **hurđa**; half — and half awake, **bađna wa hurdai, ba đna wa so jedai**; he is fast —, **hurda wein bu ku jira.**

aspect, *n.*, **muḫ,—hi**; at the — of his master, he is out of countenance, **kolka muḫha sahebki u arko, yu baḫda.**

aspersion, *n.*, **saïdis,—ki.**

aspirate, *v.tr.*, **neifso.**

aspire (to *or* after), *v.tr.*, **dama', ku taba'.**

aspire to *or* after, *v.tr.*, **dama'**, **ku taba'**.

ass, *n.*, (in general) **dameiro,—ihi**; he —, **dameir,—ki**; she —, **dameir,—ti**; young — (ass's foal), **dameir yar**; wild —, **dabeir dibaded,—ki**, or **gumburi,—gi**.

assail, *v.tr.*, **dagalan, dirir, werar**; — unexpectedly, **gād**.

assassin, *n.*, **layan,—ki**.

assault, *n.*, **dirir,—ti, werar,—ki**.

assemblage, *n.*, **iss ku daran,—ki**; — of tents, **rer,—ki**.

assemble, *v.tr.*, **iss ku dar, iss u gei, ururi**.

assembled, *a.*, **urursan**; be —, **urur, urursanada**.

assembly, *n.*, **urur,—ki, kulan,—ki, shir,—ki, guto,—adi**; — of men, **rahan,—ti**; — for prayer, **jama',—ha**; have an —, **shira, so shira**; go to the —, **shirka tag**.

assent, *n.*, **heshis,—ki, oggolan,—ti**.

assent, *v.i.*, **la heshi, ku heshi, oggolai, oggolaw**; —, *v.c.*, **heshishi, oggolaisi**.

assert, *v.tr.*, (affirm) **dabai**; he asserts his history with such a boldness that everyone believes it, **shekadisi sidu u dabainaya, dadki o dami** or **dan ba rumaistai**.

assertion, *n.*; this may suffice to vindicate my assertion, **wahan ku fila hadalkaiga o an rumainaya**, or **in hadalkaigu run nohda**, or **run idin ku muhda**.

asseverate, *v.tr.*, **so daro, dar so mari**; asseverate that you have not done that, **inanad wahha falin so daro**.

assimilate, *v.tr.*, (make like) **u ekaisi**; (compare) **iss u eg**.

assist, *v.tr.*, **la 'awi, 'awin, la habo, la had, u gargar**; (in the fight) **hili**.

assistance, *n.*, **'awin,—ti, 'awimad,—di, hil,—ki**.

assistant, *n.*, **'awis,—ki, hiliya,—hi**.

associate, *n.*, **jāl,—ki, mushrik,—gi**.

associate with, *v.tr.*, **la dawaiso**, (**dawaista**), **la wah'atan**, (**wah'atama**), **la wah'ad hado**.

association, *n.*, **dawo,—adi, wah'ad,—di**.

assume, *v.tr.*, **had** (*plur.* **hada**), **hado** (*plur.* **hata**); (arrogate), he assumes too much to himself, **isagu wa iss ku tara**.

assurance, *n.*, (certitude) **dab,—ti**; (firmness) **adkan,—ti**.

assure, *v.tr.*, (assert) **dabai, rumai**; (be sure) *v.i.*, **hub**.

astern, *ad.*, **markabka harkisa dambe**.

asthma, *n.*, **haho,—adi**.

astonish, *v.tr.*, **yabi**; be —, **yabsanaw, la yabsanaw**.

astonishing, astonished, *a.*, **yaban, yabsan, la yabsan, yab haba**.

astonishment, *n.*, **la yab,—ki**.

astound, *v.tr.*, **kaga nihi**; be —, **nah**.

astray, *ad.*, **halloh**; go —, **ambo**,

habab; lead —, ambi, hababi;
they were led — from the
right worship of God, 'ābud-
ninti Ilaḥhai e tosnaid ba
iyagá laga ambiyai.

astrologer, *n.*, geda goiyai,—hi
(*m.* and *f.*), hariyan,—ki (*m.*),
—ti (*f.*).

astrology, *n.*, geda goiyo,—adi.

astronomer, *n.*, hedigiyai,—hi.

asunder, *ad.*, kala; put it —,
kas iss ka dig.

at, *prp.*, ku; — sea, baddu ku
so jira or baddu so so'oda;
— home, aḥalki bu joga, —
your house, aḥalkagi bu joga;
— hand, dowyahai; — leisure,
gortanan haul kaleh lahain;
— ease, baraḥ; — a stand,
wan weirweirsanahai; — a
loss, wan rāgsanahai; we are
— odds, 'oll bannu nahai, or
her bannu lehnahai, or wannu
iss honsana, or honsimad ba
na deh yal; — this moment,
iminkadan, gortan, haddatan,
gortatan o kaleh; — this day,
malintan, darartan o kaleh,
'ana malkan; — that time,
gortasa, kolkasa; — one
time or other, mar ama mar
kaleh; — that time or the
other, gorta ama gortedahan;
— no time, kolla, kolna, had-
na, gorna; — last, kolki dambe se; — first, kolki horai;
— the very first, gorti ugu
horaisai; — the first coming
of the governor, serkalka
imadkisi horai; — once, mar

keliah; all things are ordered
— the will of God, waḥ waliba haulka Ebbahai bai ku
so'odan or ba hagajiya.

atheist, *n.*, gal,—ki.

atmosphere, *n.*, ne'aw,—di, dabail,—shi.

atone, *v.tr.*, (reconcile); Jesus
atoned us to God, 'Issa Ebbehen ino geiyai or heshisiyai.

atone for, *v.i.*; if you wish to be
in peace atone for your sins,
hadad donaisid inad nabad
gashid dembigagi hanun iss
kaga bii or ka tobad ken.

atonement, *n.*, tobad,—di.

attack, *n.*, dagal,—ki, dagalan,
—ki, dirir,—ti, werar,—ki,
mag,—gi, jalalaḥa,—hi; —
of another tribe, dulan,—ki;
unexpected —, gādnin,—ti.

attack, *v.tr.*, dagalan, dirir,
werar, mag, jalalaḥ, dūl, gād,
ku guluf (gulfa, plur.).

attain, *v.tr.*, hel; *v.i.*, (arrive at)
is he wise who hopes to — the
end without the means? ma
miyirsan yahai kan iss lihi
inu aḥirtanka darajalaan ku
heli dona?

attend, *v.tr.*, (serve) 'awi, la jir, la
jog; (wait for, accompany)
weheli, sug, ra'; (yield, give
attention) *v.i.*, yel; yield to
his saying, hadalkisa yel; — a
woman during her confinement,
v.tr., ka umuli; *v.i.*, iss ka
umuli.

attendance, *n.*, sugnin,—ti; give
attendance to your master,

sāhebka sugnin u ḥabo or **ninka ku taliya yel.**
attendant, *n.*, **ḥadan,—ki, mididin,—ki, nin la joga, sebiyan, —ki.**
attention, *n.*, **feyigan,** or **foyigan,** or **fojigan,—ti.**
attentive, *a.*, **feyig, foyig** or **fojig**; be —, **foyigow**; be an — man, **nin fojiganahaw.**
attest, *v.tr.*, (certify) **dabai, fur, marḥati ku fur**; — to, **u fur**; — against, **ku fur.**
attestation, *n.*, **marḥati,—gi.**
attract, *v.tr.*, **ku kaḥai, ku jido**; (allure) **sasab, ḥalḥal, dufso**; bad actions or deeds attract youth to bad, **falnin ḥun,** or **ḥumi dalinyaro waḥ ḥun bai ku jidata,** or **jar bu ku tura**; good deeds attract youth to good, **falnin wanaksani dalinyaro waḥ wanaksan bu ku jita.**
attractive, *a.*, **waḥ dufsanaisa.**
attribute, *n.*, (quality adherent) as **mamus,** reputation, respect.
attribute, *v.i.*, (suppose) **u malai, ku sheg.**
auction, *n.*, (open sale) **ḥarash, —ki.**
augment *and* augmentation, *n.*, **korod,—ki, kordis,—ki.**
augment, *v.tr.*, **badni, badnai, kordi, kordiso.**
aunt, *n.*, (paternal) **eddo,—adi**; maternal —, **habaryar,—ti.**
aurora, *n.*, **aroriyo,—adi, aroriyo hore.**
authority, *n.*, **ḥukum,—ki.**
authorize, *v.tr.*, **idin**; be authorized, **ha lagu idmo.**
of no avail, *n.*, **wa waḥ an waḥba tarain.**
avoid, *v.tr.*, (keep away from) **iss ka daur**; he avoids me, **wa iss ka ka i dauraya.**
avow, *v.tr.*, (confess) **ḥado, ḥiro.**
avowal, *n.*, **ḥir,—ti.**
await, *v.tr.*, **daur, u jed.**
awake, *v.i.*, **ka‘, sara ka‘, tos**; remain —, **so jed, ‘awai.**
awake, awaken, *v.tr.*, **ke‘i, tosi, ka ke‘i.**
awaking, *n.*, **tosnin,—ti.**
be aware of, *v.i.*, **foyigow** or **fojigow, ogow.**
away (with this), *prp.*, **la tag kan,—kas**; they went —, **wa maḥan yihin.**
awkward, *a.*, **bassar ḥun.**
awry, *a.*, **ḥallohan, janjedah**; *ad.*, **ḥalloh, janjed**; be —, **janjed**; put —, **janjedi.**
axe, *n.*, (crooked one) **gudumo** or **gudimo,—adi.**
azure, *n.*, **madow ‘adan.**

B.

babble, babbling, *n.*, **daudar,—ki.**
babble, *v.i.*, **daudar.**
babbler, *n.*, **nin daudarah,—ki**; **ninki daudarkaaha,** the babbler.

babe, baby, *n.*, **ilmo,—hi, jaḥa, ihi, murjo', hi.**

bachelor, *n.*, (unmarried man) **dōb,—ki.**

back, *n.*, **ḍabar,—ki** (gen. name), **jirjir,—ki** (this word is especially used for the back of man and generally for designating the hinder part of anything); all the —, **jirjir'ad,—ki**; fall on your —, **jirjira'dká u da'**; carry a person on your —, **ḍabarká ku siḍ**; — of animals, **dul,—shi**; — behind the camel's hump, **maraḥsar,—ki.**

back, *ad.*, **ḍabarka, dabada, dib**; be —, **noḥo**; at one o'clock I will be back in the office, **kowdan hafiska ku noḥon**; come —, **so noḥo**; give — to, **u'eli**; go —, **dib u noḥo**; keep —, **dib u joji** or **hai**; pull —, **dabada**, or **ḍabarka**, or **dib u jid**; send —, **dib u dir**; take — to you, **'esho.**

backbite, *v.tr.*, **ḥano.**

backbiting, *n.*, **ḥan,—ti, ḥamasho,—adi.**

backbiter, *n.*, **nin ḥan badan.**

backbone, *n.*, **laf ḍabar,—ti, —ka.**

backside, *n.*, **dabo,—adi.**

backslide, *v.tr.*, (in religion) **dinta jahad, kāfar, tarak.**

backslider, *n.*, (an apostate) **kafir, —ki, tarik,—gi.**

backward, —s, *ad.*, **dib**; go —, **dib u so'o**; go — and forwards, **hore iyo diba u so'o.**

bad, *a.*, **ḥun, bas, darran**; be —, **ḥumaw**; do — to, **u ḥumai**; make (him, it) —, **ḥumai.**

bad state, bad thing, *n.*, **belo,—adi.**

badge, *n.*, **alif,—ki, astan,—ki.**

badger, *n.*, (a kind of) **bauna,—hi**; (honey-eater) **ḥor,—ki**; (kind of small pig living under ground) **ḥarendi,—di.**

bag, *n.*, **joniad,—di**; — made of skins, **hashin,—ti, jirab,—ki, oḥli,—gi**; — of dates, **min,—ki, gosarad,—di**; half a bag of dates, **min gohi**; (purse) **kish,—ki**; long — used to go into the country, **madad, —ki**; (of cows, udder) **'ando, —adi.**

baggage, *n.*, **alabo,—di, ḥalab,—ki.**

bail, *n.*, (surety) **'arbun,—ti, damin,—ti, 'udal,—shi.**

bail, *v.tr.*, (be surety for some one) **damino, rahan.**

bait, *v.tr.*, (a lure to entice fish ...) **la'af,—ti.**

bake, *v.tr.*, **bislai, mufai.**

baker, *n.*, **'ajinleh,—ihi, ḥabbas, —ki.**

bakery, *n.*, **muḥbasad,—di.**

balance, *n.*, (scales) **misan,—ki.**

balance, *v.tr.*, (weigh) **mis.**

bald, *a.*, (without hair) **bidarleh, nin bidarleh**; — head, **daka'ad**; **dakadi 'adaid,** the bald head.

baldness, *n.*, **bidar,—ti.**

bale, *n.*, (of goods) **ḥidmo alaboah,—madi.**

ball, *n.*, (any round body) **kubad, —di, gu'unso,—di.**
ballast, *n.*, **farmi,—gi.**
ballast, *v.tr.*, **faram.**
bamboo, *n.*, **jara',—i'hi.**
band, *n.*, (a tie) **bohor,—ki**; belly— for camels or other animals, **hain** or **'ain,—ti**; for horses, **wegered,—ki.**
bandit, *n.*, (highwayman) **dalin, —ki, dalin bilad,—ki, saruh, —hi.**
bandy, *n.*, **tukubai,—ihi.**
bandy, *a.*, **halloh.**
bane, *n.*, (poison) **dunkal,—shi, wabayo,—adi.**
bane, *v.tr.*, **dunkal si, wabayai.**
baneful, *a.*, **wabayaisan.**
bang, *v.tr.*, (thump, beat) **tanton, tumujai.**
bang, *n.*, **tantomo,—adi.**
banish, *v.tr.*, **safiri, masafiri.**
banishment, *n.*, **safiris,—ki, masafiris,—ki.**
bank, *n.*, (hillock) **gumbur,—ti, bur,—ti**; (shore) **heb,—ti.**
banquet, *n.*, **diafad,—di.**
barber, *n.*, **rais,—ki.**
bare, *a.*, **hawan.**
barefoot, *a.*, **kabala**; the barefooted man, **ninki kabahalaa.**
bareness, *n.*, **hawanan,—ti.**
bare, *v.tr.*, **hawi.**
bargain, *n.*, **baya'ad,—di**; a — is a —, **baya'adba baya'adah.**
bark, *n.*, (rind of a tree) **dir,—ki**; 2nd — used for making ropes, **dub,—ki, maidah,—di**; — producing red dye, **asal,—ki.**

bark, *v.tr.*, (take off the bark) **dil, dir.**
bark, *v.i.*, (to bay) **'ei** or **'i.**
barking, *n.*, **'i,—di.**
barm, *n.*, (yeast) **hamir,—ki.**
barrack, *n.*, **himad,—di.**
barrel, *n.*, (cask) **barmil,—ki.**
barren, *a.*, **ma dalais,—ki** (*m.*), **—ti** (*f.*); for all females, **galof,—ti.**
barrow, *n.*, (hand-barrow) **rarab, —ti.**
barter, *v.tr.*, **dafi, dafso, dori, dorso.**
barter, bartering, *n.*, **dafsasho,—di, dafsis,—ki.**
base, *a.*, **fudud.**
baseness, *n.*, **fudaid,—ki.**
bashful, *a.*, (shy) **fulaah, fulai, —ihi** (also *n.*).
bashfulness, *n.*, **fulanimo,—adi.**
basin, *n.*, **hedo,—adi**; large oval —, **habal,—ki.**
bask, *v.tr.*, (warm) **diri, kululai**; — in the sun, **duksi.**
bask, *v.i.*, **iss diri**; — yourself in the sun, **duksiso.**
basket, *n.*, **kolai,—gi, sambil,—ki**; — used for carrying rubbish, **alol,—ki.**
bastard, *n.*, **gara',—ri'hi, wa'al** or **we'el,—ki.**
baste, *v.tr.*, (to beat) **ul la da'**; (to sew slightly) **hodob, iss ku hodob.**
bat, *n.*, (flitter mouse) **fidmer,—ti.**
bate, *v.tr.*, (lessen) **din, iga din.**

bateful, *a.*, **hori dableh.**
bath, *n.*, **muhurasho,—adi.**
bathe, *v.i.*, **muhuri, badda biyaha ku so habojiso.**
batten, *v.tr.*, (fatten) **shishlai, nāhi**; (to grow fat) *v.i.*, **shishlow, nah.**
battle, *n.*, **dagal,—ki, dirir,—ti, werar,—ki, harbi,—gi.**
bawd, *n.*, (a procurer) **fatal,—ki** (*m.*), **fatalad,—di** (*f.*), **hawad,—ki** (*m.*), **hawadad,—di** (*f.*).
bawl, *v.i.*, (cry loudly) **dowdowlai.**
bawler, *n.*, **dowdowleh,—hi.**
bay, *n.*, **jori.**
bazaar, *n.*, **suh,—hi.**
be, *v.i.*, **ah** (*affix*), **ahaw** (*see* Gram.); what is it to me? **aniga mahai i la tahai?** he is to be killed, **in la dila bu lehyahai**; you are to speak, **hadalka ada leh** or **inad hadasha bad lehdahai**; it is day, **wa darar, malin**; it was night, **habein bai ahaid**; it is over, **damatai**; how is it with you? **simai, side ku la tahai?** it is so with me, **sidasai i la tahai** or **aniga wa i la sida**; what is the matter? **wa side?** so it is, **wa sida**; let it be so, **sida u da**; so be it, **sida ha ahato**; I am to go thither, **halkasan inan tago lehahai**; it is good being here, **wa wanag in halkan la jogo**; it was better being there, **ti ba tan ka wanaksanaid**, or **ti ba tan dantai**, or **halko ba si wanaksanaid**; there is, there are, there was, there will be, **wah jira** (*sing.* and *plur.*), **wah jirai, wah jiri dona**; there are many men, **niman badan ba jira** or **niman badni wa jiran**; here he is, **halku joga**; there is one, **wa mid**; this is the reason why I did it, **eddi an wahha ku samaiyai wa tá.**
bead, *n.*, **mid,—di.**
beam, *n.*, (wood) **dogob,—ki.**
beams, *n.*, (of the sun) **falladaha horahda,—ihi horahda.**
bear, *v.tr.*, (carry) **had, sid**; (bring forth) **dal, bihi, yelo.**
beard, *n.*, **gad,—ki**; bearded, **gadleh**; beardless, **gad la** or **gad ma lahita.**
bearer, *n.*, (porter) **hamal,—ki, nin wah hada** or **sida.**
beast, *n.*, **dugag,—gi**; wild —, **bahal,—ki**; wild — good for eating, **ugad,—di**; tame —, **marabi,—di**; tame — become wild, **bubal,—shi**; tame — flying away, **aïmad,—ki.**
beat, *v.tr.*, **dil, la, ku dufo, ku dug**; — hard, **sug**; — repeatedly, **la da', gara', ul la da'.**
beaten, *a.*, **la dilai, sugan.**
beautiful, *a.*, **bahsan, hurohsan, huroh badan, huroh wanaksan.**
beautify, *v.tr.*, **hurhi**; *v.r.*, **hurhiso.**
beauty, *n.*, **huroh,—di.**

because, *c.*, **haddeh.**

become, *v.i.*, (be made) **noḥo**; what will — of me? **tolow! maḥa i dambain?**

bed, *n.*, **sarir,—ti, gogol,—shi**; go to —, **hurda dono** or **tag**; he is a—, **wa jifa, wa hurda**; he lies sick a—, **bukan** or **ḥanun bu la jifa**; put him out of his —, **sarirtisa ka tosi**; he is on his death—, **wa ugu dambaistisi**; —side, **sarirti gesteda**; he that goes to — thirsty rises healthy, **ninki harad ku seḥada, āfimad bu ku so tosa**; it is — time, **hurda jogta**; —stead, **ḥoriyo sarired.**

bed (of a river), *n.*, **dei'** or **diḥ, —di, doh,—hi**; dry — of a river, **gof,—ki.**

bedding, *n.*, **gogol,—shi**; prepare the —, **gogoshi gogol.**

bedew, *v.tr.*, (moisten gently) **yar ḥo, yar ḥoi.**

bee, *n.*, **shini,—di.**

beef, *n.*, **hilib lo'ad, hilibki lo'da.**

beetle (coleopterous insect), *n.*; the stinking black one, **ḥar walwal,—ki.**

befall (to happen to), *v.i.*; it befell me, **waḥ ba igu da'ai**; the worst that can — me is to die, but I do not fear, **waḥha ugu ḥun e igu da'a** (or **di'i dona**) **wa mot, ka se biḥi mayo.**

before, *prp.*, **hore, horai, horta**; — noon, **duḥurka hortisa**; I will die — I behave so, **waḥ**

ban ḍiman intanan aslubta yelan; — and behind you, **hortada iyo dabadada ba**; — the face of the whole town he was hanged, **dadki magalada jogai hortodi ba lugu deldelai**; I love you — myself, **anigu adan ka ja'lahai**; *ad.*, **awal** or **awel**; long —, **beri horai.**

beg, *v.tr.*, **bari**; — earnestly, **dalab, dalbo**; — for alms, **dawirso**; they — for peace, **iyagu heshis (nabad) bai raban**, or **iyagu bari yai raban.**

beget, *v.tr.*, **dal, yelo.**

beggar, *n.*, **dagag,—gi, nin dagagah, dawaro,—di, miskin,—ki** (*m.*), **miskinad,—di** (*f.*)

begging, *n.*, **bariyo,—di, dawarsi, — gi.**

begin, *v.tr.*, **kaga ḥabo**; — quick, **daḥso ugaga ḥabo, u ḥalḥal.**

beginning, *n.*, **horan,—ti**; the — of the world, **dunida horantedi.**

begone! *int.*, (go away!) **tag! iss ka tag! iss ka baḥ! iga** or **naga tag!**

beguile, *v.tr.*, (delude) **dufso, ḥalḥal.**

behalf, *n.*, **awo,—adi, darad,—di**; on my —, **awadai, daraddai.**

behave (well), *v.i.*, **aslubnaw**; he behaves ill, **wa aslub ḥun yahai.**

behaviour, *n.*, **abur,—ki, aslub, —ti.**

behead, *v.tr.*, **gowra'**.

beheading, *n.*, **gowra',—i'hi**.

behind, *ad.* and *prp.*, **dib**; leave —, **dambaisi**; go —, **ka dambai**; remain —, **dambai, dib u hað**; ride —, **aga dambai ka ful**; she came —, **dibai u so ka'dai**; he came —, **dibu u so ka'ai**; before and —, **hor iyo dabo**; is there yet anything — ? **weli dabada waḥ ma jiran**.

behold, *v.tr.*, (look) **arag, dai, daur, eg, jedali**.

being, *n.*, (a creature) **ūn,—ki**.

belay, *v.tr.*, (place in ambush) **ku hatati, ðumi**.

belch, *n.*, **da'o,—di**.

belch, *v.i.*, **da'**.

belief, *n.*, **amin,—ti, rumaisad, —ki**.

believe, *v.tr*, **āmin, rumaiso**.

believer, *n.*, **nin amina**, or **amina yal**.

bell, *n.*, **gando,—adi**; little —, **dawan,—ki**.

bellow, *v.i.*, **'ei** or **i'**.

bellowing, *n.*, **bana'ei,—gi**.

bellows, *n.*, **buffimo,—adi**.

belly, *n.*, **'alol, shi, ur,—ki**; upper part of the —, leg,—**gi**; under part of the —, **gumar, —ki**; —ache, **alol hanun**, or **ur hanun,—ki**; my — aches, **alosha i hanunaisa**; open the —, **doḥ**; opening of the —, **dohnin,—ti**.

belong, *v.i.*; the word **leh** ordinarily expresses the meaning of "belong": I — to God, **Ilaḥ-** hai ba i leh; it belongs to me, to him, **ana leh, isaga leh**.

beloved, *a.*; God has sent to us his beloved son. **Ebbehen wuḥu ino so dirai inankisi u ja'ala**.

below, *ad.* and *prp.*, **dāf, dāfta, hos, hosta**; is he —? **dāfta** or **hosta ma jira?**

belt, *n.*, (man's) **sun,—ki**; (woman's) **boḥor,—ki**.

bend, *v.tr.*, (make crooked) **ḥallohi**; — a bow, **ḥanso so god**; — the body, **jidka forori**; — the knee, **rugga so lab**, or **jilibka ðig**; — the stick against the wall, **usha derbiga ku tiri**, — the brow, **huruf**; — yourself, bow, *v.i.*, **fororso, tirso**; — on, **ku tirso**; — to drink water, **raḥ**.

bending, *n.*, **forar** or **foror,—ki**; (being off the perpendicular) **ḥalloh,—hi**; — of the brow, **huruf,—ki**.

beneath, *ad.*, **dāf, hosta**; put —, **hosaisi**.

benediction, *n.*, **barakad,—di, du'o,—adi**; he has been blessed, **du'adi ku da'dai**.

benefactor, *n.*; it is my —, **wa nin i deḥsiah**; it is our —, **wa nin no ron**, or **ninkasi wa no tolmon yahai**, or **wa nin waḥ no tara**.

beneficence, *n.*, **deḥ,—di**.

beneficent, benevolent, *a.*, **deḥ badan, ga'an badan**.

benefit, *n*, (profit) **fayido,—adi, helin,—ki**.

bent, *a.*, **ḫalloḫan, forarsan, forara.**

benumbed (person), *n.*, **damad, —ki.**

benumbed, *a.*, **damadsan.**

bequeath, *v.tr.*, (leave by will) **dardaran.**

bequeathment, bequest, *n.*, **dardaran,—ki.**

beseech, *v.tr.*, (implore) **bari, dalbo**; I — you, sir, pardon me, **sab, bari yan ka dalbadai e i 'affi,** or **waḫan ka bariyai e i 'affi**; I — your attention, **fojigantadan weidisanaya,** or **ka bariyaya.**

beside, besides, *prp.*, **ges, gesta, ag,—ta, dow**; sit — him, **ag** or **ges fadi** or **fadiso.**

besmear, *v.tr.*, **uskagai, wasaḫai.**

bespatter, *v.tr.*, **dulduli.**

bespattering, *n.*, **duldul,—ki.**

besprinkle, *v.tr.*, **rushai, ku saïd.**

best, *a.*; this is the best, **waḥhasa ka wada wanaksan** or **ugu wanaksan**; it is the — for you, **adiga sidasa ku wada danta,** or **adiga sidasa lagu ḫatai**; I will do the — I can, **inta tägtai tahai ban yeli** or **ban samain** or **ban tari.**

bestow, *v.tr.*, **u dib, si.**

bestride, *v.tr.*, **dada'.**

bet, *n.*, **sharad,—ki.**

bet, *v.tr.*, **la sharatan.**

betray, *v.tr.*, **ḫawaisi, dag.**

betrothe, *v.tr.*, (affiance) **don, la ballan.**

betrothed, *a.*, **donan.**

betrothing, *n.*, **donin,—ki, donanan,—ti.**

better, *a.*, **dāma** (*m.*), **dānta** (*f.*), **ka ron, ka wanaksan**; he, she is — than you, **isagu wa ku dāma, iyadu wa ku dānta**; make —, **wanaji**; grow —, **si wanaksan u baḥ** or **noḥo**; he grows — in health, **wa afimadaya.**

between, *prp.*, **deḥ, deḥda**; go —, **deḥ gal**; come —, **so deḥ gal, so daḥai.**

bevy, *n.*, (flock of birds) **shir, —ki, shirkoda.**

beware, *v.i.*, (be cautious) **feyigaw** or **fojigow.**

bewilder, *v.tr.*, (to lose in pathless places) **hababi, ambi**; *v.i.*, **habab, ambo.**

beyond, *prp.*, **shishai,—di.**

Bible, *n.*, **torad iyo injil, toradka iyo injilka.**

bid, *v.*; do as you are bid, **fal sida lugu leḥyahai** or **dega nuglow** (obey); when we are bidden to great feasts, we must take our fine clothes, **marka 'id wein nailo ku yedo, dar wanaksan an so huwano** or **an so ḫarragono**; I bade him go home, **aḫalki ḫabo ban ku idi**; — him come in, **aḫalka hor u so mar ku deh** or **so gal ku deh**; I am bidding you farewell, **nabad geliyo ayan ku odonaya.**

bier, *n.*, (wooden frame to carry a dead body) **rarab,—ti.**

big, *a.*, **wein**; make —, **weinai.**

bile, *n.*, **da'ar,—ti.**
bilious, *a.*, **da'araisan.**
bill, *n.* (any written paper) **warhad,—di**; — of goods, **hisab,—ti**; here is the —, **wa ta hisabti**; — of passage, **tiked,—ki.**
billet, *n.*, (log of wood) **hulad** or **hulod,—ki.**
bind, *v.tr.*, (tie) **hid**; he was bound hand and foot, **ga'an iyo lug ba wa ka hidna**; — yourself by promise, **ballan iss ku hid** or **ku tasho.**
bird, *n.*, **shimbir,—ti**; birds in general, **hād,—di**; (fowls) **doro,—adi**; kinds: **dorei,—di, fin,—ti, gallow,—gi** ... (*see* Som.-Eng. Voc.).
birth, *n.*, **dalnin,—ti**; give —, **dal, umul**; come to —, **dalo.**
biscuit, *n.*, **biskut,—ki.**
bison antelope, n., **bi''id,—ki.**
bit, *n.*, (small piece) **in yar**; — of a bridle, **hakamai,—mihi, hilhad** (*see* curb).
bitch, *n.*, **eiyad,—di.**
bite, biting, *n.*, **haninyo,—adi.**
bite, *v.tr.*, **hanin**; *v.r.*, **iss hanin.**
bitter, *a.*, **hadad, danan.**
bitterness, *n.*, **hadad,—ki, danan,—ki.**
black, *n.*, **madow,—gi**; *a.*, **madow, madowba.**
blacken, *v.tr.*, **madowbai.**
blacksmith, *n.*, **tumal,—ki.**
bladder, *n.*, **kadsha hais,—ti.**
blade-bone *or* shoulder-bone, *n.*, **laf garab,—ti, —ki.**
blame, *n.*, **masabidnimo,—adi.**
blame, *v.tr.*, **masabid, hanib.**
blameable, *a.*; he is —, **nin la masabido waiyai**; thou art —, ... **wa tahai.**
blamer, *n.*, **masabid,—ki.**
blanket, *n.*, **busta,—hi, kumbul,—ki.**
blaspheme, *v.tr.* and *v.i.*, **Ilah 'aï, Ilah inkar.**
blasphemer, *n.*, **nin Ilah 'aïa.**
blaze, *n.* (flame) **belbel,—ki, hallow,—gi, olol,—ki.**
blaze, *v.i.*, **olol.**
bleed, *v.i.*, (lose blood) **dig bah**; my wound is bleeding, **hontaida dig ka bahaya** or **ka imanaya.**
bleed, *v.tr.*, (let blood) **dig ka si da.**
bleeding, *n.*, **dig bah** or **bihi**; — of the nose, **goror,—ki.**
blemish, *n.*, **'eib,—ti.**
blemish, *v.tr.*, (stain) **'eibai.**
bless, *v.tr.*, **barakadai, du'ai, hadei, sahal.**
blessed, *a.*, **barakadaisan, du'a haba.**
blessing, *n.*, **barakad,—di, du'o,—adi, hair,—ki.**
blessedness, bliss, *n.*, **raho,—adi, rahad,—di.**
blind (roller), *n.*, **alol,—ki.**
blind, *a.*, **indala.**
blindness, *n.*, **indalaan,—ti.**
blister, *n.*, **ga'anti biyo i galai, 'agti wa i biyotai.**
block, *n.* (stem of a tree) **dogob,—ki.**
blockhead, *n.*, **dohon,—ki, na's,—ki.**

blood, *n.*, **dig,—gi.**
bloody, *a.*, **digleh**; a — man, **nin layanah.**
bloom, blossom, *n.*, **ubaḥ,—biḥi, man,—ki.**
blot, *n.*, (obliteration) **babiis,—ki.**
blot out, *v.tr.*, **babii, bii, ka bii, tir, ka tir.**
blow, *n.*, (stroke) **nabar,—ki**; — with the flat of a sword, **ballad,—ki**; — with the fist, **tantomo,—adi, tumujo,—adi**; — with the hand, **darbaḥ,—hi.**
blow, *v.i.*, (to move with a current of air) **dabaishi wa da'aisa,** or **dabail ba ina haisa**; — with the mouth, *v.tr.*, **afuf**; — with bellows, **bufi**; — your nose, **iss ka simi** or **sinso,** or **sinka iss ka tir**; (winnow) **huf**; — out the lamp, **siradka baẖti** or **seḥi.**
blue (colour), *n.*, **madow 'adan,—ki.**
blunder, *n.*, **ẖatalad,—di.**
blunder, *v.tr.*, **ẖatal**; *v.i.*, **ẖatalan, iss ẖatal.**
blunt, *a.*, **af darran.**
boar, *n.*, **dofar,—ki, dofar lab, dofar ki lab.**
board, *n.*, (plank) **loḥ,—hi.**
boast, *v.i.*, **bu, fan.**
boast, boasting, *n.*, **fan,—ka.**
boat, *n.*, (a small one) **seḥimad** or **siḥimad,—di**; (a large one) **doni,—di, baẖlad,—di.**
boat-hook, boat-staff, *n.*, **bagad,—ki.**
boatman, *n.*, **baḥri,—gi.**
body, *n.*, **jid,—ki**; a dead —, **miyid,—ki.**
bog, *n.*, **doḥbo,—adi.**
boil, *n.*, (ambury) **dullah,—liḥhi.**
boil, *v.tr.*, **kari**; (to be agitated by heat) *v.i.*, it boils, **kar, distigi kar**; the water boils, **biyihi wa karayan.**
boiled, *a.*, **karsan**; give me the — water, **biyaha karsan i si**; — meat, **hilib karsan.**
boiler, *n.*, (a kettle) **digsi,—gi, disti,—gi, deri,—gi, adar,—ki.**
boiling, *n.*, **kar,—ki**; *a.*, give me boiling water, **biya karaya i si.**
bold, *a.*, **gesiah, ẖodah, lab**; *n.*, **gesi,—gi, rifai,—fihi, rifakal** (*plur.*).
boldness, *n.*, **gesinimo,—adi.**
bone, *n.*, **laf,—ti.**
book, *n.*, **kitab,—ki**; the written or sacred —, **'ilmi,—gi.**
boot, *n.*, **kab,—ti.**
booty, *n.*, (plunder) **bob,—ki, boli,—gi.**
border, *n.*, (a selvage added to a skin dress) **darur,—ki**; — of cloth, **daraf,—ti, godi,—gi.**
bore, *n.*, (hole made by boring) **dalol,—ki.**
bore, *v.tr.*, **daloli, ku maroji.**
born, *a.*, **dashai**; a new— boy, **wil dowan dashai**; be —, **dalo.**
borrow, borrowing, *n.*, **amaḥ,—di.**
borrow, *v.tr.*, **amaḥo, so yelo.**
borrower, *n.*, **dein ẖad,—ki.**
bosom, *n.*, **lab,—ti, nas,—ki.**
botch, *n.*, (ulcer) **bōg,—ti**; (a

piece of cloth stitched to old clothes) **karin,—ti.**

botch, *v.tr.*, (mend clumsily) **kar.**

both, *prn.*, **labada ba**; on — sides, **labada gesod ba.**

bother, *v.tr.*, **dali.**

bottle, *n.*, **ḫarurad,—di.**

bottle, *v.tr.*; — the wine, **ḫaruradaha ḫamri ka buḫbuḫi.**

bottom, *n.*, **daf,—ti, gun,—ti**; — of a vessel, **sal,—ki.**

bottomless, *a.*, **gun ma leh.**

bough, *n.*, (large shoot of a tree) **lan,—ti.**

bought, *a.*, **ibsan**; be —, **ibsanaw**; not —, **ma ibsana.**

bounce, *v.i.*, (leap) **bod.**

bouncing, *n.*, **bodo,—adi, botin, —ti.**

bound, boundary, *n.*, **dal,—ki.**

bound, *a.*, **ḫidan, nin ḫidan.**

bounteous, *a.*, **deḫsiah, nin deḫsiah.**

bounty, *n.*, **deḫ,—di.**

bow, *n.*, (act of reverence) **forar** or **foror,—ki, rako',—di, sujud, —di.**

bow, *n.*, (weapon) **ḫanso,—adi.**

bow, *v.tr.*, (bend) **ḫallohi**; — your knees, **jilba dig**; — your head, **madahhaga forori**; — your body, **jidkaga ḫallohi** or **forori.**

bow, bow down, *v.i.*, **iss forori, fororso.**

bowel, *v.tr.*, **uslahada ka so biḫi** or **difo** or **jid** or **gur.**

bowels, *n.*, **uslaho,—adi, uslahais, —ti.**

bowl, *n.*, (vessel for drinking) **fujan** or **fijan,—ki.**

box, *n.*, (of bark *or* a small one of wood ...) **abḫad,—di**; (wooden) **saharad,—di, sanduḫ,—hi.**

box, *n.*, (blow given with the hand) **tantomo,—adi, tumujo, —adi, darbaḫo,—adi.**

box, *v.tr.*, **tumujai, darbaḫ, faragorgor.**

boy, *n.*, **wil,—ki, inan,—ki, kurai,—gi, mudakar,—ki**; little —, **ilmo,—ihi, ku yar, ki yara**; boys, small boys, **inamo,—adi, 'arur,—ti, maḫal,—shi, maḫaldad,—ki.**

bracelet, *n.*, **dugagad,—di**; wooden —, **haïmboro,—adi**; — of silver, **sindi,—gi, waḫfi,—gi.**

brag, *n.*, (boast) **ḫawayad,—di, ḫalalif,—ti.**

brag, *v.i.*, **ḫawaisi**; *v.tr.*, **ḫalalif ku shub**; *v.c.*, **ḫalalif ka shub.**

braid (of hair), *n.*, **tidei',—di'hi**; (a texture) **tida'sho,—adi.**

braid, *v.tr.*, (weave together) **tidi'**; *v.r.*, **tido'o.**

braided, *a.*, **tida'an**; the — hair, **timaha tida'an, timahi tida'na.**

brain, *n.*, **maskaḫ,—di.**

brambles, *n.*, (in a valley beside a dry river) **ḫid.**

branch, *n.*, **lan,—ti**; branches put in a tent during the time of rain, **daragad,—di.**

brand, *n.*, **ḫori dableh, ḫoriga dabkaleh**; the —, **duḫul dableh, duḫul dambasleh.**

brand, *v.tr.*, (mark with a branding-iron) **gub.**

brandy, *n.*, **brandi,—gi.**

brass, *n.*, **naḥas,—ti, sufur,—ki.**

brave, *a.*, **(nin) gesiah, gesi,—gi, ḫodah, lab, (nin) ragah.**

bray (as asses), *v.i.*, **'i, madar**; the ass brays, **dameirku wa madara.**

bread, *n.*, **kibis** or **kimis**; hot —, **kibis kulul**; new —, **kibis diran**; stale —, **kibis ḫabow.**

breadth, *n.*, **ballad,—di.**

break, *v.tr.*, **burburi, bururi, jebi, jejebi**; — the stick, the glass, **usha, galaska jebi**; — the bottles, **ḫaruradaha jejebi**; — your neck, **ḫorta iss jebi**; — silence, **wa hadli kartan**; — the wall down, **derbiga burburi**; — the eggs, **ugaḥhan bururi**; — the eyes, **isha ka bururi**; — the picture, **sawirka bururi**; — open the door, **albabka burburiya** or **burbursha** or **jida** or **iss ka jida** or **ku dufta**; — the prison, **ḥabsiga jebi**; — (quell) that horse, **faraská i tababar** or **jarra bar**; — his back, **dabada ka la da'**; — the head, **daḥar, ka dangalashi**; (violate) **kufso.**

break, *v.i.*, (burst) **burbur, burur, jejeb, jab, ka jab**; the ice breaks, **barafku wa burbura** or **jajaba**; the ice broke, **barafki jejeb**; the glass broke, **galaski jejeb** or **burbur**; when the wave breaks, **kolka mawjaddu burburto**; I broke my leg, **lug ban ka jabai** (*lit.* I was broken of my leg); — your leg, **lug ka jab**; my eye burst, **il ba i bururtai.**

break (of the day), *n.*, **aroryo,—adi.**

breakfast, *n.*, **afuro,—adi.**

breakfast, *v.i.*, **afur.**

breaking, *n.*, **jab,—ki, jabnin,—ti.**

breast, *n.*, **lab,—ti.**

breath, *n.*, **neif,—ti**; last —, **ugu dambais,—ti**; shortness of —, **hinrag,—gi.**

breathe, *v.i.*, **neifso.**

breech, *n.*, **dabo,—adi, sal,—ki.**

breed, *v.tr.*, (produce) **yelo, dal**; that child is cutting teeth, **inanka ilkihisi ba u so baḥaya**; (bring up) **kori.**

breeding, *n.*, **koris,—ki.**

breeze, *n.*, **ne'aw,—di.**

brew, *v.tr.*, (to prepare, as a liquor, from several ingredients) **ḫosh, iss ku ḫosh, iss ku dar.**

brick, *n.*, (baked) **ājurad,—di**; (not baked) **leben,—ki.**

bridal, *n.*, (wedding) **aros,—ki.**

bride, *n.*, (newly-married woman) **arosad,—di.**

bridegroom, *n.*, **aros,—ki.**

bridge, *n.*, (of the nose) **sanḫaror,—ki**; (of the sole) **raïs magado,—adi.**

bridle, *n.*, **ḥakamai** or **ḥakama,—ihi.**

bright, *a.*, **dalalaya** (*m.*), **dalalaisa** (*f.*).
brighten, *v.tr.*, **'adai, kaga dalali, iftimi.**
brightness, *n.*, **dalal,—ki.**
brim, *n.*, (edge) **girgir** or **jirjir, —ki.**
brimstone, *n.*, (sulphur) **kebrid, —ki.**
bring, *v.tr.*, (fetch) **ken, ka ken, gei, la kalai**; — to me, — to us, **i ken, no ken** or **i, no la kalai**; — to him, her, them, **u gei**, or **u la tag**; — me a coach, **gadi i ken**; — Ali with you, **Ali so kahai**; — to light, **dal, yelo**; she brought a child into the world, **inan bai ifka kentai**; — him into debt, **ḥan geli**; — into danger, **'absi geli**; — him to do it, **ha falai e waḥhas u gei**; — back *or* again, **so 'eli**; — back to, **u eli**; — to life again, **nolai, nolaisi**; — away, **si ḥad, so sar, ka so sar**; — the boy down, **wilka dafta u so rog**; or **so deji**; — forward, **horo u ken, horo u jid, horo u so jid**; — in, **so geli**; — here, **halka ken, la kalai, so gur**; — out, **tus, dibadda u sar**; — out your story, **shekadada so sar**; — that man out of trouble, **war! ninka ḥumanta ka biḥi**; he was brought forth before the time, **shinku dalad ma aha**, or **shinki ma dalan**, or **shinki ma gadin**; he was brought forth at his time, **shinki ku dalan**; the she-camel brought forth a young one, **hashi nerig bai abah ku dashai** or **dalatai** or **dalisai**: — up (educate ...) **kori**; help to — up, **la kori**; be brought up, **kor**; be brought up with, **la kor**; your bad conduct will — mischief upon you, **aslubtada ḥumi mel darran bai ka ridi** or **ka turi.**
brink, *n.*, (edge) **fiḥ,—hi**; — of a mountain, **jar,—ki**; — of a river, **dan,—ki.**
brisket, *n.*, (of a horse) **geddo, —adi.**
brittle, *a.*, **jilai'san.**
brittleness, *n.*, **jila'** or **jilai',—lihi.**
broad, *a.*, **balladan.**
broaden, *v.tr.*, **balladi.**
broil, *v.tr.*, (dress meat on coals) **dub, sol.**
broken, *a.*, **burbursan**; be —, **burbur, jab, jajab**; a — language, **af burbursan, afki burbursana.**
broke, *v.i.*, (contract business for others) **dilal, dilal noḥo.**
broker, *n.*, **dilal,—ki.**
brokerage, *n.*, (fee for promoting bargains) **ma'ash,—ki.**
broom, *n.*, **minfiḥ,—di**; (a piece of wood used as a broom) **digahad,—ki.**
broth, *n.*, **fud,—ki.**
brother, *n.*, **walal,—ki.**
brotherhood, *n.*, **walalnimo,—adi.**
brow, *n.*, **kod,—ki**; (forehead) **fod,—di.**

brown (colour), *n.* and *a.*, **marrin,** —**ki**; light —, **'asusleh, owlan.**

browse, *v.i.*, **daḥ**; the cow browses, **lodi wa daḥaisa**; the sheep browse, **adigi wa daḥaya.**

bruise, *n.*, (contusion) **lāban,**—**ki.**

bruised, *a.*, **laban.**

brush, *n.*, **burush,**—**ki.**

brushwood, *n.*, (brambles) **ḥanan,** —**ki.**

brutal, *a.*, **bahalah.**

brute, *n.* and *a.*, **bahal,**—**ki.**

bubble, *n.*, **ḥumbo,**—**adi.**

bucket, *n.*, **baldi,**—**gi, barmil yar;** leathern —, **naḍ,**—**ki, wadan,**—**ti;** rope and — for drawing water, **dowlis.**

buckle, *n.*, (a ring with a tongue) **ḥadabo,**—**adi.**

buffet, *n.*, (a blow with the hand) **dirbaho** or **darbaho,**—**adi.**

buffet, *v.tr.*, **dirbaḥ.**

bug, *n.*, **kutan,**—**ti.**

bugbear, *v.tr.*, (frighten) **baji.**

bugalow, *n.*, (large boat) **baḥlad,** —**di, dōni,**—**di, ḥanyad,**—**di.**

build, *v.tr.*, **ḍis, ḍiso;** — for, **u ḍis, aḥalka u samai.**

building, *n.*, **disnin,**—**ti, samain,** —**ti.**

built, *a.*, **ḍisan.**

bull, *n.*, **ḍibi,**—**gi.**

bullet, *n.*, **jalilad,**—**di.**

bullock, *n.*, **dibi yar.**

bum, *n.*, (the buttocks) **sal,**—**ki.**

bump (bunch), *n.*; (a hard lump) **tur,**—**ti.**

bunch (bundle), *n.*; (a number of things tied together) **guntin,** —**ti, ḥidmo,**—**adi.**

bunch, *n.*, (of hair) **ḍor,**—**ki.**

buoy, *n.*, **boyad,**—**di.**

burden, *n.*, **ḥamil,**—**ki, rar,**—**ki, rarmo,**—**adi.**

burial, *n.*, **asnin,**—**ti.**

burn, *n.*, (heat caused by fire) **gubnin,**—**ti;** — made on sheep (brand) **hanjid,**—**di.**

burn, *v.tr.*, **gub;** *v.r.*, **gubo;** — him alive, **nolanta ku gub;** — to ashes or carbonize, **hurunshai;** *v.i.*, **gubo;** he burns like fire, **dab o kalu u gubanaya.**

burnt, *a.*, **guban;** a — thing, **hurunsho,**—**adi.**

burr, *n.*, (the round kotob of horn next the deer's head) **kod,**—**ki;** — of the ear (lobe), **dahal,**—**shi;** (upper part of the lobe) **ḥurdan,**—**ki.**

burrow, *n.*, (hole made in the ground by rabbits) **god,**—**ki.**

burst, *v.i.*, **ḥaraḥ, burur, dila';** *v.tr.*, **bururi.**

bury, *v.tr.*, **ās.**

bush, *n.*, (thick shrub) **ḥanan,**—**ki;** a sour —, **darān,**—**ti;** a kind of — with a milky sap, **dibow,**—**gi.**

business, *n.*, **haul,**—**shi, dan,**—**ti.**

bustard, *n.*, **'elal jog** or **jog jog,** —**ti, salalmodleh,**—**lihi.**

busy, *a.*, **haul badan, haulaisan, haushoda.**

but, *c.*, **lakin, se** (used as an *affix*).

butcher, *n.*, **adi ẖal,—ki.**
butcher, *v.tr.*, **gowra', ẖal.**
butler, *n.*, (servant in charge of liquors, head servant) **buder, —ki** or **ninka sorta frenjiga u diga.**
butt, *n.*, (mark to shoot at) **ẖiyas, —ti, dug,—ti**; the — end or extremity of a thing, **'aro,—adi.**
butter, *n.*, **bur'ad,—ki**; melted —, **siḥin,—ti**; —milk, **īr,—ti.**
butterfly, *n.*, **balanbālis,—ti.**
buttock, *n.*, **sal,—ki.**
button, *n.*, **bádan,—ki.**
buy, *v.tr.*, **ibi, so ibi, ibso, so ibso, sosi, siso, ka ibi.**
buzz, *v.i.*, (hum) **guẖ, ẖin.**
by, *prp.*, **agta, gesta**; — my side, **agtaidi, gestaidi.**

C.

c, third letter of the English alphabet.
cabbage, *n.*, **kobi,—gi.**
cable, *n.*, **hadig wein,—i—a.**
cackle, *n.*, (of fowls) **'i,—di.**
cackle, *v.i.*, **'i.**
cadaver, *n.*, **baẖti,—gi, miyid,—ki, raẖ,—di.**
cage, *n.*, (for birds) **sab,—ki.**
cake, *n.*, (Arab one) **ḥalwad,—di.**
calculate, *v.tr.*, **tiri, tirso, ḥisab.**
calculation, *n.*, **tiro,—adi, ḥisab, —ti.**
calf, *n.*, (young of a cow) **weil,—ki**; (in general) **weilo,—ihi**; (fleshy part of the leg behind, below the knee) **muruẖ,—ki.**
call, *n.*, (vocal address) **yed,—ki, yednin,—ti.**
call, *v.tr.*, (to name) **u biḥi, ugu yed**; (to invite) **u yed**; call after him, **ād u yed**; — again *or* back, **so'eli**; — aloud from, **ka yed**; — him aside, **goni ugu yed**; — him out, away, **dibada u sar**; — at that place, **mesha si mar**; — back your word, **hadalkági ku noẖo**; the governor calls for you, **serkalki ba ku yedaya** *or* **donaya**; do you — for drink? **ma waḥad 'abtid bad donaisa?** — for dinner, **sorta hagaji** or **sorta kala hagaji**; — forth, **u yed**; — in, **so geli**; — in your money, **la'agtadá ha ku so gasho**; — him off from that bad thing, **ninka waẖha ẖun** or **dauga ẖun uga yed**; I am called off from my studies, **barashadaidi ba la iga yedai**; — on, — to, — unto, — upon, **bari, dalbo**; — him to help, **'awimad ugu yed**; — over the names of the assembly, **nin walba magiḥisa ugu yed**; — him to witness, **marẖati ugu yed**; — to remembrance, **hus usi**; — together, **iss u kalada**; — him up in the morning, **arorta hore so tos.**

call to prayer, *v.tr.*, **adin.**
calling to prayer, *n.*, **adimad,—di, edan,—ki.**
caller, *n.*, (the man calling to prayer) **muadin,—ki, nin adimaya.**
callousness, *n.*, **gandafil,—shi**; — of the camel's hind legs, **gorof leged,—ki**; — of the camel's chest, **shaf,—ki.**
be callous, *v.i.*, **gandafilow**; my hand will become callous, **ga'anti i gandafilodai.**
calm, *n.*, (at sea) **ḥawāl,—shi.**
calm, *v.tr.*, **ḥabowji.**
calumniate, *v.tr.*, **edai, ku edai, hafar, ḥano.**
calumniator, *n.*, **nin ed badan, hafar badan, ḥabas,—ki.**
calumny, *n.*, **hafar,—ki, ḥan,—ti, ḥabasnimo,—adi.**
camel, *n.*, **gel,—i, gelal,—shi** (*plur. com. gen.*), **aur—ki** (*m.s.*), **aur—ti** (*plur. com. gen.*), **rati,—gi** (*m.*), **hal,—shi** (*f.*); (stallion) **barḥab,—ki**; castrated —, **gol,—ki**; a kind of large —, **koron,—ki**; young —, **nirig, gi** (*m.*) **—ti** (*f.*); young she —, **ḥalin,—ti**; — water-bearer, **dān,—ki**; —not tamed, **aïmad,—ki, laïli,—gi**; — without load, **adaïsimo,—adi**; — accustomed to carry loads, **ḥamil ḥad.**
camelopard, *n.*, **gerri,—gi, halgerri,—di.**
camp, *v.i.*, **deg, hoio.**
camphire, camphor, *n.*, **kanfur,—ki.**

can, *v.i.*, (be able) (*defective* and *auxiliary verb*) **kar**; he — read and write; **wa aḥri kara o ḥori kara**; I will do it if I —, **wan samain hadan karo**; he does all he —, **wuḥu kara bu fala**; I cannot, **ma karo, kari mayo**; he cannot come, **ma iman karo.**
cancel, *v.tr.*, (efface) **babihi.**
cancer, canker, *n.*, **hudai** or **huda,—ihi.**
cancerous, *a.*, **hudai.**
candle, *n.*, **shimai'** or **shama',—ihi.**
cane, *n.*, (kind of reed) **dūr,—ki.**
canine tooth, *n.*, **mi'i,—di.**
cannibal, *n.*, **dadḥal,—ki** (*m.*), **dadḥalato,—adi** (*f.*).
cannon, *n.*, (gun) **madfa',—i'hi.**
canon, *n.*, (rule, law) **ḥainun,—ki.**
canter, *v.i.*, (gallop gently) **hardaf.**
cap, *n.*, **kofiad,—di.**
capable, *a.*, **kara**; be —, **kar.**
capableness, capability, *n.*, **karnin,—ti.**
cape, *n.*, (a headland) **rasi,—gi.**
captive, *n.*, (a prisoner of war) **ninki dagal ba lagu ḥabtai**; **nagti wai la haden** or **nagtasu wa la ḥabtai**; (a slave) **adon,—ki, bidai,—hi, bidad,—di.**
caravan, *n.*, **ḥafila,—di, safar,—ki.**
cards, *n.*, **turub,—ki** (*sing.* and *plur.*); play at —, **turub 'ayar.**

care, *n.*, (solicitude, heed) **foyigan** or **fojigan,—ti, ilalo,—adi**; take —, **iss ka eg, ilali jir, ogow**; *v.r.*, **iss jir, iss ka jir, iss ogow.**

care, *v.i.*, (be anxious); what — you? **maḥad u dan ledahai** or **maḥad u fojigantahai?** he cares for nobody, **nin na dan u ma leh.**

careful, *a.*, **aminah, foyig, feyig** or **fojig**; be —, **aminahaw.**

carefulness, *n.*, **aminimo,—adi.**

careless, *a.*, **(nin) fojigla, mudāya',—i'hi.**

carelessness, *n.*, **fojiglaan,—ti.**

caress, *n.*, **salaḥid, -di.**

caress, *v.tr.*, **salaḥ.**

cargo, *n.*, **mal,—ki, sheḥnad,—di**; bring your —, **so nawil, sheḥnadda nawila.**

carpenter, *n.*, **najar,—ki** or **nijar, —ki.**

carpet, *n.*, **firash,—ki**; a Somali —, **kebed,—di.**

carriage, *n.*, **gadi** or **gari,—gi.**

carried, *a.*, **(nin) la sido.**

carrier, *n.*, (porter) **ḥamal,—ki.**

carry, *v.tr.*, (convey) **ḥad, sid, sido**; — for, **u ḥad, u sid**; — a child, **hambar**; — thy child, **hambaro**; — yourself well, **si wanaksan u so'o**; he carries himself well, **aslub tolmon** or **waḥan bu lehyahai**; — about you, **sido**; — away, **la tag, dibada u la baḥ**; — away by force, **ka difo**; — back, **dib u 'eli**; — down, **hosta gei**; — out your design, **dama'haga** or **dantada wado**; — over the child, **inanka durdurka ka talabi.**

cart, car, *n.*, **gawadi,—di.**

cartouche, cartridge, *n.*, **rasas, —ti.**

carve, *v.tr.*, (to cut wood) **ḥarad.**

carved, *a.*, **ḥardan.**

carving, *n.*, **ḥarad,—ki.**

cascade, cataract, *n.*, **biya garbaha ka so dulai, garbo,—ihi.**

case, *n.*, (box) **abḥad, saharad, —di**; judicial —, **ḥujad, —di**; — of complaint derived from any transgression of the Somali customs or traditions, **ḥer,—ki.**

cash (ready money), *n.*; (of silver) **shola boli,—di**; (of brass) **'adadi,—di.**

cask, *n.*, (a vessel) **barmil,—ki.**

cast, *v.tr.*, (throw) **tur, rid**; — a spear, **waranka rid**; — yourself at his feet, **hortisa iss ku tur**; — away, **ḥor**; — behind, **dambaisi, daba joji**; — down, **hosaisi**; — headlong, **madaḥha u tur, so weidafi.**

castaway, *n.*, (rejected) **nin inkaran, nin la na'ai.**

caste, *n.*, **ḥigal,—ki, ḥolo,—adi, tol,—ki**; the high castes, **gob, —ki**; the low castes, **sab,—ti**; the three low castes: **tumal, —ki, midgan,—ki, yibir,—ki.**

castor-plant, *n.*, **bu'a'ad, bu'amadow.**

castrate, *v.tr.*, **dufan, tun.**

castrated, *a.*, **dufanan, tuman**; a gelded animal, **dugag tuman.**

castration, *n.*, **dufan,—ki.**

cat, *n.*, **bissad,—di, dinad,— di**; male —, **huri,—gi**; wild —, **dinad habishi**; civet —, **dinad sabad,—di**; small —, **dinad yar.**

cataplasm, *n.*, (a poultice) **damoḥ, —hi**; apply a —, **damoḥ.**

catarrh, *n.*, **durai,—gi.**

catch, *v.tr.*, (hold on to) **ḥabo, ḥabso, heji**; — hold of, **ka ḥabo, ka ḥabso**; — with, **ku ḥabso**; — the truth, **runta ḥab**; the wood will — fire, **ḥabadu wai guban**; he has caught a distemper, **udur bu ḥadai** or **ḥabsadai** or **wu bukodai.**

catching, *n.*, **ḥabasho.**

caterpillar, *n.*, **dirindir,—ti.**

caterwaul, *n.*, (of cats) **shiddo, —adi.**

caterwaul, *v.i.*, **shiddai.**

Catholic, *a.*, **katholik,—gi, nin katholigah.**

cattle, *n.*, **holo nol,—ki, fof,—ki, darer,—ki, sof,—ki**; neat *or* black —, **lo',—di.**

cause, *n.*, (reason ...) **ed,—di, sabab,—ti.**

cause, *v.c.*; this is expressed by using the causative form of the verb (*see* Gram.).

cauterise, *v.tr.*, **gub.**

cautery, *n.*, (burning application) **dab,—ki.**

caution, *n.*, (sponsion) **damin, —ti.**

cautious, *a.*, **foyig**; be—. **fojigow.**

cavalry, *n.*, **fardoleh,—di.**

cave, cavern, *n.*, **boran,—ti, god, —ki.**

caw, *v.i.*, (cry as the rook) **'ei** or **'i.**

cease, *v.tr.*, (discontinue) **da, iss ka da.**

celebrate, *v.tr.*, (praise) **aman**; (solemnise) **'id.**

cement, *n.*, **simid,—ki.**

cemetery, *n.*, **ḥabalo,—lihi, ḥabur,—ti, hawal,—shi.**

censure, *v.tr.*, (blame) **hanib.**

centre, *n.*, **deh,—di.**

century, *n.*, **boḥol sanadod.**

certain, *a.*, (sure) **la huba**; — news, **war la huba**; it is —, **wa dab, wa run, wa la huba**; be —, **huḥ**; make —, **dabai, kaga dabai, rumai, run la huba sheg.**

certain, *a.*, (some one) **hebel, waḥ ba.**

certainty, certitude, *n.*, **dab,—ti, run,—ti.**

certify, *v.tr.*, (assure) **dabai, fur, marḥati ku fur, rumai.**

chafe, *n.*, (heat caused by rubbing) **gomod,—ki**; (rage, fury) **'ado, —adi.**

chafe, *v.tr.*, (make hot) **kululai**; (make angry) **kaga 'adaisi**; (make warm by rubbing) **gomodi.**

chafe, *v.i.*, (rage) **'ado**; (to be sore or galled by riding) **gomod.**

chain, *n.*, **silsilad**; — of mountains, **buro iss ku yal, buraha iss ku yal, buraha garbohoda.**

chain, *v.tr.*, (tie with chains) **silsilad ku hid** or **ku jebi.**

chair, *n.*, **kursi,—gi.**

chalk, *n.*, **malas,-ti, dareyo,-adi.**

challenge, *n.*, (invitation to fight) **dandansid** or **dandansis,—ki**; (a demand for something due) **dignin,—ti, ḥanan,—ki.**

challenge, *v.tr.*, (call to fight) **dandanso**; (claim) **ḥanan, ninki dignin u dir.**

chamber, *n.*, (apartment) **ḥollad,—di.**

chameleon, *n.*, **jirjiroleh,—lihi.**

champ, *v.tr.* and *v.i.*, (chew, bite) **'alasho**; the horse champs his bit, **farasku hakamihi yu 'alashanaya.**

chance, *n.*, (luck) **ayan,—ki.**

change, *n.*, (alteration, novelty) **bedalad,—di**; — of money, **sarrif,—ki.**

change (a thing), *v.tr.*; (barter, exchange) **dafi, iss dafi, dafso, dori, dorso**; — money, **sarrif**; — your shirt, **ḥamiskaga iss ka dig o mid kaleh gasho** or **huwo**; — your hat with mine, **kofiadada taida i dafi** or **igu dori**

channel, *n.*, (canal) **doḥ,—hi.**

chant, *n.*, (vocal music) **hes,—ti.**

chant, *v.tr.* and *v.i.*, (sing) **hes.**

chap, *n.*, (chink, cleft) **dila',—hi**; — of the ground, **bohol,—shi**; — of the skin, **safan,—ki.**

chaplet, *n.*, (garland, string of beads) **tusbaḥ,—hi.**

chapter, *n.*, **surad,—di.**

character, *n.*, (mark) **sumad,—di**; an indelible —, **sumad an weliged biḥin**; (personal qualities, particular constitution of mind) **'amal,—ki.**

charcoal, *n.*, **duḥul,—shi.**

charge, *n.*, (custody, care) **ilalo,—adi**; (burden) **ḥamil,—ki, rar,—ki, rarmo,—adi.**

charitable, *a.*, **naḥsan.**

charity, *n.*, (love) **ja'ail,—ki**; (mercy) **naḥadin,—ti.**

charm, *n.*, (words or characters imagined to have some magical power) **fāl,—ki**; (amulet) **ḥirsi,—di, ḥardas,—ti, ma'fo,—adi.**

charm, *v.tr.*, (enchant) **fāl.**

chase, *n.*, (hunting) **ugadsi,—gi, dabnin,—ti.**

chase, *v.tr.*, (hunt) **ugadso, dab, dabo.**

chastise, *v.tr.*, (punish) **ḥanuji, tababar.**

chat, chatter, chattering, *n.*, **daudar,—ki.**

chat, *v.i.*, (babble) **daudar.**

chatterer, *n.*, **nin daudarah.**

cheap, *a.*, (at a low rate) **jaban, gana' jaban**; rice is —, **bariski jeb**; sell —, *v.tr.*, **gana' jaban,** or **yar si,** or **ku ibi**; buy —, **gana' jaban so si,** or **ku ibi.**

cheapen, *v.tr.*, (lessen) **gana' jebi.**

cheat, *n.*, (deceit, fraud) **hadig,—gi, dulun,—ki, ḥelad,—di, ḥiyan,—ki, ḥayano,—adi.**

cheat, *v.tr.*, (defraud) **da', dulun, ḥayanai, ḥiyanai.**

cheater, *n.*, **nin dulunah, hadig badan, ḥiyanah, ḥayano leh.**

cheek, *n.*, **'an,—ki, daban,—ki**; chubby —, **'an bur,—ki.**

cheer, *n.*, (entertainment) **diafad,**

—di ; (cheerfulness, gaiety) **baḍaḍ,—ki, raïn,—ti.**
cheer, *v.tr.*, (make cheerful) **kaga baḍaḍi, kaga rairaisi, kaga baḍbaḍaḍi** ; (grow cheerful) *n.i.*, **baḍaḍ, rai, rairai.**
cheerful, *a.*, **baḍaḍsan.**
cheese, *n.*, (dry curd) **fär,—ki.**
chest, *n.*, (a wooden box) **saharad,—di, sanduḥ,—hi** ; (breast) **lab,—ti.**
chew, *v.tr.*, (masticate) **'alali, 'alasho, rabso** ; — the cud, *v.i.*, (ruminate) **'alalnaḥso.**
chewing, *n.*, **'alal,—ki, alalis,—ki, rabsi,—gi** ; — cud, **alalnaḥsi,—gi.**
chide, *v.tr.*, (rebuke) **dagal.**
chief, *n.*, (a commander) **aḥil or aḥal,—ki, garad,—ki, ugas,—ki** ; (chieftain, leader) **abban dulai,—lihi** ; — in a government office, **taliya,—yihi, ḥakin,—ki** ; vice —, **gudi,—di, —gi.**
child, *n.*, **arur,—ti, ḍalan,—ki** (*sing.* and *plur.*), **da yar,—di,—aid, ku yar, ki yara, ilmo,—ihi** ; chubby —, **ilma koba'ai** ; sucking —, **ilma nasaha jaḥa** ; spoiled —, **ilma ḍalimaḥ** ; corrupted —, **ilma ḥun.**
childhood, *n.*, **arurnimo,—adi, da yar, yaran,—ti.**
chill, chilly, *a.*, **daḥamodai, nin daḥamodai** ; be —, **daḥamow, or daḥamod.**
chin, *n.*, **dan,—ki, lafta gadka.**
chink, *n.*, (crevice) **dila',—hi.**
chink, *v.i.*, (to sound by striking

each other) **danan** ; the money shines and chinks, **la'agtu wa ḍalasha o dananta.**
chip, *n.*, (a small piece of wood) **ḥanfaf,—ki, ḥanshar,—ki, ḥushash,—ki.**
chip and chop, *v.tr.*, (cut into small pieces) **gogo, jarjar.**
chirp, *n.*, (the voice of birds) **'ei or 'i,—di.**
chirp, *v.i.*, **'i** ; the bird chirps, **shimbirtu wa 'ida.**
chita, *n.*, (hunting one) **arim'ad,—ki.**
choice, *n.*, **dor,—ki, dorasho,—adi** ; I leave it to your choice, **wa adigi iyo dorashada** ; it is in my choice, **aniga dorashada leh,** or **aniga dorashada ban lehahai.**
choice, chosen, *a.*, **dorsan, naḥwa.**
choke, *v.tr.*, (suffocate) **'abūd, siriri** ; *v.r.*, **jogso** ; be choked, **'abūdan.**
choking, *n.*, **siririn,—ti, siriris,—ki.**
cholera, *n.*, **da'un,—ki, haḥleh,—ihi.**
choose, *v.tr.*, **dori, doro, ka doró, ka naḥai, ka naḥaiso, ka ḥulo.**
chowter, *v.i.*, (grumble) **gunus** ; that child does nothing but —, **wilkasi waḥ kaleh ku arki maisid an gunus ahain.**
Christ (the Saviour of the world), *n.*, **Kristos.**
christian, *n.*, **kristan,—ki.**
church, *n.*, **kinisad,—di.**
churl, *n.*, (rustic man) **jingeli or jangali,—gi.**

cicatrice, *n.*, (scar) **nabar,—ki, dahar,—ki.**
cigar, *n.*, **sigarad, shirud** or **shurud,—ki.**
cinnamon, *n.*, **harfa** or **karfa,—di.**
circle, *n.*, **gobo,—adi, gobabin,—ti**; make a —, **gobai, gobabi.**
circular, *a.*, **gobaban, hersan.**
circulate, *v.i.*, **ku wareg**; the blood circulates, **diggu wa dalala,** money should —, **la'agtu** or **la'agi wa waregi lahaid.**
circumcise, *v.tr.*, **gūd, balagta ka go, haranta ka go, buryada ka go, halalai.**
circumcision, *n.*, **gūdnin,—ti.**
circumcised, *a.*, **gūdan.**
circumstances, *n.*, (state, condition) **dan,—ti**; I am in better —, **dantaidi hore ka ron yan wa ta.**
cistern, *n.*, (a reservoir) **berked** or **berkad,—di.**
cite, *v.tr.*, (summon) **amarhadur u sar.**
citation, *n.*, **amarhadur,—ki.**
city, *n.*, **magalo,—adi.**
civil, *a.*, (polite) **amusan, wayelah.**
claim, *n.*, **gar,—ti, hanan,—ki.**
claim, *v.tr.*, **gar u shego, hanan shego**; give the things he claims, **gar mari, gar si.**
clamour, *n.*, (bustle) **buh,—hi, bulhan,—ki, —ti** (for the past), **gurhan,—ki, sawahan,—ki, dawah,—hi, hailo,—adi.**
clamour, *v.tr.*, **buh, dawah, haili.**
clang, *n.*, (a sharp noise) **bikel** or **bigil,—ki.**
clap (your hands), *v.tr.*, **saabada iss ku difo** or **dufo, dirbah.**
clap, *n.*, **darbaho** or **dirbaho,—adi, saab,—ki**; (crack) **ba',—di.**
clash, *v.i.*, (strike one against another) **iss tun, iss jid.**
clatter, clattering, *n.*, **shido,—adi.**
clatter, *v.i.*, (make noise) **shidai.**
claw, *n.*, **'iddi,—di.**
clay, *n.*, **dohbo,—adi.**
clay, *v.tr.*, (cover with clay) **dohb, dohbai, dohbo ku dohb.**
clean, *a.*, **'adaisan, safaisan, safiah, maïdan, miran, nadifsan.**
clean, cleanse, *v.tr.*, **'adai, safai, hal, maïd, maïdo, tir, ka tir, iss ka tir, nadifi, nadif ka dig**; — up, **hor.**
cleanness, *n.*, **nadif,—ti, safi,—gi.**
clear, *a.*, **miran, safiah**; a — day, **wa darar dalalaisa.**
clear, *v.tr.*, (make bright) **'adai, mir**; — a business, difficulty, **hagaji, wanaji**; — the account, **hisabta hagaji**; be —, **miran.**
cleft, *n.*, (a crevice) **bohol,—shi, dila',—hi, jeh,—hi.**
clement, *a.*, **nahsan**; be —, **nah.**
clemency, *n.*, **nahdin,—ti, naharis,—ki.**
clever, *a.*, **wah yahan, fi'an, faridah, farsamo badan, farid,—ki, fi',—hi**; be —, **fi'anaw.**

cleverness, *n.*, **farsamo,—adi, fi'-nan,—ti.**
client (of a man in power), *n.*, **singal,—ki, deris,—ki.**
cliff, *n.*, (a steep rock) **jar,—ki.**
climb, *v.tr.* and *v.i.*, (ascend) **ful, kor, dusha u baḥ, ka baḥ, burta ka baḥ.**
clinch, *v.tr.*, (hold fast) **ḥeji.**
clip, *v.i.*, (to swallow words) **ḫud-ḫudi**; you swallow the words, **adigu hadalkaga wa ḫudḫu-disa.**
clippspringer, *n.*, **ba'ïr,—ki, —ti.**
clock, *n.*, **sa'ad,—di.**
clód, *n.*, (a lump of earth) **fud 'arraah,—ki, 'arradaaha.**
close, *n.*, (an enclosure) **ḥero,—adi, od,—di.**
close, *v.tr.*, (shut) **abud, ḥid**; — in, **ku ḥid.**
close, *a.*, **abudan, ḥidan.**
close to, *ad.*, **u dow.**
closet (water-), *n.*, **aḫal har,—ki, kakus,—ki, madar,—ki.**
cloth, clothes, *n.*, **dar,—ka**; here I have meat, clothes and drink, **halkan ku haista 'unnadi iyo darki iyo biyihi ba.**
clothe, *v.tr.*, **huwi, waḥ u geli**; *v.r.*, **huwo, gasho.**
cloud, *n.*, **darur,—ti**; roving clouds, **'adar,—ki.**
cloudy, *a.*, **daruran, 'usub.**
clout, *n.*, **ḫarḫad,—di.**
clove, *n.*, (spice) **ḫurunful,—ki.**
club, *n.*, (a heavy stick) **bud,—ki.**
clutch, *v.tr.*, (hold in the hand) **ka difo.**

coach, *n.*, **gadi,—gi**; — horse, **faras gadi jida,—ki, gadigi jedi jirai**; — man, **gadiwa-leh,—hi.**
coagulate, *v.tr.*, **fadisi.**
coal, *n.*, **duḫul,—shi**; live or burning —, **duḫul nol.**
coarse, *a.*, (rude) **ḫalafsan**; be —, **ḫalaf.**
coast, *n.*, **ḥeb,—ti.**
coat, *n.*, **garba galai,—ihi.**
cobweb, *n.*, **bul'aro,—adi.**
cock, *n.*, **dig,—gi, digag,—gi, dora,—ihi** (both genders).
cocoanut, *n.*, **narjin,—ti, nara-jin,—ti, narjil,—shi.**
cod, *n.*, (husk) **ḫolof,—ti, jilif,—ti.**
coffee, *n.*, (berry) **bun,—ki**; — husks, **ḫashir** or **ḫashar,—ki, ḫawa,—ihi**; — pot, **ibriḫha ḫahwaah**; Arabic —, **jemelad,—di**; — shop, **maḫayad,—di**; — house keeper, **maḫawi,—gi.**
coffin, *n.*, **kafan,—ti.**
cohabit, *v.i.*, (ninka) **la jog**; **wa-da joga** (*plur.*); we cohabit, **wannu wada jogna.**
coiffure (of Somali women), *n.*, **gambo,—adi.**
coition, *n.*, (copulation) **galmo,—adi, warmo.**
cold, coldness, *n.*, **daḥan,—ti, ḫabow,—gi**; severe —, **gaba-dano,—adi**; disease caused by —, **durai,—gi**; — fit, **had-hadyo,—di**; take or catch a —, **daḥamow, daḥan ḫad**; I caught a —, **durai ban ḫadai.**

cold, *a.*, **ḥabow, gabadano wein.**
colic, *n.*, **alol ḥanun, ur ḥanun, —ki.**
collect, *v.tr.*, **iss u gei, iss u ken, ururi, ku so gur.**
college, *n.*, **madrasad,—di.**
collyrium, *n.*, **inda kul,—shi.**
colour, *n.*, **ranji,—gi, midab,—ki.**
colt, *n.*, (suckling) **dal,—ki, darman,—ki.**
column, *n.*, **tir,—ki.**
comb, *n.*, (man's) **fiḋin,—ki**; — for the beard, **gaḋ feḋ,—ki**; woman's —, **saḥaf,—ti.**
comb, *v.tr.*, **feḋ, feḋo, iss u feḋo.**
combat, *v.tr.* and *v.i.*, **dagalan, werar.**
combat, *n.*, **dagal,—ki, werar,—ki.**
combustible, *n.*, **ḥabo,—adi.**
come, *v.i.*, **imo**, (commonly) **kalai**; how comes that? **war! waḥas maḥa sidas ka ḋigai?** or **war! wa side sasi?** — about, **ku so wareg**; — again, back, **so noḥo, so lāban**; — after, **radi, raḋ gur**; — along, **so ra'**; — along the shore, **ḥebta so ra'**; — away, **ka so baḥ, ina ken**; — by, **so mar**; — down, **so deg, hosta kalai, so ḋaḋa**; — down from, **ka so deg**; — for, **u kalai**; — forth, **so baḥ**; — forward, **wad**; — from, **ka kalai**; — in, **so gal**; — in for, **u so gal**; — into, **ka da'**; — into trouble, **jar ka da'**; — near, **so ḋowow, so durug**; — next, **ku ḥig**; that comes of my doing, **waḥhasi waḥai waḥha ku noḥden wa waḥ anigu an samaiyai**, or **kasu wa shuḥulkaigi**; how did you — off? **war! side u so baḥsatai?** do you think to — off so? **war! ninyohow sida ku baḥsan maisid ha modin**, or **ma u malainaisa inad sida ku baḥsatid?** my hair comes off, **timihi iga so hodai**; the moon comes out, **dayiḥhi wa ka so baḥaya**; — to, **so so'o, so gaḋ, gaḋ**; — to me, **i so gaḋ** or **baḥ**; he came to a shameful end, **si ḥun bu dintai**; it came to pass, **waḥai noḥotai**; — to and fro, **so noḥo, si noḥo**; — together, **issa so ra'a**; — with, **so ra'**; — life, — death, I will go alone, **ama an dinto, ama an nolado, keligai ban so'on**; — between, **so daḥai, no daḥai, so na deḥ gal**; — quick, **so daḥso, so orod**; — up, **so kor, dusha u kalai, dusha u so baḥ**; let —, **so da**; when old age comes upon you, you cannot do anything, **markad dā wein gaḋid**, or **markad odaiowdid waḥba ma kari dontid.**
coming, *n.*, **imatin,—ki.**
comfort, *n.*, (ease) **haulyari,—di, ladnan,—ti.**
comfortable, *a.*, **ladan.**
command, commandment, *n.*, **ḥukun,—ki, ḥainun,—ki, ḥaul,—ki, wasiad,—di.**
command, *v.tr.*, (order) **ḥukun,—**

ki; *v.i.*, (have the supreme authority) **ka sarrai.**

commend, *v.tr.*, (praise) **aman**; everybody commends him, **nin waliba wa amana**; (commit) **aman**; — your spirit to God, **naftada Ilaḥhai ku aman** or **amanaiso.**

commerce, *n.*, **bo'shirad** or **bo'shurad,—di.**

commit, *v.tr.*, (intrust) **aman, amanaiso, amano u ḋib**; I committed that business to you, **shuḥulkas adan hugu amanaistai**; (do, perpetrate) **fal.**

communicate, *v.tr.*, **la hadal, ogaisi, u sheg, warsi, u warran.**

communication, *n.*, **war,—ki.**

communion, *n.*, (union in the common worship or faith) **iss ku daran,—ki**; (participating in the blessed sacrament) **tanaul,—ki.**

companion, *n.*, **sahīb,—ki, wehel, —ki.**

company, *n.*, **dāwo,—adi, waha'd,—di.**

compare, *v.tr.*, **iss u eg.**

compass, *n.*, **dirad,—di.**

compassion, *n.*, (pity) **naḥdin,—ti.**

compensation, *n.*, **dornin,—ti.**

compendium, *n.*, **gabnin,—ki.**

complain, *v.i.*, (lament) **baroro, hasuso, musanaw**; — in law, **ashtakai, ashtako, gar shego, gar u shego, garan, la garan.**

complaint, *n.*, (a lament) **baror, —ti, hasus,—ti, musanaw,—gi**; — in law, **ashtako,—di, gar,—ti.**

complete, *v.tr.*, **ḋamai, idlai.**

complete, *a.*, **ḋan, ḋami, damaid, idil, idli, leil, leili.**

completely, *ad.*, **ḥaib.**

completion, *n.*, **ḋamad,—ki, ḋaman,—ti.**

complexion, *n.*, **'amal,—ki, midab,—ki.**

compliance, *n.*, **oggolan,—ti.**

comply, *v.i.*, **oggolaw.**

comprehend, *v.tr.*, (comprise) **garo, ḥabso.**

comprehensive, *a.*, **eraigas wa la garan kara.**

comprehension, *n.*, **garasho,—adi.**

compress, *v.tr.*, (force into a narrow compass) **dis, ku dis, tuji.**

compunction, *n.*, (repentance) **ala'al,—ki, taubad,—di.**

conceal, *v.tr.*, **ḋumi, ḥari**; *v.r.*, **ḋumo.**

concealment, *n.*, **ḋumasho,—adi, ḥaris,—ki.**

conceive, *v.tr.* and *v.i.*, (be pregnant) **ḋal, yelo.**

conception, *n.*, **ḥabal,—ki** (Arabic).

concern, *n.*, **arrin,—ki, —ti, yel, —ki.**

concession, *n.*, (grant) **ḋibnin,—ti.**

conciliate, *v.tr.*, **heshisi.**

conclude, *v.tr.*, (make an end) **ḋamai, idlai.**

concord, *n.*, (agreement) **nabad, —di, heshis,—ki.**
concubine, *n.*, **adōn,—ti.**
concupiscence, *n.*, **shahwad,—di.**
condemn, *v.tr.*, (**ninka**) **u tali**; the judge condemned me, **ninki dauladed ba igu garaiyai**; God will — you, **Ebbahai wu ku 'adabi.**
condition, *n.*, (state) **dan,—ti.**
conduce, *v.i.*, **ka rid, gei, kaḥai.**
conduct, *n.*, (management) **talo, —adi**; (behaviour) **abur,—ki, aslub,—ti.**
confess, *v.tr.*, (avow) **ḥiro, ḥado.**
confession, *n.*, **ḥir,—ti.**
confide in, *v.tr.*, **aman, yesho, ḥadari.**
confidence, *n.*, **yeshod,—ki.**
confine, *v.i.*, (limit); Somaliland confines Abyssinia, **dul Somalied, dul Abashied bu ku yal** or **ku idlada**; *v.tr.*, (shut up) **ḥid.**
confinement, *n.*, **ḥidnan,—ti.**
confirm, *v.tr.*, (put past doubt) **dabai, rumai**; (strengthen) **adkai.**
conflict, *n.*, **dirir,—ti.**
conflict, *v.tr.*, **dirir.**
confluence, *n.*, (concourse) **buḥ,—hi, urur,—ki.**
conform with, *v.i.*, **oggolaw**; — to the will of God, **talada Ebbahai oggolaw.**
congeal, *v.tr.*, **fadisi**; *v.i.*, the milk congeals, **'anihi fadistai.**
congratulate, *v.tr.*, I came to — you, **inan adiga kaga badadiyo yan u imi.**
congregate, *v.tr.*, **ururi, so ururi, iss ugu ken, iss ugu gein.**
congregation, *n.*, **jama',—hi.**
conjuration, *n.*, **fal,—ki.**
conjure, *v.tr.*, **dalbo, ka don, ka dono**; — up, **fal**; (exorcise) **ka sar, eri.**
conjurer, *n.*, **nin waḥ fala.**
conquer, *v.tr.*, **ka ḥad, ka hel.**
consecrate, *v.tr.*, **ḥodus ka samai** or **ka dig.**
consent, *n.*, **oggolan,—ti.**
consent to, *v.i.*, **oggolaw, 'ajibi.**
consequence, *n.*, **dog,—ti.**
consequently, *ad.*, **haddaba.**
consider, *v.tr.*, (examine) **hubso, tasho, aloshada la tasho.**
consideration, *n.*, **hubsad,—ki, tashi,—gi.**
consist, *v.i.*, (subsist); God is before all things, and by him all things —, **Ilah ba walba ugu horaiya, o wah waliba isaga ku noliyihin**; our life consists in the union betwixt the body and the soul, **nolantenu wa jidkena iyo naftena iss ku yal**; the land consists of plains, valleys and mountains, **berrigu wa banan iyo faro iyo buro.**
consolidate, *v.tr.*, **adkai, tāg, ad u tāg.**
constancy, *n.*, **adkan,—ti, samir, —ki.**
constellation, *n.*, **urur ḥidigaah.**
constipation, *n.*, **'alol ingegnan, —ti.**
constipated, *a.*, **'alol ingegan, nin 'alol ingegan leh.**

construct, *v.tr.*, **ḋis, samai.**
construction, *n.*, **ḋisnin,—ki,** — **ti, ahal samais,—ki.**
consult, *v.tr.* and *v.i.*, **la faḫ, weidi, weidiso** ; — your strength, **itālkaga la tasho.**
consultation, *n.*, **faḫ,—hi.**
consume, *v.tr.*, **babihi, lumi** ; time consumes everything, **gor ba waḥ walba babihisa.**
consumption, *n.*, (disease) **ḫaho, —adi, lahaw,—gi.**
contemn, *v.tr.*, **fududai.**
contempt, *n.*, **fudaid,—ki.**
contemptible, *a.*, **fudud, gun** ; — person, **gumais,—ti.**
content, contentment, *n.*, **badad, —ki, raḥo,—adi.**
contest, *v.tr.* and *v.i.*, (dispute) **ha la heshin, ha heshinina** (*plur.*); we will —, **innagu heshin donno.**
continue, *v.tr.* and *v.i.*, **hor u so'o, wad.**
contract, *v.tr.*, (shorten) **gabi, yarai, yaraisi** ; get or — a disease, **'udur ba kugu di'i** ; — a bad habit, **aslub ḥun ba kugu di'i.**
contradict, *v.i.*, (not to keep your word) **hadalkaga beinai** ; (oppose verbally) **asarar.**
contradiction, *n.*, **asarar,—ki.**
contradictor, *n.*, (**nin**) **asarar badan, asarar wein, asarar miḋanah.**
contrary, *n.*, (reverse) **edis,—ti.**
contrite (be), *v.pr.*, **ḫomamai.**
contrition, *n.*, **ḫomamais,—ki.**
contrivance, *n.*, (device) **ḥigmad** or **ḥikmad,—di.**
contumacy, *n.*, (a wilful disobedience to any summons) **didnin, —ti.**
canvalescence, *n.*, **ladnan,—ti.**
conversation, *n.*, **hasawai,—ihi.**
converse, *v.i.*, **hasaw.**
convey, *v.tr.*, (carry) **so ḫad, so sid.**
convict, *v.tr.*, (prove guilty) **ku garai** ; be convicted, **ka gar hel, garow.**
convoke, convocate, *v.tr.*, **so ururi** ; — to that place, **meshas iss ugu gei, rag o ḋan u yed.**
convulsion, *n.*, (spasm in children) **abodi,—gi.**
cook, *n.*, **deriya karis, sor karis, —ki.**
cook, *v.tr.*, **bislai.**
cooked, *a.*, **bisil** ; not —, **ma bisla, 'edin, 'edinah.**
cool, *a.*, **ḫabow.**
cool, *v.tr.*, (make cool) **ḫabowji** ; *v.i.*, (grow cool) **ḫabow** ; *v.r.*, **ḫabojiso.**
copper, *n.*, **naḥas,—ti.**
copulation, *n.*, (coupling) **galmo, —adi, warmo,—adi** ; — of camels, **abaho,—adi** ; — of neat cattle, **ofno,—ihi.**
copulate, *v.tr.*, (couple) **u kaḥai ha ofiyaie** ; *v.i.*, **saro.**
copy, *n.*, (a transcript) **ḥadilad, —di.**
copy, *v.tr.*, **ḥadil.**
coral, *n.*, (white) **sha'ab** or **sha'b, —ki.**
cord, *n.*, **haḋig,—gi.**

cork, *n.*, **fur.**

cork, *v.tr.*, (stop with a cork) **abud.**

corn, *n.*, (wheat) **saren,—ki, messego,—adi.**

cornea, *n.*, **indaha 'aloshada'ad, haïd,—di** ; — of the eye, **isha haïdeda.**

corporal, *n.*, (of police) **'awaldar, —ki, kabul,—ki.**

corpse, *n.*, **baḥti,—gi, miyid,—ki, raḥ,—di.**

correct, *v.tr.*, **tababar.**

corrupt, *v.tr.*, (spoil) **ḥudmi, ka bii, dil, u ḥumai** ; (become rotten) *v.i.*, **ḥudun.**

corrupted, *a.*, **ḥudunsan, ḥudmai.**

corruption, *n.*, **ḥudun,—ki.**

cost, *n.*, (price of a thing) **gana', —di.**

cotton, *n.*, **udbi,—gi.**

cough, *n.*, **ḥufa',—fi'ḥi, durai.**

cough, *v.i.*, **ḥufa'.**

council, *n.*, **shir,—ki** ; go to the —, **shirka tag.**

counsel, *n.*, **talo,—adi, wano,—adi.**

count, *v.tr.*, **hisabi, ḥisabo, tiri, tirso.**

countenance, *n.*, **jah,—hi.**

country, *n.*, **miyi,—gi, magalo, —adi, bilad,—ki, ardal,—ki.**

courage, *n.*, **gesinimo,—adi, bili, —gi.**

courageous (man), *a.*, **gesi,—gi, gesiah, kelliya badan, kelliya leh, bilileh.**

course of life, *n.*, **'emri,—gi.**

court-house, *n.*, **hakamad or mahakamad,—di.**

cousin, *n.*, (paternal) **ina ader, —ki** ; (maternal) **ina abti.**

covenant, *n.*, (contract) **ahdi,—gi.**

cover, *v.tr.*, (overspread) **huwi** ; *v.r.*, **huwo, dabol** ; — with the sheet, **ded** ; — the head to warm him, **huri** ; — the face to hide him, **u hagog, u hagoji** ; *v.r.*, **u hagogo** ; — with the shield, **gabo.**

cover, *n.*, (anything used to cover) **dabol,—ki** ; — of a boiler, **dabol deri, sāb,—ki.**

covered, *a.*, **dabolan.**

covet, *v.i.*, **dama'.**

covetous, *a.*, **dama'san.**

covetousness, *n.*, **dama',—hi.**

cow. *n.*, **sa',—hi** ; herd of cows, **lo',—di** ; a milch —, **irman, —ki** ; **gabān,—ki, sa' gabānah** ; — no longer milked, **han,—ki.**

cow, *v.tr.*, (dispirit) **baji.**

coward, *n.*, **fulai or fula,—ihi, hād,—ki.**

cowardice, *n.*, **bajis,—ki, fulanimo,—adi.**

crab, *n.*, (crustaceous fish) **'arsanyo,—adi.**

crack, *n.*, **ba',—di.**

crack, *v.i.*, (burst, split) **burur, dila', harah.**

cramp, *n.*, (spasm or contraction of the nerves) **kabuliyo,—adi.**

crawl, *v.i.*, (creep) **berka ku so'o, bogga ku so'o.**

cream, *n.*, **laben,—ti.**

create, *v.tr.*, **abur, ūn**; be created, **aburan, umanow.**
created, *a.*, **aburan, ūman.**
creation, *n.*, **aburnin,—ti.**
creature, *n.*, **ūn,—ki.**
credit, *n.*, (belief) **amin,—ki**; (reputation) **mamus** or **namus,—ti**; taking on —, **dein,—ki.**
creditor, *n.*, **ninka gashiga kugu leh.**
creed, *n.*, (faith) **āmin,—ki, aminad,—di**; (rule of faith) **ḥainunka aminadda**; the Apostles' Creed, **ḥainunka rassulyada.**
crepuscle, *n.*, **fid,—ki, maḥrib,—ki, gabbal da',—di'hi.**
crescent, *n.*, **bil,—shi.**
crib, *n.*, (manger) **ḥabal,—ki.**
crier (public), *n.*, **ḥarash,—ki.**
crime, *n.*, **ḥujad,—di, ḥujad hun, dembi,—gi.**
criminal, *a.*, **ḥujadleh, ḥujad ba ḥabsatai.**
crimson, *n.*, **gudud, gududan.**
cripple, *n.*, (person) **orjujun,—ki, laḥad la,—ki—a, lug laan**; congenital —, **alan,—ki, alanad,—di**; — by accident or sickness, **'uriyan,—ki, 'uriiyanad,—di.**
crocodile, *n.*, **jaḥas,—ti.**
crook, *n.*, (any crooked instrument) **hangol,—ki.**
crooked, *a.*, **ḥalloḥan**; a man with — legs, **nin luga ḥalloḥan,** or **nin dalba leh,** I have seen the woman with — legs, **nagti dalbaha lahaid ban arkai.**
crookedness, *n.*, **ḥalloḥ, ḥalḥalloḥ,—hi**; — of the legs, **dalbo,—ihi.**
crop, *n.*, (craw of fowls) **'alal,—ki.**
cross, *n.*, **salib,—ki, iss ku talab,—ti**; make a —, **iss ku talab samai.**
cross, *a.*, (peevish) **iss ku talabsan, ḥun, waḥ yela badan.**
cross, *v.tr.*, (lay, or go across) **ka talab, deḥ mar, weidaro**; *v.c.*, **weidari**; why do you — me thus? **mahad sidas iga ḥanunjinaisa?**
croup, *n.*, (buttocks of a horse) **fan,—ki.**
crouch, *v.i.*, (stoop low) **dukus.**
crow, *n.*, (bird) **tukai** or **tuka,—ihi.**
crowd, *n.*, (multitude) **buḥ,—hi, urur,—ki.**
crown, *n.*, (of hair, left on girls) **ḥerar,—ki.**
crucify, *v.tr.*, **salibka ku musmar.**
crude, *a.*, (raw) **'edinah, 'edin.**
cruel, *a.*, **'adow,—gi, bahal,—ki, baan.**
cruelty, *n.*, **'adownimo,—adi.**
crupper, *n.*, (for a camel's saddle) **daba gelis,—ki.**
crush, *v.tr.*, (squeeze) **burburi.**
crutch, *n.*, (for a cripple) **tukubai,—bihi.**
cry, *n.*, (clamour) **dawaḥ,—hi, ḥailo,—adi, 'i,—di, orr,—ki**; (lamentation) **baror,—ti, musanow,—gi, oin,—ki.**
cry, cry out, cry aloud, *v.i.*, **ḥaïli,**

'i, **dawaḥ, orri, yed**; (weep) **baroro, musanow, oi**; *v.c.*, **kaga barori, kaga oi**; — the auction of the camels, **ibka gela la ibinayo ku dawaḥ.**

cubit, *n.*, (measure) **dudun,—ki.**

cuckoo, *n.*, (a bird) **guguleh,—lihi, gumais,—ti.**

cucumber, *n.*, **ḥiyar,—ki.**

cud, *n.*, (of ruminants) **'alalnaḥsi,—gi, alya 'elis,—ki.**

cudgel, *n.*, (a heavy stick) **ḥarai** or **ḥara,—ihi.**

cultivate, *v.tr.*, **beir.**

cultivation, *n.*, **beir,—ti.**

cunning, *a.*, **ḥiyanah, ḥiyana leh, nejis,—ki.**

cunningness, *n.*, **ḥiyan,—ki, nejisnimo,—adi.**

cup, *n.*, (a small drinking vessel) **fujan** or **finjan,—ki.**

cup, *v.tr.*, (to bleed by scarification and a cupping-glass) **tob.**

cupping, **tobnin,—ti.**

cupping-glass, or the horn (cornet) used in the place of it, **tobin,—ki.**

cupper, **nin waḥ toba, nag waḥ tobta**; the cupper, **ninki waḥ tobijirai, nagti waḥ tobi jirtai.**

cupboard, *n.*, **kabad,—ki.**

curb, *n.*, (part of a bridle) **durmad,—di, hilḥad,—di.**

curd, *n.*, (coagulated part of milk) **gadod,—ki.**

curdle, *v.tr.* and *v.i.*, **fadisi, gadodi.**

cure, *n.*, (restoration to health) **boksis,—ki, boksin,—ti, boski,—gi.**

cure, *v.tr.*, (restore to health) **boksi**; be cured, **bokso**; he is cured, **boksadai.**

curiosity, *n.*, **fudul,—shi, gulad,—di.**

curious, *a.*, **gulawa,—ihi, fudul badan, fuduliah, fuduli,—gi.**

curl, *n.*, (a ringlet of hair) **sunarad,—di.**

curl, *v.tr.*, (form into ringlets) **maroji, marori, soh.**

curled, *a.*, **marorsan, sohan.**

curry, *v.tr.*, (dress leather) **yel naḥ**; (a kind of sauce used in India) **sanunad,—di** (*see* **kahri** *in* Suppt.).

curse, *n.*, **habar,—ki, inkar,—ti, na'lad,—di** or **na'dal,—shi.**

curse, *v.tr.*, **habar, inkar, na'dal**; *v.i.*, **Ilaḥ 'aï, Ilaḥ inkar.**

cursed, *a.*, **habaran, habar ḥaba, inkaran, inkar ḥaba, na'lad ḥaba.**

custom, *n.*, (habit) **dastur,—ti**; (tax) **'ashur,—ti.**

cut, *n.*, (a gash) **sarmo,—adi, sarsar,—ki.**

cut, *v.tr.*, **go, jar**; — into two parts, **kala go** or **goi**; — into many parts, **gogo, kala gogo**; — into small pieces (chop), **kidif**; — the skin, **sar, sarsar**; — meat, **ḥal**; *v.r.*, **iss go**; — for yourself, **goso, gogoso**; be —, **go.**

D.

dabble, *v.i.*, (in water) **galgalo.**

dagger, *n.*, (short sword) **bilawa** or **bilawai,—ihi.**

daily, *ad.*, **gor** or **kol walba**; every day, **'asho** or **malin walba.**

dale, *n.*, (a valley) **far,—ti.**

dam, *n.*, (a mole, a bank) **deir,—ki, ḥer,—ki.**

damage, *n.*, **da'an,—ki, ḫasaro,—adi.**

damn, *v.tr.*, (condemn to eternal torments in the future world) **'adab**; a damned man, **nin la 'adabai.**

damp, *a.*, (wet) **ḫoiyan.**

damp, *v.tr.*, (moisten) **ḫoi** or **ḫo.**

dance, *n.*, **'ayar,—ti**; a kind of —, **sa'ab,—ki.**

dance, *v.i.*, (move with measured steps) **'ayar**; *v.c.*, **'ayarsi.**

danger, *n.*, **'absi,—di, shil,—ki.**

dangerous, *a.*, **'absileh**; not —, **'absila, shilla.**

dare, *v.i.*, (be not afraid of) **ha biḫin, sababo**; do not —, **ka hisho, baḫ.**

dark, darkness, *n.*, **gudḥur,—ki.**

dark, *a.*, **gudḥur, gudḥuraḥ, madowba.**

dart, *n.*, (javelin) **waran,—ki.**

date, *n.*, (time of an event) **ayan,—ti**; (the fruit of the — tree) **timir,—ti**; nice and clean —, **barni,—di, hallawi,—gi, sa'maran,—ti**; wild dates, **maïdo,—adi.**

daughter, *n.*, **inan,—ti**; the — of Ali, **ina Ali.**

dawn, *n.*, (the break of day) **aroryo,—adi, gabbal so baḥ,—ki so beḥ.**

day, *n.*, **'asho,—adi, ayan,—ti, ḋarar,—ti, malin,—ti, 'ana mal,—ki, manta**; — and night, **haben iyo ḋarar**; make that in the —, **ḋararti waḥha fal**; a holiday, **ayan,—ti**; Sunday is not a work —, **aḥaddi ayan hauled ma aha**; — by —, **malin walba**; the next —, the following —, **malinta dambe, malintan so so'ota**; the third —, *or* the — after to-morrow, **sā dambe**; every other —, **malin daf**; to-day, this —, **manta, ḋararta, malinta**; all the — long, **manto leili**; the — before yesterday, **dorrād**; this many a —, **beri hore waḥa jirai**; this — week, **malintan totobadkeda**; the — after the — after to-morrow, **sākub** or **sākun.**

day-break, *n.*, **aroryo,—adi**; — light, **gabbal,—ki.**

dead, *a.*, **nin goai, nag godai**; he is —, **go**; the — men, **dadki ḋintai.**

deaf, *a.*, **ḋegala.**

deafness, *n.*, **ḋegalaan,—ti.**

dear, *a.*, (costly) **adag, gana' adag.**

death, *n.*, **ḋimad,—ki, ḋimasho,—adi, gēri,—di, mot,—ki**; (for beasts) **baḫti,—gi.**

debauch, *v.tr.*, (corrupt) **ḥumai, hatal, lumi.**
debauchee, *n.*, **nin ambabai** or **lumai** or **lunsan** or **iss lumiyai.**
debaucher, *n.*, **lumiyai,—yihi.**
debt, *n.*, **gashi,—gi, han,—ti.**
debtor, *n.*, **nin gashiyaisan** or **hamaisan.**
decalogue, *n.*, **tobanka wasiadod.**
decapitation, *n.* (*see* beheading).
decay, *v.i.*, (decline); his strength decays, **italkisa waḥba ka da'a.**
deceit, *n.*, (fraud) **hiyan,—ki, hiyano,—adi, hayan,—ki, halhal,—ki, hawayad,—ki.**
deceitful, *a.*, **hiyanah, hiyanaleh.**
deceive, *v.tr.*, **hiyanai, hayanai, hawaisi, halhal, hatal, dufi, dufso.**
deceived, *a.*, (man) **nin la hayanaiyai, halhalan**; be —, *v.i.*, **hawai, hatalan.**
deceiver, *n.*, (misleader) **mahawi, —gi.**
decide, *v.tr.*, (determine) **da'wadda no mari**; — our dispute, **honsigayaga ku tali.**
decision, *n.*, **talo,—adi.**
deck (of a ship), *n.*, **salaḥ,—hi.**
declivity, *n.*, (slope) **aror,—ki, babaḥ,—hi, gol,—shi, sibibaḥ,—di.**
decollate, *v.tr.* (*see* behead).
decrease, *v.tr.*, **din, hosaisi, yarai**; (grow less) **diman.**
decree, *n.*, (edict) **ḥukun,—ki**; what God has decreed, we must submit to, **waḥha Ebbahai ina yidahdo inainu yella bainu lehnahai.**
deed, *n.*, (action) **falnin,—ki,** or **—ti.**
deep, *a.*, **der, husur.**
deepen, *v.tr.*, **si derai.**
defamation, *n.*, **'eib,—ti, kashif, —ki.**
defame, *v.tr.*, **'eibai, kashif, mamus jebi.**
defeat, *v.tr.*, **eri.**
defence, *n.*, **beḥnin,—ti.**
defend, *v.tr.*, (protect) **ka 'eli, karaw**; *v.r.*, **iss karaw, iss ka guluf.**
defendant, *n.*, (in law) **mudali, —gi.**
defer, *v.tr.*, (refer to) **gābi, raji**; *v.i.*, **gāb, rāg.**
defile, *v.tr.*, (make foul) **doḥbai, uskagai, wasahai.**
defiled, *a.*, **uskagaisan, wasahaisan, hallawsan.**
defraud, *v.tr.* (*see* cheat).
defy, *v.tr.*, (challenge) **dandanso**; you must never — a fool, **nin wallan ha dandansan.**
deject, *v.tr.*, (cast down) **ka hulbi, hulubsi**; be dejected, **wahan, hulub, hulubsanaw.**
dejected, *a.*, **hulubsan, nin wahamai** or **ruhmai.**
dejection, *n.*, (melancholy) **hulub, —ki, wahan,—ki.**
delation, *n.*, **dignin,—ti.**
delay, *n.*, (deferring) **rāgnin,—ti.**
delay, *v.i.*, **rāg, gab**; *v.tr.*, **rāji, gabi.**
delectation, *n.*, **farḥad,—di, raḥo, —adi.**

delegate, *v.tr.*, (send) **dir.**

delight, *n.*, **farah,—hi, farhad, —di, raho,—adi.**

delight, *v.tr.*, (please) **ka farhi, rahaisi, rairaisi**; *v.i.*, (take — in) **farhi, raho, rahaiso, rairai, badad.**

delightful, *a.*, **farahsan.**

deliver, *v.tr.*, (give) **bihi**; (set free) **iss ka si da**; — up, **magalada iss ka bihi.**

delivery, deliverance, *n.*, (of goods) **dibnin,—ti**; (birth of a child) **umusho,—adi.**

delude, *v.tr.*, **dufi, dufso, halhal, hatal.**

deluge, *n.*, **dād,—ki, biyihi 'arrada rogai.**

demand, *v.tr.*, (ask) **sual, weidi, weidiso**; (claim) **hanan, shego.**

demand, *n.*, (question) **sual,—ki, weidis,—ki**; (claim) **hanan,—ki.**

demon, *n.*, (a spirit) **jini** or **jinni, —gi**; (the devil) **shaidan,—ki.**

demoniac, *n.*, **nin derderan.**

demonstrate, *v.tr.*, **rumai, tus.**

den, *n.*, (cavern) **boran,—ti, god, —ki.**

denial, *n.*, (negation, refusal) **dafirad,—di, didnin,—ti**; self-—, **iss ne'ban,—ti.**

denigrate, *v.tr.*, **hano, 'eibai.**

denominate, *v.tr.*. **maga' u bihi.**

denounce, *v.tr.*, **dein ka tur.**

denouncer, delator, denunciator, *n.*, **dein ka tur,—ki.**

denudate, *v.tr.*, **hawi.**

denunciation, *n.*, **dignin,—ti.**

deny, *v.tr.*, **dafir, did, ha la heshin, ha yelin**; he denied his God, **Ilahhisu dafirai.**

depart, *v.i.*, **tag, ka tag, gur**; when he departed, **gortu gurai** or **tagai.**

depart, departure, departing, *n.*, **gurnin,—ki, tegnin,—ki.**

deposit, *n.*, **amano,—adi.**

deposit, *v.tr.*, **aman, amano u dib, amano ku reb.**

deposition, *n.*, (in law) **marhati, —gi.**

deprive, *v.tr.*, (take off) **ka had, farhad iss u did**; be deprived, **'ala'al, da'anaw ha laga hado, bel.**

depth, *n.*, **derer,—ki, deran,—ti.**

descend, *v.i.*, **deg, so deg, ka so deg.**

descent, *n.*, (coming down) **degnin,—ti**; (process of lineage) **holo,—adi.**

desert, *n.*, **'idla,—di, 'idla'irsila, —di, miyi,—gi**; *a.*, **'idla, 'idlaah.**

design, *n.*, (a purpose) **dama',—hi.**

design, *v.tr.*, (purpose) **dama'.**

desire, *n.*, **donin,—ti, weidis,—ki.**

desire, *v.tr.*, **don, rab.**

desist, *v.i.*, **da, iss ka da.**

despair, *n.*, (loss of hope) **husad, —ki**; *v.i.*, **huso, iss ka huso.**

desperate, *n.*, **nin iss ka hustai.**

despatch, *v.tr.*, (send) **dir, dahso u dir.**

despise, *v.tr.*, **fududai.**

despoil, *v.tr.*, **ka ḩad, ka ḩad, rog.**
despoliation, *n.*, **rognin,—ti.**
despond, *n.* (*see* despair).
destiny, *n.*, (fate) **ayan,—ki, wed,—ki.**
destitute, *a.*, **nin la na'ai.**
destroy, *v.tr.*, **babihi, bii.**
destruction, *n.*, **babiis,—ki.**
detach, *v.tr.*, **kala kaḩai.**
detain, *v.tr.*, (stop, keep) **joji**; — him prisoner, **ninka ḩabsiga ku raji**; (hinder) **u dib.**
deter, *v.tr.*, **'absi, baji.**
determine, *v.tr.*, (decide) (**waḩhas**) **ku tali**; (influence the choice) **ugu tali**; *v.i.*, **dama'.**
determinate, *a.*, **nin dama'san,—ki, dama'sana.**
determination, *n.*, **talo,—adi.**
detest, *v.tr.*, (hate) **na'.**
detestation, *n.*, **ne'ban,—ti.**
detraction, *n.*, **ḩan,—ti.**
devastate, *v.tr.*, **rog.**
devastation, *n.*, **rognin,—ti.**
develop, *v.tr.*, **fur.**
deviate, *v.i.*; reason often deviates, **miyirku ḩajeila dauga wanaksan bu ka dua.**
device (*see* contrivance).
devil, *n.*, (evil spirit) **shaidan,—ki, 'ifrid,—ki.**
devotion, *n.*, **'ibādad,—di.**
devout, *a.*, **'ibādad ja'el, 'ibādad badan.**
dew, *n.*, **ďarab,—ki, sayaḩ,—hi.**
dewy, *a.*, **ďarabsan, sayaḩsan.**
dewlap, *n.*, (flesh hanging down from the throat of oxen) **'al,—shi** or **'ad,—di, ma'al,—shi.**
dialect, *n.*, **af,—ki.**
dialogue, *n.*, **hadal,—ki.**
diamond, *n.*, **almas,—ki, deman, —ki.**
diarrhoea, *n.*, **dabaḩau,—di**; this man has —, **ninkasi dabaddu ka baḩaya.**
dice, *n.*, **lafo,—ihi.**
die, *v.i.*, (lose life) **ďimo, go, bahti.**
difference, *n.*, (disparity) **kala mid,—di**; (dispute), what is the —? **maḩa idin deḩaiga?**
different, *a.*, **kala mid.**
dig, dig up, *v.tr.*, **ḩod.**
digging, *n.*, **ḩodnin,—ki.**
dik-dik, *n.*, (sand antelope) **sakaro** or **sagaro,—adi.**
dike, *n.*, (mound) **deir,—ki, ḩer, —ki.**
dilacerate, *v.tr.*, **dila'i.**
dilapidate, *v.tr.*, **lumi.**
diligent, *a.*, **hauled.**
diminish, *v.tr.*, **ďin, gābi, yarai, yaraisi, yaraiso.**
dine, *v.tr.*, **ďararo, ḩadai.**
dinner, *n.*, **ďararad,—ki, ḩadimo, —adi, 'unno,—adi.**
dip, *v.tr.*, (immerge) **ḩusi, dar, so dar**; (wet) **ḩoi.**
direct, *a.*, (straight) **ḩuman, tosan.**
direct, *v.tr.*, **tos u wad, tos u kaḩai**; — that letter to the governor, **warḩadda serkalka u gei** or **ku tosi.**
direction, *n.*, (line of motion) **ges,—ti, ďan,—ki.**
dirge, *n.*, (funeral song) **dikri,—di.**

dirt, *n.*, **uskag,—gi, wasaḥ,—hi, nijas,—ti, saboh,—di, doro, —adi**; — of the teeth, **huro, —adi.**
dirt, dirty, *v.tr.*, (foul) **uskagai, wasaḥai, sabai.**
dirty, *a.*, **uskagleh, uskagaisan, wasaḥaisan, nijasah, doro wein, saboh badan.**
disagree, *v.i.*, **did.**
disappear, *v.i.*, **libid.**
disappoint, *v.tr.*, **luggo.**
disappointed, *a.*, **nin lugoai**; be —, **lugo.**
disappointment, *n.*, **luggoyo,—adi.**
disarm, *v.tr.*, **furo, ninka furo, hubka ka ḥad.**
discern, *v.i.*; — between truth and falsehood, **run iyo bein kala so'o.**
discharge, *v.tr.*, (unload) **fur, ka so gur, ka so rog**; *v.r.*, **ka baḥ**; (dismiss) **eri.**
disciple, *n.*, **radis,—ki.**
discipline, *n.*, **ḥainun,—ki.**
discontent, *a.*, **weirweirsan**; be discontented, **weirweir**; *v.tr.*, **weirweiri.**
discontent, discontentment, *n.*, **weirweir,—ki.**
discontinue, *v.tr.*, **da, reb.**
discord, *n.*, **ḥonsimad,—ki.**
discourage, *v.tr.*, (dispirit) **ḥulubsi, ka ḥulbi**; be discouraged, **ruḥan.**
discouragement, *n.*, **ḥulub,—ki, wahan,—ki.**
discourse, *n.*, **hadal,—ki, hasawai,—ihi**; religious —, **masalo,—adi.**
discover, *v.tr.*, (disclose) **fur, ka ḥad, dabolka ka ḥad**; (make known) **ogaisi**; (find out) **hel.**
discovery, *n.*. **muḥ,—hi.**
discreet, *a.*, **fi'an, fojig.**
discretion, *n.*, **fi'nan,—ti, fojigan,—ti**; age of —, **garad,—ki.**
discussion, *n.*, (debate) **masalo,—adi**; an aggressive —, **ḥonsi,—gi.**
disease, *n.*, **bukan,—ki, 'udur,—ki**; contagious —, **saboh,—di** — of cows, **sambab,—ki**; — of sheep, **mindi 'iris dab**; — of lambs, **haḥlei**; — of kids, **jaḥleh**; — of sheep and goats, **dogor rugmad,—ki.**
disembowel, *v.tr.*, **doḥ.**
disembark, *v.i.*, **deg, so ḋaḋa'**; *v.tr.*, **deji, ka so deji, rog, ka so rog, ka so ḋaḋi'i, ka so gur.**
disgrace, discredit, dishonour, *n.*, **ḥishod,—ki**; *v.tr.*, **'eibai, ḥil.**
disguise, *v.tr.*, **midab dori** or **rog**; *v.r.*, **iss dori.**
disgust, *n.*, **yiḥyiḥsi,—gi, balaf,—ki**; *v.tr.*, **kaga yiḥyiḥsi.**
disgusted, *a.*, **yiḥyiḥsodai**; be —, **yiḥyiḥso, na'.**
disgusting, *a.*, **yiḥyiḥsan.**
dish, *n.*, (a vessel) **wel,—ki, se'ni,—gi**; — of wood, **ḥedo,—adi**; large —, **ḥedo balladan**; small —, **ḥobad,—di.**
dishonest, *a.*, **ḥayanoleh, ḥishodla.**
disherit, disinherit, *v.tr.*, **dairi.**
disjoin, *v.tr.*, **fuji, kala fuji.**

dislike, *n.*, **ma ja'alan,—ti**; — of food, **balaf,—ki**; *v.tr.*, **ha ja'alan, balfi.**
dismay, *n.*, (fright) **bahdin,—ti, nahadin,—ti**; *v.tr.*, **baji, kaga nihi.**
dismiss, *v.tr.*, **eri.**
dismount, *v.i.*, (alight) **deg.**
disobedience, *n.*, **dega adkan,—ti, asi,—gi.**
disobedient, *a.*, **dega adag, 'asiah.**
disobey, *v.tr.*, **'asi, did, ha mahlin, ha yelin.**
disperse, *v.tr.*, **firdi.**
display, *v.tr.*, (exhibit to sight or mind) **tus, ogaisi, muji.**
disprove, *v.tr.*, (confute) **beinta ku rumai, beini.**
dispute, *n.* (*see* discussion).
disrespectful, *a.*, **amus darran.**
disseminate, *v.tr.*, **firdi, iss ka saïd.**
dissension, disunion, *n.*, **honsimad,—di.**
dissolve, *v.tr.*, (melt) **dahaji, dalali**; *v.i.*, **dalal.**
dissuade, *v.tr.*, **ka du.**
distance, *n.*, **fogan,—ti**; a short —, **odrogad,—ki.**
distant, *a.*, **fog, shishai**; a — place, **mel fog.**
distinct, *a.*, **so'an, kala so'an, kala mid.**
distinction, *n.*, **sa'din,—ti.**
distinguish, *v.tr.*, **kala garo, kala so'o.**
distract, *v.tr.*, **jedi.**
distress, *n.*, (calamity) **ayan humo,—adi.**
distribute, *v.tr.*, **haibi, u haibi, sisi.**
distribution, *n.*, **haib,—ti.**
district, *n.*, (a quarter) **hafad,—di.**
disturb, *v.tr.*, **dāli.**
ditch, *n.*, (a trench) **hatah,—di, boran,—ti.**
dive, *v.i.*, **hus, muhur.**
divert, *v.tr.*, (entertain) **ayarsi, jalbebi**; *v.r.*, **jalbebo.**
divide, *v.tr.*, **kala go, haibi.**
divine, *a.*, **hodusah.**
division, *n.*, **haib,—ti.**
divorce, *n.*, **furnin,—ti**; *v.tr.*, **fur.**
divorced, *a.*, **furan**; a — woman, **nag furan.**
dizziness, *n.*, (whirl in the head) **madah wareir,—ki.**
dizzy, *a.*, **hof maduhhu warerayo**; (make giddy) **wareri.**
do, *v.tr.*, **fal, samai, yel**; all is done, **gidi damadai**; I know not what to — with them, **anigu wahan ku falo garan mayo.**
doctor, *n.*, (in physic) **hakim,—ki, dahdar,—ki.**
doctrine, *n.*, **dabta,—hi.**
dog, *n.*, **eï,—gi**; hyæna, **yeyi, di.**
dogma, *n.*, **dab,—ti.**
dolour, *n.*, **hanun,—ki.**
dome, *n.*, **kubad,—di.**
domestic (*see* servant).
doom, *n.*, **hisab,—ti.**
door, *n.*, **albab,—ki, illin,—k dah,—hi.**
double, *v.tr.*, **labai.**

doubt, *n.*, **mala,—ihi, wiswis,—ki**; *v.tr.*, **malai.**
doubtful, *a.*, **malaisan.**
dough, *n.*, **'ajin,—ti.**
dove, *n.*, **ḫamam,—ki**; turtle —, **ḫolli,—di.**
down, *n.*, (of birds) **hād,—di.**
down, *prp.* and *ad.*, **dāf,—ta, hos,—ta**; fall —, **ku da'**; go — the hill, **burta hos uga deg,** or **burta dāf,** or **burta hos u dāf**; go — the stream, **dur-durka si ra'**; come —, **so deg, ka so deg**; lie —, **jifso**; sit —, **fadiso**; the wind is —, **dabaishi da'dai**; the moon is —, **dayiḫhi de'**; the sun is —, **ḫorahdi da'dai**; up and —, **dul iyo hos, dushiyo hosta ba warwareg**; get —, **dada'**; make him get —, **so dadi'i.**
downcast, *a.*, (dejected) **nin ruḫ-mai**; be —, **ruḫan.**
dozen, *n.*, **derjin,—ki**; a — of eggs, **derjin ugaḫhanah.**
draff, *n.*, (sweepings) **ḫushash,—ki.**
drag, *v.tr.*, (draw) **so jid.**
dragon, *n.*, **mas dula, mas la-yanah.**
drain, *v.tr.*, (draw off water) **bi-yaha gudi** or **go** or **liḫ.**
draught, *n.*, (drinking at once) **antugo,—adi**; I drank it at a —, **antugo kelian ku liḫai.**
draw, *v.tr.*, (pull) **jid, jidjid, so** or **si jid, so jidjid, ka so biḫi**; — up water, **dowli**; — back, **dib u 'eli, dib u noḫo**; the night draws on, **habenki wa so so'oda**; my fate draws nigh, **geridaidi wa so so'ota** or **dowdahai**; (represent by picture) **sawir.**
drawing, *n.*, **sawir,—ki.**
dread, dreadfulness, *n.*, **baḫdin** or **baḫnin,—ti.**
dread, dreadful, *a.*, **'absileh, laga 'abso, laga boḫo.**
dream, *n.*, **dadab,—ki, riyo,—adi, riyod,—ki, tamanta,—ihi**; *v.i.*, **dadab, riyo.**
dress, *n.*, (cloth) **dar,—ki**; Somali —, **maro,—adi, ḫaili,—gi**; *v.tr.*, **huwi, ḫamiska u geli**; — yourself, **huwo, gas-ho.**
drink, *v.tr.*, **'ab, dan, fūd**; *v.c.*, **'absi, dansi**; — liquors, wine, **iss ku dufo**; do you — wine? **ma iss ku dufata?**
drive, *v.tr.*, (guide) **jid**; — away, off, **eri**; (compel) **ku eri**; — the nail in the table, **musmar-ka miska ku eri**; — out, **ka eri.**
drizzle, drizzling rain, *n.*, **'adar,—ki**; it drizzles, **'adar dah,** or **'irku wa 'adar dahaya.**
drogman, *n.*, **af ayen,—ki.**
drone, *n.*, (male bee) **ḫunḫani,—di.**
drop, *n.*, **dibi',—di, tifiḫ**; a — of water, **tifiḫ biyaah.**
dropsy, *n.*, (sickness) **bararshai,—ihi.**
drought, *n.*, **abār,—ti.**
drown, *v.tr.*, **hafi**; *v.r.*, **iss hafi**; be drowned, **hafo.**
drowning, *n.*, **hafin,—ti.**

drowsy (sleepy), *a.*, (**nin**) **hurda, damadsan, gama'san, lulo badan.**
drowsiness, *n.*, **lulo,—adi.**
drum, *n.*, **durban,—ki.**
drunk, *a.*, **saḫransan, liḫsan**; be —, **saḫran**; make him —, **kaga saḫrami**; make yourself —, **iss ku dufo.**
dry, *a.*, **ḫalalan, ingegan**; be —, **ḫalal, ingeg**; *v.tr.*, **ḫalaji, ḫalali, ingeji.**
duck, *n.*, **badag,—gi**; *v.tr.*, (immerse) **ḫusi, muḫuri.**
ducking, *n.*, **muḫurasho,—adi.**
due, *a.*; it is money —, **la'agtan amaḥ ba la igu lehyahai**; come in — time, **gor gorah kalai**, or **gor wanaksan kalai**; that letter is written in — form, **warḫadas si wanaksan ba la ḫorai**; *n.*, give everyone his —, **nin walba waḥhisa ha la siyo**; we must give the devil his —, **shaidanka wuḥhu lehyahai an sino.**
dug, *n.*, (udder, nipple) **'ando,—adi.**
dull, *a.*, **ḫulabsan, doḫon,—ki, sila'n** (for work); to make dictionaries is a — work; **iss ku daranka eraiyada wa shuḫul sila'n.**
dumb, *a.*, (mute) **'arrabla**; deaf and —, **'arrab iyo degа ba la**, or **'arrab lo dega la.**
dumbness, *n.*, **'arrablaan,—ti.**
dung, *n.*, (excrement) **har,—ki, saḫaro,—adi, us,—ki**; of camels, horses and cattle, **fanto,—adi, fulul,—ki** (when dry) and **falti,—di** (when liquid); — of camels, sheep and goats, **sālo,—adi.**
dust, *n.*, **amud,—di, habas,—ki, sesa** or **sisa,—di, sigo,—adi, sufur,—ti.**
duty, *n.*, (tax) **'ashur,—ti.**
dwarf, *n.*, **'ilin,—ki** (*mas.*), **'ilimad,—di** (*fem.*).
dwell, *v.i.*, **fadi, jir, jog, rugaiso.**
dwelling, *n.*, **rug,—ti, fadi,—gi, guri,—gi, jog,—gi.**
dye, *n.*, **sibaḥ,—hi**; *v.tr.*, **sibaḥ.**
dyer, *n.*, **nin sibaḥah.**
dying, *a.*, (expiring) **nin dimanaya**; he is in a — state, **wa nin hai ka si baḥaisa.**
dysentery, *n.*, **dabadig,—ti, ḥundur,—ti**; — of horses and cattle, **darfa', 'ihi.**

E.

each, *a.prn.*, **walba, waliba**; — one, **mid waliba, middiba, min.**
eager, *a.*, **daḫso badan.**
eagle, *n.*, **baḫaiya,—ihi**; (a kind of) **kolambai,—badi.**
ear, *n.*, **deg,—ti**; — lap, **dahal,—shi.**
early morning, *ad.*, **wā beri.**
earn, *v.tr.*, **ḫogso**; — your bread, **naftada u ḫogso.**
earnest, *a.*, **ḫog badan.**
earring, *n.*, **ilḫad,—di.**

earth, *n.*, amud,—di, 'arro,—adi,
'id,—di, ḍul,—ki, il,—ki,
dunyo,—adi, duni,—di, berri,
—gi; — quake, ḍul garir,—
ki.

earthen, *a.*, 'id laga samaiyai;
an — pot, adār,—ki.

ease, *n.*, haulyari,—di, ladnan,
—ti, barah,—hi; live at —,
haulyari ku jir; take your —,
barah u faḍi; give him some
—, inu naso u fasaḥ.

ease, *v.tr.*, (relieve) sahal; this
will — you, tan wa ku tadna-
hai.

easy, *a.*, sahalan.

east, *n.*, bari,—gi.

eat, *v.tr.*, 'un; be eaten, lugu
'un; it is eaten, la 'un.

ebb, *n.*, (low tide) 'ari,—di; *v.i.*,
'ari; the sea ebbs, baddi 'aridai.

echo, *n.*, dayan or diyan,—ki;
v.i., diyan or dayan.

eclipse (of the sun), *n.*, hosis or
hosas,—ki.

economize, *v.tr.*, daḥ, daḥo.

edge, *n.*, (cutting part of any
instrument) af,—ki; (brink)
girgir or jirjir,—ki, darur,—
ki, faraḥ,—hi.

educate, *v.tr.*, bar, kori, u tali;
be educated, kor; educated
with, la kor.

education, *n.*, barnin,—ti, koris,
—ki.

eel, *n.*, (a fish) ḥud,—ki.

efface, *v.tr.*, babihi, bii.

egg, *n.*, beid,—ki, ugaḥ,—hi,
ugaḥan,—ti.

eight, *num.*, sided,—di; eighth,
sidedad; one-eighth ($\frac{1}{8}$), fallad, rima'.

eighteen, *num.*, sided iyo toban,
—ki.

eighty, *num.*, sidehtan,—ki.

either, *prn.*, ama; either ... or
not, hadi ... iyo hadikaleh.

elbow, *n.*, ḥusul,—ki.

elder, *a.*, ka wein, kan kaleh ka
wein.

eldest, *a.* and *n.*, (first-born)
'urad,—ki.

elephant, *n.*, marodi,—gi.

eleven, *num.*, kowb iyo toban,—
ki; eleventh, kowb iyo tobnad,—ki, —ti.

eloquent, *a.*, af yaḥan,—ki, nin
af yaḥanah.

else, *a.*; Hassan or any one —,
Hassan ama nin kasta; no-
body — will come, nin kaleh
iman mayo, or nin kaleh o
ḍami ...; he did that when he
had nothing — to do, wuhu
falai kolku wuhu ḥabto o ḍan
wahyai; nowhere —, mel kaleh o ḍan tegi mayo; *ad.*,
ama, hadikaleh se; go your
ways, or — I will beat you,
daugaga ḥabso, hadikaleh se
ban usha ku la do'o.

emasculate, *v.tr.*, ḍufan.

embark, *v.i.*, dof, ful; *v.tr.*, dofi,
dofsi, fuli.

embarkation, *n.*, dof,—ki.

embassador (of peace), *n.*, ergo,
—adi; embassy, ergo,—adi

embers, *n.*, dambas kulul, raran,
—ki.

emblem, *n.*, **sumad,—di.**
embrace, *v.tr.*, (take a full hand) **ka buhso.**
emetic, *n.*, **dawada ka mantajisa.**
employ, *v.tr.*, (for work) **ninka shuhul u habo, shuhul si.**
employment, *n.*, **haul,—shi**; unemployed, **haul la, shuhul la.**
empty, *a.*, **babah, madan**; be —, **mado**; *v.tr.*, **madi.**
enchant, *v.tr.*, **fāl.**
enchanter, *n.*, **nin wah fal, nag wah fasha** (*fem.*).
enchantment, *n.*, **fāl,—ki.**
enclose, *v.tr.*, **od.**
enclosure, *n.*, **hero,—adi**; small —, **mahal herais,—ki, —ti**; make an —, **hero od.**
encourage, *v.tr.*, **la tosi, la hagaji, gesinimo u yel.**
end, *n.*, **ahir,—ki, idlan,—ti**; last — or breath (death), **ugu dambais,—ti**; the — of the year, **sanadda ahirkedi** or **idlanti**; go to the further — of the street, **surinku meshu ku go o tag**; he draws towards his —, **ugu dambaistisi bu dowyahai**; the ultimate — is death, judgment, heaven or hell, **kolki ugu dambaisai,** or **dugta ugu dambaisa wa gerri, iyo hisab, iyo janno ama' 'adab.**
endeavour, *v.i.*, **hausho, haul gal.**
endless, *a.*, **an idlan lahain, an idlan ahain.**
endure, *v.tr.*, (support) **hado, u samir.**
enemy, *n.*, **'adow,—gi, 'oll,—ki**; become, be — with, **la 'ollow** (*sing.*), **'olloba** (*plur.*).
energetic, *a.*, **nin hauled, hog badan.**
engage, *v.tr.*, (stake as a pledge) **u dibo, rahan**; (employ, enlist) **habso**; — in a bad way, **halhal, hatal.**
English, *a.*, **ingris,—ki**; an Englishman, **nin ingrisah**; — language, **af ingris.**
engrave, *v.tr.*, **harad.**
enlarge, *v.tr.*, **balladi, weinai.**
enlighten, *v.tr.*, **iftimi, shid, sirad, dabka bihi.**
enmity, *n.*, **'ollad,—di.**
enough, *ad.*, **bas**; that is —, **intasa ku filan**; — for me, **aniga igu filan**; — for us, **annaga nogu filan**; not —, **diman, nagu ma filla.**
enquire, *v.tr.*, **weidi.**
enrage, *v.tr.*, (provoke) **kaga 'adaisi.**
ensign, *n.*, **'alan,—ki**; — staff, **hori 'alan,—ki.**
enslave, *v.tr.*, **bidai ka dig.**
entangle, *v.tr.*, **iss ku mergi**; be entangled, **iss ku mereg.**
entanglement, *n.*, **mereg,—gi.**
enter, *v.i.*, (come or go in) **gal, so gal**; — for, **u so gal**; *v.c.*, **geli, so geli.**
entertain, *v.tr.*, (converse) **hasawi**; (treat at table) **hadaisi**; (amuse) **jalbebi.**
entertainment, *n.*, **hasawai,—ihi; diafad,—di, jalbeb,—ti.**
entice, *v.tr.*, **dufso, halhal, hatal, sasab.**

enticement, *n.*, **dufsasho,—adi, ḫalḫal,—ki, sasabasho,—adi.**
entire, *a.*, **daman, dan, dami, idil, leil.**
entrails, *n.*, **uslaho** or **usloho,—adi, uslahais,—ti.**
entrance, *n.*, (entry) **illin,—ki.**
entrap, *v.tr.*, (ensnare) **dab.**
entreat, *v.tr.*, (solicit) **bari.**
enumerate, *v.tr.*, **midmid u tiri.**
envelop, *v.tr.*, **dudub.**
envelope, *n.*, (a cover, wrapper) **kish,—ki.**
envious, *a.*, **ḥasid,—ki.**
envy, *n.*, **ḥasidnimo,—adi, ḥisti,—gi.**
epilepsy, *n.*, **suḥdin,—ti**; have a fit of —, **suḥ.**
epiploon, *n.*, **haïd alolo,—adi, haïd mindi'iro,—adi.**
epithet, *n.*, **nanaïs,—ti.**
epoch, epocha, *n.*, **ayamo,—ihi, tariḫ,—hi.**
equal, *a.*, **iss ku mid, iss ku siman, iss leh eg**; not —, **iss ku mid ma aha, iss ma leh eka.**
eradicate, *v.tr.*, **ruji.**
eradication, *n.*, **rujin,—ti, rujis,—ki.**
eremite (hermit), *n.*, **nin goniah, 'idla fadiya, 'idla degah.**
err, *v.i.*, **ḫatalan, iss ḫatal, ḫawai.**
error, *n.*, **ḫatalad,—di.**
escape, *n.*, **baḥsad,—ki, ya',—hi**; *v.tr.*, **ka baḥso**; we cannot — temptation, **ḥuffinta ka baḥsan kari maino**; *v.i.*, **baḥso, ya'a** (used in the *plur.*).
espouse, *v.tr.*, **gurso.**
espousals, *n.*, **gur,—ki, gursad, ki.**
espy, *v.tr.* and *v.i.*, **so ilalai, ilalo tag.**
establish, *v.tr.*, **ka so sar**; — the true religion, **dinta runtaah ka so sar.**
esteem, *n.*, **murwad,—di**; *v.tr.*, **murwad.**
estimate, *n.*, (value set) **ḫadari,—gi.**
eternal, *a.*, **had iyo gor, dayim.**
eternity, *n.*, **dayiman** or **dayimis,—ki.**
European, *n.*, **frenji,—gi.**
eunuch, *n.*, **nin dufanan, koron,—ki.**
evaporate, *v.tr.* and *v.i.*, **galibiḥi**; the sun evaporates water, **ḫorahdu biyaha wa galibiḥisa**; the fire evaporates water, **dabku biyaha wa galibiḥiya** or **galibasha.**
evaporation, *n.*, **galibaḥ,—ihi.**
evening, *n.*, **galab,—ti, 'asar,—ki, maḫrib,—ki**; come at —, **galab** or **galabta kalai.**
ever, *a.*, **weli.**
everlasting (*see* eternal).
every, *a.*, **kasta, walba**; everywhere, **mel kasta, mel walba.**
evidence, *n.*, **marḫati,—gi.**
evident, *a.*, **muḫda, muḫata** (*fem.*).
evil, *n.*, **ḥuman,—ti, shar,—ki**; — doer, **layan,—ki**; do — to him, **u ḥumai**; what — have I done to you? **maḥan kugu ḥumaiyai?**

ewe, *n.*, **lah̤,—di, sabein,—ti.**
examine, *v.tr.*, **beji, hubso, tasho, so tasho, si tasho.**
except, *prp.*, **mahae, mahe.**
exchange, *n.*, **d̈afsasho,—adi, d̈afsis,—ki**; *v.tr.*, **d̈afi, d̈afso, dori, dorso.**
excoriation, *n.*, **diran,—ki**; excoriated, **diran.**
excrement, *n.*, **us,—ki.**
excrescence, *n.*, (of flesh in a sore) **ad̈ad̈,—ki.**
excuse, *n.*, **samah̤,—ihi, h̤al, —ki**; (pardon) *v.tr.*, **'affi, samah̤.**
exhaust, *v.tr.*, (drain) **gud̈i, mad̈i**; be exhausted, **ruh̤an.**
exhibition, *n.*, **tusnin,—ti, mujnin,—ti.**
exile, *v.tr.*, **dairi**; *n.*, **dairis,—ki**; exiled, **dairsan.**
exist, *v.i.*, **jir**; the soul is certain of her existence, **naftu wa h̤ubta inai jirto.**
existing, *a.*, **nol.**
expect, *v.tr.*, (wait for) **sug, u jed, u kadi, u jog, u jogso, ninka d̈aur.**
expectation, *n.*, **sugnin,—ti.**
expel, *v.tr.*, (drive away) **eri, safiri** or **masafiri, ka sar**; expelled, **safirsan.**
expend, *v.tr.*, **bih̤i.**
expense, *n.*, **bih̤is,—ki, h̤araj, —ki**; useless —, **h̤asaro,—adi.**
experience, *n.*, **ah̤li,—gi.**
experiment, *n.*, **bejis,—ki.**
expiate (*see* atone).
expiation, *n.*, **tobad ken,—ki.**
expire, *v.tr.*, **ugu dambaistada neifso.**
explain, *v.tr.*, **muji.**
explaining, explanation, *n.*, **mujnin.**
explicate, *v.tr.*, (disentangle) **furfur.**
explorator, *n.*, **nin magalada so deh̤ mara o ilalaiya,** or **nin magalada ilalaiya.**
explore, *v.tr.*, **ilali, so ilalai.**
explosion, *n.*, **h̤arah̤,—ihi.**
export, *v.tr.*, **magalada ka sar o Aden u sar.**
exportation and importation, *n.*, **wah̤ha magalada so gala iyo wah̤ha magalada ka baha.**
expose, *v.tr.*, (show) **muji, tus**; — a child, **dabsi**; — your life, **naftada ku sabab.**
exposure, *n.*, (of goods) **mujis,—ki.**
express, *v.tr.*, **u sheg.**
expressly, *ad.*, **ogan u**; I did that —, **ogan ban u falai.**
expulse (*see* expel).
expulsion, *n.*, **masafiris,—ki.**
extend, *v.tr.*, (stretch out) **so bih̤i, tikso**; (enlarge) **weinai**; *v.i.*, **gad̈**; the Somali country extends as far as the Abyssinian, **dulka Somalida kan Abshantu gad̈a.**
exterior, *n.*, **dibad,—di.**
extinction, *n.*, **idlan,—ti, babiis, —ki.**
extinguish, *v.tr.*, **bah̤ti, babii, id̈lai.**
extort, *v.tr.*, **ka dufo, ka h̤ad, ka h̤og, muh̤uni.**

extortion, *n.*, **muḥuno,—adi.**
extract, *v.tr.*, **ka so biḥi.**
extraordinary, *a.*, **yaban, yabsan, yablch, yab ḥaba.**
eye, *n.*, **il,—shi**; eyes, **indo,—ihi**; — ball, the pupil, **isha inankeda,** or **isha wilkeda, indaha wilkoda** (*plur.*); — beam, glance, **daimo,—adi, egmo,—adi**; — brow, **kod,—ki**; — drop, **ilmo,—adi.**
black-eyed, *a.*, **nin inda madow**; pink-eyed, **nin inda yaryar**; grey-eyed, **nin inda owlan**; one-eyed, **ḥof'awaran, illa.**
one-eyed person, *n.*, **'awar, —ki.**
be one-eyed, *v.i.*, **'awarnaw, 'awarahaw, 'awaran, 'awar noḥo.**
eye-lash, *n.*, **isha balkedi, indaha balkoda** (*plur.*).
eye-lid, *n.*, **ḥirib,—ti**; upper —, **ḥirib sarai,—ti**; lower —, **ḥirib hosai.**
eye-sight, *n.*, **arag,—gi.**
eye-sore, *a.*, **isha bog ku leh.**
eye-tooth, *n.*, **mi'i,—di**; — teeth, **mi'iyo, mi'iyihi.**
iris of the eye, *n.*, **buh,—di, isha buhdeda, indaha buhdoda.**
cornea of the eye, *n.*, **isha 'alosheda 'ad, indaha 'aloshoda 'ad** (*plur.*).

F.

face, *n.*, **weiji,—gi, hagag,—gi, jah,—hi, fayo,—ihi.**
facile, *a.*, **jilai'san, shuḥul jilai'san, saḥalan.**
fagot, *n.*, **ḥidmo ḥabaah,—adi, ḥabaha ahaid.**
fact, *n.*, **falnin,—ti, waḥ la falai**; take him in the — (act), **runta ku ḥabo**; matter of —, **đab,—ti**; it is a matter of —, **wa đabti.**
fail, *v.i.*; he has failed to do his duty, he must be dismissed, **waḥ hun bu falai e shuḥulka ha laga saro**; the day begins to —, **đarartu wa damanaisa** or **libdaisa.**
faint, *a.*, **suḥsan, weidsan**; *v.i.*, **weïdow, suḥ.**
fainting, *n.*, **weïd,—ki**; — fit, **suḥdin,—ti.**
fair, *a.*, **baḥsan, ḥuroḥsan, shuban**; — sex, **dumar,—ki.**
fairness, *n.*, **'adan,—ti, —ki.**
fairy, *n.*, **ḥuliad,—di.**
faith, *n.*, (belief) **amin,—ki, din, —ta**; (fidelity) **đar,—ti.**
faithful, *a.*, **amina,—ihi, nin aminah.**
faithless, *a.*, **đar jiđ,—ki.**
fakir, faquir, *n.*, **fakir,—ki**; go and beg always for the same thing, **ku si fakirow.**
fall, *n.*, **kufnin,—ti**; heavy —, **hambaro,—adi**; he is dead of his —, **kufnintisi bu u đintai**; *v.int.*, **da', kuf**; — on the

ground, **dulka ku da'**; — forward, **hor u kuf**; — backward, **dib u kuf**; — headlong, **madah u** or **ku kuf**; — from, **ku so da'**; that fell into his mind, **wahhasi u da'dai**; — in, on, **ku da', ku dufo**; — heavily, **hambarow**; *v.c.*, **kufi leged, ku rid, hambarai.**

fallacious, *a.*, **hiyano leh.**

falling, *n.*, (of the fleece or hair of animals) **dogor rugmad,—ki**; (of a man knocked down) **gagab,—ki.**

fallow beast, *n.*, **ugad,—di.**

false, *a.*, **beinah**; prove —, **beini.**

falsehood, falseness, *n.*, **bein,—ti, halalif,—ti, hawayad,—di.**

falter (*see* stammer).

family, *n.*, **has,—ki, rer,—ki.**

famine, *n.*, **abār,—ti, dihal,—ki.**

famish, *v.tr.*, (starve) **abārai, dihali**; *v.i.*, (die of hunger) **abār** or **abarow, dihalanow.**

fan, *n.*, **marawahad,—di**; (instrument for winnowing grain) **masaf,—ki.**

fancy, *n.*, **husus,—ti, miyir,—ki.**

fang, *n.*, (tusk) **mi'i,—di.**

fantasia, *n.*, **dabaldeg,—gi.**

far, *ad.*, **fog, mel fog**; farther, **ka fog**; farthest, **ugu fog**; go so —, **sidas u fogow**; you must learn so —, **sidas u baro**; so — as I can guess, **sidas u malain karo**; how —? **intai jirta?** how — is it thither? **meshasi intai ino jirta?** do you know how — he has gone away? **intu fogadai ma garanaisa?** go —, **fogow**; go farther, **si fogow**; — off, away, **jidai.**

farewell! *int.*, **amana Allah! nabad gelyo! salamad!**

fart, *n.*, **duso,—adi**; *v.i.*, **dus.**

fashion, *n.*, **dastur,—ti**; this is our —, **haragadayada wa 'ainka.**

fast, *n.*, (fasting) **son,—ki**; *v.i.*, **son**; *a.*, (firm) **adag**; as — as a mountain, **sida bur o kalehah u adag**; (speedy) **dahso u so'o**; a — *or* deep sleep, **hurdo wein**; he is in a — sleep, **hurdo wein bu ku jira**; *ad.*, hold —, **heji, ād u heji**; boil —, **ād u kari**; do not write so —, **dahso ha u horin.**

fasten, *v.tr.*, **adkai, hid.**

fastening, fastness, *n.*, **adkan,—ti.**

faster, *n.*, (a fasting man) **saïm,—ki, nin saïmah, nin soman.**

fat, *a.*, **shilis, buran, nahsan**; become —, **nah**; *n.*, **barur,—ti**; **dayi,—gi**; the — of the tail, **badi,—di.**

fate, *n.*, (destiny) **ayan,—ki, wed,—ki.**

father, *n.*, **abba,—ihi**; (for religious or priests) **badri,—gi**; — in-law, **soddog,—gi.**

fatigue, *n.*, **'ato,—adi, dāl,—ki.**

fatigued, *a.*, **'ataisan, dālan, dashan**; be —, **'atow, dāl.**

fault, *n.*, **hatalad,—di, tahsir,—ti, dembi,—gi.**

favour, *n.*, (partiality) **eho,—adi, ehasho,—adi**; *v.tr.*, (be partial) **eho, ka eho.**

fawn upon, *v.tr.*, **ḥayaḥayai.**
fawning, *n.*, (flattery) **ḥayoḥayo, —adi.**
fear, *n.*, (dread) **'absi,—di, baḥdin,—ti**; *v.i.*, (be afraid) **'abso, baḥ**; *v.tr.*, (frighten) **'absi, ka baḥo** or **boḥo, baji.**
fearless, *a.*, **'absila.**
feast, *n.*, **'id,—di, siyaro,—adi, siyarad,—di**; make a —, **'id, siyar.**
feather, *n.*, **bāl,—ki.**
feature (*see* face).
fecal matters, *n.*, **saḥaro,—adi, ḥar,—ki.**
fecundity, *n.*, **dalasho,—adi.**
feed, *n.*, (food) **sor,—ti, sabbar, —ki, soryo,—adi, masruf** or **musruf,—ki**; *v.tr.*, **sor, sabbar, sabbaro**; — the cattle, **daḥgei, daji**; — your family, **masruf**; *v.i.*, he lives on fruits, **mido bu ku nolyahai**; he lives like a Somali, **sida dadka Somalied bu u 'una.**
feel, *v.i.*, **tabo**; *v.c.*, **tabsi**; *v.tr.*, I — a great pain, **hanun ḥun ba i haya**, or **ād ban u ḥanunsanaya**; how do you — yourself? *or* how do you do? **sidad tahai? maḥad jogta? maḥad falaisa.**
feeling, *n.*, **tabasho,—adi**; having the same feelings, **iss ku talo**; have a bad — against, **ḥonso.**
felicitate (*see* congratulate).
felicity, *n.*, **faraḥ,—ihhi, raḥo,—adi, raḥad,—di.**
fell, *v.tr.*, (cut down) **go, jifi, leged.**
fellow, *n.*, **wehel,—ki.**
female, *n.*, **didig** or **dadig,—gi** *a.*, **didig.**
fence, *n.*, **ḥero,—adi, od,—di** *v.tr.*, (inclose) **od.**
ferment, *n.*, **ḥamir,—ki.**
ferocious, *a.*, **dadḥunah.**
ferocity, *n.*, **dadḥun,—ki.**
fertile, *a.*, **barwaḥaisan**; fertile place, **ramash,—ki.**
fertility, *n.*, **barwaḥo,—adi.**
fervent, *a.*, **kulul, 'ibādad badan.**
fester, *v.i.*, (grow virulent) **'alid** or **'alir.**
fetch, *n.*, (device) **ḥikmad,—di**; *v.tr.*, **so ḥad, la kalai, ken, gei.**
fetid, *a.*, **ḥudmun, ur ḥudmun.**
fetter, *v.tr.*, (bind) **silsiladai, silsilad ku jebi, ḥeg, dabdabar, shekal, ḥofali, iss weidari, settai.**
fetters, *n.*, (trammels) **ḥofal,—ki, dabar,—ki, ḥeg,—gi, shekal** or **shakal,—ki, setto,—adi, iss weidar,—ki.**
feud, *n.*, **dirir,—ti, ḥonsi,—gi, 'ollad,—di.**
fever, *n.*, **daḥan,—ti**; a violent or burning —, **fallad ḥun** or **kulul**; fit of —, **ḥadḥadyo,—adi.**
field, *n.*, **doho,—adi, ḥaḥlad,—di.**
fiend, *n.*, (devil) **'ifrid,—ki.**
fierce, *a.*, **dad'una**; a — camel, **rati dad'unah,—gi, dad 'unka aha.**
fife, *n.*, **bibileh,—ihi.**
fifteen, *num.*, **shan iyo toban,—ki.**

fifth, *num.*, **shanad,—ki, —di.**
fifty, *num.*, **konton,—ki**; fiftieth, **kontomad,—ki, —di.**
fig, *n.*, **berde** or **berda,—ihi, darai,—gi.**
fight, *n.*, **dagal,—ki, dirir, werar,—ki, ḥarbi,—gi**; *v.tr.* and *v.i.*, **dirir, dagalan, werar, ḥarbi, la dirir, la dagalan, la ḥarbi waḥ ka werar**; — for, **ku taba'.**
figure, *n.*, (shape) **surrad,—di, midab,—ki**; — of a calf, **maḥar,—ki**; — of a camel, **maharsar,—ki**; *v.tr.*, (form into a shape) **midab u yel.**
file, *n.*, (tool) **sofa,—ihi**; *v.tr.*, **sofai.**
fill, *v.tr.*, **buḥi, buḥso, so ɗami, dar, so dar.**
filled, *a.*, **buḥsan**; be —, **buḥsan, buḥsanow.**
filly, *n.*, **darman,—ti.**
film, *n.*, (of the brain) **ḥub,—ki**; our brain is hidden by a thin pellicle, **mas ka'denu ḥub bai ku ḥarsontahai.**
filter, *n.*, (strainer) **ɗarur,—ti**; *v.tr.*, **ɗarur.**
filth (*see* dirt).
fin, *n.*, **bāl,—ki.**
find, *v.tr.*, **hel**; do not —, **wah**; — out thy food, **helhel, ḥab.**
fine, *a.*, **baḥsan, huroḥsan, ḥurohbadan**; *n.*, (penalty) **ḥasir,—ki**; *v.tr.*, set a — upon, **ḥasir.**
finger, *n.*, **far,—ti**; the fore —, **murdiso** or **murudsato,—adi**; middle —, **far doḥo,—adi**; ring —, **'awo,—adi, fadumo,—adi**; little —, **far yaro,—adi.**
finish, *v.tr.*, **ɗamai, ɗamaiso, idlai, ḥalas, lāso.**
finished, *a.*, **ɗamā, ɗamān, ḥalas**
fire, *n.*, **dab,—ki**; a great —, **og,—ti**; — brand, **ḥori dableh, duḥul dambasleh**; light of the —, **ilais,—ki**; *v.tr.*, set on —, **dabka shid**; — that house, **aḥalka gub**; set on —, **dabka belbelli** or **ololi** or **nolai.**
fire-stone, *n.*, **dardar,—ki**; the three stones on which they place the boiler are called, **dardaro,—adi.**
fire-tongs, *n.*, **birrḥab,—ki.**
firm, *a.*, **adag, tāgan**; be —, **tāgnow, adkaw, iss adkai.**
firmness, *n.*, **adkan,—ti, tāg,—ti.**
firmament, *n.*, **'ir,—ki.**
first, *num.*, **kowad,—ki, —di, horai, kan horai**; the — covenant, **aḥdigi horai**; the — man of the town, **ninka magalada ugu horaiya**; be the —, **ugu** or **u horai**; go —, **horai**; *ad.*, **horta, hor, gorti horai**; go —, **hor u so'o**; — begot, *or* — begotten, **'urad,—ki, ki u hor ɗashai.**
fish, *n.*, **kalun,—ki**; saw —, **daba safan,—ki**; *v.tr.*, catch —, **jilab, so jilab, jilabo**; where did you catch that —? **haggad ka so jilabatai tā?**
fisher, fisherman, *n.*, **sayad,—ki.**
fishing, *n.*, **jilabasho,—adi.**

fishing-boat, *n.*, **kalumaisato,—adi.**

fist, *n.*, **tantomo,—adi, tumujo, —adi**; *v.tr.*, **tanton, tumujai.**

fistula lacrymalis, *n.*, **il yaro,—adi.**

fit, *a.*; he is — for that employment, **isagu hausha wa ḥaban kara**; it is not — for you to speak so, **adigu inad sida u hadashid ku ma eka**; he is — for war, **dagal wa ka adag yahai**; *v.tr.*, (suit); that shirt fits me very well, **ḥamiskasi wa i leh egyahai**; *n.*, sudden — of burning fever, **ḥando,—adi.**

five, *num.*, **shan,—ti.**

fix, *v.tr.*, (make fast) **dab, tāg**; — a day, **malin ballan**; — your dwelling there, **fadigaga halká ka d's** or **ka sar**; — a handle, **dāb ku joji.**

fixity, *n.*, **tāg,—ti.**

flag, *n.*, **'alan,—ki**; — staff, **ḥori 'alan,—ki.**

flagellation, *n.*, **karbash,—ki, ulais,—ki, sergad,—di, gara-'is,—ki.**

flageolet, *n.*, **bibileh,—lihi.**

flake, *n.*, (flock of wool) **rifan,—ki**; — of fire, **dinbil,—shi, bilig,—ti.**

flame (*see* blaze).

flash (of lightning), *n.*, **danab,—ki.**

flask, *n.*, (kind of bottle) **weiso, —adi.**

flat, flatten, *v.tr.*, **banai, sin, iss ku sin**; *a.*, **banan, siman.**

flatter, *v.tr.*, **sasab, sasabo, ḥaya-ḥayai.**

flattery, *n.*, **sasab,—ki**; **sasaba-sho,—adi.**

flavour, *n.*, **dadan,—ki.**

flay, *v.tr.*, (strip off) **dubka ka biḥi, haragga** or **santa ka mudhi.**

flea, *n.*, **injirbodo,—adi, takfi,—gi.**

flee, *v.i.*, (to fly) **baḥ.**

fleece, *n.*, **dogor,—ti.**

flesh, *n.*, **hilib,—ki, 'ad,—ki, jid,—ki, jimid,—ki.**

flexibility, *n.*, **lih,—hi.**

flexible, *a.*, **liḥah**; a — stick, **ul liḥah.**

flier, *n.*, **nin 'araraya, nin baḥ-sanaya.**

flight, *n.*, **'arar,—ki, baḥsi,—gi, ya',—hi.**

fling, *v.tr.*, **rid, rido, ku rid.**

flint (silex), *n.*, **dagaḥ madow, —gi, du'un,—ti.**

float, *v.i.*, **sabai**; floating, *n.*, **sabais,—ki.**

flock, *n.*, (of people) **guto,—adi, urur,—ki, fadi,—gi**; a — of horses, **fadi fardaah,** or **kadin fardaah**; a — of cows, neat cattle, **fadi lo'ah,** or **kadin lo'ah**; (they say a'so for) a — of horses, **fardo,—ihi**; a — of cows, **lo',—di**; a — of goats and sheep, **adi,—gi**; a — of wild *or* fallow beasts, **raḥan,—ti**; a junction of flocks, **iss ku daran,—ki**; a — of young sheep, **maḥal,—shi**; — of wool, **rifan,—ki**; *v.i.*, (gather into flocks) **urur, iss urur.**

flog (beat), *v.tr.*, **dengadai, ḥawdi,**

karbash, ḫaisaramai, serwanai, jedal, lamai sergadai, ulai.

flogging, *n.*, **denged,—ki, ḥawdis, —ki, karbash,—ki, jedal,—ki, sergad,—ki, sergan,—ti.**

flood, *n.*, **dād,—ki.**

floor, *v.tr.*, **loḥyada aḫalka ku sarab.**

flooring, *n.*, **alwaḥda sarabkeda.**

flour, *n.*, **bur,—ki, daḫir,—di, saren,—ki.**

flourish (bloom, blossom), *v.i.*, **ubaḥaiso, uboḥo**; this tree is blooming, **gedkasi wa ubaḥnaya.**

flow, *v.i.*, **baḥ, dādi**; the bucket flows (leaks), **baldigi wa dādinaya**; the tears —, **ilma ka horaisa** or **ka dareiraisa** or **ka da'aisa**; the tide flows and ebbs, **mayaddu wa buḥsanta o 'arida.**

flower, *n.*, **ubaḥ,—ihi, man,—ki.**

flue (soft down or fur), *n.*, **yiliḥ, —di.**

flux and reflux, *n.*, **maujad,—di, mayad,—di.**

fly, *n.*, (an insect) **diḥsi,—gi**; *v.i.*, (flee, run away) **'arar, baḫo, baḥso, ya'a** (*plur.*); (for beasts) **bub**; *v.tr.*, sleep flies the wretched, **hurdo dad ḥun wa daaisa**; he was fain to — the Somali land, **wa la muḥurunshai inu bilad Somalied ka yimado.**

foal, *n.*, (of horses) **darman,—ki** or **—ti**; (of cows and camels) **ḫan,—ki.**

foam (froth), *n.*, **ḥumbo,—adi, abur,—ki**; *v.i.*, the camel foams, **aurku abur bu ke'inaya** or **ke'iya**; make —, **kaga ḥumbaisi.**

fog, *n.*, **'iro,—adi.**

foggy, *a.*, **'iraisan.**

foist, *n.*, **duso,—adi**; *v.i.*, **dus.**

fold, *n.*, (enclosure for sheep) **ḥero,—adi**; small —, **edeg,—gi**; (a plait) **labnin,—ti, dubnin,—ti**; *v.tr.*, (double, plait) **dub, lab, lablab**; (gather sheep into the —) **kuriyai**; — in form of a ball, **kus.**

folk *or* folks, *n.*, **dad,—ki.**

follow, *v.tr.*, **ra', so ra', radi, ninka radkisa gur**; *v.i.*, **daba so'o, ka daba kalai, ka dambai.**

follower, *n.*, **radis,—ki.**

following, *a.*, **dambai.**

folly, *n.*, **walli,—di, iss walwal, —ki**; the follies of the world, **iss walwalka dunida.**

food, *n.*, **sor,—ti, 'unno,—adi, sabbar,—ki, masruf,—ki, hambo,—adi, soryo,—adi.**

fool, *n.*, foolish, *a.*, **nin wallan, washa, walwallan, doḫon,—ki, na's,—ki, miyirla.**

foolishness, *n.*, **miyirlaan,—ti**; he plays the fool, **wa iss walwallaya.**

foot, *n.*, **'ag,—ti**; from head to —, **'agti ila madaḥha**; he walks barefooted, **kabalaan bu ku so'oda**; go on —, **'aga ku so'o**; — by —, **talabo-talabo**; at the —, **'agta**; put your feet in, **illo**; the — of the mountain, **burta 'agteda**; broad-footed, **nin 'aga wein**; — path, *n.*, **dau,—gi, jid,—ki, marin, —ki**; sole of the —, *n.*, **'agta 'ad, 'agti 'adaid**; —step, *n.*, **rad,—ki**; sound of the steps, **jān,—ti.**

for, *prp.*, **u**; — your sake, **daradda, awada**;—us, **daradden, awaden**; — fear, he did not do that, **bahdin bu waḥ la ḥaban wahyai**; — the present we have enough, **haddadan jogta nagu filan**; — ever, **gor iyo galab, weligi**; they left him — dead, **inu dintai ba la modai, o la iss kaga yimi**; how much did you sell it —? **imisad sisai?** whom are you —? **kuma** or **aya ku leh?** *conj.*, do not meddle with him, for he is a cheat, **ha ra'in ninka, wa nin ḥiyanahah.**

forbear, *v.i.*, (abstain) **iss ka da**; — to swear, **iss ka da darta.**

forbearance, *n.*, (patience) **dulḥadasho,—adi.**

forbid, *v.tr.*, **u did.**

forbidden, *a.*, **waḥ la iss u didai, waḥ la iss ka ḥukumai.**

force, *n.*, (vigour) **adkan,—ti, tāg,—ti**; (violence) **ḥog,—gi, ḥasab,—ti, muḥuno,—adi**; (power) **itāl,—ki**; the — of truth, **itālka runta**; *v.tr.*, (oblige) **ḥasab, muḥuni**; obtain by —, **dufo, so dufo**; — down, **hos u muḥuni**; — out, **ka muḥuni.**

ford, *n.*, **gudubsino,—adi**; look for a —, **gudubsi.**

fore-arm, *n.*, **dudun,—ki.**

forebode (*see* foretell).

forefather, *n.*, **abbayal,—shi.**

fore-finger (*see* finger).

foregoing, *a.*, **horai.**

forehead, *n.*, **fod,—di, jah,—hi.**

foreigner, *n.*, **marti,—di, nin rerod,—ki, shishaiyai,—ihi, nin shishaiyaiah.**

fore-leg, *n.*, **jeni,—gi.**

forenoon, *n.*, **barḥin,—ti, barḥad,—di, barḥo,—adi, gelin hore.**

forepart, *n.*, **bar,—ki,** or **barki sarai.**

foresaid, *a.*, **horai lo yidi.**

forest, *n.*, **dud,—di, sharer,—ki, mel shareran, meshi sharereraid**; plant a —, **shareri.**

foretell, *v.tr.*, **waḥ sheg, fali.**

foreteller, *n.*, **waḥ sheg,—gi, nin waḥ shega.**

foretelling, *n.*, **waḥ sheg,—gi.**

forfeit, *v.tr.*, **hallai**; that girl has forfeited her honour, **gabaddasi namuskedi hallaisai.**

forge, *v.tr.*, **tun**; forged, **tuman.**

forget, *v.tr.*, **ilaw, ilow.**

forgetfulness, *n.*, **ilowsho,—ihi.**

forgive, *v.tr.*, **'affi, samaḥ.**

forgiveness, *n.*, **'affi,—gi, samaḥ, —di,** or **samḥad,—di.**

fork, *n.*, **muda',—'ihi, faudal faroleh.**

forlorn, *a.*, **la na'ai.**

form, *n.*, (shape) **midab,—ki**; (way, manner) **si,—di.**

form, *v.tr.*, (frame) **samai.**

former, *a.*, **hore, horai.**

formerly, *ad.*, **beri horai, kolki horai, wā hore.**
formula, *n.*, (form of prayer) **ayad,—di.**
fornicate, *v.i.*, **ka sinaiso, was.**
forsake, *v.tr.*, (leave, depart from) **dairi**; he forsook his word, **hadalkisi bu na'ai.**
forsaker, *n.*, (of God) **nin Ilah na'ai.**
forswear, *v.tr.*, **dafir**; he forswore his religion, **dintisi bu dafirai**; *v.i.*, (swear falsely) **bein ku daro.**
fort, fortification, *n.*, **'alḫad,—di.**
forth, forward, *ad.*, **hor**; step —, **hor u so'o**; bring —, **hor u ken, hor u la kalai, hor u la so'o**; come —, **so baḥ**; go —, **dibada u baḥ**; and so —, **o sida u wad.**
fortify, *v.tr.*, **adkai, itāl u yel, gesinimo u yel.**
fortitude, *n.*, **adkan,—ti, gesinimo,—adi.**
fortnight, *n.*, **afarr iyo tobnad,—ki**; **shan iyo tobnad,—ki.**
fortune, *n.*, **ayan,—ki**; ill —, **ayan ḥumo,—adi**; — teller, **tawila,—ihi.**
forty, *num.*, **afarrtan,—ki.**
forward, *ad.*, **hor, horai**; the man who does not go —, goes backward, **ninki an horai u so'onini, dibu u so'oda**; from this time —, **gortan inta ka dambaisa.**
foul (*see* dirty).
foulness, *n.*, **doro,—adi.**
found, *v.tr.*, (establish) **ka ɗis.**
foundation, *n.*, (basis) **sal,—ki.**
founder, *v.i.*, (stumble as a horse) **turonturo**; *v.tr.*, **'ataisi**; **faraska ha 'ataisin,** do not founder the horse.
fountain, *n.*, **ib,—ti, il,—shi.**
four, *num.*, **afarr,—ti**; fourth, **afrad,—ki, —di.**
fourteen, *num.*, **afarr iyo toban, —ki**; fourteenth, **afarr iyo tobnad,—ki, —di.**
fowl, *n.*, **doro,—adi, hād,—di.**
fox, *n.*, **dawa'o,—a'adi**; male —, **dawa',—hi**; a kind of —, **golla waraba.**
fracture, *n.*, **jabnin,—ti.**
fragile, *a.*, **jilai'san.**
fragility, *n.*, **jila'** or **jilai',—li'hi.**
fragrance, *n.*, **udgon,—ki.**
fragrant, *a.*, **udgon.**
frame, *n.* The frame of a Somali tent is composed of two **udub** or **kaballo** of a **dig ɗoho,** of some **ɗigo,** and of **ɗig lola** crossing the **ɗigo.**
frankincense, *n.*, **beyo,—adi.**
fraternity, *n.*, **walalnimo,—adi.**
fraud (*see* cheat).
free, *a.*, **furan**; I am —, **an iyo naftaida,** or **aniga iyo naftaidu**; thou art —, **adiga iyo naftada**; he is —, **isagi iyo naftisi,** or **wa nin iyo nafti**; *v.tr.*, (set at liberty) **sarraḥi.**
free-will, *n.*, **ḥushi,—gi.**
freeze, *v.tr.* and *v.i.*, **baraf ka ɗig**; cold freezes the water, **gabadanadu biyaha baraf bai ka ɗigta**; water freezes, **biyuhu baraf bai noḥdan.**
freight, *n.*, **mal,—ki**; *v.tr.*, (load a ship) **sheḥnad** or **sheḥmad.**

French, *a.*, **fransis,—ki, nin fransisah.**
frenzy, *n.*, **walli,—di.**
fresh, *a.*, **ḫabow, ma'an, 'usub.**
fret, *v.tr.*, (wear away by rubbing) **hoḫ, haḫuḫ**; *v.i.*, (be angry) **'ado.**
Friday, *n.*, **jima'** or **jimai',—i'hi.**
friend, *n.*, **abban,—ki, jal,—ki, sahīb,—ki, wehel,—ki**; become —, **abbanso, wehesho.**
fright, *n.*, **baḫdin,—ti, 'absi,—di.**
frighten, *v.tr.*, **'absi, baji.**
frightful, *a.*, **laga 'absado, laga baḫo.**
fringe, *n.*, **da'al,—ki, daraf,—ti, shash,—ki**; — of silk, **faraḫ, —hi.**
fro, *ad.*; go to and —, **hore iyo dib u so'o,** toss to and —, **lul.**
frog, *n.*, **rah, rihhi** (the frog).
from, *prp.*, **ka**; go — him, **ka tag**; he comes — the jungle, **miyi bu ka so galaya** or **ka imanaya**; — time to time I take fever, **gor ka gor da'anti igu da'da**; — the creation of the world, **halki iyo malinti dunida la umai**; — my childhood, **halkiyo arurnimadaidi**; — top to toe, **kugta ila sulka**; do not speak — above, **dusha ha ka hadlin**; they brought it — afar, **mel fog ba laga kenai**; they caught him — amidst the crowd, **buḫhi ba lugu deḫ ḫabtai**; they come — behind, **wa iga daba yimaden**; I hear a voice — beneath, **'od ban hosta ka maḫlaya**; — beyond, **mel ka shishaisai**; — whence do you come? **hagge bad ka timid.**
front, *n.*, **hor,—ti**; — to —, **wa iss hor jogan,** or **wa iss egayan**; in — of, **horta**; — tooth, **fol,—ki.**
frontier, *n.*, **dal,—ki.**
frost, *n.*, **gabadano,—adi.**
froth, *v.i.*, **dobi, ḫoḫ**; that camel froths, **aurkasi wa dobinaya** or **wa ḫoḫaya**; *n.*, **humbo,—adi.**
frown, *v.i.*, **jahha ururi, jahḫur.**
fructify, *v.i.*, **mido yelo (yesha,** *plur.*), **so bah.**
frugal, *a.*, **'ir yar.**
fruit, *n.*, **mid,—ki, ḫadab,—ki, arah**; eat fruits, **ḫadabaiso**; a — eater, **ḫadabaisato,—adi, nin ḫadabaisatoah**; a seeker of fruits, **arah donato,—adi.**
fruitless, *a.*, **ma dalai, an dalin, fayidala**; a fruitless labour, **haul fayida la.**
frustrate (*see* disappoint).
fry, *v.tr.*, **shil, shilo**; fried, **shilan**; frying man, **deriya shil, —ki**; a woman ..., **shilato,—adi**; frying pan, **dawa,—ihi.**
fuel, *n.*, **ḫabo,—adi.**
fugitive, *n.*, **ḫof 'ararai, ḫof ka bahsadai.**
fulfil, *v.tr.*, **damai, shuḫulkisi damai.**
fulfilment, *n.*, **damad,—ki.**
fulgency, fulgor, *n.*, **dalal,—ki.**
full, *a.*, **buha, buhai.**
fun, *n.*, **kaftan,—ki.**
funeral feast, *n.*, **aḫan,—ki.**

funk, *v.i.*, **baḫ**; cause to —, **baji**.
funnel, *n.*, **masaf,—ki.**
fur, *n.*, **yiliḥ,—di, dogor,—ti.**
furnace, *n.*, **mufo,—adi.**
furniture, *n.*, **alabo,—adi.**
further, *ad.*, **shishai**; go —, **si fogow**; the — side, **gesta shishai.**
furthest, *ad.*, **ugu fog, ugu shishai**; go to the — part of the world, **dunida halka ugu fog tag.**
furuncle, *n.*, (ambury) **dullaḥ,—hi, māl, mashi, ka so baḥ,—ihi.**
fury, *n.*, **'ado, 'adadi** (the ...).
future, *n.*, **kolka dambe, marka dambe.**
fy! *int.*, **maga'ha be!**

G.

gabble, *n.*, (loud talk) **daudar,—ki.**
gad fly, *n.*, **dameira galib,—ki, gebni,—gi, takar,—ti.**
gag, *v.tr.*, **af dub**; gagging, *n.*, **af dub,—ki.**
gain, *n.*, (profit) **fayido,—adi, helin,—ki, kordis,—ki, korod,—ki, ma'ash.**
gait, *n.*, (manner of walking) **talabo,—adi.**
galaxy, *n.*, (milky way) **waḫ habar,—ki.**
gale, *n.*, **dabail,—shi.**
gall, *n.*, (bile) **'ameiti,—di**; (rancour) **ur ḫumo,—adi, ḫonsimad,—ki.**
gall, *v.tr.*, (hurt by fretting the skin) **hoḫ, gomodi.**
gallop, *n.*, **hardaf,—ki**; — at full speed, **ka'din,—ti, jeni ḥor,—ki**; *v.i.*, **hardaf**; *v.c.*, **hardafi.**
gamble, *v.i.*, **ḫamar**; — with, **la ḫamar.**
gambling, *n.*, **hamar,—ki.**
game, *n.*, **'ayar,—ti, jalbeb,—ti**; kind of —, **kor u bodo,—adi, shaḥ,—di.**
gangrene, *n.*, **hudai,—ihi.**
gap, *n.*, (deep, between two rocks) **bohol,—shi**; (an opening) **dila',—hi**; — in the front teeth, **fanaḥ,—hi.**
gape, *v.i.*, (yawn) **afka kala ḫad, afka kala hai.**
gaping, *n.*, **af kala ḫad,—ki, af kala hais,—ki.**
garden, *n.*, **beir,—ti, bustan,—ki**; *v.i.*, **ḫagaf.**
gardener, *n.*, **ḫagaf,—ki, nin beirta ḫagafaya.**
gargle, gargarism, *n.*, **luḫluḫasho,—adi**; —, gargarize, *v.tr.*, **luḫluḫo.**
garland, *n.*, (for horses) **sitaḥ,—hi.**
garlic, *n.*, **ton,—ti.**
garment, *n.*, **dar,—ki**; skin — for men, **ḫaïran,—ki**; — for women, **dū,—gi.**
gash, *n.*, **sarmo,—adi.**
gasp, *n.*, **ḫamansi,—gi**; the last —, **hamansigi ugu dambaiyai**; *v.i.*, **ḥamanso.**

gate, *n.*, **albab,—ki, illin,—ki, dah,—hi.**

gather, *v.tr.*, **iss ku dar, ururi, so ururi, iss u gei, kuriyai, iss u ken, iss u gur**; *v.i.*, **iss u urura, iss u taga**; the clouds —, **daruruhu iss u ururayan**; they gathered together, **wa iss u ururen.**

gathered, *a.*, **urursan, la iss u gurai**; — fruits, **mido la iss u gurai.**

gathering, *n.*, **ururis,—ki.**

gaunt, *a.*, (lean) **weidsan, weida.**

gay, *a.*, **nin farahah.**

gaze, *n.*, **egmo,—adi**; *v.i.*, (stare) **isha ku 'adai, indo ku tol.**

gazelle, *n.*, **dero,—adi**; he —, **der,—ki**; Semmeringe's —, **'aul,—ki, —shi.**

geld (*see* castrate).

gem, *n.*, (precious stone) **johorad, —di.**

gender, *n.*, (sort) **'ain,—ki, tol, —ki.**

genealogy, *n.*, **abtirsinyo,—yihi**; give thy —, **abtirso**; give a —, **abtiri.**

generally, *ad.*, **asalba.**

generate, *v.tr.*, **dal, yelo.**

generation, *n.*, **dalasho,—adi.**

generosity, *n.*, **deh,—di.**

generous man, *a.*, **dehsi,—gi, nin dehsiah, nasab,—ki, ron.**

genital, *a.*, **hod,—di.**

genitals, *n.*, **hodo,—dihi.**

genius, *n.*, (bad spirit) **jini** or **jinni,—gi.**

gentile, *n.*, (heathen) **gal,—ki**; the gentiles, **galo,—adi.**

gentle, *a.*, **habow.**

gentleman, *n.*, **hawaja,—ihi, serkal,—ki.**

genuflexion, *n.*, **jilba jog,—gi.**

get, *v.tr.*, **hel**; — your bread, **kibistada hogso**; — your pardon, **samhaddada weidiso**; — a wife, **nag dono**; — a cold, **dahan had**; — a place, **shuhul dono**; — an ill habit, **dastur hun baro**; — money of him, **la'ag hado**; he gets the praise of all the world, **isagu aman dad o dan bu lehyahai**; we must be contented with such as we can —, **hadba wahainu lehnahai an ku farahno**; he got a good servant, **hadan wanaksan bu lehyahai**; I could not — him to come, **ninki inu yimado ka wahyai**; — it made, **u samaisi, u damaisi**; I will — a spear made for you, **waran dan wad iga heli**; I got her to go, **eriyai**; — you gone, **iss ka tag**; — ready, **diar ha ahato, diar garai**; — yourself ready, **diar ahaw**; — more, **iss ku tar**; — abroad, **dibada u so sar, eri, war gei**; — the news, **warki wa la baranaya**; — away, *v.tr.*; — the boys away from my room, **ahalkaiga inamada dibadda uga sar**; — the box away, **sanduhha la tag**; — away, *v.i.*, **yur!** he gets away, **wa tagaya, wa si so-'oda**; — yourself back, **noho**; — down, **so deg**; — down the stairs, **salanka so deg**; —

down from, **ka deg, ka so deg**; — from, *v.tr.*, **ka so bihi, ka had**; I could not — from him, *v.i.*, **ka tegi kari wahai**; — in, *v.tr.*, **so geli**; — your money in, **la'agtada so geli**; *v.i.*, **so gal**; they got into Berberah, **Berberah galai**; — off, — him off from jail, **habsiga ka so sar**; he could not — off, *v.i.*, **bahsan kari wah**; — off from your horse, **faraskaga ka deg**; — out, *v.tr.*, **dibadda u sar**; — out that nail, **musmarkas ka so bihi**; — out, *v.i.*, **dibadda tag, dibadda u bah**; — out from, **ka so bah**; — to the shore, **hebta u deg**; — to the top of the hill, **burta fihheda gad**; — together all the pieces, **inaha o dan iss u ken**; — in that place, **halkas iss ugu gei**; — up, *v.tr.*; — up the wood, **horiga had**; — him up, **ke'i, tosi**; *v.i.*, **ka', sara ka', so ka', tos**; it is time to — up, **wa gorti la ke'i jirai**; — up the stairs, **sallanka kor**; — up again, **sallanka kor misna**; — up again, *v.i.*, **ka' misna**; — up to your father, **ka' o abbahá u tag**; his rage gets above your anger, **'adadisu tada ka hun**; he gets before him, **isagu wa dulmaraya**; he gets well again, **wa boksanaya misna**.

ghost, *n.*, **naf,—ti, ruh,—hi.**

Holy Ghost, the, *n.*, **ruhha hoduskaah.**

giant, *n.*, **nin der, ninki dera** (the ...), **torog,—gi.**

giddiness, *n.*, **warer,—ki, madah warer,—ki**; be troubled with —, *v.i.*, **warer**; *v.c.*, **wareri, madah wareri.**

giddy, *a.*, **warersan.**

gift, *n.*, **hadiad,—di, sin,—ti**; — by will, **ahan,—ki**; first — before the marriage, **gabati,—gi**; the second — ..., **yarad, —ki.**

gild, *v.tr.*, (cover with gold) **biyo dahabah mari.**

gimlet, *n.*, (awl) **kaba tola** or **tolai,—ihi.**

ginger, *n.*, **sinjibil,—shi.**

gingerly, *ad.*; go gingerly, **gād.**

gingerness, *n.*, **gādnin,—ti.**

giobberti, *n.*, (sweeper) **har gur, —ki.**

giraffe, *n.*, **gerri,—gi, halgerri, —di.**

gird, *v.tr.*, (bind round) **gunti**; *v.r.*, **gunto, sunka hido.**

girdle, *n.*, **sun,—ki, bohor,—ki, gunti,—gi.**

girl, *n.*, **gabad,—di, inan,—ti, ugub,—ti**; girls in general, **hablo,—ihi, ugubod,—ki.**

girth, *n.*, (strap for a saddle) **wegered,—ki.**

give, *v.tr.*, **si, u dib, bihi**; — him the lie, **ninka beini**; — thanks, **mahadi, mahad u nah**; — answer, **jawab, u 'eli**; — to everyone his due, **nin walba wihhisa si**, or **wuhhu lehyahai si**; — evidence, **marhati ku fur**; — a good and faithful account, **ḥisab wanaksan o aminah si**; God gives me grace so to do, **Ilaḥhai ba i la ḥabanaya**, or **Ilaḥhai ḥair i siyai inan sida ku yelo**; I gave him credit, **wan rumaistai**; — the oath, **ɗaro**; — trouble, **dāli**; the boys — me trouble, **arurtu wa i dalisa**; — hopes, **la ballan**; — a call, **yeɗ, ḥaïli**; — a guess, **malai, garo**; — joy, war, **kaga baɗbaɗi** or **badbaɗaɗi**; — leave, **fasaḥ**; — judgment, **ḥukum**; — ground, **durug, ka durug**; — place, **u banai, ka baïd**; — notice, **dignin dir, ogaisi**; — heed, **iss ka eg, ilali, ogow**; — challenge, **dandanso**; — to suck, **nuji**; — a look, **so arag**; I gave way to his wise proposal, **wanadisi fi'anaid ban degaistai**; he gave way to melancholy, **iss ḥulbiyai**; the ground gave way under my feet, **amuddi 'agtaida hosteda ka dustai**; — away, **na'**; he gives all away, **wa wada na'aya gidi**; I gave up my money for lost, **la'agtaida wan ka samra**; they gave him up for dead, **ka ḥustai**; — back again, **'eli, so 'eli, u 'eli, dib u si**; — into his mind, **taladisa ra'**; — for, **ɗafi**; do not —, **ka 'esho, u did**; — off, — out, — over, **iss ka da, na'**.

giver, *n.*, **basha,—ihi, ɗiba,—ihi, deḥsi,—gi, siya,—yihi.**

giving, *n.*, **ɗibnin,—ti, ɗibasho, —adi.**

gizzard, *n.*, **bog,—gi.**

glad, *a.*, **baɗaɗan, baɗaɗsan**; be —, **baɗaɗsanaw, iss ka rai, rairai.**

glaire, *n.*, **ḥako,—adi.**

glance, *n.*, **daïmo,—adi, egmo, —adi.**

glass, *n.*, **galas,—ki.**

gleam, *n.*, (phosphorescent) **galabildan** or **garabildan,—ki.**

glean, *v.tr.*, **gur.**

gleet, *n.*, (venereal disease) **jabti, —di.**

glisten, glister, glitter, *v.i.*, **ɗalal.**

globe, *n.*, **kuriyaisnan,—ti.**

gloom, *n.*, **wahan,—ki, ḥulub,—ki**; *v.i.*, (be sad) **wahan, ḥulub.**

gloomy, *a.*, **ḥulubsan**; be —, **ḥulubsanaw.**

glorify, *v.tr.*, **aman**; — yourself, **bu.**

glory, *n.*, **aman,—ti.**

glow, *n.*, (shining heat) **olol,—ki**; *v.i.*, **olol**; glowing irons, **bir ololaisa.**

glue, *n.*, **habag,—ti**; *v.tr.*, **ku nab.**

glutton, *n.*, **'anda der,—ki, hunguri wein, 'ir wein.**

gluttony, *n.*, **hunguri weinan,—ti, 'ir weinan,—ti.**

gnash, *v.i.*, **jiriḥso**; *v.c.*, **kaga jiriḥi.**

gnashing, *n.*, **jiriḥsi,—gi.**

gnat, *n.*, **kane'o,—adi, ɗunyalai, —ihi.**

gnaw, *v.tr.*, **feno, fenfeno, rug.**

gnawing, *n.*, **fenfenasho,—adi, fenfenad,—ki.**

go, *v.i.*, **tag, so'o, baïd**; — together, **iss ra'a**; let us — together, **an iss ra'ano**; I cannot —, **ma tegi karo**; he is gone, **teg**; they are gone, **tagai**; — that way, **hagga' u ka', dauga ḥabso**; — on foot, **lug ku so'o**; he has gone a journey, **wa sod'alai**; how goes your health? **afimadkaga ka warran?** so the world goes, **dunida sidasah**, or **dunidu wa sida**; how — your concerns? **iss ka warran?** so the report goes, **warku wa sida**; he went unpunished, **ḥasirad laan bu ku tagai**; let —, **si da**; let — the anchor, **barosinka si da**; — about, **wareg so wareg, so warwareg**; — about the world, **dunida so wareg**; I shall — about it, **wan kaga ḥaban**; — about your business, **orod o shuḥulkaga ḥabso**; such a report goes abroad, **warkas mel walba gadaya** or **ka baḥaya**; thou art able to — against him, **ninka wa iss ka 'adadin karta** or **wa ḥabili karta**; — along, **mar**; — along the house, **aḥalka daf**, or **aḥalka hor mar**; — along with ..., **ninka si ra'**; he goes aside, **ges bu u baïdaya**, or **dauga ḥun bu ḥabsanaya**; he goes astray, **wa iss hallainaya**; they — asunder, **wa kala so'odan** or **so'onayan**; — away, **tag, iss ka tag, iss ka baḥ, gur, ina kala wad**; he went away with a thing, **waḥ bu la tagai**; — back, **noḥo**; — back with, **la noḥo**; he goes back from his word, **hadalkisi bu asararaya** or **dafiraya**; — backward, **dib u noḥo, dib u so'o**; — before, **hor so'o, hor u mar, ka horai** — behind, **dambai, ka dambai** — between, **deḥ gal**; I went between them, **anigu wa deḥ galai**; — beyond, **ka shishai**; — beyond the hill, **burta shishadeda mar**; they went beyond my hopes, **intan sugayai yai i dulmartai**; — by, **ag mar**; I will see the prisoners — by, **maḥabisti o i ag maraisa arki dona**; the time goes by, **gortu daḥso u so'onaisa**; the wind goes contrary to us, **dabaishi ba ina haisa**; — down, **hosta u deg, hosta tag, u daf**; — down the stairs, **sallanka si mar, sallanka ka so deg**; — down again, **deg mar kaleh**; no meat will — down with him, **midna** or **waḥba ka degi mayo**; the sun goes down, **ḥorahdi wa da'aisa**; — first, **horaí, hor u so'o, si tag, si so'o**; — for, **u ka'**; — for help, **haïla gei**, or **ma'awinad u ka'**; — for the governor, **serkalka don** or **u yed**; he goes for a robber, **tug ba la moda**; that goes for nothing, **waḥba ku ma fila**; he went forth, **tamashlai teg**;

the news went forth yesterday, **shala lugu warramai**; he went forth last week, **todobadki bu dashai**; — forward, **horo u wad**; he goes forward in learning, **barashadisi wa wadanaya**; — from, **ka tag**; he goes from the service (work), **shuhulki bu ka tagaya**; — in, **gal, u daf**; — near, **u durug, ag tag, u dowai**; I went near to be devoured, **in la igu liho ban u dowadai**; he went off yesterday, **shalai bu dintai**; these goods will never — off, **holahasi kolleh ibsami mayan**; hear the great guns — off, **mahal! madafi'adi la rid**; — on, **so'o, wad**; he goes on an embassy, **ergu u ka'aya**; — on your way, **dantada ra'**; — on board the ship, **markabka ful**; — on as you have begun, **sidad ugaga habatai u wad**; how does your business — on? **danta** or **hausha ka warran?** — over the river, **durdurka ka talab**; he goes out of the way, **daugi bu ka baïdaya, daugi an tosnain bu maraya**; the fire goes out, **dabki wa bahtiyaya**; — through the crowd, **buhha deh mar**; he went through many dangers, **'absi badan bu si deh marai**; — through the town, **magalada hul** or **so hul**; — round, **her, mer, so mer, ku so wareg, meraiso**; make him — round, **meri, mermeri**; — to, **tag, u tag, u bah, gad, u ka', u so'o**; — to Bulahar, **Bulahar habo**; I shall not — to that price, **gana'da gadi mayo**; — up, **sarai u bah, dusha tag**; — up and down, **dul iyo hos ba mar**; — upon him, **amin**; — with, **ra'**.

goat, *n.*, **riyo,—ihi** (gen. name); a he —, **orgi,—gi**; a she —, **ri,—di.**

gob, *n.*, (small quantity of food) **antugo,—adi.**

God, *n.*, **ebba** or **ebbai,—ihi, ilah, Allah, wehel,—ki, rabbi, —gi, lilah,—hi**; — bless you, **hair Allah ha ku siyo**; — save you, **Ilahhai ha ku sahalo**; thanks to —, **mahad Allah**; he makes a — of his belly, **'aloshisi bu Ebba ka digaya**; — willing, I shall come back next week, **hadi Allah idmo todobadka damban so nohon**; — helping, **hadi Ilah i gargaro**, or **hadi Ilahhai i la habto**; — forbid! — avert! **Ilahhow naga hai! Ilahhow ha no kenin!**

Godsend, *n.*, **'awo,—adi.**

goggle, *v.i.*, **indaha ashhar**; — eyed, **ashharah, ashhar,—ki.**

going, *n.*, **tegnin,—ki.**

gold, *n.*, **dahab,—ki.**

goldsmith, *n.*, **sayah,—hi.**

gonorrhœa, *n.*, **jabti,—di.**

good, *a.*, **wanaksan, fi'an, ron, tolmon, wa'an, san, ād**; be —, **wanaksanaw, tolmonow, ronaw, fi'anaw, samo**; be —,

v.c., **ronaw, tolmonai, wanaji, hagaji**; depart from evil and do —, **waḥha ḥun ka durug, o wah san fal**; for your —, **awada, daradda.**
good bye! *int.*, **amana Allah.**
goodness, *n.*, **wanag,—gi, tolimo, —adi.**
goods, *n.*, **alabo,—adi, holo,—ihi, saman,—ki.**
goose, *n.*, **badag,—gi.**
gospel, *n.*, **injil,—ki.**
gourd, *n.*, **dubbo,—ihi, ubo,—adi.**
govern, *v.tr.*, **ḥukum.**
government, *n.*, **hukum,—ki, serkal,—ki.**
governor, *n.*, **ḥakin,—ki, serkal sarrai.**
grace, *n.*, **karamad,—di.**
grain, *n.*, **inin,—ti, messego,—adi.**
grammar, *n.*, **naḥwi,—gi.**
grandfather, *n.*, **awow** or **awowai, —ihi.** This word is also used for grandson and daughter.
grandmother, *n.*, **ayaiyo,—adi, muḥuyo** or **muḥayo, — adi.** Also used for grandson and daughter.
grant, *n.*, **dibnin,—ti.**
grape, *n.*, **'armo,—adi.**
grasp, *n.*, **ḥabasho,—adi**; *v.tr.*, (hold in the hand) **ḥeji, ḥabso.**
grass, *n.*, **gedo,—ihi, 'aus,—ki, diḥi,—di, daremo,—adi, dog, —ti, —gi.**
grateful, *a.*, **abalgudah**; be —, **abal u ḥab, u abalgud, abalmari.**
gratefulness, gratitude, *n.*, **abal, —ki.**
grave, *n.*, **ḥabal,—shi, ḥabri,—gi.**
gravel, *n.*, **ḥururoḥ,—hi.**
gravy, *n.*, (juice) **da'an** or **de'an, —ki.**
gray, grey, *a.*, **'irroleh**; — beard and hair, *n.*, **'irro,—di**; — horse, **maïdal,—ki**; whitish — horse, **'ainab,—ki.**
graze, *v.tr.*, **daḥgei, daji, barḥi**; take to —, **fofi, so fofi**; — the horses at night, **so mirr**; *v.i.*, **daḥ.**
grazing, *n.*, **daḥnin,—ki, —ti, mirr,—ki, —ti.**
grease, *n.*, **subag, —gi, dufan,—ki, ḥaid,— di, ḥuko,— adi, badi,—di.**
great, *a.*, **der, wein**; a — city, **magalo balladan**; a — multitude, **rag badan**; a — wind, **dabail wein**; a — deal, **waḥ badan**; be —, **weinow**; make —, **weinai, so weinai**; greater, **ka wein**; greatest, **ka wada,** or **ugu wein.**
greatness, *n.*, **weinan,—ti**; — of God, **amar,—ki.**
greedy (*see* glutton and gluttony).
green, *a.*, **owlaled**; — trees and grass, **magol,—ki.**
greet, *v.tr.*, (salute) **baridi, salam.**
grey (*see* gray).
gridiron, *n.*, (stick used instead of) **solai,—gi.**
grief, *n.*, **weirweir,—ki, ḥuman, —ti, ḥulub,—ki, sile'i, i'hi.**
grieve, *v.tr.*, **ka ḥulbi, weirweri**;

that grieves me, **wahhasi wa iga ḥulbinaya**; *v.i.*, **ḥulub, weirweir.**
grill, *v.tr.*, (broil) **sol, dub.**
grind, *v.tr.*, **budli, tun, raḥad.**
grindstone, *n.*, **lissin,—ki.**
groan, *v.i.*, **tah.**
groaning, *n.*, **tah,—hi.**
groin, *n.*, **sar'an,—ti.**
groom, *n.*, **farasjir,—ki.**
gross, *a.*, (thick) **ḥalafsan.**
ground, *n.*, **ḋul,—ki, 'arro,—adi**; what — have you for believing that? **inad waḥha ku rumaisatid sal mad u haisata?** it is the — I went upon, **wa ka salki an ku faḋistai**; I did not send him away without —, **aniga gar darro ku ma eriyin**; rising —, **gumbur,—ti, bur,—ti**; —work, **sal,—ki**; —rent, **ardiad,—ki.**
grow, *v.i.*, **baḥ, so baḥ**; the grass grows, **geduhu wa baḥan**; that boy grows bigger every day, **inankasi malin walba wa koraya**; — in grace, **karamad ku kor**; I shall — here, if I stay longer, **halkan wan ku kori, hadi an si jogo** or **faḋiyo** or **hadi an ku si rāgo**; the tree grows again, **gedku wa si baḥaya**; he grows better, **wa si wanaksanaya,** or **wil wanaksan bu noḥonaya**; he grows big, **wa koraya**; he grows childish, **wa arurowbaya**; the water grows cold, **biyuhu wa ḥabowbayan**; the rice grows dear, **baris ku wa gana' adkanaya**; I — easy, **haulyari ban ḥaba**; that boy grows fat in flesh, **inankasi wa shishlanaya**; that small girl grows handsome, **gabaḋda yari wa huroḥ badnanaisa**; he grows lazy, **'ajis bu noḥonaya**; it grows late, **wa rāgaisa**; he grows lean, **wa weidowbaya**; the money grows less, **la'agti wa ḋinmaisa**; you — old, **wa gabowbaisa**; we — poor, **wa dagagowbaina**; that man grows rich, **ninkasi hodanowbaya**; that boil grows ripe, **dullaḥhasi wa bislanaya**; the days — short, **ḋararuhu wa ḋinmayan**; — long, **wa ḋeranayan**; that boy grows sleepy, **wilkasi wa lulonaya;** he grows stupid, **doḥon bu noḥonaya,** or **wa doḥonowbaya,** or **doḥominu ku koraya**; he grows strong, **wa ḥogaisanaya** or **italaisanaya**; the lion grows tame, **libaḥhu af yaḥan bu noḥonaya**; he grows ugly, **wilki wa fol ḥumanaya**; I — weary with the boys, **inamada wa ku dalaya**; he grows well, **wa buksanaya**; the fire goes out, **ōgti wa bahaisa**; that cloth goes out of use, **darkasi wa idlanaisa**; — up, **baḥ.**
growing, *n.*, **korrin,—ki.**
growl, *v.i.*, **olol**; the camel growls, **gelu wa olala.**
grub, *v.tr.*, (dig up) **ḥod o so rid.**
grudge, *n.*, **'ollad,—di.**
grumble, *v.i.*, (gruntle) **gunus.**

grumbling, *n.*, (grunt) **gunus,—ki.**
grunting, *n.*, (of a camel) **'abad,—ki.**
guard, *n.*, **kor jir,—ki, kor jog,—gi, ilalo,—adi**; *v.tr.*, **ilali, jir.**
guess, *n.*, (conjecture) **malais,—ki**; *v.tr.*, **malai, garo.**
guest, *n.*, **abban,—ki, marti,—di.**
guide, *n.*, **abban,—ki, jid yaḥan.**
guile (*see* cheat).
guilt, *n.*, **ḥujad,—di, taḥsir,—ti.**
guilty, *a.*, **gar darran, ḥujadleh, ḥujad wein, taḥsir leh.**
guinea fowl, *n.*, **digirin,—ki, digirin 'as, digirin madow,—ki madowbai.**
gullet, *n.*, (the food pipe) **hunguri madow,—gi.**
gully, *v.i.*, **fuḥfuḥso.**
gulp, *n.*, **'antugo,—adi**; *v.tr.*, (swallow eagerly) **'antug.**
gum, *n.*, (the hard, fleshy substance covering the jaws and investing the teeth) **ḥirid,—ki**; (the vegetable secretion of trees and plants) **ḥabag,—ti**; black —, **baḥbaḥ,—hi**; a kind of —, **ḥanjo,—adi**; liquid —, **duḥsin,—ti**; take the liquid —, **duḥso**; a — tree, **muđayo** or **murayo,—adi.**
gun, *n.*, **bunduḥ,—hi**; — powder, **barud,—di.**
gush, gushing, *n.*, **ḥautan,—ki.**
gush, *v.i.*, (flow out) **hautan**; the blood gushed from my wound, **diggi nabarki ka hautamai.**
gust, *n.*, (taste) **đađan,—ki**; (a blast) **seso, sisa, sigo,—adi.**
gut, *n.*, **uslaho,—adi**; the small —, **mindi'ir,—ki**; the great —, **gana',—ihi, ḥabsin,—ki**; *v.tr.*, (to eviscerate) **doḥ.**

H.

habit, habitude, *n.*, **dastur,—ti**; (dress) **dar,—ki.**
habitation, *n.*, **fađi,—gi, rug,—ti.**
haft, *n.*, (a handle) **dāb,—ki**; *v.tr.*, **dabka ku deji.**
hail, *n.*, (frozen rain) **dagaḥ rob, robka dagihisi** (the ... ...); (health !) **salam !** — to you ! **salam alekum ! war afimad !**
hair, *n.*, **tin,—ki, timo,—ihi**; — of animals, **dogor,—ti**; — of the tail, **gamello,—adi.**
half ($\frac{1}{2}$), *n.*, **bađ,—ki, jeḥ**; (part) **go,—hi**; — a glass, a pot, **mugi.**
halloo ! *int.*, **'ar ! 'ar ! war ! war hoi !** ...
hallow, *v.tr.*, (make holy) **ḥodus u samai, ḥodus ka đig**; be hallowed, **samo.**
halt, *n.*, (a stop during a march) **jog,—gi**; *v.tr.*, **jog, jogso**; — at night, **hoio.**
halter, *n.*, (of a camel) **hogan,—ki**; (of a horse) **jarrai,—ihi, shakamad,—di.**
hamlet, *n.*, **bulal,—shi.**

hammer, *n.*, **dubbai,—ihi.**

hand, *n.*, **ga'an,—ti**; the right —, **midigta**; the left —, **bideḥda**; he has a — in it, **ga'an bu ku la jira**; my — is in, **ga'an ban ku la jira**; my — is out, **ga'an ku la ma jiro**; he is my right —, **wa ga'antaida midig**; the two men go — in —, **labada nin wa iss ku ga'an**; —writing, **far,—ti.**

hand, *v.tr.*, (give) **u ḍib**; you handle the oar well, **sebka ād bad u wadda.**

hand-barrow, *n.*, **rarab,—ti.**

handful, *n.*, **ḥantobo,—adi.**

handkerchief, *n.*, **masar,—ki.**

handle, *n.*, **dāb,—ki.**

handsome, *a.*, **ḫuroḥ badan,** or **ḫuroḥ wanaksan, baḥsan, shuban.**

hang, *v.tr.*, **deldel, alaḫ**; *v.i.*, (be suspended) **lalad, ka lalad.**

happen, *v.i.*, **noḫo**; it happens, **waḥai noḫota**; so it happened, **sidasai noḫotai.**

happy, *a.*, **badadsan, raḥaisan, ayan leh.**

happiness, *n.*, **raḫo,—adi, farḥad,—di, badad,—ki.**

harbour, *n.*, **deked,—di.**

hard, *a.*, **adag, hog badan, kulul**; — working men have — skins, **nimanka shuḫiyintaihi wa dub adag yihin**; *ad.*, it grows —, **wa adkanaisa**; strike him —, **si adag ugu dufo**; the wind blows —, **dabaishu ād bai u da'aisa.**

harden, *v.tr.*, (make hard) **adkai.**

hardness, *n.*, **adkan,—ti.**

hard-hearted (man), *a.*, **nin 'alol adag, ninki 'alosha adka** (the ...).

hard-working (man), *n.*, **ḍibtan,—ki.**

hare, *n.*, **bakaïla,—ihi**; —lipped man, **nin faruran.**

harlot, *n.*, **ḍillo,—adi.**

harem, *n.*, **dumar,—ki.**

hark! *int.*, **maḫal! degaiso!**

harm, *n.*, **waḥ yello,—adi**; *v.tr.*, **u ḫumai, ḫon yel.**

harness, *n.*, **hensai,—sihi.**

harsh, *a.*, **ḫun.**

hartebrest, *n.*, (cow antelope) **si'g,—gi.**

haste! (be quick!), **daḫso!**

hasten, *v.i.*, **daḫso, degdeg.**

hat, *n.*, **kofiad,—di.**

hate, hatred, *n.*, **ne'ban,—ti**; feeling of —, **ur ku talo,—adi.**

hate, *v.tr.*, **na', ne'baw.**

haughtiness, *n.*, **amar,—ki, amar weinan,—ti.**

haughty, *a.*, **amarsan, amar wein.**

haunch, *n.*, **missig,—ti, sin,—ti.**

have, *v.tr.*, **hai, haiso, ḫab.**

hawk, *n.*, **hadka adag, — ti**; species of —, **baḫalya,—yihi.**

hay, *n.*, **gedo,—ihi, 'aus,—ki.**

hazard, *n.*, **nasib,—ki.**

haze, haziness, *n.*, **shuḥ,—hi, shululu'**; the sky is hazy, **'irku wa shululu'aya.**

he, *prn.*, **isagu, wu, bu, yu.**

head, *n.*, **madaḥ,—hi**; —ache, **madaḥ ḫanun,—ki**; the — of the bed, **sarrirta madaḥḥeda**; be the —, **u madaḥahaw.**

heal, *v.tr.*, **buksi, u buksi** or **boksi**; be healed, **bukso.**

healing, *n.*, **boksis,—ki, boksin, —ti.**

health, *n.*, **afimad,—di.**

healthy, *a.*, **nin afimad ḥaba, ninki afimadka ḥabai.**

heap, *n.*, **tul,—ki, rasais,—ki**; *v.tr.*, **tul, rasai, mos.**

heapy, *a.*, **tulan, rasaisan.**

hear, *v.tr.* and *v.i.*, **degaiso, maḥal, aḥbal, ka aḥbal**; *v.c.*, **mahashi.**

hearing, *n.*, **máḥal,—ki.**

heart, *n.*, **wadna** or **wadnai,—ihi, ḥalbi,—gi, 'alol,—shi.**

hard-hearted man, *n.*, **mudal,—ki.**

heartless, *a.*, **wadnala.**

hearten, *v.tr.*, (animate) **gesinimo u yel.**

hearth, *n.*, **mufo,—adi.**

heat, *n.*, **hur,—ki, kul,—ki**; *v.tr.*, (make warm) **kululai.**

heathen, *n.*, (gentiles) **galo,—adi.**

heave, *v.tr.*, (lift up) **sarai u ḥad, lal**; *v.i.*, (pant) **hinrag.**

heaven, *n.*, **janno,—adi, 'ir,—ki.**

heavy, *a.*, **'ulus, 'usla.**

heaviness, *n.*, **'ulais,—ki, 'ulusnimo,—adi.**

hedge, *n.*, **od,—di.**

hedge-hog, *n.*, **ḥidig,—ti.**

heed, *n.*, **fojigan,—ti.**

heel, *n.*, **'idib,—ti.**

heifer, *n.*, **ḥalin,—ti, weil,—shi.**

height, *n.*, **derer,—ki.**

heighten, *v.tr.*, **derai, dereri.**

heir, *n.*, **nin daḥalah, ninki daḥalka aha** (the ...).

hell, *n.*, **'adab,—ti, nar,—ti**; — fire, **dab 'adabed, dab nared.**

helm, *n.*, **shukan,—ti.**

help, *n.*, **'awin,—ti, 'awimad,— di, gargar,—ki, hil,—ki**; *v.tr.*, **la 'awi, 'awin, gargar, u hili, la ḥabo**; God — you, **Ebbahai ha ka 'awino**; it is a thing we cannot —, **wa waḥainan iss ka karain**; go for —, **hailo, haila gei, ma 'awinad u ka'.**

helper, *n.*, **'awis,—ki, hiliya,— yihi, 'idan,—ki.**

hem, *n.*, **darur,—ki, serji,—gi.**

hemorrhage, *n.*, **diggi hawtankisi.**

hen, *n.*, **digãga,—di, luki,—di, tujad** or **tijad,—ki.**

henceforth, henceforward, *ad.*, **manta dabaded.**

her (*see* Grammar).

herb, *n.*, **ged,—ki.**

herd (*see* flock).

here, *ad.*, **haggan, halkan, meshan.**

hereafter, *ad.*, **aminka dabadded, hadda ka dambow.**

heritage, *n.*, **dahal,—ki.**

hermit (*see* eremite).

hero, *n.*, **nin diran**; be a —, **diranaw.**

herpes, *n.*, (tetters) **'ambar,—ti.**

hesitate, *v.i.*, **ka jog.**

hiccough, *n.*, **higgo,—adi.**

hide, *n.*, (skin) **harag,—gi**; — of camels, **mera,—ihi**; — of neat cattle, **san,—ti**; — of antelope, **idin,—ti.**

hide, *v.tr.*, (conceal) **dumi, hari, harso**; *v.r.*, **dumo, iss hari.**
hidden, *a.*, **harson.**
hiding, *n.*, **dumasho,—adi, haris, —ki**; — place, **mel harson, meshi harsonaid.**
high, *a.*, **der**; — water, **baddi wa buhda.**
highwayman, *n.*, **layan,—ki.**
hill, *n.*, **bur yar,—ti —aid, karin,—ti, kur,—ti, kurun,—ti, mos,—ki**; *v.tr.*, (heap up) **mos.**
hilt, *n.*, **dāb,—ki.**
hind, *n.*, (part of the arm) **'udud, —di**; — leg, **lug,—ti.**
hinder, *v.tr.*, **u did**; you — me, **wahtigaigi ba i didaisa.**
hinge, *n.*, (of a door) **kelbad,—di.**
hint, *n.*, (signal) **bah,—hi.**
hip, *n.*, (haunch) **sin,—ti.**
hippopotamus, *n.*, **jer,—ki.**
hire, *n.*, **kiro,—adi**; *v.tr.*, **kirai.**
his (*see* Grammar).
hiss, *n.*, **fori,—di**; *v.tr.* and *v.i.*, **fori, u fori.**
history, *n.*, **sheko,—adi**; tell a —, **shekai, sheko u mari.**
hit, *n.*, (strike) **nabar,—ki.**
hit, *v.tr.*, **ku dufo**; — the mark, **la dugo, la togo.**
hither, *ad.*, **halkan**; hitherto, **ila halkan.**
hive, *n.*, (cell of bees) **dahb,—ki**; empty —, **dahb madan**; full —, **dahb buha.**
ho! hoa! *int.*, **war hoi! na hoi!**
hoarse, *a.*, **habeibsan.**
hobble, *v.i.*, (go lamely) **duti.**
hoe, *n.*, (an instrument) **magarafad,—di.**
hog, wart hog, *n.*, **dofar,—ki.**
hoist, *v.tr.*, (raise up on high) **dofi.**
hold, *n.*, **habasho,—adi**; — of a ship, **hani,—gi**; he let go his —, **ninku wa deinaya**; get —, **habso**; they could not take — of his words, **hadalkisi hejin kari wahyai.**
hold, *v.tr.*, (keep in the hand) **ho, heji, habo**; — him fast, **ād u heji**; he held the dagger to his throat, **isaga o bilawihi horta kaga haya**; I — him but a fool, **ana haya hof wallan ban se u ahan**; *v.i.*, (stand, adhere) **ku deg**; — up, **sarrai u tāg**; — in false security, **dag.**
hole, *n.*, **boran,—ti, dalol,—ki, god,—ki, hog,—gi, galsho,—adi.**
holiday, *n.*, **ayan,—ti.**
holiness, *n.*, **hodus,—ki.**
holla! *int.*, **war! na! war ya! war hoi! na hoi! war ya hoi!**
hollow, *n.*, (a cavity) **bohol,—shi**; *a.*, **madan.**
holy, *a.*, **hodusah.**
homage (*see* honour).
home, *n.*, **ahalka, guri,—gi**; go —, **ahalka habo, hoio.**
homicide, *n.*, **dil,—ki.**
homily, *n.*, **hadis,—ki.**
honest, *a.*, **amin,—ki, aminah**; be —, **aminahaw.**
honesty, *n.*, **aminimo,—adi.**
honey, *n.*, **malab,—ki**; —comb, **dahb,—ki.**

honour, *n.*, **mamus,—ki, —ti, murwad,—di**; *v.tr.*, **mamus, murwad, murwai.**
hoof, *n.*, (of camels) **gomod,—di**; (of horses, asses, oxen ...) **ḥob,—ki**; (of goats or sheep) **ḥanjaful, raf,—ki.**
hook, *n.*, (wooden one) **hangol,—ki**; a fishing —, **jilib** or **jilab,—ki.**
hoop, *n.*, **giringir,—ti.**
hoopoe, *n.*, **gulai,—di.**
hoot, *n.*, (clamour) **ḥailo,—adi, buḥ,—hi.**
hop, *v.i.*, (jump) **bod.**
hop! hop! *int.*, **ayai! ayai!**
hope, *n.*, **sugnin,—ti**; my — is in God alone, **sugnintaidu Ilahhai keliah ku tal**; *v.tr.*, **sug**; I — in God, **Ilahhai ban sugaya.**
horizon, *n.*, **mesha 'irka iyo dulku iṣs ka hayan** or **iss kaga yalin** or **iss ka kala hayan.**
horn, *n.*, **ges,—ki, gesas,—ki,** or **geso,—ihi** (*plur.*).
hornet, *n.*, (male bee) **imir,—ki.**
horror, *n.*, **naḥadin,—ti**; the — of hell, **narta naḥadinteda.**
horse, *n.*, **faras,—ki, fardo,—ihi**; male —, **sanga** or **sangai,—ihi**; (stallion) **korma** or **kormai,—ihi,** or **faras ḥod ḥabah**; herd of horses, **fadifardaah**; white —, **hai,—gi**; red —, **ashkar,** or **ashkir,—ki**; black —, **tukai,—ihi**; chestnut —, **hamar,—ki**; grey —, **maïdal,—ki**; whitish-grey —, **aïnab,—ki**; —back, **adaḥ,—di**; — croup, **fan,—ki**; — boy, **sebiyan,—ki**; — dealer, **faṛas jir,—ki**; — shoe, **na'al,—ki**; — tail, **ḥanān,—ti.**
hospitable, *a.*, **deḥsiah, deḥsi,—gi.**
hospitality, *n.*, **soryo,—adi**; keep —, **soryai.**
host, *n.*, **abban,—ki, ninki i soryaiyai.**
hot, *a.*, **kulul, kulail, hūr wein**; cause to be —, **huri**; feeling —, **hursan**; — sand, **raran,—ki.**
hotel, *n.*, **hudel,—ki.**
hour, *n.*, **sa'ad,—di**; half an —, **sa'ad badked**; a quarter of an —, **sa'ad waḥded.**
house, *n.*, **aḥal,—ki**; stone —, **dar,—ti**; wooden —, **gembissa,—di**; coffee —, **maḥayad,—di**; public —, **dukan,—ki**; — front, **aḥal horti.**
hovel, *n.*, (shed) **wab,—ti, bul,—ki.**
how? *ad.*, **side?** — do you do? **sidad tahai? iss ka warran?** — goes the world? **dunida ka warran?** he gave us an account — it was, **sidai ahaid yu noga warramai**; you see — I love you, **wad arkaisa sidan ku ja'lahai**; — many fools there are in the world! **imisa waḥ wallan dunida joga!** or **Ebbohow maḥa waḥ wallan dunida joga!** — far? **halkai jirtai? intai fogtahai** or **jirta?** — old is he? **wa imisa jir?** — far is it thither? **halka ila halkoi**

imisai iss u jiran? — far it is thither! **halkasi foga!** — long have you been here? **imisad halkan jogtai?** — long will you abuse my patience? **imisan ku dafi?** — is that? **waḥhasi wa side?** tell me — I may speak to him? **i sheg si an u la hadlo?** God knows — to deliver us, **Ilahhai ba og si ainnu ku baḥsano** or **si u ino-gu sahalo.**

however, *ad.*, **si kasta**; — it be, **si kastai ahato** or **noḥoto**; — he be, **mid un** or **mid kasta ha ahado.**

howl, *v.i.*, (cry as a wolf) **ḥaraidi.**

howling, *n.*, **ḥaraidis,—ki.**

hoy (*see* bugalow).

huddle, *v.tr.*, (throw in confusion) **ḥalad, iss ku ḥalad.**

huff, *v.i.*, (swell with anger) **'il u surun.**

hulk, *n.*, (careen) **tabaḥad,—di,** or **dabaḥad markabka.**

hull, *n.*, (husk) **ḥolof,—ti, jidif** or **jilif,—ti, laf,—ti.**

hum, *v.i.*, (buzz) **ḥin, guḥ.**

humanity, *n.*, **ninnimo,—adi.**

humble, *a.*, **amusan.**

humbug, *n.*, (sham) **ḥalalif,—ti**; *v.tr.*, **ḥalalif ka shub.**

humectate, *v.tr.*, **yar ḥo.**

humour, *n.*, (of the body) **de'an,—ki**; (of the nose) **duf,—ki, sin,—ki**; (temper) **abur,—ki,—ti.**

hump, hunch, *n.*, **tur,—ti**; — backed, **turleh, ninki turtalaha**; — of camels, **kurus,—ki.**

hunch, *n.*, (a knock with the fist) **tantomo, tumujo,—adi**; *v.tr.*, (push) **riḥ.**

hunger, *n.*, **gajo,—adi**; — fit, **gaja ḥun,—di ḥumaid, harḥad,—di.**

hungry, *a.*, **gajaisan, ninki gajaisna**; he is always —, **had iyo gor wa gajaisanyahai**; be —, **gajo**; I am —, **wan gajonaisa** or **gaja i haisa**; I feel a — fit, **gaja ḥun ya i haisa.**

hundred, *num.*, **boḥol,—ki, tiro,—adi.**

hunt. *v.tr.*, **dab, ugadso.**

hunting, *n.*, **dabad,—ki, ugadsi,—gi.**

hunter, *n.*, **dabad,—ki.**

hurl, hurly-burly, *n.*, **shiddo,—adi.**

hurrah! *int.*, **hirro! hirro!**

hurricane, *n.*, **baḥailad** or **maḥaïlad,—di.**

hurry, *n.*, **haul badan**; the man is in a —, **ninki hausha badna**; *v.tr.*, **degdeg u ḥabo**; *v.i.*, **degdeg.**

hurt, *n.*, **'awar,—ki, ḥon,—ti, nabar,—ki**; *v.tr.*, **'awar, ḥanuni, ḥon yel**; *v.r.*, **ḥon iss yel**; *a.*, **'awaran**; be —, **'awaran** or **'awarnaw.**

husband, *n.*, **nin aḥalleh.**

hush! *int.*, (silence!) **amus! amusa!**

husk (*see* hull).

hut, *n.*, **bul,—ki**; — of one family, **jes,—ki**; — of several families not agglomerated, **jesas,—ki.**

hyæna, *n.*; striped —, **didar,—ki, ḥabal furai,—rihi**; spotted —, **'andad̄er,—ki, —ti, durwa,—gi, ḥoror,—ki, waraba, —ihi, wera,—ihi.**
hydropic, hydropical, *a.*, **bararleh,** (**nin**) **bararsan.**
hymn, *n.*, **hes,—ti.**

I.

I (*see* Grammar).
ice, *n.*, **baraf,—ki.**
idea, *n.*, **ogan,—ti.**
idiot, *n.*, **doḥọn,—ki, bahahim.**
idle, *a.*, **'ajis,—ki, 'ajisah, wahsan**; be —, **'ajisnaw, wahso.**
idleness, *n.*, **'ajisnimo, — adi, wahsi,—gi.**
idol, *n.*, **sanam,—ki.**
if, *conj.*, **hadi, bal in.**
ignominy, *n.*, **mamus jab,—ki.**
ignorance, *n.*, **oḥon laan,—ti, arurnimo,—adi.**
ignorant, *a.*, **oḥon darran, oḥonla, arur,—ti, juhula,—ihi.**
ill, *a.*, (bad) **ḥun**; (sick) **buka**; be —, **ḥumaw**; *n.*, that boy returns — (bad) for good, **inankasi sharku wanag u 'esha**; he speaks — of everyone, **isagu nin walba wa ḥil leh bu ka shega.**
illness, *n.*, **bukan,—ti.**
illegal, *a.*, **gar la.**
illegitimate, *n.*, **gara',—i'hi.**
image, *n.*, **sawir,—ki**; (figure) **surrad,—di.**
imitate, *v.tr.*, (copy) **mid u eg samai**; (endeavour to resemble) **isaga kaleh noḥo.**
immediately, *ad.*, **aminkada, iminkada, markiba, haddada, haddadatan.**
immense, *a.*, **wein.**
immerse, *v.tr.*, **ḥusi.**
immodest, *a.*, **ḥishodla.**
immortal, *a.*, **au d̄iman karin.**
impatient, *a.*, **kadsan la, sugnin la.**
impede, *v.tr.*, (hinder) **joji.**
impel, *v.tr.*, (force) **muḥuni.**
impenetrable, *a.*, **haud.**
impenetrability of a forest, *n.*, **haud,—ki.**
impenitence, *n.*, **taubad** or **tobad laan,—ti.**
imperfect, *a.*, **an d̄amain.**
impertinent, *a.*, **amusla.**
implore, *v.tr.*, **bari**; — for us, **noga ḥad.**
importunity, *n.*, (looking at some one when eating) **ḥud,—ki.**
impose, *v.tr.*, **sar**; — a fine, **ḥasir**; — taxes, **ashur sar.**
impossible, *a.*, **la ma kar, la ma karo**; it is —, **waḥ wa la ma karaḥ.**
imposture, *n.*, **bein,—ti.**
impostor, *n.*, **beina leh,** or **beina was,—ki, nin muḥalḥalah.**
impotent, *a.*, **an d̄ali karin.**
impure, *a.* and *n.*, **maḥnud,—ki.**
impurity, *n.*, **maḥnudnimo,—adi, wasmo,—adi**; commit —, **was.**
in, *prp.*, **ku, gudihi.**
incalculable, *a.*, **la ma tirin karo.**
incantation, *n.*, **fāl,—ki**; make an —, **fāl.**

incantator, *n.*, **nin waḥ fāla, nag waḥ fāsha.**
incapable, *n.*, (of fighting) **hashin, —ti, nin hashinah.**
incense, *n.*, **ḥanjo,—adi, foḥ,—hi, ḥa',—hi.**
incise, *v.tr.*, **sar, sarsar.**
incision, *n.*, **sarsar,—ki, sarmo, —adi.**
inclination, *n.*, **foror,—ki, 'uskis, —ki**; profound —, **rako',—di, sujud,—di.**
incline, *v.tr.*, **forori, 'uski**; — on, **ku tiri.**
incline, *v.i.*, **fororso, 'usko, tirso**; — on, upon, **ku tirso, rako'**; inclined to evil, **nin waliba waḥ ḥun bu u jeda.**
include, *v.tr.*, **ku ḥid.**
incomplete, *a.*, **an damain.**
incomprehensible, *a.*, **an la garan.**
incorruptible, *a.*, **ma ḥudmin.**
increase, *v.tr.*, **badi, badnai, kordi**; *v.i.*, **badnaw.**
increase, *n.*, (augmentation) **kordis,—ki.**
incur, *v.tr.*, **galabso.**
indebt, *v.tr.*, **ḥan geli.**
indebted, *a.*, **ḥamaisan.**
indeed, *ad.*, **waiyai** or **weiyei.**
indelible, *a.*, **(sumad) an la babiin karin.**
independent, *a.*, **iss baḥ.**
indigent, *a.*, **'aïd,—di.**
indignant, *a.*, **'adaisan.**
indignation, *n.*, **'ado,—adi.**
indignity, *n.*, **'aï,—di.**
indigo, *n.*, **sibaḥ madow 'adanah.**
indirect, *a.*, **ḥalloḥan, jidki ḥalloḥna.**
individual, *n.*, **ḥof,—ki, 'id,—di.**
India, *n.*, **ard al hindi.**
Indian, *n.*, **hindi,—gi.**
indocile, *a.*, **'asi,—gi, 'asiah.**
indolence, *n.*, **'ajisnimo,—adi.**
indolent, *a.*, **'ajis,—ki.**
induce, *v.tr.*, **sasab.**
indulge, *v.tr.*, **'amalkis ḥun bu oggolyahai.**
indurate, *v.tr.*, **adkai.**
inebriate, *v.tr.*, **kaga saḥrami.**
ineffable, *a.*, **la ma hadli karo.**
infallible, *a.*, **ma beinain karo, bein ma shegi karo, ma ḥatalmi karo.**
infamous, *a.*, **mamus la.**
infamy, *n.*, **mamus jab,—ki.**
infancy, *n.*, **arurnimo,—adi.**
infant, *n.*, **ilmo,—ihi, murjo',—hi.**
infectious, *a.*, (contagious) **la iss ka ḥad, saboh.**
inferior, *a.*, **nin hosai, in hosai.**
infidel, *n.*, **gal,—ki.**
infidels *or* infidelity, *n.*, **galo,—adi.**
inflame, *v.tr.*, **belbelli, ololi, shid.**
inflict, *v.tr.*, **u sar.**
inform, *v.tr.*, **war gei, war ken, warran, ogaisi**; *v.r.*, **iss ka warran.**
informant, *n.*, **war kena,—ihi.**
information, *n.*, **war,—ki.**
ingratitude, *n.*, **abal darri,—di.**
inhabit, *v.i.*, **fadi, jog.**
inhabitant, *n.*, **deris,—ki.**
inheritance, *n.*, **daḥal,—ki.**
inherit, *v.tr.*, **daḥal.**
inhospitable, *a.*, **baḥail,—ki.**
inhospitability, *n.*, **morti ḥadis, —ki.**

inhuman, *a.*, **adow,—gi.**
inhumanity, *n.*, **adownimo,—adi.**
injure, *v.tr.*, **'aï, bii, waḥ yel.**
injurious, *a.*, **waḥ yellaleh, (erai) an la iss odan.**
injury, *n.*, **'aï,—di, waḥ yello, —di, na'dal,—shi.**
injustice, *n.*, **gar darri,—di.**
ink, *n.*, **ḫad,—ki.**
inkstand, *n.*, **dawād,—di, madad, —ki.**
inn, *n.*, **das,—ki.**
innocence, *n.*, **ḫujad laan,—ti, taḫsir laan,—ti.**
innocent, *a.*, **ḫujadla, taḫsirla, an taḫsir lahain.**
inoffensive, *a.*, **(wa bunduḫ) an 'idna waḥ yelin.**
inquietude, *n.*, **weirweir,—ki.**
inquire, *v.tr*, **weidi, don.**
inscribe, *v.tr.*, **ku ḫor, waraḫda ku dig.**
insert, *v.tr.*, **ku rid.**
inside, *n.*, **gudaha, gudihi.**
insnare, *v.tr.*, **dab.**
insolence, *n.*, **amar weinan,—ti.**
insolent, *a.*, **af ḥun, amusila.**
instant, *n.*, **'abbar,—ki.**
instep, *n.*, **boḫon horai.**
instruct, *v.tr.*, **bar, wani.**
instruction, *n.*, **barnin,—ti, barasho,—adi.**
instructor, *n.*, **bara,—ihi.**
insult (*see* injure).
intangible, *a.*, **an la taban karin.**
integral, *a.*, **daman.**
intellect, intelligence, *n.*, **aḫli,—gi, garasho,—adi, miyir,—ki.**
intelligent, *a.*, **'arrab jila'san, miyirsan, miyir ḫaba.**

intend, *v.tr.*, **dama'**; what do you — to do, **mahad dama'santahai.**
intention, *n.*, **dama',—hi.**
intercede, *v.i.*, **deḥ gal, u ga'an geli.**
intercept, *v.tr.*, **joji.**
intercourse, *n.*, **warmo,—adi.**
interest, *n.*, **awo,—adi, darad,—di.**
interfere, *v.tr.*, (interpose) **ga'an geli.**
interior, *a.*, **gudahaah.**
interjection (of inticing), **'ar! 'ar!** (of pain) **ha!** (of calling) **war hoi! na hoi!** (for parents) **aiya abbe! aiya hoyo!**
interpret, *v.tr.*, **ka af'eli, u kala af'eli.**
interpretation, *n.*; that — is not good, **kala af'eliskasi ma tosna.**
interpreter, *n.*, **afayen,—ki, af'elis,—ki, türjuman,—ki.**
interrogate, *v.tr.*, **weidi, sual.**
interrogation, *n.*, **sual,—shi, weidis,—ki.**
interrogative (particle), **ma? e?** (as an affix).
interrupt, *v.tr.*, **ḫulḫuladai.**
intervene, *v.i.*, **deḥ gal, la tali.**
intervention, *n.*, **talo,—adi.**
intervert, *v.tr.*, **gesta kaleh u dig** or **u rog.**
intestine, *n.*, **uslahais,—ti, uslaho** or **usloho,—adi**; long —, **ḫidmo,—ihi, mindi'ir,—ki.**
intimate, *n.*, (a familiar friend) **saḥib runah** or **saḥib dabah.**
into, *prp.*, **ku.**

intoxicate, *v.tr.*, **kaga saḥrami.**

intrepid, *a.*, **'absila, bilileh, gesi, —gi, ragah.**

intrepidity, *n.*, **bili,—gi, gesinimo,—adi.**

introduce, *v.tr.*, **geli, ku kaḥai, abur, sinif.**

intrust, *v.tr.*, **aman, amanaiso, u dibo.**

inundation, *n.*, **dād,—ki, biyihi 'arrada rogai.**

inutile, *a.*, **an waḥba tarain, waḥ ma tarai.**

invade, *v.tr.*, **dul, so da'.**

invaluable, *a.*, **ib ma laha.**

invariable, *a.* **an rogman karin.**

invent, *v.tr.*, **hindis.**

invention, *n.*, **hindisad,—di.**

investigate, *v.tr.*, **hubso.**

investigation, *n.*, **hubsad,—ki.**

invidious, *a.*, **hasid,—ki.**

invincible, *a.*, **an laga adkan karin.**

invisible, *a.*, **la ma arko, an la arki karin; God is —, Ilah wa waḥ an la arki karin.**

invite, *v.tr.*, **u yed.**

iris of the eye, *n.*, **isha buhdeda.**

iron, *n.*, **birr,—ti, sulub,—ki; — wire, hasau,—di; *v.tr.*, (smooth the clothes with) birrta mari.**

irregular, *a.*, **janjedah; make —, janjedi.**

irregularity, *n.*, **janjed,—ki.**

Islam, Islamism, *n.*, **nin islamed, dinti islamed.**

island, isle, *n.*, **gashirad,—di.**

issue, *v.i.*, **baḥ; issued, baḥ.**

itch, itching, *n.*, **'addo,—adi, 'adanyo,—adi; *v.i.*, 'adanyo.**

ivory, *n.*, **fol marodi, folki marodi,** the ...

J.

jabber (*see* babble, chatter).

jackal, *n.*, **dawa' dulmadowah, golli,—di, golli warabais,— ki, hor,—ki.**

jail, *n.*, **habsi,—gi.**

jar, *n.*, (vessel) **dil,—shi, gog,— gi, han,—ti, ḥumbo,—adi, mardaban,—ki.**

javelin, *n.*, **dagalai or degelai,— di, waran,—ki.**

jaw, *n.*, **dan,—ki.**

jealous, *a.*, **hasid,—ki; be —, hasid, gubo.**

jealousy, *n.*, **hasidnimo,—adi.**

jeer, *n.*, (scoff) **luḥuf,—ki; *v.tr.* and *v.i.*, luḥufi or luḥfi, ku ḥosol; mahad i luḥufinaisa?** why are you (laughing or) jeering at me?

jeerer, *n.*, **luḥufi,—gi, nin luḥufiah.**

jerk, *v.tr.*, **ruḥruḥ, tur.**

jest, *n.*, **ayar,—ti, kaftan,—ki.**

Jesus, *n.*, **'Issa.**

Jew, *n.*, **yuhudi,—gi; yuhud,— di (*plur.*).**

Jewess, *n.*, **yuhudiyad,—di.**

job, *n.*, **haul,—shi, shuḥul,—ki.**

join, *v.tr.*, **iss ku dar, iss u gei, iss ku hid, iss ku ḥodob, iss ku samai, iss ku tol.**

joining, *n.*, **iss ku daran,—ki, iss ku samais,—ki.**

joint, *n.*, **ḥubin,—ti, fanah,—hi**; he has put his arm out of —, **ga'antisi wa fuduḥdai.**

joke, *n.*, **kaftan,—ki**; *v.i.*, **kaftan, 'ayar.**

journey, *n.*, **kabadai,—ihi, sod'al, —ki**; half day's —, **daldalasho,—adi**; camel day's —, **gedi,—gi**; *v.i.*, **kabadai, sod'al.**

joy, joyfulness, *n.*, **badad,—ki, raïn,—ti, faraḥan,—ki, farḥad,—di, raḥo,—adi.**

joyful, joyous, *a.*, **badadan, badadsan, raḥaisan, faraḥanah, faraḥsan.**

joyousness, jubilation, *n.*, **badad, —ki** ...; give joy, **kaga badbadi** or **badbadadi.**

judge, *n.*, **daulad,—di, nin dauladed, ḥakin,—ki**; *v.tr.*, **ḥisab ḥukum, gar goi.**

judgment, *n.*, **gar,—ti, ḥukum, —ki, ḥisab,—ti.**

jug, *n.*, (vessel) **kusad,—di.**

juggler, *n.*, **maḥawi,—gi.**

juice, *n.*, **de'an,—ki.**

jujube, *n.*, **gob,—ki, hohob,—ti.**

jump, *n.*, **bodo,—adi, botin,—ti**; *v.i.*, **bod.**

junction, *n.*, **iss ku daran,—ki.**

jungle, *n.*, (desert) **'idla,—di, 'idla'ir sila,—di, miyi,—gi.**

just, *a.*, **hagagsan, haḥ, tagan, ḥuman, ragah, tolmon.**

just now, *ad.*, **aminkada, iminkada, haddadatan.**

justice, *n.*, **gar,—ti.**

jowari *or* jowaree, *n.*, (kind of corn) **hadud** or **harud,—ki**; — plant, **kassab, ḥassab,—ki, salol,—ki.**

K.

kahri *or* curry, *n.*, **sanunad,—di**; — stuff, **ḥawaj,—ki**; make the —, **sanunadda samai**; mix — with rice, **sanunadai.**

keel, *n.*, (of a ship) **herab,—ki.**

keep, *v.tr.*, **ho, hai, haiso, ḥabo**; — for you, **digo, ḥado**; — your promise, **hadalkaga daso** or **ḥejiso**; — asunder, **kala baïdi**; — away, off, **fogai, ka fogai**; — back, **dib u 'eli**; — down, **hos u hai**; — under your temper, **amalkaga iss ka hosaisi**; — where you are, **halkad jogtid jog**; — off, **du, naga du.**

keeping, *n.*, (act of) **haisi,—gi.**

kerchief, *n.*, **malḥamad,—di.**

kettle, *n.*, **digsi** or **disti,—gi, deri,—gi, adār,—ki.**

key, *n.*, **mufta,—hi.**

kick, *n.*; — of man, **lad,—ki**; — in a kind of game, **hurdun, —ki**; — of a horse, ass, mule ..., **biḥlai** or **biḥlo,—ihi, dambabud** or **dambabid,—ki**; — of a camel, **harati,—di**; *v.tr.*, **lad, hurdan.**

kid, *n.*, **wahar,—ti.**

kidney, *n.*, **kelli,—gi.**

kill, *v.tr.*, **dil, nafta ka ḫad, kaga 'aḫbal, ka kausi, ka kudi.**
kiln, *n.*, **mufo,—adi.**
kind, *a.*, (good) **wanaksan, tolmon**; *n.*, (sort) **aïn,—ki, tol,—ki**; of the same —, **iss ku tol.**
kindness, *n.*, **ja'lan,—ti, wanag, —gi, tolimo,—adi.**
kindle, *v.tr.*, **shid.**
kindred, *n.*, (kin) **ḥidid,—ki**; become —, **la ḥidid.**
king, *n.*, **boḫor,—ki, malik,—gi, suldan,—ki, ugas,—ki.**
king's evil, *n.*, **hudai** or **huda,—ihi, māl,—shi.**
kingdom, *n.*, **mulki,—gi.**
kiss, *n.*, **đunkad,—ki, đunkasho, —adi**; *v.tr.*, **đunko.**
kitchen, *n.*, **gali,—gi.**
kite, *n.*, (a bird) **đuryo,—adi**; (a toy) **diyarad,—di.**
kitten, *n.*, **dinad yar,—di, —aid.**
klipspringer, *n.*, **alakud** or **alikud, —di.**
knave, *n.*, **ḥarami,—gi, tug,—gi, nin ḥaramiah.**
knead, *v.tr.*, **'ajin, ḫosh.**
knee, *n.*, **jilib,—ki, rug,—gi**; — pan, **kurankur,—ti**; bend the —, **jilibka đig.**
kneel, *v.i.*, **jilba jogso**; remain kneeling, **jilba jog, jilba yara đig**; — and make the profound inclination, **sujud**; — (in speaking to the camel), **arun, tu**; make the camel —, **arumi, tui.**
kneeling, *n.*, (genuflexion) **jilba jog,—gi.**
knife, *n.*, **mindi,—di.**
knock, *n.*, (at the door) **garā',—hi**; — with a club, **gagab,—gi, kau,—di**; *v.tr.*, **garā'**; — down, **bŭđai, ka dufo, gagabi, ka kausi.**
knot, *n.*, **guntin,—ti, gunti,—gi, gar,—ki**; *v.tr.*, **gunud, garai, garaiso.**
know, *v.tr.*, **garo, ogow, oḫon, og**; I do not —, **moji**; *v.c.*, **ogaisi.**
knowledge, *n.*, **oḫon,—ti, 'ilmi, —gi.**
known, *a.*, **la yaḫan**; well —, **ma'ruf,—ki**; a well — man, **nin ma'rufah.**
knuckle, *n.*, **fanah,—hi, hubin, —ti.**
koodoo, *n.*, (antelope in general) **aderyo,—adi**; lesser —, **aderyo 'ari,—gi**; male —, **godir, —ki.**
koran, *n.*, (alcoran) **furḫan,—ki.**

L.

labour, *n.*, **haul,—shi, shuḫul,—ki**; *v.tr.*, **shaḫai, haul ḫabo, hausho, ḫoji.**
labourer, *n.*, **shaḫi,—gi, nin shaḫiah.**
laborious, *a.*, **hauled, haushoda, ḫog wein.**
lac, *n.*, (100,000 rupees, in India) **lak, boḫol kun o rubod, lak rubiadod.**
lactation, *n.*, **'ana nujis,—ki.**

lad, *n.*, inan,—ki, wil,—ki.
ladder, *n.*, sallan,—ki.
lade (*see* load).
laden, *a.*, raran.
ladle (*or a vessel with a handle*), *n.*, ḍura, ḥudda,—ihi, tebeda dara,—ihi.
lady. *n.*, afo,—adi, nag,—ti, úri, —di.
lag, *v i.*, (stay behind) dambai, rāg.
lamb, *n.*, barār,—ki ; she —, naïl,—shi ; he —, wan bararah.
lame (of one leg), *n.*, dutiyai, --yihi ; — woman, dutiso,—adi ; go —, duti.
lament, *n.*, baror,—ti, musanow, —gi, oin,—ti ; *v.i.*, baroro, oi, musanow ; *v.c.*, ka barori.
lake, *n.*, biyo gal,—ki, biyo galen,—ki.
lamp, *n.*, (lantern) sirad,—ki ; night —, ilais, - ki.
lance, *n.*, (long spear) waran,—ki.
land, *n.*, berri,—gi, ḍul,—ki.
land, *v.i.*, (put ashore) deg ; *v.tr.*, deji, rog, so rog, alabadada rog.
landing, *n.*, degnin,—ti, rognin, —ti.
language, *n.*, af,—ki.
languid, *a.*, ataisan, weidsan.
languish, *v.i.*, 'atow, weidow.
languor. *n.*, 'ato,—di, weidnimo, —adi.
lantern, *n.*, fanus,—ki.
lap, *n.*, ḍab,—ti.
lap, *v.tr.*, (lick up) raḥ.

lapidate, *v.tr.*, shīd.
lapidation, *n.*, shīd,—ki.
large, *a.*, balladan, wein ; footed, kabo wein.
largeness, *n.*, ballaḍ,—ki, weinan, —ti ; — of feet or sandals, kabo weinan.
lark, *n.*, hedin ḥeto,—adi.
larva, *n.*, dirḥi,—gi ; — of gnats, lunlumai,—ihi.
lash (*see* flog, flogging).
lass, *n.*, gabad,—di.
lassitude, *n.*, dāl,—ki.
last, *a.*, (utmost) ugu dambaiyai, ugu dambaisai ; at —, aḥirtanka.
last, *v.i.*, (endure) rāg.
lasting, *a.*, adag.
latch, *n.*, albabka ilḥaḍisa.'
late, *a.*, rāgsan; (deceased) dintai (*m.*), dimatai (*f.*); be —, rāg ; was it so — ? ma sidasai u ragen ? he came —, wa so rāgai.
lately, *ad.*, beri dowed.
latitude, *n.*, (breadth) ballad,—ki.
lattice-work, *n.*, sāb,—ki.
laugh, laughter, *n.*, ḥosol,—ki.
laugh, *v.i.*, ḥosol ; — at, ku ḥosol.
launch, *v.tr.*, (to force a ship into the sea) kawir.
launderer, *n.*, dhobi,—gi, dar ḥasal,—ki.
lavish, *a.*, (prodigal) lumai, nin lumai ; *v.tr.*, lumi.
law, *n.*, haul,—ki, ḥaïnun,—ki, ḥaïd,—ki.
lawful, *a.*, ḥalal ; make him —, ḥalalai.

lawfulness, *n.*, **ḥalal,—shi.**
lawsuit, *n.*, **da'wad,—di.**
lay, *v.tr.*, (place) **dig**; — aside, **daḥ, daḥo, digo**; — away, **reb**; — before, open out, **muji, tus**; — over, **dusha ka sar**; — on, **ku reb**; — down, **u dibo**; — hold of, **ho.**
laziness, *n.*, **ajisnimo,—adi, wahsi, —gi.**
lazy, *a.*, **'ajis,—ki, 'ajisah, wahsan**; be —, **'ajisnow, wahso.**
lead, *n.*, (a metal) **rasas,—ti.**
lead, *v.tr.*, (guide) **badbādi, kaḥai**; — from, out of, **ka badbādi**; — to, **u kaḥai**; — the dance, **'ayarta hagaji**; — the prayer, **ina tuki** or **tuji.**
leader, *n.*, (of the prayer) **iman, —ki.**
leaf, *n.*, **'alen,—ti**; — of a palm-tree, **au,—di.**
leak, *n.*, **dalol,—ki**; *v.i.*, **dalol**; the kettle leaks, **distigi wa dalola.**
lean, *n.*, (of meat) **jid,—ki, jimid, —ki.**
lean (animal), *n.*, **abaḥ,—hi**; *a.*, **abaḥah**; be —, **abaḥ**; *v.c.*, **abaḥi.**
lean, *a.*, **'ataisan, weïdsan**; be —, **'atow, weïdow**; *v.c.*, **weïdai.**
lean, *v.tr.*, (incline) **tiri, 'uski**; *v.i.*, **tirso, 'usko**; — upon, **ku tiri, ku tirso.**
leanness, *n.*, **'ato,—adi, weïdnimo,—adi.**
leap, *v.i.*, (jump) **bod**; *n.*, **bodo, —adi, botin,—ti.**

learn, *v.tr.*, **baro, digo.**
learning, *n.*, **barnin,—ti.**
least, *a.*, **ka wada yar, ugu yar.**
leather, *n.*, **ḥod,—ki, jan,—ti, harag,—gi.**
leave, *n.*, (permission) **fasaḥ,—hi.**
leave, *v.tr.*, (let go) **da, na'**; — aside, **mel digo**; — out, **ka ḥadi**; — behind, **dambaisi**; — on, **ku reb**; *v.i.*, **iss ka da, iss ka reb.**
leaven, *n.*, **ḥamir,—ki.**
lecture, *n.*, **ḥadis,—ki.**
ledge, *n.*, **aror,—ki.**
leech, *n.*, **'ula'ul,—shi.**
leer, *n.*, (an oblique look) **gatin, —ti.**
left (hand), *n.*, **bideḥ,—di**; to the —, **bideḥda**; — handed, **gurai,—gi.**
leg, hind-leg, *n.*, **lug,—ti**; fore —, **jeni,—gi**; — below the knee, **kub,—ki, shansho,—adi**; — of a chair, **rukun,—ki.**
one-legged man, *n.*, **nin lugla, luglawai,—ihi.**
legacy, *n.*, **dardaran,—ki.**
legal (*see* lawful).
legumen, *n.*, **ḥudrad,—di.**
leisure, *n.*, **haulyari,—di.**
lemon, *n.*, **lin danan,—ti —aid.**
lend, *v.tr.*, **amaḥi.**
lending, *n.*, **amaḥ,—di.**
length, *n.*, **derer,—ki.**
lengthen, *v.tr.*, **derai, dereri**; — by adding to, **iss ku dereri.**
Lent, *n.*, **waḥtega sonka.**
leopard, *n.*, **shabel,—ki, horgumo, —adi, nimmer,—ki.**

leper, *n.*, **bar'asleh,—ihi.**
leprosy, *n.*, **bar'as,—ki.**
less, *a.*, **diman, ka yar.**
lessen, *v.tr.*, **din, yarai, yaraiso.**
lesson, *n.*, **ma'shar,—ki.**
let, *v.i.*, **da**; — me alone, **i da**; — me go out, **dibadda i si da**; why do you — him come in? **maḥad gudaha ugu so dainaisa?** — the boys sleep, **arurta da ha seḥatai**; — down, **hosaisi**; — in, into, **so geli, so da**; — go, **si da, so da**; — me see, **bal an arko**; — him speak, **ha hadlo**; — it be so, **ha ahato, sida ha ahato**; I have let a house, **aḥal ban kiraistai.**
letter, *n.*, (of alphabet) **ḥaraf,—ki**; (an epistle) **warḥad,—di.**
level, *v.tr.*, **banai, sin, iss ku sin.**
level ground, *n.*, **ban,—ki, gegi,—di, tamuḥ,—di, mel tamuḥah.**
liar, *n.*, **beinaleh,—ihi, beinawas,—ki.**
license, *n.*, (permission) **fasaḥ,—hi.**
lick, *v.tr.*, **lef.**
lid, *n.*, **dabol,—ki, hadub,—ki, hadub gal,—ki, gorof,—ki, dabaḥ,—hi.**
lie, *n.*, **bein,—ti, ḥalalif,—ta.**
lie, *v.i.*, (tell a lie) **bein sheg.**
lie, *v.i.*, (rest) **jif, jifso, oll**; he lies along upon the ground, **dulku yal, dulku yil.**
life, *n.*, **nolan,—ti, rubad,—ki, naf,—ti**; —time, **'emri,—gi**; next —, **nolanta aḥiro** or **nolanta dambai.**
lifelessness, *n.*, **nafo,—ahi.**
lift, *v.tr.*, **hinji, kor** or **sarai u ḥad.**
light, *n.*, **if,—ki, iftin,—ki, ilais,—ki**; — of the day, **gabal,—ki**; *v.tr.*, **iftimi, sirad, shid, ololi.**
light, *a.*, (bright) **dalalaya**; (not heavy) **fudud.**
lighten, *v.tr.*, **iftimi**; it lightens, **'irku wa hilāaya.**
lightning, *n.*, **hilā,—hi.**
like, *a.*, (resembling) **leh eg, intas o kaleh, intas leh eg**; — father — son, **abbaha inankuna u eg yahai**; make —, **u ekaisi**; in — manner, **sidi o kaleh.**
like, *v.tr.*, (love) **ja'alaw**; do you — his advice? **taladisa ma ja'ashahai?** do you — it? **ma ja'ashahai** or **je'eshahai?**
likely, *ad.*, (probably) **malaha**; he is — to die of hunger, **malaha gaja dili donta**; we are — to have war, **dagal bainu downahai.**
likeness, *n.*, **ekan,—ti.**
liking, *n.*, (inclination); having the same —, **iss ku talo.**
limb, *n.*, **adin,—ki, laḥad,—ki.**
lime, *n.*, **dareyo,—adi, malas,—ti**; quick-—, **dagaḥ gubtai.**
limit, *n.*, **dal,—ki.**
limp, *v.i.*, **duti**; *n.*, **dukis,—ki.**
limpid, *a.*, (clear) **miran.**
line, *n.*, **dilin,—ti, sadar,—ki, taḥ, tihhi**; the —, lines of the hand, **herro** or **herriyo,—adi**; range in —, **taḥ, iss ku taḥ.**

linen, *n.*, **dar,—ki.**
linger, *v.i.*, **rag.**
lion, *n.*, **libaḥ,—hi**; male —, **ār,—ki**; female —, **gōl,—shi.**
lip, *n.*, **bushin,—ti, dibin,—ti, farur,—ti.**
listen, *v.i.*, **degaiso, maḥal, yel**; — to, **aḥbal, ka aḥbal.**
lit, *a.*, **siradan, shidan.**
little, *a.*, **yar, gabanah, gibinah, gaban**; *ad.*, **waḥ hoga** or **wuh hoga** or **woḥhoga, yar, ḥunyar.**
litany, *n.*, **ḥunud,—di**; recite the —, **ḥunudda mari.**
live, *v.i.*, (be alive) **nolaw, jir**; (dwell) **fadi, jir, jog, oll, rugaiso.**
liver, *n.*, **ber,—ti**; — of camels, **waslado,—ihi.**
living, *a.*, (alive) **nol**; — property, **holo nol,—ihi, —a.**
lizard, *n.*, **ḥorato,—adi, gelka abadis, ror,—ki, masso** or **monso,—adi.**
lo! *int.*, **eg! ega!**
load, *v.tr.*, **rar, sheḥnad, 'abai**; *n.*, **ḥamil,—ki, rar,—ki, rarmo,—adi.**
loading, *n.*, (freight) **sheḥnad,——di.**
loaded, laden, *a.*, **raran, 'abaisan, sheḥnadan, buḥa.**
loaf, *n.*, **kibis,—ti.**
loan, *n.*, (a thing lent) **amaḥ,—di.**
loathe, *v.tr.*, (abhor) **na'**; he loathes every meat, **hilib walba wa ka yiḥyiḥsanaya**; *v.i.*, (create disgust) **yiḥyiḥsi.**
loathsome, *a.*, **yiḥyiḥsan.**
lobe, *n.*, (of the ear) **dahal,—shi, degta dahasheda**; upper part of —, **ḥurdan** or **ḥurjan,—ki.**
lock, *n.*, **ḥuful,—ki.**
locust, *n.*, **ayaḥ,—hi, koronkoro,—adi.**
log of wood, *n.*, **dogob,—ki, jirid,—di.**
loin, *n.*, (reins) **kelli,—di**; — cloth, **maḥawis,—ki, go,—hi, haïd,—ki.**
loll, *v.i.*, **ku tirso.**
long, *a.*, **der**; — in prayer, **du'a ku rag,—gi**; — disease, **udur rāgai**; you are very — in coming, **wad rāgta**; — after, *ad.*, **gor dambow**; how — is it since? **imisa ka dambayai** or **dambaisai?**
long, *ad.*, — ago, **beri horai**; not long before, **ayamo dowed**; ere long, **gor dowba**; I will come ere long, **gor dowba wa iman dona**; as long as I live, **inta an nolahai**; as long as he is virtuous he will be admired, **intas u wanaksanyahai wa la la yabi**; all my life long, **intan jirai o dan**, or **intan nola o dan**, or **intan nola o idil**; all day long, **malin o idil.**
long, *v.tr.*, (desire earnestly) **ka rag**; I — to see him, **araggagi ban ka ragsanahai**, or **inan arko wan donaya**; — for, **tabalaisnaw**; he longs for this place, **meshatanu u tabalaisanyahai.**
look, *n.*, **egmo,—adi, arag,—gi, daïmo,—adi.**

look, *v.i.*; he looks very well, **wa afimad ḫaba**; that looks well, **wa wanaksanyahai** or **wanaksantahai**; — about you, **iss eg, iss jir**; — after, to the boy, **inanka eg** or **ilali** or **jir**; — at, **dai, bal eg**; — out, — for, **don, bād**; what do you — for? **maḥad donaisa**, or **maḥad radinaisa**? I have long looked for him, **in badan ban sugayai**; — into, over, **hubso**; — there, at, **u jed, u jeso, hagga u jeso**; let me — at the ship they speak of, **bal an ego markabka la shegayo**; — at a man eating, **ḫud**; looking at a man when eating, *n.*, **ḫud,—ki.**
look, *v.tr.*, **arag, eg, dai, jedāli, dugo.**
looking-glass, *n.*, **murayad,—di.**
loose, loosen, *v.tr.*, **deb'i**; *a.*, **deb'isan.**
lord, *n.*, **saheb,—ki.**
lose, *v.tr.*, **ḥor, ambi, hababi, hallai, lumi, bel**; *v.i.*. **ala'al, ambo, habab, hallaw, lun.**
loss, *n.*, **hallau,—gi**; suffer a —, **ed**; suffering of a —, **edis,—ki**; — of a person, **habab,—ki.**
lost, *a.*, **hababsan, hallabai.**
lounge, *v.i.*, (to idle) **ku tirso**; do not —, **ha ku tirsan.**
louse, *n.*, **injir,—ti.**
love, *n.* **ja'ail,—ki, ja'alan,—ti**; *v.tr.*, **ja'alaw**; do not —, **ha ja'alan.**
low, *a.*, **hosai**; be —, **hosai**; *ad.*, **hos, hosta**; speak —, **hos u hadal.**
lower, *v.tr.*, (bring low) **hos u ḫabo, hos u hai.**
lowing, *n.*, (of cows) **bana'ei,—gi.**
luck, *n.*, **ayan,—ki, nasib,—ki**; good —, **'awo,—adi**; bad —, **ayan ḫumo**; wish him good —, **ḫalib.**
lucky, *a.*, **ayanleh, ḫaliban.**
luggage, *n.*, **alabo,—adi.**
lull, *v.tr.*, **seḥi.**
lump, *n.*, (a mass) **fud,—ki, kus,—ki**; a — of sugar, **fud sunkorah.**
lunacy, *n.*, **walli,—di.**
lunatic, *a.*, **wallan, walla.**
lungs, *n.*, **sambab,—ki.**
lure (*see* allure).
luxation, *n.*, **fuduḥ** or **furuḥ,—hi.**
lynx, *n.*, **gududona,—gi.**

M.

machine, *n.*, **dawar,—ki.**
mad, *a.*, **wallan**; become —, **wallo.**
madden, *v.tr.* and *v.i.*, **wal, iss walwal.**
madness, *n.*, **walli,—di.**
magician, *n.*, **nin waḥ fala, nag waḥ fasha.**
magistrate, *n.*, **daulad** or **dowlad,—di.**
magnanimity, *n.*, **raganimo,—adi.**
Mahometan, *n.*, **muslim,—ki.**

maid, *n.*, **gabad,—di, ugub,—ki, gashan,—ti.**
maim, *v.tr.*, **adin go**; *a.*, **adin la.**
make, *v.tr.*, **samai, waḥai**; — well, **ād u ḥabo** or **samai**; — again, **ku lāban.**
made, *a.*, **la waḥai, samaisan**; — of, **ka samaismai**; be —, **samaisan, samaisnaw.**
maker, *n.*, **samais,—ki.**
making, *n.*, **samain,—ti.**
male, *n.*, **labod,—ki, ḥododi**; *a.*, **lab, ḥodah.**
maledict, malediction (*see* curse).
malefactor, *n.*, **layan,—ki.**
malevolent, malignant, *a.*, **ḥamiti, —gi, ḥamitiah, ḥamitigaha.**
malevolence, malignancy, *n.*, **ḥamidnimo,—adi.**
mallet, *n.*, (wooden hammer) **ḥori dubbaah.**
malice, *n.*, **histi,—gi.**
man, *n.*, **nin,—ki, rag,—gi**; he is grown a —, **wa gad madowbai**; — of prudence, wisdom, **farid,—ki, nin faridah**; — of war, **markab ḥarbiah.**
manage, *v.tr.*, **tali, ku tali**; — that office, **hafiska u tali.**
management, manage, *n.*, **talo,—adi.**
manager, *n.*, **taliya,—yihi, ḥakin, —ki.**
manducation, *n.*, **'alal,—ki, rabsi, —gi.**
mane, *n.*, (of a horse) **gūd,—ki**; hair of the —, **saïn,—ti.**
manhood, *n.*, **ninnimo,—adi, raganimo,—adi.**
mangouste (greyish-red), *n.*, **shaushugā,—ihi**; (red) **sogur,—ki.**
mankind, *n.*, **dad,—ki.**
manliness, *n.*, **raganimo,—adi.**
manner, *n.*, **si,—di, bassar,—ki**; in this —, **sidan**; do in the same —, **sidi lo samaiyai u samai**; in what —? **side?** (custom) **dastur,—ti**; having the same manners, **iss ku talo.**
many, *a.*, **badan, tiro badan.**
map, *n.*, **warḥadda dunidu ku sawirantahai.**
marble (for playing), *n.*, **fatari, —gi**; **fatatir,—ti** (*plur.*).
march, *v.i.*, **so'o, talab, baïd**; *v.c.*, **so'odsi, talabi**; *n.*, **so'od,—ki, talabo,—adi.**
mare, *n.*, **genyo,—adi.**
mark, *n.*, **'alan,—ki, astan,—ti, sumad,—di, ḥanjid,—di**; *v.tr.*, **'alamadi, sumad.**
market, *n.*, **suḥ,—hi.**
marriage, *n.*, **gūr,—ki, gūrsad, —ki, aros,—ki.**
married, *a.*, **gūrsadai**; a — man, **nag la gūrsadai**; a — woman, **nag ninleh**; a new- — man, **aros,—ki.**
marrow, *n.*, **duḥ,—hi.**
marry, *v.tr.*, **u guri, u dis, iss u guri, meri**; — your daughter to me, **gabaddada i meri**; *v.i.*, **gurso**; *v.r.*, **merso**; marry your sister-in-law in a second marriage, **dumal.**
marsh, *n.*, **rubad,—ki.**
marvel, *n.*, **yab,—ki.**
marvellous, *a.*, **yaban, yableh, la yabsan.**

masculine, *n.*, (sex) **rag,—gi.**
mason, *n.*, **bani,—gi.**
mass, *n.*, (lump) **fud,—ki**; (heap) **tul,—ki.**
Mass, *n.*, (holy sacrifice) **ḫaddas, —ki.**
mast, *n.*, **daḫal,—ki.**
master, *n.*, **saheb,—ki, maḫadin, —ki**; school- —, **mu'alim,—ki, fiḫi,—gi, bara,—ihi.**
master, *v.tr.*, **u tali**; (subdue) **jar'a bar, laïli, dastur ḥun karaw.**
masticate, *v.tr.*, **'alali, rabso.**
mastication, *n.*, **'alal,—ki, 'alalis, —ki, rabsi,—gi.**
masturb, *v.tr.*, **ka'si**; *v.r.*, **ka'so.**
masturbation, *n.*, **ka'si,—gi.**
mat, *n.*, **dermo,—adi, ḫarar,—ki, kebed,—di.**
match, *n.*, (lucifer) **ḫaraf,—ki, kebrid,—di.**
mate, *n.*, (companion) **wehel,—ki.**
maternity, *n.*, **hoyanimo,—adi.**
matrice, *n.*, (womb) **rimai,—gi, ur,—ki.**
matrimony, *n.*, **gūr,—ki.**
matter, *n.*, (pus) **de'an,—ki, malaḥ,—di**; (cause) **sabab,—ti, ed,—di**; what is the — ? **eddu wa maḥai? or maḥad lehdahai?** I make no — of it, **yelkisa!**
maturate, *v.tr.*, **bislai.**
mature, *a.*, **bisil.**
maturity, *n.*, **bisail,—ki**; age of —, **gan,—ki**; the man at the age of —, **gaḋ madowbai.**
maw, *n.*, (stomach of birds) **bog, —gi.**
maxim, *n.*, **mahmah,—di.**

may, *aux.v.*, **kar**; you — if you wish, **hadad rabtid wa karta**; if it — be, **hadai jiri karto**; if I — say so, **hadan sida odan karayo**; as much as — be, **intad kartid.**
meadow, *n.*, **doḥo,—adi.**
meal, *n.*, **'unno,—adi, haḋimo,—adi, suḥur,—ti, afur,—ki**; take your —, **suḥuro.**
mean, *a.*, (base) **fuḋud.**
meaning, *n.*, **ma'nai,—ihi**; what is the — of this word? **eraiga ma'nihisu wa mahai?**
meanness, *n.*, **fudaid,—ki.**
means, *n.*; by all —, **kolleh**; by no —, **sina.**
measure, *n.*, **gedka lugu ḫiyaso, mailin,—ki**; take the —, **ḫiyas**; *v.tr.*, **ḋuḋumi, dira'.**
meat, *n.*, **hilib,—ki, jimid,—ki, 'ad,—ki, muḫmad,—di, kumbis,—ki, jiḋ,—ki**; fat of —, **barur,—ti.**
meddle, *v.tr.*, **ga'an geli.**
mediate, *v.tr.*, **ga'an geli, heshisi, tali.**
mediation, *n.*, **heskis,—ti, talo, —adi.**
mediator, *n.*, **taliya,—ihi.**
medicament, *n.*, **daïmo,—adi.**
medicine, *n.*, **dawo,—adi, sanaḥo,—adi**; give —, **dawai.**
medicinal tree, *n.*, **gugubod,—ki.**
meditate, *v.i.*, **hubso.**
meditation, *n.*, **hubsad,—ki.**
medley, *n.*, **iss ku daran,—ki.**
meek, mild, *a.*, **ḫabow.**
meet, *v.tr.*, **la kulan**; *v.i.*, **iss urura.**

meeting, *n.*, kulan,—ki, shir,—ki, urur,—ki; have a —, shira, so shira.

melancholy,*n.*,wahan,—ki,ḥulub, —ki.

melancholic, *a.*, ḥulubsan; be —, wahan, ḥulub.

melon, *n.*, bartiḥ,—hi; water- —, ḥabḥab,—ki; wild —, unun, —ki.

melt, *v.tr.*, ḍalali, daḥaji; — in, ku ḍalali.

melted, *a.*, shuban.

member, *n.*, adin,—ki, laḥad,—ki.

membrum virile, *n.*, gus,—ki, ḥodo,—ihi, buryo,—adi.

memory, *n.*, ḥusus,—ti, fahmad, —di.

mend, *v.tr.*, (repair) kar, ḥor, kab, ḥodob.

menses, *n.*, ḍig,—gi, haïl,—ki.

mention, *v.tr.*, sheg; do not —, ha ba shegin.

merchandise,*n.*,alabo,—adi, holo, —ihi, mod,—ki, saman,—ki.

merchant, *n.*, baya mushtari,—gi, dilal,—ki.

merciful, *a.*, naḥarisleh, rahim, —ki, nin rahimah.

mercy, *n.*, naḥadin,—ti, naḥaris, —ti, rahmad,—di; have —, nah, naḥariso.

merit, *v.tr.*, galabso; *v.c.*, galabsi.

merry, *a.*, badaḍsan, faraḥanah.

mesh, *n.*, god, hog; there was plenty of fish in the meshes of the net, godadka shabagga kalun badan ba ku jirai.

message, *n.*, war,—ki.

messenger, *n.*, war ḥad,—di, war kena,—ihi.

Messiah, *n.*, elmessieh, Kristos, 'Issa el messieh.

method, *n.*, hagajis,—ki.

mewing, *n.*, dogor rugmad,—ki.

mid-day, *n.*, had,—di, duḥur,—ki.

middle, midst, *n.*, deh,—di; go in the —, u daḥai.

midwife, *n.*, umuliso,—adi.

might, *n.*, ḥog,—gi, ital,—ki; *aux.v.*, kari laha.

mighty, *a.*, ḥog wein, ḥuwad leh.

migrate, *v.i.*, gur.

migration, *n.*, gurnin,—ki.

milk, *n.*, 'ano,—ihi; fresh —, daï,—di; — of ewe, 'ana idad; — of goat, 'ana riad; fresh camel's —, ḥor,—ki; sour —, 'ano ḍanan; sour — of camels, karur,—ti; turned —, baḥ; the — has turned, 'anaha baḥai; curdle —, ga-ḍoḍ,—ki; butter —, īr,—ti; — and water mixed, badaḥ,—hi; — and butter— mixed, buḥbuḥod,—ki, weildo,—adi.

milk, *v.tr.*, liss, so liss, mal, so mal, maḥar ku mal, ḍarar mal.

million, *num.*, toban boḥol o kun.

mind (see intellect).

mind, *v.tr.*, hubso, foyigow; — well what I say, waḥan ku lehahai āḍ u hubso; — your business, dantada foyigow;

— your health, **afimadka daur**; I shall — the boy, **wilkan jiri**; *v.r.*, **iss ka daur, iss ka eg, iss ka jir, nin fojigan ahaw**; *v.tr.*, (put in —) **ḥususi.**
mine (*see* Grammar).
mingle, *v.tr.*, (mix) **iss ku dar, ḫosh, walaḫ.**
minute, *n.*, **minit,—ki.**
miracle, *n.*, **waḥ an la karin.**
mire, *n.*, (mud) **doḥbo,—adi.**
mirror, *n.*, **biladaya,—ihi, murayad,—di.**
misadventure, *n.*, **ayan humo,—adi.**
misbehave, *v.i.*, **abur humaw.**
misbehaviour, *n.*, **abur ḥun.**
misbelief, *n.*, **amin ḥun.**
miscarriage, *n.*, **ilma ka ḫoman, —ki.**
miscarry, *v.i.*, **ilma iss ka ḫon**; *v.c.*, **ilma ka ḫon.**
mischief, *n.*, **histi,—gi, waḥ yello,—adi**; do some —, **waḥ yel.**
mischievous, *a.*, **waḥ yellaleh**; *n.*, **waḥ yel,—ki.**
miser, *n.*, **baḥail,—ki, baḥailad, —di, dabḫal,—ki, masug,—gi, mudal,—ki.**
misfortune, *n.*, **ayan ḥumo,—adi.**
mislead, *v.tr.*, **ḫatal, ḫalḫal**; be misled, **ḫatalan.**
misleader, *n.*, **maḫawi,—gi.**
mist, *n.*, **'iro,—adi.**
misty, *a.*, **'iraisan.**
mistake, *n.*, **ḫatalad,—di, ilowsho,—ihi**; be mistaken, **ḫatalan.**
misunderstand, *v.tr.*, **si ḥun garo.**
mix, *v.tr.*, **ḫalad, iss ku ḫalad.**
mixture, *n.*, **ḫalad,—ki.**
moan, *n.*, **tah,—hi**; *v.i.*, **tah.**
mob, *n.*, **buḫ,—hi.**
mock, *v.tr.*, **luḫufi** or **luḫfi, ku ḫosol**; mockery, *n.*, **luḫuf,—ki.**
mode, *n.*, **si,—di.**
modest, *a.*, **ḥil** or **ḥishod badan**; be —, **ḥisho.**
modesty, *n.*, **ḥishod,—ki, ḥil,—ki.**
modify, *v.tr.*, **bedel.**
moist, *a.*, **ḫoiyan.**
moisten, *v.tr.*, **ḫoi.**
molar tooth, *n.*, **gows,—ki.**
molest, *v.tr.*, **dāli, kaga 'eisi, ḥanuji.**
moment, *n.*, **'abbar,—ki.**
Monday, *n.*, **isnin,—ti.**
money, *n.*, **la'ag,—ti**; — box, case, or linen — bag, **kish,—ki**; leathern purse, **kishad,—di.**
monition, *n.*, **wano,—adi.**
monk, *n.*, **wadad,—ki.**
monkey, *n.*, **dayer,—ki.**
monsoon (N.E.), *n.*, **bad furan, —ki**; (S.W.) **bad ḥidan,—ki.**
month, *n.*, **bil, bishi,** the ...
monthly, *ad.*, **bil walba**; I go to Aden —, **bishi ba mar ban Aden taga.**
moon, *n.*, **dayaḥ,—hi**; — light, **'addo,—adi**; half —, **dayaḥ badki**; full —, **dayaḥ d̈an, dayiḥhi d̈ama**; new —, **dayaḥ 'usub**; quarter of the —, **bil, —shi.**
moor, *n.*, (marsh) **rubad,—ki.**

more, *a.*, **ka badan, ka ron**; will you have —? **ma ka badsanaisa?** *ad.*, once —, **mar kaleh**; no —, never —, **in, inta ka dambaisa.**

moreover, *ad.*, **weli ba.**

morning, *n.*, **aror,—ti, subaḥ,—iḥhi**; this —, **saka**; early —, **aroryo,—adi.**

morning star, *n.*, **ḥidig aroryo, ḥidigti wa beri.**

morrow, *n.*, **berri,—di**; to—, *ad.*, **berri, berrito**; until to—, **halkiyo berri.**

mortal, *a.*, **nafta dila.**

mortar, *n.*, (to grind in) **malkad,—ki**; — of wood, **moya** or **moyai,—ihi**; (lime and sand mixed) **nurad,—di.**

mosquito, *n.*, **kane'o,—adi.**

most, *a.*, **ka wada badan, ugu badan.**

mother, *n.*, **hoyo,—adi**; — -in-law, **soddoh,—di.**

motive, *n.*, **ed,—di, sabab,—ti.**

moulting (*see* mewing).

mound, *n.*, **dud,—ki, gumbur,—ti.**

mount, mountain, *n.*, **bur,—ti.**

mount, *v.i.*, (go up) **kor, ful.**

mourn, mourning (*see* lament).

mouse, *n.*, **jir yar,—ki, —a**; a small —, **bara dubleh.**

moustache, *n.*, **sharub,—ti.**

mouth, *n.*, **af,—ki.**

mouthful, *n.*, **'antugo,—adi, luḥmad,—di**; give a —, **'antuji.**

move, *v.tr.* and *v.i.*, **daḥdaḥaḥ, baïd, du, durug, so'o, lul, walaḥ**; — from, off, **ka baïd, ka durug, ka du, ka so'o.**

movement, *n.*, **daḥdaḥaḥ,—hi, walaḥ,—hi.**

much, *a.*, **badan**; as —, so —, **inta, intas, inta o kaleh.**

mud, *n.*, **doḥbo,—adi, doḥbo haredad.**

muddy, *a.*, **doḥbo badan, saboh**; — place, **didi,—gi.**

mug, *n.*, **kalaḥ,—hi.**

mule, *n.*, **baḥlad,—di**; he —, **baḥlad lab.**

multiplication, *n.*, **tarin,—ki.**

multiply, *v.tr.*, **tar**; be multiplied, **taran.**

multitude, *n.*, **dad badan, buḥ,—hi, urur,—ki.**

murder, *v.tr.*, **dil.**

murderer, *n.*, **dila,—ihi.**

murmur, mumble, *v.i.*, **gunus, hos u guḥ**; *n.*, **gunus,—ki.**

muscle, *n.*, **merji,—gi.**

mushroom, *n.*, **warik,—ti.**

music, *n.*, **hes,—ti.**

musk deer, *n.*, **beïra,—ihi.**

musulman, *n.*, **muslim,—ki.**

mute (*see* dumb).

mutton, *n.*, **hilib idad,—ki, idaha.**

muzzle, *n.*, **gafur,—ki, afuf,—ti**; *v.tr.*, **afuf**; (only tying) **ganaf.**

myope, *a.*, **arag darran, imamowsan**; be —, **imamowsan.**

myopy, *n.*, **imamowsi,—gi.**

myrrh, *n.*, **malmal,—ki**; — tree, **didhin,—ki**; false — tree, **habaghadi,—gi.**

my, *p.prn.* (*see* Grammar).

mystery, *n.*, **waḥ an la garan, waḥ an la karin.**

mystification, *n.* **uggoyo,—adi.**

N.

nail, *n.*, (of the finger) **'iddi,—di;** iron —, **mismar** or **musmar,—ki.**

nail, *v.tr.*, **musmar.**

naked, *a.*, **ḫawan.**

nakedness, *n.*, **ḫawanan,—ti.**

name, *n.*, **maga',—hi;** *v.tr.*, **u biḥi, ugu yed.**

nape, *n.*, (joint of the neck) **sagan-madon,—ti.**

narrate, *v.tr.*, **sheko u mari, u shekai.**

narrative, *n.*, **sheko,—adi.**

narrow, *a.*, **'edidi.**

narrowness, *n.*, **'edidi,—gi.**

nasty (*see* dirty).

nation, *n.*, **ḫabilo,—adi.**

nativity, *n.*, **dalnin,—ti.**

natural child, *n.*, **wa'al,—ki.**

nature, *n.*, **dunyo,—adi;** (temper) **abur,—ki, —ti.**

naughty, *a.*, **ḥun.**

nausea, *n.*, **yiḫyiḫsi,—gi.**

navel, *n.*, **ḥundur,—ti;** — string, **ḥudun,—ti.**

navigate, *v.i.*, **dof.**

navigation, *n.*, **dof,—ki, dofnin, —ti.**

nayword, *n.*, (refusal) **dafirad,—di.**

near, *ad.* and *prp.*, **ag, agta, dow, sokai, ḥigta;** be —, **dowow, ḥig;** come —, **so dowow, so durug;** go —, **u dowow, u durug;** put —, **so dowai, u dowai, iss ku dowai.**

nearness, *n.*, **dowan,—ti.**

neat, *a.*, **shuban.**

neck, *n.*, **ḫor,—ti.**

necklace, *n.*, **ḫorḥid,—ki, kul,—shi, jilbad,—di.**

need, *n.*, (want) **dan,—ti, tabalo, —adi;** (poverty) **băho,—adi.**

needy (man), *a.*, (**nin**) **'aïdah, 'aïd,—ki.**

needle, *n.*, **irbad,—di;** big —, **maḥad,—ki.**

negligence, *n.*, **fojiglaan,—ti.**

negligent, *a.*, **mog, mogai.**

negotiate, *v.tr.*, **deḥ-gal.**

negro, *n.*, **sawaḥili,—gi, adon,—ki, —ti, bidai,—ihi.**

neigh, *v.i.*, **danan;** neighing, *n.*, **danan,—ki.**

neighbour, *n.*, **deris,—ki.**

neighbourhood, *n.*, **derisnimo,—adi.**

neither, *ad.*, **midna.**

nephew, *n.*, **inanki** or **ina walalkai, walalkai ba dalai, walashai ba dashai.**

nest, *n.*, **bul,—ki.**

net, *n.*, **shabak,—gi.**

nettle, *n.*, **ged ḥajin,—ki.**

nettle-rash, *n.*, **addo,—adi, ḥajin, —ti.**

neutral tint, *a.*, **owlaled.**

never, *ad.*, **abadan, abkai, abidkaina, weligai;** — mind, **yelkisa, yelkeda.**

nevertheless, *c.*, **ha ahato, ha ahataie.**

new, *a.*, **'usub, 'usba.**

news, *n.*, **war,—ki;** good —, **nabad,—di;** bring —, **war gei** or **ken;** bring — from, **ka war ken;** a man receiving —, **warḫab,—ki.**

next, *a.*, ɗow, sokai, higa; the
— house, aḥalka sokai or ɗow
or ḥiga; the — month, bisha
dambe; the — day, berri;
tell me the — word, eraiga ka
shishaiya i sheg; I will do
better — time, mar dambe wan
ka wanagi; be — to, ḥig.

nib, *n.*, 'aro,—adi.

nice, *a.*, bahsan, ād, dor, shuban,
wanaksan.

nicely (make), *v.tr.*, ḥorḥi, horoḥ
u yel, wanaji, hagaji.

niceness, *n.*, wanag,—gi.

nickname, *n.*, nanaïs,—ti.

niece, *n.*, (my) gabaɗdi or inanti
walalkai or walashai.

night, *n.*, habein,—ki; (time of
sleeping) saḥ,— di; mid —,
saḥ dehe; to—, 'awa; last
—, ḥalai; go at —, gud.

nightmare, *n.*, awawi,—gi.

nine, *num.*, sagal,—ki.

nineteen, *num.*, sagal iyo toban,
—ki.

ninety, *num.*, sagashan,—ki.

ninth, *num.*, sagalad,—ki, —di.

nip, *n.*, (pinch) ḥanjido,—adi;
v.tr., ḥanjidi.

nipple, *n.*, (teat of the breast) ib,—ti.

no, *ad.*, maya, maha.

nobody, *n.*, 'iddina.

noise, *n.*, sanḥad,—di, ḥab or
habḥab,—ti, ḥad, wa',—di,
ḥau,—di, baf! fof,—ki; make
a —, kaga sanḥadi.

nomad, *ad.* and *n.*, rer gura,—
gi; Somals are a — people,
dadka Somalied wa dad an
mel la ku hadin.

none, *prn.*, midna, middina.

noon, *n.*, duhur,—ki, had,—di;
after—, duḥurka dabaddisa.

noose, *n.*, (running knot) suryo,
—adi.

noose, *v.tr.*, suryai.

north, *n.*, jaḥ,—hi.

nose, *n.*, san,—ki; flat —, san
balladan; wipe your —, sinso,
iss ka tir, iss ka simi.

nostril, *n.*, dul,—ki.

not, *ad.*, an, ma; there is —, ma
jiro; is it —? so ma aha?

nothing, *ad.*, babah, waḥba.

notice, *n.*, war,—ki.

notify, *v.tr.*, ogaisi, warran.

nourish, *v.tr.*, sabbar, sorsi, sabbaro.

now, *ad.*, aminka, iminka, haddai, hadder; — a-days, hatan;
just—, iminkada, haddadatan.

now, *c.*, haddaba, haddeh.

number, *n.*, (mark) sumad,—ki;
(sum) tiro,—adi; a certain —,
daur,—ki.

numbness, *n.*, kabubiyo,—adi.

numerous, *a.*, badan, tiro badan.

nuptial, *n.*, aros,—ki.

nurse, *n.*, umuliso,—adi.

nut, *n.*, (cocoa-nut) narajin,—ti;
earth — (arachis), los,—ki.

O.

oar, *n.*, seb,—ki.

oath, *n.*, ɗār,—ti, imán,—ti, aḥdi,—gi.

obedience, *n.*, đega nugail,—ki, đega nuglan,—ti.

obedient, *a.*, đega nugul.

obey, *v.tr.*, (be obedient) đega nuglow, đegaiso, yel.

objurgation, *n.*, masabidnimo,—adi.

oblige, *v.tr.*, (compel) ḫāsab, muḫuni.

oblique, *a.*, ḫallohan, ma tosna, ma shubna.

obliterate, *v.tr.*, babihi.

oblivion, *n.*, ilowsho,—ihi.

observe, *v.tr.*, indai.

observation, *n.*, indo,—ihi.

obstruct, *v.tr.*, ōd.

obstructed, *a.*, ōdan.

obtain, *v.tr.*, hel, ma'ash.

occident, *n.*, galbed,—ki.

occupation, *n.*, haul,—shi, shuḫul,—ki.

occupy, *v.tr.*, shaḫaisi; *v.r.*, haushada ḫabso.

occur, *v.i.*, noḫo; it occurs, waḫhai noḫotai.

ocean, *n.*, bad,—di.

odor, *n.*, ur,—ti.

odoriferous, *a.*, udgon.

of, off (*see* Grammar).

offence, *n.*, taḫsir,—ti, dembi,—gi.

offend, *v.tr.*, 'ai.

offer, *v.tr.*, u bihi.

offering, *n.*, sadaḫad, sadaḫad Ebbahai lo gubai.

office, *n.*, (place, ...) hafis,—ki.

often, *ad.*, gor, kol, mar badan, daur gor, ḫajaila, yala.

oil, *n.*, salid,—di.

old, *a.*, gabow, duḫah, dugah; — man, odai,—gi, islan,—ki, wadad,—ki, wayel,—ki; — woman, habar,—ti, islan,—ti, wadadad,—di; — age, dā wein, gabow,—gi; — people, dad gabowbai, nin da wein, duḫ,—di; — thing, dug; grow, be —, *v.i.*, gabow; — times, beriyihi horai.

omen, *n.*, fal,—ki.

omit, *v.tr.*, iss ka da, ka ḫadi; be omitted, ka ḫad.

omnipotence, *n.*, ḫuwad,—di.

on, *prp.*, ku, dul, dusha.

onager, *n.*, (wild ass) gumburi,—gi.

once, *a.*, (one time) mar; (formerly) beri,—gi, wā,—gi, beri horai, wa horai, kolki horai, kolki; it was —, beri or wa waḫha jirai.

one, *num.*, kow,—di, mid,—ki, —di; — by —, mid mid; less —, mid la; it is all —, gidi wa iss ku wada mid; it is all — to me, gidi wa iss ugu kai mid; it is all — as if you threw your money into the river, gidi wa mid sidad la'agtadi durdurka ku ridai; every —, mid walba; they eat — another, wa iss 'unan; — handed, ga-'an keliah leh.

onion, *n.*, basal,—shi.

only, *a.*, (single) keliah; *ad.*, un.

open, *v.tr.*, fur; *a.*, banan, furan.

opening, *n.*, furnin,—ti.

opinion, *n.*, **talo,—adi, tashi,—gi.**
opposite, *a.*, **hor, horti.**
opposition, *n.*, **asarar,—ki, didnin,—ti.**
oppression, *n.*, **'eḥo,—adi, 'eḥasho,—adi.**
opulent, *a.*, **hodanah, holo badan.**
or, *c.*, **ama, amase, mase, mise.**
orange, *n.*, **lin ma'an,—ti, —aid.**
order, *n.*, (command) **ḥukum,—ki**; (regular disposition) **hagajis,—ki**; *v.tr.*, (command) **u dir**; (regulate) **hagaji, wanaji, hagajiso, wanajiso.**
orient, *n.*, **bari,—gi.**
origin, *n.*, **horan,—ti.**
ornaments, *n.*, (for women) **siyaḥad,—di.**
orphan, *n.*, **agon,—ki** (*mas.*), **—ti** (*fem.*), **rajai,—gi.**
oryx, *n.*, (beisa antelope) **bi''id,—ki.**
ostrich, *n.*, **gorayo,—adi**; male —, **gorai,—gi, halda,—gi.**
other, *a.*, **kaleh**; the —, **ki kaleh, kan kaleh**; another, **mid kaleh.**
otherwise, *c.*, **hadikaleh.**
our (*see* Grammar).
out, *prp.*, **dibad, dibadda.**
outcast, *a.*, **dairsan, la na'ai.**
outcry, *n.*, **dawaḥ,—hi, ḥailo,—adi, sawaḥan,—ki.**
outside, *ad.*, **dibadda**; *n.* and *ad.*, **duled,—ki**; he is —, **isagu duledku joga.**
oven, *n.*, **mufo,—adi.**
over, *prp.*, **dul, dusha, gud, gudka, kor**; — again, **weliba**; be —, **ka sarrai.**
overcome, *v.tr.*, **ka adkaw, dulmar.**
overseer, *n.*, **mukadam** or **maḥadim,—ki.**
overtake, *v.tr.*, **gād.**
overthrow, *v.tr.*, **dumi, ka dādi.**
owe, *v.tr.*; I — you money, **la'ag bad igu lehdahai.**
owl, *n.*, **shimbir libaḥ,—di**; small —, **'iow,—di.**
own, *v.tr.*, **ḥiro**; *a.*, (*see* Gram.).
owner, *n.*, **nin aḥalka leh.**
ox, *n.*, **dibi,—gi.**

P.

pace, *v.i.*, (step) **talab**; *n.*, **talabo,—adi.**
pacha, *n.*, **basha,—ihi.**
pacific, *a.*, **ḥabow, nabdiya.**
pacify, *v.tr.*, **nabdi.**
pack, *v.tr.*, **ḥid**; (packet) **ḥidmo,—adi.**
pack-saddle, *n.*, (camel's) **heriyo,—adi.**
pagan, *n.*, **gal,—ki.**
page, *n.*, (of a book) **bāl,—ki.**
pail, *n.*, **baldi,—gi**; — of skin, **dandul,—shi, dowlis,—ki, gorof,—ki, wadān,—ti.**
pain, *n.*, (penalty) **taḥsirad,—di**; (ache) **ḥanun,—ki, silei',—hi, ta'ab,—ki.**
pain, *v.tr.*, (afflict) **ḥanuni, ḥanuji, sili'i**; *v.imp.*, **ḥanun.**

painful, *a.*, **ḥanunsan, silei'san.**
paint, *v.tr.*, **ranji**; *n.*, (colour) **ranji,—gi.**
pair, *n.*, **laba, labada,—di.**
palate, *n.*, **danḥanag,—gi, dangalaḥ,—hi, hardad,—ki.**
palm, *n.*, (of the hand) **baba'o,—adi, ala'al** or **ala'anal,—shi, saab,—ki.**
palpitate, *v.i.*, **ror.**
palsy, *n.*, **'urian,—ki.**
pan, *n.*, **dawa,—ihi.**
panca, *n.*, **bankad,—di.**
pant, *v.i.*, **hinrag.**
panting, *n.*, **hinrag,—gi.**
panther, *n.*, **shabel,—ki, horgumo,—adi, nimmer,—ki.**
pap, *n.*, (nipple) **ib,—ti.**
paper, *n.*, **warḥad,—di, waraḥ, —di.**
parable, *n.*, **mathal,—ki.**
paradise, *n.*, **janno,—adi.**
parallel, *a.*, **siman**; they are —, **bai iss u wada jiran.**
paralytic, *a.*, **'urianah.**
parasol, *n.*, **dallayad,—di.**
parcel, *n.*, **ḥidmo,—adi.**
parchedness, *n.*, (of the mouth) **lun,—ki.**
pardon, *n.*, **samaḥ,—di, 'affi,—gi**; *v.tr.*, **samaḥ, 'affi**; — each other, **iss 'affiya.**
parent, *n.*, **walid,—ki.**
park, *n.*, (zariba) **saribad,—di.**
parricide, *n.*, **walad-inkar,—ki.**
part, *n.*, **in,—ti, ḥaib,—ti**; (half) **go,—hi**; (party), take his —, **la mel noḥo.**
part, *v.tr.*, (partake) **ḥaib, kala go**; — with, **kala gosta.**
part, *v.i.*, (quit) **tag, ka tag**; we must —, **an tagno, an kala tagno.**
partial, *v.i.*, (be) **ka 'eḥo**; — sentence, **gar 'eḥo,—ti, 'eḥadaahaid.**
partiality, *n.*, **'eḥo,—adi, 'eḥasho,—adi.**
participate, *v.tr.*, **haibso.**
particle, *n.*, **in yar,—ti, —aid.**
partner, *n.*, **mushrik,—gi.**
party, *n.*, (faction) **ḥolo,—adi.**
pasha, *n.*, **basha,—ihi.**
pass, *v.i.*, **daf, mar**; he passed by our door, **albabkayagu marai**; — away, **daf**; — along the shore, **ḥebta si mar**; *v.tr.*, — the river, **durdurka ka talab**; we shall — the winter in the town, **guga an magalada ku hadno**; — near, **ag mar, iss ku du**; — by the side, **ges ka mar**; — across, **deḥ mar.**
passage, *n.*, (on board ship) **dof, —ki.**
passenger, *n.*, **rakab,—ki.**
pat, *v.tr.*, **salaḥ**; *n.*, (light blow) **salaḥid,—di.**
patch, *v.tr.*, **kar**; *n.*, **karrin,—ti.**
paten, *n.*, **se'ni,—gi.**
path, *n.*, **dau,—gi, jid,—ki, marin,—ki.**
patience, *n.*, **dulḥadasho,—adi, kadsi,—gi, sabir** or **samir,—ki, sugnin,—ti**; have —, *or* be patient, **daur, sug, samir, dulḥado, kadso.**
patient, *a.*, **dulḥadasho badan, kadsileh, sugninleh.**
patriarch, *n.*, **batriyark,—gi.**

patron, *n.*, **abban,—ki.**
pause, *n.*, **nasad,—ki.**
paw, *n.*, **baba'o,—adi.**
pawn, *n.*, **ḋibasho,—adi, rahmad, —di**; *v.tr.*. **rahan.**
pay, *v.tr.*, **biḥi**; *n.*, (payment) **def,—ti, ḫaḫai,—gi, mushaharo,—adi.**
peace, *n.*, **nabad,—di**; **heshis,—ki, baraḥ,—hi**; be in —, **nabad gal, nabad ḫab, nabad geliyo**; they are living in —, **baraḥ ba lo yal**; make —, *v.i.*, **heshi, la heshi**; make — between them, *v.tr.*, **nabad ḫado, heshisi, nabdi.**
peak, *n.*, **'aro,—adi, fiḫ,—hi.**
pearl, *n.*, **lul,—ki.**
peasant, *n.*, **rer miyi,—gi.**
pebble, *n.*, **dagaḥ diḥed,—ki, ḫururoḥ,—hi.**
pedler, *n.*, **kabadai,—ihi.**
peel, *n.*, (rind) **ḋir,—ki**; *v.tr.*, **ḋil, ḋir**; the act of peeling, **ḋirin,—ki.**
peeled, *a.*, **ḋiran.**
peevish, *a.*, **ḥun.**
peg, *v.tr.*, (fasten with a peg) **didib**; *n.*, **didib,—ki.**
peg-top, *n.*, **druan,—ki.**
pellicle, *n.*, **holob,—ti, tohob,—ti.**
pen, *n.*, **ḫalim,—ki.**
pencil, *n.*, **ḫalim rasased.**
penance, *n.*, **tobad** or **taubad,—di**; make —, **tobad ken, tobad yelo.**
penetrate, *v.i.*, **gal**; — into, **waren, geli.**
penknife, *n.*, **mandil** or **madil,—shi.**
penitence, *n.*, **tobad,—di, ala'al, —ki.**
penitent, *n.*, **tobad-ken,—ki, ala'alsan.**
pensive (be), *v.i.*, **wahan.**
pensiveness, *n.*, **wahan,—ki.**
penury, *n.*, **'aïdnimo,—adi.**
people, *n.*, **dad,—ki.**
pepper, *n.*, **filfil.—shi.**
perceive, *v.tr.*, **arag, daren.**
perfect, *a.*, **ḋan**; the — work, **shuḫulki ḋama.**
perfection, *n.*, **ḋamad,—ki.**
perfidious, *a.*, **maḫawiah, dadka daga.**
perforate, *v.tr.*, **daloli, ku maroji.**
perform, *v.tr.*, **fal**; he performs his duties, **dantisa ād bu ḫabta.**
perfume, *n.*, **udgon,—ki**; act of perfuming, **unsi,—gi**; — of incense, **umis,—ki**; *v.tr.*, **udgonai, umi**; *v.r.*, **iss udgonai, unso**; be perfumed, **udgonow**; it is perfumed, **la udgonai.**
perhaps, *ad.*, **malaha, mindah, sow, show.**
peril, *n.*, **'absi,—di, baḫdin,—ti.**
perilous, *a.*, **'absileh.**
period, *n.*, (of time) **mudad,—di, madal,—ki.**
perish, *v.i.*, **baḫti**; I — with hunger, **gajan la baḫtiaya.**
perjure (yourself), *v.tr.*, **bein ku ḋaro.**
perjurer, *n.*, **ḋār jid,—ki.**
perjury, *n.*, **bein,—ti.**
permanent, *a.*, **adag.**
permission, *n.*, **fasaḥ,—hi, ruḫsad, —di.**

permit, *v.tr.*, **fasaẖ, ruẖsad si.**
permute, *v.tr.*, **iss đafi, la iss đafi.**
perpendicular, *a.*, **ẖumatiah.**
perpetrate, *v.tr.*, **fal.**
perpetual, *a.*, **weligi đamanain, weligi idlanain.**
persecute, *v.tr.*, **sili'i.**
persecution, *n.*, **silei',—ihi.**
perseverance, *n.*, **sabir** or **samir, —ki.**
persevere, *v.i.*, **sabir** or **samir.**
persist, *v.i.*, **adkaw, si adag u wad.**
person, *n.*, **ẖof,—ki, 'id,—di, ẖud,—di**; a nice and good —, **ẖulyad,—di.**
perspective, *n.*, **muẖ,—hi.**
perspicacity, *n.*, **nejisnimo,—adi.**
perspiration, *n.*, **đidid,—ki**; being in —, **hursan, đididsan.**
perspire, *v.i.*, **đidid.**
persuade, *v.tr.*, **sasab.**
persuasion, *n.*, **sasab,—ki, sasabnin,—ti.**
pertinacious, *a.*, (obstinate) **đega adag, rifaiah.**
perverse, *a.*, **ḥun.**
pest, pestilence, *n.*, **kud,—ki.**
pestle, *n.*, **moyai-tumai,—ihi**; wooden —, **tib,—ti.**
petition, *n.*, **arji,—gi, ardal ḥal, —ki.**
phalanx, *n.*, **konton madafto,—adi.**
phantasma, *n.*, **muhasho,—adi.**
phenomenon, *n.*, **umur,—ti, yab, ki.**
phosphorescent gleams of the sea, *n.*, **galabildan** or **garabildan, —ki.**
photograph, *n.*, **sawir,—ki.**
phthisic *or* phthysis, *n.*, **ẖaẖo,—adi, laḥau,—gi**; — of cattle. **sambab,—ki.**
phthisic, phthisical, *a.*, **nin laḥau ẖaba.**
physic, *n.*, (medicine) **dawo,—adi, daïmo,—adi**; practice —, **dawai.**
physician, *n.*, **daẖdar,—ki, ḥakim, —ki, sanaḥ,—hi.**
physiognomy, *n.*, **weiji,—gi, jah, —hi.**
pice (money=4 pies), *n.*, **beisad, —di.**
pick, pick up, *v.tr.*, **gur**; — for, **u gur**; — for yourself, **guro, gurguro.**
pick-tooth, *n.*, **findi'il gura,—ihi.**
picture, *n.*, **sawir,—ki**; *v.tr.*, **sawir.**
pictured, *a.*, **sawiran.**
pie (Indian money), *n.*, **ardi,—ġi, aradi,—di** (*plur.*).
piece, *n.*, **in,—ti, ḥubin,—ti**; little —, **in yar**; — of cloth, **karrin,—ti**; — of meat, **'ad, —ki.**
piece, *v.tr.*, (mend) **kar, kab.**
pier, *n.*, (a column) **tir,—ki**; (mole) **deked,—di.**
pierce, *v.tr.*, **daloli, ku maroji, ku joji, waren.**
piety, *n.*, **'ibādad,—di.**
pig, *n.*, **dofar,—ki.**
pigeon, *n.*, **ḥamam,—ki.**
pile, *n.*, **tir,—ki.**
piles, *n.*, (hæmorrhoids) **kintob, —ki.**
pilgrim, *n.*, **ḥaji,—gi.**

pilgrimage, *n.*, **ḥaj,—ki**; make a —, **ḥaji, so ḥaji.**
pillage, *n.*, **bob,—ki, da', di'hi** (the pillage).
pillow, *n.*, **barkimo,—adi**; a wooden —, **barki,—gi.**
pimento, *n.*, **basbas** or **bisbas,—ki.**
pimple, *n.*, **fin,—ki, dululuḥ,—hi.**
pin, *n.*, **irbad,—di**; hair—, **ḥarmil.**
pincers, *n.*, **birrḥab,—ki.**
pinch, *v.tr.*, **ḥanjidi**; *n.*, **ḥanjido,—adi.**
pine, *v.i.*, (languish) **weïdow**; *v.tr.*, **weïdai**; *v.r.*, **iss weïdai.**
pipe (of wood, used for blowing), *n.*, **gobais,—ki.**
pirogue, *n.*, **huri,—gi.**
piss, *v.i.*, (urinate) **kādi, so kādi**; *n.*, **kadi,—di.**
pistol, *n.*, **tumujad,—di.**
pit, *n.*, **gun,—ti, 'el,—ki, gof,—ki, god,—ki**; — of the stomach, **labḥo,—adi**; — of the knee, **hagal,—shi**; — of the arm, **kilkilo,—adi.**
pitch, *v.tr.*, (fix) **dab, rid.**
pitcher, *n.*, **jalaḥad,—di, kussad,—di.**
pith, *n.*, (marrow) **duḥ,—hi.**
pitiful, *a.*, **naḥsan**; be —, **naḥ.**
pity, *n.*, **naḥadin,—ti, naḥaris,—ti**; have —, **naḥariso.**
place, *n.*, **mel,—shi, hal,—ki, hag,—gi**; in another —, **mel kaleh**; put everything in its right —, **waḥ walba meshisa hagagsan dig**; there is no — for them, **mel u ma haino**; in all places, **mel walba**; in some —, **mel un**; the first — is due to him, **meshu ugu sarraisa isaga leh**; a — trodden by camels, **gelgelin**; a — out of reach, **harar,—ti**; a — in which to hide stolen articles, **rar,—ti**; — in a boat, **sallaḥ,—iḥhi**; a clean — become dirty, **sabo,—di**; a — prepared on a camel for small children, **guro,—adi.**
place, *v.tr.*, **dig**; — on, **sar, rar**; — for yourself, **digo.**
plague, *n.*, **kud,—ki.**
plain, *n.*, **ban,—ki, banan,—ki, gegi,—di, wasa'a,—hi, mel wasa'ah doho,—adi, jan,—ki**; — surface, **baraḥad,—di**; *a.*, **banan, siman**; *v.tr.*, **banai, banai, sin, iss ku sin.**
plaint, *n.*, (in justice) **gar,—ti, ashtako,—adi**; make a —, **gar u shego.**
plait, *n.*, (a fold) **dubnin,—ti**; — of hair, **tidei',—ihi**; plaiting (mats), **falag,—gi**; *v.tr.*, **dub**; (weave) **falki, tidi'.**
plan, *n.*, **tadbir,—ti.**
plane, *n.*, (surface) **siman,—ki, sinin,—ti.**
plank, *n.*, **loḥ,—hi, alwaḥ,—di.**
plant, *n.*, **beir,—ti, ged,—ki**; *v.tr.*, **beir.**
plaster, *v.tr.*, **nurad mari.**
plate, *n.*, **se'ni,—gi, su'un,—ti.**
platter, *n.*, (wooden) **hedo,—adi, ḥedo sibidi**; make a —, **ḥedo samai.**

play, *n.*, **'ayar,—ti, jalbeb,—ti**; kind of —, **sar,—ki, sa'ab,—ki, walo,—adi.**
play, *v.i.*, **'ayar, jalbebo**; — at cards, **turub 'ayar, la walaiso**; *v.tr.*, (make play) **'ayarsi, jalbebi, walaisi.**
pleasant, *a.*, **farahan, farahah.**
please, *v.tr.*, **'ajibi.**
pleasure (*see* delight).
pledge, *v.tr.*, (pawn) **ámano u dib, rahan**; *n.*, **amano,—adi, rahmad,—di, dibasho,—adi.**
plentiful, *a.*, **barwahaisan.**
plenty, *n.*, **barwaho,—adi.**
pliable, *a.*, (flexible) **lilaisa**; the — stick, **ushi lilaisai.**
pluck, *v.tr.*, (pull with force) **so jid**; — off the feathers, plume a bird, **rif.**
plunder, *n.*, **bob,—ki, da',—di'hi, jalalaha,—ihi**; *v.tr.*, **bob, da', jalalah.**
plunge, *n.*, **husid,—di, muhurasho,—adi**; *v.i.*, **ku da', hus, muhur**; *v.tr.*, **husi, muhuri.**
pock, *n.*, **furuh**; — hole, — mark, **furuhdon,—ki.**
pocket, *n.*, **kishad,—di.**
poem, poesy, *n.*, **gabai,—gi.**
poet, *n.*, **gabaya,—gi.**
point, *n.*, **'aro,—adi, fih,—hi, dul,—shi.**
point, *v.tr.*, (sharpen) **dub, fih**; — out, **tus, muji.**
pointed, *a.*, **fihan.**
poison, *n.*, **dunkal,—shi, sun,—ki, urgumo,—adi, wabayo,—adi.**
poisonous plant, *n.*, **waba** or **wabai,—gi.**
pole-star, *n.*, **hedig jah,—ti,—ha.**
police-station, *n.*, **tshoki,—gi.**
policeman, *n.*, **askari,—gi, subaihi,—gi.**
polish, *v.tr.*, **'adai, hoh.**
polite, *a.*, **edibsan, amusan, bassar wanaksan,** (nin) **wayelah**; be —, **edibsanaw**; cause to be —, **edbi.**
politeness, *n.*, **edib,—ti, amusnan,—ti.**
poll, *n.*, (head of a tree) **bar,—ki.**
pollute (*see* defile).
polygamist, *n.*, **nin hilo badan.**
pond, pool, *n.*, **balli,—gi, dog,—ti, biya gal,—ihi, biya galen,—ki.**
poop, *n.*, **har dambai,—ki.**
poor, *a.* and *n.*, **aïd,—di, dagag,—gi, dawaro,—adi, sabol,—ki, nin dan darran, nin bar ma leh.**
porcupine, *n.*, **'anahub,—ti.**
pork, *n.*, **dofar,—ki.**
porringer, *n.*, **hobad,—di.**
port, *n.*, (harbour) **dekad** or **deked,—di.**
porter, *n.*, **hamal,—ki.**
portion, *n.*, **haib,—ti.**
possess, *v.tr.*, **hai, haiso, lahaw**; I —, **ana leh.**
possession, *n.*, **lahan,—ti.**
possible, *a.*, (**wahhasi**) **wa nohon** or **wa jiri kara.**
post, *n.*, **dabal,—ki**; — office, **dabal hafis,—ki**; —man, **badiwaleh,—ihi.**
posterior, *a.*, **wah gor dambe di'i dona.**

posterity, *n.*, ḥolo,—adi.
postscript, *n.*, warḥadda waḥ ku dar.
pot, *n.*, **wel**,—**ki**, **dasad**,—**di**, **deri**,—**gi**, **adār**,—**ki**.
potato, *n.*, **baḍaddo**,—adi.
pot-bellied, *a.*, **alol wein**.
potsherd, *n.*, **burbur**,—**ki**, **jab**,—**ki**, **jajab**,—**ki**.
potter, *n.*, **derya samais**,—**ki**.
poultice (*see* cataplasm).
poultry, *n.*, (fowls) **hād**,—**di**.
pound, *n.*, (weight) **rodol**,—**ki**; (money) **guini**,—**gi**.
pound, *v.tr.*, (grind) **budli**, **tun**.
pour, *v.tr.*, **shub**, **ḥub**; — in, **ku shub**; — water on the boy's head, **inanka madaḥha biyo kaga shub**.
pout, *n.*, (a bird) **una'as**,—**ti**.
pout, *v.i.*, (look sullen) **dud**; pouter, **nin dudma badan**.
pouting, *n.*, **dudmo**,—adi.
poverty, *n.*, **dan darro**,—adi, **sabol**,—**ki**.
powder, *n.*, (gunpowder) **barud**,—**di**.
power, *n.*, **ḥuwad**,—**di**.
powerful, *a.*, **ḥuwad leh**.
pox, *n.*, (small- *or* chicken-pox) **ged 'anod**,—**ki**, **fanto**,—adi, **furuḥ**,—**hi**.
praise, *v.tr.*, **aman**; *n.*, **aman**,—**ti**.
prank, *n.*, **luggoyo**,—adi; play a —, **luggo**.
prate, prattle (*see* babble).
pray, *v.tr.*, **bari**, **do'ai** *or* **du'ai**, **du'aiso**, **tuko**, **so tuko**; — for, **u tuko**.

prayer, *n.*, **bariyo**,—adi, **du'o**,—adi, **salād**,—di, **tukasho**,—adi.
preach, *v.tr.*, **wani**, **abḥi**; *v.r.*, **iss abḥi**.
preaching, *n.*, **wano**,—adi, **hadis**,—**ki**.
precede, *v.tr.*, **horai**, **naga horai**.
precept, *n.*, **ḥaul**,—**ki**.
precipice, *n.*, **ḥarar**,—**ti**, **jar**,—**ki**.
precipitate, *v.tr.*, **ka tur**.
predecessor, *n.*, **ka horaiyai**.
predication, *n.*, **wano**,—adi.
predict, *v.tr.*, **fali**, **waḥ sheg**.
prediction, *n.*, **waḥ sheg**,—**gi**.
predictor, *n.*, **waḥ-sheg**,—**gi**, **nin waḥ shega**.
prefer, *v.tr.*, **ja'alaw**.
pregnant, *a.*, **ur leh**.
prepare, *v.tr.*, **kala hagaji**, **dig**.
prepuce, *n.*, (foreskin) **balag**,—**ti**.
prerogative, *n.*, (privilege) **sado**,—adi.
presbyte, *a.*, **il ḍer**.
presbyopy, *n.*, **il ḍeran**,—**ti**.
presence, *n.*, **jog**,—**gi**.
present, *a.*, **joga**, **ḥadir**; God is — everywhere, **Ebbahai mel walba wa joga** *or* **wa ku ḥadir**.
present, *n.*, (time) **aminka**, **iminka**; (gift) **hadiad**,—**di**, **sin**,—**ti**.
present, *v.tr.*, (offer) **si**, **u dib**, **u bihi**.
preserve, *v.tr.*, (save) **daḥ**, **daḥo**, **ka badbādi**.
preside, *v.tr.*, **u sarrai**, **u tali**.
president, *n.*, **taliya shirka**.
press, *v.tr.*, **'adadi**, **dis**, **tuji**, **iss ku tuji**.
pressed, *a.*, **disan**.

pressing, *n.*, **'adadis,—ki, disin, —ti.**
presume, *v.tr.*, (be confident) **iss fani.**
presumption, *n.*, **fan,—ki, amar weinan,—ti.**
presumptuous, *a.*, **fan badan, amar wein.**
pretence, *n.*, (false excuse) **ḥelad, —di.**
pretty, *a.*, **baḥsan, fayo wanaksan, ḫorisho wanaksan.**
prevail, *v.tr.*, **ka adkaw.**
prevent, *v.tr.*, (hinder) **u did.**
previous, *a.*, **horai.**
price, *n.*, **gana',—di, ib,—ki.**
prick, *v.tr.*, **mud.**
pricking, *n.*, **mudnin,—ti.**
prickly heat, *n.*, **ḥararad,—di, ḥajin,—ti.**
pride, *n.*, **amar,—ki, amar weinan,—ti, falaḥ,—hi, kibir,—ki.**
prince, *n.*, **amir,—ki, ugas,—ki.**
print, *n.*, (mark) **astan,—ti, sumad,—di.**
print, *v.tr.*, **daba'.**
printed, *a.*, **daba'an.**
printing, *n.*, **daba',—i'hi.**
prison, *n.*, **ḥabsi,—gi, ḥabis,—ki.**
prisoner, *n.*, **nin ḥidan, mid maḥabistaah**; prisoners, **maḥabis, —ti.**
private, *a.*, **ḫarson**; talk in —, **faḫ.**
prize, *n.*, **def,—ti, abal,—ki.**
probably, *ad.*, **malaha.**
proceed, *v.i.*, **so'o, hor u so'o.**
process, *n.*, (suit) **arin,—ti.**
proclaim, *v.tr.*, **war gei, ogaisi.**
procreate, *v.tr.*, **ďal, yelo.**
procure, *v.tr.*, **u hel.**
prodigal, *a.*, **lumai, nin lumai.**
prodigy, *n.*, **umur,—ti, yab,—ki.**
produce, *v.tr.*, **abur, yelo, ďal, sinif.**
profess, *v.tr.*, (declare openly) **ḫiro.**
profit, *n.*, **fayido,—adi, koroď,—ki.**
profligate, *a.*, **lumiyai.**
profound (reverence), *n.*, **sujud,—di, rako',—a'di.**
profundity, *n.*, **ḫusur,—ki, ḫusurnimo,—adi.**
prohibit, *v.tr.*, **u did, ka hukun.**
prolific, *a.*, **ďal badan.**
prolong, *v.tr.*, **ďerai, ďereri.**
promise, *v.tr.*, **ballan.**
prompt, *a.*, (quick) **fudfudud.**
promulgate, *v.tr.*, **ogaisi.**
prone, *a.*; we are — to evil, **shar bainu ḥigna.**
prong, *n.*, (fork) **muda',—hi.**
pronounce, *v.tr.*, **ďeh.**
proof, *n.*, **marḫati,—di.**
prop, *n.*, (support) **tir,—ki, udub, —ki.**
propagate, *v.tr.*, **firďi.**
propagated, *a.*, **firďisan.**
propagation, *n.*, **firiď,—ki.**
propel, *v.tr.*, **horo u wad, hor u muḫuni.**
proper, *a.*, **hagagsan.**
property, *n.*, **holo,—ihi, mal,—ki, mod,—ki**; living —, **holo nol,—ihi, —a.**
prophecy, *n.*, **nubuwad,—di.**
prophesy, *v.tr.*, **fali, waḥ sheg.**
prophet, *n.*, **nebi,—gi.**

propitiate, *v.tr.*, **heshisi, 'ada tir**; — for, **tobad ken.**
propitiator, *n.*, **hof heshisiya.**
prostitute, *n.*, **dillo,—adi, hahabad,—di; hahabo,—ihi** (*plur.*); *v.tr.*, **dillo** or **hahabad ka dig.**
prostrate, *v.tr.*, **berka dulka u sar.**
protect, *v.tr.*, **ilali, jir, karaw.**
protection, *n.*, **ilalo,—adi.**
protector, *n.*, **abban,—ki.**
protract, *v.i.*, (delay) **rāg.**
protuberance, *n.*, **ka-so-bah,—ihi.**
proud, *a.*, **amarsan, amar wein, falahah, kibirsan**; be —, **kibir.**
prove, *v.tr.*, **garai, marhati ku fur**; — against, **ku garai.**
proverb, *n.*, **mahmah,—di.**
provide, *v.tr.*, **masruf, sabbar.**
providence, *n.*, **hekmad,—di.**
provision, *n.*, **ji'sin,—ki, sahai, —di.**
provocation to fight, *int.*, **'ar! 'ar! i dil.**
provoke, *v.tr.*, **ka 'adaisi.**
prow, *n.*, (forepart of a ship) **har horai,—ki.**
prudence, *n.*, **foyigan,—ti, miyir, —ki.**
prudent, *a.*, **foyig, miyirsan, miyir haba.**
pruriency, *n.*, **hajin,—ti.**
psalm, *n.*, **sabur,—ki.**
puberty, *n.*, **baluhnimo,—adi.**
public house, *n.*, (stew) **sheklad, —di.**
publish, *v.tr.*, **war gei, ogaisi.**
puddle, *n.*, (muddy standing water) **didi,—gi, dirih,—di.**
puff, *v.tr.*, (blow) **afuf, bufi**; (pant) *v.i.*, **hinrag.**
puffing, *n.*, (short breathing) **hinrag,—gi.**
pull, *v.tr.*, **difo** or **dufo, jid, jidjid, wad**; — to me, **so jid, so wad**; — from me to ..., **si jid**; — up, **kor u jid.**
pulsation, *n.*, **dahdahah,—hi.**
pulse, *n.*, **hidid.**
pulverize, *v.tr.*, **budli.**
pumpkin, *n.*, **dubbai,—ihi**; (vessel) **baro,—adi.**
punish, *v.tr.*, **tahsir, hanuni.**
punishment, *n.*, **tahsir,—ti.**
pupil, *n.*, (scholar) **barad,—ki**; the — of the eye, **isha inankeda** or **wilkeda.**
purchase (*see* buy).
pure, *a.*, **miran.**
purgation, *n.*, **dabib,—ki**; effect of a —, **shuban,—ki.**
purge, *v.tr.*, **dabib**; *v.i.*, **shuban** or **dabada ku shuban.**
purgatory, *n.*, **'adab yar,—ti, —aid.**
purpose, *n.*, **dama',—hi**; purposely, **baga, hushi**; *v.tr.*, **dama', don.**
purse, *n.*, **kish,—ki**; leathern —, **kishad,—di.**
pursue, *v.tr.*, **eri, ra'dai.**
pursuit, *n.*, **ra'do,—adi.**
pus (of a sore), *n.*, **de'an,—ki, did, malah,—di.**
push, pushing, *n.*, **rih,—hi**; *v.tr.*, **rih**; — back, **dib u rih**; — hard, **dis.**
put, *v.tr.*, **dig**; — aside, **digo, dah, daho**; — out, away, **eri**;

— before, **horaisi, horta ḍig**;
— after, **dambaisi, dabadda
ḍig**; — between, **deḥdoda ḍig**;
— in, **gudaha geli, ku shub,
ku rid**; — down, **hosta ḍig,
dumi**; — on, upou, **sar**; —
more, **korḍi**; — one over the
other, **sarsar**; — out (extinguish), **baḥti, seḥi**; — up,
dusha sar.

putrefaction, *n.*, **ḥuḍun,—ki**.

putrify, *v.tr.*, **ḥuḍmi**; *v.i.*, **ḥuḍun**.

Q.

quadruped, *n.*, **nef,—ki**; a herd
of quadrupeds, **rahan,—ti**;
kadin,—ki.

quail, *n.*, (a bird) **una'as,—ti**.

quake, *v.i.*, (shiver) **garir**.

quality, *n.*, **aslub,—ti**.

quarrel, *n.*, **dagal,—ki, dirir,—
ti, housi,—gi, housimad,—ki,
ilaḥ,—ti**; *v.i.*, **dirir, dagalan,
u ḥonso, ilaḥtan**.

quarrelsome, *a.*, **baan**.

quarter (¼), *num.*, **waḥ,—di**; —
of the moon, **bil,—bishi**.

quarter, *n.*, (of a town) **ḥafad,—
di**.

queen, *n.*, **malikad,—di, raniyad,—di**; — at cards, **rani,
—di**.

quell, *v.tr.*, (subdue) **taba bar,
jarra bar, laïli, dastur hun
karaw**.

quench (your thirst), *v.r.*, **iss
harad tir, iss on tir**.

question, *n.*, (query) **sual,—shi**;
v.tr., **suāl**.

quick (be), *v.att.*, **daḥso, deg deg**;
— to fight, **baan**; *a.*, **deraiyai**.

quid, *n.*, (of tobacco) **noshug,—
gi**.

quiescent (lie, remain), *v.i.*, **oll**.

quiet, *a.*, **amusan**; be —, **amus,
amusnaw**; *v.c.*, **amusi**.

quietness, *n.*, **amusnan,—ti**.

quietude, *n.*, **nasasho,—adi**.

quill, *n.*, **bāl,—ki**.

quit, *v.tr.*, **da, na'**.

quiver, *n.*, (for arrows) **gaboyai,
—ihi**.

quoit, *n.*, (palet) **lif** or **luf,—ki**;
play at —, **luf, lif la ayar**.

R.

rabbit, *n.*, **bakaïla** or **—lai,—ihi**.

race, *n.*, **has,—ki, holo,—adi,
jilib,—ki, rer,—ki, tol,—ki**;
(running) **baratan,—ki**.

racket, *n.*, **buḥ,—hi**.

radiance, radiancy, *n.*, **dalal,—ki**.

radish, *n.*, **baḥal,—ki**.

rag, *n.*, **'alal,—ki, harḥad,—di,
suf,—ki**.

rage, *n.*, **'aḍo,—adi, 'il,—ki**; *v.i.*,
**'aḍo, 'adaisnaw, 'ilow, 'is ho,
'il u ḥab, 'il u surun**; —
against, **u 'aḍo, u 'isho**.

raillery, *n.*, **luḥuf,—ki**.

rain, *n.*, **rob,—ki**; long and lasting —, **mayai** or **ma'ai,—gi**;
— water, **hared,—di**; — is

over, **robki had**; *v.i.*, **dah**; it rains, **dah, 'irki dah.**
rainbow, *n.*, **daigan,—ti, jegan, —ti.**
raise, *v.tr.*, **kor u had, sarai u had, sara ke'i, tosi.**
ram, *n.*, **wan,—ki.**
ramble, *v.i.*, **warwareg, so warwareg**; *v.c.*, **warwariji**; *n.*, **warwareg,—gi.**
rancour, *n.*, **ur humo,—adi.**
range, *n.*, (of mountains) **har,—ki, buro iss ku yal, buraha garbohoda.**
range (*see* arrange).
rank, *v.tr.*, **tah, iss ku tah.**
rap, *v.tr.*, (snatch away) **da', ka had, ka difo.**
rapid, *a.*, **deraiyai**; a — man, horse, **nin, faras deraiyai.**
rascal, *n.*, **tug,—gi, nejis,—ki, nin hayano leh, harami,—gi.**
rat, *n.*, **jir,—ki**; a small —, **jir yar.**
rate, *n.*, **gana',—i'hi.**
rattan, *n.*, **haisaran,—ti.**
ravage, *v.tr.*, **da', ka da'.**
rave, *v.i.*, **wallo.**
raven, *n.*, **tuka** or **tukai,—ihi.**
ravenous (*see* glutton).
ravish, *v.tr.*, (take away) **kufso.**
raw, *a.*, **'edin, 'edinah**; a — fruit, **gahaïd, gahaïr,—ki.**
rawness, *n.*, **'edin,—ki.**
rays, *n.*, (of the sun) **'ad'ed,—di.**
razor, *n.*, **mandil** or **madil,—shi, mus,—ki.**
reach, *n.*, **gadnin,—ti**; *v.tr.*, **gad, so gad**; make —, **gadsi.**
read, *v.tr.*, **ahri, nah, nahso.**
ready, *a.*, **dan, daman**; make —, **diyar garai**; get — for, **u halhal.**
reality, *n.*, **run,—ti**; it is real, **wa runti.**
realize, *v.tr.*, **abur, samai.**
reap, *v.tr.*, **ururi.**
rear, *n.*, **dambais,—ki, gutada dabadeda**; (raise up) **dis**; (educate) **kori.**
reason, *n.*, (faculty) **miyir,—ki**; (cause) **ed,—di, sabab,—ti.**
reasonable, *ad.*, **miyirsan, miyir haba**; be —, **miyir hab.**
rebel, *n.*, **hasid,—ki**; *v.i.*, **hasid, 'asi.**
rebound, *v.i.*, **dib u bod.**
rebuke, *v.tr.*, **huruf.**
receive, *v.tr.*, **ahbal, ka ahbal, ka habo, ka hado.**
recent, *a.*, (new) **'usub**; recently, *ad.*, **gor dowed.**
recess, *n.*, **mel harson.**
reckon, *v.tr.*, **tiri.**
recline, *v.i.* and *v.tr.*, **ku tiri, ku tirso.**
recognize, *v.tr.*, **hiro, hususo.**
recollect, *v.tr.*, **hususo**; — every day the things seen, heard and read, **wihhi ad aragtai, ama mahashai ama ahridai 'asho walba aloshada ka la tasho.**
recompense, *n.*, **def,—ti, abalgud,—di, abal,—ki, ajar** or **ajir,—ki**; *v.tr.*, **u abalgud, abalmari, abal u hab.**
reconcile, *v.tr.*, **heshisi, nabdi.**
reconciliation, *n.*, **heshis,—ki.**
reconnoitre, *v.tr.*, **so ilalai.**
record, *v.tr.*, **hor.**

recover, *v.tr.*, **mar kaleh hel** or **don**; *v.i.*, **bokso.**
recreate, *v.tr.*, **'ayarsi, jelbebi.**
recreation, *n.*, **jelbeb,—ti.**
rectify, *v.tr.*, **ḥumati u dig, hagaji.**
rectitude, *n.*, **hagag,—gi.**
red, *a.*, **'as, gudud.**
redden, *v.tr.*, **'asai.**
reddish, *a.*, **'asusleh, owlan**; — colour, **'asus,—ti.**
redness, *n.*, **'asan,—ki.**
reduce, *v.tr.*, **din, yarai**; (to bring to a state or condition) **ka dig, ka samai.**
reed, *n.*, **dur,—ki, —ti**; a white —, **'aus salol,—ki, jara',—'ihi.**
re-establish, *v.tr.*, **so 'eli, ku so 'eli.**
refection, *n.*, **afur,—ki.**
refine, *v.tr.*, (purify) **mir.**
reflect, *v.tr.*, **hubso, aloshada la tasho, iss weidi.**
reflexion, *n.*, **hubsad,—ki.**
reflux, *n.*, **'ari,—di.**
reform, *v.tr*, **aburta ḥun hagaji** or **tosi.**
refrain, *v.tr.*, (repress) **jarra bar, tababar, amal ḥun iss karaw.**
refresh, *v.tr.*, **ḥabowji.**
refusal, *n.*, **didnin,—ti, dafirad, —di, inkirad,—di,**
refuse, *v.tr.*, **dafir, did, inkir.**
refute, *v.tr.*, **beini.**
regard, *n.*, (respect) **mamus** or **namus,—ki, —ti, murwad,—di**; he does not — what you say, **isagu hadalkaga ma degaisto** or **yelo.**
regret, *n.*, **'ala'al,—ki, ḥomamais,—ki, ur ku talo,—adi**; *v.tr.*, **u 'ala'al, iss ḥanuji, ḥomamai, ur ku talo.**
regular, *a.*, **ḥun.**
reign, *v.tr.*, **ḥukun.**
rein, *n.*, **ḥakamai,—ihi, 'ainan, —ki.**
reiterate, *v.tr.*, **hadalka ku noḥo.**
reject, *v.tr.*, **eri, na', iss ka na', iss ka tur.**
rejoice (*see* cheer).
relapse, *v.i.*, (fall back) **haddana ku kuf.**
relate, *v.tr.*, (tell) **sheg, u sheg, ka shekai.**
be related to, *v.i.*, **ḥig.**
relation, relative, *n.*, **ḥigal,—ki, ga'al,—ki, ḥigto,—adi, ḥolo, —adi.**
relax, *v.tr.*, **debi'.**
release, *v.tr.*, **so furo.**
relegate, *v.tr.*, **masafiri.**
relegation, *n.*, **masafiris,—ki.**
relent, *v.i.*, **dīman**; the heat relents, **hurki wa dinmaya.**
relief, *n.*, **hil,—ki.**
relieve, *v.tr.*, **hili, 'awin.**
religion, *n.*, **din,—ti.**
relish, *n.*, **dadan,—ki**; *v.tr.*, **dadami.**
rely upon, *v.i.*, **iss ku halai.**
remain, *v.i.*, **had, jog, jogso**; — behind, **dambai**; — with, **la had, la jog**; *v.c.*, **joji, iss ka reb**; act of remaining, **hadnin, —ti**; the remaining behind, **dambais,—ki**; the remaining part, **hadki hadai** (*sing.*), **hadadki hadai** (*plur.*).

remainder, *n.*, **had,—ki.**
remedy, *n.*, **daïmo,—adi** or **daï-mai,—ihi.**
remember, *v.i.*, **ḥususo, ḥusus-naw, ogow.**
remind, *v.tr.*, **ḥususi, ogaisi.**
remission, remit (*see* forgive *and* forgiveness).
remnants, *n.*, (of food around the mouth) **dufan,—ki**; (in the teeth) **findi'il,—ki**; pick off the —, **findi'ilo.**
remove, *v.tr.*, **durki, du, ka du, fogai, shuḥulkisa ka ḥad**; *v.i.*, **durug, gur, ka baïd, ka durug.**
remuneration (*see* recompense).
rend, *v.tr.*, **dila'i, jeḥ**; — into pieces, **jeḥjeḥ.**
rendezvous, *n.*, **shir,—ki**; go to the —, **shirka tag.**
renounce (*see* forsake).
renowned, *a.*, (famous) **lo ya-ḥan.**
rent, *n.*, (laceration) **dila',—hi**; (revenue) — of a house, **kiro, —adi**; — of ground, **ardiad, —ki.**
repair, *v.tr.*, (an injury) **halmari, so ḥalmari**; (mend) **samai.**
reparation, *n.*, **ḥal,—ki.**
repeat, *v.tr.*, **mar kaleh deh, ku lāban.**
repel, *v.tr.*, (drive back) **dib u 'eli, dib u eri.**
repent, *v.r.*, **iss ḥanuji, u ala'al, ala'alsanaw.**
repentant, *a.*, **ala'alsan.**
repine, *v.i.*, **gubo.**
reply, *v.tr.*, **waḥ u 'eli.**
report, *n.*, (account) **shati,—gi**; *v.tr.*, **u sheg.**
reprehend, reprimand, reproach, *v.tr.*, **dagal, hanib, masabid.**
represent, *v.tr.*, (exhibit) **muji.**
reprimand, *n.*, **masabidnimo,—adi.**
reprobate, *a.*, **inkaran, inkarsan, nin la 'adabai**; *v.tr.*, **'adab, hanib.**
reprove (*see* reprehend).
reptile, *n.*, **bahal hosai, waḥha bog ku so'da.**
repugnance, *n.*, (of food) **balaf,—ki, yiḥyiḥsi,—gi.**
repulse, *v.tr.*, **durki, huruf, eri.**
repulsive, *a.*, **bas.**
reputation, *n.*, **mamus,—ki, —ti, namus,—ti, —ki**; of good —, **mamusleh.**
request, *n.*, **weidis,—ki, arji,—gi**; — of a country, **ardal ḥal, —ki**; *v.tr.*, **weidi weidiso, bari, dalbo, ka dalbo.**
require, *v.tr.*, **don.**
requital (*see* recompense).
rescind (*see* abrogate).
resemblance, *n.*, **ekan,—ti.**
resemble, *v.tr.*, **u ekow**; — each other, **iss u ekada, iss leh ekada.**
residence (*see* dwelling).
resign, *v.tr.*, **da, na'.**
resist, *v.tr.*, **iss ka 'eli, ḥabil, iss karaw, u adkaiso.**
resolution, *n.*, **talo,—adi.**
resound, *v.tr.*, **diyan.**
respect, *n.*, **namus,—ti, murwad, —di**; *v.tr.*, **mamus, murwad.**
respectable, *n.*, (man) **gob,—ki.**

respiration, *n.*, **neif,—ti.**
respire, *v.i.*, **neiftiro, naso, neifso.**
respite, *n.*, **rāgnin,—ti.**
respond for, *v.i.*, **damino.**
respondent, *n.*, **damin,—ti.**
rest, *n.*, **nasad,—ki, nasasho,—adi**; *v.i.*, **jif, iss ka jif, naso, neiftiro**; make him —, **nasi, jifi.**
restitution, *n.*, **helis,—ki, helin, —ti.**
restore, *v.tr.*, **so 'eli, ku so 'eli, heli, so heli.**
restrain (*see* refrain).
result, *n.*, **dog** or **dug,—ti**; bad —, **edis,—ti.**
resurrection (the), *n.*, **sarraka'ha jidka, sarraki'hi jidki, tosninta jidka.**
resuscitate, *v.tr.*, **nolai, nolaisi.**
retain, *v.tr.*, **hai, haiso.**
retaliate, *v.tr.*, **ḫisas.**
retaliation, *n.*, **ḫisas,—ti.**
retard (*see* delay).
retch, *v.i.*, **hunḫa'**; *n.*, **hunḫa'o, —adi.**
retire, *v.i.*, **dib u jogso, ka tag, 'ari**; — from business, **danta ka tag**; *v.tr.*, (take from) **ka ḫad.**
retract, *v.tr.*, **'esho**; — your words, **hadalkaga 'esho.**
retribution (*see* recompense).
return, *n.*, **so noḫod,—ki**; *v.i.*, **so noḫo, so lāban, ku lāban**; *v.tr.*, **dib u si, 'eli, iss ka 'eli, heli, so heli.**
reunion (*see* assembly).
reunite, *v.tr.*, **ururi, iss ku dar.**
revenge, *n.*, **ḫisas,—ti, 'ollad,—di, ur ku talo,—adi**; *v.tr.*, **ḫisas, 'olladi, ur ku talo.**
revere, *v.tr.*, **murwad.**
reverse, *v.tr.*, **forori, rog.**
review, *n.*, **ḫadiris,—ki.**
revindicate, *v.tr.*, **mar kaleh ḫanan.**
revive, *v.tr.*, **nolaisi**; — those exhausted men, **dadká goai so nolaisi** or **so tosi**; *v.i.*, (return to life) **so nolaw.**
revolt (*see* rebel).
revolve, *v.tr.*, **wareji**; *v.i.*, **wareg.**
revolver, *n.*, **tumujad,—di.**
reward (*see* recompense).
rheumatism, *n.*, **ḫushashad,—di.**
rhinoceros, *n.*, **wiyil,—ki.**
rib, *n.*, **feid,—di.**
rice, *n.*, **baris** or **beris** or **barid, —ki.**
rich, *n.*, (man) **hodan,—ki, hodanah, holo badan.**
riches, *n.*, **duyo,—adi.**
rid, *v.tr.*, **ka eri, ka bādbadi**; get — of a boy, **ambi.**
ride, *v.i.*, **ful**; *v.c.*, **fuli.**
ride, riding, *n.*, **fulimad,—di.**
ridge, *n.*, **adaḥ,—di.**
rifle, *n.*, *see* gun; *v.tr.*, (ransack) *see* plunder.
rift (*see* cleft).
rig, *n.*, (top of a mountain) **jar,—ki.**
right, *a.*, (not left) **midig**; — hand, **midig,—ti**; — side, **gesta midig.**
right, *a.*, (not crooked) **ḫumati, ḫuman, tosan, shuban**; (upright) **hagagsan, tāgan, wanaksan**; be upright, **hagag,**

hagagsanaw, tosnaw, ḩumanaw; make —, **hagaji, ḩumi, tosi**; all —! *or* all is —! **haurarsan! hayai!** it is —, **wa tos, wa run.**

rigid, *a.*, (severe) **ḩalbi adag.**

rim, *n.*, (margin) **girgir** or **jirjir, —ki**; — of a glass, **ḩarḩar,—ki.**

rind, *n.*, (bark) **dir,—ki, jilif,—ti, ḩolof,—ti**; *v.tr.*, **dil, dir.**

ring, *n.*, (for a finger) **katun,—ki.**

ring, *v.tr.*, (to sound, as a bell) **gara', ku dufo**; — the bell, **gandadi gara'** or **ku dufo.**

ringlet, *n.*, (of hair) **ran,—ti, sunarad,—di.**

rip, *v.tr.*, (tear, lacerate) **dila'i, jeḥ, jeḥjeḥ.**

ripe, *a.*, **bisil.**

ripen, ripe, *v.tr.*, **bislai**; the fruit ripens *or* grows ripe, **midki bislanaya.**

rise, *v.i.*, **ka', sarra ka', tos.**

rise, rising, *n.*, **tosnin,—ti.**

risk, *v.tr.*, **sasab**; *n.*, **baḩdin,—ti, sasab,—ti.**

river, *n.*, **durdur,—ki, wadi,—gi**; dry —, **doḥ,—hi, tog,—gi.**

road, *n.*, **dariḩ,—hi, hilin,—ki, jid,—ki.**

roam (*see* ramble).

roar, *n.*, (of the lion) **jibad,—di**; *v.i.*, **u jibad.**

roast, *v.tr.*, **dub, dubo, shil.**

roasted, *a.*, **duban.**

rob, *v.tr.*, **ḥad, bob, da'**; be robbed, **da'an, da'anaw.**

robber, *n.*, **tug,—gi.**

robbery, *n.*, **tugo,—adi, bob,—ki.**

rock, *n.*, **dagaḥ wein, dagiḥhi weina, dakab,—ki, gumbur, —ti.**

rod, *n.*, **ul,—shi, lan,—ti, denged,—di, sergad,—ki.**

roebuck, *n.*, (Clarke's) **dabatag, —ti.**

rogue, *n.*, **ḥarami,—gi, nin ḥaramiah, tug,—gi.**

roll, *v.tr.*, **giringiri**; — up, **dūb, dūdub.**

roller-blind, *n.*, **alol,—ki.**

roof, *n.*, **saḩaf,—ki.**

room, *n.*, **aḩal,—ki, maḩsin,—ki, gurgur,—ki, ḩollad,—di, rar, —ti.**

root, *n.*, **jirid,—di, gun,—ti, ḥidid,—ki.**

rope, *n.*, **ḥadig,—gi**; — for fastening a camel's neck and leg, **ḩarḩarsi,—gi.**

rosary, *n.*, **tusbaḥ,—hi.**

rot, *v.i.*, (grow putrid) **ḩudun**; *v.c.*, (cause to —) **ḩudmi.**

rotten, *a.*, **ḩudunsan.**

rottenness, *n.*, **ḩudun,—ki.**

rough, *a.*, **amal ḥun, baan, ḥun, ḩalafsan.**

round, *a.*, **ḥersan, kuriyaisan, gobaban**; make —, **gobabi, kuriyai.**

round, *n.*, **gobabin,—ti, gobo,—adi, kuriyaisnan,—ti**; *ad.*, **harero,—aha**; move —, **ku wareg, waregaiso**; go —, **ku so wareg**; *prp.*, **harero,—ihi**; go — the world, **dunida ku so wareg**; I went — the world, **dunida harereheda yan so marai**; surround, *v.tr.*, **ḥerai.**

rouse, *v.tr.*, (*see* raise); *v.i.*, **bararug, tos.**
rove (*see* ramble).
roving clouds, *n.*, **'adar,—ki.**
row, *n.*, (a line) **sadar,—ki, taḥ, tiḥhi**; *n.*, (tumult) **shiddo,—adi, buḥ,—hi**; make a —, **shiddai.**
row, *v.tr.*, (impel a boat) **wad.**
rub, *v.tr.*, **dug, mari**; — off the skin, **ḥago, ḥagḥago.**
rubbish, *n.*, **ḥushash.**
rude, *a.*, **ḥalafsan.**
ruin, *n.*, **jajab,—ki, rognin,—ti.**
rule, *n.*, **ḥainun,—ki.**
ruminant, *n.*, **alalnaḥsi,—gi.**
ruminate (*see* chew).
rump (*see* croup).
run, *v.i.*, **'arar, orod, ror**; whither do you — so fast? **haggad daḥsaha ugu ordaisa?** he ran upon me, **igu so 'ararai**; — to his help, **orod ou hili**; the river runs by the mountain, **durdurku burtu so mara**; time runs insensibly, **waḥtigu ḥun yar bu so'oda**; his tongue runs perpetually, **gor iyo galab afka iss ku dari mayo**; — away, **ka 'arar, ya'a**; — after, **ka daba tag, radi.**
rupee, *n.*, **rubiad,—di, rubad,—di**; half —, **rubi,—gi.**
rupture, *n.*, (hernia) **doḥnin,—ti.**
rust, *n.*, **merid** or **mirid,—ki.**
rustic, *n.*, **badow,—gi, nin badowah.**

S.

Sabbath, *n.*, **sabti,—di.**
sack, *n.*, (bag) **joniad,—di**; leathern —, **ḥalḥala,—ihi**; (pillage) **da'nin,—ti.**
sad, *a.*, **ḥulubsan**; grow —, **ḥulub, wahan**; be —, **ḥulubsanaw**; make —, **ḥulbi, ḥulubsi.**
sadness, *n.*, **ḥulub,—ki, wahan,—ki.**
saddle, *v.tr.*, **korai**; *n.*, **kora** or **korai,—ihi**; — bag, **ḥalḥala,—ihi**; camel's pack —, **heriyo,—ihi.**
safe, *a.*, **'absila, shilla, aminah**; be —, **barī**; are you —? **ma barīden?** be —, **nabad ḥab.**
saffran (*see* turmeric).
sagacious, *a.*, **fi'an, faridah, foyig.**
sage, *n.*, **aḥil,—ki, nin aḥilah, nin herribleh.**
sailor, *n.*, **baḥri,—gi.**
sail, *n.*, **shira',—hi, shiraḥ,—hi**; *v.i.*, **dof.**
saint, *n.*, **nebi,—gi, weli,—gi, auliad,—di** (*fem.*).
sake, *n.*, **awo,—adi, darad,—di**; for the — of, **daradda, awada.**
salary, *n.*, **def,—ti, haḥai,—gi.**
sale, *n.*, (by auction) **ḥarash,—ki.**
saliva, *n.*, **alyo,—adi, dareir,—ki**; thickness of —, **lun,—ki.**
salt, *n.*, **'usboḥ,—di, miliḥ,—hi**; *v.tr.*, **'usbai**; *a.*, **'usbaisan, danan.**
salutation, *n.*, **salamad,—di**; kind of —, **mot! mot!**
salute, *v.tr.*, **salam, baridi.**

same, *a.*, iss leh eg, o kaleh, iss la, iss ku mid.

sample, *n.*, midab,—ki.

sanctify, *v.tr.*, ḥodus ka dig ; be sanctified, samo ; hallowed be, ha samado.

sanctity, *n.*, ḥodus,—ki.

sand, *n.*, amud,—di, 'id,—di ; salted —, 'arro,—adi ; — storm, 'iro,—adi, sesa, sisa, sigo,—adi.

sandal, *n.*, kab,—ti ; old and bad —, jān,—ti ; wooden —, hadafi',—hi.

sane, *a.*, (healthy) (mel) afimad leh.

sap, *n.*, de'an,—ki.

sash, *n.*, (girdle) gunti,—gi.

Satan, *n.*, shaidan,—ki, 'ifrid,—ki.

satiate, *v.tr.*, ḍergi ; be satiated, ḍereg, ḍeregsanaw.

satiate, satiated, *a.*, ḍeregsan.

satiety, *n.*, ḍereg,—gi.

satisfaction, *n.*, raḥo, —adi, rahad, —di.

satisfactory, *a.*, (sufficient) filan.

satisfy, *v.tr.*, (content) rahaisi ; (reward) u abalgud ; (make payment) tobad ken.

Saturday, *n.*, sabti,—di.

sauce, *n.*, (remaining in …) murud, —ki ; lick up the …, murdi.

savage, *a.*, baan, bahal.

save, *v.tr.*, (preserve) biḥi, ka so biḥi ; God — you, Ilah ku baḍbaḍiyo ; I saved your life, naftada ana baḍbaḍiyai ; (spare) daḥ, daḥo, digo ; (do not spend) ha biḥin, ha ku ayarin.

saving, *n.*, dahasho,—adi.

savour, *n.*, dadan,—ki.

saw, *n.*, (tool) minshar,—ki ; *v.tr.*, jar, go.

say, *v.i.* and *v.tr.*, oḍo (commonly) deḥ, sheg, u sheg.

saying, *n.*, mahmah,—di.

scab, *n.*, ḥolof,—ti.

scabbard, *n.*, gal,—ki.

scald, *n.*, (burning) gubnin,—ti ; — head, madaḥ 'adai.

scale, *n.*, (balance) misan,—ki.

scanty, *a.*, (narrow) 'edidi.

scar, *n.*, nabar,—ki, daḥar boksadai, ḥon boksatai.

scarabæus, *n.*, (black and stinking one) harwalwal,—ki.

scarce, *a.*, yar.

scare, *v.tr.*, (frighten) 'absi, baji.

scarlet, *a.*, gudud, gududan.

scatter, *v.tr.*, firḍi ; — on, ku firḍi.

scattered, *a.*, firḍisan.

scent, *n.*, udgon,—ki, ur,—ti.

scent, *v.tr.*, (perfume) udgonai, umi.

schism, *n.*, kago,—hi.

scholar, *n.*, barad,—ki, ardai,—gi.

school, *n.*, ma'lamad,—di.

schoolmaster, *n.*, bara,—ihi, fiḥi, gi, mu'alim,—ki.

science, *n.*, oḥon,—ti.

scissors, *n.*, manḥas,—ki.

scoff (*see* mock).

scold, *v.tr.*, dagal.

scold, *n.*, (a brawler) ḥof dagal badan.

scolding, *n.*, **dagal,—ki.**
scope, *n*, (aim, end) **dama‘,—hi, dug,—ti.**
scorch, *v.tr.*, **gub**; *v.i.*, **gubo.**
scorn (*see* contempt).
scorpion, *n.*, **hangarara,—ihi, hangaraleh,—ihi, dib ḥalloḥ, —hi.**
scoundrel (*see* rascal).
scourge (*see* flog).
scout, *v.i.*, **ilalo tag, so ilalai.**
scowl (*see* pout, pouting).
scrag (*see* lean).
scrape, *v.tr.*, **hoḥ**; — off the skin, **ka hoḥ**; — out a word, **babii.**
scratch, *v.tr.*, **ḥago, ḥagḥago**; *v.r.*, **iss ḥago.**
scream, *v.i.*, **dawaḥ, ḥaili**; *n.*, **dawaḥ,—hi, ḥailo,—adi.**
screen, *n.*, **iliḥid,—ki.**
scribe, *n.*, **karani,—gi.**
scribble, scribbling, *n.*, **hariḥ,—di**; *v.i.*, **hariḥ, harhariḥ.**
scripture, *n.*, **ḥorin,—ti, ḥorin ḥodusah.**
scrofula, *n*, **hudai** or **huda,—ihi, māl,—shi.**
scrub, *v.tr.*, **ād u dug, ād u hoḥ.**
scud, *v.i.*, (run away) **‘arar.**
scuffle, *n.*, (for women) **iss ku bod,—ki**; (for men) **dirir,—ti.**
sculpture, *v.tr.*, **ḥarad.**
scurf, *n.*, (dry mealy scab) **‘anbar, —ti.**
sea, *n.*, **bad,—di.**
sea-gull, *n.*, **‘ofai,—di.**
seal, *v.tr.*, **daba‘**; *n.*, **daba‘,—i‘hi.**
sealed, *a.*, **daba‘an.**
seam, *n.*, **tolnin,—ti.**
search, *v.tr.*, **bad, don**; *n.*, **donin, —ti.**
season, *n.*, **ḥeli,—gi, waḥti,—gi**; hot —, **ḥaga,—gi**; dry —, **jilal,—ki**; cold —, **gu,—gi**; the beginning of cold —, **daïr, —ti**; — before the S.W. monsoon, **kalil,—shi.**
second, *num.*, **labad, kan ki labad.**
secrecy, *n.*, **faḥ goniah, mel ‘idla ah.**
secret word, *n.*, **faḥ goniah, hadal ḥarson.**
sect, *n.*, (Mohamedan one) **shafi‘i, —gi.**
secure, *a.*, (safe) **shilla.**
security, *n.*, (caution) **‘arbun,—ti, raḥmad,—ki, ‘udal,—shi**; give for —, **raḥan**; hold in false —, **dāg**; false —, **dāgnin, —ti.**
sedition, *n.*, **ḥasidnimo,—adi.**
seduce (*see* deceive).
see, *v.tr.*, **arag, eg, dai, dugo, jedāli**; let him —, **da ha arkaie.**
seed, *n.*, **inin,—ti.**
seek, *v.tr.*, **bad, don.**
seem, *v.i.*, **mod**; it seems, **wa la moda, wa muḥata.**
see-saw, *v.i.*, (play at) **iss misan.**
seethe, seether (*see* boil and boiler).
segregate (*see* separate).
seize, *v.tr.*, **ḥabo.**
seizing, *n.*, **ḥabasho,—adi.**
select (*see* choose).
self, *refl.p.*, **iss, iss,—ki**; *n.*, **naf, —ti, ḥud,—di.**
selfish, *a.*, **iss ja‘el.**

selfishness, *n.*, **iss ja'alan,—ti.**
sell, *v.tr.*, **ibi, so ibi, ibso, so ibso.**
seller, *n.*, **nin waḥ ibiya** or **ibsha.**
selvage, selvedge, *n.*, **darur,—ki.**
semen, *n.*, **ḫorud,—ki, biya baḥ, —hi.**
sempiternal, *a.*, **dayim, silei' dayimah.**
send, *v.tr.*, **dir**; — to, **u dir**; — to me, **i so dir.**
senna-plant, *n.*, **jelelo** or **jalelo, —adi.**
sensation, *n.*, **daren,—ki.**
sense, *n.*, (good) **garad,—ki**; a man of —, **garadleh**; (meaning) **ma'nai,—ihi.**
sentence, *n.*, (judgment) **arin,—ti, gar,—ti.**
sentinel, *n.*, **kor jir,—ki, kor jog,—gi, ilalo,—adi.**
separate, *v.tr.*, **fuji, kala fuji, kala kaḥai, kala 'eli, so', kala so', dabsi.**
separation, *n.*, **so'din,—ti, dabsin, —ti.**
sepoy, *n.*, **subaihi,—gi; subaihin,—ti** (*plur.*); **askari,—gi; askar,—ti** (*plur.*).
sepulchre (*see* grave).
sepulture (*see* burial).
serjeant, *n.*, (of police) **hawaldar, —ki.**
sermon, *n.*, **wano,—adi.**
serpent, *n.*, **mas,—ki.**
servant, *n.*, **mididin,—ki, 'idan, —ki, ḫadam,—ki, sebiyan,—ki, nin la joga.**
serve, *v.tr.*, **haul ḫabo**; — God, **Ilah 'ābud**; *v.i.*, **la jir.**
service, *v.i.*, (render a) **tar.**
servitude, *n.*, **adonimo,—adi.**
set, *v.tr.*, **dig, sar, ku deji**; — in order, **hagaji, wanaji**; — a fine, **ḫasir**; — a price, **ḫimad ku sheg**; — on shore, **deji, rog**; — aside, **ges u dig**; — pen to paper, — down, **ḫor, warḫadda ku dig**; — the house on fire, **aḫalka dab geli**; he cannot — one foot before another, **so'on kari mayo**; — a time, **ballan**; — the bone, **lafta tosi**; — abroad, **ogaisi**; he had — my mind against you, **isagu wa igu ka 'adaisi**; — apart, **goni u dig**; — aside, **daḫ, doḫo**; — at work, **shaḫaisi**; — away, **la tag**; — forward, **horo u kaḫai, horo u rih, horo u wad**; — on, **sar**; (fix) **dab, 'as**; (fall below the horizon) *v.i.*, the sun sets, **ḫorahdu wa daḫaisa**; — out, **baḥ**; — upside down, **rog**; be — upside down, **rogan, rogmo**; *a.*, **saran.**
settle, *v.tr.*, **tali, ku tali, heshisi, u si tali, ku dar, iss la tali.**
settlement, *n.*, **talo,—adi, heshis, —ki.**
seven, *num.*, **todoba,—di.**
seventeen, *num.*, **todob iyo toban, —ki.**
seventh, *num.*, **todobad,—di.**
seventy, *num.*, **todobatan.**
several, *ad.*, **ḫar,—ki, daur,—ki.**
severe, *a.*, (nin) **ḫadad.**
sew, *v.tr.*, **tol**; — slowly, **gatanur**; — the sandal ties, **yel.**
sewing, *n.*, **tolnin,—ti.**

shade, shadow, *v.tr.*, **hadai**; *n.*, **had,—ki**; evening —, **had hodal,—ki.**
shady, shadowy, *a.*, **hadaisan.**
shaft, *n.*, (an arrow) **fallad,—di, gantal,—shi**; (the wooden part of an arrow) **gamun, ki, leb,—ki**; a poisonous —, **hamis,—ki.**
shagged, shaggy, *a.*, **halableh** (*m.n.*).
shaggedness, *n.*, **halab,—ti.**
shake, shaking, *n.*, **lulin,—ti, ruhnin,—ti.**
shake off, *v.tr.*, **hurguf**; — to and fro, **lūl, ruh.**
shake, *v.i.*, **ruho, garir**; his head is shaking, **madihhisa gariraya** or **ruhanaya.**
shaken, *a.*, **ruhan.**
sham (*see* deceit); — crying, **bihimbih.**
shame, *v.tr.*, **hil**; *n.*, **hil,—ki.**
shampoo, *v.tr.*, **dūg**; — with the feet, **ku jogjogso.**
shampooing, *n.*, **jogjogsi,—gi.**
shank, *n.*, **shansho,—adi**; — of camels, **dudun,—ki.**
shape, *n.*, **midab,—ki** (*see* figure); *v.tr.*, **midab u yel**; — a pencil, **hor.**
shaping, *n.*, **hornin,—ti.**
share, *n.*, **haïb,—ti**; *v.tr.*, **u haïbi, kalago, sisi**; *v.i.*, **la haibso**; you shall — with me in my riches, **holahaiga yad ila haïbsan.**
sharer, *n.*, **haibiya** or **haïbsanaya.**
shark, *n.*, **libah baded,—hi baded.**
sharp, *a.*, **af badan, lissan, fihan.**
sharpen, *v.tr.*, **lis, sofai, fih, dub.**
sharpness, *n.*, **af badnan,—ti, fihnan,—ti.**
shave, *v.tr.*, **u hir.**
shaved, shaven, *a.*, **hiran.**
shaver, *n.*, **rais,—ki.**
she, *pers. prn.* (*see* Grammar).
sheaf, *n.*, (of arrows) **hidmo gantalah.**
sheath, *n.*, **gal,—ki.**
shed, *n.*, (a hovel) **balballo,—adi, wab,—ti, bul,—ki**; make the —, **balballai.**
shed, *v.tr.*, (pour out) **dādi, hub.**
shedding, *n.*, **dādis,—ki.**
sheep, *n.*, **ido,—ihi.**
sheer, *a.*, (pure) **miran, safaisan, safiah.**
sheet, *n.*, (of paper) **bāl,—ki**; winding —, **kafan,—ti.**
shell, *n.*, **alel,—shi, laji,—gi** or **lajo,—adi.**
shelter, *n.* (*see* shed); — against cold, **duksi,—gi.**
shepherd, *n.*, **adi jir,—ki.**
shepherdess, *n.*, **adi jir,—ti.**
shield, *n.*, **gashan,—ki**; — maker, **gabariyel,—ki, gashamo samaïs,—ki.**
shift, *n.*, **hikmad,—di.**
shin, *n.*, **hog,—gi.**
shine, *v.i.*, **dalal**; shining, *n.*, **dalal,—ki.**
ship, *n.*, **markab,—ki**; (a boat) **sehimad,—di.**
shipping, *n.*, **dof,—ki.**
shipwreck, *n.*, **hashwad,—di.**
shirt, *n.*, **garba galai,—ihi, hamis,—ki** (*sing.*); **hamsan,—ti.**

shiver, *v.i.*, **garir, ḥadḥad, kurbo.**
shivering, *n.*, **kurbad,—ki**; a — fit, **ḥadḥadiyo,—adi.**
shock, *n.*, (conflict) **ḥardi,—gi**; *v.tr.*, **ḥardi.**
shoe, *n.*, **kab,—ti**; horse —, **na'al,—ki.**
shoot, *n.*, (branch) **lan,—ti, daragad,—di, ya'aï,—gi, 'urdan, —ki.**
shoot, *v.tr.*, (cast forth) **kaga rid.**
shop, *n.*, **das,—ki, dukan,—ki.**
shore, sea-shore, *n.*, **ḥeb,—ti.**
short, *a.*, **gāban, yar.**
shorten, *v.tr.*, **gābi, yarai, yaraiso.**
shortness, *n.*, **gāb,—ki, gābnin, —ti.**
shot, *n.*, **ḫururuḥ,—hi, rash,—ki.**
shoulder, *n.*, **garab,—ki**; — blade, **laf garab,—ta —ka.**
shout, *v.i.*, **ḫaili, madar, orri**; *n.*, **dawaḥ,—hi, gurḫan,—ki, orr,—ki, ḫailo,—adi.**
shove (*see* push).
show, *v.tr.*, **tus, so tus, muji**; *n.*, **tusnin,—ti, mujis,—ki, mujnin,—ti.**
shriek, *v.i.*, (shrill) **dawaḫ**; *n.*, **dawaḫ,—hi.**
shrink, *v.i.*, **dib u jogso, naḥ.**
shrub, *n.*, **ḥanan,—ki, daran,—ti.**
shudder (*see* shiver).
shut, *a.*, **dabolan, ḥidan, ōdan**; *v.tr.*, **ḥid, abud, dabol**; — your eyes, **il iss ku ḫabo.**
shy, *a.*, **ḥil badan**; be —, **ḥisho.**
sick, *a.*, **buka, 'udur haba**; be —, **bukow, 'udur ḫad.**

sicken, *v.tr.*, **bukaisi.**
sickness, *n.*, **bukan,—ki, 'udur, —ki.**
side, *n.*, **barbar,—ki, dan,—ki, ges,—ti, harer,—ti**; on all sides, **harero,—ihi**; by the —, **iss garab.**
sieve, *n.*, **golab,—ki.**
sift, *v.tr.*, **golab.**
sigh, *v.i.*, **hinrag, waraḫ, oi, musanow**; *n.*, **hinrag,—gi, oin, —ti, waraḫ,—hi, musanow, —gi, bihimbih,—hi.**
sight, *n.*, **arag,—gi**; (show) **muḫ, —hi**; short —, **habenno,—adi**; long —, **il deran,—ti.**
sighted, *a.*; good —, **il fiḫan**; long —, **il der.**
sign, *n.*, **bar,—ti, sumad,—di, 'alamad,—di**; — of the camel's anger, **dob,—ti**; *v.tr.*, (mark) **'alamadi, sumad**; (ratify by hand) **saḥeḥ.**
signal, *n.*, **baḫ,—hi.**
signature, *n.*, **saḥeḥ, hi.**
signification (*see* meaning).
silence, *v.tr.*, **amusi**; *n.*, **amusnan, —ti**; *int.*, **us! amus! amusa!**
silent, *a.*, **amusan**; be —, **amus, amusnaw.**
silex, *n.*, (flint) **du'un,—ti.**
silk, *n.*, **harir,—ti.**
silly, *a.*, (simpleton) **na's,—ki** (*n.*).
silver, *n.*, **la'ag,—ti, fiddad** or **foddad,—di.**
similitude, *n.*, **ekan,—ti.**
simple, *a.*, (sincere) **hagagsan**; be —, **hagag.**
sin, *n.*, **dembi,—gi.**
since, *adv.* and *c.*, **halkiyo gorti**;

— you saw him, **halkiyo gortad aragtai.**
sinful, *a.*, **dembileh.**
sinner, *n.*, **dad dembileh, dadka dembigaleh.**
sincere, *a.*, **lilahiah, aminah.**
sinew, *n.*, **seid,—di, bohon,—ti, bohon hore, bohon dambe, hanjid,—ki.**
sing, *v.tr.* and *v.i.*, **gabai, hes.**
singer, *n.*, **gabaya,—ihi.**
singing, *n.*, **hes,—ti.**
single, *a.*, (sole) **goniah, keliah, hud, hudah.**
sink, *v.i.*, **deg, dus, ka dus**; *v.tr.*, **deji, ka dusi.**
sip, *v.tr.*, **fihso**; *n.*, **fihsi** or **fuhsi, —gi.**
sir, *n.*, **saheb,—ki.**
sister, *n.*, **walal,—shi**; —in-law, **dumashi,—di.**
sisterhood, *n.*, **walalnimo,—adi.**
sit, *v.i.*, (down) **fadiso, salka dig, fadi**; — still, **si fadi.**
sitting, *n.*, **fadi,—gi.**
six, *num.*, **leh,—di**; — fold, **leh jer o min lehah,** or **leh jer o leh wada ah.**
sixteen, *num.*, **leh iyo toban,—ki.**
sixth, *num.*, **lehad, kan lehad.**
sixty, *num.*, **lehdan,—ki.**
size, *n.*, **hiyas,—ti, dumo',—di.**
skilful, *a.*, **fi'an, farsamo badan, wah haban og.**
skill, *n.*, **farsamo,—adi, fi',—hi, fi'nan,—ti.**
skim, *v.tr.*, **usarka ka safai.**
skimmer, *n.*, **hudda,—ihi.**
skin, *n.*, **dub,—ki, harag,—gi, sān,—ti**; — sewn to carry children, **dereb,—ti, furad,—ki**; — sewn to make a couch, **weilalis,—ti**; — placed for a shed, **gibil,—shi.**
skin, *v.tr.*, (flay) **dubka** or **haragga** or **sānta ka bihi** or **ka mudhi.**
skull, *n.*, **indolai,—ihi**; upper part of the —, **dako,—adi, kug,—ti**; each side of the —, **ges,—ti.**
sky, *n.*, **'ir,—ki.**
slab, *n.*, (a puddle) **dirih,—di, didi,—gi.**
slabber, *v.tr.*, (smear with spittle) **alyo muruh ku dādi**; *v.i.*, (drivel, slaver) **alyo muruh iss ka buhi.**
slabberer, *n.*, **nin alyo muruh wein leh,—ki, — — weina.**
slack, *v.tr.*, (unbend) **deb'i**; *a.*, (loose) **deb'isan.**
slake, *v.tr.*, (extinguish) **bahti**; (quench) **iss harad tir, iss on tir.**
slander, *v.tr.*, **'eibai, hano, hafar**; *n.*, **han,—ti, 'eib,—ti.**
slap, *v.tr.*, **darbah**; *n.*, **darbaho, —adi, faragorgor,—ki.**
slate, *n.*, (used in school) **loh,—hi.**
slaughter, *v.tr.*, **gowra', kaga kudi, ka kausi, kaga hawi, dil**; *n.*, **gowra',—ihi.**
slave, *n.*, **adon,—ki** (*mas.*), **adon, —ti** (*fem.*), **bida** or **bidai,—ihi** (*mas.*), **bidad,—di** (*fem.*), **sawahili,—gi.**
slavery, *n.*, **adonimo,—adi.**
slay (*see* slaughter).

sleep, *v.i.*, **hurud, iss ka hurud, seho, so seho, gama', jifso**; *v.c.*, **sehi, jifi**; *n.*, **hurdo,—adi, gama',—hi, sehasho,—adi.**

sleeper, *n.*, **nin hurda, nin gama'-san.**

sleepless, *a.*, **gami' wah.**

sleepy, *a.* and *n.*, (drowsy) **da-madsan, luloleh, damad,—ki.**

sleepiness, *n.*, **lulo,—adi.**

slice, *n.*, **luf,—ki.**

slide, *v.i.*, (slip) **simbiririho, si-sibo, sibiboho**; *n.*, **mel sibiba-hah.**

slight, *v.tr.*, (disregard) **fududai**; *a.*, **fudud, weïdsan.**

slightness, *n.*, **fudaïd,—ki, weïd,—di.**

slime, *n.*, (glaire) **dareir,—ki, alyomuruh,—hi**; — mixed with blood in dysentery, **a'al,—shi.**

sling, *v.tr.*, **wadfi**; *n.*, **wadaf,—ki.**

slink, *v.i.*, (sneak) **'arar, bahso**; she slank, **shinki ma ai dalin.**

slip, *v.i.*, (*see* slide); *v.c.*, (cause to —) **sibibihi, sisibi, simbiri-rihi**; *n.*, (act of slipping) **sim-biririho,—adi, sisib,—ti, sibi-boho,—adi.**

slipper, *n.*, **kab,—ti.**

slippery, *a.*, **sibibahah.**

slit, *v.tr.*, **jehjeh, dildila'i**; *v.i.*, **dila', dildila'**; *a.*, **dila'san, jehan**; *n.*, (a narrow opening) **dila',—hi, jeh,—hi.**

slope, *n.*, (declivity) **didib,—ti, aror,—ki, sibibah,—di, ba-bah,—hi.**

sloth (*see* laziness).

slouch, *n.*, (a clumsy boy) **hoga-sho,—adi**; *v.i.*, (have a down-cast look) **hogo.**

slough, *n.*, (a deep, miry place) **limad,—ki**; (of a snake) **hub,—ki.**

sloven (*see* dirty).

slow, *a.*, **rāga, rāgi jirai.**

slowly, *ad.*, **ayar** or **adyar, hun-yar**; walking —, **dukis.**

slowness, *n.*, **rāgnin,—ti.**

sly, *a.*, (cunning) **nejis,—ki, ne-jisah.**

small, *a.*, **gaban, gibin, yar.**

smallness, *n.*, **gab,—ki, gabnin,—ti, yaran,—ti.**

small-pox (*see* pox).

smash, *v.tr.*, **burburi.**

smell, *n.*, **ur,—ti, udgon,—ki**; bad —, **ur hudmun**; *v.tr.*, **urso**; *v.c.*, **ursi**; *v.i.*, **ur**; the meat smells, **hilibku wa uraya.**

smile, *v.i.*, **hosol**; *n.*, **hosol,—ki.**

smite, *v.tr.*, (strike) **tun**; *v.i.*, **kurbo**; my knees — together, **jilbahaigu wa kurbanaya.**

smith, *n.*, **tumal,—ki.**

smoke, *n.*, **hih,—hi**; where there is — there is fire, **meshi hih lihi dab bai lehdahai**; *v.i.*, **dabku wa hihaya,** or **hih ba ka bahaya**; (use tobacco) **fūd, 'ab**; *v.tr.*, (dry in —) **gawadi**; — meat, **hilibka gawadi**; — dried, **la gawadiyai.**

smooth, *v.tr.*, **mari, salah, iss ku sin**; *a.*, **salahan, siman.**

smother (*see* suffocate).

smuggle, *v.tr.*, **hayanai.**

smut (*see* dirt).

snake, *n.*, **mas,—ki**; kind of —, **'abeiso,—adi, abguri,—di.**

snare, *n.*, **debin,—ki**; the making or placing of a —, **dabnin,—ki.**

snarl, *v.tr.*, (entangle) **iss ku merji**; *v.i.*, (growl) **abad**; the camel is snarling, **aurki wa abadaya.**

snatch, *v.tr.*, **dufo** or **difo.**

sneak, *v.i.*, (creep) **bogga ku so'o.**

sneer, *v.i.*, (laugh with contempt) **ẖubiḥi**; *n.*, **ẖuḥub,—ki.**

sneeze, *v.i.*, **hindis.**

sniff, *v.tr.* and *v.i.*, **sin 'esho, sariẖo.**

snore, snort, *v.i.*, **ẖuri**; snorting, **ẖuro,—adi.**

snot, *n.*, (mucus of the nose) **duf,—ki.**

snout, *n.*, **gafur,—ki.**

snuff, *n.*, (powdered tobacco) **nashug,—gi, buri,—gi**; — box, **ẖasa'ad,—di**; *v.tr.*, (to draw in with the breath) **urso.**

snuffle, *v.i.*, (speak through the nose) **sanẖada ka hadal.**

snuffler, *n.*, **nin sanẖoleh.**

so, *a.*, **sida, sidas, sidi, sā.**

soak, *v.tr.*, **ẖoi.**

soap, *n.*, **sabun,—ti**; *v.tr.*, **sabunta mari.**

sob, *n.*, (convulsive sigh) **hiẖlai,—ihi**; *v.i.*, **hiẖlai.**

socket, *n.*, (any hollow) **gof,—ki**; the — of the eye, **isha gofkedi.**

sodomy, *n.*, **kud,—ki, maẖnudnimo,—adi**; commit —, **kud.**

sodomite, *n.*, **maẖnud,—ki.**

soft, *a.*, **jilai'san, ẖabow.**

soften, *v.tr.*, **jilai'i** or **jili'i, u tud, salaḥ**; *v.i.*, **jilai'.**

soil, *n.*, (earth) **'arro,—adi, 'id,—di**; *v.tr.*, (stain, besmear ...) **doẖbai.**

sojourn, *v.i.*, **hoio.**

solace, *n.*, **tudad,—di, tudnin,—ki.**

solder *or* soder, *v.tr.*, **iss ku deji, iss ku nab.**

sold, *a.*, **ibsan**; be —, **ibsanaw**; not —, **ma ibsana.**

sole, *n.*, (of the foot) **'agta 'ad.**

solicit, *v.tr.*, **bari, dalbo.**

solicitude, *n.*, **aminimo,—adi.**

solid, *a.*, **adag.**

solitary, *a.*, **goniah, keliah.**

solitude, *n.*, **mel goniah, 'idla 'irsila,—di.**

some, *a.*, **in,—ta, waḥ, waḥẖoga, har,—ki**; —body, **nin un**; —how, **si un**; —thing, **waḥ un**; —times, **kolkol, marmar**; —where, **mel un.**

son, *n.*, **ina, inan,—ki, wil,—ki**; sons, **arur,—ti, dalan,—ki.**

song, *n.*, **gabai,—gi, gerar,—ki, hes,—ti**; — or elegy of lamentation, **digri,—gi.**

soon, *ad.*, **gor dow**; it is too —, **wad so daẖsatai.**

soot, *n.*, **madun,—ki.**

soothe (*see* soften).

sophisticate, *v.tr.*, **bedel.**

soporific, *a.*, **seẖiya.**

sorcerer, *n.*, **nin waḥ fala, ẖariyan,—ki, ẖadaẖata** or **ẖataẖata,—ihi, yibir,—ki.**

sore, *n.*, **bog,—ti, hon,—ti**; a small —, **hon gibina**; — becoming worse, **dila'**; a person having a —, **bogaleh,—ihi.**

sorrow, *n.*, **'ala'al** or **alaana'l,—ki, human,—ti, weirweir,—ki, hulub,—ki, wahan,—ki**; *v.i.*, **weirweir, hulub, ala'al, wahan.**

sorrowful, *a.*, **hulubsan, ala'alsan, wahan.**

sort, *n.*, (species) **'aïn,—ki, tol,—ki.**

sot, *a.*, **na'asah.**

soul, *n.*, **naf,—ti.**

sound, *v.i.*, (make a noise) **kaga sanhadi**; *n.*, **sanhad,—di.**

soup, *n.*, **fūd,—ki.**

sour, *a.*, **danān, hadad.**

sourness, *n.*, **hadad,—ki.**

source, *n.*, (spring) **ib,—ti, il,—shi.**

south, *n.*, **hodub** or **hudub,—ki.**

sow, *v.tr.*, (scatter seed) **ininaha ku dādi** or **firdi** or **ku firdi.**

space, *n.*, **hawo,—adi.**

span, *n.*, **dāko,—adi.**

spare, *v.tr.*, **daur, ha ku ayarin, dah, doho**; — something for the poor, **masakinta wah u diga.**

spark, sparkle, *n.*, **bilig,—ti, biligbilig,—ti, dinbil,—shi.**

sparkling, *a.*, **biligbiligleh.**

spatter, *v.tr.*, **duldul.**

spawl, *v.i.*, **tūf**; *n.*, **anduf** or **andufo,—adi, hāko.**

speak, *v.i.*, **hadal**; *v tr*, **deh, sheg**; *v.i.*, — in sleep, **awawi.**

speaking, *n.*, (in sleep) **awawi,—gi, tamanta,—ihi.**

speaker, *n.*, (in a meeting) **gudi,—di.**

spear, *n.*, **waran,—ki**; different kinds of spears, **'aradub,—ki, bagaf,—ki, be'idi** or **bihidi,—gi, dohana,—ihi, sallado,—adi, teri,—gi, weidar,—ki.**

species (*see* sort).

speck, *n.*, (spot) **dibi',—di.**

spectacles, *n.*, **ohad,—di.**

spectre, *n.*, **muh,—hi.**

speech, *n.*, **hadal,—ki.**

speed, *n.*, **'arar,—ki, orod,—ki.**

spell, *v.tr.*, (charm) **gedago**; (read by naming letters singly) **harafka walba goni u deh,** or **harafyadan mid ba gonidis u deh**; *n.*, (a charm) **gedagoiyo,—adi.**

spend, *v.tr.*, **bihi**; (waste) **lumi, babihi.**

spendthrift, *n.*, **mudaya',—hi.**

spew, *v.i.*, (vomit) **hunha.**

sphere, *n.*, **kuriyaisnan,—ti.**

spherical, *a.*, **kuriyaisan.**

spider, *n.*, **'aro,—adi.**

spike, *n.*, **hudum,—ki.**

spill, *v.tr.*, **hub, dādi, ku dadi, rog.**

spilt, *a.*, **dadsan, shuban, rogan.**

spin, *v.tr.*, **wareji**; *v.i.*, **wareg.**

spine, *n.*, (backbone) **adah,—di.**

spirit, *n.*, (breath) **neif,—ti**; (an immaterial substance) **ruh,—hi.**

spit, *v.i*, (spawl) **tuf.**

spite, *n.*, (malevolence) **hamidnimo,—adi.**

spittle, *n.*, **tufnin,—ti, andufo,—adi, alyomuruh, dareir,—ki.**

splash, *n.*, **duldul,—ki**; *v.tr.*, **dulduli, nab, mari, marso.**
spleen, *n.*, (milt) **ber yaro,—adi.**
split (*see* slit).
spoil, *n.*, (robbery) **tugo,—adi, bob,—ki**; (corruption) **ḫudun, —ki**; *v.tr.*, (*see* rob); (corrupt) *see* corrupt.
spoon, *n.*, **fandal,—ki.**
sport, *n.*, **'ayar,—ti, jalbeb,—ti.**
spot, *n.*, (a blot) **bar,—ti, dibi',—di**; some spots, **barbar**; (a place) **mel,—shi**; *v.tr.*, **bar u yel.**
spotted, *a.*, **baraleh.**
sprain, *v.tr.*, **murku'i, murku'o**; *n.*, **murku'asho,—adi, lāban, —ki.**
sprained, *a.*, **lāban.**
spray, *n.*, **dibi',—di, 'urdan,—ki, yurub,—ki.**
spread, *v.tr.*, **firdi**; *a.*, **firdisan, firdadsan, firdadan.**
spreading, *n.*, **firid,—ki, firdis, —ki.**
spring (*see* fountain).
spring up, *v.i.*, **baḫ.**
sprinkle, *v.tr.*, **saïd**; — over, **ku saïd.**
sprinkling, *n.*, **saïdis,—ki.**
spurn, *n.*, (a kick) **lad,—ki.**
spy, *v.tr.*, (watch) **so ilalai**; *n.*, **ilalo,—adi**; send a —, **ilalo dir**; — glass, **hoḫad,—di.**
squander, *v.tr.*, **hub, lumi.**
squanderer, *n.*, **mudāya', i'hi, lumiyai,—ihi.**
squat, *v.i.*, (sit upon the heels) **kadalob, kadalobso.**
squatting, *n.*, **kadalob,—ki.**
squeamish, *a.*, **yiḫyiḫsan.**
squeeze, *v.tr.*, **dis, ku maroji, tuji**; *n.*, **disin,—ti.**
squint, *n.*, **'awar,—ki**; — eyed, **il maḫalub, ashḫarah**; *v.i.*, **indaha ashḫar.**
squirrel, *n.*, earth —, **daba galla, —ihi**; rock —, **walo,—adi.**
stab, *n.*, (of a sword) **fajaso,—adi**; — with the flat of a sword, **ballad,—ki**; *v.tr.*, **fajas.**
stable, *n.*, **ḫero,—adi, gola,—ihi.**
stack (*see* heap).
staff, *n.*, **ul,—shi, ḫori,—gi**; — of a spear, **samaï,—di**; — of an arrow, **gamun,—ki, leb,—ki**; bended staves used for making a Somali hut, **dig,—ti, dig doḫo,—adi, dig lolah,—ihi, kabal,—ki, kaballo,—adi, lol,—ki, lau,—ti.**
stagger, *v.i.*, (reel) **tukub.**
stagnant water, *n.*, **gelgelin biyaha.**
stain, *n.*, **dibi',—di, bar,—ti**; *v.tr.*, (maculate) *see* corrupt.
stair, staircase, *n.*, **sallan,—ki.**
stake, *n.*, **udub,—ki, hensarar,—ki.**
stale, *a.*, (old) **gabow, dug.**
stalk (*see* staff).
stammer, *v.i.*, **haghago.**
stammerer, *n.*, **nin haghagleh, nin labla.**
stammering, *n.*, **haghag.**
stamp, *n.*, (for letters) **tiked,—ki.**
stanch (stop) *v.tr.*, **joji**; stanch the blood, **digga joji.**

stand, *n.*, **jog,—gi, nasad,—ki**; make a —, **jog, naso.**

stand, *v.i.*, **tagnow, hagag, hagag u jogso**; — still, **ha daḥdaḥa-ḥin**; my watch stands still, **sa'adaidi wa jogsanaisa**; the bargain stands, **baya'addi wa jogta** or **weliba tāgan tahai**; this house stands very well, **aḥalka mel wanaksan bu ka disanyahai**; a great many people — about him, **dad badan ba ku mersan**, or **dad badni wa ku mersanyahai**; — against, **iss ka ḥeji, iss karaw**; God will — by us, **Ebbehena wa ina karebi**; I stood by when Ali killed the man, **anigu wa so jogai kolki Ali ninka dilai**; I — for that office, **anigu ḥafiskasan u joga**; God stands for us, **Ebbehen innagu ina la jira**; that letter stands for ..., **ḥaraf-kasi ... bu u jira**; I — in need of a camel, **aur ban u dan lehahai**; you — in my light, **iftinkaigi bad iga fa-dida**; — off, **dib u jogso**; — out (resist), **ḥabil, u adkaiso**; — out of the way, **dauga ka baïd**; — out of my sight, **araggaiga ka libid**; — to your word, **hadalkaga ḥejiso**; — up, **tāgnaw**; — with, **la heshi.**

stand, *v.tr.*, **ḥabil, u samir.**

standing, *a.*, **tāgan**; *n.*, — up (during Mahomedan prayers), **faral,—ki.**

standard, *n.*, (flag, ensign) **'alan, —ki.**

star, *n.*, **ḥidig,—ti.**

stare, *n.*, (a fixed look) **egmo,—adi**; *v.i.*, **isha ku 'adai, indo ku tol.**

start, *n.*, **naḥadin,—ti**; *v.i.*, **naḥ, dib u naḥ**; (begin to run) **ka gur, ka so'o.**

startle, *v.tr.*, **kaga niḥi, baji.**

starvation, *n.*, **dihal,—ki, ma'alul, —shi.**

starve, *v.i.*, **dihalanaw, abaḥ**; *v.tr.*, **dihali, abiḥi.**

starving, *a.*, **dihalan, abaḥah.**

starveling, *n.*, (thin and weak animal) **abaḥ,—hi.**

state, *n.*, (condition) **dan,—ti**; bad —, **dan darran,—adi**; good —, **ladnan,—ti**; *v tr.*, (*see* settle).

statement, *n.*, **talo,—adi.**

stay, *n.*, **fadi,—gi, jog,—gi, rug, —ti**; (delay) **rāgnin,—ti**; *v.i.*, **fadi, jog, rugaiso, rāg**; *v.tr.*, (delay) **raji.**

steady, *a.*, **adag, tāgan.**

steal, *v.tr.*, (rob) **ḥad.**

stealth, *n.*, (act of stealing) **ḥad-nin,—ti.**

stealthily, *v.i.*, (go) **u dukus.**

steam, *n.*, (vapour) **umis,—ki.**

steel, *n.*, **birr,—ti**; — of a tinder box, **du'un dableh.**

steep, *n.*, (precipice) **harar,—ti, jar,—ki**; *a.*, **mel sibibaḥah**; *v.tr.*, (soak) **ḥoi.**

stem, *n.*, **jirid,—di, lan,—ti.**

stench, *n.*, **ḥudmun,—ki, ur ḥud-mun**; *v.tr.*, (make to stink) **ḥudmunai.**

stenching, *a.*, **ur ḫudmun.**
step, *n.*, **talabo,—adi**; sound of the —, **jan,—ti**; *v.i.*, (make a —) **talabso, so talab**; — over, out, **ka talab, ka talabso**; cause to —, **talabi.**
step-mother, *n.*, **ayo,—adi.**
sterile, *a.*, **ma dalais, (ged) an mido lahain.**
stern, *n.*, (of a ship) **ḫar dambe.**
sternutation, *n.*, **hindisad,—di.**
stick, *n.*, **ul,—shi, lan,—ti** (*see* rod); *v.tr.*, **ku dab, ku mud, ku deji**; (pierce) **waren, ku joji**; *v.i.*, **ku deg.**
stiff, *a.*, **adag, ḫalafsan.**
stiffen, *v.tr.*, **ḫalafi**; *v.i.*, **ḫalaf.**
stifle (*see* suffocate).
still, *a.*, **amusan**; *ad.*, **ila iminka**; — more, **weliba.**
sting, *n.*, (a sharp point) **'aro,—adi**; *v.tr.*, **mud, ḫanin.**
stinging, *n.*, **mudnin,—ti, ḫaninyo,—adi.**
stink, *n.*, (bad smell) **ḫudmun,—ki, ur ḫudmun**; *v.i.*, **ḫudmunahaw.**
stinking, *a.*, **ur ḫudmun.**
stipulate, *v.tr.*, **ka ballan.**
stipulation, *n.*, **ballan,—ki.**
stir, *v.tr.*, **daḫaji, walaḫ**; *v.i.*, **daḫdaḫaḫ.**
stirring, *n.*, **walaḫ,—hi.**
stirrup, *n.*, **rakāb,—ki.**
stitch, *n.*, **mudnin,—ti**; *v.tr.*, **mud, tol.**
stock, *n.*, (body of a plant) **jirid,—di**; (store) **jawan,—ki**; *v.tr.*, (store) **si dig, si ḫado.**
stomach, *n.*, **'alol,—shi**; pit of the —, **labḫo,—adi.**

stone, *n.*, **dagaḫ,—ihhi**; big —, **dakab,—ki, dadab,—ti**; fire —, **dagaḫ madow**; a very hard —, **kured,—ki**; — used to grind corn ..., **midḫin**; grindstone, **lissin,—ki**; — of fruits, **laf,—ti**; the three stones on which they put the boiler, **dardar,—ki**; *v.tr.*, (lapidate) **shīd, dagiḫi.**
stool, *n.*, **barjin,—ki, gambad,—ki, kabad,—ki.**
stoop, stooping, *n.*, **foror,—ki, 'uskis,—ki**; *v.i.*, **fororso, 'usko**; *v.tr.*, **forori, 'uski.**
stop, *n.*, **jog,—gi, ragāsho,—adi**; (end) *see* end; *v.i.*, **jog, jogso, sug, iss tāg, kadi**; *v.tr.*, **joji**; — thief, **tugga joji**; — the bottle, **ḫaruradda furai** or **abud.**
store (*see* stock).
storm, *n.*, **dabail wein,—shi, —aid, baḫailad,—di, duf,—ki.**
story, *n.*, (history) **sheko,—adi**; (fiction) **ḫalalif,—ti.**
stout, *a.*, **buran, shilis, ḫogwein**; — man, **torog,—gi.**
stoutness, *n.*, **ḫog,—gi, adkan,—ti, gesinimo,—adi, bili,—gi, ital,—ki, tāg,—ti.**
strabism (*see* squinting).
straggle (*see* ramble).
straight, *a.*, **hiyas, ḫun, ḫumati, shuban, tosan**; be placed —, **ḫoton**; put it —, **ḫumati u tāg**; make it —, **ḫiyas ka dig, humi**; place it —, **ḫotomi**; be —, **ḫumanaw.**
strain, *n.*, (a sprain) **murkuasho,—adi**; *v.tr.*, (filter) **darur.**

strainer, *n.*, (filter) **darur,—ti.**
strait, *n.*, (a narrow pass) **'edidi, —gi**; *a.*, **'edidi, 'edidsan.**
straiten, *v.tr.*, **'edidi.**
strange, *a.*, **yaban, yab ẖaba, yableh.**
stranger, *n.*, **marti,—di** (*see* foreigner).
strangle, *v.tr.*, **siriri, 'una ẖabatai.**
strangulation, *n.*, **siririn,—ti, siriris,—ki.**
strap, *n.*, **yel,—shi, baïd,—di, lid,—ki.**
stratagem, *n.*, **ẖigmad,—di.**
straw, *n.*, **'aus.**
stream, *n.*, **doẖo,—adi, durdur, —ki.**
street, *n.*, **dariẖ,—hi, surin,—ki.**
strength, *n.*, **ẖog,—gi, adkan,—ti, itāl,—ki, tāg,—ti**; give —, **itāl u yel.**
strengthen, *v.tr.*, **adkai, tāg.**
stretch out, *v.tr.*, **biẖi, so biẖi, tikso, ẖoranso**; the birds — their wings, **hādi ba iss kala jida**; — your legs, **didibso.**
stretching out, *n.*, **tiksi,—gi.**
strew (with), *v.tr.*, **firdi, ku firdi.**
stride, *n.*, **dada',—hi**; *v.i.*, *v.tr.*, **dada', ka dada'.**
strife (*see* quarrel).
strike, *v.tr.*, **dil, ku dufo, la**; — down, **ka dangalaẖsi, budai**; — upon, **ku tun**; — to break, **fajas.**
string, *n.*, **ẖadig yar, ẖadig dumo' yar, sefari,—gi.**
strip, *v.tr.*, (make naked) **ẖawi**; — off, **dir, mudẖi.**
stripped, stript, *a.*, **diran, ẖawan.**
stripe, *n.*, **alif,—ki, dilin,—ti**; *v.tr.*, **alif ku jid, alifiyai, dilimo u yel.**
strive, *v.i.*, **hausho, haul gal.**
stroke, *n.*, (blow) **nabar,—ki**; rub gently, *v.tr.*, **salaẖ.**
stroll (*see* ramble).
stroller, *n.*, **nin warwareg badan.**
strong, *a.*, **adag, ẖog wein, ẖog badan**; be —, **adkaw, ẖabil.**
struggle, *v.i.*, **hausho, ẖogso, iss muẖuni.**
stubble, *n.*, **'aus,—ki, gargor,—ki, 'aus salol,—ki.**
stubborn, *n.*, (strong-headed) **'asi, —gi, rifai,—ihi.**
study, *n.*, **barasho, hubsad,—ki**; *v.tr.*, **baro.**
stumble, *n.*, **turonturo,—adi**; *v.i.*, **turonturo.**
stump, *n.*, (of a tooth) **fallid,—ki**; — of a tree, **jirid,—di, kurtun,—ki.**
stun, *v.tr.*, **kaga niẖi**; be stunned, **naẖ.**
stunning, *n.*, **naẖadin,—ti, ẖau, —di.**
stupefaction (*see* astonishment).
stupid, *a.*, (sluggish) **doẖon,—ki, na's,—ki, miyirla, bahahim.**
stupidity, *n.*, **miyirlaan,—ti.**
stutter (*see* stammer).
sty, *n.*, (inflamed tumour) **fin,—ki.**
subdue, *v.tr.*, **iss ka hosaisi, taba bar, dasturtada ẖun iss karaw.**
subject, *n.*, **deris,—ki, nin hosai.**
submit, *v.tr.*, (*see* subdue and subject); *v.i.*, **yel, degaiso.**
subterfuge, *n.*, **ẖelad,—di.**
succeed, *v.i.*, (prosper) **dama' hel,**

mar o hel; (follow) **meshisa ahaw.**
succession, *n.*, **dambais,—ki.**
successor, *n.*, **ninki ka dambaiya.**
succour, *n.*, (*see* help); *v.tr.*, **'idami** (*see* help).
succourer, *n.*, **'idan,—ki.**
such, *prn.*, **kas o kalehah, hebel.**
suck, suckling, *n.*, **jaha,—ihi, nujis,—ki**; *v.tr.*, **nug, mudso, jah**; sucking child, **ilma nasaha jaha**; — up, **fihso.**
suckle, *v.tr.*, **nuji.**
suddenly, *ad.*, **marki ba.**
suet, *n.*, **barur,—ti.**
suffer, *v.tr.*, (permit) **u samir, fasah**; — a loss, **ed**; *v.i.*, **hanunso, silei', ta'ab**; — in mind, **ur ku talo**; — for, **u hanunso, ka tobad ken**; cause to —, **hanuni, hanuji, sili'i, sug, hanun.**
suffering, *n.*, **hanun,—ki, silei',—hi, ta'ab,—ki**; — of the soul and of the body, **'araraf,—ki.**
suffering, *a.*, **nin sila'san, sugan, hanunsan.**
suffice, *v.i.*, (be sufficient) **filow, ku filow.**
sufficient, *a.*, **ku filan.**
suffocate, *v.tr.*, **'abūdi, 'abūd, buhuji, 'iji**; be suffocated, **abudan, abudnaw, 'ihsanaw**; suffocated, **'abūdan, 'ihsan.**
suffocation, *n.*, **'ih,—di.**
sugar, *n.*, **sonkor** or **sunkor,—ti.**
suicide, *v.i.*, (commit ...) **iss dil.**
suit, *v.tr.*, (be fitted to) **leh eg**; it suits me, **wa i lehegyahai**; it suits you, **wa ku lehegyahai**; *n.*, — at law, **arin,—ti, gar,—ti**; a man gaining the —, **nin gar leh**; a man losing the —, **nin gar la.**
sulky (*see* pout).
sullen, *a.*, **hulubsan, dudma badan**; be —, **wahan, hulub.**
sullenness, *n.*, **wahan,—ki, hulub,—ki.**
sully, *v.tr.*, **dohbai, wasahai, uskagai.**
sulphur, *n.*, **kebrid,—ki.**
sultan, *n.*, **suldan,—ki.**
sum, *n.*, **hisab,—ti, tiro,—adi**; — given monthly to the Somali chiefs, **miri,—di.**
summit, *n.*, **aror,—ki.**
summon, *v.tr.*, (cite) **amarhadur u sar.**
summons, *n.*, **amarhadur,—ki.**
sun, *n.*, **horah,—di, 'ad'ed,—di**; morning —, **horah subah**; evening —, **horah galbed.**
sunbeam, *n.*, **'ad'ed.**
Sunday, *n.*, **ahad,—di.**
sunless, *a.*, **mel an horah lahain, horah la.**
sunny, *a.*, **horah leh, mesha horah ba kugu haisa.**
sunrise, *n.*, **horah so bah,—bihi.**
sunset, *n.*, **horah da',—di'hi.**
sunshine, *n.*, **milei',—ihi, sudi',—gi.**
sup, *n.*, **fihsi,—gi**; *v.tr.*, **fihso.**
superior, *n.*, **nin u madahah, nin horai, nin sarrai.**
supine, *a.*, (lying on the back) **jirjir'ad.**
supper, *n.*, **'asho,—adi**; take your —, **'ashai.**

supply, *n.*, (maintenance) **masruf, —ki**; *v.tr.*, (maintain) **musruf.**
supplice, *n.*, **silei',—hi, ta'ab,—ki.**
support, *n.*, (prop) **tir,—ki, udud, —ki**; (help) **hil,—ki**; *v.tr.*, **u dulhado, hili, habil.**
suppose, *v.tr.*, (think) **malai.**
supposition, *n.*, **mala,—ihi.**
sure, *a.*, **huba**; be —, **hub.**
surety, *n.*, (security) **'arbun,—ti, 'udal,—shi.**
surface, *n.*, **barahad,—di, dul,—shi.**
surpass, *v.tr.*, **dul mar.**
surprise, *v.tr.*, **gād.**
surrender, *v.i.*, **so baho, u so gal.**
surround, *v.tr.*, **herai, mermeri, ka buhso.**
suspect, *v.tr.*, **malai, tuhun.**
suspected, *a.*, **la tuhmai (nin).**
suspicion, *n.*, **tuhun,—ki.**
suspicious, *a.*, **tuhunsan.**
sustain, *v.tr.*, (bear) **had, sid, tiri**; (maintain) **sabbar, sabbaro**; (suffer) **ed, u samir.**
swad, *n.*, (for babies) **dereb,—ti.**
swallow, *v.tr.*, **lih, hudhudi.**
swallowing, *n.*, **hudhudis,—ki.**
sway, *v.tr.*, (rule) **ka sarrai.**
swear, *v.i.*, **daro, iman si, ahdi.**
swearing, *n.*, (oath) **ahdi,—gi.**
sweat, *v.i.*, **didid**; *n.*, **didid,—ki.**
sweep, *v.tr.*, **fih, hād.**
sweepings, *n.*, **hushash,—ki.**
swept, *a.*, **fihan.**
sweet, *a.*, **ma'an**; — thing, **ged ma'an.**
sweeten, *v.tr.*, **ma'anaiso.**
sweets, *n.*, **nana,—ihi.**
swell, *v.i.*, **barar**; cause to —, **barari.**
swelling, *n.*, **barar,—ki.**
swim, *v.i.*, **dabbalo**; — over, **ka dabbalo.**
swimming, *n.*, **dabbal,—shi.**
swine, *n.*, **dofar,—ki.**
swing, *n.*, **ruhan,—ki, lalad,—ki, ruhnin,—ti**; *v.tr.*, **ruh, ruhruh**; *v.i.*, **ruho, lalad.**
swoon, *v.i.*, **suh, weïdow**; *n.*, **suhdin,—ti.**
sword, *n.*, **bilawa** or **bilawai,—ihi, seif,—ti.**
syphilis, *n.*, **habad.**

T.

tabernacle, *n.*, **balballo,—adi, bul,—ki, rug,—ti, guri,—gi.**
table, *n.*, **mis,—ki.**
tabour, *n.*, (drum) **durban,—ki.**
tack, *v.tr.*, **hodob, iss ku hodob, iss ku tol.**
tail, *n.*, **dabo,—adi**; — of goats, **dib,—ki**; — of sheep, **dilif,—ki**; fat — of the sheep, **badi, —di**; lifting up the —, **hanan, —ti.**
tailor, *n.*, **dar tol,—ki, derji,—gi.**
take, *v.tr.*, **ho, hai, haiso, hab, habo, had, hado, habso**; I took the cup at his hand, **fujanki ga'antisan ka hadai**; — that malefactor, **layanká habso**; they took the town,

magaladi ḥatai; if I can — him, **hadan ḥadan karo**; — the meat out of the pot, **'adka ka so biḥi distiga**; — that physic, **dawada ḥado**; it has taken root, **ḥididai lehdahai**; — hold of that, **waḥhas ḥabso** or **ḥejiso**; — a snuff, **nashug urso**; we took the longest way, **daugi ugu dera bannu ḥabsanai** or **ra'nai**; — the shortest way, **dauga ugu gaban ḥabso**; — care, heed, **iss karaw, fojigow, iss ka eg, iss ka daur**; — you no care of that, **dan adigu ha u gelin**; let your friends — part with you, **u da sahibyadadu ha ku la wadagenai**; he took alarm at the noise, **sanḥaddi bu ku naḥai**; — a good resolution, **tala āda ḥado**; I — you at your word, **hadalkagan ku dainaya**; — that word in good part, **hadalka ha ḥonsan**; — him in a lie, **bein ku ḥabo**; — in a bad deed, **falnin ḥun ku ḥabo**; — pity on him, **u naḥariso**; I took a great affection to him, **ja'ail wanaksan ban u ḥabai**; I shall — it as a great favour, **sidi sado wanaksan ban kaga aḥbali**; I will — that affair at my own peril, **haushas sababtaidu ku ḥadan dona**; what course shall I — now? **dau ma an ḥabsanaya?**; I — it to be the best way, **sidi ugu wanaksanaid ban u wada** or **u sida**; he took offence at that, **waḥhasi 'ai u ḥatai**; — an account of the suit, **arinti war noga ken**; — my word for it, **hadalkaiga rumaiso**; — time, **waḥti ḥado, dulḥado**; — and keep, **ho o ḥado**; — again, **mar kaleh ḥado**; — back again, **'esho**; — him along with you, **si kaḥaiso**; — that asunder, **baïdi**; — away, **mesha ka ḥad, ninka ka kaḥai** or **ka sar**; — away his flock, **adigisa kala tag**; — that down, **waḥhas deji**; — him down, **iss ka hosaisi, iss ka joji**; I shall — his pride down, **amarkisa wan jebin** or **bassarin**; I took him for another, **nin kalan modai**; — from, **ka dufo, ka ḥabo, ka ḥad, so dufo**; — of, **la tag**; — off the skin, **haragga** or **dubka iss ka jar** or **go**; — off your hat, **kofiadda iss ka dig**; — him off from his work, **shuḥulkisa ka sar**; — out that tooth, **iligga so biḥi** or **so jid**; — to pieces, **jeḥjeḥ**; — to, **kaḥai, so kaḥai**; — up arms, **hub ḥata**; that will — up a good deal of time, **haul badan ba igaga biḥi donta**; — up the book, **kitabka ḥad.**

tale, *n.*, (story) **sheko,—adi**; he is always telling stories (tales), **ḥalalif bu ka shekanaya**; (oral report) **dirandiro,—adi**; — bearer, **nin ḥamasho badan**; — bearing, **ḥamasho,—adi, dirandiro,—adi.**

talisman, *n.*, **ḫardas,—ti, ḫajolad, —di.**
talk, *v.i.*, *v.tr.*, **hadal, hasaw**; — with, **la hadal, la hasaw**; *n.*, **hadal,—ki, hasawai,—ihi.**
tall, *a.*, **der.**
tallow, *n.*, (suet) **barur,—ti, dayi, —gi, haïd,—di.**
tamarind, *n.*, **ḥamar,—ti, gedad ḥamarah.**
tame, *a.*, **af yaḫan, la 'arbiyai**; — beast, **marabi,—di**; — beast flying away, **bubal,—shi**; *v.tr.*, **'arbi.**
tank, *n.*, **berkad,—di.**
tar, *n.*, **damur,—ki**; *v.tr.*, **damur mari.**
taste, *n.*, **dadan,—ki**; *v.tr.*, **dadami.**
tatter, *n.*, (rag) **suf,—ki.**
tattle (*see* babble).
taunt, *n.*, **'ai,—di**; *v.tr.*, **'ai**; why do you — him? **mahad u 'aiaisa** or **'aïtamaisa?**
taw, *n.*, (a marble to play with) **fatari,—gi.**
tax, *n.*, **'ashur,—ti**; *v.tr.*, **dadka 'ashur.**
tea, *n.*, **shah,—hi, 'alen,—ti.**
teach, *v.tr.*, **bar, u dig, wani.**
teacher, *n.*, **bara,—ihi.**
tear, *n.*, **ilmo,—adi**; (rent) **dila', —hi, jeḥ,—hi**; *v.tr.*, (lacerate) **dila'i, jeḥ, jeḥjeḥ, kidif.**
tease, *v.tr.*, **dāli.**
teat, *n.*, **ib,—ti.**
telegraph, *n.*, **tar,—ki.**
telescope, *n.*, **hoḫad,—di.**
tell, *v.tr.*, **deh (odo), u sheg, ogaisi.**

temper, *n.*, **abur,—ki** or **—ti, 'amal,—ki.**
temperance, *n.*, **'ir yaran,—ti.**
temperate, *a.*, **'ir yar.**
temperature, *n.*, **waḫti,—gi.**
tempest, *n.*, **duf,—ki, dabail wein.**
temples, *n.*, (of the head) **dafor, —ki.**
tempt, *v.tr.*, **ḥuffi.**
temptation, *n.*, **ḥuffin,—ti, ḫawayad,—di.**
tempter, *n.*, **maḫawi,—gi.**
ten, *n.c.*, **toban,—ki.**
tenth, *n.o.*, **tobnad,—ki.**
tend, *v.tr.*, (watch) **ilali, jir, la jog.**
tendon, *n.*, (sinew) **seid,—di, ḫanjid,—ki, boḫon,—ti.**
tent, *n.*, (for travel) **balballo,—adi**; (in an enclosure) **ḫois,—ki**; (not in an enclosure) **ḫoḫob,—ki**; (an abode) **rug,—ti, bul,—ki, guri,—gi.**
term, *n.*, (limit) **dal,—ki**; (a word) **erai,—gi.**
terminate, *v.tr.*, **damai, idlai.**
terrible, *a.*, **laga 'absado, laga boḫo.**
terror, *n.*, **baḫdin,—ti.**
testicle, *n.*, **ḫinin,—ti.**
testify, *v.tr.*, **rumai, marḫati ku fur.**
testimony, *n.*, **marḫati,—di.**
tetter, *n.*, (white blight) **'anbar, —ti.**
than, *c.*, **ka.**
thank, *v.tr.*, **mahadi, mahad u naḫ.**
thanks, *n.*, **mahad,—di.**
that, *a.* and *prn.* (*see* Grammar); *c.*, **an, in, bal an, ha.**

thatch, *n.*, **'aussalol,—ki.**
the, *art.* (*see* Grammar).
theft (*see* thief).
their, they, *pos.prn.* (*see* Gram.).
then, *ad.*, **gortas, gorti**; *c.*, **haddai.**
there, *ad.*, **hagga, haggas, halka, mesha.**
therefore, *c.*, **haddaba.**
these, *dem.prn.* (*see* Grammar).
thick, *a.*, **adag, buran, ẖalafsan, ẖara wein.**
thicken, *v.tr.*, **adkaisi, ẖalafi.**
thickness, *n.*, **ẖaro,—adi.**
thief, *n.*, **tug,—gi**; theft, **tugo, —adi, ẖadnin,—ti.**
thieve, *v.tr.*, **ẖad.**
thigh, *n.*, **baudo** or **bowdo,—adi.**
thin, *a.*, **jilai'san, weïdsan, dumo' yar.**
thine, *pos.prn.* (*see* Grammar).
thing, *n.*, **ged,—ki, bahal,—ki, —shi, waẖ,—hi.**
think, *v.i.*, **tasho, malai**; — of, **ka tasho**; — well, **aloshada la tasho, malai, mod.**
third, *num.*, **sadeẖad,—ki**; one — (⅓), **salol,—ki.**
thirst, *n.*, **harad,—ki, on,—ki.**
thirst, *v.i.*, (be thirsty) **harad, omanaw.**
thirsty, *a.*, **haradsan.**
thirteen, *num.*, **sadeẖ iyo toban, —ki.**
thirteenth, *n.o.*, **sadeẖ iyo tobnad.**
thirty, *num.*, **sodon,—ki.**
this, *a.*, (*see* Grammar).
thither, *ad.*, **halka.**
thong, *n.*, (string of leather) **indal,—shi.**
thorn, *n.*, **ẖodaẖ,—di.**
thorny, *a.*, **ẖodaẖ leh.**
those, *dem.a.* (*see* Grammar).
thou, *pers.prn.* (*see* Grammar).
thought, *n.*, **tashi,—gi, fīkir,—ki, mala,—ihi.**
thousand, *num.*, **kun,—ki.**
thread, *n.*, **dun,—ti, miẖ,—hi.**
three, *num.*, **sadeẖ,—di.**
throat, *n.*, **hunguri,—gi, 'una,—ihi, bo',—hi**; the thyroid body or kernel, **rubad,—di.**
throng (*see* crowd).
throttle, *n.*, (wind-pipe) **bo',—hi.**
through, *prp.*, **deẖdis, deẖdeda.**
throughout, *prp.*, **o dan.**
throw, *v.tr.*, **ẖor, rid, tur, iss ka saïd**; — away, **tur, iss ka tur**; — down, **hosta u ẖor, hosta u tur, ka dādi**; — in, at him, **ku rid, ku ẖor, ku tur**; — upon, **lāl, ku lāl**; — the child, **dabsi.**
throwing down, *n.*, (at once) **dādis,—ki.**
thrown, *a.*, **la tur, dādsan.**
thrust in, *v.tr.*, (a nail) **ka rid, ka dusi.**
thumb, *n.*, **sul,—ki.**
thump, *v.tr.*, **tumujai**; *n.*, **tumujo,—adi, tantomo,—adi.**
thunder, *n.*, **onkod,—ki**; it thunders, **wa onkodaisa.**
thunderbolt, *n.*, **hilā,—hi.**
Thursday, *n.*, **ẖamis,—ki.**
thus, *ad.*, **sida, sidas, sidi.**
thy, *pos.prn.* (*see* Grammar).
tick, *n.*, (insect) **gafanai,—ihi, shilin,—ti.**
ticket, *n.*, **bas,—ki, tiked,—ki.**

tickle, *v.tr.*, **ḥadatai, kilkilai.**
tickling, *n.*, **ḥadato,—adi.**
tide, *n.*, (time, season) **waḥti,—gi, ḥeli,—gi**; (ebb and flow of the sea) **mayad,—di**; high —, **buḥ,—hi**; low —, **'ari,—gi, —di.**
tidings, *n.*, (news) **war,—ki.**
tie, *v.tr.*, **ḥid, ḥido**; — the she-camel's teats, **mar**; — one side, **hasha ka agmar.**
tight, *a.*, **adag.**
tile, *n.*, **ājurad,—di.**
till, *prp.*, *c.*, **tan iyo gortan, had iyo intan, ila, ilama.**
timber, *n.*, (every large tree) **damas,—ki, damal,—shi, ged damalah.**
time, *n.*, **āmin,—ki, —ti, gor,—ti, had,—di, kol,—ki, jir, jer, mar,—ki, da,—di, mu,—gi, sa,—ki, wa,—gi, ya,—di, gelin,—ki**; a short —, **'abbar, —ki, in gibinah**; after a —, **hadow, hadowto**; a long —, **buran, ḥeli,—gi, waḥti,—gi, gu,—gi**; — past, **awal**; the present —, **gortan jogta**; the — to come, **kolka dambe**; appoint a fixed —, **ballan.**
timid, *a.*, **(wil) fulaah.**
tin, *n.*, **tanag,—gi**; — pot, **dāsad,—di.**
tip, *n.*, (of the ear) **degta dahasheda.**
tire, *v.tr.*, (make weary) **dāli**; *v.i.*, (fall with weariness) **dāl, 'atow, 'ataisnaw.**
tired, *a.*, **'ataisan, dalan, dashan.**
to, *prp.*, **u.**
toad, *n.*, **rah, rihi** (the ...).
toast, *v.tr.*, **dub.**
tobacco, *n.*, **buri,—gi**; a kind of —, **hamumi,—gi**; a man in want of —, **ḥamunsan**; be in want of —, **ḥamunsanaw.**
toe, *n.*, **sul,—ki, far,—ti.**
toil, *v.tr.*, **ḥoji, ḥogso.**
tomb, *n.*, **ḥabal,—shi.**
tongue, *n.*, **'arrab,—ki.**
tooth, *n.*, **ilig,—gi**; — stick or brush, **adai,—gi, rumai,—gi**; — pick, **findi'el gura,—ihi.**
top, *n.*, (highest part of a thing) **'aro,—adi, aror,—ki, dul,—shi, guro,—adi, jif,—ti**; — of the head, **dalo,—adi, kug, —ti**; peg —, **druan,—ki.**
torment, *n.*, **silei'—i'hi, ta'ab,—ti**; *v.tr.*, **'adab, 'adib, kaga-'eisi.**
tormented, *a.*, **silei'san.**
torrent, *n.*, (dry) **tog,—gi.**
tortoise, *n.*, **din,—ki.**
torture (*see* torment).
toss, *v.tr.*, (agitate) **lul, ruḥ**; be tossed, **lulan,—ruḥo.**
tossed, *a.*, **lulan, ruḥan.**
touch, *n.*, **tabasho,—adi**; *v.tr.*, **tabo**; make him —, **tabsi**; — in pressing, **tuji.**
tough, *a.*, (stiff) **ḥalafsan.**
tow, *n.*, **ḥig,—gi, ḥaskul,—shi**; — used for closing the camel's teats, **maraḥ,—hi.**
tower, *n.*, **nobab** or **nobiad,—di.**
town *n.*, **magalo,—adi.**
trace, track, *n.*, **rad,—ki**; *v.tr.*, **radi, radkisa gur**; lose the —, **rad go.**

trade, *n.*, **boshirad** or **boshurad,—di.**

trader, *n.*, **ba'ya mushtari,—gi.**

tradition, *n.*, **sheko,—adi.**

train up (*see* educate).

tramp, trample, *v.tr.*, **ku jogso.**

tranquil, *a.*, **amusan, ḫabow.**

transact, *v.tr.*, **la samai, wanaji.**

transfix, *v.tr.*, **ka mud biḫi, daloli, musmar ku daloli.**

transform, *v.tr.*, **midab kaleh u rog.**

translate, *v.tr.*, (transfer) **ka kaḫai, ka gur**; (interpret) **u kala af 'eli.**

transmigrate, *v.i.*; that family transmigrated from his town into another, **ḫaskasi magaladisa ka taga o magalo kaleh u ka'a.**

transport, *v.tr.*, **gur, u sid.**

trap, *n.*, (a snare) **dabin,—ki**; *v.tr.*, **dab.**

trapper, *n.*, **dabad,—ki.**

travel, *v.i.*, **daḫ, so daḫ, sod'al, safar**; *n.*, **sod'al,—ki, dof,—ki.**

traveller, *n.*, **kabadai,—ihi, safanleh,—ihi, nin sod'alah.**

traverse, *v.tr.*, **ka talab, mar.**

tread upon, *v.tr.*, **ku jogso.**

treasure, *n.*, **ḫasanad,—di.**

treat, *v.tr.*, **ballan**; — with, **la ballan.**

treaty, *n.*, **ballan,—ki, aḥdi,—gi.**

tree, *n.*, **beir,—ti, ged,—ki**; (in general) **dir,—ti**; — used to shut the enclosure, **da'an,—ti.**

tremble, *v.i.*, **garir, kurbo**; (fear) **baḫ, baḫo.**

trespass, *n.*, **dembi,—gi, ḥujad,—di.**

tresses, *n.*, **tidei',—hi.**

tress, *v.tr.*, **tidi', tido'o.**

trial, *n.*, **bejis,—ki.**

tribe, *n.*, **toll,—ki, ḫolo,—adi, jilib,—ki.**

tribulation, *n.*, **ḥuman,—ti, weirweir,—ki.**

tribunal, *n.*, **ḫakamad,—di.**

tribute, *n.*, **bād,—di**; pay the —, **bādda biḫi.**

trick, *n.*, (mischievous) **ḥisti,—gi** (*see* cheat); — in game, **sir,—ki**; play a —, *v.tr.*, **u ḥisti.**

trickle, *v.i.*, **tifiḫso.**

trip, *n.*, (in wrestling) **ḫonof,—ki**; (a stumble) **turonturo,—adi**; (a journey) **kabadai,—ihi**; take a —, **ku so wareg.**

trot, *n.*, **kadlo,—adi**; *v.i.*, **kadlai.**

trouble, *n.*, **dāl,—ki, ḥuman,—ti, weirweir,—ki**; *v.tr.*, **dāli, ḫulḫuladai, weirweiri, rog.**

troublesome, *a.*, **ḫulḫulad badan.**

troublesomeness, *n.*, **ḫulḫulad,—di.**

trousers, *n.*, **surual,—ki.**

true, *a.*, **sal, wa sal, wa run, wa runtis, wa runted.**

trunk, *n.*, (of a tree) **jirid,—ki**; (a box) **sanduḫ,—hi**; (elephant's) **ga'an,—ti.**

trust, *n.*, **yeshod,—ki, amano,—adi**; *v.tr.*, **amano u dib, aman, amanaiso**; *v.i.*, **yesho, ku yesho.**

truth, *n.*, **run,—ti, lilahi,—di, dab,—ti**; confirm the —, **rumai.**

truthful, *a.*, **lilahiah.**
try, *v.tr.*, **beji, iss beji**; *v.i.*, (endeavour) **hausho.**
tube, *n.*, (wooden) **gobais,—ki.**
Tuesday, *n.*, **salasa,—di.**
tumble, *n.*, (a fall) **ḥambaro,—adi, kuf,—ki**; *v.i.*, **ḥambarow, kuf.**
tumult, *n.*, **ḥailo,—adi**; **dawaḥ, —hi.**
turban, *n.*, **imāmad** or **amāmad, —di**; arrange his —, **u imāmad.**
turd, *n.*, **us,—ki**; *int.*, **bus!**
Turk, *n.*, **tukri,—gi, rumi,—gi.**
Turkey, *n.*, **rum.**
turmeric, *n.*, (Indian safran) **hurūd,—di.**
turn, *n.*, **wareg,—gi**; *v.tr.*, **rog, jedi, wareji**; — upside down, **forori, rog**; *v.i.*, **jeso, so jeso, wareg, iss ka wareg**; — back, **dib u jeso, dib u noḥo**; — by, **ku wareg**; — aside from, **il iss ku ḥabo.**
turtle, *n.*, (sea tortoise) **din baded, —ki**; — dove, **ḥolli,—di.**
tusk, *n.*, **mi'i,—di**; — of the wart hog, **kalad,—di.**
twang, *n.*, **gango,—adi, sanḥo, —adi.**
twelve, *num.*, **lab iyo toban,—ki**; twelfth, **lab iyo tobnad, —ki, —di.**
twenty, *num.*, **labatan, — ki**; twentieth, **labatanad,—ki,** or **—di.**
twice, *num.*, **laba gor.**
twilight, *n.*, **gabal da',—di'hi, fid,—ki, maḥrib,—ki.**
twin, *n.*, **matan,—ki** (*mas.*), **—ti** (*fem.*).
twine, *n.*, **sefari,—gi.**
twink, twinkle (*see* glance).
twist, *n.*, (*see* string); *v.tr.*, **maroji** or **marori, soh, tidi'.**
twisted, *a.*, **marorsan, sohan, tida'an.**
twitch, *n.*, (a quick pull) **difad** or **dufad,—ki**; *v.tr.*, **dufo, jid.**
two, *num.*, **laba,—di.**
tyranny, *n.*, **dulam,—ki.**

U.

udder, *n.*, **'ando,—adi.**
ugly, *a.*, **ḥun.**
ulcer, *n.*, **bog,—ti.**
umbilical string, *n.*, **ḥudun,—ti.**
umbrella, *n.*, **dallayad,—di.**
unable, *a.*, **ma karo.**
unarmed, *a.*, **hubla.**
uncle, *n.*, (paternal) **ader,—ki**; (maternal) **abti,—gi.**
under, *prp.*, **dāf, dāfta, hos, hosta**; be —, **hosai**; put —, **hosaisi**; go —, **hos gal, hos u gal.**
understand, *v.tr.*, **garo**; do you —? **ma ku da'dai?** I —, **i da'dai.**
understanding, *n.*, **aḥli,—gi, garasho,—adi.**
undress, *v.tr.*, **ḋarka iss ka ḋig** or **iss ka biḥi.**
undulation, *n.*, **godgod,—ki.**
unemployed, *a.*, **haulla, shuḥulla.**
unequal, *a.*, **kala mid, iss ku mid maaha.**

unfit, *a.*, **ma galo.**
unfold, *v.tr.*, **furfur.**
unfortunate, *a.*, **ayan hun**; be —, **ayan humaw.**
ungenerous, *a.*, **deh darran.**
ungratefulness, *n.*, **abaldarri,—gi.**
unhappy (be), *v.i.*, **ba.**
uninhabited, *a.*, **'idla.**
unintelligible, *a.*, **an la garan, wah an la karin.**
union, *n.*, **iss ku darran,—ki.**
unit, *n.*, **mid,—ki.**
universe, *n.*, **duni,—di, dunyo,—adi.**
unjust, *a.*, **gar darran.**
unjustice, *n.*, **gar darro,—adi.**
unkind, *a.*, **naharis la, naharis (ba) ma yahan.**
unlawful, *a.*, **haran.**
unlawfulness, *n.*, **haran,—ti.**
unleavened bread, *n.*, **kibis,—ti, kidar,—ki, muhbasad,—di.**
unload, *v.tr.*, **deji, fur.**
unlucky, *a.*, **ayan hun.**
unripe, *a.*, **'edin.**
unsafe, *a.*, **'absileh, shilleh.**
unsafety, *n.*, **'absi,—di, shil,—ki.**
unseen, *a.*, **harson.**
unsheath, *v.tr.*, **ka bihi.**
until, *prp.*, **inta, ila inta.**
untruth, *n.*, **bein,—ti.**
up, *prp.*, **dul, dusha, gud, gudka, kor**; — to, **ila, ilama.**
upon, *prp.*, **dusha, gudka, ku, sarai u.**
upper, *prp.*, **dusha sarai.**
upright, *a.*, **hagagsan, tāgan, tosan, humati**; be —, **hagagsanaw, hagag u so'o, humati u so'o, tāgnow**; make —, **hagaji, tosi, humati u tāg.**
uprightness, *n.*, **hagag,—gi, humati,—gi, tāg,—gi, —ti.**
uproar, *n.*, **hailo,—adi, dawah,—hi.**
uproot, *v.tr.*, **ruji, fuji, so fuji**; — this tree, **gedká fuji.**
upset, *v.tr.*, **forori, rid, rog.**
upside down, *a.*, **rogan, fororsan.**
upwards, *ad.*, **dusha gestedi.**
urethra, *n.*, **ib,—ti.**
urge, *v.tr.*, **muhuni.**
urine, *n.*, **kádi,—di**; *v.i.*, **kádi, so kádi.**
us, *prn.*, (*see* Grammar).
usage, *n.*, **dastur,—ti.**
use, *n.*, **wah tar,—ki**; be of —, **wah tar**; of no —, **ma taro.**
useful, *a.*, **wah tara** (*mas.*), **wah tarta** (*fem.*).
useless, *a.*, **wah ma tarai.**
uselessness, *n.*, **wah ma tarai,—rihi.**
utensil, *n.*, **wel,—ki.**
utility, *n.*, **wah tar,—ki.**
utter, *v.tr.*, **deh, hadal yedi.**
uvula, *n.*, **hilib dalhai,—hihi.**

V.

vaccinate, *v.tr.*, **sarsar.**
vaccination, *n.*, **sarsarmo,—adi.**
vagina, *n.*, **sil,—ki.**
vale, *n.*, **far,—ti.**
valley, *n.*, **bohol,—shi, doho,—adi.**
value, *n.*, **gana',—di.**

valuable, *a.*, **gana' adag.**
van, *n.*, (fan) **masaf,—ti.**
vanity, *n.*, **falaḥ,—hi, kibir,—ki.**
vanquish, *v.tr.*, **ka adkaw.**
vapor, *n.*, **umis,—ki** ; — clinging to the lid, **umi,—gi.**
variety, *n.*, **kala mid,—di.**
vase, *n.*, (vessel) **wel,—ki** ; — in which incense is burnt, **idan, —ki.**
vast, *a.*, **balladan.**
vegetable, *n.*, **ḫudrad,—di.**
veil, *n.*, **hijad,—di, malḫamad, —di.**
vein, *n.*, **ḥidid,—ki.**
vengeance, *n.*, **'ollad,—di** ; take —, **'olladi.**
venom, *n.*, **sun,—ki, urgumo,—adi, wabayo,—adi.**
venomous, *n.*, (liquid) **urgumo,—adi.**
venture, *v.tr.*, **sasab.**
veranda, *n.*, **ardah,—gi.**
verdant, *a.*, **osob.**
verdure, *n.*, **osob,—ki.**
verse, versification, *n.*, **gabai,—gi.**
versify, *v.i.*, *v.tr.*, **gabai.**
vertigo (*see* giddiness).
very, *ad.*, **badan.**
vessel, *n.*, (utensil) **wel,—ki, gurgur,—ki** ; earthen — used for cooking, **deri,—gi** ; bark —, **āgan,—ti** ; — made of a large gourd, **baro,—adi, dubbo,—adi, ubo,—adi** ; — made of a camel's skin, **tebed,—di** ; — with a handle, **ḫudda,—ihi, tebeda dara,—ihi** ; — used for ablutions before prayer, **weiso,—adi.**
vex, *v.tr.*, **kaga 'eisi** or **'isi, kaga 'ili.**
vice-chief, *n.*, **gudi,—di.**
victory, *n.*, **adkan,—ti.**
view, *n.*, **muḫ,—hi.**
vigilance, *n.*, **ilalo,—adi.**
vigour, *n.*, **ital,—ki, ḥog,—gi.**
vile (*see* abject).
village, *n.*, **rer,—ki.**
vinegar, *n.*, **ḫal,—ki.**
violate, *v.tr.*, **kufso** ; violated, **kufsan.**
violent, *a.*, **fallad ḥun.**
violence, *n.*, **ḥog,—gi, muḫuno, —adi.**
viper, *n.*, **jilbis,—ki.**
virgin, *n.*, **ugub,—ki** ; (in general) **ugubod,—ki.**
virile (membrum), *n.*, **gus,—ki.**
virtuous, *a.*, **tolmon** ; be —, **tolmonow.**
visage, *n.*, **weiji,—gi, jah,—hi, fayo,—ihi.**
viscous matters mixed with blood in dysentery, *n.*, **aḥal,—shi.**
visible, *a.*, **la arka, muḫda** (*m.*), **muḫata** (*f.*).
vision, *n.*, (actual sight) **muḫ,—hi** ; (the thing seen) **muḫad,—ki, muḫasho,—adi.**
visit, *v.tr.*, **ka war don, inu nabad ḫabo so dai.**
visitor, *n.*, **marti,—di.**
voice, *n.*, **luḫ,—di, 'od,—ki.**
void, *a.*, **madan.**
vomit, *v.tr.*, **hunḫa', mantag.**
vomiting, *n.*, **hunḫa'o,—adi, mantag,—gi.**
vowel, *n.*, **ḥaraf,—ki.**

voyage, *n.*, **dof,—ki**; *v.i.*, **dof**; *v.c.*, **dofi, dofsi.**
vulture, *n.*, **gorgor,—ki, homādai,—ihi, hunsho,—adi.**

W.

wages, *n.*, **mushaharo,—adi.**
waist, *n.*, **deḥ,—di**; — band, **sun,—ki.**
wait, *v.i.*, *v.tr.*, **jog, jogso, ɗaur, sug**; — for, **u kadi**; — a moment, **'abbar jog.**
waiting, *n.*, **egmo,—adi.**
wake, waken, *v.i.*, **barārug, ka', sara ka', so ka', so jed.**
wakeful, *a.*, **gami' waḥ.**
walk, *v.i.*, **so'o, talab, baïd**; take a —, **tamashlai**; — on, **mar**; — on all fours, **gurguro**; — on the breech, **kurkurso**; — with difficulty, **tukub**; *n.*, **so'od,—ki, tamashlai,—ihi**; — on all fours, **gurgurasho,—adi**; — on the breech, **kurkuris,—ki.**
wall, *n.*, **derbi,—gi, gidar,—ki.**
wallow, *v.i.*, **galgalo**; *n.*, **galgalasho,—adi.**
wander, *v.i.*, **ku so wareg**; — about, **warwareg, so warwareg**; *v.c.*, **warwareji, so warwareji.**
wanderer, *n.*, **nin warwarega.**
wandering, *n.*, **warwareg,—gi.**
want, *n.*, **tabalo,—adi, sabol,—ki**; a man in —, **nin bāhan** or **nin waḥ u bāhan**; *v.i.*, (be deficient) **tabalaisnaw**; (wish for) **don.**
wanty, *n.*, **wegered,—ki.**
war, *n.*, **dagal,—ki, 'ollad,—di.**
ward, *n.*, (a division of a town) **ḥafad,—di**; *v.tr.*, (guard) **ilali, karaw.**
warlike, *a.*, **dagal ja'el.**
warm, *a.*, **(wa) kulul, kulail**; feeling —, **hursan**; *v.tr.*, **diri, kululai**; — yourself, **kulāl, duksiso**; — at the sun *or* prepare a warm place, **duksi**; — at the fire, **ku ɗalal.**
warmth, *n.*, (of the sun's rays) **dalo',—a'di.**
warn, *v.tr.*, **dig** (with **u** or **ku**).
warning, *n.*, **dignin,—ti**; send a —, **dignin dir.**
warrior, *n.*, **gashan ḥad,—ki, hub ḥad, gesi,—gi, rakab,—ki.**
wart, *n.*, **burobahalad,—di.**
wary, *a.*, (prudent) **foyig** or **fojig.**
wash, *v.tr.*, **ḥal, ḥasal, maïd, so maïd, 'adai**; *v.r.*, **maïdo**; — the hands, **faraḥal**; — the face, **foldaḥ**; — hands, face, *v.r.*, **faraḥalo, foldoḥo.**
washed, *a.*, **maïdan.**
washerman, *n.*, **ɗar ḥasal,—ki, dhobi,—gi.**
washing, *n.*, **maïdasho,—adi**; — of the hands, **faraḥal,—ki**; — of the face, **foldaḥ,—diḥhi.**
waste, *v.tr.*, **ku 'ayar, lumi**; — money, **'idlai**; do not waste, **ha ku 'ayarin**; (expend needlessly) **hor, ḥub.**
watch, *n.*, **ilalo,—adi**; — word,

baḥ,—hi; (pocket timepiece) **sa'ad,—di.**
water, *n.*, **biyo,—ihi** (*plur. n.*); fresh —, **biyo ma'an**; sour —, **biyo ḍanan** or **biyo ḥaḍaḍ**; salt —, **biyo 'usbaah**; rain —, **biyo rob** or **hared,—di**; well —, **weyer,—ki**; river —, **biyo durdur**; — course, **tog,—gi**; — fall, **biyo garbada ka so dulai**; — bag, **sibrar,—ki**; *v.tr.*, **warabi**; — the flock, **aror, arori**; — before the house, **rushai.**
watering, *n.*, **aror,—ki.**
wave, *n.*, **maujad,—di, tarshad, —di.**
wax, *n.*, **ḥaujo,—adi, shama'** or **shimai',—ihi.**
way, *n.*, **dau,—gi, jid,—ki, marin,—ki, hilin,—ki, dariḥ,—hi.**
weak, *a.*, (feeble) **weïdsan, 'ataisan.**
weakness, *n.*, **weïd,—di.**
we (*see* Grammar).
wealth, *n.*, **dunyo,—adi, ḥolo,—ihi.**
wealthy, *a.*, **ḥolo badan, rawi,—gi, rawiaḥ, baḍaḍah.**
wean, *v.tr.*, **ka guḍi**; be weaned, **guḍ, ha laga guḍiyo.**
weapon, *n.*, **hub,—ki.**
wear, *v.tr.*, **sid, sido.**
weary, *a.*, **dālan, dāshan**; be —, **dal, dālanaw**; *v.tr.*, **ḍāli.**
weariness, *n.*, **dāl,—ki.**
weather, *n.*, **dabaïl,—shi, ḥeli, —gi**; bad —, **dabail ḥun**; cold —, **dabaïl ḥabow**; fair or fine —, **dabaïl wanaksan**; hot —, **haufi,—gi, kalil,—shi.**
weave, *v.tr.*, **ḍar samai.**
weaver, *n.*, **ḍar samais,—ki.**
web-footed birds, *n.*, **badag,—gi.**
wedding, *n.*, **aros,—ki, 'ayar, ti.**
wedge, *n.*, **bishil,—ki.**
Wednesday, *n.*, **arbaḥa,—di, rabuḥ,—hi.**
week, *n.*, **todobad,—ki.**
weep, *v.i.*, **oi.**
weeping, *n.*, **oin,—ti.**
weigh, *v.tr.*, **mis, misan.**
weight, *n.*, **misan,—ki.**
weighty, *a.*, **'ulus.**
welfare, *n.*, **awo,—adi, darad,—di.**
well, *n.*, **'el,—ki, gof,—ki**; *a.*, **ladan, bed ḥaba, waḥsan**; *ad.*, **ād** (with **u**), **haurarsan, wa waḥsan.**
welt (*see* border).
wen, *n.*, **buro,—adi.**
went (*past of* 'to go'), *v.i.*, **teg.**
west, *n.*, **galbed,—ki.**
wet, *a.*, **ḥoiyan**; be —, **ḥoiyanaw**; — land, **raïs,—ki**; *v.tr.*, **ḥoi.**
whale, *n.*, **nibiri,—gi.**
wharf, *n.*, **deked,—di.**
what? *prn.*, **ya?** (*see* Grammar).
whatsoever, *a.*, **waḥ un.**
wheat, *n.*, **saren,—ki.**
wheel, *n.*, **giringir,—ti, shag,—gi.**
when, *c.*, **gorta, kolka, marka**; *interrog. ad.*, **gorma? hadma? kolma? marma?**
whence, *ad.*, **halka, hagga** (with **ka**); *int.*, **hagge? halke?**

whenever, *ad.*, **gor kasta, gor walba.**
where? *ad.*, **hagge? me? meyai?** (*mas.*), **medai?** (*fem.*).
wherever, *a.*, **mel kasta, mel walba.**
whet, *v.tr.*, (sharpen by friction) **lis, afai.**
whetstone, *n.*, **lissin,—ki.**
whether (*see* Grammar).
whey, *n.*, **ir,—ti.**
which (*see* Grammar).
while, *n.*, **gor,—ti, kol,—ki**; (a short time) **'abbar,—ki**; *ad.*, **gorta.**
whine, *v.i.*, **waraḥ**; *n.*, **waraḥ, —hi.**
whip, *n.*, **jedal,—ki**; *v.tr.*, **jedal.**
whirl, *v.i.*, **wareg.**
whirlpool, *n.*, **biya iss ku waregaya.**
whirlwind, *n.*, **sisa, sigo,—adi.**
whisper, *v.i.*, **hos u hadal**; — to him, **hos u la hadal.**
whistle, *v.i.*, *v.tr*, **fori**; *n.*, **fori, —di.**
white, *a.*, **'ad**; be —, **'adaw**; remain —, **'adaisnaw.**
whiten, *v.tr.*, **'adai.**
whiteness, *n.*, **'adan,—ki, —ti.**
who? *int.prn.*, **ayo? aya? ya?**
whosoever, whomsoever, *prn.*, **nin un.**
whole, *a.*, **dan, gidi**; *n.*, **daman, —ti.**
wholesome, *a.*, **wanaksan.**
why? *ad.*, **maḥai u, mu? wayo?**
wick, *n.*, **dubalad,—di.**
wicked, *a.*, **ḥun, baan, bās.**
wide, *a.*, **balladan.**
widen, *v.tr.*, **balladi.**
wideness, width, *n.*, **ballad,—ki.**
widow, *n.*, **'armali,—di.**
wife, *n.*, **afo,—adi, nag,—ti, islan,—ti, úri,—di, hilo,—ihi**; — of the father (stepmother), — of a paternal or maternal uncle, **ayo,—adi.**
wild beast, *n.*, **bahal,—ki, bubal,—shi.**
wilful, *a.*, **oganah.**
wilfully, *ad.*, **ogan u.**
wilfulness, *n.*, **ogan,—ti.**
will, *n.*, **ḥushi,—gi, ogan,—ti, ḥaul,—ki, umur,—ti, oggolan, —ti**; it is my —, **baga! ḥushigai.**
willing, *a.*, **oggol**; be —, **oggolaw.**
win, *v.i.*, *v.tr.*, **ka adkaw, dul mar.**
wind, *n.*, **dabail,—shi**; windless, **dabail laan.**
windpipe, *n.*, **bo',—hi, hunguri, —gi.**
wind up, *v.tr.*, **wareji.**
winding, *n.*, **wareg,—gi.**
window, *n.*, **dahad,—di**; (of a Somali hut, a kind of hole) **fod,—ki.**
wine, *n.*, **ḥamri,—gi.**
wing, *n.*, **bāl,—ki.**
wink, *v.i.*, **il iss ku ḥabo**; *n.*, **il iss ku ḥabasho,—adi.**
winnow, *v.tr.*, **ḥuf.**
winter, *n.*, (or time of rain) **gu, —gi.**
wipe, *v.tr.*, **ka biḥi**; — your lips, **aftiro.**
wire, *n.*, **ḥasau,—di.**

wisdom, *n.*, **garad,—ki, herrib, —ti, miyir,—ki.**
wise, *a.*, **fi'an, garadleh, herribleh, miyirleh.**
wish, *v.tr.*, **don, rab**; *n.*, **donin, —ti.**
whiskers, *n.*, **timihi damanka.**
wit, *n.*, **ahli,—gi, kaftan,—ki.**
witch, *n.*, **nag wah fasha, nag fal tahan, nagti falka tihin** (the ...); *v.tr.*, (bewitch) **fāl.**
with, *prp.*, **ku, la.**
wither, *v.i.*, **ingeg.**
within, *prp.*, **gudaha.**
without, *prp.*, **laan, laan,—ti.**
witness, *n.*, **marhati,—gi**; *v.tr.*, (give testimony) **fur, marhati ku fur.**
woman, *n.*, **nag,—ti.**
womankind, *n.*, **dumar,—ki, nagnimo,—adi.**
womb, *n.*, **halus,—ki, rimai,—gi, ur,—ki.**
wonder, *n.*, **'ajeb,—ti, yab,—ki, la yab,—ki, umur,—ti**; *v.* (wonder at) **la 'ajeb, yab, la yab, la yabsanaw**; cause to —, **'ajebi, yabi.**
wonderful, *a.*, **yaban, yab haba, yab leh, yabsan, la yabsan.**
woo, *v.tr.*, **ashah.**
wood, *n.*, **hori,—gi**; fire —, **habo, —adi, hatab,—ki**; hard —, **hori haroleh.**
wooden, *a.*, **horiah, hori laga samaiyai.**
woodpecker, *n.*, **daudaula,—ihi.**
wool, *n.*, **dogor,—ti.**
word, *h.*, **erai,—gi, haul,—ki**; bad —, **heb,—ti.**
work, *n.*, **shuhul,—ki, shahi,—gi. haul,—shi**; hard —, **dibtan, —ki**; *v.tr.*, **haul habo, hausho, hoji, shahai**; — hard, **dibtan**; *v.c.*, **shahaisi**; — for yourself, **shahaiso.**
workman, *n.*, **shahi,—gi, nin shahiah**; hard-working man, **dibtan,—ki.**
world, *n.*, **duni,—di, dunyo,—adi.**
worm, *n.*, **dirhi,—gi.**
worry, *v.tr.*, **dali.**
worse, *a.*, **ka hun**; become —, **ka si dar.**
worship, *n.*, **'abudnin,—ti.**
worst, *a.*, **ka wada hun, ugu hun.**
worth, *n.*, **gana',—di.**
wound, *n.*, **nabar,—ki, dahar,—ki, hon,—ti, awar,—ki**; a new —, **dahar 'usub, daharki 'usba** (the ...); *v.tr.*, **dahar, hon, nabar yel.**
wounded, *a.*, **daharleh, honleh, nabarleh**; mortally —, **dinsan.**
wrap, *v.tr.*, **lablab, dudub.**
wrath, *n.*, **'ado,—adi, 'il,—ki.**
wreck, *n.*, **hashwad,—di.**
wrestle, *n.*, **legdan,—ki, tab,—ti**; *v.i.*, **legdan**; — with, **la legdan.**
wretch, *n.*, **lumiyai,—ihi, Allah habai,—gi, nin Allah habaiah.**
wring, *v.tr.*, **maroji** or **marori.**
wrinkle, *n.*, **dubnin,—ki, godgod, —ki.**
wrist, *n.*, **'ur'ur,—ki, dudun,—ki.**
write, *v.tr.*, **hor, warhadda ku dig.**

written, *a.*, **ḫoran.**
writer, *n.*, **ḫora,—gi.**
writing, *n.*, **ḫorin,—ki**; hand —, **far,—ti.**
wrong, *a.*, **gura'an, gura'na, ḫalloḫan.**
wrongness, *n.*, **gura',—i'hi.**

Y.

yawn, *v.i.*, **afka kala ḫad, afka kala hai.**
yawning, *n.*, **af kala ḫad,—ki, af kala haïs,—ki.**
yea, *ad.*, **ha, waiyai.**
yean, *v.tr.*, **yelo, ḋal.**
year, *n.*, **sanad,—di, gu,—gi, kal,—ki**; last —, **kal horai, sanad horai**; next —, **kal dambe, gu dambe**; past —, **sanad ḋowed**; the coming —, **sanadda so so'ota**; the being in years, **gan,—ki, ḫan,—ki.**
yearn, *v.i.*, **tabalaisnaw.**
yeast, *n.*, **ḫamir,—ki.**
yellow, *n.*, **wob,—ki.**
yes, *ad.*, **ha.**
yesterday, *ad.*, **shalai, shalaito**; the day before — **dorad**; — night, **ḫalai.**

yet, *a.*, **weli.**
yield, *v.tr.*, (produce) **yel**; (grant) **biḫi, si**; *v.i.*, **oggolaw.**
yon, yonder, *ad.*, **halká, halko, mesha, mesho, shishai, u shishai** (the farthest).
you, ye, *pers.prn.*, (*see* Grammar), **ow, yow** (used as affixes).
young man, *n.*, **baḫsi, —gi, barbar,—ki, ḋalinyaro,—adi, mudakar,—ki**; younger son, **'uradḫigai,—ihi**; the youngest, **kan ugu yar, gar u ḋambais.**
youngling, *n.*, **ḋal,—ki.**
your, *pos.prn.* (*see* Grammar).
youth, *n.*, **da yar,—di, —aid, dalinyaro,—adi, barbar,—ki.**

Z.

zariba *or* zereba, *n.*, **ḫero,—adi**; — of thorns, **ḫero ḫodaḫleh**; make a —, **ḫero od.**
zeal, *n.*, **kul,—ki.**
zebra, *n.*, **farow,—gi.**
zero, *n.*, **gobabin,—ti.**
zigzag, *n.*, **baïdbaïd,—ki**; walk in — (as a snake), *v.i.*, **baïdbaïd.**

SUPPLEMENT

TO

SOMALI-ENGLISH VOCABULARY.

U

SUPPLEMENT

TO

SOMALI-ENGLISH VOCABULARY.

A.

'abid, *f.n.*, drinking.—**di** (*see* **'ab**, drink).

abar, *v.i.*, aim at, go straight to.

abārai, *v.tr.*, famish, starve (*see* **abār**, drought).

abārow, *v.i.*, starve, die of hunger.

abārdaur, *f.n.*, a fertile place, neither wet nor dry.—**ti.**

Abbaha, *n.*, the Father (first Person of the blessed Trinity).

abbayal, *n.pl.*, forefathers.—**shi.**

abbarihi, *ad.*, about; **abbarihi lab iyo tobanki yu no yimi**, he came to us at about 12 o'clock.

abur, *m.n.*, foam, froth.—**ki.**

'adabai, *a.*; **nin la 'adabai**, a damned man, reprobate (*see* **'adab**, hell).

'adib, *m.n.*, torment.—**ki.**

'adiban, *v.p.*, be tormented.

u adkaiso, *v.tr.*, resist.

adkan, *f.n.*, firmness, hardness, victory, Confirmation (sacrament of).—**ti.**

'adawad, *f.n.*, enmity.—**di.**

aḥal, *f.n.*, viscous matter mixed with blood in dysentery.—**shi.**

aḫan, *m.n.*, funereal feast.—**ki.**

'aïnan, *m.n.*, rein, kidney.—**ki.**

ajar, *m.n.*, indulgence.—**ki.**

'ala'al, *m.n.*, remorse.—**ki.**

'alal, *m.n.*, crop (the first stomach of a fowl).—**ki.**

'alamad, *f.n.*, sign, mark.—**di.**

'alamadi, *v.tr.*, mark.

alḫad, *f.n.*, fort, fortification.—**di.**

Allah ḫabai, *m.n.*, reprobate, abject man, wretch.—**gi**; **nin Allah ḫabaiah.**

almas, *m.n.*, diamond.—**ki.**

aluhiyad, *f.n.*, divinity.—**di.**

alwaḫ, *f.n.* (*plur.* of **loḫ**), planks.—**di**; **alwaḥda sarabkeda**, flooring.

alyo muruḫ, *m.n.*, slaver or spittle drivelling from the mouth.—**hi** (*see* **alyo**, saliva).

alyo muruḫ iss ka buḫi, *v.i.*, slabber, slaver, drivel, besmear with saliva.

alyo muruḫ ku dādi, *v.tr.*, slabber, smear or wet with saliva.
(nin) alyo muruḫ weinleh, *m.n.*, slabberer; **ninki alyo muruḫ weina,** the slabberer.
ambabai (nin), *a.v.*, a debauchee.
aminad, *f.n.*, belief, creed, faith. **—di.**
amir, *f.n.*, prince, chief.**—ki.**
arah donato, *f.n.*, a seeker of fruits in the jungle.
'araraf, *m.n.*, affliction, suffering. **—ki.** This word is used when the pain of the soul or of the body is so intense that it would be preferable to die.
a'taraf, *m.n.*, confession.**—ki.**
a'tarafo, *v.r.*, confess yourself.
'awai, *v.i.*, do not sleep, remain awake and chat.**—ya, wan —n.**
'awais, *m.n.*, time from 8 p.m. to midnight.**—ki.**
'awaldar, *m.n.*, sergeant or corporal (of the police).**—ki.**
ayad, *f.n.*, formula, form of prayer.**—di.**
ayanta Issa, *n.*, Christmas.
ayanta 'ided, *n.*, holiday, solemnity (*plur.* **ayamaha 'ided**).
ad̈yar (*see* **āyar**), *ad.*, slowly; **ad̈yar iyo ad̈yar,** little by little.

B.

bād, *f.n.*, tribute.**—di.**
badag, *m.n.*, duck.**—gi.**
kaga bad̈bad̈i or **bad̈bad̈adi,** *v.c.*, cheer, rejoice.
badiwaleh, *m.n.*, postman.**—hi.**
bad̈ow, *m.* and *f.n.*, rustic (coming directly from the jungle).**—gi, —di; nin, nag bad̈owah,** a rustic man, woman.
ka so baḥ, *m.n.*, a protuberance. **—hi.**
bahahin, *m.n.*, idiot.**—ki.**
baḫbaḫ, *m.n.*, blackish gum.**—hi.**
baïd (*root*), walk, march, go; **ka —,** give place ...
baïr, *m.n.*, clippspringer (with long ears but smooth hair of the same colour as those of a gazelle).**—ki.**
u banai, *v.i.*, give place for, to.
bar ma leh, *a.*, poor (without any money); **ninkasi bar ma laha,** this man is quite poor.
bar, *m.n.*, top, head, poll of a tree. **—ki; dirta barkoda.**
bar or **barka sarai,** *m.n.*, forepart.
bara dubleh, *m.n.*, small mouse (a kind of kangaroo rat).
(nin) baraḥah, *a.*, accommodated.
barar, *v.i.*, swell.
barari, *v.tr.*, swell, dilate.
baratan, *m.n.*, race (running).**— ki.**
baridi, *v.tr.*, greet, salute (*see* **bari,** be safe).
baya'ad, *f.n.*, bargain.**—di.**
bedelan, *v.p.*, be changed; **bedelma, wan bedelmi.**
boḫon, *f.n.*, the great sinew over the heel.**—ti; — horai,** instep.
boyad, *f.n.*, buoy.**—di.**
bog, *m.n.*, acclamation.**—gi.**

burambur, *v.tr.*, sing (used only for women).

buro', *m.n.*, a mound of sand; **bura'ha.**

buro iss ku yal, *m.n.*, a range of mountains; **burihi iss ku yil** (*plur.*), the ...

burush, *m.n.*, brush.—**ki.**

D.

da'nin, *f.n.*, sack (of a town), pillage.—**ti.**

ɖab, *f.n.*, lap.—**ti.**

ɖab, *f.n.*, certainly.—**ti.**

ɖabai, *v.tr.*, affirm, assure; **kaga** —, make certain.

ɖabain, *f.n.*, affirmation.—**ti.**

dabah, *v.tr.*, sacrifice.

dabīḥad, *f.n.*, sacrifice, victim.—**di.**

dad'unah, *a.*, fierce, wild.

dadki dintai, *m.n.*, the dead.

daghi or **dagiḥi**, *v.tr.*, lapidate, stone.

daḥa, *ad.*, often.

an dal lahain, *locution*, without limit.

ɖalan, *m.n.pl.*, children.—**ki.**

dalaẖ, *f.n.*, divorce (*see* **fur**).—**di.**

dalaẖ, *v.tr.*, divorce; **sadeḥda dalaẖod bad igaga furaisantahai** (a kind of swearing by which they pledge themselves to divorce).

dalo, *f.n.*, top of the head.

dalol, *m.n.*, (numeral) one-third.

damoẖ (*see* **ku damoẖ**), *v.tr.*, put on a plaster, poultice.

damoẖ, *m.n.*, cataplasm, poultice. —**hi.**

damur, *m.n.*, tar, pitch.—**ki.**

dan (*see* Part I.); **wa dantisi**, or **wa isagi iyo danti**, it is his concern; **aya dan leh?** who has anything to say? **ana dan leh**, I have something to say; **nin o ɖan u ma lihi**, I care for nobody.

dardar, *m.n.*, the three stones on which they put their boiler.—**ki.**

daren, *v.tr.*, perceive; **darema, wan daremi.**

daren, *f.n.*, perception, sensation. —**ti.**

darfa', *m.n.*, dysentery (in horses and cattle).—**i'hi.**

wa ɖebai, *locution*, he has committed fornication, adultery; **wa i ɖebai**, he has committed adultery with me. These expressions are used in the Ogaden, and by the Dulbanteh and Darod.

deg (*see* Part I.); **ku dega, ku degta**, *a.*, adhesive.

ɖegta dahasheda, *locution*, the tip of the ear.

dein, *f.n.*, omission, leaving.—**ti.**

dein ka tur, *m.n.*, delator, denunciator.

deman, *m.n.*, diamond.—**ki.**

dembab, *v.i.*, sin, commit a sin.

dembabi, *v.c.*, make him sin.

si ɖerai, *v.tr.*, deepen (sink far below the surface).

derai, *v.i.*, run quick (as a gazelle).
deraiyai, *a.v.*, rapid, swift, quick in running.
dergi, *v.tr.*, satiate, make him abound, give him as much as he wishes.
derjin, *m.n.*, a dozen.—**ki.**
didi, *m.n.*, muddy place.—**gi.**
didi, *m.n.*, the getting angry, wild in playing.—**gi.**
didi, *v.i.*, get angry; **didiya, wan didiyi.**
didib, *f.n.*, declivity, slope (so abrupt that it is impossible to stand on).—**ti.**
didibso, *v.i.*, stretch out the legs.
didibsan, *a.*, having the legs extended, stretched out.
ḍif, *num.*, few, a little.
difad or **dufad**, *m.n.*, a twitch, a quick pull.—**ki.**
dignin, *f.n.*, denunciation.—**ti.**
digri, *m.n.*, elegy, song of lamentation.—**gi.**
dilid, *f.n.*, murder.—**di**; or **dil**, *m.n.*, homicide.—**ki.**
dillo ka ḍig, *v.tr.*, prostitute.
ḍiman, *v.i.*, decrease, grow less; **ḍinma, wan ḍinmi.**
(nin) ḍimanaya, *a.*, dying man.
an ḍiman karin, *a.*, immortal.
dina', *m.n.*, fillet (the loins of oxen, horses, &c.—**ki,** —**yo** (*see* **sarar**).
dira', *v.tr.*, measure; *a.*, **wan —i.**
ḍiran (nin), *a.*, a hero, a man never afraid; **ninki ḍirana,** the hero.
ḍiranaw, *v.att.*, be a hero.
dirandiro, *f.n.*, oral report about somebody.
diriḥ, *f.n.*, puddle or muddy standing water.—**di.**
dog, *f.n.*, consequence.—**ti.**
dol, *f.n.*, the second tooth (upper and under one).—**shi,** —**o.**
iss u don, *v.tr.*, affiance, betroth.
donanan, *f.n.*, affiance, betrothing. —**ti.**
du, *v.tr.*, remove, keep off; —**a, wan —i; ka —**, keep from, dissuade.
ḍuban, *a.*, long, acute (*see* **ḍer**); **san ḍuban**, a long nose; **sanki ḍubna**, the ...
duf, *m.n.*, storm, tempest.—**ki; duf ba dahaya**, there is a storm.
iss ku dufo, *v.tr.*, drink liquors, wine, make yourself drunk (*lit.* beat yourself).
ku dug, *v.tr.*, beat.
dugo, *v.i.*, look; **dugta, wan dugan.**
dugtan, *v.p.*, be aiming at; **dugtama, wan dugtami.**
dūl mar, *v.tr.*, win, overcome.
dumal, *v.tr.*, marry your sister-in-law, marry a second time.
dumo', *f.n.*, size.—**di;** — **wein,** big; — **yar,** thin, small.

E.

edeg, *m.n.*, a small fold for lambs and kids (within the enclosure). —**gi.**

ekan, *f.n.*, likeness, resemblance. —**ti.**

ku eri (*see* Dictionary), *v.tr.*, drive into; **musmar ku eri**, drive in a nail; **ka eri**, drive out.

ergo (*see* Dictionary), *f.n.*, embassy.

F.

fadilad, *f.n.*, virtue.—**di.**

fadi (*see* Dictionary); **fadi fardaah**, a herd of horses; **fadi lo'ah**, a herd of neat cattle.

fag, *v.tr.*, take off the warp or the woof of cloth to make thread.

fahmad, *f.n.*, memory.—**di.**

fakir, *m.n.*, a Mussulman fakir.—**ki.**

fakirow, *v.tr.*, beg (alms); **si** —, beg always; **ninkasi wa fakiranyahai**, this man is always doing the same work.

falahnimo, *f.n.*, pride.

falau, *m.n.*, means.—**gi.**

fali, *v.tr.*, foretell, predict; **ninki ba i faliyai inan gor dow dimanaya**, the man foretold me that I was to die soon.

fallid, *m.n.*, stump of a tooth.—**ki.**

iss fani, *v.i.*, presume of yourself, boast.

fanah gara'is, *m.n.*, beating repeatedly on the knuckles.—**ki.**

farrin, *f.n.*, the word said.—**ti**; **farrin igu gei**, go and tell him what I said to you.

fayo, *m.n.pl.*, features, face.—**ihi**; **fayo wanaksan**, nice features; **fayihi wanaksana**, the ... (*see* **horisho**).

fenfenad or **fenfenasho**, *m.n.*, *f.n.*, gnawing.—**ki**, —**di.**

fid, *m.n.*, first part of the night, from sunset to 8 o'clock.

fihnan, *f.n.*, sharpness, acuteness. —**ti.**

fuhsi, *m.n.*, drinking.—**gi.**

fuhfuhso, *v.i.*, gully, make noise with the lips in drinking (*see* **kalo**).

fuji or **so fuji**, *v.tr.*, separate, take out (*see* **ruji**); **kala** —, separate (two things joined).

G.

gabil, *f.n.*, a skin of a cow or a camel used to shade children when on camels.—**shi.**

gahaïd or **gahaïr**, *m.n.*, raw fruit. —**ki.**

galibah, *m.n.*, evaporation.—**hi.**

galibihi, *v.tr.*, *v.i.*, evaporate.

gamod, *m.n.*, water coming from the **gadod**, curdled milk.—**ki.**

gamun, *m.n.*, stick of an arrow, —**ki.**

gana', *m.n.*, the great gut.—**i'hi.**

gantal, *f.n.*, arrow.—**shi.** (When the stick and the arrow are joined they form the arrow, which is called **fallad, gantal, degalai.**)

ka gar hel or **garow,** *v.p.*, be convicted.
gara'is, *m.n.*, flagellation.—**ki.**
gawadi, *f.n.*, cart, car.—**di.**
geiso (*see* **gei**), *v.r.*, bring your part.
gidihan, *indef. num.*, general.
giringiri, *v.tr.*, roll up.
gunanad, *m.n.*, agony, last moments.—**ki.**
guro, *f.n.*, a place prepared on camels for small children.

H.

ḥab, *v.tr.*, clean a plate by eating what remains on it.
habeibsan, *a.*, hoarse.
habo, *v.tr.*, gather fuel, firewood.
had hodal, *m.n.*, evening shadow. —**ki.**
ḥadir, *a.*, present; **wa ku ḥadir,** he is present.
ḥadiri, *v.tr.*, pass the review.
ḥadiris, *m.n.*, review.—**ki.**
ḥag Ebbehen or **Ebbahai,** *locution*, towards God, for the sake of God.
haga or **hagi,** *ad.*, all right; **wa hagi,** it is all right, good, well, it is so.
haghago, *v.i.*, stammer; **haghagta.**
haḫnimo, *f.n.*, justice.
ḥajolad, *f.n.*, talisman (made of silver, and ordinarily tied to the upper part of the arm).—**di.**
iss ku halai, *v.r.*, rely upon.
haleil, *v.tr.*, catch, reach.
ḥamasho, *f.n.*, backbiting.—**di.**
hangarara, *m.n.*, a kind of centipede.—**ihi** (*see* Dictionary).
ḥaransan; waḥ waliba iga ḥaransan, an oath often used by the Somalis. (By this oath they bind themselves to a divorce.)
hardi, *m.n.*, shock.—**gi.**
ḥardi, *v.tr.*, shock.—**ya**; **wan ḥardiyi.**
ḥasakab, *m.n.*, accent (sign).—**ki.**
ḥashwad, *f.n.*, wreck, shipwreck. —**di.**
ḥaskul, *f.n.*, tow (made from the bark of trees).—**shi.**
kaga hawi, *v.tr.*, slay, beat without mercy.
hig, *m.n.*, tow.—**gi** (*see* **ḥaskul**).
higto, *f.n.*, relation.—**adi.**
hiḫlai, *m.n.*, sob, convulsive sigh. —**hi.**
hiḫlai, *v.i.*, sob.
ḥishod, *m.n.* (*see* Dictionary); *means also* disgrace, discredit, dishonour.
ḥilo, *m.n. sing.* and *pl.*, wife, wives.—**hi; ḥilaaigu wa sadeḥdi dalaḫadod inaiyan aḫalka ku jirahain,** I divorce you by three divorces (oath having the same meaning as that of the word **dalaḫ,** *which see*).
ḥilo badan, *a.*, polygamist.
hogo, *v.i.*, slouch; **hogta, wan hogan.**
hogasho, *f.n.*, slouch.—**adi.**
ḥub, *m.n.*, slough of a snake.—**ki.**

hubal, *a.*, certain, sure.
ḥundur, *f.n.*, dysentery.—**ti.**
ḥunguriyai, *v.tr.*, envy.—**ya,** —**n.**

Ḫ.

ḫa, *m.n.*, incense.—**hi.**
ḫabil, *m.n.*, skins sewn together and used as cradles for babies. —**ki.**
ḫaḥabad, *f.n.*, prostitute.—**di; ḫaḥabo,**—**ihi** (*plur.*), prostitutes.
ḫaḥabad ka d̄ig, *v.tr.*, prostitute.
ḫado, *f.n.*, dinner.
ḫaibai, *a.*, adulterated; **wa rubiad ḫaibaiah** or **ḫaibaah,** this rupee is adulterated, is false.
ḫaisaran, *f.n.*, ratan (cane).—**ti.**
ḫaisaramai, *v.tr.*, flog.
ḫalab, *f.n.*, shagginess.—**ti.**
ḫalab leh, *a.*, shagged, shaggy, hairy, rough, having long hair.
ḫamir, *m.n.*, ferment, yeast.—**ki.**
ḫamis, *m.n.*, poisonous arrow; **kolka fallad̄du doḥbantahai waḥha la yid̄ahda ḫamis,** when the arrow is poisoned they call it **ḫamis.**
ḫamri, *m.n.*, liquor, wine.—**gi.**
ḫasanad, *f.n.*, treasure.—**di.**
ḫodus ka d̄ig, ka samai, *v.tr.*, sanctify, consecrate.
ḫon, *v.tr.*, wound, hurt.
ḫoranso, *v.tr.*, stretch out.
ḫoris ho, *m.n.pl.*, features.—**ihi.**
ḫud, *f.n.*, person, nature, self.—**di.**
ḫudum, *m.n.*, spike, stake.—**ki.**
ḫuḥub, *m.n.*, sneer, ludicrous scorn.—**ki.**
ḫubiḥi, *v.tr.*, sneer, scorn.
ḫumbaho, *v.i.*, fall sick again; **ḫumbahda, wan ḫumbahan.**

K.

ka'anut, *m.n.*, holy order.—**ki.**
kabo, *v.i.*, gully.
kabul, *m.n.*, corporal (of police). —**ki.**
kanfur, *m.n.*, camphor.—**ki.**
katholik, *m.n.*, Catholic.—**gi; katholigaah,** a Catholic.
kidif, *v.tr.*, tear or cut into small pieces; **kidfa, wan kidfi.**
kilkilai, *v.tr.*, tickle.
korban, *m.n.*, Eucharist, Communion.—**ki.**
Kristos, *prop.n.*, Christ.
kudmo, *f.n.*, sodomy (*used also for* fornication; *see* **wasmo**).
kurtun, *m.n.*, stump of a tree become dry.

I.

idan, *m.n.*, authority, dominion. —**ki.**
idan or **u idin** (*see* **u idin** in Dictionary).
ifḫaristiya, *m.n.*, Eucharist.—**ihi.**
iḫ, *f.n.*, suffocation, smothering, —**di.**
iḫsan, *a.v.*, suffocated.

iḫsanaw, *v.att.*, be suffocated.
'iji, *v.tr.*, suffocate, smother.
ilaḫ, *f.n.*, quarrel, strife.—**ti.**
Inanka, —**i**, —**u**, *n.*, the Son (Second Person of the Blessed Trinity).
ina, *a.*, any (*see* **in**, part, piece).

J.

jawan, *f.n.*, stock, store.—**ti.**
ha i ged or **jed min**, do not distract me.
dinta jaḥad, *v.tr.*, backslide (in religion), apostatize.
jidḫadasho, *f.n.*, incarnation.
jirso, *v.i.*, be old; **wilkasu todoba jirsai** or **jirsadai**, this boy is seven years old; **so** —, take shelter; **aḫalka so jirso.**
jori, *f.n.*, bay.—**di.**
junub, *f.n.*, pollution during sleep.—**ti**; **iss ku** —, have a pollution during sleep.

L.

labḫo, *f.n.*, pit of the stomach.
lalad, *m.n.*, a swing.—**ki.**
lilah, *m.n.* (*see* Dictionary), God. —**hi.** This word means especially 'the truth.'
limad, *m.n.*, slough, a deep miry place.—**ki.**
liturgiyad, *f.n.*, liturgy.—**di.**
lol, *v.i.*, play.
loli, *v.tr.*, amuse, cause to play.
lol, *m.n.*, boughs used in making the Somali hut (*see* **dig lola**). —**ki.**
lul, *v.i.*, hang.

M.

madal, *m.n.*, a measure of uncooked rice.—**ki.**
madowbow, *v.p.*, be black.
mahawi, *m.n.*, tempter, misleader (in religion only).—**gi.**
maïd, *v.tr.* (*see* Dictionary), baptize.
maïdasho, *f.n.*, baptism.
maïrun, *m.n.*, chrism.—**ki.**
masar, *m.n.*, handkerchief.—**ki.**
masḫad, *f.n.*, ointment, unction. —**di**; **masḫadda aḫirah** or **masḫadda ḋadka buka**, Extreme Unction.
ma'shar, *m.n.*, lesson.—**ki.**
meri, *v.tr.*, marry.
merso, *v.r.*, marry (yourself).
mestira, *m.n.*, mystery.—**hi.**
midmid u tiri, *v.tr.*, enumerate.
midnimo, *f.n.*, unity.
minḋa? *part. int. neg.*, is it not?
miran, *a.v.*, clear, limpid.
iss misan, *v.i.*, swing, see-saw.
miskinad, *f.n.*, beggar (woman). —**di.**
salibka ku mismar, *v.tr.*, crucify.
mot, *m.n.*, death.—**ki.**
mud, *m.n.*, the place after the **shaf** in the camel's chest.—**ki.**
ka mud biḋi, *v.tr.*, transfix.

muḥallis, *m.n.*, Saviour.—**ki.**
mulk, *m.n.*, throne.—**gi.**
mulki, *m.n.*, kingdom.—**gi.**
murwai, *v.tr.*, honour, respect.

N.

iss na', *v.r.* (*see* **na'**, Dictionary), abnegate, renounce yourself.
iss ne'bahan, *f.n.*, abnegation. —**ti.**
nab, *v.tr.*, splash; **timaha nab**, splash your hair flat with lime or mud; **ku** —, glue.
nabar yel, *v.tr.*, wound, hurt.
nabid or **nebid**, *m.n.*, wine.—**ki.**
naḥsan, *a.v.*, charitable, merciful.
dab nared, *m.n.*, hell-fire.—**ki.**
niyed, *f.n.*, conscience.—**di.**
nolol, *f.n.*, life.—**shi.**

O.

oḥon daran or **oḥon la**, *a.*, ignorant.
ori or **'uri**, *f.n.*, wife, lady, woman. —**di.**

R.

Rabbi, *m.n.*, God.—**gi.** This word means especially 'the Lord.'
ra'id, *f.n.*, the accompanying, going along with.
du'a ku rāg, *m.n.*, ascetic, praying a long time.—**gi** (*see* **rāg**, delay ...).
rash, *m.n.*, shot (any kind of shot, as dust-shot ...).—**ki.**
rassul, *m.n.*, Apostolic.—**gi**; **dịnta rassuligaah**, the Apostolic religion.
raya, *ad.*, right.
rido, *v.r.*, pitch, throw, upset yourself; **ridda, wan ridan.**
biyihi 'arrada rogai, *locution*, the Deluge (*see* **dād**).
(**nin**) **rogmai**, *a.*, abashed.
u ronaw, *v.tr.*, benefit, do good to.
ruḥ, *m.n.*, spirit, mind.—**hi.**
ruḥha ḥoduskaah, *prop. n.*, the Holy Ghost (Third Person of the Blessed Trinity).
rumaisi, *m.n.*, affirmation.—**gi.**
rutbah, *m.n.*, ceremony, rite.—**hi**; **rutab.—ti** (*plur.*).

S.

Sadeḥmidnimada, —**i**, *prop. n.*, the Trinity (of God).
sahalan, *a.v.*, easy.
seg, *v.tr.*, miss, omit; **saladdi ban segai**, I omitted, missed the prayer.
segasho, *f.n.*, omission.
shahawad, *f.n.*, passion (of the soul).—**di.**
shirud or **shurud**, *m.n.*, cigar.—**ki.**
sig or **la wah**, *v.tr.*, miss in aiming at.

sigarad, *m.n.*, cigar, cigarette.—**ki.**
sir, *v.tr.*, cheat, deceive, trick (in playing).
sir, *f.n.*, a cheating in a game, trick.—**ti.**
sirra, *m.n.*, sacrament.—**hi**, —**yal.**
sunarad, *f.n.*, curl (a ringlet of hair).—**di.**
surad, *f.n.*, chapter.—**di.**

T.

tegid, *f.n.*, the going ...—**di** (*see* **tag**, go).
taḥadiska dabiḥadda, *n.*, consecration (at Mass).
iss ku talabsan, *a.v.*, crossed, lying across.
tambuk, *m.n.*, tent (of Europeans). —**gi.**
tarak, *v.tr.*, apostatize, backslide (in religion).
tarik, *m.n.*, apostate, backslider. —**gi.**
tarbiyad, *f.n.*, operation.—**di**; **tarbiyad ḥun**, awkwardness.
taubadlaan, *f.n.*, impenitence.—**ti.**
tawila, *m.n.*, fortune-teller.—**hi.**
a tosi, *v.tr.*, encourage (*see* **tos**, right).
tulan, *a.v.*, accumulated, heaped.
iss tun (*see* **tun**, forge), *v.i.*, clash; **ku tun**, strike upon.
tumin, *f.n.*, show, exposure.—**ti.**

U.

udbi, *m.n.*, cotton.—**gi.**
ugadsi, *m.n.*, chase, hunting.—**gi.**
ugadso, *v.tr.*, hunt.
ulaka', *f.n.*, will.—**di**; **ninka ulaka'disu wa mid baan**, the will of that man is a bad one.
ulaka' ... u, *ad.*, wilfully.
ulaka'ah, *a.*, wilful.
umasho, *f.n.*, creation.
'unid, *f.n.*, eating.—**di.**
ur, *v.i.*, smell.—**a**, **wan** —**i.**
urur ḥidigaah, *m.n.*, constellation.—**hi.**
usar, *m.n.*, scum.—**ki**; **usarka ka safai**, skim.

W.

wabayaisan, *a.v.*, baneful, poisonous.
wado (*see* **wad**), *v.r.*, go on (for yourself).
wadi', *v.tr.*, preach; —**ya**, **wan wadi'i.**
waḥtiga sonka, *locution*, Lent, the quadragesimal fast.
wajib. This word means 'must,' 'obliged,' 'necessary'; it is used as follows: 1st pers., **igu wajib**, I must, I am obliged, it is necessary for me; 2nd pers., **kugu wajib**; 3rd pers. sing. and plur., **ku wajib**; 1st pers. plur., **ina ku wajib**; 2nd pers. plur., **idin ku wajib.**

wal (*root*), *v.tr.*, *v.i.*, madden, to become mad.

walaḥ, *f.n.*, thing.—**di.** This word is especially used for invisible things.

tobanka wasiyadod, decalogue.

waslado, *m.n.*, liver (of camels). —**hi.**

weidafi, *v.tr.*, throw, cast headlong; **so** —, **iss** —, throw yourself.

weisweis, *v.tr.*, distract.

weisweis, *m.n.*, distraction.—**ki.**

wer, *m.n.*, a linen surrounding the head (emblem of mourning).—**ki.**

wer, *v.tr.*, surround the head ... on account of mourning.

wero, *v.r.*, surround your head ...; **werta, wan weran.**

waḥ ka werar, *v.tr.*, fight with.

wiswis, *m.n.*, doubt, uncertainty.

wiswislaan, *f.n.*, without any doubt, certainty.

Y.

yala, *ad.*, often (*see* **ya**).

yel naḥ, *v.tr.*, curry (dress tanned leather).

LONDON:
PRINTED BY GILBERT AND RIVINGTON, LIMITED
ST. JOHN'S HOUSE, CLERKENWELL, E.C.

CPSIA information can be obtained
at www.ICGtesting.com
Printed in the USA
BVOW06s2138070717
488814BV00008B/140/P

9 781482 097504